Private Military and Security Contractors

Private Military and Security Contractors

Controlling the Corporate Warrior

Edited by Gary Schaub Jr. and Ryan Kelty

ROWMAN & LITTLEFIELD
Lanham • Boulder • New York • London

Published by Rowman & Littlefield
A wholly owned subsidiary of
The Rowman & Littlefield Publishing Group, Inc.
4501 Forbes Boulevard, Suite 200, Lanham, Maryland 20706
www.rowman.com

Unit A, Whitacre Mews, 26-34 Stannary Street, London SE11 4AB,
United Kingdom

British Library Cataloguing in Publication Information Available

Library of Congress Cataloging-in-Publication Data

Names: Schaub, Gary, 1969– editor. | Kelty, Ryan, 1971– editor.
Title: Private military and security contractors : controlling the corporate warrior / edited by Gary Schaub and Ryan Kelty.
Description: Lanham, Maryland : Rowman & Littlefield, 2016. | Includes bibliographical references and index.
Identifiers: LCCN 2016007297 (print) | LCCN 2016007467 (ebook) | ISBN 9781442260214 (cloth : alk. paper) | ISBN 9781442260221 (pbk. : alk. paper) | ISBN 9781442260238 (electronic)
Subjects: LCSH: Private military companies (International law) | Private military companies—Law and legislation. | Private security services—Law and legislation.
Classification: LCC KZ6418.5 .P75 2016 (print) | LCC KZ6418.5 (ebook) | DDC 341.6—dc23
LC record available at http://lccn.loc.gov/2016007297

∞ ™ The paper used in this publication meets the minimum requirements of American National Standard for Information Sciences Permanence of Paper for Printed Library Materials, ANSI/NISO Z39.48-1992.

Printed in the United States of America

Contents

Chapter One

From Making to Buying

Controlling the Coercive Capacities of the Corporate Warrior

Gary Schaub Jr. and Ryan Kelty

On 20 March 2003, the United States and a coalition of allies invaded Iraq with the intention to quickly overthrow the Ba'athist government of Saddam Hussein, install new leadership, and transition to supporting that regime as it reformed the institutions of the state in ways amenable to liberal democratic ideals. The initial combat phase of the operation went as planned, with President George W. Bush declaring an end to "major combat operations" on 1 May 2003. Unfortunately for the coalition, decisions made in this period enabled a protracted insurgency that required the sustained presence of coalition military forces to provide security while Iraqi state institutions were rebuilt.[1]

The US military had not sufficiently planned for this contingency.[2] Nor was it structured to sustain the continuous deployment of its forces—particularly after the downsizing and reorganization of its force structure in the 1990s.[3] In that period, the majority of the support structure was retained in the active duty force, greatly reduced in the reserve force, and eliminated from the National Guard.[4] The Army's Logistics Civil Augmentation Program (LOGCAP) was established to "augment Army forces" by means of private firms that kept "a list of willing and qualified personnel" that they could recruit on short notice to deploy when called upon.[5] When the Army needed to rotate its forces in Iraq in 2004 and introduce reserve and guard forces to replace them, LOGCAP was activated and tens of thousands of contractors surged to support US forces.

Original plans for utilizing contractors for more than logistical support focused primarily on using them to prepare the new Iraqi government's security forces to assume their responsibilities—a mission set that private firms had successfully performed in Croatia, Bosnia, and elsewhere.[6] Furthermore, civilian agencies had planned to use private companies to rebuild Iraq's infrastructure "in an environment with little threat from insurgents or terrorists."[7] The degradation of the security environment necessitated reconsideration of these assumptions.[8] In particular, armed security services were required for Department of State personnel and civilian contractors engaged in reconstruction efforts. After a short period wherein US Army personnel provided a modicum of security for State Department officials, civilian agencies contracted with private security providers, such as DynCorp, that had performed that task in conflict zones since 1994.[9] The civilian agencies redirected at least $766 million from their reconstruction budgets—more than 15 percent—to security provision in 2004 and the number ballooned thereafter.[10] By mid-2005, the Defense Department estimated that there were at least 60 private military and security companies (PMSCs) in Iraq employing as many as 25,000 security personnel.[11] By September 2007, when the Department of Defense (DOD) began officially tracking the number of contractors employed in its area of operations, there were 154,825 DoD contractors total in Iraq, of which 9,952 were private security contractors, both armed and unarmed.[12]

The spark that crystallized the need for such tracking was the 16 September 2007 shooting of 35 unarmed noncombatants—17 fatally—by Blackwater contractors providing security for a convoy of State Department personnel.[13] Although the incident undermined the counterinsurgency strategy of the US-led coalition[14] and provoked outrage, Iraqi diplomatic protests,[15] congressional scrutiny,[16] the resignation of the director of the State Department's Bureau of Diplomatic Security,[17] and the assertion of DoD oversight over all private security contractors co-deployed with US military or civilian agency personnel in areas of combat operations,[18] the Department of State did not terminate Blackwater's contract. Indeed, US officials—including President George W. Bush—praised Blackwater's performance in general[19] and renewed its contract in April 2008, reluctantly terminating it in January 2009 when the Iraqi government refused to license the company.[20] Furthermore, the difficulties encountered in holding the Blackwater personnel accountable encouraged the Iraqi government to insist that all American contractors working in Iraq be subject to Iraqi legal jurisdiction, a position subsequently enshrined in the US-Iraq Status of Forces Agreement of January 2009.[21] Despite the difficulties, a surge of private security contractors entered the country during the final years of direct American involvement to provide security for the American civilian personnel that remained.[22]

The increased role of private contractors to provide essential support and services for the US military was a trend that the United States could not stop. "At the height of Operation IRAQI FREEDOM, contractor numbers well exceeded the military footprint; a similar situation is occurring in support of Operation ENDURING FREEDOM [in Afghanistan]. I do not expect this to change now or in future contingency operations," wrote Secretary of Defense Robert Gates to his subordinates in January 2011.[23] Indeed, although he expressed concern over the "risks introduced by our current level of dependency," the balance of contractors to military forces continued to tilt toward the former in Iraq and Afghanistan, as shown in figures 1.1 and 1.2.[24]

As can be seen in figure 1.1, the number of contract personnel was on average equal to the number of uniformed personnel in Iraq through the period. Furthermore, private security contractors (PSCs), a subset of contractors responsible for providing armed and unarmed security for persons and places, numbered over 10,000 for most of the period and reached a maximum of 15,279 in June 2009. In Afghanistan, figure 1.2 shows that contractors outnumbered military personnel for the entire period except during the Afghan surge from September 2010 to September 2011. The number of PSCs was greater than in Iraq, hovering around 20,000 from 2010 to 2012 and reaching a maximum of 28,686 in June 2012.

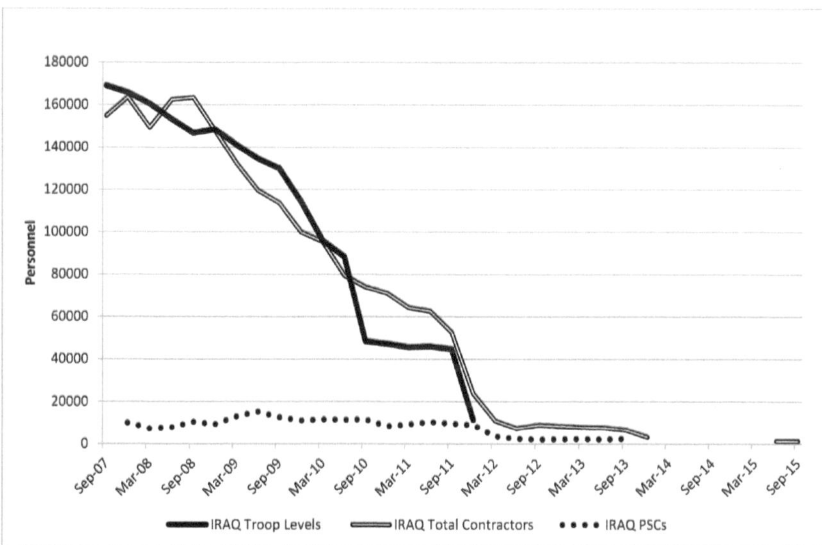

Figure 1.1. Troops, Contractors, and Private Security Contractors (PSCs) in Iraq 2007–2013

The wars in Iraq and Afghanistan made it clear that the most powerful state on the planet had constructed its armed forces in terms of a roughly equal mix between traditional military forces and those generated by the private sector. That it had not entirely meant to do so did not necessarily matter. Nor did its relative lack of success in using these military forces to achieve its political objectives in distant countries. As the leading state in the international system, its behavior provided a model for others to follow.[25] Its choice to acquire significant portions of its force structure on the market from private actors on an ad hoc basis is a clear signal that a significant change is occurring in the manner in which states have organized themselves to acquire and control coercive means.

RETAINING CONTROL OVER A BROKEN MONOPOLY

Exercising meaningful control over violence and utilizing it for productive purposes has been—and continues to be—one of the central challenges facing mankind. Establishing orderly relations so that people may be in some measure secure against violence is elementary to civilization. Such relations require controlling those persons whose particular attributes make them proficient in the ways of violence and, furthermore, harnessing their skills for the good of the community. Communities, societies, and polities have adopted different institutional forms to accomplish this over the centuries.

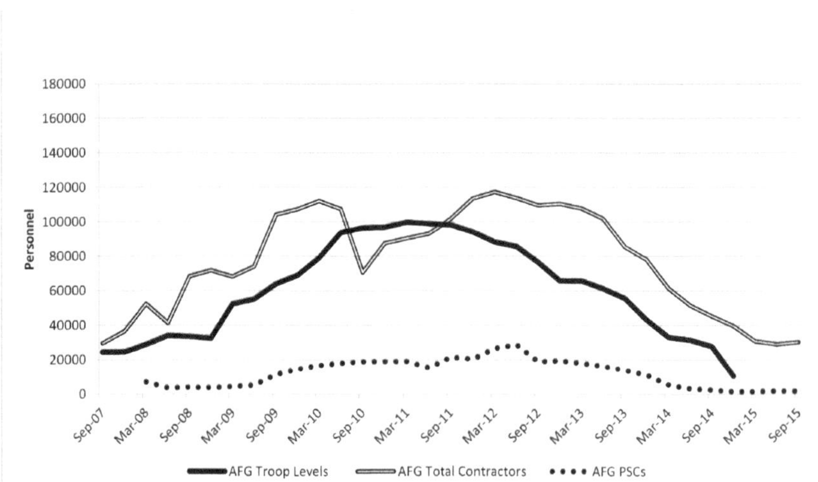

Figure 1.2. Troops, Contractors, and Private Security Contractors (PSCs) in Afghanistan 2007–2014

Armed forces have consisted of popular militias and feudal hosts made up of members of the community pressed into service by circumstance or obligation, mercenary companies employing foreign volunteers contracted on a temporary basis, "subsidy troops" consisting of foreign military forces leased from their home sovereign on a permanent basis, citizens conscripted into service on behalf of the state, and citizen volunteers paid by the state on a permanent basis.[26] These ways of populating an armed force vary in terms of whether the people are members of the community or not, whether they are organized on a temporary or permanent basis, whether they serve voluntarily or are coerced, and whether they are paid directly for their services by the state or by a third party.

Throughout the past 150 years, most advanced states have settled on armed forces populated by citizens on a permanent basis and paid directly by the state. The largest shifts have been in whether their labor was appropriated through conscription or through voluntary accession.[27] But, as indicated above, this has begun to change during the past quarter century. States have begun to acquire personnel for their armed forces indirectly, hiring citizens and foreigners on a temporary basis, paid by a private firm that in turn is paid by the state. This trend began with the recognition that there was significant overlap in the skills required for many military and civilian positions—particularly in technical, support, and administrative areas[28] —and, in the United States in particular, the shift from conscription to an all-volunteer force. Outsourcing non-core functions from the military as an institution—i.e., those not directly tied to using and managing organized violence—was seen as the next logical step.[29] As the American experience in Afghanistan and Iraq indicates, even core military functions have been performed by private entities.

Theories of international relations and, indeed, most state practice throughout the past century would not lead us to expect such occurrences. Over the past few centuries, the sovereign territorial state has been the primary institution organized to use violence in a legitimate manner.[30] Indeed, its ability to assert a monopoly over the legitimate use of physical force to enforce its will is perhaps the primary defining criterion for statehood.[31] The idea that the state's role as the exclusive provider of security would be displaced or require supplementation from private actors poses "a basic challenge to the structure of the entire international system."[32]

What are the implications of breaking this monopoly? In the rest of this introductory chapter, we construct a framework for engaging this question. First we define and describe the characteristics of these new actors—private military and security companies (PMSCs)—and the functions that they have undertaken on behalf of states and other clients. Then we turn to the contours of the market for their services during its formative period from 1990 to 2007. Significant shifts occurred in the types of services demanded by states, the manner in which these private actors were used by states, and the scope of their activities as the market rapidly developed. The scope and scale of the market highlighted that the appearance of these actors and their use by states was not a minor phenomenon. Rather its rapid growth indicated the utility of this method of acquiring coercive capacities and posed significant philosophical, legal, ethical, political, financial, and policy issues for the leaders of the interstate system.

The burgeoning market for force made it apparent that key states were reevaluating their choice between producing their own coercive capacities and acquiring them on the market. By doing so they were choosing between agents for whom a tapestry of social and political institutions had been erected to ensure that they could be meaningfully controlled and utilized purposively to wield violence on behalf of the state and agents for whom that tapestry did not yet exist.

To capture that choice, in the third section we use principal-agent theory to elaborate upon the institutional and normative mechanisms that states use to develop and control their military forces and to ensure that their preferences are consonant with those of state leaders, their behaviors are monitored, and deviations from expected and appropriate behavior are disciplined. These mechanisms range from the socialization and indoctrination of the individual soldier, to sociocultural norms and expectations, to the hierarchical total institution in which they are employed, state laws and regulations regarding appropriate civil-military relations, and the enforcement of the interstate oligopoly over the legitimate use of violence through the institutions of international law. These mechanisms have been developed over centuries to ensure that state principals can avoid the hazards of investing coercive powers in agents that may misuse them and endanger the polity and/or citizenry or simply perform poorly when needed.

In the final section, we turn to comparing these institutions with those available to regulate behavior of private military and security companies. In doing so, we introduce three uncertainties that employing private actors as coercive agents raises for states. In what ways can we expect the preferences of these private agents to differ from those of the state leaders who hire them? How have states endeavored to monitor and control the PMSCs with which they contract for services? To what degree can we expect the personnel employed by PMSCs to be inclined to perform their duties in ways that replicate those of regular military forces? In all, how have states attempted to exercise meaningful control over PMSCs so that they responsibly wield coercive power on the state's behalf?

Our contributors address these questions with robust analyses of the microfoundations of the market that address the social and role identities adopted by individual contract employees, the scope, manner, and degree to which they are accepted as legitimate members of the military profession by regular forces, and the tensions that can arise between them. They address the ways and degree to which key states—South Africa, the United States, Canada, the United Kingdom, and Israel—have built institutions and practices to structure their contractual relations with PMSCs so that their functional preferences will align as much as possible with what the state desires. Furthermore, our contributors address the ability and willingness of these states to monitor and enforce discipline in response to any deviations from expected and appropriate behavior by PMSC personnel. Our contributors also analyze the ability of the industry to regulate itself. Finally, they assess the efforts to construct a nascent international legal regime to reinforce efforts by states and the industry to define and encourage effective practices and appropriate behavior, punish inappropriate behavior, and shape the market so that its participants advance the causes of peace and security while minimizing the dangers in loosening states' oligopolistic control over the means of legitimate organized violence. We conclude with an analysis of where and how this tapestry of controls has been successful and suggestions for how it may be improved. Together, we produce a theoretically informed synthesis of many concerns and arguments raised in the literature that produces new insights into different aspects of the challenges of controlling PMSCs and how they relate to one another as states change the manner in which they make and acquire their coercive capacities.

THE CORPORATE WARRIOR

First we must define these actors that have stepped into the breach. What are private military and security companies? The literature has labeled these entities "mercenaries," "mercenary companies," "corporate mercenary firms," "private military companies," "private military firms," "private military and security companies," and "private security companies," as well as terms such as "contingency contractors" and "stability operations companies," among others. The variance indicates the degree to which the industry is contested, amorphous, and ever-changing.

In this volume, we generally opt for the term "private military and security company" (PMSC), although at times the contributors to this volume have chosen more specific language to address subsets of these actors. The Montreux Document provides the most widely endorsed definition of the term:

> Private business entities that provide military and/or security services, irrespective of how they describe themselves. Military and security services include, in particular, armed guarding and protection of persons and objects, such as convoys, buildings and other places; maintenance and operation of weapons systems; prisoner detention; and advice to or training of local forces and security personnel.[33]

There are a number of dimensions in this definition that ought to be highlighted and expanded upon. First and foremost, PMSCs are *private entities* or *nongovernmental* organizations. This means that they are not formal instruments of the state, nor are they under the direct positive control of government authorities absent additional mechanisms, such as contracts. Second, these organizations are *legal business entities*, meaning that they *sell* services to their clients with the intent to make a profit. Furthermore, they engage in overt contractual dealings with their clients. Thus they must follow "laws requiring registration, periodic reporting, and licensing of foreign contracts."[34] Many have adopted a hierarchical corporate structure, with their owners tied to stock and financial markets, publicly advertise their services, and openly recruit their personnel.[35] Third, these services relate to *military and/or security* functions, which at their base entail *the threat, use, or control of violence*. Such services are equivalent to tasks typically provided by governmental entities, such as the military or policing organizations. Fourth, these services involve the employment of *personnel that utilize esoteric skills and knowledge* on behalf of their clients, not the selling of materiel. Arms manufacturers and arms dealers are a different type of actor.[36] Fifth, they are *organizations*, not individual freelancers, although their business model may entail calling upon such individuals as part of a cadre system.[37] This—and the lacunae of the restrictive formal definitions of *mercenaries* in international law—is what differentiates them from private actors who sold military-like services in the past.[38]

Some of the disputes over what PMSCs are derived from the wide array of services that they offer under the rubric of "military and security services." Indeed, private military and security companies have been extremely entrepreneurial in responding to the demands of strong states, weak states, and other entities. Peter Singer's classic typology distinguishes between *types of firms* based upon their functions in terms of how proximate they are to the use of organized violence. "Military provider firms . . . focus on the tactical environment, . . . provide services at the forefront of the battlespace, by engaging in actual fighting, either as line units or specialists, . . . and/or direct command and control of field units."[39] Executive Outcomes' role in the Angolan civil war, discussed below, provides a classic illustration. "Military consulting firms . . . provide advisory and training services integral to the operation and restructuring of a client's armed forces," much as MPRI did in Croatia and Bosnia.[40] Finally, "military support firms . . . specialize in secondary tasks" that are not the core competencies of military forces, including "logistics, intelligence, technical support, supply, and transportation."[41] Numerous companies provided these services to coalition forces in Afghanistan and Iraq.

Yet because the industry is constantly evolving, some firms have remained niche service providers while others have diversified their service offerings across all of these categories. This suggests that perhaps a functional typology would be more useful for capturing the size, shape, and evolution of the private military and security marketplace. For our purposes the typology used by the Private Security Database (PSD), presented in table 1.1, serves quite well.[42]

THE SHIFTING CONTOURS OF THE MARKET FOR FORCE

A good deal of the literature on PMSCs is built upon anecdotal evidence, vignettes, and case studies. The amorphous and ever-shifting market for force has made it difficult to capture systemic trends in their proliferation, their use, the types of tasks that they perform, and changes in these dimensions over time. The Private Security Database (PSD) provides a means of addressing some of these questions.[43]

Table 1.1. Typology of PMSC Tasks

Task	Description
Combat and military operations	Direct involvement in military operations and fighting
Military assistance	Military training and consulting (e.g., tactics)
Operational support	Operation and/or maintenance of combat-related goods (e.g., weaponry, satellites) and/or fulfilling certain functions in the command and control chain
Logistics support	Transportation of soldiers and/or combat-related goods
Intelligence	Risk assessments, reconnaissance, translation services, interrogations
Quasi-police tasks (prevention) and border patrol	Provision of safety of public places and/or protection of state and local borders
Security/protection (individuals and facilities)	Mobile or stationary security for individuals and/or facilities; this task refers to protective services details
Police advice and training	Training and/or consulting to police forces
Demining	Destruction and removal of land and/or naval mines
Humanitarian aid	Provision by private actors of armed material or logistical services for humanitarian purposes, such as transportation of food in crisis zones
Weapons disposal/ destruction	Removal, destruction, and disposal of warfare-related goods and facilities
Facility and infrastructural buildup	Construction of infrastructure such as military bases

The project focused on the activities of PMSCs in 32 fragile states in the period 1990–2007.[44] These states displayed "deficits in the effective control of territory, the monopoly of violence and the ability of state actors to enforce and implement political decisions" during at least one year in this period.[45] The PSD includes "every instance in which public actors (governments or international organisations) hired PMSCs between 1990 and 2007" as "aggregated contractual relationships" for different tasks in each country each year.[46] Each "contract event" consists of a client, a location, a task, and the number of companies contracted to perform that task or its variants in a given year. Each instance in the dataset therefore may aggregate contracts with multiple companies to perform the same task.[47] The tasks are those defined in the typology in table 1.1. Furthermore, the PSD indicates whether the task was contracted by the contracting state for itself or on behalf of a third party, which allows analysis of assistance through PMSCs as a separate category of events. While the PSD does not capture PMSC activity across the entire interstate system—there were 189 states represented in the United Nations in the year 2000[48] and the PSD covers only the 32 fragile states among them—it does permit us to gain purchase over the PMSC market in the regions that both theory and anecdotal evidence suggest have been most salient to its development and evolution.[49]

Perhaps the most obvious place to begin is with the number of PMSCs. Figure 1.3 indicates the number of companies operating in fragile states during the period under observation. The figure shows, for example, that in 1999 there were 27 companies working in 10 fragile states at the behest of 5 contracting states. At the end of the Cold War there was but one PMSC relationship captured in the PSD data: that of the American contract with International Charter Incorporated of Oregon to support the Economic Community of West African States (ECOWAS) peacekeeping contingent in Liberia.[50] From this humble beginning, the number of companies operating in fragile states increased significantly, with gradual and then accelerating growth. This is especially the case at the turn of the millennium, with a vast expansion of the industry occurring shortly after 9/11. The number of companies reaches its maximum (in the dataset) in 2007, with 142 PMSCs operating in 13 fragile states at the behest of 7 contracting states.

In contrast, the number of states within which they were operating increased slightly through the mid-1990s, reaching 13 in 1995 and remaining at about that level through the remainder of the period. Thus while the number of companies increased, their operations did not expand geographically at a similar pace. In general, this indicates that an increased number of companies were performing more security-oriented services within a finite number of states in any given year. This is borne out in figure 1.4, which shows that the actual number of fragile states suffering from significant instability in the PSD dataset varies throughout the period as some states overcome their

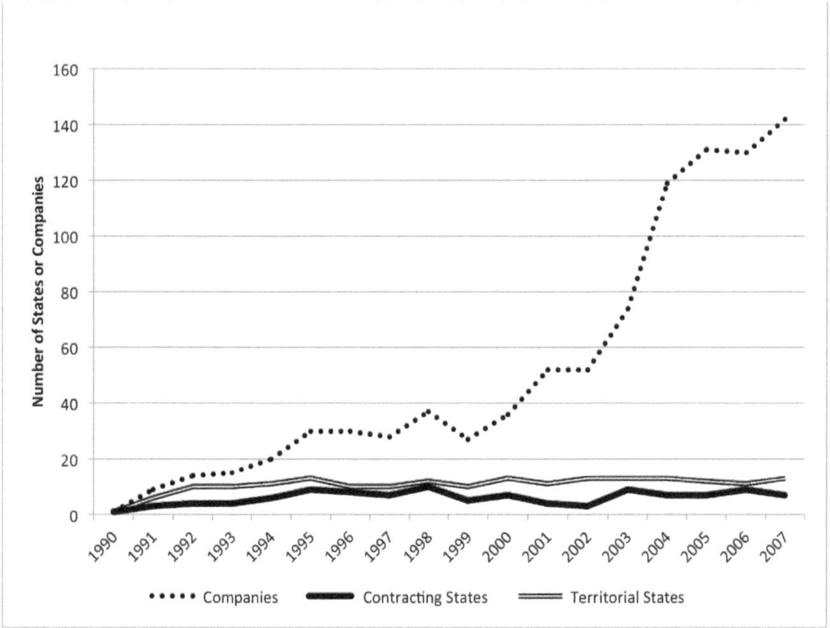

Figure 1.3. PMSCs, Client States, and Territorial States

crises and others experience new traumas.[51] But overall, the number of fragile states increases early on in the post–Cold War period and then declines in a step-like fashion thereafter. The shaded area of figure 1.4 mimics the "location states" line in figure 1.3 and gives more detail on the distribution of PMSC activities in those states. PMSCs were active in 186 of the 576 state-years covered by the PSD dataset. The level of PMSC activities initially follows the increase in unstable fragile states, remains stable through the mid-1990s, and declines along with the number of unstable fragile states until the increase after 9/11. What is notable, however, is the growth of PMSC activity in fragile states before and mostly *after* they have gained a measure of stability. PMSCs remain in these states for a period of time to provide services that these states cannot yet provide effectively for themselves. This is consistent with the thesis that PMSCs "establish themselves not only as providers of security services but as security experts defining which services are needed."[52] It is also consistent with the thesis that PMSCs can be utilized to consolidate state institutions. Indeed, only Angola, the Ivory Coast, Sierra Leone, and the Philippines experienced continued instability after the end of the PMSC presence. Furthermore, the data are not consistent with the thesis that PMSCs cause instability. Only Nigeria had a

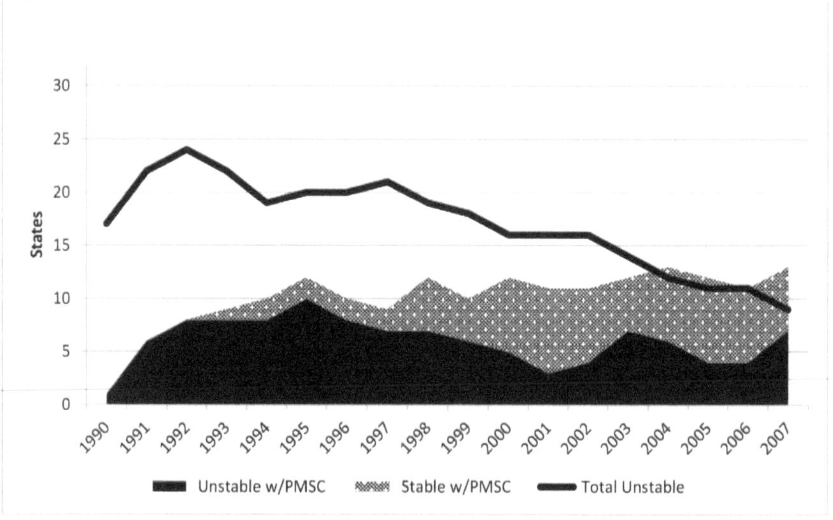

Figure 1.4. PMSCs and Unstable Fragile States

PMSC presence before it experienced the crisis that merited it the status as a fragile state in the PSD dataset, although that crisis occurred three years after the PMSC presence ended.

Turning our attention now to who has hired these PMSCs, we find that they first garnered significant attention through their ability to supplement or replace national military and/or police forces within the sovereign boundaries of the state (see textbox 1.1 on Angola). If this was their only, or even primary, use, then the number of client states and territorial states in the zone of instability would be equal. Figure 1.3 shows that the number of client states—those that hired the PMSCs to perform tasks in these fragile environments—is consistently fewer than the territorial states. This is an indication that PMSCs are not domestic actors, selling their services to fragile states that are able to pay for them.

VICTORY FOR HIRE

Wars of national liberation and state consolidation are often tragic affairs. The wars in Angola proved no different. After 14 years of struggle, the efforts of the primarily urban People's Movement for the Liberation of Angola (MPLA), the primarily rural National Front for the Liberation of Angola (FNLA), and the primarily rural National Union for the Total Independence of Angola (UNITA) abruptly succeeded when the 1974 "Carnation Revolution" in Portugal resulted in a new government that was determined to liquidate its African colonial empire.[1] Despite Portuguese efforts to establish a transitional unity government between the three liberation movements, fighting began between them prior to formal independence.[2] The MPLA established and maintained control of the government and most of the country with the backing of the Soviet Union and the intervention of Cuban military forces.[3] The FNLA and UNITA in particular continued to fight with assistance from South Africa and Zaire, as well as support from the United States.[4] The civil war continued through the Cold War and wound down near its end as foreign troops from Cuba, South Africa, and Zaire were withdrawn as part of the New York Accords of December 1988.[5]

In the wake of the Cold War, external support for the MPLA regime fell rapidly and its strength relative to UNITA diminished. A peace agreement was signed in May 1991 and multiparty elections were held in September 1992. A dispute over the fairness of the outcome reignited the civil war between the MPLA and UNITA.[6] UNITA achieved rapid successes and by 1993 controlled 80 percent of Angolan territory, including the towns of Kefekwena and Soyo, which contained oil production facilities that were a major source of revenue for the struggling MPLA government.[7]

Absent its Soviet patron, the MPLA turned to a new ally, a private corporation that offered military advice, training, and paramilitary combat services for a price: Executive Outcomes.[8] Staffed by former South African commandos who had fought with UNITA against the MPLA just a few years earlier, it was an unlikely choice. In its first combat mission, a force of 80 men ejected UNITA's forces from the Soyo oil facilities in a week of fierce fighting.[9] This initial success was followed by a one-year, $40 million contract to train the Angolan army and direct front-line operations.[10] Executive Outcomes personnel openly flew Angolan air force Mig-27 and Su-25 combat aircraft, Mi-17 Hind attack helicopters, and armored fighting vehicles in support of Angolan forces.[11] Twenty months and 20 contractor fatalities later, the combined Angolan military/Executive Outcomes units had beaten UNITA forces so thoroughly that they signed a peace accord with the Angolan government.[12] UNITA was so impressed by Executive Outcomes' ability to magnify the combat ability of the MPLA government's forces that it insisted that the company be withdrawn as a condition of its agreement.[13] Executive Outcomes withdrew and was replaced by a United Nations peacekeeping force that failed to prevent renewed fighting.

> The ability of a private entity to so thoroughly affect the outcome of a long-standing civil war by providing crucial military expertise, skilled personnel, and small but extremely effective combat forces to a weak, unstable, and less developed state "sent shockwaves around the region."[14] Its ability to repeat its performance in Sierra Leone demonstrated that it was not a fluke.[15] Its unique form of organization, its relative openness in its activities, and its political and business links endowed it with a level of legitimacy heretofore unseen for a "mercenary" company. Finally, its willingness and ability to perform "tasks which both African and Western governments have approved of, but have hesitated to attempt themselves because of financial or political costs" established the possibility that such private actors could be a much-needed force for stability, able to fill the gap where states or the United Nations feared to tread.[16]

Rather, it demonstrates that PMSCs can also be used as proxies to intervene in fragile states. Many originally feared that "mercenary" companies would foment coups and revolutions at the behest of their clients.[53] PMSCs have been useful instruments and proxies independent of overt military intervention. At times they have served to directly complement the military forces of the fragile state, as in the American use of PMSCs to help the government of Colombia fight narcotraffickers and the Fuerzas Armadas Revolucionarias de Colombia (FARC).[54] Such missions are primarily oriented toward building partner capacity in the fragile state, however. This sort of relationship characterized the use of MPRI by the United States to intervene in the wars of Yugoslav disintegration in the 1990s (see textbox 1.2 on Croatia). Figure 1.5 indicates that regardless of their function, PMSCs have been used independently at a fairly consistent rate of two to four interventions each year in these fragile states.[55]

TO END A WAR

The dissolution of Yugoslavia was one of many crises that occupied Western leaders in the aftermath of the Cold War. The changed security environment enabled and accelerated ethnic, religious, social, and political tensions that were exploited by successors to Josip Broz Tito looking to consolidate their political position. Yugoslavia's constituent republics—particularly Slovenia and Croatia—sought greater autonomy while Serbia sought to consolidate its leadership of the Yugoslav Federation. Serbian president Slobodan Milosevic encouraged and provided material support to ethnic Serbs in other republics to unify and resist moves toward autonomy undertaken by their governments. While Slovenia's succession from Yugoslavia proceeded with relatively little difficulty,[1] Serbia encouraged uprisings in the Krajina region of Croatia to hinder its autonomy. Political conflict and ethnic violence led to declarations of independence—of Krajina from Croatia and Croatia from Yugoslavia—as well as the displacement of 330,000 Croats and other non-Serbs over the course of 1990–1991.[2] The conflict was temporarily settled in January 1992 with a cease-fire, de facto autonomy for the Krajina Serb statelet, and the deployment of United Nations peacekeepers.[3] International recognition of Croatia and Slovenia as sovereign states soon followed.[4] Croat President Franjo Tudjman realized that emulating Serbian tactics could yield territorial gains in Bosnia-Herzegovina and he made common cause with Milosevic to partition their neighbor along ethnic lines.[5] The result was the civil war in Bosnia.[6]

Until this point, American and European leaders alike viewed the breakup of Yugoslavia as a tragic "European problem that could and should be settled by Europeans."[7] But by 1994 the Clinton administration chose to become more involved. The Americans concluded that the Serbs were primarily responsible for the conflict in Bosnia and, rather than threatening to sanction Croatia for supporting its partisans, instead offered aid to abandon them and make common cause with the Bosnians against the Serbs.[8] The aid package included military assistance that would help reform the Croatian Army, which suffered from low morale, "poor leadership and an unprofessional organizational structure," as well as little institutional means to overcome these shortcomings.[9] The challenge was that such aid, as well as arms sales, was prohibited by the 1991 United Nations arms embargo on all warring parties.[10]

Deputy Secretary of Defense John Deutch suggested to the Croatian minister of defence that they hire Military Professional Resources Incorporated (MPRI), an American private military and security company (PMSC) led by retired US Army general officers, to help reform his military.[11] The request was made[12] and "Assistant Secretary of State for European and Canadian Affairs Richard Holbrooke persuaded the State Department to license MPRI to provide training to the Croatian Army."[13] Two contracts were approved in December 1994 to make Croatia a potential candidate for the fledgling NATO Partnership for Peace program by helping restructure its defense institutions and to educate its personnel "in democratic principles and civil-military relations."[14] No military training whatsoever was included in the MPRI contracts.[15] Yet the Croatian minister of defense "told MPRI representatives [retired General] Carl Vuono [former Chief of Staff of the US Army] and [General Crosbie] Butch Saint [the retired former commander of US Army Europe] that he wanted a revamped military to 'drive the Serbs out of my country,'" by which he meant the Krajina.[16]

Over the next seven months, the war in Bosnia intensified. Bosnian Serb offensives increasingly targeted UN peacekeeping forces.[17] They culminated in the spring of 1995 when Serb forces began capturing and using UN peacekeeping personnel as human shields against UN-NATO air strikes,[18] overran the UN "safe areas" of Srebrenica and Zepa, and massacred at least 8,000 Muslims.[19] In late July, 10,000 Croat troops and air support crossed the border to support Bosnian forces in intense combat with Serb forces in western Bosnia. Furthermore, Croat forces launched Operation Storm on 3 August to reconquer the Krajina.

In both they were surprisingly successful. The 20,000-strong Krajina Serb forces collapsed in the face of the Croat offensive and fled into Bosnia, followed by over 200,000 ethnic Serb civilians from the region.[20] Operation Storm "established an ethnically homogenous Croat region in the west, and simultaneously exposed the Bosnian Serb stronghold in northwestern Bosnia."[21] Croat and Bosnian Muslim forces were able to capitalize on this opening due to the Bosnian Serbs' inability to bring their forces to bear where and when necessary given the NATO air campaign that began on 30 August.[22] When the Dayton talks began on 1 November 1995, Croat forces controlled 20 percent of Bosnia.[23]

An effective Croatian military had been essential to American strategy. As Richard Holbrooke put it, "as diplomats we could not expect the Serbs to be conciliatory at the negotiating table as long as they had experienced nothing but success on the battlefield."[24] As Ivo Daalder, then director for European affairs on the National Security Council staff responsible for coordinating Bosnia policy, wrote, "Operation Storm . . . provided an important boost to the diplomatic track of the U.S. strategy, not least because it temporarily put the Serbs on the defensive."[25]

The rather remarkable performance of Croat forces "shocked observers."[26] Throughout the campaign, Croat forces demonstrated previously unseen skill combining "air[power], mobile infantry, artillery, and shock tactics" in a manner similar to a NATO force "to destroy Serbian communication and command centers . . . [and] render[] the Bosnian Serb army combat ineffective."[27] They demonstrated a level of "military expertise that could only have been derived from their increasingly congenial relationship with the United States."[28] Canadian Army Colonel Andrew Leslie, the chief of staff to the commander of the Southern Sector of the United Nations in Croatia, observed that "it was a textbook operation, though not a JNA [Yugoslav National Army] textbook. Whoever wrote that plan of attack could have gone to any NATO staff college in North America or Western Europe and scored an A-plus."[29] His boss, Canadian Army Major General Alain Forand, credited MPRI for the vast improvement in Croat capabilities: "I don't think it was the Croats themselves that did that."[30] A French commander concurred: "If they are not involved in military planning, then what are they doing there? Are we supposed to believe that [recently retired Major General John] Sewall [of MPRI, whose previous position had been "the Pentagon's special advisor to the Muslim-Croat federation"[31]] and his people are tourists?"[32] Indeed, despite official denials from US government officials and MPRI executives,[33] analysts concluded that MPRI's contract was part of a larger covert effort to quickly improve the combat capability of the Croat military despite the UN arms embargo.[34] Impressed by the results, the Bosnian government made the provision of a similar training program a condition to its agreeing to the Dayton Accords.[35]

As with Executive Outcomes in Angola, MPRI's work in Croatia demonstrated that the combat effectiveness of institutionally weak and unprofessional military forces could be increased substantially in a short period of time through the use of a private entity. MPRI's status as a private firm enabled the US government to use it to pursue its strategic objectives in the Balkans without flagrantly violating the UN arms embargo.[36] Its success guaranteed further business would be had for PMSCs—both in the Balkans and elsewhere.

But perhaps the most prominent role of PMSCs shown in figure 1.5 is to complement national military forces. Indeed, as discussed above, this was the formal role accorded to private contractors in American military doctrine and plans under LOGCAP in the 1990s. This trend is increasing: figure 1.5 shows that strictly military interventions have decreased in the post–Cold War period. More and more national military forces are accompanied by PMSC supplementary and auxiliary forces. From a policy perspective, the challenges raised by these co-deployments, including the deconfliction, coordination, and cooperation of these different agents, have been significant.[56] As instruments of foreign policy, PMSCs appear to have quickly evolved into a complementary good rather than a substitute for national military forces.

To suggest that co-employment of state military forces and PMSCs in military interventions is increasing does not mean that the balance between states utilizing them as complements and those using them as substitutes has remained constant throughout the period. Figure 1.6 shows that this has not been the case. In the 1990s fragile states increasingly used PMSCs within

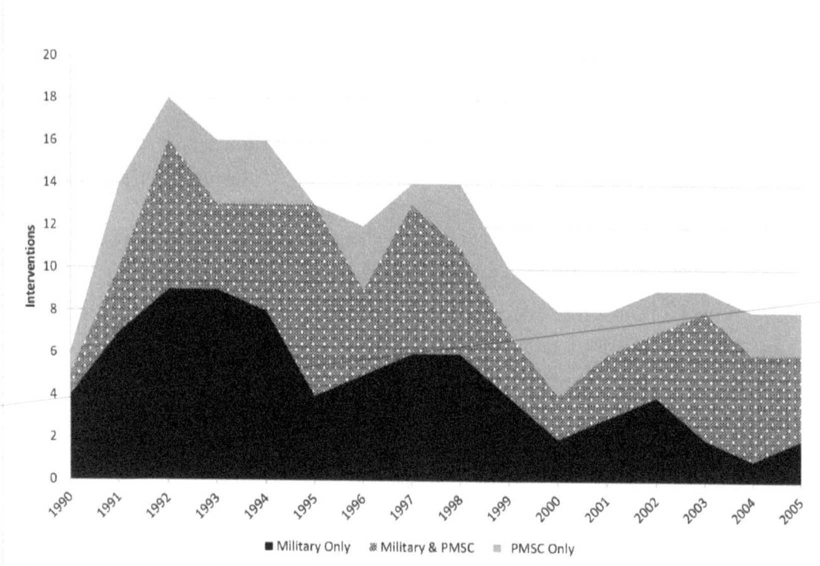

Figure 1.5. Force Mix by Intervention 1990–2005

their own territories, catching up with and even surpassing their use by external clients engaging in intervention. The phenomenon was heavily concentrated in Africa, with Angola, Congo, Liberia, Mozambique, Sierra Leone, and Rwanda contracting with PMSCs as Executive Outcomes' effectiveness became known. But Croatia and then Bosnia joined their ranks, utilizing MPRI and other American PMSCs as they consolidated their institutions after the peace settlement at Dayton in 1995.

This dimension of the market declined significantly in these fragile states beginning in 1999 and throughout the rest of the period under study. Direct employment of PMSCs by fragile states was eclipsed by the steep increase in PMSCs contracted with external states and utilized in an expeditionary manner. It is possible that some of this shift occurred because external powers began to pay for the services originally contracted by weak states in an effort to sustain their development. As Deborah Avant noted with regard to MPRI, "The Croatian government . . . gradually paid less of the bill. The US Defense Department's contributions to these efforts grew from $105,000 in 1995 to $6,000,000 in 2003."[57] It is also in this period that the mix of military forces and PMSCs in interventions begins to increase in number (as shown in figure 1.3) and size with the interventions in Yugoslavia, Afghanistan, and Iraq.

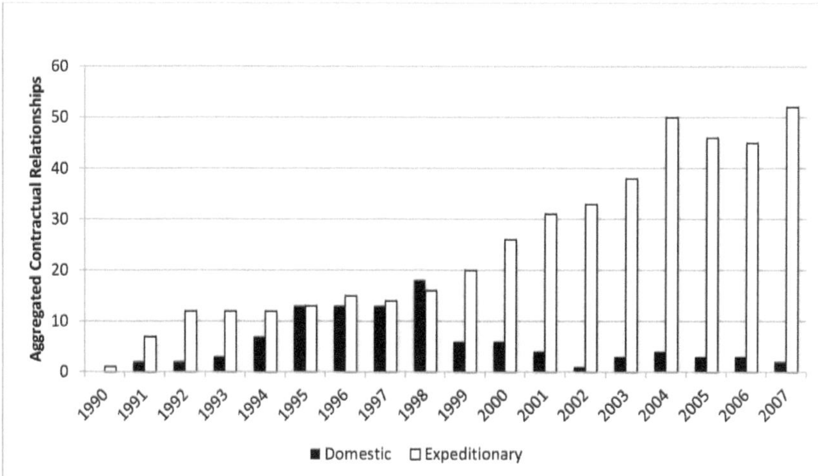

Figure 1.6. PMSC Use in Fragile States

What has also evolved over the course of the period is the mix of services provided by PMSCs, regardless of whom they are working for. In figure 1.7, we have aggregated the functions delineated in the typology above into categories similar to those used by Singer to get at the degree to which core military services of the state have been provided by private actors. As can be seen, PMSCs have provided core services to states at a fairly constant level throughout this period. Core services include combat and military operations, military assistance, and operational support—functions typically performed by state military forces. The second category encompasses functions that are near the core of state security functions, including logistical support for military forces, intelligence services (collection and analysis), quasi-policing tasks and border control, securing individuals and property, and providing advice and training to police forces. These services have seen the greatest increase in the private security market in fragile states. It is likely that this reflects changes in military doctrine among the liberal democratic states that have engaged in military interventions in this period, with their focus on producing stability and effective governance rather than combat. Finally, support functions such as demining, providing humanitarian aid, disposing and destroying weapons, and construction of buildings and infrastructure have also increased over the period, perhaps reflecting the propensity of external states to continue to utilize PMSCs in post-conflict environments.

Although the PSD data is limited to demand originating from the zone of instability that has more and more come to occupy the national security agenda of the stable liberal democracies in the zone of peace, it does provide

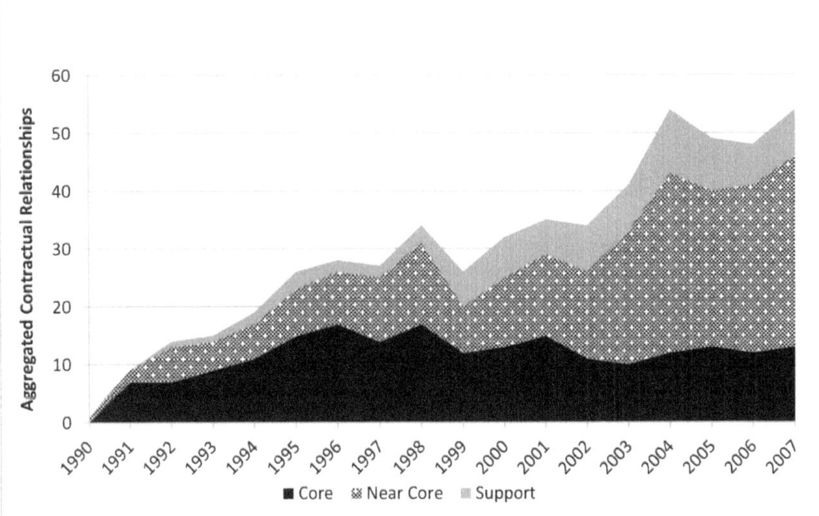

Figure 1.7. PMSC Tasks in Fragile States

a significant overview of how the market for force has grown and evolved from its point of origin through the first 18 years of the post–Cold War era. It shows that the numbers of firms have grown significantly over this time, that the clients of these firms have shifted, from external actors using them for expeditionary purposes to fragile states directly employing them within their territory to external actors and expeditionary operations again in the company of their formal military forces, and that the mix of services demanded and supplied has also shifted toward the middle of the continuum ranging from core military functions through those near the core to those that only support them.

What it does not show is how the rapid development of a global market for private actors that were organized, able, and ready to effectively provide a far greater range of support services to state militaries—indeed, to provide effective combatants—raised significant philosophical, legal, ethical, political, financial, and policy issues for the leaders of the interstate system. One of the primary purposes of understanding these trends is to better enable the development of theory and policy. The availability of new actors that states can use to pursue their policies through the use of organized violence and associated mechanisms requires thought on both. In the following section, we begin to address how the contributors to this volume consider the problem of controlling the corporate warrior.

TO MAKE OR BUY COERCIVE CAPACITY?

It is clear that a significant change has occurred in the manner in which many states have organized themselves to acquire and control coercive means domestically and internationally. This reflects in part a reevaluation of the heretofore preferred method of producing their security themselves to now allow other, private institutions to organize to recruit and deliver personnel trained to support, manage, and use military force on behalf of the state on an as-needed basis. Understanding the implications of these new agents for the meaningful control and purposeful use of military force by state actors requires a comparison with its traditional agent: the military.

State leaders have historically faced a dilemma in controlling the agents upon which the state relies for external defense and internal security: ensuring that the coercive power inherent in a military force is used for the common good, as defined by the leadership, and is not used to destroy the state, control the state, or prey upon the society that it is to protect.[58] Much of the history of the development of the state has hinged upon the solutions to this dilemma. When state institutions were weak and their leaders did not "control the chief concentrated means of coercion within well-defined territories" or "exercise priority in some respects over all other organizations operating within those territories," they had to rely upon a system of decentralized suppliers of organized coercive capability.[59] Whether these capabilities were supplied by mercenary companies as in Italy and the Netherlands, or feudal lords as in Prussia and Russia, state leaders had to guard against two possibilities. The first was that these actors would use their coercive powers to usurp authority over part or all of the territory within the state. The second was that they would not perform their duties as agreed. These relational and functional risks proved to be too great and over the course of centuries states progressively co-opted these actors and created institutions to perform these duties themselves.[60] In essence, they chose to make, rather than buy, their own security apparatus.[61]

The primary problem to be overcome was that of creating an agent whose preferences did not diverge from those of state leaders on these essential conditions. Preference divergence was addressed—at least in most developed states—through building institutions that would socialize, indoctrinate, and professionalize both the leadership of these military agents—officers—as well as their troops, that would monitor their behavior closely, and that would enforce appropriate behavior through rewards and punishments. The result has been tremendous:

> As the military became consolidated as a symbol of national unification and supremacy, and has developed into an instrument of the state rather than individual power-holders (such as feudal chiefs), the ideology of the officer

> corps gradually changed. Soldiers' loyalty to the military system was insured not on the basis of pay, as in the older, internationally recruited mercenary forces, but on the basis of attachment to the common national cause, and with the aid of new laws of general conscription.[62]

The primary concern of the military professional became the security of the state.[63] National defense against actual or potential enemies—not the seizing of profit or political power—was accepted as the primary reason for the existence of military forces.

This alignment was not only task-oriented, but also one of identity. States have invested significant resources in selecting as officers personnel who will be likely to identify with their role.[64] They have developed institutions to systematically professionalize them, including military academies and other institutions of higher learning.[65] These institutions engage in "professional socialization, that is, the . . . individual, micro-level changes in outlooks and behavior among the members of the profession . . . [which] involves the indoctrination and internalization of certain values, outlooks, and behavior elements."[66] Officers learn that their role is that of guardian of the state and this prototype is reinforced through almost every aspect of the military member's existence: uniforms, rituals, emblems, and oaths, as well as interactions with others that elicit and reinforce their identity.[67]

Therefore, at least in mature and stable states, the relational preferences of the military agent and state leaders align to an exceptional degree.[68] The primary question for most of the literature that addresses civil-military relations in these states is not whether those who control the means of organized coercion will seek to control the state, but rather the alignment of functional preferences—that they perform their duties in ways that accord with the wishes and expectations of state leaders. Even then, the concern is within a fairly narrow band of behavior regarding the expert advice offered by the military in terms of resource requirements and courses of action while maintaining civilian preeminence within an "unequal dialogue."[69]

Moreover, significant organizational structures have been erected to monitor and control the performance of military personnel in those duties. Indeed, militaries are organizations whose members are trained to kill people and destroy property under carefully circumscribed circumstances. In order to legitimate such behavior, militaries exert pervasive control over their members' work and private behavior so as to ensure their integrity.[70] Militaries are a mix of "total" and "greedy" institutions that rely upon physical and "non-physical mechanisms to separate the insider from the outsider and to erect symbolic boundaries between them."[71] Within this overarching institution, militaries are highly stratified and hierarchical structures.[72] To ensure that orders will be followed in the heat of combat, "the organizing principle of authority is domination—the issuing of direct commands."[73] Each member is trained to respect the chain of command, every subordinate is monitored by a direct superior, and those superiors are responsible for the behavior of their subordinates, up and down the chain of command.[74] Such interlocking mechanisms of command and control ensure appropriate behavior. Perhaps more so than other bureaucracies, militaries struggle to impose order upon a messy reality. They do so through the development of institutionalized procedures—doctrine—for virtually all behaviors. This is especially the case with regard to the use of force, which is highly regulated in the field by rules of engagement. Deviations from expected, appropriate, and indeed, prescribed behavior are most readily observed and noted—and referred for disciplinary action.

Finally, states erected significant and reinforcing mechanisms to enforce the implementation of orders and policies. Virtually all incentives point members of the military toward compliance with the mission, standards, and values of the institution. Most Western militaries have been long governed by justice systems separate from those of civilian society.[75] At the center of the military justice system is the commanding officer for whom it is one of his primary tools to maintain discipline within the ranks. Immediate commanders are generally empowered to punish infractions as they have proximate knowledge about the performance of their subordinates. Furthermore, military members are primarily dependent upon the evaluations of their direct superiors for their career development and progression, thus giving commanders the ability to reward compliance and obedience as well as punish disobedience. The decentralization of both monitoring and enforcement within a total and greedy institution composed of members who have been indoctrinated, socialized, and professionalized makes for a very coherent agent for the state to entrust with its coercive powers.

Furthermore, states have erected an oligopolistic society that limits the right to legitimately use organized violence only to themselves.[76] These restrictions have been codified in treaties, agreements, international law, and customary practice. The idea that only states may engage in the legitimate use of force against one another is so fundamental to international law that the International Court of Justice "maintains the position expressed in the Nicaragua Case judgment, that only acts attributable to a State can constitute an 'armed attack.'"[77] Moreover, "regulation of the forcible activities of these non-state actors is still through the criminal law, of both a domestic and international nature."[78] But beyond this restriction of legitimate actors, the resort to force by states has become highly regulated as well. Restrictions apply not only to the behavior of states, but also to their agents—that is, those who can lawfully engage in combat. Not only do they enjoy privileged status, their behavior is subject to the law of armed conflict: "every member of the armed forces, whatever his or her rank, has a personal responsibility to comply with the law of armed conflict, to ensure that it is complied with by others and to take action in the event of violations."[79] With its emphasis on the legal responsibilities of individual combatants, their commanders, and their states, the law of armed conflict—and international law more generally—provides an additional source of control for states to exercise over those who wield organized violence at the level of the interstate system.

CONTROLLING THE CORPORATE WARRIOR

Yet despite—or perhaps because of—the substantial investment that states have made in producing their own coercive agents, strong and stable states have permitted and enabled private entities to reenter the market for force as suppliers of services heretofore restricted by the state's monopoly. Weaker states have accepted the legitimacy of these private actors and have utilized them to increase their own capacity to provide security. By procuring these services on the market rather than producing them themselves, states have abandoned the elaborate tapestry of controls developed over the last 400 years—from the individual through the institution to the state itself and international law—that they have used to ensure that the preferences of their agents coincide precisely with their own. They have instead begun to create new structures and institutions to control these actors. But these institutions are nascent, incomplete, and rely upon instruments that may not exist or be effective.

The current lack of clear controls introduces uncertainties into states' relationship with their agents, uncertainties that may undermine the effective management and purposive use of military force by the state. These uncertainties are of three kinds. The first is the degree to which the *relational and functional preferences* of these private corporate agents will coincide with those of their state principals. The second is the degree to which the state can *monitor and control* the PMSCs with which it contracts for services. The third is the degree to which the *personnel* employed by PMSCs will be *inclined to perform their duties* in ways that can substitute for the functions of military forces. These uncertainties underlie the challenges faced by state principals, as well as the analyses and insights generated by the contributors to our volume.

RELATIONAL AND FUNCTIONAL PREFERENCES

The first set of uncertainties arises from the degree that the relational and functional preferences of these agents diverge from those of the state leaders that hired them. Because the state does not produce these actors itself, it must search for actors with the qualities it desires in the marketplace. Each time the state selects an agent from the market it faces the problem of *adverse selection.*[80] States want to select an agent that is capable of delivering the desired outcome and whose relational and functional preferences most coincide with their own, but must make the effort to collect information about the agents offering their services. Such research is costly in time and effort—and will not yield perfect information about the preferences and diligence of the available agents. This is in part because agents have incentives to misrepresent their true preferences: they overpromise and underdeliver.[81] It is also in part because the market for security is inscrutable: the buyer and seller have difficulty discerning the quality of their service beforehand.[82] Unable to truly discriminate between agents, the state offers "fair" compensation for the task to be done, compensation that is likely below that which would attract higher-quality agents. The inability of the state to differentiate between potential suppliers crowds out those whose services are more expensive and, presumably, of higher quality. Thus states generally select from a range of suppliers that are disproportionately of lower quality in their ability and willingness to deliver services than they would prefer.[83]

Furthermore, the primary concern of such agents is not the security of the state. Rather, agents have their own interests and pursue their principal's objectives only to the extent that doing so is advantageous.[84] Early in the post–Cold War period, many states and observers feared that PMSCs might harbor serious ambitions to directly influence or displace the political leadership of the state through extra-constitutional means. Such dangers arising from different relational preferences were quite salient in weak and unstable states and their neighbors.[85] Indeed, in chapter 2, Shannon Bosch, Marelie Maritz, and Matthew Kimble argue that South Africa built its entire approach to PMSCs in response to this danger. The industry's South African genesis during the period when the African National Congress (ANC) was attempting to consolidate power after the transition to majority rule led the government to adopt a rigid and restrictive approach to these new actors.

On the other hand, some states have not reacted to the challenge that PMSCs supposedly pose to state control over organized violence. They do not anticipate that the relational preferences of PMSCs will pose a problem. In chapter 3, Guy Seidman considers the case of Israel, where the control of private military actors, either corporate or individual, has yet to enter the policy agenda. In this, it reflects the common belief among the leaders of states with well-developed regulatory cultures that they have significant processes for selecting, monitoring, and controlling private agents in other spheres.[86]

Likewise, the ability of states to control private actors when they supplement military forces in limited contingencies has been the underlying premise of the use of PMSCs in maritime commerce. In chapter 4, Christopher Spearin argues that states, the United States in particular, have encouraged private commercial shipping companies to undertake greater responsibility for their own protection when shipping goods through potentially insecure waters. They have done so because PMSCs in the maritime environment pose little threat to the state's monopoly over the use of force and can reduce the demand to exercise it extraterritorially. As a result, to the degree that states and shippers express concern, it is centered upon the functional preferences of PMSCs.

MONITORING AND ENFORCEMENT

This pushes the problem of adverse selection to the implementation phase, where it becomes an issue of misrepresenting actual performance. State principals have to monitor the behavior of their agents and enforce appropriate behavior when deviations occur. The problem of *moral hazard* arises from the inability to directly observe an agent's performance in the field and the necessity to instead rely upon proxy indicators. The agent then has incentives to pursue the proxy measures rather than the more abstract goals and objectives that underlay the state's reasons for hiring them.[87] While this can be a more general phenomenon for any individual or organization, whether a private or public entity, it expresses itself in particular ways when bridging the public-private divide.

Private commercial enterprises exist to make profits, not serve the state. As Lindsay Cohn put it, "the management of a private firm has no imperative to subordinate its interests in profit to the government's interest in effectiveness."[88] They will therefore give precedence to the former objective over the latter. This will change their behavior from that expected from regular military forces. First, private agents will seek to minimize the resources devoted to achieving the objectives specified by the contract under which they operate. Expenditures beyond the point where marginal cost equals marginal product while meeting the minimum requirements of the contract reduce profits. Firms therefore have greater incentives to accept the risk of mission failure than to maximize the chances of mission success. In this they differ from military forces in two ways. First, they are less likely to share the preference for "overwhelming force" in order to achieve a decisive outcome.[89] Second, they need not fight to win. In the event that a particular operation or service becomes unprofitable, either due to underestimation of the true costs of implementation or because of changing conditions, the company can renegotiate its contract or quit.[90] For example, a 1997 contract between Sandline and the government of Papua New Guinea to render an insurgent force "combat ineffective" within three months explicitly stated that "the achievement of the primary objective cannot be deemed to be a performance measure for the sake of this agreement if it can't be demonstrated that for valid reasons it cannot be achieved within the timescale and with the level contracted resources provided."[91] By contrast, regular military forces that attempted to shirk in this manner could be tried for treason.

Moreover, PMSCs have incentives to limit their activities to performing only tasks specified in their contract—or, rather, maximizing the indicators of performance specified in the contract. Private, profit-seeking entities agree to deliver a service for a fee and are held to account for doing so. But "when the proxy is not perfectly linked to what is really desired, the agent may be motivated to deliver the one at the expense of the other."[92] As Tom Ricks noted of PSCs employed by the Department of State's Bureau of Diplomatic Security in Iraq, "Fundamentally, the bodyguard's mission was different from that of the US military. . . . The contractor was hired to protect the principal. He had no stake in pacifying the country."[93] Therefore the considerations shaping their behavior differed considerably from those of the military forces that shared the battlefield. Thus the difference in motivation, reinforced through market competition, directly reduces the overlap between the functional preferences of state principals and private agents hired to perform military and security functions.

PMSCs are not state agencies designed to pursue the interests of the state, nor are they located within an overarching hierarchical structure that disciplines their behavior through regular oversight and enforcement processes, and so functional uncertainties are introduced into the relationship between the state and its agents. How have states attempted to construct their contractual relations with PMSCs so that their functional preferences will align as much as possible? What does this look like in the operational context of the battlefield? And what approaches have states taken in general to impose oversight and enforcement mechanisms on corporate warriors?

In chapter 5, David Strachan-Morris addresses the use of contractors on the battlefields of Iraq and Afghanistan. He analyzes the mechanisms through which attempts were made to control PMSCs on the battlefield in Iraq. These included legislation and regulations, a monitoring system to track the movements of PMSCs and render assistance when necessary, and intelligence to enable PMSCs to plan their movements to avoid potential trouble spots, in the hope that this would reduce the likelihood of armed confrontations with the civilian population.

Increasing the ability of states to manage their contractual relations with PMSCs has been a primary topic of the policy literature.[94] How can states adopt a more strategic approach to contracting? In chapter 6, David Perry analyzes the efforts of the United States and Canada to erect regulatory mechanisms that would ensure that contracts and contractors are properly managed and coordinated, provide oversight and transparency for contracts, and integrate the use of PMSCs into national policy and doctrine so as to establish an effective legal regime for contracted PMSCs.

The regulatory commitment of some states is low because PMSCs are neither based nor active in these states or because the governments of these states, for various reasons, simply do not accept the argument that PMSC regulation is required. The United Kingdom offers such a case. The United Kingdom has taken a more lenient approach to controlling PMSCs, argue Eugenio Cusumano and Christopher Kinsey in chapter 7. British officials judged direct regulation too costly and prohibitively difficult to implement and instead have relied upon "old boy networks" and the "nod and wink business practice approach" to industry regulation.[95] The lack of salient incidents of misbehavior enabled the government to work with the industry to help it regulate itself and to support the efforts of international bodies to provide regulatory guidance.

A theme throughout each of these chapters is that the market for force grew faster than states' desires and attempts to regulate it. A dearth of appropriate international and domestic regulations, and especially enforcement, produced incentives for other sets of actors to fill the void. In this environment, the industry sought to regulate itself. Our volume contains two evaluations of these efforts. In chapter 8, Surabhi Ranganathan analyzes the principal associations in the PMSCs industry—the International Stability Operations Association (ISOA), the British Association of Private Security Companies (BAPSC), and the now defunct Private Security Company Association of Iraq (PSCAI)—in terms of their legitimacy, accountability, and effectiveness as regulatory bodies. She argues that these qualities are dependent upon the structure of these organizations, their membership, the efforts that they have undertaken to promote and disseminate best practices, standards of performance and adherence to norms among their members, and their cooperation with other regulatory entities.

In chapter 9, Doug Brooks, the founder and former president of ISOA, Andrew Koch, and Gary Schaub Jr. delve more deeply into the efforts of ISOA to play the role of an informal regulator of the international private security industry. They argue that industry self-regulation can effectively enable firms to address problems that concern them all, including establishing and enforcing standards of performance, controlling entry to the industry, and mitigating the uncertainty and costs that accompany operating under multiple domestic regulatory regimes. Yet success varies with the degree of homogeneity of an industry, the ability of firms to cooperate as well as compete among themselves, and their endowing an external body such as a trade association with sufficient resources and power to propagate standards and independently assess and sanction violations of agreed practices. Brooks, Koch, and Schaub evaluate the performance of ISOA given the heterogeneity of the private security industry and the limited resources and powers invested by the industry in ISOA.

Those efforts at regulation at the interstate level resulted in the 2008 Montreux Document, the first major international undertaking to address the use of companies that offer security services for hire. In chapter 10, Ian Ralby analyzes the Montreux Document, locating it within a growing body of "soft law" initiatives that utilize quasi-legal instruments to clarify how states ought to conduct their affairs. He argues that its most significant functions are clarification regarding the application of international law to PMSC contracting and the potential it has to form the basis of binding customary international law. These efforts are no substitute for the vast array of international law that has been developed by states to constrain the behavior and conduct of their armed forces, but rather are indicative of the ways that states and other stakeholders are adapting their practices to these new private actors.

PERSONNEL

Ultimately, however, it is the individual contractor that acts as the agent of the state. They are the ones who are held responsible for their behavior, facing penalties as individuals rather than as part of the corporate entity that employs them.[96] Indeed, one of the key innovations that the industry adopted to enable it to take advantage of the conditions of supply that prevailed in the initial post–Cold War period and to act nimbly in response to demand for services was to adopt a cadre structure. Many PMSCs have minimal management structures and a temporary workforce—a striking contrast with the strict hierarchical structure of state militaries that favor long career patterns and the long-term development of personnel.[97]

By design, firms lack a tight hierarchical structure and the bureaucratic overhead necessary to conduct detailed oversight of their employees' behaviors.[98] Because of this lax institutional environment, many firms relied upon the quality of their employees and the degree to which they could be entrusted to perform the tasks at hand with professional skill. In particular, some of the most prominent firms in the 1990s made a point of highlighting the limited pool from which they would recruit personnel for specific projects. The employees of Executive Outcomes were primarily veterans of the South African special forces known to one another to ensure their quality.[99] Likewise, MPRI was staffed exclusively by retired US military personnel and their positions in the company's structure reflected their former rank and specialty.[100] Blackwater also limited its recruitment to former US military and police personnel with requirements for their training and position detailed by their contracts with the US government.[101]

Following the practices of these early entrants into the market for force, a general claim is often made that many of the individuals working for PMSCs typically have a military background, particularly those from Western countries.[102] These individuals have undergone socialization, disciplining, education, and training in the military for years—quite often for many years. Thus, they have been exposed to military culture, both formal and informal.[103] They are familiar with national and international law, the restraints on military activity due to regulations and norms, and they may have developed strong notions of military professionalism, honor, and military ethos. Unprofessional behavior is attributed to "a few bad apples."[104] The regulation potential of the individual contractor, then, rests in the assumption that their exposure to military culture, to its organizational values, norms and rules, has a lasting effect in the sense that military culture still influences and perhaps even determines their present behavior.[105]

Yet these individuals face different incentives than they did when they were in the military. The incentive to minimize costs while maximizing measured performance incentivizes individual private contractors as well as their parent companies. Members of the military are socialized, trained, and indoctrinated to accept that they may face the "unlimited liability" of risking life and limb in the service of their country.[106] Although thousands of contractor personnel have been killed or injured in Iraq and Afghanistan,[107] such "sacrifice has no place in the cost-benefit analysis that is at the heart of commercial soldiering."[108] Thus their incentives are structured to more readily shift risks from themselves and onto others, such as noncombatants in the area. For instance, "Blackwater maintained a relatively bellicose military culture that . . . motivated its personnel to use violence quite freely against anyone suspected of posing a threat."[109] While force protection also motivates state military forces,[110] commanders have at times ordered their forces to reduce its priority in order to achieve tactical, operational, and strategic objectives.[111] Furthermore, unlike a soldier who could be tried and severely punished for desertion, relatively little prevents an individual contractor from quitting their job and leaving before the completion of their company's contract.[112] The lack of oversight, discipline, and enforcement inherent in PMSC organizational structures provides far fewer incentives for individual contractors to perform their duties to the utmost.

To what degree do PMSC personnel *possess the inclination to perform their duties* as if they were regular military personnel? To what degree do they reflect any previous indoctrination that they received if they served in a state military? To what extent has their status as private employees adulterated their identity? How have they resolved the conflicting incentives that they face? What is the content of the identity of these personnel? Is it as homogenous as some claim? Or is it too heterogeneous to be considered a single identity? Are these private actors recognized as military professionals by members of state militaries? Or are contractors characterized as an "other" or out-group whose presence disrupts the military profession in the performance of their duties? The last three chapters in this volume address these questions.

In chapter 11, Volker Franke examines the occupational self-conceptions and motivations of a sizable sample of individuals who have been employed by private security firms to assess whether there is an emerging professional identity among them. In contrast to approaches intended to formally regulate the industry, he focuses on the merits and limitations of informal regulation through social group norms and identifications. Informal regulation in this context refers to the norms, rules, and values that are internalized by individuals as a central element of their very sense of "selfness" and identity and that, as a result, guide behavior through continual self-surveillance and self-regulation instead of the threat or use of external sanctions. He utilizes social identity theory as a conceptual frame to develop a typology of contractor identities based on the degrees of formal and informal regulation shaping them.

In chapter 12, Gary Schaub Jr. extends this analysis. He argues that a key factor that affects the likelihood that Western PMSC personnel will adopt the norms of the military personnel whom they supplement is the degree to which they are accorded status as members of the military profession by traditional members of the military profession, in particular officers who are responsible for maintaining the ethos and identity of the profession. The greater their acceptance into the profession of arms the more likely PMSC personnel will behave like military professionals. He draws upon two aspects of identity—role and social—to assess the manner and degree to which contractors may be accepted as brothers-in-arms by a large sample of elite field-grade officers.

In chapter 13, Ryan Kelty extends the analysis even further. He assesses whether and to what extent uniformed personnel perceive contractors as legitimate actors within the military's "total force." Avant argued that "the tensions between PSCs and active-duty soldiers may undermine the loyalty, initiative, and fighting power of soldiers."[113] Kinsey and others have argued that state militaries will "become a recruiting ground" for PMSCs and recruits will see their time in service as merely training for a more lucrative career in the private sector.[114] Kelty uses the concept of social comparisons and attitudes toward contractors across several highly salient work-related factors as the foundation for assessing these claims and for assessing the impact of contractor integration among uniformed personnel. Kelty discusses the implications of this analysis in the context of needs to control when, how, and how much to use contractors through better regulation, oversight, and program evaluation.

In the final chapter, Gary Schaub Jr. draws together the arguments made by the contributors to the volume. He synthesizes their insights in terms of the three uncertainties that the resort to private actors introduces to the state's ability to control and meaningfully utilize violence: that deriving from the divergence of preferences between the state and PMSCs, the looser oversight and enforcement mechanisms used to discipline the behavior of PMSCs, and the degree to which PMSC personnel are suitable substitutes for regular military personnel. He then turns to the gaps that remain in the tapestry of control that states have woven to regain their collective oligopoly over the legitimate use of force internationally and offers brief suggestions for addressing them. Finally, he summarizes the overall argument of the volume: that the different efforts taken by states have resulted in an uneven patchwork of imperfect mechanisms to effectively control the corporate warrior.

Overall, this volume provides a unique contribution to the literature through the depth and breadth of its coverage of this multifaceted topic as well as an examination of the interaction between the micro and macro levels of analysis. By addressing the views and identities of the actual persons involved in the delivery of military services—officers, enlisted, and contractors—we are able to gain some leverage over their similarities and differences, how they view one another, and the tensions that may underlie their interactions in a theoretically informed and empirically based manner that few others have attempted.

In particular we argue that PMSCs are not militaries, their employees are not soldiers, and the former are imperfect substitutes for the latter. When states acquire coercive capacities on the market rather than producing them themselves they bypass the comprehensive institutions for managing those who utilize violence on their behalf that have been developed over the centuries. At the micro level, individual contractors conceive of their social and role identities differently than do military personnel, face different incentive structures and mechanisms of oversight and enforcement, and are recognized as a related but separate other by military forces. This lack of coherence on the ground increases uncertainties for all in deployed environments and highlights the requirement for additional monitoring and enforcement mechanisms. At the state level our coverage illustrates the spectrum of approaches taken by strong states: South Africa has not accepted the legitimacy of these new actors; the United States and Canada have accepted their legitimacy and taken similar approaches to regulating their behavior, albeit with different levels of vigor; the United Kingdom accepts their legitimacy and places great trust in their propriety; and finally Israel—a heavily militarized state where these actors have yet to emerge on the policy agenda. The contrasts here highlight the difficulties that efforts to gain consensus at the interstate level have encountered and demonstrates the importance of harmonizing instruments such as the Montreux Document to educate and socialize states, corporations, and individuals in their responsibilities and obligations. Finally, two critical analyses of the attempts by PMSCs themselves to organize and regulate their own industry, including the reflections of the founder of a key trade association, enable us to draw inferences about the scope and limits of institutions and regulatory mechanisms originating from these new actors themselves. The challenge of controlling the corporate warrior has engendered two decades' worth of scholarship that has addressed many of these issues, and more, individually. We believe this volume offers a uniquely holistic, theoretically informed synthesis that produces new insights into different aspects of the problem of controlling PMSCs and indicates the complexities that arise as they interact.

NOTES

1. Michael R. Gordon and Bernard E. Trainor, *Cobra II: The Inside Story of the Invasion and Occupation of Iraq* (New York: Pantheon Books, 2006), pages 475–96; Thomas E. Ricks, *Fiasco: The American Military Adventure in Iraq* (New York: Penguin, 2006), pages 149–202; James Fallows, *Blind into Baghdad: America's War in Iraq* (New York: Vintage Books, 2006).

2. Nora Bensahel, Olga Oliker, Keith Crane, Rick Brennan Jr., Heather S. Gregg, Thomas Sullivan, and Andrew Rathmell, *After Saddam: Prewar Planning and the Occupation of Iraq* (Santa Monica: RAND Corporation, 2008). On the inadequacy of planning for the use of contract personnel, see United States General Accounting Office, *Military Operations: Contractors Provide Vital Services to Deployed Forces but Are Not Adequately Addressed in DoD Plans*, GAO-03-695 (Washington: General Accounting Office, June 2003).

3. Ronald E. Sortor, *Army Active/Reserve Mix: Force Planning for Major Regional Contingencies* (Santa Monica: RAND Corporation, 1995); David McCormick, *The Downsized Warrior: America's Army in Transition* (New York: New York University Press, 1998).

4. Mark Cancian, "Contractors: The New Element of Military Force Structure," *Parameters* 38, 3 (Autumn 2008), page 68.

5. Cancian, "Contractors," page 66.

6. Deborah D. Avant, *The Market for Force: The Consequences of Privatizing Security* (Cambridge: Cambridge University Press, 2005), pages 121–22.

7. William M. Solis, *Rebuilding Iraq: Actions Needed to Improve Use of Private Security Providers*, GAO-05-737 (Washington: Government Accountability Office, July 2005), page 1.

8. Christopher Kinsey, *Private Contractors and the Reconstruction of Iraq: Transforming Military Logistics* (London: Routledge, 2009).

9. Solis suggests that the US military was tasked to protect only its own personnel (Solis, *Rebuilding Iraq*, page 3). Cusumano and Kinsey argue, however, that the US Army provided security details for State Department officials in 2003 but the details were unwilling to follow State Department preferences for keeping a low profile, for accommodating abrupt changes in itinerary, or for protecting low-level officials or static sites (Eugenio Cusumano and Christopher Kinsey, "Bureaucratic Interests and the Outsourcing of Security: The Privatization of Diplomatic Protection in the United States and the United Kingdom," *Armed Forces and Society* 41, 4 [October 2015], pages 601–3).

10. Solis, *Rebuilding Iraq*, page 1.

11. Solis, *Rebuilding Iraq*, page 8.

12. Heidi M. Peters, Moshe Schwartz, and Lawrence Kapp, *Department of Defense Contractor and Troop Levels in Iraq and Afghanistan: 2007–2014* (Washington: Congressional Research Service, 22 July 2015), page 5, table 4.

13. Spencer S. Hsu, Victoria St. Martin, and Keith L. Alexander, "Four Blackwater Guards Found Guilty in 2007 Iraq Shootings of 31 Unarmed Civilians," *Washington Post* (22 October 2014), available at https://www.washingtonpost.com/world/national-security/verdict-expected-in-blackwater-shooting-case/2014/10/22/5a488258-59fc-11e4-bd61-346aee66ba29_story.html, accessed 11 August 2015; Erik Prince with Davin Coburn, *Civilian Warriors: The Inside Story*

of Blackwater and the Unsung Heroes of the War on Terror (New York: Portfolio/Penguin, 2013), pages 207–31.

14. Ricks, *Fiasco*, pages 370–73; Sudarsan Raghavan and Thomas E. Ricks, "Private Security Puts Diplomats, Military at Odds in Iraq Fuel Debate," *Washington Post* (26 September 2007), available at http://www.washingtonpost.com/wp-dyn/content/article/2007/09/25/AR2007092502675.html, accessed 14 October 2015; Sue Pleming and Andrew Grey, "Gates Takes Swipe at Security Contractors in Iraq," Reuters (19 October 2007), available at http://www.reuters.com/article/2007/10/19/us-iraq-usa-blackwater-idUSN1842593420071019, accessed 3 August 2015; Peter W. Singer, *Can't Win with 'Em, Can't Go to War without 'Em: Private Military Contractors and Counterinsurgency*, Policy Paper 4 (Washington: Brookings Institution, September 2007); Frank G. Hoffman, "Neo-classical Counterinsurgency?" *Parameters* 37, 2 (Summer 2007); Jeffrey S. Thurnher, "Drowning in Blackwater: How Weak Accountability over Private Security Contractors Significantly Undermines Counterinsurgency Efforts," *The Army Lawyer* (July 2008); Molly Dunigan, *Victory for Hire: Private Security Companies' Impact on Military Effectiveness* (Palo Alto: Stanford University Press, 2011), pages 71–72.

15. James Glanz and Alissa J. Rubin, "Blackwater Shootings 'Murder,' Iraq Says," *New York Times* (8 October 2007), available at http://www.nytimes.com/2007/10/08/world/middleeast/08blackwater.html?, accessed 14 October 2015.

16. *Blackwater USA: Hearing before the Committee on Oversight and Government Reform, House of Representatives, One Hundred Tenth Congress (October 2, 2007)*, serial number 110-89 (Washington: Government Printing Office, 2008), available at https://house.resource.org/110/org.c-span.201290-1.1.pdf.

17. John M. Broder, "State Dept. Official Resigns; Oversaw Blackwater and Other Private Guards," *New York Times* (25 October 2007), available at http://www.nytimes.com/2007/10/25/washington/25griffin.html?_r=0, accessed 14 October 2015.

18. Ashton Carter, Under Secretary of Defense for Acquisition, Technology, and Logistics, *Department of Defense Instruction 3020.50: Private Security Contractors (PSCs) Operating in Contingency Operations* (Washington: Department of Defense, 22 July 2009).

19. George W. Bush, "The President's News Conference. October 17, 2007," *The American Presidency Project*, available at http://www.presidency.ucsb.edu/ws/index.php?pid=75943, accessed 18 October 2015; "U.S. Ambassador Praises Blackwater Bodyguards," *USA Today* (26 October 2007), available at http://usatoday30.usatoday.com/news/world/iraq/2007-10-26-iraq-news_N.htm, accessed 15 October 2015; Jeremy Scahill, *Blackwater: The Rise of the World's Most Powerful Mercenary Army*, revised and updated edition (New York: Nation Books, 2008), page 16; Scott Fitzsimmons, *Private Security Companies during the Iraq War: Military Performance and the Use of Deadly Force* (London: Routledge, 2016), page 3.

20. Dana Hedgpeth, "State Department to Renew Deal with Blackwater for Iraq Security," *Washington Post* (5 April 2008), available at http://www.washingtonpost.com/wp-dyn/content/article/2008/04/04/AR2008040403449.html, accessed 14 October 2015; "Controversial Blackwater Security Firm Gets Iraq Contract Extended by State Dept," *CBS News* (30 January 2009), available at http://www.cbsnews.com/news/us-nixes-blackwater-contract-for-iraq/, accessed 14 October 2015.

21. James Risen and Timothy Williams, "U.S. Looks for Blackwater Replacement in Iraq," *New York Times* (29 January 2009), available at http://www.nytimes.com/2009/01/30/world/middleeast/30blackwater.html, accessed 14 October 2015; Dunigan, *Victory for Hire*, page 72; Prince with Coburn, *Civilian Warriors*, pages 229–30.

22. Jeremy Scahill, "Iraq Withdrawal? Obama and Clinton Expanding US Paramilitary Force in Iraq," *The Nation* (22 July 2010); Prince with Coburn, *Civilian Warriors*, pages 230–31; Bruce E. Stanley, *Outsourcing Security: Private Military Contractors and U.S. Foreign Policy* (Lincoln: Potomac Books, 2015), pages 8–9.

23. Robert M. Gates, "Strategic and Operational Planning for Operational Contract Support (OCS) and Workforce Mix," memorandum for the secretaries of the military departments et al. (Washington: Office of the Secretary of Defense, 24 January 2011), page 1.

24. Data for figures 1.1 and 1.2 are drawn from the following sources: For data from September 2007 to December 2013 for Iraq and December 2014 for Afghanistan, see Peters,

Schwartz, and Kapp, *Department of Defense Contractor and Troop Levels in Iraq and Afghanistan*, pages 5–6, tables 3–4. For data in 2015, see United States Deputy Assistant Secretary of Defense for Program Support, *Contractor Support of U.S. Operations in the USCENTCOM Area of Responsibility* (Washington: Department of Defense, quarterly), posted at the Private Security Monitor, "Data and Statistics: CENTCOM Data," Sié Chéou-Kang Center for International Security and Diplomacy of the University of Denver website, available at http://psm.du.edu/articles_reports_statistics/data_and_statistics.html, accessed 19 December 2015.

25. Joao Resende-Santos, "Anarchy and the Emulation of Military Systems: Military Organization and Technology in South America, 1870–1914," in Benjamin Frankel, editor, *Realism: Restatements and Renewal* (London: Frank Cass, 1996); Emily O. Goldman and Richard B. Andres, "Systemic Effects of Military Innovation and Diffusion," *Security Studies* 8, 4 (Summer 1999); Theo Farrell, *The Sources of Military Change: Culture, Politics, Technology* (Boulder: Lynne Rienner Publishers, 2002).

26. Lars Mjøsetand and Stephen Van Holde, "Killing for the State, Dying for the Nation," in Lars Mjøsetand and Stephen Van Holde, editors, *The Comparative Study of Conscription in the Armed Forces* (Amsterdam: JAI, 2002), page 8; Samuel E. Finer, "State- and Nation-Building in Europe: The Role of the Military," in Charles Tilly, editor, *The Formation of National States in Western Europe* (Princeton: Princeton University Press, 1975), pages 93–102.

27. Mjøsetand and Van Holde, *The Comparative Study of Conscription in the Armed Forces*; Perti Joenniemi, editor, *The Changing Face of European Conscription* (Aldershot: Ashgate, 2006); Curtis L. Gilroy and Cindy Williams, editors, *Service to Country: Personnel Policy and the Transformation of Western Militaries* (Cambridge: MIT Press, 2006).

28. Morris Janowitz, *The Professional Soldier: A Social and Political Portrait* (New York: The Free Press, 1960), pages 64–74.

29. Mark Erbel and Christopher Kinsey, "Privatizing Military Logistics," in Rita Abrahamsen and Anna Leander, editors, *Routledge Handbook of Private Security Studies* (New York: Routledge, 2016), pages 70–73; Christopher Kinsey, "Transforming Supplying War: Considerations and Rationales behind Contractor Support to Future UK Overseas Military Operations in the 21st Century," *International Journal* 69, 4 (December 2014), page 498; Matthew Uttley, *Contractors on Deployed Military Operations: United Kingdom Policy and Doctrine* (Carlisle: Strategic Studies Institute, September 2005); Allison Stanger, *One Nation under Contract: The Outsourcing of American Power and the Future of Foreign Policy* (New Haven: Yale University Press, 2009), page 85.

30. Hedley Bull, *The Anarchical Society: A Study of Order in World Politics* (London: Macmillan, 1977), page 8; William H. McNeill, *The Pursuit of Power: Technology, Armed Force and Society since AD 1000* (Chicago: University of Chicago Press, 1982); Hendrick Spruyt, *The Sovereign State and Its Competitors: An Analysis of Systems Change* (Princeton: Princeton University Press, 1994); Charles Tilly, *Coercion, Capital, and European States, AD 990–1992* (Cambridge: Blackwell, 1992); Barry Buzan and Richard Little, *International Systems in World History: Remaking the Study of International Relations* (Oxford: Oxford University Press, 2000); Brian M. Downing, *The Military Revolution and Political Change: Origins of Democracy and Autocracy in Early Modern Europe* (Princeton: Princeton University Press, 1992); Everett C. Dolman, *The Warrior State: How Military Organization Structures Politics* (New York: Palgrave, 2004); Robert O. Keohane and Joseph S. Nye Jr., *Power and Interdependence* (New York: Longman Publishing Group, 2001), page 20.

31. H. H. Gerth and C. Wright Mills, translators and editors, *From Max Weber: Essays in Sociology* (New York: Oxford University Press, 1946), pages 82–83; Bull, *The Anarchical Society*, pages 8–9; Robert I. Rotberg, "Failed States, Collapsed States, Weak States: Causes and Indicators," in Robert I. Rotberg, editor, *State Failure and State Weakness in a Time of Terror* (Washington: Brookings Institution and World Peace Foundation, 2003), page 3.

32. Robert Mandel, *Armies without States: The Privatization of Security* (Boulder: Lynne Rienner Publishers, 2002), page ix.

33. Confederation of Switzerland Department of Foreign Affairs and the International Committee of the Red Cross, *The Montreux Document on Pertinent International Legal Obligations and Good Practices for States related to Operations of Private Military and Security Companies during Armed Conflict*, UN Document A/63/467-S/2008/636 (Geneva: International Com-

mittee of the Red Cross, 2008), preface ¶ 9(a), available at http://www.eda.admin.ch/psc, accessed 5 May 2015.

34. Peter W. Singer, *Corporate Warriors: The Rise of the Privatized Military Industry* (Ithaca: Cornell University Press, 2003), page 46.

35. This is not to say that these companies are indiscreet and transparent, however.

36. However, PMSCs may facilitate the purchase or transfer of armaments. See Malcolm Hugh Patterson, "Private Military and Security Companies and the International Trade in Small Arms and Light Weapons," in Andrew T. H. Tan, editor, *The Global Arms Trade: A Handbook* (London: Routledge, 2014).

37. Singer, *Corporate Warriors*, pages 102–3, 120.

38. As the Montreux Document explains, "Article 47 of Protocol I additional to the 1949 Geneva Conventions, applicable in international armed conflicts, describes a mercenary as someone who: (1) is especially recruited in order to fight in an armed conflict; (2) in fact takes a direct part in hostilities; (3) is motivated essentially by the desire of private gain; (4) is neither a national of a party to the conflict nor a resident of territory controlled by a party to the conflict; (5) is not a member of the armed forces of a party to the conflict; (6) has not been sent by a State which is not a party to the armed conflict on official duty as a member of its armed forces. That definition excludes most PMSC personnel, most of whom are not contracted to fight in military operations. Many are nationals of one of the parties to the conflict. Moreover, it is difficult to prove the motivation of private gain; presumably, not all of them are thus motivated. Lastly, while some private contractors are reportedly very highly paid, it would be very difficult to verify if they receive a substantially higher wage than soldiers. This being said, PMSC employees do sometimes meet the conditions for definition as mercenaries. If that is the case, they are not entitled to combatant or prisoner-of-war status in an international armed conflict" (Montreux Document, page 40).

39. Singer, *Corporate Warriors*, page 92.

40. Singer, *Corporate Warriors*, page 95.

41. Singer, *Corporate Warriors*, page 97.

42. Adapted from Zeljko Branovic, *The Privatisation of Security in Failing States: A Quantitative Assessment*, Occasional Paper 24 (Geneva: Geneva Centre for the Democratic Control of Armed Forces, April 2011), page 21, table 5.

43. The Private Security Database was initiated and implemented under the umbrella of the "Privatization and Commercialization of Security" project of the Collaborative Research Center Berlin with financial support from the German Science Foundation/Deutsche Forschungsgemeinschaft (DFG). The dataset is described in Branovic, *The Privatisation of Security in Failing States*, and version 4 is available at the Data on Conflict and Security website, http://www.conflict-data.org/psd/Data_Download/index.html.

44. The sample includes the following states: Afghanistan, Albania, Algeria, Angola, Azerbaijan, Bosnia, Burundi, Cambodia, Colombia, Congo-Brazzaville, Congo-Kinshasa, Croatia, Ethiopia, Georgia, Guatemala, Guinea-Bissau, Iraq, Côte d'Ivoire, Lebanon, Liberia, Mozambique, Nepal, Nigeria, Peru, Philippines, Rwanda, Sierra Leone, Somalia, Sudan, Tajikistan, Uganda, and Yugoslavia (Serbia + Kosovo). See Branovic, *The Privatisation of Security in Failing States*, page 18, table 2.

45. Branovic, *The Privatisation of Security in Failing States*, pages 17–18, describes the coding rules for selecting the sample. It is important to note that the sample remains constant; one cannot see whether a state became more or less fragile during the period covered without additional data. Therefore determinations of the effect of PMSC involvement on any state's stability cannot be made.

46. Branovic, *The Privatisation of Security in Failing States*, page 19.

47. There were 621 instances of contracts, but these were consolidated into 580 cases of "contractual relationships" by combining those where multiple companies performed similar tasks.

48. United Nations, "Growth in United Nations Membership, 1945–Present," United Nations website, available at http://www.un.org/en/members/growth.shtml, accessed 18 October 2015.

49. One key aspect of the PMSC market that is not addressed by the PSD data is their use by strong and stable states in the course of their daily peacetime operation. Many of these support functions are not "inherently governmental tasks" and therefore pose fewer control issues for state principals. See Philip A. Odeen, chairman, *Report of the Defense Science Board Task Force on Outsourcing and Privatization* (Washington: Office of the Under Secretary of Defense for Acquisition and Technology, August 1996); John R. Luckey, Valerie Bailey Grasso, and Kate M. Manuel, *Inherently Governmental Functions and Department of Defense Operations: Background, Issues, and Options for Congress*, R40641 (Washington: Congressional Research Service, 15 June 2009).

50. Oldrich Bures, "Private Military Companies: A Second Best Peacekeeping Option?" *International Peacekeeping* 12, 4 (Winter 2005), page 538.

51. Of the 576 state-years covered in the data, states were unstable in 309 of them.

52. Anna Leander, "The Market for Force and Public Security: The Destabilizing Consequences of Private Military Companies," *Journal of Peace Research* 42, 5 (September 2005), page 612.

53. Singer, *Corporate Warriors*, pages 196–97.

54. On Colombia, see Pedro Ruz Gutierrez and E. A. Torriero, "U.S. Pilots Risk Their Lives in Colombia's Drug War," *Fort Lauderdale Sun Sentinel* (19 September 2000), available at http://articles.sun-sentinel.com/2000-09-19/news/0009190123_1_pilot-error-daredevil-pilots-colombia/2, accessed 19 October 2015; Eugene B. Smith, "The New Condottieri and US Policy: The Privatization of Conflict and Its Implications," *Parameters* (Winter 2002–2003), page 110; Jim Rochlin, "Plan Colombia and the Revolution in Military Affairs: The Demise of the FARC," *Review of International Studies* 37, 2 (April 2011); Anders Sømme Hammer, *The Control of Private Security Companies: A Study of the Relationship between the United States and Private Actors in Plan Colombia*, master's thesis (Oslo: University of Oslo, May 2006).

55. This figure is derived from figure 11 in Branovic, *The Privatisation of Security in Failing States*, page 33. In this part of his analysis, Branovic combined the PSD data with that of the Military Intervention dataset to determine when PMSC use by external clients was accompanied by their military forces. See Jeffrey Pickering and Emizet F. Kisigani, "The International Military Intervention Dataset: An Updated Resource for Conflict Scholars," *Journal of Peace Research* 46, 4 (July 2009), for details pertaining to the Military Intervention dataset.

56. As David Strachan-Morris discusses in chapter 5. Also see Dunigan, *Victory for Hire*, pages 52–76; Ulrich Petersohn, "The Effectiveness of Contracted Coalitions: Private Security Contractors in Iraq," *Armed Forces and Society* 39, 3 (July 2013).

57. Avant, *The Market for Force*, page 107.

58. Peter D. Feaver, "The Civil-Military Problematique: Huntington, Janowitz, and the Problem of Civilian Control," *Armed Forces and Society* 23, 2 (Winter 1996), pages 155–56.

59. Tilly, *Coercion, Capital, and European States*, page 19.

60. "The destructive and coercive nature of [the soldier's] particular attributes makes him the one force society has to come to terms with, to harness or bribe into public service" (Maury D. Feld, *The Structure of Violence: Armed Forces as Social Systems* [Beverly Hills: Sage, 1977], page 13).

61. Ronald Coase, "The Nature of the Firm," *Economica* 4, 16 (November 1937), pages 386–405.

62. Bengt Abrahamsson, *Military Professionalization and Political Power* (Beverly Hills: Sage, 1972), page 152; C. Wright Mills, *The Power Elite* (New York: Oxford University Press, 1959), chapter 8.

63. Samuel P. Huntington, *The Soldier and the State: The Theory and Politics of Civil-Military Relations* (Cambridge: Belknap Press of Harvard University Press, 1957), page 65.

64. Karl Demeter (Angus Malcolm, translator), *The German Officer-Corps in Society and State: 1650–1945* (New York: Frederick A. Praeger, 1965); Arnold Eisendorfer and Martin S. Bergmann, "The Factor of Maturity in Officer Selection," *Psychiatry* 9, 1 (1946); Ben S. Morris, "Officer Selection in the British Army, 1942–1945," *Occupational Psychology* 23, 4 (October 1949); Stanley B. Williams and Harold J. Leavitt, "Methods of Selecting Marine

Corps Officers," in George A. Kelley, editor, *New Methods in Applied Psychology* (College Park: University of Maryland Press, 1947); John W. Masland and Laurence I. Radway, *Soldiers and Scholars: Military Education and National Policy* (Princeton: Princeton University Press, 1957); George A. Kourvetaris and Betty A. Dobratz, "Social Recruitment and Political Orientations of the Officer Corps in a Comparative Perspective," *Pacific Sociological Review* (1973); John A. Fitzgerald, "Changing Patterns of Officer Recruitment at the US Naval Academy," *Armed Forces and Society* 8, 1 (Fall 1981); William P. Snyder, "Officer Recruitment for the All-Volunteer Force: Trends and Prospects," *Armed Forces and Society* 10, 3 (Spring 1984); Ian McAllister and Hugh Smith, "Selecting the Guardians: Recruitment and Military Values in the Australian Corps," *JPMS: Journal of Political and Military Sociology* 17, 1 (Summer 1989); Cathy Downes, *Special Trust and Confidence: The Making of an Officer* (New York: Routledge, 2013).

65. Sanford M. Dornbusch, "The Military Academy as an Assimilating Institution," *Social Forces* 33, 4 (May 1955); Corelli Barnett, "The Education of Military Elites," *Journal of Contemporary History* 2, 3 (July 1967); Bengt Abrahamsson, *Military Professionalization and Political Power* (Beverly Hills: Sage, 1972), page 60; John P. Lovell, "Professionalism and the Service Academies," *American Behavioral Scientist* 19, 5 (May/June 1976); Giuseppe Carforio, editor, *The European Cadet: Professional Socialisation in Military Academies—A Cross-national Study* (Baden-Baden: Nomos Verlagsgesellschaft, 1998); Karl W. Haltiner, "Athens versus Sparta: The New Missions and the Future of Military Education in Europe," in Harry Kirkels, Wim Klinkert, and Rene Moelker, editors, *NL ARMS: Netherlands Annual Review of Military Studies* (Breda: Netherlands Defence Academy, 2003); Randall Wakelam, "One Officer Factory: The Royal Military College and Officer Education since 1955," *Historical Studies in Education* 26, 1 (Spring 2014).

66. Abrahamsson, *Military Professionalization and Political Power*, pages 16–17. Also see Joseph L. Soeters, Alise Weibull, and Donna Winslow, "Military Culture," in Giuseppe Caforio, editor, *Handbook of the Sociology of the Military* (New York: Kluwer Academic, 2004).

67. Nathan Joseph and Nicholas Alex, "The Uniform: A Sociological Perspective," *American Journal of Sociology* 77, 4 (January 1972); Talcott Parsons, *The Social System* (New York: The Free Press, 1951); Robert K. Merton, *Social Theory and Social Structure* (New York: The Free Press, 1957); Neal Gross, Ward S. Mason, and Alexander W. McEachern, *Explorations in Role Analysis* (New York: Wiley, 1958); Peter J. Burke and Jan E. Stets, *Identity Theory* (Oxford: Oxford University Press, 2009); Michael A. Hogg, *The Social Psychology of Group Cohesiveness: From Attraction to Social Identity* (Washington Square: New York University Press, 1992).

68. Mills, *The Power Elite*, chapters 8–9; Jonathan Powell, "Determinants of the Attempting and Outcome of Coups d'État," *Journal of Conflict Resolution* 56, 6 (December 2012); John B. Londregan and Keith T. Poole, "Poverty, the Coup Trap, and the Seizure of Executive Power," *World Politics* 42, 2 (January 1990); Peter D. Feaver, *Armed Servants: Agency, Oversight, and Civil-Military Relations* (Cambridge: Harvard University Press, 2003), pages 10–11.

69. Eliot A. Cohen, *Supreme Command: Soldiers, Statesmen, and Leadership in Wartime* (New York: The Free Press, 2002); Deborah D. Avant, "Are the Reluctant Warriors Out of Control? Why the U.S. Military Is Averse to Responding to Post–Cold War Low-Level Threats," *Security Studies* 6, 2 (Winter 1996/1997); Deborah D. Avant, "Conflicting Indicators of 'Crisis' in American Civil-Military Relations," *Armed Forces and Society* 24, 3 (Spring 1998); Andrew J. Bacevich, *The New American Militarism: How Americans Are Seduced by War* (Cambridge: Oxford University Press, 2005); Richard K. Betts, *Soldiers, Statesmen, and Cold War Crises* (Cambridge: Harvard University Press, 1977); Richard K. Betts, "Are Civil-Military Relations Still a Problem?" in Suzanne C. Nielsen and Don M. Snider, editors, *American Civil-Military Relations: The Soldier and the State in a New Era* (Baltimore: Johns Hopkins University Press, 2009); Peter D. Feaver, "Civil-Military Relations," in Nelson W. Polsby, editor, *Annual Review of Political Science* 2 (1999); Peter D. Feaver, *Armed Servants: Agency, Oversight, and Civil-Military Relations* (Cambridge: Harvard University Press, 2003); Dale R. Herspring, *The Pentagon and the Presidency: Civil-Military Relations from FDR to George W. Bush* (Lawrence: University Press of Kansas, 2005); Kenneth W. Kemp and Charles Hudin, "Civil Supremacy over the Military: Its Nature and Limits," *Armed Forces and Society*

19, 1 (Fall 1992); Daniel Bessner and Eric Lorber, "Toward a Theory of Civil-Military Punishment," *Armed Forces and Society* 38, 4 (October 2012).

70. Kurt Lang, *Military Institutions and the Sociology of War: A Review of the Literature with Annotated Bibliography* (Beverly Hills: Sage, 1972), page 55.

71. Erving Goffman, "The Characteristics of Total Institutions," in *Symposium on Preventive and Social Psychiatry, Walter Reed Army Institute of Research, Washington, D.C. 15–17 April 1957* (Washington: Government Printing Office, 1958); Lewis A. Coser, *Greedy Institutions: Patterns of Undivided Commitment* (New York: The Free Press, 1974), page 6.

72. Robert D. Miewald, "Weberian Bureaucracy and the Military Model," *Public Administration Review* 30, 2 (March/April 1970); G. Dearborn Spindler, "The Military: A Systematic Analysis," *Social Forces* 27, 1 (October 1948), page 86.

73. Morris Janowitz, "Military Elites and the Study of War," *Conflict Resolution* 1, 1 (March 1957), page 14; Huntington, *The Soldier and the State*, pages 74–76.

74. Lang, *Military Institutions and the Sociology of War*, page 62; Guénaël Mettraux, *The Law of Command Responsibility* (New York: Oxford University Press, 2009).

75. William Winthrop, *Military Law and Precedents*, 2nd edition (Washington: Government Printing Office, 1920); Louis B. Nichols, "The Justice of Military Justice," *William and Mary Law Review* 12, 3 (1971); Edward F. Sherman, "Military Justice without Military Control," *Yale Law Review* 82, 7 (June 1973); Stephen S. Strickey, "'Anglo-American' Military Justice Systems and the Wave of Civilianization: Will Discipline Survive?" *Cambridge Journal of International and Comparative Law* 2, 4 (2013).

76. Bull, *The Anarchical Society*, page 19; Stephen D. Krasner, *Sovereignty: Organized Hypocrisy* (Princeton: Princeton University Press, 1999), page 47.

77. Karl Zemanek, "Armed Attack," in Rüdiger Wolfrum, director, *Max Planck Encyclopedia of Public International Law* (October 2013), available at http://opil.ouplaw.com/view/10.1093/law:epil/9780199231690/law-9780199231690-e241, accessed 1 November 2015.

78. Christian Henderson, "Non-state Actors and the Use of Force," in Math Noortmann, August Reinisch, and Cedric Ryngaert, editors, *Non-state Actors in International Law: Studies in International Law* (Oxford: Hart Publishing, 2015), page 77; Nicholas Tsagourias, "Non-state Actors and the Use of Force," in Jean d'Aspermont, editor, *Participants in the International Legal System: Multiple Perspectives on Non-state Actors in International Law* (Abington: Routledge, 2011).

79. *The Law of Armed Conflict: Basic Knowledge* (Geneva: International Committee of the Red Cross, June 2002), page 5-1.

80. Terry M. Moe, "The New Economics of Organization," *American Journal of Political Science* 28, 4 (November 1984), pages 754–55; Oliver E. Williamson, *Markets and Hierarchies* (New York: The Free Press, 1975).

81. Keith Hartley, "The All-Volunteer Force: An Economic Perspective," in Gwyn Harries-Jenkins, editor, *Recruitment to the All-Volunteer Force* (Fort Belvoir: US Army Institute for the Behavioral and Social Sciences, March 2001), page 42.

82. Diego Gambetta, "Inscrutable Markets," *Rationality and Society* 6, 3 (July 1994), page 354; Christopher Kinsey, *Corporate Soldiers and International Security: The Rise of Private Military Companies* (London: Routledge, 2006), page 158.

83. The ability to choose a quality agent will vary with the ability of the state to discriminate between the potential performance of agents, to select from among many, and to determine when their performance is more easily measured (Moe, "The New Economics of Organization," page 759).

84. Moe, "The New Economics of Organization," page 756.

85. Ian Douglas, "Fighting for Diamonds: Private Military Companies in Sierra Leone," in Jakkie Cilliers and Peggy Mason, editors, *Peace, Profit or Plunder? The Privatisation of Security in War-Torn African Societies* (Pretoria: Institute for Security Studies, 1999); Avant, *The Market for Force*, pages 95–98; Leander, "The Market for Force and Public Security"; Simon Chesterman and Chia Lehnardt, "Introduction," in Simon Chesterman and Chia Lehnardt, editors, *From Mercenaries to Market: The Rise and Regulation of Private Military Companies* (Oxford: Oxford University Press, 2007).

86. J. Eric Fredland, "Outsourcing Military Force: A Transactions Cost Perspective on the Role of Military Companies," *Defence and Peace Economics* 15, 3 (June 2004), page 216.
87. Moe, "The New Economics of Organization," page 755.
88. Cohn, "It Wasn't in My Contract," page 391.
89. Betts, "Are Civil-Military Relations Still a Problem?" page 14.
90. Lindsay P. Cohn, "It Wasn't in My Contract: Security Privatization and Civilian Control," *Armed Forces and Society* 37, 3 (July 2011), page 389.
91. Quoted in Fredland, "Outsourcing Military Force," page 211.
92. John Donahue, *The Privatization Decision: Public Ends, Private Means* (New York: Basic Books, 1989), page 42.
93. Ricks, *Fiasco*, page 370.
94. James Jay Carafano, *Private Sector, Public Wars* (Westport: Praeger Security International, 2008); Kinsey, *Private Contractors and the Reconstruction of Iraq*; Stanger, *One Nation under Contract*; Moshe Schwartz and Jennifer Church, *Department of Defense's Use of Contractors to Support Military Operations: Background, Analysis, and Issues for Congress*, CRS Report R43074 (Washington: Congressional Research Service, 17 May 2013); Laura A. Dickinson, *Outsourcing War and Peace: Preserving Public Values in a World of Privatized Foreign Affairs* (New Haven: Yale University Press, 2011). Furthermore, state regulation is the primary vehicle pursued by international mechanisms such as the Montreux Document, as we discuss later.
95. Kinsey, *Corporate Soldiers*, page 154.
96. For instance, when the United States Attorney announced the indictments of the six Blackwater employees in the Nisour Square incident, he said, "It bears emphasis that today's indictment is very narrow in its allegations. Six individual Blackwater guards have been charged with unjustified shootings on September 16, 2007, not the entire Blackwater organization in Baghdad" (quoted in Erik D. Prince, "How Blackwater Serves America," *Wall Street Journal* [16 December 2008], page 23). Although, even then, enforcement is rare: according to the Department of Justice, only 20 cases of wrongdoing were prosecuted under the Military Extraterritorial Jurisdiction Act between 2000 and 2014 (Charles Dunlap, "Civilianizing Military Justice? Sorry, It Can't—and Shouldn't—Work," *War on the Rocks* [8 October 2015]). Also see Dickinson, *Outsourcing War and Peace*, chapter 4.
97. Singer, *Corporate Warriors*, pages 101–4, 119–23; David Isenberg, *Soldiers of Fortune Ltd.: A Profile of Today's Private Sector Corporate Mercenary Firms* (Washington: Center for Defense Information, November 1997), *passim*.
98. Katherine E. McCoy, "Beyond Civil-Military Relations: Reflections on Civilian Control of a Private, Multinational Workforce," *Armed Forces and Society* 36, 4 (July 2010), page 679.
99. David Shearer, *Private Armies and Military Intervention*, Adelphi Paper 316 (Oxford: Oxford University Press, 1998), page 41.
100. Singer, *Corporate Warriors*, page 120.
101. Prince, "How Blackwater Serves America," page 23.
102. Petersohn, "The Effectiveness of Contracted Coalitions," page 471. This claim does not extend to third country nationals or host nation nationals, however, and they constitute the vast majority of the PMSC workforce.
103. Petersohn, "The Effectiveness of Contracted Coalitions," page 469.
104. Chris Hendershot, "The Commercial Military and Security Services Industry: A Canadian Consideration?" in Rosalind Warner, editor, *Unsettled Balance: Ethics, Security, and Canada's International Relations* (Vancouver: University of British Columbia Press, 2015), page 91.
105. Sebastian Drutschmann, "Informal Regulation: An Economic Perspective on the Private Security Industry," in Thomas Jäger and Gerhard Kümmel, editors, *Private Military and Security Companies: Chances, Problems, Pitfalls and Prospects* (Wiesbaden: VS Verlag für Sozialwissenschaften, 2007), page 454.
106. John Hacket, *The Profession of Arms* (London: Times Publishing Company, 1963), page 63. Also see Huntington, *The Soldier and the State*, page 15.
107. According to the US Bureau of Labor 1,627 contractors were killed in Iraq between January 2001 and June 2015, with another 18,392 sustaining serious injuries, defined as requir-

ing four or more days' absence from work. See United States Department of Labor, Office of Workers' Compensation Programs, "Defense Base Act Case Summary by Nation," United States Department of Labor website, available at http://www.dol.gov/owcp/dlhwc/dbaallnation.htm, accessed 24 September 2015. Also see Steven L. Schooner, "Why Contractor Fatalities Matter," *Parameters* 38, 3 (Autumn 2008); Steven L. Schooner and Collin D. Swan, "Contractors and the Ultimate Sacrifice," *Service Contractor* (September 2010); Molly Dunigan, Carrie M. Farmer, Rachel M. Burns, Alison Hawks, and Clause Messan Setodji, *Out of the Shadows: The Health and Well-Being of Private Contractors Working in Conflict Environments* (Santa Monica: RAND Corporation, 2013).

108. Deane-Peter Baker, "To Whom Does a Private Military Commander Owe Allegiance?" in Paolo Tripodi and Jessica Wolfendale, editors, *New Wars and New Soldiers: Military Ethics in the Contemporary World* (Surrey: Ashgate, 2011), page 197.

109. Fitzsimmons, *Private Security Companies during the Iraq War*, page 4.

110. Daniel Ward, "Assessing Force Protection Risk," *Military Review* 77, 6 (November–December 1997); Jeffrey Record, "Force-Protection Fetishism: Sources, Consequences, and (?) Solutions," *Aerospace Power Journal* (Summer 2000); Jeffrey Record, "Collapsed Countries, Casualty Dread, and the New American Way of War," *Parameters* 32, 2 (Summer 2002); Paul Cornish, "Myth and Reality: US and UK Approaches to Casualty Aversion and Force Protection," *Defence Studies* 3, 2 (May 2003); Hugh Smith, "What Costs Will Democracies Bear? A Review of Popular Theories of Casualty Aversion," *Armed Forces and Society* 31, 4 (Summer 2005).

111. Sarah Sewall, "Modernizing US Counterinsurgency Practice: Rethinking Risk and Developing a National Strategy," *Military Review* 86, 5 (September–October 2006); John A. Nagl, James F. Amos, Sarah Sewall, and David H. Petraeus, *The US Army/Marine Corps Counterinsurgency Field Manual*, number 3-24 (Chicago: University of Chicago Press, 2008); David Kilcullen, *Counterinsurgency* (New York: Oxford University Press, 2010); Stanley A. McChrystal, "ISAF Commander's Counterinsurgency Guidance" (Kabul: Headquarters International Security Assistance Force, 2009); Stanley A. McChrystal, "Tactical Directive" (Kabul: Headquarters International Security Assistance Force, 2 July 2009).

112. Sarah Percy, *Regulating the Private Security Industry*, Adelphi Paper 384 (London: Routledge, 2006), page 17; Caroline Holmqvist, *Private Security Companies: The Case for Regulation*, Policy Paper 9 (Stockholm: Stockholm Institute for Peace Research, 2005), page 29; Steven J. Zamparelli, "Contractors on the Battlefield: What Have We Signed Up For?" *Air Force Journal of Logistics* 23, 3 (Fall 1999), page 18.

113. Avant, *The Market for Force*, page 261.

114. Kinsey, *Corporate Soldiers*, page 155; Dunigan, *Victory for Hire*, pages 63–68; Sarah K. Cotton, Ulrich Petersohn, Molly Dunigan, Q. Burkhart, Megan Zander-Cotugno, Edward O'Connell, and Michael Webber, *Hired Guns: Views about Armed Contractors in Operation Iraqi Freedom* (Santa Monica: RAND Corporation, 2010), pages 21–24.

NOTES TO "VICTORY FOR HIRE" BOX

1. Phillippe C. Schmitter, "Liberation by Golpe: Retrospective Thoughts on the Demise of Authoritarian Rule in Portugal," *Armed Forces and Society* 2, 1 (November 1975); Juan J. Linz and Alfred Stepan, *Problems of Democratic Transition and Consolidation: Southern Europe, South America, and Post-Communist Europe* (Baltimore: Johns Hopkins University Press, 1996), pages 118–23; Franz-Wilhelm Heimer, *The Decolonization Conflict in Angola, 1974–76: An Essay in Political Sociology* (Geneva: Institut Universitaire de Hautes Études Internationales, 1979); W. G. Clarence-Smith, "Review Article: Class Structure and Class Struggles in Angola in the 1970s," *Journal of Southern African Studies* 7, 1 (October 1980).

2. In "Angola . . . there was no pretence at a dignified surrender of power. The Portuguese simply transferred sovereignty 'to the Angolan people' and left local nationalists and foreign interventionists to slog it out" (Stuart A. Notholt, "Review: *The Decolonization of Portuguese Africa: Metropolitan Revolution and the Dissolution of Empire* by Norrie MacQueen; *Mozam-*

bique since Independence: Confronting Leviathan by Margaret Hall, Tom Young," *African Affairs* 97, 387 [April 1998], page 277).

3. William J. Durch, "The Cuban Military in Africa and the Middle East: From Algeria to Angola," *Studies in Comparative Communism* 11, 1–2 (Spring–Summer 1978); M. R. Bhagavan, *Angola's Political Economy, 1975–1985* (Uppsala: Scandinavian Institute of African Studies, 1986), page 7; Mark Webber, "Soviet Policy in Sub-Saharan Africa: The Final Phase," *Journal of Modern African Studies* 30, 1 (March 1992); Edward George, *The Cuban Intervention in Angola, 1965–1991: From Che Guevara to Cuito Cuanavale* (London: Frank Cass, 2005); Piero Gleijeses, "Moscow's Proxy? Cuba and Africa 1975–1988," *Journal of Cold War Studies* 8, 2 (Spring 2006).

4. Prexy Nesbitt, "Terminators, Crusaders and Gladiators: Western (Public and Private) Support for RENAMO and UNITA," *Review of African Political Economy* 15, 43 (1988); George V. Wright, "US Foreign Policy and Destabilisation in Southern Africa," *Review of African Political Economy* 16, 45–46 (1989); William Minter, "The US and the War in Angola," *Review of African Political Economy* 18, 50 (1991); Inge Tvedten, "U.S. Policy towards Angola since 1975," *Journal of Modern African Studies* 30, 1 (March 1992); Martin Meredith, *The Fate of Africa: From the Hopes of Freedom to the Heart of Despair—A History of Fifty Years of Independence* (New York: PublicAffairs, 2005), page 316.

5. Inge Tvedten, *Angola: Struggle for Peace and Reconstruction* (Boulder: Westview, 1997), pages 38–39; W. Martin James III, *A Political History of the Civil War in Angola: 1974–1990* (New Brunswick: Transaction Publishers, 2011).

6. Anthony W. Pereira, "The Neglected Tragedy: The Return to War in Angola, 1992–93," *Journal of Modern African Studies* 32, 1 (March 1994).

7. David Shearer, *Private Armies and Military Intervention*, Adelphi Paper 316 (London: Institute of Strategic Studies, 1998), page 46; Peter W. Singer, *Corporate Warriors: The Rise of the Privatized Military Industry* (Ithaca: Cornell University Press, 2003), page 108; Herbert M. Howe, "Private Security Forces and African Stability: The Case of Executive Outcomes," *Journal of Modern African Studies* 36, 2 (June 1998), page 311.

8. Slightly different accounts of the arrangement can be found in Shearer, *Private Armies*, page 46; David Isenberg, *Soldiers of Fortune Ltd.: A Profile of Today's Private Sector Corporate Mercenary Firms* (Washington: Center for Defense Information, November 1997), page 5; Khareen Pech, "Executive Outcomes: A Corporate Conquest," in Jakkie Cilliers and Peggy Mason, editors, *Peace, Profit or Plunder? The Privatisation of Security in War-Torn African Societies* (Pretoria: Institute for Security Studies, 1999), pages 83–86; Howe, "Private Security Forces and African Stability," pages 311–12; Singer, *Corporate Warriors*, page 108.

9. Singer, *Corporate Warriors*, page 108.

10. Isenberg, *Soldiers of Fortune Ltd.*, page 5; Howe, "Private Security Forces and African Stability," page 312; Singer, *Corporate Warriors*, page 107.

11. Singer, *Corporate Warriors*, page 106.

12. Isenberg, *Soldiers of Fortune Ltd.*, page 5; Singer, *Corporate Warriors*, page 109.

13. Shearer, *Private Armies*, page 48; Singer, *Corporate Warriors*, page 110.

14. Singer, *Corporate Warriors*, page 108.

15. Isenberg, *Soldiers of Fortune Ltd.*, pages 5–6; Singer, *Corporate Warriors*, pages 110–15; Avant, *The Market For Force*, pages 82–92.

16. Shearer, *Private Armies*; David Shearer, "Outsourcing War," *Foreign Policy* (Fall 1998), pages 75–76; Doug Brooks, "Write a Cheque, End a War," *Conflict Trends* 6 (July 2000); Doug Brooks, "Messiahs or Mercenaries? The Future of International Private Military Services," *International Peacekeeping* 7, 4 (Winter 2000); Christopher Spearin, "Private Security Companies and Humanitarians: A Corporate Solution to Securing Humanitarian Spaces?" *International Peacekeeping* 8, 1 (Spring 2001); United Kingdom House of Commons Foreign Affairs Committee, *Private Military Companies. Ninth Report of Session 2001–02. Report, Together with Proceedings of the Committee, Minutes of Evidence and Appendices*, HC 922 (London: The Stationery Office, 1 August 2002); Oldrich Bures, "Private Military Companies: A Second Best Peacekeeping Option?" *International Peacekeeping* 12, 4 (Winter 2005).

NOTES TO "TO END A WAR" BOX

1. Sabrina Petra Ramet, "Slovenia's Road to Democracy," *Europe-Asia Studies* 45, 5 (1993); Anton Bebler, "Slovenia's Smooth Transition," *Journal of Democracy* 13, 1 (January 2002).

2. John Ashbrook and Spencer D. Bakich, "Storming to Partition: Croatia, the United States, and Krajina in the Yugoslav War," *Small Wars and Insurgencies* 21, 4 (December 2010), pages 538–40.

3. Ashbrook and Bakich, "Storming to Partition," page 540; Mile Bjelaja and Ozren Žunec, "The War in Croatia, 1991–1995," in Charles W. Ingrao and Thomas Allan Emmert, editors, *Confronting the Yugoslav Controversies: A Scholars' Initiative* (West Lafayette, Indiana: Purdue University Press, 2009), pages 167–68.

4. Roland Rich, "Recognition of States: The Collapse of Yugoslavia and the Soviet Union," *European Journal of International Law* 36, 1 (1993); Peter Viggo Jakobsen, "Myth-Making and Germany's Unilateral Recognition of Croatia and Slovenia," *European Security* 4, 3 (Autumn 1995); Beverly Crawford, "German Foreign Policy and European Political Cooperation: The Diplomatic Recognition of Croatia in 1991," *German Politics and Society* 13, 2 (Summer 1995); Beverly Crawford, "Explaining Defection from International Cooperation: Germany's Unilateral Recognition of Croatia," *World Politics* 48, 4 (July 1996); David H. Bearce, "Institutional Breakdown and International Cooperation: The European Agreement to Recognize Croatia and Slovenia," *European Journal of International Relations* 8, 4 (December 2002); Bjelaja and Žunec, "The War in Croatia, 1991–1995," pages 167–69.

5. Dusko Doder, "Yugoslavia: New War, Old Hatreds," *Foreign Policy* 91 (Summer 1993), pages 18–19; Ashbrook and Bakich, "Storming to Partition," page 541.

6. Ashbrook and Bakich, "Storming to Partition," page 541. Of course, the war resulted from a complex of causes. See Laura Silber and Allan Little, *Yugoslavia: Death of a Nation* (New York: Penguin, 1997); Misha Glenny, *The Fall of Yugoslavia: The Third Balkan War*, 3rd revised edition (New York: Penguin, 1996); Susan L. Woodward, *Balkan Tragedy: Chaos and Dissolution after the Cold War* (Washington: Brookings Institution Press, 1995).

7. Madeleine Albright with Bill Woodward, *Madam Secretary: A Memoir* (New York: Miramax Books, 2003), page 226; Kenneth I. Juster, "Discussant," in Meena Bose and Rosanna Perotti, editors, *From Cold War to New World Order: The Foreign Policy of George H. W. Bush* (Westport: Greenwood Press, 2002), pages 299–300.

8. Ashbrook and Bakich, "Storming to Partition," pages 542–44; Silber and Little, *Yugoslavia*, pages 322–23; Molly Dunigan, *Victory for Hire: Private Security Companies' Impact on Military Effectiveness* (Palo Alto: Stanford University Press, 2011), page 93. "US policy, at least since late 1993, appears to have been oriented consistently towards shifting the regional balance of power in favor of Croatia and the Bosnian government" (Karl Mueller, "The Demise of Yugoslavia and the Destruction of Bosnia: Strategic Causes, Effects, and Responses," in Robert C. Owen, editor, *Deliberate Force: A Case Study in Effective Air Campaigning. Final Report of the Air University Balkans Air Campaign Study* [Maxwell Air Force Base: Air University Press, January 2000], page 28).

9. Deborah D. Avant, *The Market for Force: The Consequences of Privatizing Security* (Cambridge: Cambridge University Press, 2005), page 101. "As it stands now [in early 1994], the HV [Hrvatska Vojska, or Croatian Armed Forces] would not be able to wage the offensive operations necessary to liberate its territory and crush the Serbian (Croatian Serbs) insurgency. It is also questionable whether or not the HV would be capable of effective defensive operations in response to combined Serbian forces from Croatia and Bosnia and Herzegovina were they to wage an all-out offensive" (Ozren Zunec, "Democracy in the 'Fog of War': Civil-Military Relations in Croatia," in Constantine P. Danopoulos and Daniel Zirker, editors, *Civil-Military Relations in the Soviet and Yugoslav Successor States* [Boulder: Westview, 1996], page 222).

10. Established by United Nations Security Council Resolution 713 of 25 September 1991. As Avant argues, "given the awkward nature of sending U.S. military assistance to Croatia during a U.N. arms embargo, a private contract between the Croatian government and MPRI

allowed U.S. expertise to flow to Croatia without direct U.S. government involvement" (Avant, *The Market for Force*, page 104).

11. Ashbrook and Bakich, "Storming to Partition," page 547.

12. Roger Cohen, "U.S. Cooling Ties to Croatia after Winking at Its Buildup," *New York Times* (28 October 1995); Jakkie Cilliers and Ian Douglas, "The Military as Business: Military Professional Resources, Incorporated," in Jakkie Cilliers and Peggy Mason, editors, *Peace, Profit and Plunder? The Privatisation of Security in War-Torn Societies* (Pretoria: Institute for Security Studies, 1999), pages 114–15.

13. Dunigan, *Victory for Hire*, page 93.

14. Singer, *Corporate Warriors*, pages 125–26.

15. MPRI vice president and former director of the Defense Intelligence Agency Lieutenant General (retired) Ed Soyster stated, "One, we don't teach in the battlefield skills. We do that in other places. We didn't, we didn't teach that in Croatia. That's not what we were asked to do. . . . And as a contractor you do what the contract says. We were not licensed to do that, and the Croatians never asked us to do that" (quoted in David Isenberg, "MPRI Couldn't Read Minds: Let's Sue Them," *Huffington Post* [19 August 2010]).

16. Ashbrook and Bakich, "Storming to Partition," page 547.

17. Jan Willem Honig and Norbert Both, *Srebrenica: Record of a War Crime* (New York: Penguin, 1997), pages 141–59; Derek H. Chollet, *The Road to the Dayton Accords: A Study of American Statecraft* (New York: Palgrave Macmillan, 2005), pages 1–2.

18. Frederick H. Fleitz, *Peacekeeping Fiascoes of the 1990s: Causes, Solutions, and U.S. Interests* (Westport: Praeger, 2002), pages 141–43; Tracy Wilkinson, "U.N. Troops Held as Human Shield: Bosnia—Ukrainian Peacekeepers in Zepa 'Safe Area' Detained by Serbs to Ward off NATO Air Strikes. Rebel Advance Slows as Government Soldiers Strongly Resist," *Los Angeles Times* (18 July 1995).

19. United Nations International Criminal Tribunal for the Former Yugoslavia, "The Conflicts," International Criminal Tribunal for the Former Yugoslavia website, available at http://www.icty.org/sid/322, accessed 6 October 2015; Honig and Both, *Srebrenica*, pages 48–67; W. R. Smyser, *The Humanitarian Conscience: Caring for Others in the Age of Terror* (New York: Palgrave Macmillan, 2003), page 144; Kirsten Nakjavani Bookmiller, *The United Nations* (New York: Chelsea House, 2008), page 81; Christopher Paul, Colin P. Clarke, and Beth Grill, *Victory Has a Thousand Fathers: Sources of Success in Counterinsurgency* (Santa Monica: RAND Corporation, 2010); Marlise Simons, "Mladic Arrives in the Hague," *New York Times* (31 May 2011).

20. Mueller, "The Demise of Yugoslavia," page 27.

21. Jutta Paczulla, "The Long, Difficult Road to Dayton: Peace Efforts in Bosnia-Herzegovina," *International Journal* 60, 1 (Winter 2004–2005), page 261.

22. Mark C. McLaughlin, "Assessing the Effectiveness of Deliberate Force: Harnessing the Political-Military Connection," in Owen, *Deliberate Force*, page 193.

23. Avant, *The Market for Force*, page 103.

24. Richard Holbrooke, *To End a War* (New York: Random House, 1998), page 73.

25. Ivo H. Daalder, *Getting to Dayton: The Making of America's Bosnia Policy* (Washington: Brookings Institution, 2000), page 173.

26. Mueller, "The Demise of Yugoslavia," page 27.

27. Ashbrook and Bakich, "Storming to Partition," page 549.

28. Silber and Little, *Yugoslavia*, page 357.

29. Silber and Little, *Yugoslavia*, page 357. Singer misidentifies Colonel Leslie as a British officer (Singer, *Corporate Warriors*, page 127).

30. "Croatian Atrocities Being Forgotten," *CBC Report* (21 July 2003), available at http://www.globalresearch.ca/articles/CHO307D.html, accessed 6 October 2015.

31. Ken Silverstein and Daniel Burton-Rose, *Private Warriors* (New York: Verso, 2000), page 171.

32. Singer, *Corporate Warriors*, page 278, note 10.

33. MPRI vice president Harry E. "Soyster says that MPRI, like the U.S. government, knew the attack on the Krajina would take place and that perhaps half a dozen officers who graduated from its training seminars took part in the operation. Otherwise, he insists, the

company played no role in the Krajina campaign. 'It's impossible, no matter how good you are, to turn around an army in a few months,' he says. 'But it's a great myth. It's good for our business'" (Ken Silverstein, "Mercenary, Inc?" *Washington Business Forward* [26 April 2001]).

34. Tim Ripley and Paul Beaver, "Analysis: Operation Storm," *Jane's Sentinel: The Balkans Newsletter* 2, 8 (no date), pages 2–3; Roderick de Normann, "Operation Storm: Attack on the Krajina," *Jane's Intelligence Review* (November 1995), pages 495–98; David Halberstam, *War in a Time of Peace: Bush, Clinton, and the Generals* (New York: Scribner, 2001), pages 335–36; Sabrina P. Ramet, *The Three Yugoslavias: State-Building and Legitimation, 1918–2005* (Indiana University Press, 2006), pages 453–54.

35. Singer, *Corporate Warriors*, page 126.

36. "Whether MPRI violated the terms of the United Nations arms embargo is a murky issue" (Matthew J. Gaul, "Regulating the New Privateers: Private Military Service Contracting and the Modern Marque and Reprisal Clause," *Loyola of Los Angeles Law Review* 31, 4 [June 1998], page 1490). On the embargo, see Mark Bromley, *United Nations Arms Embargoes: Their Impact on Arms Flows and Target Behavior. Case Study: Former Yugoslavia, 1991–96* (Stockholm: Stockholm International Peace Research Institute, 2007).

Chapter Two

Mercenaries or Legitimate Actors?

South African Regulation of PMSCs

Shannon Bosch, Marelie Maritz,
and Matthew Kimble

South Africa has played a key role in the development and regulation of the marketplace for private military and security company (PMSC) services. The South African apartheid-era military was large, well trained, highly motivated, and experienced in nonconventional conflicts.[1] The transition from the apartheid regime required "the integration of the old, apartheid-era South African Defence Force (SADF) with the former guerrilla armies of the African National Congress (ANC) and the Pan-Africanist Congress (PAC), as well as the armed forces of each of the four 'homelands' (Transkei, Ciskei, Venda, and Bophuthatswana)."[2] This was facilitated by a largely Afrikaner officer corps with "a tradition of commitment to apartheid."[3] While those who remained went to great lengths to demonstrate their allegiance "to South Africa's duly constituted, ANC-led government," many left after "what they saw as rough treatment by the South African transitional government," who saw their service in "the former regime's dirty wars . . . [as] a source of embarrassment."[4] Indeed, key units that specialized in low-intensity conflict were summarily disbanded.[5] These formed a pool of highly skilled former military personnel who constituted the nucleus for a new type of military actor: PMSCs.[6]

Almost overnight, South Africa became a major home to companies that offered professional military and security services in ongoing African conflicts. Indeed, the prototypical PMSC, Executive Outcomes (EO), was founded by former South African special forces and its leadership saw ample opportunities to market their skills to the many fragile governments in Africa—many of whom they had actively opposed during their service in the South African military. In its heyday, Executive Outcomes provided a wide range of services, including training African government forces, clearing mines, medical and welfare services, and rebuilding infrastructure. Its services contributed significantly to the stabilization of Angola in 1994 and Sierra Leone in 1996.[7] It was a profitable business, worth $20 million–$100 million per annum.[8]

Yet the existence of a well-organized, well-trained, and well-equipped group of military personnel that had formerly opposed the men and women of the new South African government posed a dilemma. Would they one day oppose the government? Many feared that these "unemployed upholders of the old order could derail political reforms and subsequent majority rule."[9] Could they be co-opted to serve as an adjunct to, or enabler of, the state's other military, security, and foreign policy institutions? Or would their very existence indicate an inability on the part of the government to secure a monopoly over the legitimate use of force within the state's territory?

Upon taking office in April 1994, the ANC-led National Unity Government had to consider such questions for both domestic and international reasons. Domestically, PMSCs could be seen as providing disaffected former military personnel with a productive outlet for their skills and talents where they were less likely to ferment trouble during the period of consolidation and reconciliation.[10] On the other hand, they could also be seen as undermining the state at the very time that it was struggling to demonstrate the effectiveness and professionalism of the police and military. Indeed, the "South African Defence Force (SADF) regard[ed] the loss of trained personnel [to Executive Outcomes], pilots especially, as crude poaching" that undermined their quality and effectiveness.[11]

Internationally, their leadership position in southern Africa influenced the ANC-led government's answers. African states had endured the activities of mercenaries for decades and had acted to prohibit them through the Organization of African Unity Convention for the Elimination of Mercenaries in Africa, the creation of Article 47 of Protocol I additional to the Geneva Conventions, and the United Nations International Convention against the Recruitment, Use, Financing, and Training of Mercenaries.[12] Although previous mercenaries had proven generally incompetent and ineffective at achieving their goals,[13] Executive Outcomes' 1993 feat capturing the oil facilities in Soyo Angola from UNITA rebels with a force of 80 men astonished observers and "sent shockwaves around the region."[14] Furthermore, that these men were former SADF personnel who had previously fought against the Angolan government and alongside UNITA emphasized their mercenary character in "providing military services for hire to the highest bidder."[15] Such actors "stood in direct opposition to the great project of self-determination" in Africa, "not only because they often literally fought against it, but also because the idea of fighting for money was disturbing in an environment where the other players were deeply motivated by a belief in national liberation."[16]

These actors could also taint the new South African government and reduce its symbolic and actual power. Not only did they represent "exactly the phenomenon newly independent states were fighting against,"[17] but they could also be seen as an instrument of South African imperialism. The previous regime had engaged its special operations forces to undermine the stability of many of these states, assassinate opponents of apartheid abroad, and commit atrocities.[18] Many of these personnel formed the leadership and core of the new South African PMSCs.[19] If the ANC-led South African government permitted these businesses to incorporate in South Africa, to operate from its territory, and to recruit their personnel from among South African citizens, then it could be seen as complicit in the previous regime's policies and damage its credibility among its fellow African states. Indeed, that the largest and most visible clients of Executive Outcomes were the governments of Angola and Sierra Leone—allies of the ANC-led government—was not seen as a happy coincidence by some observers.[20] Rather, there was speculation that the services of Executive Outcomes were coordinated with the government—an allegation that it vehemently denied.[21] Furthermore, the activities of these PMSCs began to attract the attention of the United Nations (UN) special rapporteur for the Working Group on the use of mercenaries as a means of violating human rights and impeding the exercise of the right of peoples to self-determination.[22] The special rapporteur, inter alia, raised questions about their influence and particularly their access to the natural resources in Angola and diamond fields in Sierra Leone as partial payment for their service.[23] Together, these domestic and international factors reduced the enthusiasm that the ANC-led government felt for the new and innovative private security actors in its midst.

These domestic and international factors led South Africa to take a unique approach to the regulation of PMSCs. Rather than treat these new entities as legitimate providers of security, whose behavior was to be regulated by the state, the ANC-led government chose to treat PMSCs and their employees as akin to mercenaries and effectively moved to prohibit them and their activities. Yet the government demonstrated an inability to enforce these prohibitions in practice. In the following sections we address how the South African government has sought to regulate the industry, the government's motivations for adopting a very restrictive approach, and the impact felt by South African nationals and corporations involved in the private security industry. We conclude by discussing how the South African approach demonstrates the difficulties that one state, even a key one, can have enforcing its will upon nonstate actors if its approach is out of step with the prevalent trends in the international community.

SOUTH AFRICA'S APPROACH

In the 1990s, the new South African government faced a growing number of PMSCs whose incomes, reputation for effectiveness, and slick corporate identities differentiated them and their services from those of traditional mercenaries.[24] These new actors emphasized their ability to act as "stabilizing forces"[25] for weak and fragile governments in the region to gain legitimacy and win lucrative contracts from governments as well as "publicly listed companies."[26] Against this effort stood the political realities of their services. "The decision to intervene and to take sides in an armed conflict is a political one, whether it is made by an international organization, a regional organization, a coalition of states, or a single state. When private individuals and companies are allowed to make such decisions, the concept of international law loses all meaning," argued two analysts for the South African Institute for Security Studies.[27] They reflected the interest of the government in establishing a legal regime to regulate and control this burgeoning industry before it caused irreparable damage to South Africa's interests. This regime has had three phases: the prohibition on members of the South African military from engaging in "mercenary" activity under the Defence Act of 1957, the extension of this prohibition to all South African civilians and entities except by explicit approval under the Foreign Military Assistance Act of 1998 (FMA) and the Prohibition of Mercenary Activities Act of 2006 (PMA), and the extension of this regulation to all forms of organized conflict behavior by South African civilians under a proposed 2010 amendment to the South African Citizenship Act of 1995.

Prior to 1998 and the promulgation of the FMA, members and auxiliary members of the South African Defence Forces were prohibited under section 121A of the Defence Act 44 of 1957 from serving as mercenaries, although the act itself did not define the term.[28] Section 121A prohibits these individuals from encouraging others or "render[ing] services as a mercenary." The act imposed penalties of a fine not exceeding 10,000 SA Rands, imprisonment for a maximum of five years, or both. Moreover a court vested with penal jurisdiction was authorized to try such an offense even though the act that constituted the offense was committed outside the Republic of South Africa, although there are no reported cases of any such prosecutions.[29]

The Defence Act's focus on SADF members and their reserve staff indicates that prior to 1994 the apartheid government seldom had to deal with South African citizens rushing to take up mercenary careers. That all changed in 1994, when special operations units were summarily disbanded[30] and a large cohort of white, highly skilled former military personnel found themselves without an employment future in South Africa.[31] One of the primary and urgent objectives of the FMA was to extend this prohibition against mercenarism beyond the membership of the SADF to all South

African civilians.[32] The FMA is also constitutionally mandated in terms of section 198(b) of the South African Constitution Act 200 of 1993, which states: "The resolve to live in peace and harmony precludes any South African citizen from participating in armed conflict, nationally or internationally, except as provided for in terms of the Constitution or national legislation."[33]

THE REGULATION OF FOREIGN MILITARY ASSISTANCE ACT OF 1998

The FMA was drafted at a time when the South African private military and security industry was experiencing a boom, with lucrative contracts from the governments of Angola, the Central African Republic, Rwanda, and Sierra Leone, as well as mining companies and a variety of international nongovernmental organizations (NGOs) operating in these states.[34] The contracts were to provide troops, intelligence, advice, training, "operational support, logistics support, site security and crime prevention services."[35] Initially there was speculation that a post-apartheid ANC government might award newly established local PMSCs contracts for similar services, and Executive Outcomes is alleged to have even been offered a contract to train the armed branch of the ANC, "Umkhonto weSizwe," as "a bridging exercise."[36] However, the post-apartheid government had good reason to be suspicious of these predominantly white, Afrikaner men who had been trained to fight the ANC and who now offered their services. The only contracts that PMSCs secured on South African soil were from "private citizens and businesses."[37] South African PMSCs looked instead to foreign governments for contracts.[38]

The FMA entered into force in 1998. It was the first and most direct piece of domestic legislation of its type in the world,[39] and it is unapologetically hard-line and couched in "anti-mercenary" rhetoric.[40] Broadly speaking the FMA has two functions: 1) to ban mercenary activity, and 2) to regulate military assistance provided by South African citizens outside of South Africa. The FMA is activated by the declaration of an armed conflict.[41]

The FMA defines "prohibited activities" in section 2 as "recruitment, use, training or financing of mercenary activities," and then goes on to define "mercenary activities" as the "direct participation as a combatant in armed conflict for private gain."[42]

The FMA goes further in section 3 to prohibit the rendering of any "foreign military assistance" without prior authorization from the National Conventional Arms Control Committee (NCACC)—a body established by the FMA. The FMA defines "foreign military assistance" as "military services or military-related services, or any attempt, encouragement, incitement or solicitation to render such services, in the form of":

a. military assistance to a party to the armed conflict by means of—

   i. advice or training;
   ii. personnel, financial, logistical, intelligence or operational support;
   iii. personnel recruitment;
   iv. medical or para-medical services; or
   v. procurement of equipment;

b. security services for the protection of individuals involved in armed conflict or their property;
c. any action aimed at overthrowing a government or undermining the constitutional order, sovereignty or territorial integrity of a state;
d. any other action that has the result of furthering the military interests of a party to the armed conflict,
e. but not humanitarian or civilian activities aimed at relieving the plight of civilians in an area of armed conflict.

This definition includes within its ambit a range of activities traditionally undertaken by PMSCs,[43] and requires all PMSCs to first gain NCACC authorization to offer "military assistance" before entering into any contract to provide such services.[44] Once the minister of defense has granted such authorization, on the recommendation of the NCACC, each subsequent contract that the PMSC concludes must be authorized by the NCACC.[45] The NCACC has the ability to grant or reject authorization, to set conditions for each application to provide military assistance, and, in terms of sections 4(3) and 5(3), to "at any time withdraw or amend any authorisation so granted." Section 7 of the legislation lists several bases upon which the NCACC must refuse an application to offer foreign military assistance:

1. An authorisation or approval in terms of sections 4 and 5 may not be granted if it would—

   a. be in conflict with the Republic's obligations in terms of international law;
   b. result in the infringement of human rights and fundamental freedoms in the territory in which the foreign military assistance is to be rendered;
   c. endanger the peace by introducing destabilising military capabilities into the region where the assistance is to be, or is likely to be, rendered or would otherwise contribute to re-

gional instability and would negatively influence the balance of power in such region;
d. support or encourage terrorism in any manner;
e. contribute to the escalation of regional conflicts;
f. prejudice the Republic's national or international interests;
g. be unacceptable for any other reason.

Any person guilty of rendering foreign military assistance without the necessary authorization from the NCACC, or who fails to observe the conditions attached to such authorization, will be liable for a prison term and/or a fine.[46]

Right from the outset the definitions used in the FMA reveal that the drafters clearly had Executive Outcomes and its personnel in mind.[47] As Deborah Avant comments, "both PSCs and many government officials agreed that the Act's intent was to de-legitimize private security and put companies like Executive Outcomes out of business."[48] It is significant that South Africa would choose definitions that mirror closely the type of conduct prohibited under the Additional Protocol I[49] and the two Mercenary Conventions, since South Africa is not party to either the Organization of African Unity (OAU) Mercenary Convention[50] or the UN Mercenary Convention.[51] The FMA by design cast individual private security contractors (PSCs) as mercenaries through its broad definition of "foreign military assistance," and criminalized their activities until prior authorization has been obtained from the NCACC. In this way South Africa's approach to the PMSC industry was at odds with the response of other Western states that viewed PSCs as legitimate actors and focused attention on regulating the industry. Not surprisingly, South Africa's prosecuting authority struggled to secure cooperation from other states in its enforcement of the FMA for acts carried out extraterritorially, especially when these other states had been actively contracting the services of South African citizens and PMSCs.[52]

The basis upon which the NCACC must refuse an application to offer foreign military assistance set out in section 7 of the FMA has been criticized for containing exclusions that are broadly stated, extensive in their scope, and couched in vague terms, making it almost impossible for potential applicants to assess the likelihood of being granted the required authorization, or to attempt to align themselves with the requirements set out by the legislature.[53] The FMA currently places unchecked power in the hands of the NCACC (an organ of the executive branch of government) to determine the operations of PMSCs,[54] thereby determining foreign policy without parliamentary oversight.[55] This harkens back to the apartheid era when legislation gave power to the executive in order to bypass parliamentary oversight.[56] Moreover, the minister of defense can choose to "bureaucratically delay" the authorization process without having to provide any justification.[57] With the passage of the FMA, South Africa soon earned the reputation for having arguably the most aggressive regime of domestic legislation aimed at regulating the activities of PMSCs and their personnel.[58]

ATTEMPTS AT PROSECUTION UNDER THE FMA

In practice, however, South Africa's National Prosecuting Authority (NPA) largely restricted its enforcement efforts to activities easily characterized as mercenary—where individuals were accused of attempting to destabilize or overthrow governments for profit—and overlooked failures to request permission for more benign security-related activities. But even where it focused, the NPA had difficulty enforcing the law.

Richard Rouget was the first person to be charged in 2003 under the FMA for "recruiting mercenaries for the conflict in the Ivory Coast."[59] After pleading guilty, the Pretoria High Court reduced his fine to R75,000.[60] In February 2004 Carl Alberts entered a plea bargain agreement with the NPA for alleged mercenary activities in the Ivory Coast. His jail time was suspended and ultimately Alberts only paid a fine of R10,000.[61]

One month later, the infamous "Wonga coup"[62] plot to kidnap the president of Equatorial Guinea, Teodoro Objang Nguema Mbasogo, and replace him with exiled opposition politician Severo Moto,[63] saw 64 men[64] being recruited in South Africa by Logo Logistics (headed by Simon Mann) and Military Technical Services (under Nick du Toit), ostensibly to provide security for mining operations in the Congo. That a small army of men could be recruited on South African soil by PMSCs registered in the British Virgin Islands and the Bahamas indicates that the FMA's deterrent effect was limited. The daring coup attempt[65] was foiled when the South African government tipped off the Zimbabwe authorities.[66] The men were imprisoned in Zimbabwe for immigration offenses and Simon Mann was later transferred to Equatorial Guinea, where he was tried and sentenced to a further 35 years.[67] Meanwhile Nick du Toit and a further 15 men, including four South Africans, were arrested in Equatorial Guinea[68] and convicted of a range of offenses including "crimes against the head of state, government, illegal possession of arms and ammunition, terrorism and possession of explosives."[69] They were sentenced to 34 years in prison.[70] Less than five years later, in 2009, the government of Equatorial Guinea pardoned "Mann, du Toit and three other South Africans on humanitarian grounds"[71] and the other South Africans were repatriated to South Africa.[72] South African resident Sir Mark Thatcher[73] was fined and subject to suspended sentences.[74] The remaining eight accused were subject to a full prosecution in terms of the FMA, but the charges were later dismissed on the grounds that the evidence before the court suggested that the South African government had sanctioned their actions.[75] The allegation of involvement by the South African government has always been officially denied and was never proved.[76]

After the Wonga coup, it was hoped that new legislation would replace the beleaguered FMA.[77] Implementation of the Prohibition of Mercenary Activities Act (PMA) of 2006 was delayed, however, and no prosecutions were pursued until February 2013, when 20 Congolese Nationals[78] were arrested and charged with allegedly planning a coup against the government of the Democratic Republic of Congo (DRC).[79] Since the PMA had not yet become law they were charged with contravening the FMA by "engaging in mercenary activity or rendering foreign military assistance without authorization," and contravening the Riotous Assemblies Act by conspiring to commit murder.[80] The accused's lawyers brought an application to declare the FMA unconstitutional on the grounds that it was unclear and ambiguous,[81] while the state argued that South Africa must not be seen as a haven for mercenaries.[82] Judge Billy Mothle ultimately dismissed the application, but not before noting that the FMA was broad enough in its application to also cover the activities of PMSCs that have been deemed legitimate by other states.[83] Ultimately, the prosecution faltered and the charges were dismissed against 15 of the men and the remaining 5 were acquitted.[84]

Despite having adopted such a hard-line regulatory approach, the FMA had proven an insufficient basis upon which to prosecute effectively, even for those high-profile instances of alleged mercenarism.[85] Moreover, very little enforcement had resulted for those individual employees of PMSCs who were not engaged in mercenary-type activities, but who were merely flaunting the requirements of the FMA by not seeking authorization from the NCACC. For example, two South African PMSCs, Meteoric Tactical Solutions and Erinys, were both providing protection services in Iraq without NCACC authorization—and in the case of Erinys, without even having applied to the NCACC for such approval. Despite this, no action was brought against either company.[86] It did not take many unsuccessful prosecutions for the minister of defense to admit "that despite the fact that the FMA had been in operation for considerable time, very few prosecutions have been instituted in terms of the Act."[87]

THE PROHIBITION OF MERCENARY ACTIVITIES AND REGULATION OF CERTAIN ACTIVITIES IN COUNTRY OF ARMED CONFLICT ACT 27 OF 2006

Given the record of limited prosecutions for alleged instances of blatant mercenary behavior, and cabinet concern over the increased participation of South African citizens in conflicts around the world,[88] the Department of

Defence (DOD) sponsored the Prohibition of Mercenary Activities and Regulation of Certain Activities in Country of Armed Conflict Act 27 of 2006 as a replacement. The DOD made clear the government's need for a stronger deterrent of mercenary activities, to improve the FMA's definitions, and to clarify its position regarding enlistment in foreign armed forces, extraterritorial jurisdiction, presidential powers to make regulations and determine "regulated countries," appropriate penalties, and alignment with the NCACC.[89]

The PMA was intended to make it easier for the NPA to successfully prosecute mercenaries.[90] It defines "mercenaries" as citizens who provide "assistance in the form of advice, logistical support, training, security services or personnel recruitment."[91] Specifically, under section 2 of the PMA:

2. (1) "no person may within the Republic or elsewhere" may:

a. Participate as a combatant for private gain in an armed conflict;
b. Directly or indirectly recruit, use, train, support or finance a combatant for private gain in an armed conflict;
c. Directly or indirectly participate in any manner in the initiation, causing or furthering of

   i. An armed conflict;
   ii. A coup d'état, uprising or rebellion against any government; or
   iii. Directly or indirectly perform any act aimed at overthrowing a government or undermining the constitutional order, sovereignty or territorial integrity of a state.

The PMA definition brands anyone involved in any conflict for private gain as being a mercenary, even if it is just supportive or financial.[92] This definition is much broader than the definition provided for in the UN Mercenary Convention. During the parliamentary working group discussion of the PMA the DOD made it clear that in its opinion the definition of "mercenary" had to be expanded to include other forms of involvement in the security sector that fell short of armed conflict, but that might destabilize states. Therefore, the PMA made a provision for possible prosecution in these situations as well.[93] These discussions prior to the drafting of the PMA reflect the government's decision to equate PMSCs and mercenaries. In later working group discussions on the PMA, the DOD emphasized that even though there might not be a conflict in a particular country, the situation in that country might be sensitive to destabilizing forces,[94] and consequently drafted the PMA so as to make it possible to try a South African involved in situations of destabilization as a mercenary, irrespective of whether an armed conflict is declared.

The PMA also attempts to increase the jurisdictional scope of the NPA, in terms of the activities and areas of conflicts where the act is applicable.[95] The PMA states in section 11, for example, that

- "Any act constituting an offence under this Act and that is committed outside the Republic by—
    - a citizen of the Republic;
    - a person ordinarily resident in the Republic;
    - a company incorporated or registered as such under any law, in the Republic; or
    - any body of persons, corporate or unincorporated, in the Republic
- must be regarded as having been committed in the Republic and the person who committed it may be tried in a court in the Republic which has jurisdiction in respect of that offence.[96]

The net effect of section 11 is that any criminal activity by a South African committed outside of South Africa could be prosecuted in a South African court. This section is in direct response to the difficulties that the South African government faced in trying to prosecute the South Africans involved in the Wonga coup attempt.[97]

While the PMA increased the scope of the activities that could lead to prosecution, it retained several aspects of the FMA's regulatory structure.[98] First, the PMA provides that all forms of foreign military assistance must be authorized if provided to a party to an armed conflict, or in a regulated country.[99] Second, the PMA also prevents South African citizens from joining the armed forces of another country without obtaining prior permission from the South African government.[100] Third, the PMA empowers the NCACC to attach conditions to its authorization of any foreign military assistance and specifies various grounds upon which the NCACC can refuse such authorization, especially if the service to be rendered "in any manner initiates, causes or furthers an armed conflict, or a coup d'état, uprising or rebellion against a government."[101] On the other hand, the PMA also eliminates the FMA's blanket catchall condition that authorization can be denied "for any other reason." The PMA received the necessary presidential assent in November 2007, but has yet to receive the necessary presidential proclamation and regulations to make it law.[102]

THE PROPOSED AMENDMENT TO SECTION 6 OF THE SOUTH AFRICAN CITIZENSHIP ACT 88 OF 1995

The South African government announced a proposed amendment to section 6 of the South African Citizenship Act 88 of 1995 in 2010.[103] The proposed amendment would permit the government to revoke the citizenship of any South African serving in a foreign military for "engaging in a war under the flag of a country that the Government of South Africa does not support."[104] This new scheme aimed at denying citizenship to those working in the private security industry was taken when it became apparent that the PMA could not be used to prevent South African citizens from serving in the Israeli Defense Forces.[105] When the amendment was proposed, the Department of Home Affairs director general maintained that it was only aimed at naturalized South African citizens (i.e., immigrants),[106] who would be precluded from retaining their South African citizenship if they were serving in a foreign military. However, the concept of a "foreign military" was not defined and there was nothing in the proposed amendment that precluded these provisions from being applied to nonimmigrant citizens.[107] After concerns were raised about the constitutionality of denying citizenship on this basis,[108] the wording was altered to read "Section 6(3): Any person who obtained South African citizenship by naturalisation in terms of this Act shall cease to be a South African citizen if he or she engages, under the flag of another country, in a war that the Republic does not support."

The high commissioner for the UK Foreign Office expressed concern that the 800-plus South Africans who are part of the British Army would be forced to renounce their South African citizenship.[109] The ANC-led government rejected these concerns, stating that they would not "create loopholes allowing South Africans not only to join foreign armies but also become mercenaries with companies such as Aegis."[110] This policy and response demonstrated that the government continued to equate mercenaries and PMSCs and desired to gain control over all military activities pursued by South Africans. Kader Asmal, a professor of constitutional law, commented on this new tactic of the government: "We know how our government has not been able to implement the present anti-mercenary legislation because it has overreached itself. We wonder about the justification for the proposed amendments."[111]

THE SOUTH AFRICAN REGULATORY REGIME IN HINDSIGHT

If one looks over the history of attempted prosecutions under the FMA, it is telling that there have been none that resulted in a guilty verdict without some form of plea bargain.[112] Perhaps more telling is the fact that the majority of attempts at prosecution have been reserved for genuine mercenaries and coup plotters, although by law *any* PSCs engaged in unauthorized foreign military assistance were liable for prosecution.[113] Given the broad definition given to the term "foreign military assistance," which covers activities pursued by PMSCs that have been deemed legitimate by other states, it is likely that requiring PMSCs to justify their actions rather than force the NCACC to provide reasons as to why a PMSC may no longer operate will lead to constitutional challenges on the basis of the rights to freedom of trade, occupation, and profession[114] set out in section 22 of the Constitution of the Republic of South Africa 1996. Admittedly, maintaining a monopoly over the legitimate use of violence could conceivably be considered reasonable, rationally connected to a legitimate government purpose, and therefore a justifiable limitation on these constitutional rights. However, the FMA prohibits a whole range of nonmilitary activities that are carried out by the employees of PMSCs.[115] NGOs and think tanks also could find themselves in violation of the broadly worded prohibition against providing "advice and training."[116] Similarly, any company providing equipment to other militaries (backpacks, spare parts for vehicles, tents, etc.) could face prosecution for the "procurement of equipment."[117]

The very broad discretionary power of the NCACC will likely face administrative law challenges for its failure to ensure transparency in the exercise of discretionary powers, and to permit courts to review decisions of the NCACC in a timely manner. Even those reviewing applications admit a large measure of uncertainty in interpreting the provisions of the FMA.[118] On the whole, both the FMA and PMA are very broad and there is a good deal of skepticism that they would be fairly applied.[119]

ASSESSING THE IMPACT OF THE SOUTH AFRICAN REGULATORY REGIME

When it became apparent that the tension between the new ANC government and the old special operations forces of the apartheid regime, reinvented as the booming private military industry, would not be resolved, the South African PMSCs and their personnel "conducted their activities more clandestinely" so as to not attract government attention.[120] Complying with the vagaries of the NCACC made South Africa–based PMSCs painfully aware that even if they were initially successful in avoiding a section 9 denial of their application and managed to secure the NCACC's authorization, there was always the potential that the NCACC would invoke sections 4(3) and 5(3) of the FMA and simply withdraw or amend its authorization.[121] Executive Outcomes terminated its services in January 1999, citing in part public criticism and the constrictive provisions contained in the FMA.[122] With the potential threat of prosecution, South African companies that engaged in anything connected to the private security industry stepped back into the shadows,[123] "charter shopping"[124] to reincorporate themselves in a country with less onerous legislation. Lifeguard, Security Control Systems, and Saracens moved their headquarters out of South Africa, while Frederick, Nicholas and Duncan (FND) went underground.[125] They became cagey about their contracts, secretive about their employee details (especially if they were South African nationals), and guarded when eliciting legal advice or lobbying government. All this makes it particularly difficult to gather reliable data on how the industry has reacted to the FMA.

The FMA has also impacted South African nationals whose employment (even for PMSCs operating abroad) is at the mercy of the NCACC, which has the power to designate the "regulated countries" and the right to refuse applications to provide foreign military assistance, to set conditions for such permission, and to retract authorization at any time. Nathan Hodge reports that Erinys (a UK-based PMSC) preemptively retrenched 100 South African employees when the FMA was promulgated, in order to avoid the reputational damage and potential legal complications that might have resulted if the South African government chose to investigate and prosecute these individuals.[126] Many South African PSCs and PMSCs argue that they are facing unfair criminalization under the FMA, leaving them liable for prosecution for actions that international humanitarian law and anti-mercenary treaties do not prohibit,[127] solely because of their nationality. Even the OAU Mercenary Convention permits African states to hire non-nationals to perform security functions. South Africans who are already enlisted in the armed forces of another country or who are employed by foreign PMSCs would be well-advised to accept the citizenship or residency of that country, in order to avoid the risk of prosecution by virtue of their South African nationality.[128] Cobus Claassens, a former Executive Outcomes operative, now lives in Nigeria and runs the Nigerian division of Pilgrims Group, a UK-based PMSC providing "security for multinationals and the British High Commission."[129] There are many more stories like this.

In casting its net so broadly, the vague wording of the FMA might be interpreted to deny authorization to South African PSCs guarding vulnerable humanitarian NGOs, or involved in demining operations in conflict zones.[130] If the PMA does enter into force, section 5 could prohibit South Africa–based humanitarian organizations themselves from conducting their operations in conflict zones,[131] making humanitarian organizations wary of operating out of South Africa.[132]

Furthermore, it is likely that the South African government deliberately conflated the PSCs with mercenaries when drafting the FMA and PMA. The post-apartheid government wanted to effectively outlaw all forms of private security work within its borders in order to minimize the risk of losing control over its foreign policy.[133] It simply could not chance the reputational damage and possible regional destabilization that would result if South African PMSCs acted as mercenaries in Africa and the rest of the world.[134] In fact, government officials have agreed that the real intent behind the FMA was to "de-legitimize" the industry.[135]

The unintended consequence of this choice to unilaterally delegitimize the industry was that the government also lost its ability to regulate the private military and security industry once it had moved offshore or underground.[136] Despite the fact that an estimated 1,780,874 South Africans are working for PMSCs throughout the world,[137] the NPA has yet to prosecute any PMSCs or PSCs for engaging in private security work without the authorization of the NCACC. In fact, less than a handful of PSCs have ever applied for license from the NCACC to do so.[138] Instead the NPA engaged in prosecutorial discretion, targeting only the more mercenary-type activities, and resorting to plea bargaining to impose penalties, revealing perhaps the legitimate concern around the significant administrative and constitutional law challenges that could undermine prosecutions under the FMA. The FMA is largely ineffective in deterring South African citizens from participating in the private security industry, and it has proven toothless in successfully prosecuting PSCs even when they have been found in violation of the FMA. Counterintuitively, South Africa may increase its control over the industry if it chooses to loosen its regulation of it.[139]

While the government would have us believe that the FMA has limited the industry to "largely offering non-combat services,"[140] the death of a South African in Nigeria from friendly fire in March 2015 suggests otherwise.[141] Old names in the industry, like Eeben Barlow (former head of Executive Outcomes, now chairman of STTEP) and Pilgrims Africa Ltd. (another South African PMSC based in Lagos), made headlines in 2015 assisting the Nigerian government in combating Boko Haram.[142] The response from the South African government has been to condemn the actions of the South African nationals involved, and reaffirm the provisions of the FMA to suggest that any South Africans involved with offering military assistance in Nigeria will be arrested on their return to South Africa.[143] The FMA has conveniently (and perhaps intentionally) allowed the South African government to shirk its state responsibility to regulate its nationals, and instead wash its hands of these highly skilled "trouble makers," forcing them to seek employment with foreign PMSCs.[144]

GENERAL TRENDS IN THE DOMESTIC REGULATION OF PMSCS

The South African government's approach to the PMSCs is markedly different from the responses from other governments, even those like the United

Kingdom[145] and the United States[146] who are considered prolific users and producers of PMSCs. The legislation in both the US and the UK gives a strong indication of the desire to both regulate and utilize PMSCs,[147] and that the awarding of lucrative government contracts to reputable PMSCs is to be preferred over outlawing the industry.[148]

This trend is echoed by three studies[149] undertaken by the United Nations high commissioner for human rights' Working Group on the use of mercenaries as a means of violating human rights and impeding the exercise of the right of peoples to self-determination. When compared to the regulatory regimes found in the 23 states surveyed, South Africa's regulatory regime is unique in its hard-line regulation of the PMSC industry. In most of the states examined, there was no reference in the domestic legislation aimed specifically at prohibiting mercenaries,[150] unlike the South African legislation that appears to conflate individual PSCs and corporate PMSCs with mercenaries. With the sole exception of India, South Africa is the only state that regulates the industry through the extraterritorial application of its domestic legislation[151] on the basis of nationality or place of incorporation, and seeks to control, regulate, and prosecute South African registered PMSCs and PSCs, even where they are employed on foreign territory or contracted by foreign companies or governments.[152] South Africa's licensing regime is the most stringent and out of kilter with what is expected in other states,[153] requiring PMSCs to secure authorization from the NCACC before concluding each individual contract for military assistance.[154] The South African legislation imposes far harsher penalties, including incarceration, while the states surveyed only imposed administrative sanctions involving "warnings, fines, temporary suspension of the company's activities, withdrawal of authorisation, and seizure of weapons and firearms."[155]

SOUTH AFRICA'S OBLIGATIONS WITH RESPECT TO PMSCS UNDER INTERNATIONAL LAW

At the time the South African government was drafting the FMA, neither international humanitarian law treaties nor international human rights treaties—all drafted prior to the industry boom—made any specific reference to PMSCs and the contractors they employ.[156] For some, the omission of reference to the employees of PMSCs is put down to the fact that they are simply mercenaries—to be dealt with by the two international anti-mercenary treaties.[157] However, personnel of PMSCs seldom fulfill the complex definitional requirements for mercenarism,[158] although some former mercenaries have gained employment with PMSCs.[159] The official UN position, expressed through the working group established pursuant to the UN Commission on Human Rights Resolution 2005/2, was that PMSCs are operating legally in a "grey zone, which is not defined at all, or at least not clearly defined by international legal norms."[160]

Realizing that there was a gap in the existing international law, there was a flurry of international responses aimed at addressing the gray area that PMSCs inhabit, culminating in the Montreux Document (see chapter 10 in this volume),[161] the International Code of Conduct (ICoC) for Private Security Service Providers (see chapters 8 and 9 in this volume),[162] and the draft PMSC convention.[163] South Africa was one of the 17 states who jointly finalized the Montreux Document on the occasion of a concluding meeting in Montreux, Switzerland, on 17 September 2008, and the government did become a party to it.[164] To the extent that South Africa contributed to the drafting process that led to these documents it appears that its hard-line approach of criminalizing any unauthorized private actor's use of force was rejected in favor of an internationally accepted approach of regulating the industry, although some aspects of its approach are consonant with the emerging regime.[165]

According to the Montreux Document, the international humanitarian law (IHL) status of these PMSCs "depends on their exact employment and functions,"[166] as well as the time, location, and prevailing circumstances surrounding their actions.[167] The draft PMSC convention also adopts the position that "PMSCs and their employees are distinct from mercenaries,"[168] which is significant given that the draft PMSC convention came from the working group tasked with an anti-mercenary agenda. On the other hand, the Montreux Document argues that PMSCs "do not operate in a legal vacuum"[169] and, consistent with South Africa's approach, asserts that states are responsible for regulating the extraterritorial conduct of PMSC-related businesses that are registered in or operating out of their territory. Furthermore, the draft PMSC convention requires countries to assume state responsibility and control over PMSCs to ensure their personnel are held accountable, through legislative, administrative, and other measures, for any violations of international law.[170] This position did draw some sharp criticism from the major Western powers, from whence 70 percent of the private military and security services originate, who argued that the draft PMSC convention was biased against the private military and security industry and "at odds with the Montreux Document" and the ICoC.[171]

The draft PMSC convention highlights the observance of the principles of the rule of law, respect for state sovereignty, and international human rights law,[172] and establishes for the first time that there are certain "inherent state functions that cannot be outsourced"[173] while reinforcing that mercenary activities and illicit trafficking in firearms are prohibited.[174] Moreover, it states that the use of force or excessive use of firearms will be deemed illegal.[175] The draft convention further imposes criminal liability, establishes jurisdiction, and makes allowances for extradition, transfer of criminal proceedings, and mutual legal assistance in instances of contravention of the convention—this latter provision being quite helpful to the South African approach.[176] Significantly, the convention provides remedies to victims of convention offenses.[177] However, as Laurence Juma correctly points out, the draft PMSC convention still requires states to carry the burden of enforcing the regulatory regime, so there is still the need for domestic regulation, and as the preceding section attests, extraterritorial regulation of PMSCs and PSCs left to the domestic level has been problematic and sporadic.[178]

To this end, 2014 saw some interesting developments emanating from the International Organization for Standardization (ISO), which has already developed an ISO 26000 standard that addresses issues of security and risk management.[179] Taking this standard, the American National Standards body (ANSI) launched ANSI PSC 1 (a guide drafted in 2012 titled "Management System for Quality of Private Security Company Operations" that is intended to operationalize the ICoC into a "certified management system standard"[180]) and is now planning a new project committee (PC 284)[181] to deliver a certifiable standard to "which organisations (like PMSCs) can demonstrate their observance of human rights and international law and by conformance obtain accreditation through a third party certification audit."[182] When the new ISO standard is complete, it will be up to each state's domestic standards body or PMSC licensing body to elect to enforce it. Once established, PMSCs can apply to be audited by accredited certification bodies in order to determine that they meet the stipulations of the new ISO standard. It is envisaged that the accreditation authority will receive reports and conduct ISO-type audits and field inspections—calling on information from foreign offices, embassies, and the military to verify that PMSCs are adhering to the standard.[183]

What stands out from the various regulatory initiatives discussed above is that they are aimed at regulation, not criminalizing the private military and security industry. They are founded on notions of observance of international law and state responsibility for activities at odds with the internationally accepted norms. When one considers the approach taken by the South African government against this backdrop it is clear that the FMA and the proposed PMA exceed these international law obligations.[184] It would appear that the South African government sees it as its duty to establish or maintain its monopoly on the legitimate use of violence, and to strictly regulate the behavior of its citizens to whom it grants permission to use violence, even when those activities occur outside its borders. The post-apartheid government arrived at this position largely because of the history between these newly established South African PMSCs and their personnel, and their link to the apartheid-era military's special operations units. In attempting to regulate this industry out of existence and thereby avert any potential threat to the state and its foreign policy, the government has lost the battle to regulate the industry in a meaningful and effective way. It has failed to deter and successfully prosecute even mercenary-type activities. South Africa has not effectively implemented its regulatory regime because it is the lone voice that characterizes PMSCs as mercenaries in an international community that sees the industry as legitimate and in need of regulation rather than criminalization. The emerging international regulatory regime, however, may offer South African authorities more assistance than in the past to prosecute extraterritorial violations of looser international standards of behavior, those that the consensus of states has deemed beyond the pale.

CONCLUSION

The boom in the private military and security industry has ushered in a new era in international law.[185] States,[186] corporations, intergovernmental organizations, and nongovernmental organizations[187] admit that they would not be equipped to operate in conflict situations were it not for their reliance upon PMSCs.[188] In short, employees of PMSCs are fast outnumbering traditional armed forces on the ground in conflict situations, and are becoming more prevalent and mainstream.[189] It is widely acknowledged that a blanket ban on the activities of PMSCs and PSCs, in the style of the FMA and the proposed PMA, "is neither practicable nor necessary."[190] Instead, it's very likely that PMSCs and PSCs will be a permanent feature in all "humanitarian, peacekeeping, and peace-enforcement operations,"[191] and many states have given a strong indication of their desire to continue to utilize the private military and security industry.[192] South Africans with military training remain highly sought after by firms in the industry. They continue to be recruited and work clandestinely in defiance of the FMA,[193] even opting to change their citizenship.[194]

The South African government's response to the rise of Executive Outcomes and the "Wonga coup" scandal has resulted in a regulatory regime that exceeds the international and regional obligations to outlaw mercenarism and effectively sees all PSCs as tainted with the mercenary reputation.[195] This hard-line regulatory approach is exceptional compared to the general trends toward regulating the private military and security industry seen in other countries as well as internationally.

The 2014 South African Defence Review detailed a future for the SADF within Africa.[196] When addressing PMSCs, the Defence Review conceded that the involvement of PMSCs and PSCs with links to South Africa "in defence transformation, peacekeeping and peace building in conflict and post-conflict areas will continue into the foreseeable future."[197] Therefore it advocated reconsidering the regulation of PMSCs and their relationship with the SADF.[198] This appears to be a fresh view of the true nature of the private military security industry, especially within the South African and African context, and one that suggests that the FMA and PMA may be reconsidered in the future. There is no doubt that PMSCs and PSCs need to be controlled. The proper mechanism for this control rests with proper regulation through the state rather than the current legal prohibitions.

NOTES

1. Michael Evans, "The Front-Line States, South Africa and Southern African Security: Military Prospects and Perspectives," *Zambezia* 12 (1984/1985); Herbert M. Howe, "Private Security Forces and African Stability: The Case of Executive Outcomes," *Journal of Modern African Studies* 36, 2 (June 1998).
2. Jakkie Cilliers, "Security and Transition in South Africa," *Journal of Democracy* 6, 4 (1995), page 46.
3. Samuel P. Huntington, "Reforming Civil-Military Relations," *Journal of Democracy* 6, 4 (1995), page 13.
4. Peter W. Singer, *Corporate Warriors: The Rise of the Privatized Military Industry* (Ithaca: Cornell University Press, 2003), page 103.
5. Singer, *Corporate Warriors*, page 102.
6. Many of these are from the special operations divisions like the disbanded 32 Buffalo Battalion (Deborah D. Avant, *The Market for Force: The Consequences of Privatizing Security* [Cambridge: Cambridge University Press, 2005], page 158).
7. Kevin A. O'Brien, "PMCs, Myths and Mercenaries: The Debate on Private Military Companies," *RUSI Journal* 145 (2000), page 60.
8. Sarah Franklin, "South African and International Attempts to Regulate Mercenaries and Private Military Companies," *Transnational Law and Contemporary Problems* 17, 2 (Winter 2008), page 247.
9. Howe, "Private Security Forces and African Stability," page 311.
10. Avant, *The Market for Force*, page 158.
11. Jeremy Harding, "The Mercenary Business: 'Executive Outcomes,'" *Review of African Political Economy* 24, 71 (March 1997), page 89.
12. Sarah Percy, *Mercenaries: The History of a Norm in International Relations* (Oxford: Oxford University Press, 2007), page 169.
13. Percy, *Mercenaries*, pages 185–87.
14. Singer, *Corporate Warriors*, page 108.
15. Singer, *Corporate Warriors*, pages 108–9.
16. Percy, *Mercenaries*, pages 188–89; Harding, "The Mercenary Business," page 87.
17. Percy, *Mercenaries*, page 189.
18. Singer, *Corporate Warriors*, page 102.
19. Singer, *Corporate Warriors*, page 102.
20. Avant, *The Market for Force*, page 164.
21. O'Brien, "PMCs, Myths and Mercenaries," page 60.
22. Enrique Bernales Ballesteros (1987–2004); Shaista Shameem (2004–2005).
23. Fabien Mathieu and Nick Dearden, "Corporate Mercenaries: The Threat of Private Military and Security Companies," *Review of African Political Economy* 34, 114 (December 2007), page 747.
24. Joana Abrisketa, "Blackwater: Mercenaries and International Law," *Fundación para las Relaciones Internacionales y el Diálogo Exterior (FRIDE)* (October 2007), page 2.
25. Christopher H. Lytton, "Blood for Hire: How the War in Iraq Has Reinvented the World's Second Oldest Profession," *Oregon Review of International Law* 8 (Summer 2006), page 313.

26. Junio V. Palomba, "Private Military and Security Companies and the Pursuit of Legitimacy," *E-international Relations* (2 October 2009), available at http://www.e-IR.info/?p=2450, accessed 4 June 2015.
27. Mark Malan and Jakkie Cilliers, "Mercenaries and Mischief: The Regulation of Foreign Military Assistance Bill," Occasional Paper 25 (Pretoria: Institute for Security Studies, September 1997), page 1.
28. Yves Sandoz, "Private Security and International Law," in Jakkie Cilliers and Peggy Mason, editors, *Peace, Profit or Plunder? The Privatisation of Security in War-Torn African Societies* (Pretoria: Institute for Security Studies, 1999), page 215.
29. Section 121(4).
30. Singer, *Corporate Warriors*, page 102.
31. Avant, *The Market for Force*, page 158.
32. Franklin, "South African and International Attempts to Regulate Mercenaries and Private Military Companies," page 249.
33. Carlos Ortiz, "Regulating Private Military Companies: States and the Expanding Business of Commercial Security Provision," in Libby Assassi, Duncan Wigan, and Kees Van der Pijl, editors, *Global Regulation Managing Crises after the Imperial Turn* (Basingstoke: Palgrave Macmillan, 2004), page 214.
34. Avant, *The Market for Force*, page 160.
35. Avant, *The Market for Force*, page 160.
36. Avant, *The Market for Force*, pages 158, 160.
37. Avant, *The Market for Force*, page 159.
38. Avant, *The Market for Force*, page 159.
39. Raenette Taljaard, "Implementing South Africa's Regulation of Foreign Military Assistance Act," in Alan Bryden and Marina Caparini, editors, *Private Actors and Security Governance* (London: Transactions Publishers, 2006), page 167.
40. Deane-Peter Baker and Sabelo Gumedze, "Private Military/Security Companies and Human Security in Africa," *African Security Review* 16, 4 (2007), page 4.
41. Fred Schreier and Marina Caparini, "Privatising Security: Law, Practice and Governance of Private Military and Security Companies," Occasional Paper 6 (Geneva: Geneva Centre for the Democratic Control of Armed Forces, March 2005), page 107.
42. Section 1(iv).
43. Caroline Holmqvist, *Private Security Companies: The Case for Regulation*, SIPRI Policy Paper 9 (Stockholm: Stockholm International Peace Research Institute, January 2005), page 52.
44. Holmqvist, *Private Security Companies*, page 52; FMA section 4(1) or 5(1).
45. Ortiz, "Regulating Private Military Companies," page 215; FMA section 4(2) or 5(3).
46. FMA section 8(1). The FMA does not prescribe a maximum fine or maximum period of imprisonment for offenses.
47. Jakkie Cilliers and Richard Cornwell, "Africa: From the Privatization of Security to the Privatization of War?" in Jakkie Cilliers and Peggy Mason, editors, *Peace, Profit or Plunder? The Privatisation of Security in War-Torn African Societies* (Pretoria: Institute for Security Studies, 1999), page 239; Khareen Pech, "Executive Outcomes: A Corporate Conquest," in Cilliers and Mason, *Peace, Profit or Plunder*? page 96.
48. Avant, *The Market for Force*, page 162.
49. The Additional Protocol I to the Geneva Conventions, Article 47, available at http://www.icrc.org/ihl/intro/470, accessed 16 June 2015.
50. Organization of African Unity, *Convention for the Elimination of Mercenarism in Africa (Opened for Signature) 3 July 1977*, OAU Document CM/817 (29), Annex 2, Article 1 (3rd revision 1977), which entered into force on 22 April 1985. To date only 30 members of the African Union have ratified the convention.
51. United Nations, *International Convention against the Recruitment, Use, Financing and Training of Mercenaries*, UN Treaty Series 2163 (A/RES/44/34) (UN Mercenary Convention), which entered into force on 20 October 2001. Only 33 states had become party to the convention and very few of those are the major powers.
52. Avant, *The Market for Force*, pages 162–63.

53. *Dawood v Minister of Home Affairs* 2000 3 South Africa 936 (CC), paragraph 53.
54. Taljaard, "Implementing South Africa's Regulation of Foreign Military Assistance Act," pages 167, 171.
55. Malan and Cilliers, "Mercenaries and Mischief," pages 7, 10.
56. Taljaard, "Implementing South Africa's Regulation of Foreign Military Assistance Act," pages 167, 171; Schreier and Caparini, "Privatising Security," page 108.
57. Malan and Cilliers, "Mercenaries and Mischief."
58. Holmqvist, *Private Security Companies*, page 50.
59. Philip C. Jacobs, "South Africa's New Counter-Mercenary Law," *Strategic Review for Southern Africa* 30, 1 (May 2008), page 11.
60. Subsequently Rouget was alleged to be active in Iraq, a clear indication of the lack of political will to institute prosecutions against PSCs not engaging in the classic mercenary activities (Taljaard, "Implementing South Africa's Regulation of Foreign Military Assistance Act," page 175).
61. Taljaard, "Implementing South Africa's Regulation of Foreign Military Assistance Act," pages 175–76.
62. Adam Roberts, *The Wonga Coup: Guns, Thugs and a Ruthless Determination to Create Mayhem in an Oil-Rich Corner of Africa* (London: Profile Books, 2009).
63. Franklin, "South African and International Attempts to Regulate Mercenaries and Private Military Companies," pages 247–48.
64. Many were members of the disbanded 32 Buffalo Battalion and several had links to Executive Outcomes before it was disbanded.
65. James Brabazon, *My Friend the Mercenary: A Memoir* (New York: Grove Press, 2011); Roberts, *The Wonga Coup.*
66. "Timeline: E Guinea Coup Plot," *BBC News* (3 November 2009), available at http://news.bbc.co.uk/2/hi/africa/4170589.stm, accessed 6 June 2015.
67. "Timeline: E Guinea Coup Plot."
68. "Timeline: E Guinea Coup Plot."
69. "Severo Moto, condenado a 63 años de cárcel por el intento de golpe de Estado en Guinea Ecuatorial," *El Pais Internacional* (26 November 2004), available at http://internacional.elpais.com/internacional/2004/11/26/actualidad/1101423606_850215.html, accessed 10 July 2015.
70. "Timeline: E Guinea Coup Plot."
71. "Timeline: E Guinea Coup Plot."
72. "Timeline: E Guinea Coup Plot."
73. The son of the former British prime minister Margaret Thatcher.
74. Mathieu and Dearden, "Corporate Mercenaries," page 746.
75. Alex Vines, *Well Oiled: Oil and Human Rights in Equatorial Guinea* (New York: Human Rights Watch, July 2009), pages 75–76; Louis Oelofs, "Court Hears Details of Alleged E Guinea Coup Plot," *Mail and Guardian Online* (14 February 2007). The accused were R. S. Archer, V. Dracula, L. du Preez, E. Harris, M. Kashama, N. T. Mathias, H. J. Hamman, and S. Witherspoon, Pretoria Regional Court Case No. 14/4315/05.
76. Franklin, "South African and International Attempts to Regulate Mercenaries and Private Military Companies," page 248.
77. Security and Constitutional Affairs Select Committee Department, "Prohibition of Mercenary Activities and Regulation of Certain Activities in Countries of Armed Conflict Bill [B42B-2005]: Briefing," Parliamentary Monitoring Group (7 September 2006), available at https://pmg.org.za/committee-meeting/7298/, accessed 10 July 2015.
78. Including Etienne Kabila, who claimed that he was "in fact the biological son of the slain Laurent Kabila and that Joseph was an adopted child from a Rwandan family" (De Wet Potgieter and Khadija Pate, "Congo Rebels, a Kabila Family Affair?" *Daily Maverick* [12 February 2013], available at http://www.dailymaverick.co.za/article/2013-02-11-congo-rebels-a-kabila-family-affair#.VXnmzKbN7dk, accessed 6 June 2015).
79. "Etienne Kabila Charged in South Africa for DR Congo 'Plot,'" *BBC News* (12 February 2013), available at http://www.bbc.com/news/world-africa-21432981, accessed 8 June 2015.

80. Peter Fabricius, "Strange Chapter in South Africa-Congo Saga Ends," *Star* (24 February 2015), available at http://www.iol.co.za/the-star/strange-chapter-in-South Africa-congo-saga-ends-1.1823026#.VXSkmc-qqko, accessed 5 June 2015.

81. South African Press Association, "DRC Coup Plot Accused Denies Guilt," IOL News (5 August 2014), available at http://www.iol.co.za/news/crime-courts/drc-coup-plot-accused-denies-guilt-1730979, accessed 14 April 2016.

82. Ntando Makhubu, "Five DRC 'Rebels' Freed," *IOL News* (21 February 2015), available at http://www.iol.co.za/news/crime-courts/five-drc-rebels-freed-1.1821749#.VXSiA8-qqko, accessed 5 June 2015.

83. South African Press Association, "DRC Coup Plot Accused Denies Guilt."

84. "Undercover Cop Testifies in DRC Coup Plot Trial," *News 24* (11 August 2014), available at http://www.news24.com/SouthAfrica/News/Undercover-cop-testifies-in-DRC-coup-plot-trial-2014081, accessed 10 June 2015; South African Press Association, "DRC Coup Plot Continues," *IOL News* (11 August 2014), available at http://www.iol.co.za/news/crime-courts/drc-coup-plot-trial-continues-1.1733776#.VXSiCc-qqko, accessed 5 June 2015; Makhubu, "Five DRC 'Rebels' Freed," *IOL News* (21 February 2015), available at http://www.iol.co.za/news/crime-courts/five-drc-rebels-freed-1.1821749#.VXSiA8-qqko, accessed 5 June 2015.

85. J. J. Messner, "Working towards Effective Legislative and Regulatory Solutions for the Private Security Industry in Africa," in Sabelo Gumedze, editor, *Elimination of Mercenarism in Africa: A Need for a New Continental Approach* (Pretoria: Institute for Security Studies, 2008), page 152.

86. Schreier and Caparini, "Privatising Security," pages 107–8.

87. Len le Roux, "South African Mercenary Legislation Enacted," Institute for Security Studies website (21 January 2008), available at https://www.issafrica.org/topics/peacekeeping-and-conflict-management/21-jan-2008-iss-today-south-african-mercenary-legislation-enacted, accessed 10 July 2015.

88. Roux, "South African Mercenary Legislation Enacted."

89. Republic of South Africa, Department of Defence, Briefing to the Security and Constitutional Affairs Select Committee, Prohibition of Mercenary Activities and Regulation of Certain Activities in Countries of Armed Conflict Bill [B42B-2005] (Cape Town: National Assembly, 7 September 2006).

90. Franklin, "South African and International Attempts to Regulate Mercenaries and Private Military Companies," page 253.

91. Franklin, "South African and International Attempts to Regulate Mercenaries and Private Military Companies," page 251.

92. Franklin, "South African and International Attempts to Regulate Mercenaries and Private Military Companies," page 251. This approach echoes the broad antiterrorism legislations passed in the US and elsewhere.

93. Security and Constitutional Affairs Select Committee department briefing on the PMA.

94. Security and Constitutional Affairs Select Committee meeting on the PMA.

95. Franklin, "South African and International Attempts to Regulate Mercenaries and Private Military Companies," page 251.

96. FMA, section 11(1).

97. Franklin, "South African and International Attempts to Regulate Mercenaries and Private Military Companies," page 253.

98. Ortiz, "Regulating Private Military Companies," page 215.

99. A person seeking such authorization must submit an application to the NCACC, which considers the application and may either refuse it, grant the application subject to conditions as it may determine, or at any time withdraw or amend an authorization already granted (section 7[2]).

100. Franklin, "South African and International Attempts to Regulate Mercenaries and Private Military Companies," page 253.

101. Section 7(2)(g).

102. "The Prohibition of Mercenary Activities and Regulation of Certain Activities in Country of Armed Conflict Act (Act 27 of 2006) is not yet in operation pending the finalization of Regulations to this Act" (*National Assembly of South Africa Questions for Written Reply to*

Minister Jeff Radebe [Minister of Justice and Constitutional Development], Issued by Parliament [3 September 2013], available at http://www.politicsweb.co.za/archive/2006-prohibition-of-mercenary-activities-act-not-y, accessed 24 June 2015); Sabelo Gumedze, "Pouring Old Wine into New Bottles? The Debate around Mercenaries and Private Military and Security Companies," *Elimination of Mercenarism in Africa: A Need for a New Continental Approach* (Pretoria: International, July 2008), page 40.

103. B17 GG 33356 (5 July 2010); the South Africa Citizenship Amendment Act will add subsection (c) to the already existing section 6 of the South Africa Citizenship Act.

104. "South Africa to Strip Soldiers Abroad of Citizenship?" *DefenceWeb* (6 August 2010), available at http://www.defenceweb.co.za/index.php?option=com_content&view=article&id=9204:South Africa-to-strip-soldiers-abroad-of-citizenship&catid=54:Governance&Itemid=118, accessed 6 June 2015.

105. Eddie Cottle, "Will the ANC Government Ever Prosecute South Africans Serving in the Israeli Defence Force?" South African Civil Society Information Service (21 April 2015), available at http://www.sacsis.org.za/site/article/2355, accessed 2 September 2015.

106. "South Africa to Strip Soldiers Abroad of Citizenship?"

107. This bill would, however, not have any effect on South African PSCs who are not serving in a foreign military.

108. Bronwyn Manby, *Citizenship Law in Africa: A Comparative Study*, 2nd edition (New York: Open Society Foundations, 2010), page 78, footnote 205; Law Society of South Africa, "Before the Parliamentary Portfolio Committee on Home Affairs. Re: Submissions by the Law Society of South Africa in Re: SA Citizenship Amendment Bill 2010" (no date), available at http://pmg-assets.s3-website-eu-west-1.amazonaws.com/docs/100817pchomelssa_0.pdf, accessed 13 August 2015.

109. Ian Drury, "Ex-Cabinet Minister Paul Boateng Becomes a Director of a Private Military Firm after Lobbying to Water Down Anti-mercenary Legislation," *Mail Online* (9 November 2009), available at http://www.dailymail.co.uk/news/article-1226269/Paul-Boateng-director-private-military-firm-lobbying-water-anti-mercenary-laws.html, accessed 6 June 2015.

110. Jonathan Oliver, "Lobbying Row as Ex-Minister Paul Boateng Lands Defence Firm Job," *Sunday Times* (8 November 2009), available at http://www.timesonline.co.uk, accessed 6 June 2015.

111. Kader Asmal and John Peter, "Proposed Citizen Law Is an Erosion of Rights," *Business Day Live* (4 August 2010), available at http://www.bdlive.co.za/articles/2010/08/04/kader-asmal-nd-john-peter-proposed-citizen-law-is-an-erosion-of-rights;jsessionid=24E3F3651E4AA70ED5E956683BCF5E4A.present1.bdfm, accessed 24 July 2015.

112. Taljaard, "Implementing South Africa's Regulation of Foreign Military Assistance Act," page 174.

113. Erica Gaston, "Mercenarism 2.0? The Rise of the Modern Private Security Industry and Its Implications for International Humanitarian Law Enforcement," *Harvard International Law Journal* 49, 1 (Winter 2008), page 241; Nathan Hodge, "Army for Hire," *Slate* (31 August 2006), available at http://www.slate.com/articles/news_and_politics/foreigners/2006/08/army_for_hire.html, accessed 6 June 2015.

114. David Abrahams, "Brief Legal Commentary on PMSCs in South Africa" (2008), page 2, available at http://psm.du.edu/media/documents/national_regulations/countries/africa/south_africa/south_africa_legal_commentary_by_david_abrhams_2008-english.pdf, accessed 13 August 2015. This has been endorsed by the courts in *S v Lawrence*; *S v Negal*; *S v Solberg* 1997 (4) South Africa 1176 (CC), paragraph 32.

115. Avant, *The Market for Force*, page 162.

116. Avant, *The Market for Force*, page 162.

117. Avant, *The Market for Force*, page 162.

118. Avant, *The Market for Force*, page 162.

119. Avant, *The Market for Force*, page 162.

120. Avant, *The Market for Force*, page 161.

121. Section 7(2)(c).

122. Several Executive Outcomes operatives moved across to Lifeguard and continued to work in Sierra Leone (O'Brien, "PMCs, Myths and Mercenaries," page 59).

123. Holmqvist, "Private Security Companies," page 42.

124. Benjamin Perrin, *Modern Warfare: Armed Groups, Private Militaries, Humanitarian Organizations, and the Law* (Vancouver: University of British Columbia Press, 2012), page 228.

125. Avant, *The Market for Force*, page 166.

126. Hodge, "Army for Hire."

127. Nadia Ahmadou and Sabelo Gumedze, *Seminar Report on the Prohibition of Mercenary Activities and Regulation of Certain Activities in Areas of Armed Conflict Act 27 of 2006* (Pretoria: Institute for Security Studies, 22 May 2008), available at http://www.iss.co.za/uploads/RPSSREPFIN.pdfwww.iss.co.za/uploads/RPSSREPFIN.pdf, accessed 6 June 2015; *Kaunda v The President of the Republic of South Africa* 2005 (3) South Africa 235 (CC) Chaskalson CJ, paragraphs 38–40.

128. Jacobs, "South Africa's New Counter-Mercenary Law," page 11.

129. William Wallis and Katrina Manson, "Africa's Soldiers of Fortune Join Fight against Boko Haram," Financial Times (26 March 2015), available at http://www.ft.com/cms/s/0/4cda876e-d2e8-11e4-a792-00144feab7de.html#axzz45phBwmeP, accessed 14 April 2016.

130. Franklin, "South African and International Attempts to Regulate Mercenaries and Private Military Companies," page 252.

131. Even though the bill does allow for an exemption to be made for South African humanitarian organizations, there are no criteria set out determining what constitutes a "humanitarian organization" (Franklin, "South African and International Attempts to Regulate Mercenaries and Private Military Companies," page 252).

132. Peter W. Singer, "War, Profits, and the Vacuum of Law: Privatized Military Firms and International Law," *Columbia Journal of Transnational Law* 42, 2 (Spring 2004), pages 539–40.

133. Avant, *The Market for Force*, page 167.

134. Franklin, "South African and International Attempts to Regulate Mercenaries and Private Military Companies," page 252.

135. Avant, *The Market for Force*, page 162.

136. Taljaard, "Implementing South Africa's Regulation of Foreign Military Assistance Act," pages 167, 169.

137. Tom Nevin, "South Africa's Second Army," *African Business* 46, 392 (December 2012), page 37.

138. Sabelo Gumedze, *The Need for an International Code of Conduct for Private Security Actors in Africa* (Pretoria: Institute for Security Studies, 24 February 2012), available at https://www.issafrica.org/iss-today/the-need-for-an-international-code-of-conduct-for-private-security-actors-in-africa, accessed 27 July 2015.

139. Doug Brooks, "Messiahs or Mercenaries? The Future of International Private Military Services," *International Peacekeeping* 7, 4 (Winter 2000), page 136.

140. Avant, *The Market for Force*, page 161.

141. David Smith, "South Africa Mercenaries Are 'Giving Boko Haram a Hiding,'" *Mail and Guardian* (17 April 2015), available at http://mg.co.za/article/2015-04-16-South Africa-mercenaries-turn-the-tide-in-nigeria, accessed 3 June 2015.

142. Peter Fabricius, "Mercenaries Turning Tide in Nigeria," *IOL News* (12 April 2015), available at http://www.iol.co.za/news/africa/sadf-mercenaries-turning-tide-in-nigeria-1.1843796#.VXSklM-qqko, accessed 3 June 2015.

143. South African Press Association, "Arrest SA 'Mercenaries,' says Defence Boss," *IOL News* (29 January 2015), available at http://www.iol.co.za/news/africa/arrest-South Africa-mercenaries-says-defence-boss-1.1810571#.VXS4os-qqkp, accessed 3 June 2015.

144. Brooks, "Messiahs or Mercenaries?" page 136; Taljaard, "Implementing South Africa's Regulation of Foreign Military Assistance Act," pages 167, 169.

145. United Kingdom Foreign and Commonwealth Office, *Private Military Companies: Options for Regulation 2001–02*, HC 557 (London: The Stationery Office, 2002).

146. Arms Export Control Act (AECA), Uniform Code of Military Justice, US Code, Title 10, Subtitle A, Part II, Chapter 47; Military Extraterritorial Jurisdiction Act 2007 (MEJA) Public Law 106–523, International Traffic in Arms Regulations; Bureau of Political-Military

Affairs of the US State Department, Committee on Armed Services, *Inquiry into the Role and Oversight of Private Security Contractors in Afghanistan. Report Together with Additional Views* (Washington: United States Senate, 2010), available at https://www.congress.gov/111/crpt/srpt345/CRPT-111srpt345.pdf, accessed 6 June 2015.

147. Jose Gomez del Prado, "Mercenaries, Private Military and Security Companies and International Law," lecture, University of Wiscomsin Law School (31 January 2008), page 25.

148. United Kingdom Foreign and Commonwealth Office, *Consultation on Promoting High Standards of Conduct by Private Military and Security Companies (PMSCs) Internationally* (London: The Stationery Office, 2009), available at http://www.fco.gov.uk, accessed 28 May 2015; Clive Walker and Dave Whyte, "Contracting Out War? Private Military Companies, Law and Regulation in the United Kingdom," *International and Comparative Law Quarterly* 54, 3 (July 2005), pages 587, 651, 660–61.

149. (1) *Status Report on Anglophone Africa: Comprehensive Study and Analysis of National Legislation* (New York: United Nations Office of the High Commissioner for Human Rights, no date; hereinafter referred to as *Anglophone Africa*) looked at Ghana, Mauritius, Sierra Leone, The Gambia, Nigeria, Uganda, and Kenya. (2) *Analysis of Eight Francophone African Countries' National Legislation on PMSCs* (New York: United Nations Office of the High Commissioner for Human Rights, no date; hereinafter referred to as *Francophone Africa*) looked at Burkina Faso, Cameroon, Côte d'Ivoire, the Democratic Republic of Congo, Mali, Morocco, Senegal, and Tunisia. (3) *Comparative Analysis of the Regulation of Private Military and Security Companies in Eight Asian Countries* (New York: United Nations Office of the High Commissioner for Human Rights, no date; hereinafter referred to as *Asia*) looked at China, India, Malaysia, Pakistan, the Philippines, Singapore, Sri Lanka, and the United Arab Emirates. Reports are available at http://www.ohchr.org/EN/Issues/Mercenaries/WGMercenaries/Pages/NationalLegislationStudies.aspx, accessed 6 June 2015.

150. *Francophone Africa*, page 17; *Anglophone Africa*, page 38; *Asia*, page 3.

151. *Francophone Africa*, page 4; *Anglophone Africa*, page 40; *Asia*, page 32.

152. Avant, *The Market for Force*, pages 162–63.

153. *Francophone Africa*, page 6; *Anglophone Africa*, page 37; *Asia*, pages 13, 29.

154. Holmqvist, *Private Security Companies*, page 52.

155. *Francophone Africa*, page 15; *Asia*, page 15.

156. Perrin, *Modern Warfare*, page 8; International Committee of the Red Cross, *The Montreux Document on Pertinent International Legal Obligations and Good Practices for States Related to Operations of Private Military and Security Companies during Armed Conflict* (Geneva: International Committee of the Red Cross, 2008), page 37, available at http://www.icrc.org/web/eng/siteeng0.nsf/html/montreux-document-170908, accessed 5 June 2015 (hereinafter "Montreux Document").

157. Ian Ralby, "A Brief Explanation of the Private Security Regulatory Initiatives: UN Initiatives," I.R. Consilium website (17 April 2014), available at http://irconsilium.com/a-brief-explanation-of-the-private-security-regulatory-initiatives-u-n-inititatives, accessed 4 June 2015.

158. Sabelo Gumedze, "Towards the Revisions of the 1977 OAU/AU Convention on the Eliminations of Mercenarism in Africa," *African Security Review* 16, 4 (2007), page 24.

159. The security industry in Sierra Leone has a reputation for being heavily infiltrated by ex-mercenaries (*Anglophone Africa*, page 15).

160. Marina Mancini, Faustin Ntoubandi, and Thilo Marauhn, "Old Concepts and New Challenges: Are Private Contractors the Mercenaries of the Twenty-first Century?" in Francesco Francioni and Natalino Ronzotti, editors, *War by Contract: Human Rights, Humanitarian Law and Private Contractors* (Oxford: Oxford University Press, 2011), page 340.

161. International Committee of the Red Cross, Montreux Document, pages 36, 39.

162. Available at http://icoc-psp.org, accessed 18 February 2015. To date, over 500 private military security companies have signed the ICoC (John Crook, "Contemporary Practice of the United States Relating to International Law," *American Journal of International Law* 107, 1 [January 2013], page 213).

163. United Nations Office of the High Commissioner for Human Rights, "Working Group on the Use of Mercenaries as a Means of Violating Human Rights and Impeding the Exercise of

the Right of Peoples to Self Determination," available at http://www.ohchr.org/EN/Issues/Mercenaries/SRMercenaries/Pages/SRMercenariesIndex.aspx, accessed 18 February 2015; Gabor Rona, "Remarks by Gabor Rona, UN Working Group on the Use of Mercenaries, Montreux +5 Conference 11–13 December 2013," United Nations Office of Human Rights, Office of the High Commissioner, available at http://www.ohchr.org/EN/NewsEvents/Pages/DisplayNews.aspx?NewsID=14105&LangID=E, accessed 3 July 2015; Sabelo Gumedze, *Addressing the Use of Private Security and Military Companies at the International Level*, ISS Paper 206 (Pretoria: Institute for Security Studies, November 2009), available at http://www.issafrica.org/publications/papers/addressing-the-use-of-private-security-and-military-companies-at-the-international-level, accessed 6 June 2015; United Nations Office of the High Commissioner for Human Rights, "UN Working Group on Mercenaries to Launch Study on the Use of Private Military and Security Companies by the UN" (18 March 2013), available at http://www.ohchr.org/EN/NewsEvents/Pages/DisplayNews.aspx?NewsID=13154&LangID=E, accessed 13 August 2015.

164. Simon Chesterman, "Lawyers, Guns and Money: The Governance of Business Activities in Conflict Zones," *Chicago Journal of International Law* 11, 1 (Summer 2010), page 334.

165. Gaston, "Mercenarism 2.0?" page 232.

166. International Committee of the Red Cross, Montreux Document, pages 36, 39.

167. Won Kidane, "The Status of Private Military Contractors under International Humanitarian Law," *Denver Journal of International Law and Policy* 38, 3 (Summer 2010), pages 412, 419.

168. Ralby, "A Brief Explanation of the Private Security Regulatory Initiatives."

169. James Cockayne, "Regulating Private Military and Security Companies: The Content, Negotiation, Weaknesses and Promise of the Montreux Document," *Journal of Conflict and Security Law* 13, 3 (Winter 2008), page 403.

170. Article 13; Rona, "Remarks by Gabor Rona."

171. Human Rights Council, *Annual Report of the Working Group on the Use of Mercenaries as a Means of Violating Human Rights and Impeding the Exercise of the Right of Peoples to Self-Determination*, A/HRC/15/25 (New York: United Nations Office of the High Commissioner for Human Rights, 2 July 2010), paragraph 7.

172. Articles 4–7.

173. These are defined as "functions which are consistent with the principle of the State monopoly on the legitimate use of force and that a State cannot outsource or delegate to PMSCs under any circumstances. Among such functions are direct participation in hostilities, waging war and/or combat operations, taking prisoners, lawmaking, espionage, intelligence, knowledge transfer with military, security and policing application, use of and other activities related to weapons of mass destruction and police powers, especially the powers of arrest or detention including the interrogation of detainees and other functions that a State party considers to be inherently State functions" (Ralby, "A Brief Explanation of the Private Security Regulatory Initiatives").

174. Articles 9, 12.

175. Articles 10, 11, 19.

176. Articles 21–26, 28.

177. Articles 27, 29.

178. Laurence Juma, "Privatisation, Human Rights and Security: Reflections on the Draft International Convention on Regulation, Oversight and Monitoring of Private Military and Security Companies," *Law, Democracy and Development* 15 (2011).

179. Available at http://www.iso.org/iso/home/standards/iso26000.htm, accessed 25 February 2015.

180. Available at https://www.asisonline.org/Standards-Guidelines/Standards/published/Pages/Management-System-for-Quality-of-Private-Security-Company-Operations-Requirements-with-Guidance.aspx, accessed 26 March 2015.

181. Available at http://www.iso.org/iso/iso_technical_committee?commid=4857900, accessed 15 February 2015.

182. Rebecca DeWinter-Schmitt, "A New Twist to Management Standards, Bringing in Human Rights," *Private Security Monitor* (Summer 2014), available at http://psm.du.edu/commentary/index.html, accessed 4 December 2014.

183. Michael Scheimer, "Separating Private Military Companies from Illegal Mercenaries in International Law: Proposing an International Convention for Legitimate Military and Security Support that Reflects Customary International Law," *American University International Law Review* 24, 3 (2009), page 642. The British government has, together with the UK Accreditation Service, run a pilot project to develop accreditation bodies to audit PMSCs against PSC 1. Olive Group (a renowned PMSC), has, through this process, already received its PSC 1 accreditation.

184. Jacobs, "South Africa's New Counter-Mercenary Law," page 4.

185. Shannon Bosch, *The Combatant Status of Private Military and Security Contractors in International Armed Conflicts, in Light of the International Humanitarian Law Notion of Civilian Direct Participation in Hostilities*, PhD thesis (Durban: University of KwaZulu-Natal, 2013), chapter 6.

186. Notably the United States, Australia, Canada, and the United Kingdom.

187. Benjamin Perrin, *On the Edges of Conflict: Humanitarian Assistance and the Private Security Debate—An International Humanitarian Law Perspective* (no publisher, no date), page 21, available at http://www.croixrouge.ca/cmslib/general/oteoc_ben_perrin.pdf, accessed 15 December 2014.

188. Zoe Salzman, "Private Military Contractors and the Taint of a Mercenary Reputation," *International Law and Politics* 40 (2008), page 859.

189. Bosch, *The Combatant Status of Private Military and Security Contractors in International Armed Conflicts*, page 154.

190. Human Rights Council, *Annual Report of the Working Group on the Use of Mercenaries as a Means of Violating Human Rights and Impeding the Exercise of the Right of Peoples to Self-Determination*, paragraph 7.

191. Peter Singer, "Humanitarian Principles, Private Military Agents: Implications of the Privatized Military Industry for the Humanitarian Community," *Brown Journal of World Affairs* 13, 1 (Fall/Winter 2006), page 3.

192. Gomez del Prado, "Mercenaries, Private Military and Security Companies and International Law," page 25.

193. O'Brien, "PMCs, Myths and Mercenaries," pages 59–60.

194. Taljaard, "Implementing South Africa's Regulation of Foreign Military Assistance Act," page 167.

195. Shannon Bosch and Marelie Maritz, "South Africa Private Security Contractors Active in Armed Conflicts: Citizenship, Prosecution and the Right to Work," *Potchefstroom Electronic Law Journal* 14, 7 (2011), page 102.

196. Tim Murithi, "The South Africa Defence Review: A Contrarian Perspective," South Africa Foreign Policy Initiative, Policy Brief 4 (5 July 2012), page 1; Mark Paterson, rapporteur, "The South African Defence Review of 2012: Problems, Progress, and Prospects," Centre for Conflict Resolution Policy Brief 11 (3 May 2012), page 1.

197. South Africa Department of Defence, *South Africa Defence Review 2014* (Pretoria: Ministry of Defence, 2014), chapter 3, paragraph 48, which was finally published in 2014, available at http://www.gov.za/sites/www.gov.za/files/defencereview_2014_ch10-13.pdf, accessed 6 June 2015.

198. South Africa Department of Defence, *South Africa Defence Review 2014*, chapter 3, paragraph 48.

Chapter Three

Privatizing the Israeli Defense Forces

Retracing the Public-Private Divide

Guy I. Seidman

The *private-public* distinction is one of the most basic features of Western legal thinking. It suggests that there is and should be a divide between the sphere where governments exercise their powers and the private sphere where nongovernmental entities operate with significant autonomy. This is the distinction between government action and oversight under law and individual liberties. It is the basis of liberal theory and the Rule of Law.[1] Although contested,[2] "in recent decades, different versions of this distinction have attained new or renewed prominence in a wide range of disciplines and areas of inquiry, from 'public choice' economics to social history and feminist scholarship."[3] Moreover, whatever one's view of the theoretical distinction, its impact is significant: how this line is drawn decides which functions will be carried out (or overseen) by government and which will be left to private individuals and corporations. I set the topic of private military and security companies (PMSCs) and their employees in this context.

Many have expressed concern with the rising use of PMSCs to conduct an ever-increasing range of American defense functions: tasks previously carried out by the military and other official functionaries. This transfer of functions to private market entities, a form of "privatization"—to use the idiom commonly used in most Western nations—raises serious concerns. While private firms have long played a role in the provision of services to the American military, the degree of outsourcing was not public knowledge. Only in recent years did the public become aware of large numbers of PMSC personnel used in the field and of the depth and range of tasks entrusted to them. These include running spy networks, intelligence analysis, covert operations, and prisoner interrogation.[4]

In terms of drawing the line between public and private, the case seems very strong for having such functions be solely performed by official agents. One reason is that even libertarians hold national security and foreign relations to be clear examples of governmental tasks.[5] Another is that public entities have a strong claim for a monopoly on the legal use of force.[6] Furthermore, even if some use of PMSCs in the security apparatus can be accepted, surely government must retain effective control and accountability of their actions at all times.[7] All of this explains the wide discomfort over the actual use of PMSCs by the US military and the demands for more official oversight and better control and sanctioning mechanisms.

Although the United States has been central to the study of this phenomenon, Israel offers a contrasting case. Israel has been characterized as a "garrison state,"[8] one "in which the specialists on violence are the most powerful group in society" and "the distinctive frame of reference [for social policy] is fighting effectiveness."[9] Birthed in a war of independence, Israel has been in a near-constant state of conflict since its founding. It "has been compelled to allocate vast human and financial resources toward the development, maintenance, and reinforcement of a large and ever-ready military establishment."[10] As a result, the Israeli Defense Forces (IDF) have played a key role in almost all aspects of Israeli society. Mandatory conscription for all citizens save Arabs allowed the IDF to "serve as a pioneering educational force . . . which will heal tribal and diaspora divisions and implement the historic missions of the State of Israel, by building the homeland and making the deserts bloom."[11] The IDF enjoys massive public support.[12] The Israeli defense budget was 20.8 percent of public expenditures in 1960; it rose to 42.6 percent in 1970 before dropping to 29.4 percent in 1980, 22.1 percent in 1990, 15.8 percent in 2001, 15 percent in 2010, and 13 percent in 2014, the last year data are available.[13] The IDF has traditionally chosen a policy of self-reliance for its materiel requirements, carrying out as much of its own business as it could and buying from private suppliers only when necessary.

In this chapter I argue that matters have changed in Israel. I describe how the IDF leadership identified seismic shifts in Israeli political economy—the rise of neoliberalism—early on and chose to ride, albeit in a controlled fashion, the rising tide of privatization of government functions that has taken place in recent decades. But given the penetration of the IDF into many facets of the Israeli economy, and its provision of services that in many societies would be considered nonmilitary, the question to be addressed is whether privatization touched what would be considered core military functions.

My central conclusion is that, at least for now, the IDF has not devolved core military functions to the private sector. What privatization meant, initially, was the attempt by IDF leadership to curb the army's "national" functions so as to focus on the core function of national defense. More recently, privatization has come to mean the extensive purchase of goods and services from private sector firms.

I conclude the chapter with two additional notes, looking beyond the formal, legal confines of the IDF. The first concerns the Israeli military-industrial complex. Originally created to supply a self-reliant IDF, it now has a much wider scope. The Israeli government allows (but tightly controls) arms exports, and Israel has become one of the world's leading arms exporters. The second concerns the activity of Israeli PMSCs outside of Israel. It looks at how Israelis use the expertise acquired during their military service when they become civilians. While few Israelis appear to have become mercenaries or international weapons dealers, many have built upon the skills acquired in the military service, working in the high-tech industries and earning Israel the moniker "Start-Up Nation."[14] In other words, the Israeli state maintains control over PMSCs by tightly regulating what is privatized, by retaining oversight over what PMSCs actually do in its service, and, to the extent possible, also what they do in their relations with and operation in foreign nations.

ISRAEL'S PATH TO PRIVATIZATION: SOCIETAL CHANGES AND FISCAL CONCERNS

Israel has been in a near-constant state of conflict since its founding. Israelis therefore gave high priority to establishing security forces and organized much of society toward national defense. The very first legal instrument of the new state, the Law and Administration Ordinance, authorized (section 18) the establishment of land, air, and naval armed forces.[15] The IDF—the people's army and the nation's protector—became a superagency employed by the government in all national tasks. Practical reasons entwined with ideological ones. The IDF's conscripts provided a relatively disciplined, cheap, practical tool to carry out its policies. Furthermore, the socialist, collective-oriented, nation-building government of Israel's first prime minister (and minister of defense), David Ben-Gurion, used the IDF as a tool to shape the "new Israeli" and to legitimate and popularize their agenda. The IDF would "contribute to absorption of immigrants, educate for good citizenship and patriotism, and foster culture. IDF engineering units were used to construct and maintain many of the camps, which housed a large number of new immigrants who arrived in the early 1950s."[16]

The IDF's diverse roles in building the nation continued well into the 1990s, when section 18 was amended to clarify that the IDF has the power to act for the accomplishment of national security goals as well as in the defense of the nation. This language resolved any lingering doubts about the legality of soldiers' ability to agree to carry out their military service in the

Israeli police or a host of other "recognized services," including immigration absorption, education, health, homeland security, and so on. In practice, the IDF has set up small units within hospitals, educational facilities, and other public institutions where soldiers performed "national" duties, writ large. The IDF thus has played a broad role in Israeli society for over half a century and modern privatization efforts should be measured against this baseline.

FISCAL CRISES AND IDEOLOGICAL SHIFTS

In recent decades, Israel has undergone extensive social, legal, and economic changes. These have made the privatization of military functions socially acceptable, legally feasible, and economically necessary. It has also opened the door to PMSCs.

Israel once had the image of a young, egalitarian nation where the good of the nation was placed ahead of the interests of the individual, where capitalism was scoffed at, and where the kibbutz, the famous idealistic form of collective settlement, was the country's vanguard. A shift began in 1977 when the Labor-led coalition that had ruled Israel since 1948 lost power. "Chronic hyperinflation and unsustainable public-debt levels in the mid-1980s" brought about "a shift towards market-oriented structural reforms. . . . Anti-inflationary measures were particularly successful, [reducing inflation] to low, single-digit levels by the end of the [1990s]."[17] The policy shift coincided with the collapse of the Soviet bloc and the apparent victory of liberal capitalism as the dominant economic system.

Israel swung from being a socially equitable, welfare-oriented state to the other extreme, in a process more akin to a post-communist regime than to a Western social democracy.[18] A "neo liberal culture of popularity ratings began to develop, marked by personal choice, marketing commercialization and competition. The emphasis on private consumption intersected with post-materialist values that revolved around the needs, liberties, desires and body of the individual" has taken hold.[19] All major political parties in Israel, including Labor, have accepted the nation's shift in orientation toward free-market capitalism. This shift in ideology has even affected the kibbutz. The utopian settlement-form began an extensive privatization process starting in the 1990s. When the movement celebrated its 100th anniversary, it bore only "little resemblance to the ideals which once motivated [the kibbutzim]. . . . Only a quarter of kibbutzim still function as equalized cooperatives, while the rest have begun paying salaries to their members."[20]

The results are mixed. On the one hand, Israel's ruling elite have had a clear preference for privatization of government functions and a significant reduction of spending on subsidies and benefits.[21] This caused a significant shift in the Israeli economy. "The early 1990s also saw the emergence of a world-class, export-based high-tech sector specialising in computer hardware and software, medical technologies and pharmaceuticals."[22] As a result, "Israel . . . has catapulted in the past two decades from a minor state-dominated economy to a market-driven technology hothouse" and in 2010 acceded to "the exclusive club of advanced countries, the Organization for Economic Cooperation and Development [OECD]."[23] On the other hand, the social results are troubling: the attrition of the welfare state has brought a sharp rise in economic inequality and in the number of the poor.[24]

On the other hand, the OECD reported that "public social spending in Israel is 16%, some 5 percentage points below the OECD average."[25] Furthermore, while "defense spending is several percentage points of GDP higher than most OECD countries'. . . civilian spending as a share of GDP has already been whittled down to a relatively low level."[26] It may have been troubling for Israelis to find out that they are the OECD's poorest member with the widest social gaps,[27] but the trend continues. The 2015 budget "contains neither reforms that could spur economic growth nor attempts to reduce poverty and social gaps."[28]

PRIVATIZATION AND THE IDF

It is within this context that Israel's most powerful agencies—the IDF, the Ministry of Defense (MoD), and the Ministry of Finance (MoF)—came to find common ground in privatization. The professional civil servants of the MoF have taken the lead in economic matters after successfully steering the Israeli economy through the meltdown of the 1980s. Under a string of governments with a pro-market, pro-privatization, neoliberal orientation, the MoF and the Bank of Israel have "together brought Israel to balance its budget and behave conservatively and responsibly."[29] The main thrust of their policies was to curb public spending, economize, and privatize government functions to the extent possible.

The practice that has evolved is for the MoF to press the MoD to economize, and leave the IDF with the discretion over the details, that is, to decide which functions to outsource. In the rare cases of a public outcry over a privatization decision, the military can reverse course. Most often the IDF pursues the course of privatization under its own discretion, and it seems that the Israeli public feels comfortable in letting the IDF do so (bear in mind that the Israeli public also entrusts the IDF with the nation's physical survival and entrusts the IDF with its conscript sons and daughters). In recent decades, as more information on IDF failings has come to light, Israelis have a more realistic view of the military but are not significantly less supportive of it. This is why the IDF consistently polls as the most trusted public institution in Israel.[30] Given this level of trust, it is unsurprising to find the Israeli public content to leave the military to decide what functions need to be carried out in uniform and what functions can be "civilianized." Of all agencies of Israeli government, the IDF is seen as "a safe pair of hands," in its traditional meaning of "[a] reliable, if somewhat dull, person who can be entrusted not to make a mistake with a task."[31]

It is difficult to pinpoint the exact moment when the Israeli establishment began seriously considering any form of IDF privatization. The limited public records available suggest that IDF brass came up with the idea in the 1980s, the MoF embraced it, and in recent years it has been pushing the military hard to expand its use across the board. During the financial crisis of the 1980s, the IDF faced growing fiscal pressures from the civilian side of government and increasing expectations from the Israeli public for efficiency, transparency, and accountability. In an effort to retain control over its budget and professional priorities, the IDF leadership chose a policy that focused on maintaining core military functions and devolving "national" functions to other agencies and the private sector.

This began during the term of Chief of Staff Rafael Eitan (1978–1983), who initiated two seemingly contradictory policies. On the one hand he nixed the military bands, hitherto the bedrock of the Israeli entertainment world, to focus military resources on operational military capability. But he retained and expanded some of the social functions of the IDF, including the social project nicknamed "Raful's Youth" that drafts troubled youth to shape them through a socialization and education process in boot camp conditions.

Clearer statements and broader policies on the need to focus IDF resources on its core military business were made by subsequent chiefs of staff. Lieutenant General Dan Shomron (1987–1991) "communicated to a non-military audience his conviction that the IDF ought to be, as he put it, 'smaller and smarter'. . . . His remarks opened a public debate that progressively grew more intense."[32] Indeed, by the early 1990s there were additional reasons to reconsider IDF structure and training: the IDF had trouble policing mutinous civilians in the first Palestinian uprising (1987–1993), and then the Gulf War (1991) suggested that future wars would be based on technological skills and remote-control operations carried out by specialists.

It was probably during the tenure of IDF Chief of Staff Ehud Barak (1991–1995) that the Israeli public became aware that the IDF wished to narrow its role in Israeli society. Barak envisioned a new model for the IDF: a smaller, professional, mission-oriented military. This vision was coined in two oft-quoted expressions: in one he asked for a "small, smart army"; in the other he held that "anything that does not shoot will be cut off," basically vowing to turn the IDF into a modern, professional armed force fit to face the battlefield of the future, even at the price of shedding its societal functions.

During this period, a committee led by a former director general of the Israeli MoF recommended[33] more civilian oversight over military procurement, more transparency, and the taking into account in defense-economy decision making of all economic aspects, that is, considering not just the needs of the military but the full impact of any decision on the Israeli economy. The report is understood to support privatization and outsourcing of military goods, especially those relating to the Israeli military industries,[34] and an effort to make military contracting more orderly.

During this period, much IDF privatization took the form of *demilitarization* of its assets. Given its role in the development of the Israeli nation, the defense establishment has been entrusted with massive public resources ranging from land holdings,[35] to electronic bandwidth, to patents and other forms of intellectual property. These national properties are likely to remain at the disposal of the military for as long as it states a need for them. Therefore the IDF and the MoD had to be "enticed" to free resources that are no longer necessary for military operations or are economically inefficiently used by them.

The process of demilitarizing resources for use by civilian government agencies or private actors has been vigorously pursued in recent decades. Since 1993, Israeli government decisions required the IDF to move military bases out of city centers, with vacated lands to be used for civilian purposes. The expected benefits were triple: freeing prime urban real estate for civilian use, providing more than enough funds for relocation of IDF units, and strengthening the periphery of Israel. This ambitious plan applied to over 120 military installations to make 20,000 acres available for residential building at a cost of over $4 billion but with an expected gain of $7.4 billion for the state.[36] The IDF released communication bandwidth in the 1990s in favor of cellular phone companies in Israel and the Palestinian Authority.[37]

IDF privatization took the form of devolving the provision of goods or services, previously produced or carried out by the state, to a private entity—a form closer to the black-letter definition of privatization. The rationale holds that private firms usually are more efficient and more proficient at producing these goods and services than IDF servicemen. According to the Brodet Report, by 2004 the IDF had significantly privatized its transportation needs (including busing soldiers, leasing passenger cars, and maintenance of most vehicles), its construction and infrastructure projects, many of its instruction services, some airplane maintenance, air force cadet instruction, some IT services, and satellite imaging. The military also reported that it has considered privatizing dining facilities and outsourcing medical services so that they are provided by programs such as HMOs [health maintenance organizations] available to civilians.[38] The head of the IDF Technological and Logistics Directorate spoke quite frankly on this point. "What I wish to do is outsource anything that is not within our core business. . . . The factors we take into account in outsourcing are whether we have the capacity to function in emergency conditions, that there is no damage to operational capacity. . .

and of course long term economic feasibility. . . . About 90% of the Israeli Technological and Logistics Directorate activity is carried out by civilians . . . this is valued at billions of shekels."[39]

Yet the vision of Barak and the Sadan Report enjoyed only limited success. Privatization beyond demilitarization was not particularly attractive to Israelis, who had been socialized into the ethos of the "people's army" and had most often experienced military service firsthand. This may have come as a surprise to the IDF. By the 1990s Israel had undergone major social, political, and economic changes, and many of the IDF's historic "national" nonmilitary assignments had disappeared. Some were just obsolete. Others were provided by civilian (public or private) institutions. IDF chiefs possibly assumed that the public would welcome cutting the military's remaining societal functions in exchange for the promise of a more professional, cost-effective force, but this was not quite the case. IDF plans to shutter its radio station and to stop using conscripts as full-time teachers in field schools met with stiff public and parliamentary opposition.[40]

After a hiatus between the events of September 11, 2001, and the 2006 war between Israel and Hezbollah in Lebanon, the government again moved to focus the IDF on its core military functions. The prime minister appointed a commission with senior members from both sectors. The Brodet Report of May 2007 was rightly touted by the press as "the most comprehensive ever publicized on the functioning of the IDF, its structure and budget, with particularly harsh criticism of the way in which the IDF and the Defense Ministry handled military and budgetary business to date."[41] Its core findings echo the Sadan Report, calling on the IDF to undergo a management revolution and to "learn how to calculate the economic significance of its moves and . . . become more efficient."[42] After the Israeli government approved the Brodet Report, the MoD hired in 2008 the preeminent consulting firm McKinsey & Company to help it effectuate the changes required by the Brodet Report while maintaining control over their execution. The main findings of McKinsey & Co. were officially published in late 2009.[43]

The Brodet Report reveals the contours, rationales, and likely limits of the IDF privatization policy. The report provides a list of what are, presumably, IDF criteria for "civilianization" of IDF functions. These are matters (1) that are not within the core of operational activity; (2) that have long-term economic viability; (3) that have efficient competition in the civilian market; (4) that if civilianized, can still be provided for in times of emergency; (5) that do not contain unique technological know-how that needs to be preserved; (6) that offer no injury to operational capabilities; (7) that can receive security clearance, if needed; and (8) that bring about savings in military payroll costs.[44]

The commission makes two further recommendations. First, it calls for the civilianization of all functions performed in the IDF that can be performed by civilian professionals, such as economists, lawyers, mechanics, and information technology specialists. It stresses the need to bear in mind the real economic costs of such measures but does not elaborate further. Second, it calls on the entire defense establishment to examine whether they should continue executing functions that are not within their "core business." The standard the commission suggests is whether such a function directly contributes to the national defense. Here the commission intimates that many functions should be moved—with their allocated budget—from the MoD to other government agencies whose "core business" it is to police, teach, carry out construction, or assist local communities, all functions now carried out, at least in part, by the MoD and the IDF.[45]

With this endorsement, IDF privatization has begun to extend into some security functions, albeit domestically oriented ones. The IDF has the overall responsibility for Israel's security, and Israel has unusually wide security concerns. Not only must borders be well guarded, but so must institutions ranging from malls to colleges. So it is not surprising that internal security involves the civilian police, private security firms, and the IDF, with the government outlining the role of each body. Some of these functions have been shifted to private sector providers. For example, the operation of checkpoints between Israel and the Palestinian Authority has been privatized. The change occurred through a string of government decisions starting in 1999. The idea was to "civilianize" the checkpoint. At first control was shifted from the IDF to the Israeli Airport Authority and then to private contractors, who effectively operate in a policing capacity. The privatization has drawn criticism from human rights activists and Arab-Israeli spokespersons who claim that it has worsened the already uncomfortable conditions in the checkpoints.[46] On the other hand, purely military checkpoints within Palestinian territories for control of traffic have been and remain the preserve of the IDF. Furthermore, publicly available information suggests that the IDF does not use private companies to carry out actual combat activities, interrogate prisoners, gather intelligence, or perform other core military functions.

Thus privatization of IDF functions in Israel has taken a course similar to that in other countries, with the armed forces becoming more focused on the use and management of violence, devolving support functions to the private sector, and transferring nonmilitary functions to other state agencies and nonstate entities. But given the traditional role of the IDF in Israeli society, the long-term direction of the IDF leadership to professionalize the force and increase its proficiency in core military functions along with the recent shift in Israeli defense policy toward high-intensity conflict suggests that we may see further privatization of non-core functions but not combat.[47]

CONCLUSION

With the devolution of state functions to the private sector on the civilian side and the attempts to focus the IDF on its core military functions on the other, the Israeli military has faced increased public scrutiny of its perks and inefficiencies. This has meant that even major spikes in violence, such as the 2006 war against Hezbollah and major military operations in the Palestinian Territories, did not always lead to budget increases. Conversely, the Israeli defense budget remains large and seems set to increase, not decrease, at the present time. The defense budget increased from NIS 48.6 billion for 2009 to NIS 53.2 billion for 2010, and from 57.5 billion shekels to 70.5 billion in 2014.[48] The trend seems likely to continue in coming years.

In 2015 Israel experienced another round of public debate about the contours of the IDF's roles and responsibilities within Israeli society. A commission appointed to evaluate the defense budget headed by retired IDF Major General Yohanan Locker handed its report in July 2015. It made over 50 cost-saving recommendations starting with limiting manpower expenditure through eliminating pensions for noncombatants, raising retirement age, capping salaries, and reducing personnel by 11 percent. Other notable recommendations included (a) shortening the obligatory service for men from 32 months (to which it had only recently been cut from 36 months) to 24 months by 2020, providing gender equality; (b) raising the defense budget to NIS 59 billion but capping it at that level for five years; (c) "civilianizing" more IDF functions; (d) privatizating and outsourcing functions such as the production of the Merkava tank, the renovation of armored vehicles, and high-level maintenance; and (e) requiring full transparency in MoD dealings with the Prime Minister's Office, the Finance Ministry, and the National Security Council.[49]

The press viewed the report as "an indictment against the way the army was managing itself. Locker determined that the army did not know how to properly manage its manpower and did not know how to properly manage its budget."[50] It cited the report as stating that the "Israeli Army Eats Up Land, Air and Radio Frequencies."[51] It was hardly a surprise that the defense establishment lambasted the report.[52] The fate of the report's specific recommendations is in the hands of the prime minister, but its ideas are likely to have resonance in the public and political arenas for some time to come.[53]

But the devolution of state functions to the private sector that has taken place over the past three decades may be reaching its limit. A petition against the constitutionality of a 2004 statute setting up prison privatization set in motion the first major court intervention in federal privatization.[54] In 2009, a rare nine-justice panel—three-justice panels being the norm—took the exceptional step of striking down the statute. Speaking for an eight-justice majority, court president Dorit Beinisch made clear that the question before her concerned the limits of the state's power to pass on to private entities functions that were hitherto reserved for the state. Her conclusion was that the statute permitting private prisons exacerbates the constitutional infringement on personal liberties already inherent in incarceration and is unconstitutional. The lone dissenter was aware of the constitutional misgivings but even more troubled by the conditions in Israeli prisons and he would have favored judicial restraint.

The impact of this holding on government privatization policy, including in defense, has so far been minimal, but it may have impact in future cases. It is possible that the decision could bar privatization of core military functions under the argument that only the sovereign state may carry them out. This is either because of the potential of such functions to infringe on human and civil rights of people (such as IDF personnel and any persons with whom the IDF engages) or because maintaining monopoly over the use of force is one of the prime justifications for the state itself.[55]

Furthermore, although neoliberal economics has made the argument about conscription leading to the inefficient use of labor in society more respectable and powerful, the IDF's model as a "people's army" driven by mandatory conscription for both men and women enjoys wide support.[56] This holds true despite declining rates of conscription (the IDF itself warns that in the near future, perhaps only 50 percent of Israeli Jewish men will serve in its ranks),[57] concerns over growing disparities in service among subgroups of Israeli society,[58] and the potential loss of motivation for service among the general public.[59] While such trends have preceded the shift to an all-volunteer military in many Western states,[60] it took decades for them to overcome arguments about the use of the military as an institution that forms national identity. As an immigrant nation, Israeli leaders argue that Israel requires such a national institution[61] and as long as conscription is framed in this way, there will be adequate manpower available to perform the core functions of the IDF. It is unlikely that Israel will find itself in a position similar to that of the United States in 2003 when its limited reserves of manpower required the services of PMSCs to fill the gap.[62]

Finally, it seems fair to say that further privatization and outsourcing measures, as well as civilianization of resources held by the military, will take place in the context of the ongoing struggle between the civilian and military sides of government to field an effective military at a reasonable cost to Israeli society. I am relatively comfortable predicting that any measure taken will be long drawn and well judged because both the MoD and the MoF need to be in agreement and because the Israeli public is in many ways more reluctant to accept privatization in the military than the political decision makers. These natural breaks, reinforced by the lack of necessity to turn to the private sector to supply manpower for military operations, the focus on professionalizing the IDF, and the limits to devolving essential governmental functions imposed by the judiciary and the Israeli constitution, will keep Israel on one extreme of the spectrum when it comes to controlling corporate warriors.

NOTES

1. J. L. Hill, "The Five Faces of Freedom in American Political and Constitutional Thought," *Boston College Law Review* 45, 3 (2004), pages 529–30; Trevor R. S. Allan, *Constitutional Justice: A Liberal Theory of the Rule of Law* (Oxford: Oxford University Press, 2001).

2. Erwin Chemerinsky, "Rethinking State Action," *Northwest University Law Review* 80, 3 (Fall 1985), page 505; Gerald Turkel, "The Public/Private Distinction: Approaches to the Critique of Legal Ideology," *Law and Society Review* 22, 4 (1988); Michael D. Birnhack, "Book Review: Privacy in Context," *Jurimetrics: The Journal of Law, Science, and Technology* 51, 4 (Summer 2011), page 463.

3. Jeff Weintraub, "The Theory and Politics of the Public/Private Distinction," in Jeff Weintraub and Krishan Kumar, editors, *Public and Private in Thought and Practice: Perspectives on a Grand Dichotomy* (Chicago: University of Chicago Press, 1997), page 1.

4. The seminal text on this topic is Peter W. Singer, *Corporate Warriors: The Rise of the Privatized Military Contractors* (Ithaca: Cornell University Press, 2003). Other significant texts include Tim Shorrock, *Spies for Hire: The Secret World of Intelligence Outsourcing* (New York: Simon & Schuster, 2008); and Shawn Engbrecht, *America's Covert Warriors: Inside the World of Private Military Contractors* (Washington: Potomac Books, 2010).

5. Robert Nozick, *Anarchy, State, and Utopia* (New York: Basic Books, 1974).

6. In Israel this is reflected in section 6 of Basic Law: The Military, which states that "no armed force other than the Defence Army of Israel shall be established or maintained except under Law" ("Basic Law: The Military," available at http://www.knesset.gov.il/laws/special/eng/basic11_eng.htm, accessed 15 August 2015); Clifford J. Rosky, "Force, Inc.: The Privatization of Punishment, Policing, and Military Force in Liberal States," *Connecticut Law Review* 36, 3 (Spring 2004), page 885, footnote 15.

7. For extensive critique in the specific context of PMSCs see Paul R. Verkuil, *Outsourcing Sovereignty: Why Privatization of Government Functions Threatens Democracy and What We Can Do about It* (New York: Cambridge University Press, 2007); also see Mateo Taussig-Rubbo, "Outsourcing Sacrifice: The Labor of Private Military Contractors," *Yale Journal of Law and Humanities* 21, 1 (Winter 2009); Lindsay P. Cohn, "It Wasn't in My Contract: Security Privatization and Civilian Control," *Armed Forces and Society* 37, 3 (July 2011).

8. Dan Horowitz, "Is Israel a Garrison State?" *Jerusalem Quarterly* 4 (1977); Stephen Goldfield, *Garrison State: Israel's Role in U.S. Global Strategy* (San Francisco: Palestine Focus Publications, 1985); Baruch Kimmerling, "Patterns of Militarism in Israel," *European Journal of Sociology* 34, 2 (November 1993); Gabriel Sheffer, "Has Israel Really Been a Garrison Democracy? Sources of Change in Israel's Democracy," *Israel Affairs* 3, 1 (1996); Harold D. Lasswell, *Essays on the Garrison State* (New Brunswick: Transaction Publishers, 1997), page 132; Jacob Abadi, *Israel's Quest for Recognition and Acceptance in Asia: Garrison State Diplomacy* (London: Frank Cass, 2004).

9. Harold D. Lasswell, "The Garrison State," *American Journal of Sociology* 46, 4 (January 1941), pages 455, 458.

10. Alex Mintz, "Military-Industrial Linkages in Israel," *Armed Forces and Society* 12, 1 (Fall 1985), page 9.

11. Israeli Defense Minister David Ben-Gurion, quoted in Stuart A. Cohen, "From Integration to Segregation: The Role of Religion in the IDF," *Armed Forces and Society* 25, 3 (Spring 1999), page 388.

12. The IDF is trusted by 88.1 percent of Jewish Israelis, the highest of any public institution (Tamar Hermann, Ella Heller, Chanan Cohen, Gilad Be'ery, and Yuval Lebel, *The Israeli Democracy Index 2014* [Jerusalem: The Israel Democracy Institute, 2014], pages 38–39).

13. Data for 1960–2001 from Yaacov Lifshitz, *The Economics of Producing Defense: Illustrated by the Israeli Case* (Dordrecht: Kluwer, 2003), page 98, table 6.6. Data for 2010 and 2014 from Stockholm International Peace Studies Institute, "Military Expenditure by Country as Percentage of Government Spending, 1988–2014," available at http://www.sipri.org/research/armaments/milex/milex_database, accessed 9 August 2015.

14. Dan Senor and Saul Singer, *Start-Up Nation: The Story of Israel's Economic Miracle* (New York: Random House, 2011).

15. No. 1 of 5708-1948, issued on 19 May 1948—five days after Independence Day.

16. Alek D. Epstein and Michael Uritsky, "Questioning the Role of Army in Nation-Building: The Development of Critical Discourse on Civil-Military Relations in Israel," in Constantine P. Danopoulos, Dhirendra Vajpeyi, and Amir Bar-Or, editors, *Civil-Military Relations, Nation Building, and National Identity: Comparative Perspectives* (Westport: Praeger, 2004), page 169.

17. Furthermore, society is complicated, with many policy agendas rooted in ethnicity and religion (Angel Gurría, "Presentation of the Labour Market and Social Policy Review of Israel: Remarks by Angel Gurría, OECD Secretary-General, at the Roundtable with Israel's Finance Minister Yuval Steinitz. Prime Minister's Office in Jerusalem, 19 January 2010," available at http://www.oecd.org/israel/presentationofthelabourmarketandsocialpolicyreviewofisrael.htm, accessed 15 August 2015). Also see Yair Aharoni, "The Changing Political Economy of Israel," *Annals of the American Academy of Political and Social Science* 555, 1 (January 1998); on the Israeli economy in the early 1980s see Zalman F. Shiffer, "Money and Inflation in Israel: The Transition of an Economy to High Inflation," *Federal Reserve Bank of St. Louis Review* 64, 7 (August/September 1982).

18. Jonathan Nitzan and Shimshon Bichler, *The Global Political Economy of Israel: From War Profits to Peace Dividends* (London: Pluto Press, 2002); Adam Hanieh, "From State-Led Growth to Globalization: The Evolution of Israeli Capitalism," *Journal of Palestine Studies* 32, 4 (Summer 2003).

19. Uri Ben-Eliezer, "Post-Modern Armies and the Question of Peace and War: The Israeli Defense Forces in the 'New Times,'" *International Journal of Middle East Studies* 36, 1 (February 2004), pages 52–53. Israel joined the OECD in 2010 (Organization for Economic Cooperation and Development, "Israel's Accession to the OECD," available at http://www.oecd.org/israel/israelsaccessiontotheoecd.htm, accessed 7 August 2015).

20. Eli Ashkenazi, "Degania A, First Kibbutz in Israel, to Undergo Privatization," *Ha'aretz* (17 February 2007); Eli Ashkenazi, "After 100 Years, the Kibbutz Movement Has Completely Changed," *Ha'aretz* (7 January 2010).

21. Nehemia Shtrasler, "Privatization Is Good," *Ha'aretz* (8 November 2009).

22. Gurría, "Presentation of the Labour Market."

23. Ethan Bronner, "Issues Stand before Israel in Joining Elite Group," *New York Times* (20 January 2010), page A7. Nonetheless, he notes, Israel's "secretive weapons trade, patent-bending drug industry and occupation of Arab lands are raising last-minute questions."

24. Miri Endweld, Daniel Gotleib, and Refaela Cohen, *Poverty and Inequality in Income Distribution in Israel, 2006/7: Main Findings* (National Insurance Institute, Research and Planning Administration, February 2008).

25. Barak Ravid, "OECD Entrance Is 'Seal of Approval,' Netanyahu Says," *Ha'aretz* (10 May 2010); Meirav Arlosoroff, "The Most Exciting, Screwed-Up Country in the World," *Ha'aretz* (11 May 2010).

26. Ravid, "OECD Entrance Is 'Seal of Approval.'"

27. Liel Kyzer, "Israel Set to Become OECD's Poorest Member," *Ha'aretz* (20 January 2010); Dana Weiler-Polak, "Poll: Nearly 50% of Israelis Fear State Is Pushing Them into Poverty," *Ha'aretz* (17 November 2009); Rafael D. Frankel, "The Loud Awakening of Israel's Secular Middle Class," *The Atlantic* (8 August 2011), available at http://www.theatlantic.com/international/archive/2011/08/the-loud-awakening-of-israels-secular-middle-class/243263/, accessed 7 August 2015.

28. Moti Bassok, "Cabinet Approves 88 Billion Budget for 2015," *Ha'aretz* (8 October 2014).

29. Meirav Arlosoroff, "Soft Landing Israel Teaches the World a Lesson in Economics," *Ha'aretz* (15 September 2009).

30. Hermann, Heller, Cohen, Be'ery, and Lebel, *The Israeli Democracy Index 2014*, pages 38–39.

31. Gary Martin, "A Safe Pair of Hands," *The Phrase Finder*, available at http://www.phrases.org.uk/meanings/309350.html, accessed 9 August 2015.

32. Stuart A. Cohen, *Israel and Its Army: From Cohesion to Confusion* (London: Routledge, 2008), page 83.

33. Secondary sources indicate; the report itself remains unpublished.

34. Which at the time were already suffering a deep financial crisis; the massive and often economically struggling military industries have been the subject of government privatization efforts for decades, and many of them still are. See, e.g., Niv Elis, "Israel Military Industries Moving Ahead with Privatization," *Jerusalem Post* (5 March 2015); also see Guy Seidman and Eyal Nun, "Women, the Military and the Court: Israel at 2001," *Southern California Review of Law and Women's Studies* 11, 1 (Fall 2001).

35. On this, see particularly Zafrir Rinat, "How Did IDF Gain Control over Half of the Country?" *Ha'aretz* (17 November 2008), available at http://www.haaretz.com/print-edition/business/how-did-idf-gain-control-over-half-of-the-country-1.257326, accessed 15 August 2015.

36. See Brodet Commission, *Doch ha-Va'adah Libchinal Taktziv ha-Bitacho* (Jerusalem), 2007, pages 100–102. See Yuval Azulai and Lilach Weissman, "Cabinet Sets Up Company to Move IDF Bases to South," *Globes* (1 April 2015), available in Hebrew at http://www.globes.co.il/en/article-cabinet-sets-up-company-to-move-idf-bases-to-south-1000998342, accessed 15 August 2015; Noa Korsk, "Tel Aviv and Netanya Security Systems Will Pay Tens of Millions for Construction of Luxury Towers," *Ha'aretz* (16 May 2010), available in Hebrew at http://www.haaretz.co.il/hasite/spages/1169088.html, accessed 8 August 2015.

37. Brodet Commission, *Doch ha-Va'adah Libchinal Taktziv ha-Bitacho*, page 102.

38. Brodet Commission, *Doch ha-Va'adah Libchinal Taktziv ha-Bitacho*, pages 103–4.

39. Remarks of General Udi Adam in a 2004 lecture. He was later one of the first generals to resign over the failings of the Second Israeli-Lebanese War. See Idi Adam, "Transcript of The Future Structuring of Israel's Defense Industries," seminar held at the Fisher Institute for Air and Space Strategic Studies (12 September 2004), available in Hebrew at http://www.fisherinstitute.org.il/?CategoryID=23&ArticleID=121, accessed 8 August 2015.

40. The public debate in the Knesset revealed some of the figures of this scheme: in 2000 there were 1,700 soldier-teachers; the 2008 level was 1,000. Opposition Knesset member Zevulun Orlev stated that 300 fewer teachers meant the desertion of perhaps 3,000 of the weakest students in the system, but there was no real disagreement around the table. See Rebecca Anna Stoil, "Orlev Calls to Thwart Tamir's 40% Cut to National Service," *Jerusalem Post* (21 May 2008).

41. Meirav Arlosoroff, "Brodet: Slashing Army Training Was Wrong," *Ha'aretz* (30 March 2007).

42. "The commission accused the IDF of manipulating data presented to the government to increase its budget. The commission also accused the IDF of failing to consider the economic ramifications of much of its activities, which caused it to squander vast amounts of ammunition during the Second Lebanon War" (Arlosoroff, "Brodet"). The commission did, however, recommend a one-time addition to the budget, taking account of the war with Lebanon (Brodet Commission, *Doch ha-Va'adah Libchinal Taktziv ha-Bitacho*, page 19).

43. Israeli Defense Forces, "IDF to Follow McKinsey and Co.'s Recommendations for Efficiency" (25 November 2009), available at http://www.idf.il/1283-11888-en/Dover.aspx, accessed 15 August 2015.

44. Brodet Commission, *Doch ha-Va'adah Libchinal Taktziv ha-Bitacho*, page 103. The commission notes that the IDF currently does not calculate the real costs of conscript service.

45. Brodet Commission, *Doch ha-Va'adah Libchinal Taktziv ha-Bitacho*, pages 105, 106.

46. Meron Rapoport, "Outsourcing the Checkpoints," *Ha'aretz* (2 October 2007).

47. Scott C. Farquha, editor, *Back to Basics: A Study of the Second Lebanon War and Operation CAST LEAD* (Fort Leavenworth: US Army Combined Arms Center, 2009); David E.

Johnson, *Hard Fighting: Israel in Lebanon and Gaza* (Santa Monica: RAND Corporation, 2011).

48. Moti Bassok, "Defense Budget to Grow, Education Spending to Shrink," *Ha'aretz* (30 September 2009); Zvi Zrahiya, "Defense Budget for 2014 Tops 70 Billion Shekels," *Ha'aretz* (7 December 2014). Official estimates suggested that the Second Lebanon War had limited impact on the Israeli economy: see Zeev Klein, "Central Bureau of Statistics: The Second Lebanon War Will Cut Israel's GDP in 2006 by 0.7%, or NIS 5 billion," *Globes* (20 September 2006). As for operation "Cast Lead," the IDF claimed that its expenses for reservist mobilization, weapons use, and home front activities in the operation came to NIS 4 billion. See "PM Orders NIS 2.4b. to Restock IDF," *Jerusalem Post* (10 February 2009), page 6.

49. Yaakov Lappin and Yonah Jeremy Bob, "Locker Commission Calls for Massive IDF Budget Cuts Across-the-Board," *Jerusalem Post* (21 July 2015); Avital Lahav, "Locker Committee Recommends Freezing Defense Budget for Five Years," *ynetnews.com* (21 July 2015), available at http://www.ynetnews.com/articles/0,7340,L-4682560,00.html, accessed 8 August 2015; Meirav Arlosoroff, "Locker IDF Reforms: More Money, More Transparency," *Ha'aretz* (22 July 2015).

50. Alex Fishman, "The Opening Shot of the Battle for the Defense Budget," *ynetnews.com* (25 July 2015), available at http://www.ynetnews.com/articles/0%2c7340%2cL-4683778%2c00.html, accessed 8 August 2015.

51. Arik Mirovsky and Amitai Ziv, "Israeli Army Eats Up Land, Air and Radio Frequencies, Says Special Panel," *Ha'aretz* (22 July 2015). The MoD was said to have direct control over 40 percent of the country's land and some influence on planning for another 40 percent.

52. Fishman, "The Opening Shot"; Yael Klein, "Defense Minister Ya'alon: 'The Locker Commission Report Is Superficial and Unbalanced,'" *JerusalemOnline.com* (21 July 2015), available at http://www.jerusalemonline.com/news/politics-and-military/politics/israeli-defense-minister-condemns-locker-commission-report-14763, accessed 8 August 2015; Gil Cohen, "Ya'alon: Proposed IDF Reforms 'a Gamble on the Lives of Israeli Citizens,'" *Ha'aretz* (21 July 2015); Rotem Starkman, "The Profligate Israeli Army Will Fight Criticism with Every Weapon It Has," *Ha'aretz* (23 July 2015).

53. Lilach Weissman, "PM to Decide on Locker Report Defense Cuts," *Globes* (23 July 2015), available in Hebrew at http://www.globes.co.il/en/article-netanyahu-to-decide-on-locker-report-1001055175, accessed 8 August 2015; Jonathan Lis, "To Craft Defense Budget, Netanyahu to Compare Panel's Report with Military's Plan," *Ha'aretz* (28 July 2015); Moti Bassok, "Locker Does Less to Trim Army Spending than It Seems," *Ha'aretz* (24 July 2015), available at http://www.haaretz.com/beta/.premium-1.667562, accessed 15 August 2015; Amos Harel, "More than Half of Israel's Security Cabinet Wants Say in Defense Budget," *Ha'aretz* (27 July 2015); Saul Amstrdmski, "Kahlon, Netanyahu, and Others: Locker Recommendations Will Not Be Implemented in the Near Term," *Calcalist* (4 August 2015), available in Hebrew at http://www.calcalist.co.il/local/articles/0,7340,L-3666068,00.html, accessed 8 August 2015.

54. The Supreme Court Sitting as the High Court of Justice, *H.C.J. 2605/05 Academic Center for Law and Business, Human Rights Division v. Minister of Finance* (Jerusalem: 19 November 2009).

55. Joshua Horwitz and Casey Anderson, "Taking Gun Rights Seriously: The Insurrectionist Idea and Its Consequences," *Albany Government Law Review* 1, 2 (2008); on the effects of private contractors on the state see Kimo Sassi, "Committee Opinion: Private Military and Security Firms and the Erosion of the State Monopoly on the Use of Force" (Strasbourg: European Parliamentary Assembly, 27 January 2009), available at http://assembly.coe.int/nw/xml/XRef/Xref-DocDetails-EN.asp?fileid=12076&lang=EN&search=InByaXZhdGUgY29udHJhY3RvcnMiIA, accessed 15 August 2015.

56. For a general introduction to IDF conscription policies see Seidman and Nun, "Women, the Military and the Court."

57. Gil Cohen, "IDF Expanding Net of Recruits but 1 in 6 Won't Finish Service," *Ha'aretz* (9 December 2014).

58. Yagil Levi and Shlomo Mizrahi, "Alternative Politics and the Transformation of Society-Military Relations: The Israeli Experience," *Administration and Society* 40, 1 (March 2008); Yagil Levy, "Military-Society Relations: The Demise of the 'People's Army,'" in Guy

Ben-Porat, Yagil Levy, Schlomo Mizrahi, Ayre Naor, and Erez Tzfadia, editors, *Israel since 1980* (Cambridge: Cambridge University Press, 2008), page 117.

59. Amos Harel, "Discarding Their Uniform Thought," *Ha'aretz* (6 August 2004); Amos Harel, "IDF Facing Shortage of New Soldiers," *Ha'aretz* (24 February 2012).

60. Karl W. Haltiner and Tibor Szvircsev Tresch, "New Trends in Civil-Military Relations: The Decline of Conscription in Europe," in Alise Weibull and Abrahamsson Bengt, editors, *The Heritage and the Present: From Invasion Defence to Mission Oriented Organization* (Karlstad: Digitaltryck, 2008).

61. Stuart A. Cohen, "The Israel Defense Forces (IDF): From a 'People's Army' to a 'Professional Military'—Causes and Implications," *Armed Forces and Society* 21, 2 (Winter 1995); Cohen, "From Integration to Segregation"; Cohen, *Israel and Its Army*.

62. Moshe Schwartz and Jennifer Church, *Department of Defense's Use of Contractors to Support Military Operations: Background, Analysis, and Issues for Congress* (Washington: Congressional Research Service, 17 May 2013), page 4.

Chapter Four

Private Security and Somali Piracy

The Challenges of the Maritime Marketplace

Christopher Spearin

"Unprecedented." That term aptly describes the nature of Somali piracy over the past decade as well as the international community's legal, diplomatic, and military response.[1] In particular, the term applies to American recommendations, presented over a number of years, that try to shift responsibility for protecting the sea lanes onto commercial shippers. On 17 November 2008, Vice Admiral Bill Gortney, then serving as the US Fifth Fleet commander, asserted that "companies don't think twice about using security guards to protect their valuable facilities ashore. Protecting valuable ships and their crews at sea is no different."[2] When he learned that international private military and security companies (PMSCs) were considering anti-piracy contracts, Gortney's spokesperson, Lieutenant Nate Christensen, said this was "a great trend. . . . We would encourage shipping companies to take proactive measures to help ensure their own safety."[3] In his April 2009 congressional testimony, General David Petraeus, then the commander of US Central Command, argued that shippers would have to "get more serious" about their own security and consider employing private security.[4] In a similar way in October 2012, Andrew Shapiro, the assistant secretary of state for the Bureau of Political-Military Affairs, offered this strong endorsement for PMSC usage: "Perhaps the ultimate security measure a commercial ship can adopt is the use of privately contracted armed security teams."[5] In light of the heavy concentration of shipping around the Horn of Africa, let alone the maritime traffic in the Indian Ocean, this call seemingly promotes a substantial opportunity for PMSCs. What is more, the call implicitly indicates that the US Navy will not be providing further resources at sea to counter Somali piracy.[6]

This embrace of the private sector by US military commanders and others with responsibility to ensure safe passage along these sea lanes[7] raises a number of questions. What are the supply and demand dynamics? Are there unique factors related to the maritime environment that will impact the desired PMSC presence? What are the concerns regarding regulation? What might some of the implications be for maintaining freedom of navigation?

In answering these questions, I contend that while the land-oriented PMSC industry, the focus of much of this book, conditions the maritime marketplace, the very nature of the maritime environment raises distinctive issues that are material, legal, and normative in nature. When viewed as a partner alongside state naval assets, the PMSC industry can complement navies, but cannot replace navies nor execute in full the responsibilities of these navies, real or potential, in countering Somali piracy. When viewed as the prominent provider of security, PMSCs upset traditional notions of who does what with respect to maintaining freedom of navigation. This in turn presents concerns about regulation and performance.

"RESPONSIBILIZATION"

The US Navy's call for PMSC-shipper engagement has a normative underpinning—"responsibilization."[8] This recasts traditional conceptions of state/civil society responsibilities such that nonstate actors are seen "as a set of autonomous subjects both responsible for and capable of securing themselves"[9] rather than as objects whose security is provided predominantly by the state. As Anna Leander and Rens van Munster describe it, this is a process that reorients the relationship between the state and civil society and empowers nonstate actors to seek out their own security or to exist as security actors in their own right. While states can seek to shape the marketplace, security is nevertheless *conceived* as a market-based issue rather than something provided primarily or solely by the state.[10] This is, according to Pat O'Malley, "a technology of governance that removes the key conception of regulating individuals by collectivist risk management, and throws back upon the individual the responsibility for managing risk."[11]

This process differs on land versus at sea. On land, there is an ideational space for PMSC operations that overlaps and stands apart from the state security sector.[12] While somewhat similar dynamics exist at sea, there are also intervening factors related to freedom of navigation, hegemonic activism, and anti-piracy activities generally. The United Nations Convention on the Law of the Sea (UNCLOS), in its various provisions, helps ensure that the rights of states to enjoy freedom of navigation are not unduly restricted, a concept dating from Hugo Grotius' thinking in the seventeenth century.[13] Legally, ships are treated as sovereign entities and generally only a state's military/policing vessels are allowed to interfere with the travels and conduct of like flagged ships in international waters without permission or special authorization. Yet it is also historically accurate to write that navies of hegemonic sea powers over the past two centuries have traditionally backstopped this freedom of navigation for both altruistic and self-interested strategic and commercial reasons.

Because the US Navy, *the sole remaining global navy today in light of its size and forward presence*, has itself made the call for PMSC-shipper engagement to counter Somali piracy, it has implicitly bypassed flagging states, whatever their capabilities. It has also ignored whatever regulations these states may have in place about the permissibility of arms on board, and is directly focused on a nonstate actor—the shipper.

Certainly, promoting PMSC-shipper engagement has some appeal given the challenges the US Navy and other state naval forces encounter in confronting Somali piracy; even with considerable naval assets deployed, the overall anti-piracy effort has been limited in effect. Evolving pirate tactics and strategies, such as the use of long-range pirate "mother ships" and shifts in the hunting zones, have expanded the potential area of operations to 2.5 million square miles. Though as many as 60 naval vessels would be required to secure passage in the Gulf of Aden alone, the international presence is often limited to around 30 ships operating not only in the gulf, but also off Somalia, in the Arabian Sea, and out into the larger Indian Ocean.[14] Geographically localized initiatives, therefore, such as the Maritime Security Patrol Area in the Gulf of Aden and the subsequent Internationally Recommended Transit Corridor, have limited usefulness given the vastness. Compounding this challenge for state naval forces is the quickness of Somali pirates; a ship's capture can take less than 15 minutes.

As for optimization, international naval forces are often oddly both overly capable and less than adequate for anti-piracy tasks. On the one hand, they together possess expensive and sophisticated armaments designed to destroy sometimes substantial targets in the air, on and beneath the waves, and on land—a significant measure of overkill for the small pirate skiffs and even the larger mother ships. On the other hand, though some improvements have been made given the challenges posed by small craft and maritime terrorism, most major surface vessels are designed primarily to detect and confront like high-end vessels at stand-off ranges.[15]

PMSC-SHIPPER ENGAGEMENT

Private security is a client-centered enterprise that has elements familiar to both military endeavors and policing, but which also stands apart from these traditionally state-focused activities. The range of PMSC services on land includes consulting, advisement, risk assessment, training, and static and mobile security services. Above all, PMSC-applied violence is predominantly defensive and protective in orientation. Informing this stance, in part, is the desire to avoid the pejorative term "mercenary." Equally, the industry's role is to complement state security sector activities rather than actively supplant them.[16] From one angle, this is manifest in documents from earlier in this century such as the Coalition Provisional Authority's directive in Iraq. In these policies, PMSCs were not to be involved in offensive combat operations and law enforcement operations. From another angle, this is manifest in the desires of some militaries, such as those of the US, the UK, Australia, and Canada, to emphasize their combat operations and their offensive application of violence such that they wish to be seen (and to see themselves) as highly trained specialists in this particular niche. This offensive/defensive division is an extension of a wider trend across militaries to accentuate the "teeth" rather than the "tail" aspects of military operations, with the latter becoming the target of privatization.

In one sense then, the US Navy's call for PMSC-shipper engagement is in keeping with the industry's particular defensive orientation and capabilities on land. PMSCs do not control the vessel and, by default, there is not the opportunity to conduct offensive operations. Similarly, because the PMSC industry is primarily based on contractual manpower rather than on the ownership of substantial equipment, only a few maritime PMSCs at the time of writing have vessels that could be interposed between pirates and the ships they are protecting, let alone go on the offensive against pirate skiffs and mother ships.

What is more, established legal restrictions regarding violence do limit firms. For instance, Article 107 of UNCLOS details a definite state focus: "A seizure on account of piracy may be carried out only by warships or military aircraft, or other ships or aircraft clearly marked and identifiable as being on government service and authorized to that effect." This limits what PMSCs can do because through their engagement with shippers, they cannot be viewed as *under government service*. Indeed, PMSCs working under contract to commercial shippers have to be wary. They could themselves be accused of piracy as defined by Article 101: "any illegal acts of violence or detention, or any act of depredation, committed for private ends by the crew or the passengers of a private ship or a private aircraft." This means that firms are protecting commercial shipping rather than proactively hunting pirates at sea or dealing aggressively with the ramifications of piracy. This runs contrary to some calls suggesting that an unconventional threat against which the conventional military forces of states sometimes encounter difficulties, functionally and legally, should increasingly be met by a robust unconventional response.[17] PMSCs can *deter* and *counter* Somali pirates in some ways, but they cannot *combat* them.

Challenges, therefore, remain regarding how the US Navy and other naval forces can or should combat piracy and potentially capture pirates; they cannot be rectified by a forceful PMSC panacea. On the one hand, United Nations Security Council Resolution 1816 of 2 June 2008 first opened the door, with the Somali interim government's permission, for assertive naval operations extending into Somali waters (i.e., including the right of reverse hot pursuit from the high seas into territorial waters). This involves "'all necessary means' to repress acts of piracy and armed robbery at sea, in a manner consistent with relevant provisions of international law." On the other hand, navies are less adept at gathering evidence required for successful legal prosecution, some vessels may not have the capacity to detain large numbers of suspects, and the delivery of suspects may take time off station. Also, the possible lack of a timely delivery for prosecution may violate the domestic laws of the particular navy's country.[18] Extradition to Somalia is problematic due to the lack of rule of law and the strong likelihood of mistreatment. Trial in Western countries may lead to claims for political asylum. Moreover, because Resolution 1816 is to be interpreted as consistent with international law (i.e., UNCLOS), naval forces are subject to Article 110, meaning that a suspect pirate vessel cannot be fired on; it has to be visited first to determine whether it is involved in piracy before more assertive action can be taken. Only when naval forces directly witness piratical activity (note the aforementioned 15-minute window) or know conclusively that a ship has been captured by pirates can assertive action be taken.

CONCERNS REGARDING CONDUCT, ORGANIZATION, AND GOVERNANCE

No doubt, PMSC utilization by shippers reduces concerns about naval optimization and force and legal limitations noted above. Put differently, a new mind-set might develop, one premised on the "mentality" of private security as described by sociologist Les Johnston: "The practice of commercial security is informed by a risk-based mentality whose focus is instrumental, calculative, preventative, anticipatory and future-oriented. . . . In particular, risk reduction is consistent with a penal philosophy less preoccupied with inflicting punishment than with minimizing harm."[19] The US Navy and other naval forces would not have to worry about being everywhere at once or trying to respond in time as PMSC operations would be widespread enough to largely preclude assertive action or "punishment." PMSC-shipper engagement would be convoying on a micro, close, and more effective scale in a manner that is more sensitive to the demands of commercial shippers than to the timetables set by military exigencies.

In this vein, as Johnston suggests, there is the potential for admirable objectives through private, nonstate actors: "There is no reason, in principle, why commercial security—whether considered at sub-national, national, or transnational levels—should be unable to contribute to collective well-being, *provided that it is located within an appropriate governmental regime.*"[20] The word "governmental" is important because both state governments and other actors are involved, a collective concept described as security governance.[21]

The word "appropriate" is likewise important and here there is some cause for concern. It is important to recall that problems related to PMSCs operating on land in Afghanistan and Iraq caused significant political and operational ramifications for clients, state and nonstate alike, and it is only now that governance structures are becoming robust. Such governance is important. As the British government warned back in 2002, privatized violence has to be controlled in a special way because "actions in the security field have implications which go beyond those of normal commercial transactions."[22]

Building on this and in contrast to PMSC land operations, there is only a limited possibility of private backup or rapid reaction forces at sea should a *tripwire*, an intrinsically land-oriented term, be activated. In this context, since firms do not have the overkill capabilities of state navies and should the deterrence provided by the mere PMSC presence fail, then violence may have to be employed effectively, responsibly, and legally in a self-defensive manner. This means that PMSC personnel must not only be resourceful and capable, they must also be familiar with the nature of sea conditions, the specific demands of ship operations and architecture, and the usage of special maritime equipment. Not having these skills may mean a lack of mission success, accidents, and even a PMSC's commercial downfall. It may also pose negative implications for the reputations and/or bottom lines of states and shippers. As officials from Hart Security suggest, "the work at sea is very different to that on land. . . . Everything is at stake here."[23]

PMSCs on land also benefit from task divisions on the basis of abilities and cost-related decisions. In order to obtain sufficient numbers of personnel in a cost-effective manner for land operations as David Perry identifies in chapter 6 of this book, locals or third-country nationals from Asia, Africa, and South America are employed in the tens of thousands. These individuals are remunerated at rates several times lower than individuals possessing past experience from developed-world security sectors. They also often perform tasks, such as static guarding, that require less training than either their developed-world military counterparts or the developed-world PMSC employees often working in managerial posts or conducting close protection, training, and intelligence assessments.

With these factors in mind, the PMSC industry has faced challenges regarding personnel with limited maritime capabilities. With the interventions of the early twenty-first century coming to a close, PMSCs are looking for further contracts and diversification in order to remain viable. There are also start-ups looking to cash in. As one PMSC official put it, many firms are "fly-by-night companies started up around people's kitchen tables."[24] Though a firm's maritime experience may be lacking, anti-piracy operations are nevertheless an ideal opportunity.[25] As well, when looking at PMSC anti-piracy endeavors, some firms have sought out personnel with more limited skill sets that can come more cheaply in order to meet demand, but this runs the risk of mishap.

GOVERNMENTAL RESPONSE

To handle these challenges, the international response has certainly been "governmental," though the "appropriateness" of the efforts is uncertain. To explain, in September 2011, the United Nations' International Maritime Organization (IMO) reversed its policy of discouraging the arming of merchant ships in any way, though it did so in a limited manner. On the one hand, through the issuing of circulars, especially for flag states, ship owners, ship operators, and shipmasters, the IMO offered recommendations for the different actors to consider in their risk assessments, vetting, and hiring procedures regarding PMSCs. In 2012, the IMO also backed the creation of the International Organization for Standardization's Publically Available Specification 28007. This specification concerned "Guidelines for Private Maritime Security Companies (PMSC) providing privately contracted armed security personnel (PCASP) on board ships." On the other hand, the IMO asserted that PMSCs were not an "alternative to Best Management Practices" and that its recommendations were "not intended to endorse or institutionalize" PMSC involvement.[26] Also, in keeping with the IMO's character as an interstate organization, it underscored that each flag state was to determine the permissibility of PMSCs and the actual authorization requirements. Simply put, whereas the US Navy's call attempted to responsibilize shippers and revealed limits to the de facto security provided for merchants by the hegemonic sea power, the IMO reminded flagging states that they possessed de jure responsibilities in framing the security decisions to be made by shippers.

The response of flagging states has not been homogeneous vis-à-vis state regulation. This is evident in three different ways. First, some states, such as the Netherlands, have prohibited ships sailing under their respective flags from utilizing PMSCs. They do not shape the marketplace in which shippers act. Second, some states, such as Liberia, Norway, and the United Kingdom, have developed regulations but have placed among their requirements proof of risk evaluation. In this vein, it is unclear the degree to which states monitor and enforce their requirements, especially at sea, and if some of the long-standing regulatory divides between national ship registries and "flags of convenience" will arise. Third, some states have been especially "hands-on" in their approach. Cyprus, for instance, is working to facilitate PMSC vetting on the behalf of shippers. As well, Spain has trained private personnel providing security aboard Spanish-flagged fishing ships operating in the Indian Ocean.

State officials often indicate that, even with their guidance, shippers would be wise to consult their insurers regarding the appropriateness and costs associated with PMSCs. This approach reflects the aforementioned "governmental" nature of the response and the importance insurance plays more generally in maritime affairs.[27] However, the collective stance taken by the industry is far from clear. On the one hand, in some cases the industry has promoted the use of PMSCs. For instance, Swinglehurst Limited, an insurance broker, and Hart Security have together developed a product that combines PMSC personnel, security preparation measures, and discounted war risk insurance coverage. Conversely, and in particular relation to hull/machinery and protection and indemnity insurance, there is some hesitation toward the PMSC presence.[28] The US Congressional Research Service, for instance, in its survey of the insurance industry found that "despite the persistence of pirate attacks . . . [many] underwriters are reluctant to employ armed security onboard their vessels. The use of armed security may create third-party liabilities if security officers harm innocent mariners or vessels. . . . [I]nsurers contend that arming ship crews would encourage pirates to be more violent when taking a ship, increasing the risks to cargo, vessels, and crew."[29] Building upon insurers' concerns is the worry that increases in PMSC usage, especially while state regulations develop and are untested, will lead to a qualitative decrease among firms.[30]

Indeed, some shippers are worried about whether firms have the ability to employ violence responsibly and competently. Many of the concerns raised by those calling for a more aggressive approach toward Somali piracy—for instance, the fears of rising and uncontrolled violence negatively affecting trade, seafarers' lives, and environmental disaster—are also raised by those concerned about perceived deficiencies in ethical and responsible PMSC-shipper engagement.[31] Hence, rather than absorb the costs and risks linked to PMSC usage, some shippers have chosen to absorb the expense of increased fuel consumption and the virtual attrition of their fleets that comes with adding sometimes upward of three weeks to transit times.[32]

Another matter relates to those more fundamental understandings about who should be doing what on the high seas and that ensuring freedom of navigation rests with states. Peter Hinchliffe, the International Chamber of Shipping's marine director, argues, "I think what navies are forgetting, and perhaps governments are forgetting as well, is that we are not talking about the protection of an individual ship in a piece of water. What we are talking about is the fundamental obligation of nations to provide safe passage for world trade. So, therefore, it is totally unsatisfactory for naval authorities to try to devolve that responsibility to innocent merchant ships."[33] Put simply, the usage of PMSCs, called for by the US Navy no less, upsets long-standing expectations and assumptions about who provides order at sea.

This matter also points toward why another maritime body, the Baltic and International Maritime Council (BIMCO), an organization for ship owners controlling 65 percent of global tonnage, has only grudgingly changed its views on PMSCs at sea. For BIMCO, PMSC employment is to be a last resort, the preferable option being state-provided vessel protection detachments (VPDs).[34] Despite its reservations, BIMCO felt compelled to act in November 2011: "With the increasing use of armed guards on ships and the fear that second-rate security firms may take advantage of the piracy situation, BIMCO is forging ahead with the development of a standard contract for the employment of armed guards."[35] In March 2012, BIMCO similarly released guidance on the use of force by contracted security while firmly holding its nose: "In providing this Guidance it is assumed that no armed guards shall be deployed without a detailed risk assessment by the Ship owners and that the deployment of armed guards shall not be an alternative to the implementation of the current Best Management Practices (BMP) and other protective measures."[36]

The sudden normative upheaval, therefore, caused by the US's call and reflective of the tenacity of Somali pirates, puts shippers at a disadvantage in structuring their overall relationship with PMSCs. From one standpoint, understandable concerns among shippers with limited experience alongside different flag state regulations will likely hamper the shipping industry's collective ability to develop the PMSC marketplace in a manner to its liking. In a similar way, divisions among humanitarian nongovernmental organizations (NGOs) regarding PMSC services prevented them from employing their potential collective weight in the marketplace.[37] From another standpoint, as we have seen, states in the developed world have significantly shaped the PMSC market through their considerable reliance.[38] In particular, analysts like Deborah Avant argue that the United States has the ability to determine "the [private security] market's ecology"[39] but this has largely been land-centric in orientation. Not surprisingly, debate thus far has focused on whether developed-world states, especially the United States, have actually exercised their influence appropriately and effectively in structuring PMSC involvement in security governance.[40] Similarly, in terms of intragovernmental analysis in the United States, attention has focused on the differences in how the State Department, the Pentagon, and USAID—all prominent US state clients—manage their relationships with PMSCs in the land environment and to what regulatory, and ultimately structural, effect.[41] However, the concerns here are additionally vexing as client status now *befalls shippers* rather than states or the US government writ large. These states, as largely land-centric clients, have not previously shaped the maritime marketplace in any direct way.

CONCLUSION

The analysis above has mostly focused on three main actors involved in the security governance constructs pertaining to anti-piracy endeavors off the Horn of Africa: the United States, PMSCs, and shippers. Given the collective military might of the United States and its specific application in countering Somali piracy, the American call for a PMSC presence is significant. Just as in conflict environments on land, Western militaries have recognized a gap in their ability to provide security at sea and are suggesting that shippers, who stand to directly benefit, turn toward the market to provide a solution. Consideration of PMSCs is important because anti-piracy contracts are part of an evolving industry that is most often linked to contracts on land. Drawing out the exceptional nature of operations at sea is important in order to recognize the unique legal and human rights sensitivities, yet it is unclear if firms countering piracy uniformly possess this understanding. It is uncertain whether they can adapt to be appropriate agents. What is more, the chance for mishaps will likely increase as more and more firms enter the marketplace. Finally, consideration of shippers is important because the responsibility to provide for their own security, particularly of the armed variety, has been thrust upon them. Flag states and insurers, in varying and sometimes contradictory ways, try to shape the marketplace in which shippers must now make their decisions. Taken together, there is no doubt that the unprecedented US call for PMSC-shipper engagement in countering Somali piracy, and its resulting heterogeneous effects, will continue to be intriguing for analysts focused on good conduct and order at sea generally and the development and the maritime spread of the PMSC industry specifically.

NOTES

The views expressed in this chapter are those of the author and do not necessarily reflect those of the Canadian Department of National Defence or the Government of Canada.

1. For analysis of these wider developments, see James Kraska, *Contemporary Maritime Piracy: International Law, Strategy, and Diplomacy at Sea* (Santa Barbara: Praeger, 2011); David F. Marley, *Modern Piracy: A Reference Handbook* (Santa Barbara: ABC-CLIO, 2010).

2. Combined Maritime Forces Public Affairs, "Super Tanker Attacked in Arabian Sea," story number NNS081117-07 (17 November 2008), http://www.navy.mil/search/display.asp?story_id=40943.

3. Katharine Houreld, "Security Firms Join Somali Piracy Fight," *San Francisco Chronicle* (26 October 2008).

4. Tony Capaccio, "Petraeus Urges Ships to Use Armed Guards," *Boston Globe* (25 April 2009), available at http://www.boston.com/news/nation/washington/articles/2009/04/25/petraeus_urges_ships_to_use_armed_guards/, accessed 22 October 2015.

5. Andrew J. Shapiro, "Turning the Tide on Somalia Piracy: Remarks to the Atlantic Council," Department of State Bureau of Public Affairs (26 October 2012), available at http://www.state.gov/t/pm/rls/rm/199927.htm, accessed 22 October 2015.

6. Christopher Spearin, "A Private Security Solution to Somali Piracy? The U.S. Call for Private Security Engagement and the Implications for Canada," *Naval War College Review* 63, 4 (Fall 2010), page 60. At the time of writing, the U.S. Navy's operations in the Gulf of Aden now focus on monitoring Iranian naval assistance to Houthi rebels fighting in Yemen. This effort includes the engagement of an aircraft carrier, the sort of asset not employed in countering piracy. "US Warships Head to Yemeni Waters; Could Block Iran Weapons," *Stars and Stripes* (21 April 2015), available at http://japan.stripes.com/news/us-warships-heads-yemeni-waters-could-block-iran-weapons, accessed 28 September 2015; Aaron Mehta, "US Ships Still Monitoring Iranian Flotilla," *Defense News* (23 April 2015), available at http://www.defensenews.com/story/defense/policy-budget/warfare/2015/04/23/iran-ships-yemen-houthi-us-navy-flotilla-roosevelt/26241855/, accessed 28 September 2015.

7. "The Navy and Marine Corps exist to control the seas, assure access, and project power beyond the sea, to influence events and advance American interests across the full spectrum of military operations," states "Naval Power 21 . . . a Navy Vision" (Washington: Department of the Navy, October 2002), page 1.

8. This is not to suggest that in the post–Cold War Era, the "movement" of responsibility has solely been between state and nonstate actors. Note, for instance, the concept of the "Responsibility to Protect" that emphasizes the responsibility states have to respond to severe degradations of human rights in other states. See Gareth Evans and Mohamed Sahnoun, chairmen, *The Responsibility to Protect: Report of the International Commission on Intervention and State Sovereignty* (Ottawa: International Development Research Centre, December 2001); Alex J. Bellamy, *Global Politics and the Responsibility to Protect: From Words to Deeds* (London: Routledge, 2010).

9. Patrick Jerome Cullen, *Private Security in International Politics: Deconstructing the State's Monopoly of Security Governance*, unpublished PhD thesis (London School of Economics and Political Science, 2009), page 118, emphasis in original.

10. Anna Leander and Rens van Munster, "Private Security Contractors in Darfur: Reflecting and Reinforcing Neo-liberal Governmentality," *International Relations* 21, 2 (June 2007), pages 201–16.

11. Pat O'Malley, "Risk and Responsibility," in Andrew Barry, Thomas Osborne, and Nikolas Rose, editors, *Foucault and Political Reason: Liberalism, Neo-liberalism, and Rationalities of Government* (Chicago: University of Chicago Press, 1996), page 203.

12. Nils Rosemann, *Code of Conduct: Tool for Self-Regulation for Private Military and Security Companies*, Occasional Paper 15 (Geneva: Geneva Centre for the Democratic Control of Armed Forces, 2008), pages 7–8.

13. Hugo Grotius, *The Free Sea* (Indianapolis: The Liberty Fund, Inc., 2004).

14. Lauren Ploch, Christopher M. Blanchard, Ronald O'Rourke, R. Chuck Mason, and Rawle O. King, *Piracy Off the Horn of Africa*, CRS Report for the US Congress, R4-528 (Washington: Congressional Research Service, 24 April 2009), page 9.

15. Brian Reyes, "First Sea Lord Warns of al-Qa'eda Plot to Target Merchant Ships," *Lloyd's List* (5 August 2004), page 8.

16. See, for instance, Cullen, *Private Security*, page 263.

17. See, for instance, Robert Mandel, "Fighting Fire with Fire: Privatizing Counterterrorism," in Russell D. Howard and Reid L. Sawyer, editors, *Defeating Terrorism: Shaping the New Security Environment* (Guilford: McGraw-Hill/Dushkin, 2004), pages 62–73.

18. Alisha Ryu, "Shipping Industry Mulls Hiring Private Security to Fight Piracy," *Voice of America* (22 October 2008), available at http://voanews.com/english/2008-10-22-voa42.cfm?renderforprint=1, accessed 25 June 2009; "World Scrambles"; Bret Stephens, "Why Don't We

Hang Pirates Anymore?" *Wall Street Journal* (25 November 2008); J. Peter Pham, "Somali Pirates Undeterred by Naval Build-Up, but Risks Heightened," *World Defense Review* (2 April 2009); Mike Corder and Slobodan Lekic, "Dutch Navy Under Fire for 'Idiotic' Catch and Release of Somali Pirates," *Chicago Tribune* (21 April 2009); Dan Lett, "Practicalities of Pirate Prosecution Raises Questions," *Winnipeg Free Press* (22 May 2009), available at http://www.winnipegfreepress.com/breakingnews/Prosecution-of-pirates--45858172.html, accessed 1 October 2015.

19. Les Johnston, "Transnational Private Policing: The Impact of Global Commercial Security," in J. W. E. Sheptycki, editor, *Issues in Transnational Policing* (London: Routledge, 2000), page 39, emphasis in original.

20. Johnston, "Transnational Private Policing," page 39.

21. Elke Krahmann, "Conceptualizing Security Governance," *Cooperation and Conflict* 38, 1 (March 2003), pages 5–26.

22. United Kingdom Foreign and Commonwealth Office, *Private Military Companies: Options for Regulation*, HC 577 (London: The Stationery Office, 12 February 2002), page 20.

23. Marie Sophie Joubert, "Private Security Firms Benefit from Piracy," *France 24* (30 November 2008), available at http://www.france24.com/en/20081130-private-security-firms-benefit-piracy-somalia-military-blackwater, accessed 5 May 2010.

24. John T. Pitney Jr. and John-Clark Levin, *Private Anti-piracy Navies: How Warships for Hire Are Changing Maritime Security* (Plymouth: Lexington Books, 2014), page 98.

25. "Shippers Weigh Armed Response to Somali Piracy," *Hellenic Shipping News Worldwide* (4 June 2009), available at http://www.hellenicshippingnews.com/index.php?option=com_content&task=view&id=50445&Itemid=79>&task=view&id=50445&Itemid=79, accessed 5 May 2010.

26. "IMO Approves Further Interim Guidance on Privately Contracted Armed Security Personnel," intersessional meeting of the Maritime Security and Piracy Working Group of the Maritime Safety Committee, 13–15 September 2011, briefing 47 (16 September 2011), available at http://www.imo.org/mediacentre/pressbriefings/pages/47-piracyguidance.aspx, accessed 12 December 2011.

27. The author is grateful for the emphasis placed on this point by an anonymous reviewer. For a consideration of the role played by the insurance industry, see Luis Lobo-Guerrero, *Insuring Security: Biopolitics, Security and Risk* (London: Routledge, 2010), chapter 6.

28. Generally, there are three types of insurance carried by shippers: (1) war risk, which covers war, terrorism, and insurgency; (2) hull/machinery, which covers physical risks; and (3) protection and indemnity, which covers the crew.

29. Ploch, Blanchard, O'Rourke, Mason, and King, *Piracy Off the Horn of Africa*, page 41.

30. "Piracy: Issues Arising from the Use of Armed Guards" (London: Ince & Co. International LLP, 2011), page 2. The author will look with great interest as to how various interested parties will respond to the previously mentioned International Organization for Standardization's Publically Available Specification 28007.

31. See, for instance, Roger Middleton, *Piracy in Somalia: Threatening Global Trade, Feeding Local Wars*, Chatham House Briefing Paper, AFP BP 08/02 (London: Chatham House, October 2008); David Osler and Mike Grinter, "Owners Hire Armed Guards to Secure Ships against Pirates," *Lloyd's List* (12 September 2008), available at http://lloydslist.com/ll/news/owners-hire-armed-guards-to-secure-ships-against-pirates/20017570367.htm, accessed 22 October 2015.

32. There are also some combinations. The Maersk Line, for instance, has opted in some circumstances to take the longer route and in others to rely on private security. In order to handle qualitative and reputational concerns, Maersk only hires PMSCs employing former US Navy SEALs, thus reinforcing its image as the "Tiffany of shipping companies." Sandra I. Erwin, "War on Somali Pirates: Big Business and Growing," *National Defense Magazine* (14 August 2012), available at http://www.nationaldefensemagazine.org/blog/Lists/Posts/Post.aspx?ID=868, accessed 22 October 2015.

33. Ryu, "Shipping Industry Mulls Hiring Private Security to Fight Piracy." Following the shift in IMO policy and the development of nascent state regulation governing PMSCs at sea (Germany being the case in point here), Hinchliffe warned that such measures "must not create

a mechanism for governments to abrogate their responsibility under UNCLOS to protect trade routes" (Henning Gloystein and Jonathan Saul, "Germany Wants Armed Guards on Europe Ships as Piracy Costing Billions of Dollar a Year," Reuters [23 August 2011], available at http://www.alarabiya.net/articles/2011/08/23/163755.html, accessed 1 October 2015).

34. Issues regarding risk are also at play here. BIMCO notes that VPDs likely resolve "a number of the liability and legal issues albeit with the same physical risks" (The Baltic and International Maritime Council, "BIMCO's Position: Piracy, Armed Robbery, Kidnapping, Torture and Murder at Sea," available at http://www.bimco.org/Viewpoint/03_Piracy.aspx, accessed 12 September 2012).

35. Terry Hutson, "Piracy: BIMCO to Prepare Armed Guards on Ships Contract," *Ports and Ships Maritime News* (23 November 2011), available at http://www.ports.co.za/news/news_2011_11_23_01.php, accessed 14 October 2015.

36. The Baltic and International Maritime Council, "Guidance on Rules for the Use of Force (RUF) by Privately Contracted Armed Security Personnel (PCASP) in Defence of a Merchant Vessel (MV)" (no date), available at https://www.bimco.org/~/media/Chartering/Document_Samples/Sundry_Other_Forms/Sample_Copy_Guidance_on_the_Rules_for_the_Use_of_Force.ashx, accessed 14 October 2015.

37. Christopher Spearin, *Humanitarian Non-governmental Organizations and International Private Security Companies: The "Humanitarian" Challenges of Moulding a Marketplace*, Policy Paper 16 (Geneva: Center for the Democratic Control of the Armed Forces, 2007).

38. Kathleen M. Jennings, *Armed Services: Regulating the Private Military Industry*, Fafo Report 532 (Oslo: Fafo, 2006), page 24.

39. Deborah Avant, *The Market for Force: The Consequences of Privatizing Security* (Cambridge: Cambridge University Press, 2005), page 220.

40. See, for instance, Caroline Holmqvist, *Private Security Companies: The Case for Regulation*, SIPRI Policy Paper 9 (Stockholm: Stockholm International Peace Research Institute, January 2005); Christopher Kinsey, "Regulation and Control of Private Military Companies: The Legislative Dimension," *Contemporary Security Policy* 26, 1 (April 2005), pages 84–102; Dave Whyte, "Lethal Regulation: State-Corporate Crime and the United Kingdom Government's New Mercenaries," *Journal of Law and Society* 30, 4 (December 2003), pages 575–600.

41. See, for instance, Sudarsan Raghavan and Thomas E. Ricks, "Private Security Puts Diplomats, Military at Odds in Iraq Fuel Debate," *Washington Post* (26 September 2007), available at http://www.washingtonpost.com/wp-dyn/content/article/2007/09/25/AR2007092502675.html, accessed 22 October 2015; United States Department of Defense, Office of the Deputy Under Secretary of Defense (Logistics and Materiel Readiness), *Contractor Support of U.S. Operations in USCENTCOM AOR, Iraq, and Afghanistan* (Washington: Department of Defense, May 2009).

Chapter Five

Controlling the Corporate Warrior in Iraq

David Strachan-Morris

The use of private military and security companies (PMSCs) has, quite rightly, come under considerable scrutiny in the wake of the exponential growth of the industry in Iraq and, later, in Afghanistan. The behavior of the PMSCs and the apparent lack of oversight have called the use of contractors into question and have made their future use problematic for the United States government in particular. Lack of planning for the aftermath of the coalition invasion of Iraq in 2003 resulted in an insurgency that threatened to overwhelm the reconstruction effort. Instability, coupled with an insufficient number of troops to fight the insurgents and at the same time provide security for agencies engaged in reconstruction, led to a reliance on PMSCs to fill the gap. While long-established companies were quick to offer their services to potential clients, they were joined by a host of newly formed companies, some of which existed in little more than name. Estimates of the number of PMSCs and their personnel vary considerably, which in itself was, and still is, part of the problem: no agency ever knew how many contractors were in country, who they were, or who exactly they worked for. Two of the leading commentators on the PMSC industry, Peter Singer and David Isenberg, estimate that there were between 60 and 200 PMSCs in Iraq at the height of the war.[1] The Special Inspector General for Iraq Reconstruction (SIGIR) reported in October 2008 that there were 77 PMSCs and in the same year the Congressional Budget Office estimated that there were between 20,000 and 30,000 employees of PMSCs in Iraq.[2] The number of Department of Defense (DoD) contractors employed on security duties in September 2009 was estimated at 12,684—or 11 percent of the total number of DoD contractors.[3] The Private Security Company Association of Iraq (PSCAI) stated that in 2009 it had 40 members, consisting of foreign and Iraqi PMSCs, although not all PMSCs operating in Iraq are members of the association.[4]

The manner in which PMSCs conducted themselves in Iraq raised questions regarding the ethics and legality of their use. Some companies were later charged with fraud as a result of their business practices while others have come under criticism as a result of the actions of their personnel on the ground. Accusations of shady business practices and lack of discipline on the part of the PMSCs can be matched by counter-accusations of insufficient contract oversight and poor planning on the part of the government and military.[5] It is not the purpose of this chapter to rehearse these "scandals" as they are more than adequately covered in the existing body of literature, in the media, and in government reports. This chapter is intended to inform the ongoing debate about how PMSCs should be controlled in the future by analyzing how these "corporate warriors" were controlled on the battlefield in Iraq and the oversight mechanisms that were put in place. These systems were created more or less "on the fly" in reaction to incidents on the ground and evolved over time. When it became apparent there were problems with the reconstruction of Iraq the Department of Defense and Department of State (DoS) both produced doctrinal documents that focused on nation building and emphasized the need for a multiagency approach in similar situations in the future.[6] Sharing information on the security situation would likely be a key feature of interagency cooperation. There was little or no information sharing between military, government, and civilian agencies in the early days of the Iraq war, which often meant contractors operated with little or no awareness of the threats and, occasionally, hindered military operations.

There were essentially three sets of mechanisms through which attempts were made to control PMSCs in Iraq. The first was the use of legislation and regulations. The second was the use of a monitoring system to track the movements of PMSCs and render assistance when necessary. The third was the provision of intelligence products that enabled PMSCs to plan their movements to avoid potential trouble spots, in the hope that this would reduce the likelihood of armed confrontations with the civilian population. As with most other aspects of the war, though, there was no plan for the presence of so many armed contractors on the battlefield and, therefore, all of these measures were introduced as ad hoc solutions. While the issues created by the presence of PMSCs on the battlefield were resolved to a limited extent, creating solutions in the midst of operations was not ideal. Understanding these practical issues will undoubtedly assist those planning for future operations.

In this chapter I analyze each of these mechanisms in turn. The first section will examine the laws and regulations that governed the actions of the security contractors, in particular Coalition Provisional Authority Order 17, which provided immunity from prosecution by the Iraqi authorities. The second section will describe the measures that were introduced to monitor the activities of security contractors on the ground and improve accountability for their actions. The third section will discuss how a joint military-contractor intelligence system was established to improve the flow of information to contractors, with the intention that this would help them avoid known trouble spots. I conclude by discussing the initiatives that are currently under way to improve oversight of contractors on the battlefield and argue that development of contractor oversight mechanisms should be a continual process, rather than an afterthought. This chapter covers the period 2003–2011 as it seeks to analyze the difficulties involved in regulating the security industry in foreign theaters. Since 2011 the security industry in Iraq has been regulated by local legislation and a dedicated department within the Ministry of the Interior provides oversight. This department issues operating licenses, carries out inspections of company premises, and acts as the intermediary between the security industry and the government.[7]

REGULATION

Regulation of PMSCs in Iraq was a combination of international law, Coalition Provisional Authority regulations, US government legislation, military regulations, and attempts by the industry to self-regulate. This was a wholly unsatisfactory arrangement because it was never clear which laws and regulations applied or who had jurisdiction over the contractors. The contractors themselves were often citizens of third-party nations (i.e., not citizens of the United States or Iraq). This judicial vortex has led to some of the harshest criticism of the use of PMSCs, because despite the numerous apparent "violations" of one law or another, there have been very few prosecutions and even fewer convictions.

Perhaps the most well-known of the regulations that applied to PMSCs was Coalition Provisional Authority Order 17, which gave contractors immunity from prosecution under Iraqi law. This was only one of a series of sections within the order, which in its totality dealt with the entire relationship between the military, the CPA, and contractors on the one hand and the Iraqi legal system on the other.[8] The section specifically dealing with immunity read:

> Unless provided otherwise herein, the MNF, the CPA, Foreign Liaison Missions, their Personnel, property, funds and assets, and all International Consultants shall be immune from Iraq legal process.[9]

This did not, however, provide complete immunity from prosecution. The order specifically placed all personnel under the jurisdiction of their "sending state."[10] On the face of it, this was a sensible precaution in circumstances under which a fair trial could not be guaranteed for contractors within the Iraqi judicial system, even if it had been fully functional at the time. This order was also consistent with the normal form for Status of Forces Agreements (SoFAs) in other theaters, in which US troops are granted a certain amount of immunity from local prosecution. In fact, CPA Order 17 is closely modeled on existing SoFAs that the United States has with nations in which there are American troops. In 2008 there were between 80 and 115 SoFAs in place between the US and other nations, some of which provided full immunity for DoD personnel (such as the agreement with Mongolia) or shared jurisdiction (such as the agreement with NATO).[11] There was, therefore, nothing unusual about CPA Order 17 on the face of it. The difficulty, however, was that unlike almost all other SoFAs it was not supported by a coherent mechanism for exercising judicial control over contractors once immunity from local judicial process was established.

To start with, there were difficulties with even exercising jurisdiction over US citizens working as contractors for the DoD. The two main pieces of legislation that could have been used, the Uniform Code of Military Justice (UCMJ) and the Military Extraterritorial Jurisdiction Act (MEJA), needed some amendment before they could be applied to contractors. Even then, the wording of the subsequent amendments has been imprecise and ambiguous, with lawyers still debating the practicalities of conducting prosecutions under these acts.[12] This problem was exacerbated when it came to contractors from third-country nations that did not have any official representation in Iraq. The South African contractors are a case in point: they were not "sent" by their state in the sense of the definition of "sending state" in CPA Order 17, nor was South Africa part of the coalition, and there is still no official South African diplomatic representation in Iraq. Therefore there was (and still is) no organization that could provide jurisdiction over a South African contractor in the event of any allegations against them. To take Australia as an example of a nation that was a coalition partner and does have diplomatic representation in Iraq, there would seem to be a basis for Australia to exert jurisdiction over one of its citizens, as CPA Order 17 would require. Donald Rothwell, professor of international law at the University of Sydney, found that a combination of Commonwealth law and Australian legislation, in particular the Crimes (Foreign Incursions and Recruitment) Act 1978 and the Crimes (Overseas) Act 1964, provided a sound basis upon which Australian citizens could be held accountable for their actions in Iraq.[13] That said, Australia has allowed Afghanistan to try one of its citizens for murder in Afghanistan while working as a contractor.[14] Similarly, there are two examples of British citizens who have been tried in Iraq and Afghanistan for crimes committed in those countries: in Iraq Daniel Fitzsimmons was sentenced to life for the murder of two colleagues in the International Zone and in Afghanistan Bill Shaw has been jailed for two years after allegedly bribing officials.[15]

These are, however, only a minority of cases. A 2008 study of 610 incident reports filed by contractors conducted by Human Rights First found that there were 73 cases of contractors firing on civilian vehicles in Iraq between July 2004 and April 2005 with no apparent official investigations into many of the incidents beyond whatever inquiries the PMSC may have conducted internally.[16] In some cases, PMSCs have fired employees if they concluded that they may have breached the law (referred to as the "window or aisle, chicken or fish" option).[17] Some high-profile incidents were investigated by the US military—the so-called Aegis "trophy video," made by contractors working for the company in 2005 and later released on the Internet, was investigated by the US Army's Criminal Investigation Division, who determined that all the shootings shown on the video were within the rules of engagement and no further action was taken.[18]

A large part of the problem was the fact that shooting at civilian vehicles that came close to PMSC convoys appeared to be justified by the Rules of Engagement (ROE) contained within CPA Order 17, later revised as Rules for the Use of Force (RUF) under Annex C to Multi-National Force–Iraq (MNF-I) Order Number 09-109.[19] It became routine for PMSC convoys to fire at civilian vehicles that came too close because of the suicide car-bomb attacks that killed a number of PMSC employees, particularly in late 2004 and early 2005.[20] The combined effect of the apparent immunity of CPA Order 17 and the ROE led to a culture in which risk was transferred to the civilian population as the PMSCs emphasized the protection of their client over the potential harm to the local community. This was in many ways a natural consequence of the emphasis that was placed upon force protection by the US military, especially in the early years of the war in Iraq.[21] To a very large extent the PMSCs were mirroring their major client, the DoD, but with much less accountability: while few contractors have been prosecuted for their actions, the 2008 Human Rights First report noted that at least 60 military personnel had been court-martialed for the deaths of Iraq civilians.[22]

The State Department summed up the attitude of the US government toward the issue of legal jurisdiction over contractors in response to a request by a reporter who wanted background information on the legal aspects of a story he intended to file on private security details (PSDs):

> The reporter wants to have a backgrounder with someone who can explain what legal mechanisms are in place to hold private security contractors accountable in the event of wrongful death or criminal acts, but we should deny the backgrounder. Because as for the legal jurisdiction under which a PSD operates, this is where things get hazy. There is no Uniform Code of Military Justice for PSDs. Private security contractors fall under CPA General Rule 17, which grants private security contractors immunity from prosecution in Iraqi

> courts. In wrongful deaths where deadly force was authorized, if the PSD is found negligent, the only recourse is dismissal. In cases where there was clear criminal intent, a criminal case could hypothetically be pursued in U.S. federal court, but this has yet to happen out here.[23]

This email was written shortly after what became one of the most notorious incidents involving PMSCs in Iraq—the Nisour Square shootings on 16 September 2007 in which 14 civilians were killed and 20 injured by a team of Blackwater contractors working for the US State Department. This case, perhaps more than any other, typified the difficulties mentioned in the email. The initial sticking point was whether the Military Extraterritorial Jurisdiction Act (MEJA) applied to the Blackwater contractors as they were under contract to the State Department and not the Department of Defense.[24] The legal first case brought against them, in 2009, was dismissed as the judge ruled that the evidence was flawed, being based on statements offered in response for improperly offered immunity.[25] That ruling was overturned by an appeals court in 2011 and four men were eventually found guilty of various offenses relating to the shootings (mostly manslaughter) in October 2014 using Title 18, section 3228 of the US Code, which allows for prosecution in the District of Columbia (or the accused's home district) of offenses outside the jurisdiction of any state or district.[26] Legislation to extend MEJA to all government contractors is still working its way through Congress.[27]

CPA Order 17 was applied without the necessary legislative framework to support it and the unintended consequence was that the PMSCs were seen as totally unaccountable for their actions. The PMSCs contributed to the problem by adopting the same risk-transfer culture as the military. The fact that the US government appeared unaware of the legal situation, or was unwilling to be proactive on the matter, only exacerbated the situation. The next section will show how a system of monitoring security contractors was also supposed to improve accountability, by requiring PMSCs to report all serious incidents involving loss of life, injury, or damage to property.

CONTROL AND COORDINATION[28]

The multibillion-dollar reconstruction of Iraq began almost immediately after the war ended. However, the insurgency that had started slowly rapidly increased into a significant threat to the rebuilding efforts. As the security situation destabilized further there was an increase in the use of PMSCs, which led to problems because their activities were often not coordinated with coalition forces. Military units reported that individual PMSCs based within their areas of operation were able to coordinate movement and had started to establish processes for sharing intelligence with local units, but PMSCs based outside their areas and who just passed through were not able to take part in these local coordination efforts. Very often units would only be aware that a PMSC was in their area if an incident occurred.[29] There was also considerable variance in attitudes as some units were prepared to cooperate with PMSCs and others would not: this difference in attitudes was reciprocated within PMSCs.[30]

PMSCs began to suffer casualties almost as soon as the reconstruction began, having been caught out by the rapidly increasing insurgency. In the first year of operations there were 31 fatal incidents in which 42 civilian contractors were killed.[31] What was arguably the defining incident of that time occurred in Fallujah on 31 March 2004, when four contractors were murdered after their convoy entered the city and their bodies hanged from a bridge. The publicity generated by this incident brought the issue of contractor security into sharp focus and the DoD decided it was time to find a way of gaining oversight over PMSC activities and, at the same time, provide them with the security information they needed. The Project and Contracting Office (PCO), the DoD agency charged with overseeing the reconstruction of Iraq, issued a contract to Aegis Defence Services in 2004 to establish Reconstruction Operations Centers (ROC) throughout Iraq that would create a command, control, and intelligence infrastructure for PMSCs.

The Reconstruction Operations Center network consisted of a National Reconstruction Operations Center (NROC) in Baghdad and a number of Regional Reconstruction Operations Centers (RROCs) throughout Iraq. Although the ROCs served all the PMSCs and other reconstruction agencies, Aegis Defence Services provided all the personnel. What was significant is that intelligence was given as much priority as operations and there was a national-level intelligence section, supported by regional intelligence sections at each RROC. In early 2005 responsibility for the ROC system was passed from the PCO to the Gulf Region Division (GRD) of the US Army Corps of Engineers (USACE). A Multi-National Force–Iraq (MNF-I) Fragmentary Order (FRAGO) was issued in May 2005 to more firmly attach the RROCs to each of the divisions in Iraq, further enhancing the coordination between PMSCs and the military. Paragraph 3.A stated:

> Multi-National Corps–Iraq (MNC-I) will integrate the RROCs into [Major Subordinate Command (MSC)] operation centers and provide them with intelligence to pass on (once cleared) to relevant agencies. RROCs will pass information and intelligence gathered by their sources to coalition forces and act as a conduit for communication with the ROC.[32]

Under the ROC system, PMSCs submitted notification of their movements to the ROC, which passed this information on to the coalition forces. The missions were then tracked by the ROC, using transponders that had been placed on one or more vehicles in the convoy. In the event of an emergency, the transponders had an "emergency button" that, when activated, would alert the ROC. The ROC staff would then coordinate communication between the PMSC and the coalition forces to provide assistance. Between January 2005 and July 2005 the number of daily missions being tracked by the ROCs increased from fewer than 10 to an average of 110.[33] A total of 84 organizations (PMSC, military, diplomatic, and NGO) used the various ROC services, which included coordination of a quick reaction force and medical assistance to PMSCs in an emergency, as well as intelligence services, which are dealt with in the next section.[34]

The first audit of the ROCs by the special inspector general for Iraqi reconstruction (SIGIR) demonstrates some of the issues of overseeing civilian contractors in a dynamic situation. SIGIR concluded that Aegis was not in compliance with its contract to establish the ROC network because it had not established security centers in each of Iraq's 18 provinces but had only done so in the six divisional headquarters as specified in the FRAGO. SIGIR expressed concern that it was "unclear whether this structure provides adequate threat assessment and warning to PCO and reconstruction contractors or adequate safety and security to PCO and reconstruction personnel."[35] The establishment of the six ROCs was, however, in accordance with FRAGO 05-108 and the issue was addressed in a modification to the contract with Aegis that aligned it with the FRAGO.[36] The SIGIR report made no comment on the performance of the ROCs as a means of oversight of PMSCs generally.

The fact that PMSCs were effectively kept at arm's length—that is, by communicating with them through the ROCs—had a significant impact on the relationship between PMSCs and the military. While it is fair to say that good relations were possible between military units and PMSCs, mainly as the result of individual efforts, there was some institutional hostility toward the contractors. Brigadier General Karl Horst, deputy commander of the Third Infantry Division in Baghdad, made his feelings toward contractors clear in an interview with the *Washington Post*. He said, "These guys run loose in this country and do stupid stuff. There's no authority over them, so you can't come down on them hard when they escalate force. . . . They shoot people, and someone else has to deal with the aftermath. It happens all over the place."[37] For their part, the PMSCs argued that progress had been made to improve accountability. Johan Jones, director of the Private Security Company Association of Iraq, said that "whilst the behavior of a few PMSCs is unhelpful, we have to also keep in mind that 'bad apples' are present in all organizations, including the MNF-I. . . . There have been huge strides amongst the Iraqi government to regulate and maintain accountability regarding PMSCs. There have also been huge strides within the PMSC community to identify those that behave in an unacceptable manner."[38] The source of this tension was the fact that there was still no clear mechanism for PMSCs to be held accountable for their actions. One of the functions of the ROC was to report all incidents involving contractors to the coalition forces. The author is aware from personal experience that this did happen—reports were provided on a daily basis—but the coalition forces often did little more than record the incidents.[39]

The problem was that the system in place provided neither coordination nor control, but simply passive monitoring and reaction to incidents, although the military could refuse permission for PMSC movements. There was no means by which the military and the PMSCs could reconcile their two missions. While the military were trying to fight an active insurgency, the PMSCs had a responsibility toward the clients they were carrying. These clients were often unarmed civilians who needed to be transported to reconstruction sites or to meetings at Iraqi government ministries and these journeys frequently took them through trouble spots. PMSC convoys did not have the capability to stop and deal with any damage they had caused, because they lacked the support available to military units and felt that their responsibility lay in removing the client from the potential threat.[40] This was a particular bone of contention with General Horst, who believed that PMSCs should stop and ascertain the condition of the occupants of any vehicle they fired on.[41]

The ROC system was further refined in February 2008 to improve the integration of the PMSC and military operations functions, to enhance the systems for tracking PMSC movements, recording incidents, providing quick reaction forces, and medical evacuation of casualties. In the wake of the Blackwater shooting incident in September 2007, the DoD and DoS formulated a joint policy on oversight of PMSCs in Iraq. MNF-I FRAGO 07-428 established Contractor Operations Centers (CONOCs) within divisional headquarters to coordinate and monitor the movements of PMSCs who were contracted to the Department of Defense and the Department of State.[42] This meant that the staff responsible for tracking the movements of contractors moved into divisional headquarters while the remainder of the Reconstruction Operations Center functions stayed where they were, including the intelligence staff. This was because the ROCs, and the intelligence staff within them, needed to remain accessible to the wider reconstruction community. This FRAGO established an Armed Contractor Oversight Division (later the Armed Contractor Oversight Branch), putting responsibility for PMSC oversight into a single agency within the military command for the first time. The 2007 order was updated by further orders in 2009 and 2010, which put greater responsibility upon the division headquarters and incorporated a set of clauses that were to be inserted into all DoD contracts to ensure compliance with the improved coordination and accountability mechanisms for PMSCs. Perhaps the most significant change was that local commanders had input into the decision-making process. PMSC movement notification requests went through the chain of command to the tactical unit on the ground, which decided whether or not to grant the request and allow the PMSC into its area of responsibility. The tactical unit also had input into the route, so it could help the PMSC avoid potential trouble spots.[43]

As far as the PMSCs were concerned, the services provided by the CONOCs were essentially the same as the ROC. They did, however, expect some benefit in closer integration with the military, particularly with improved response times in the event of an incident.[44] The major change was the improvement in military monitoring and oversight of their activities. A SIGIR report in July 2009 noted significant improvement in oversight and monitoring of PMSCs. The report specifically stated that

> Key DoD and DoS officials responsible for controlling and coordinating PMSC operations and managing the incident reporting system generally reported to us that the recent procedural changes have improved their oversight, coordination, and control of PMSC activities. PMSC officials also believe that their coordination with the military has improved.[45]

Perhaps even more significantly, however, these changes formally established a mechanism for holding PMSCs accountable for their actions on the ground. All PMSCs were required to report serious incidents in their entirety within 96 hours to the US military and to report the incident to the Iraqi Police.[46] The contracting agency was required to carry out a full investigation and this could result in a number of outcomes that could range from a Letter of Concern to the PMSC all the way to a full criminal investigation. Furthermore, the contracting agency's investigation did not preclude investigations by the tactical commander or any other commander in the chain of command.[47] In April 2009, SIGIR found that the databases were not capturing all the incidents and that the new Armed Contractor Oversight Division was applying its own judgment as to whether an incident should be recorded and tracked. The definition applied by the Oversight Division was found to be significantly narrower than the one contained in the orders. In fact, SIGIR found that the Oversight Division had recorded only half of the serious incidents that had been reported between 1 May 2008 and 28 February 2009. Of the 47 incidents that SIGIR determined should have been investigated, it was found that only 21 were actually taken any further, with only one resulting in a criminal prosecution.[48] Two months later, in July 2009, SIGIR found that the situation had not changed significantly, with the Armed Contractor Oversight Branch (as the Armed Contractor Oversight Division had been renamed) still unable to provide documentation for 51 percent of the incidents that had been reported, including 16 in which remedial action had been taken.[49] Subsequent reports by SIGIR concentrated more on the problems PMSCs encountered during the transition to oversight by the Iraqi government rather than PMSC conduct. By July 2011 SIGIR reported that there were still problems with the reporting systems and that some of its recommendations had never been implemented, although this was partly due to other changes in the contracting oversight infrastructure. By this time, however, shooting incidents had declined to negligible levels and traffic accidents and harassment at checkpoints by Iraqi security forces were by far the most common incidents involving PMSCs.[50] It is difficult to assess whether the system to hold PMSCs accountable improved after 2008 as it was never again tested as severely as before, but the lack of documentation and continued inability to provide a comprehensive list of PMSCs operating in Iraq indicates that oversight was still by no means rigorous.

Since 2005 monitoring of PMSCs has improved considerably. The Reconstruction Operations Centers and their successors, the Contractor Operations Centers, steadily improved the monitoring and oversight of PSCs in Iraq. As coordination between the military and PSCs improved, so did the relationships between the two. Contractual control improved along with battlefield control: the military staff available to oversee contracts increased and more training was made available. The insertion of clauses requiring certain modes of behavior into contracts gave the military an important tool because it could impose penalties upon PSCs that did not comply—up to and including cancellation of the entire contract. The element that is still lacking, however, is the ability to hold PMSCs and their employees legally accountable for their actions. Although the mechanism to do this was put in place, it has failed to work because of the continued lack of connectivity between the various organizations responsible for oversight and differing interpretations of the guidelines. As a result, the crucial link between oversight and accountability was never fully made in Iraq.

INTELLIGENCE COOPERATION

One of the more unique aspects of contractor oversight and monitoring in Iraq was the establishment of an intelligence interface between the US military and PMSCs. It was created as part of the ROC system in order to provide contractors with sufficient information to allow them to plan their missions and avoid likely trouble spots. This was also one of the most heavily regulated aspects of the relationship between the military and PMSCs but also provided a model of cooperation between the two "communities," given the level of trust that developed.

The ROC provided a daily graphical intelligence report each morning, a written intelligence summary with more in-depth analysis each evening, and the basic data on incidents over the previous 24 hours in a spreadsheet format that PMSCs could import into their own databases or mapping software.

While this in itself was not quite enough for PMSCs to plan their missions in detail, it was enough for their own intelligence analysts to do this for them. The ROC also provided a wider intelligence function by allowing reconstruction agencies to submit requests for information and obtain in-depth reports on the security situation in areas where reconstruction sites were located. This information was provided via a website, to which PMSCs, nongovernmental organizations, and reconstruction agencies were granted access after their bona fides were established—as the information was still technically owned by the DoD it could not be distributed to unauthorized users outside Iraq.

The May 2005 FRAGO establishing the ROCs ordered the military to provide intelligence to them but did not describe how this should be achieved. Initially this was the result of local arrangements based on personal relationships between the divisional intelligence staffs and the ROC personnel. The intelligence interface therefore evolved from existing doctrine and guidelines produced in Iraq. The level of cooperation between the RROCs and their associated units varied a great deal, with some RROC personnel being allowed to work in the divisional headquarters itself and others simply being provided little more than a sanitized list of incidents from the last 24-hour period. Cooperation with the US military was initially easier, possibly because it had more experience dealing with civilian contractors, even if this situation was new to them.

One particularly interesting area of oversight was the problem of actually providing information to the contracting community. Many of those requiring the ROC intelligence product, such as the large South African contingent, were not able to gain access to MNF-I information because they did not have recognized security clearances and it was important that their requirements be addressed. The RROCs, therefore, had a key role in obtaining enough information from the military to generate a sufficiently useful product. The guidelines were relatively straightforward: information regarding a direct and immediate threat to contractor or client life could be disseminated almost immediately. This was the result of a reasonably high degree of trust that developed between the civilian contractors and the divisional intelligence staff. This was based on the division intelligence staff's recognition of the fact that the RROC intelligence personnel, almost all of whom had served in intelligence roles in the military before being employed as civilian contractors, were acutely aware of the need to protect classified information and could be relied upon to behave in a professional manner.[51] That there were formal intelligence-sharing agreements between the United States and the countries of origin of most RROC staff members—and that these staff members held a security clearance—also helped considerably.[52] Once proof of this clearance was established, access to information was generally granted, which facilitated the process for extracting and declassifying the information that was required by the civilian contractors engaged in reconstruction. When the US Army Corps of Engineers took over the ROC network in March 2005 this put a coherent military infrastructure around the relationships, and ROC intelligence staff had a more solid basis for developing their relationships with the divisions they were working alongside. Apart from occasional changes in the guidelines the system for providing intelligence to PMSCs and the wider contracting community remained largely unchanged until the ROCs were closed during the withdrawal of US forces in 2011.

The existence of formal contracts allowed the US military to exert oversight through the compliance mechanisms put in place, with a contracting officer's representative (COR) monitoring performance and compliance with the contract. In the event of a breach of the contract, which in the case of the ROCs would include a breach of security, the COR could decide to hold a Board of Enquiry or even open an Article 15-6 inquiry under the Uniform Code of Military Justice. The contract with Aegis required the company to provide "intelligence briefings, products and special assessments" to "support the Gulf Region Division of the US Army Corps of Engineers, MNF-I, reconstruction related agencies, and private security companies consistent with applicable Department of Defense (DoD) and MNF-I regulations." A key clause of the contract allowed the contractors to transmit classified information to PMSCs or other contractors who were about to conduct movements on the ground if that information contained "imminent threat to life."[53] The existence of contractual mechanisms and a military officer specifically tasked with oversight is an important point because it shows that whatever the criticisms of oversight in general, the ROC intelligence staff were very tightly controlled and subjected to fairly rigorous pre-employment vetting and continual review of their adherence to the regulations. From the very beginning of the contract, the ROC intelligence personnel, of all nationalities, were well aware that they were expected to work within US legislation and regulations concerning access and use of classified information, as well as those of their home nation. They were under threat of strict penalties for breaches of security, which could include loss of security clearance—something none of them wanted to risk—and, therefore, they were keen to work within whatever guidelines were in place.

Both the US Army Corps of Engineers and the Aegis contractors found the level of trust that was built up over time to be a significant factor in aiding oversight of the provision of intelligence to PMSCs. Richard Siebert, who was employed as ROC director of intelligence from 2006 to 2007, ascribed this to the ethos of the people who served on the ROC intelligence staff:

> The moral and ethical aspects of the matter cannot be under-estimated. The contractors employed come from mainly US-allied nations and had all served

> in respected military institutions. For the most part, these people brought with them the same values and moral perspectives they had while in uniform. That they are not in uniform anymore doesn't change their ethical standpoint on things. [54]

Major Kent Lightner, the US Army Corps of Engineers COR from March 2007 to March 2008, believed that having a team of contractors who had built a relationship of trust with the military managed to create a useful "buffer zone." In an interview with the author he said the ROC was often able to trap any potential security breaches, with potential compromises being spotted within the ROC intelligence offices before they leaked any further. He also made two further useful points: first, there had been no major security breaches between the time the ROC intelligence staff was established up to that point in his tour of duty; and second, the capacity for any one individual to cause harm through a security breach was very low because the type of information provided to the ROC was not of a critical nature, normally only containing details of incidents that happened in the past.[55] The ROC was not, for example, given details of future operations, current intelligence on insurgent groups, or details on methods of intelligence collection used.

Creation of the intelligence interface between the military and PMSCs achieved a number of things. First, it provided the PMSCs with the information they needed to avoid trouble spots, which should have reduced the number of shooting incidents and reduced the burden on the military. Second, it proved that proper oversight and control mechanisms could be put in place over PMSCs. Third, and most importantly, it provided a means by which the concerns and interests of those on both sides of the fence could be communicated. Members of the ROC intelligence staff were occasionally asked to act as "subject matter experts" on the PMSC community or to act as intermediaries between the military and PMSC community.[56]

CONCLUSION

PMSC contractors had a difficult and dangerous job to do in Iraq—there is no doubt about that. According to the US Department of Labor 1,627 contractors were killed in Iraq between January 2001 and June 2015, with another 18,392 sustaining serious injuries (defined as requiring four or more days' absence from work).[57] There are no reliable figures on the number of Iraqi contractors who have died or been injured. It is unfortunate that they were not well served by an oversight system that should have been able to provide greater safety (while acknowledging that complete safety was not possible and that the system did improve over time) as well as greater accountability. Perhaps the great lesson of Iraq is that so much more needed to be done prior to the conflict and that all parties involved—the military, the international community, and the PMSCs—should have been part of the solution. There are signs that this is beginning to happen.

At the top level, there are greater efforts by the international community to regulate the use of PMSCs. In March 2000 the US Department of State, the British Foreign Office, a number of leading mineral extraction companies, and NGOs such as Amnesty International and Human Rights Watch started the process of developing a set of Voluntary Principles on Security and Human Rights. These principles were intended to provide a framework within which oil and mining companies would manage their security, with due regard for the human rights of the local populations in the areas where they were working. This process has continued over the last decade, with signatories and partner organizations joining constantly.[58] The Montreux Document on Private Military and Security Companies, signed by 17 nations in September 2008, was a major step forward in that it regulates the relationship between states and the private security sector.[59] Chapter 10 in this volume explores the importance of the Montreux Document as a stepping stone to more meaningful regulation and oversight of PMSCs. Taking the Montreux Document and the Voluntary Principles on Human Rights as starting points, there is an initiative by the Geneva Centre for the Democratic Control of Armed Forces (DCAF) to produce a set of regulations to govern the relationships between commercial entities and PMSCs. In January 2010 DCAF published a discussion document containing a proposed global code of conduct for PMSCs, with the assistance of the American and British governments, among others.[60] Subsequently an International Code of Conduct for Private Security Service Providers, written under the auspices of DCAF, was signed by 708 companies by September 2013.[61] This process continues with the creation of the International Code of Conduct Association (ICoCA), formed in September 2013, which has 140 PSC members at the moment. Six governments are members as well as 13 NGOs, and there are also 15 "observer" organizations.[62] This is an important step forward as it moves the debate on from how PMSCs should behave to how oversight can be achieved. Although still voluntary, this oversight mechanism provides a means of monitoring compliance with the Code of Conduct, with limited sanctions for those that break the code, and, significantly, allows for complaints by third parties to be investigated. This independent body is an improvement upon the industry's previous arrangements, under the auspices of organizations that were also lobbying for the industry but could be strengthened by active support from national governments—possibly even with legislation requiring PMSCs to be signatories of the Code of Conduct. The International Organization for Standardization is also developing ISO PC 284, based on the Montreux Document and the ICoCA.[63]

The PMSC community has taken steps to regulate itself. The British Association of Private Security Companies (BAPSC) and the International Stability Operations Association (ISOA) both have charters or codes of conduct to which members must agree. The ISOA Code of Conduct is the more extensive of the two in that it details the international agreements that its members should adhere to as well as addressing a number of issues that arose in Iraq, not least of which were allegations of "people trafficking" and withholding travel documents of employees who wished to leave.[64] There is, of course, some debate over the advisability of allowing the industry to regulate itself. Certainly both organizations have an interest in the economic well-being of their members and promote their services, which could have a bearing upon the selection or rejection of members, but the integrity of their ability to police themselves could be called into question.[65] To answer the latter point, Andrew Bearpark (director general of the BAPSC) has proposed an independent "ombudsman" to oversee that aspect of the association's work.[66] Chapter 9 in this volume covers the ISOA in greater detail and the authors make the important point that as a "trade association" the ISOA cannot really enforce regulations or punish offenders (beyond excluding them from membership) but it can, and does, play an important role by encouraging its members and national governments to abide by or enforce the numerous laws and regulations that already exist. Chapter 7 explores the United Kingdom's approach to industry regulation, which has largely been one of self-regulation.

The US government and the US military are also taking steps to improve oversight of contracts, with the increase in contracting staff and improved education of military officers.[67] The inclusion of specific clauses in PMSC contracts with the DoD will also facilitate improved oversight and control of armed contractors. But the piece that is still lacking is the integration of the PMSCs' mission with that of the military. It is still important to ensure that the PMSCs do not interfere with the efforts of the military to conduct their operations, whether they are fighting a full-scale war, conducting counterinsurgency operations, or executing a peacekeeping mission. The need for commanders to be fully aware of contractors operating in their area is addressed in the US Army/Marine Corps Counterinsurgency Manual (FM 3-24) but arguably it is too late to do this when the unit has arrived in country.[68] The greatest lesson of Iraq is that all agencies need to work together *before* the contingency arises. Not only do there need to be legal and contractual frameworks in place, but the military and PMSCs need to make the most of opportunities to interact, possibly even engaging in joint training, and find ways to integrate their operations. Initiatives like the ROC in Iraq need to become preventions rather than cures.

NOTES

1. Peter Singer, *The Private Military Industry and Iraq: What Have We Learned and Where to Next?* Policy Paper for the Geneva Centre for the Democratic Control of Armed Forces (Geneva: Geneva Centre for the Democratic Control of Armed Forces, November 2004), page 4; David Isenberg, *Shadow Force: Private Security Contractors in Iraq* (Washington: Cato Institute, 16 February 2009), available at http://www.cato.org/pub_display.php?pub_id=9979, accessed 3 April 2010.

2. Special Inspector General for Iraq Reconstruction, *Field Commanders See Improvements in Controlling and Coordinating Private Security Contractor Missions in Iraq* (Washington: Special Inspector General for Iraq Reconstruction, July 2008), page 2.

3. Moshe Schwartz, *Department of Defense Contractors in Iraq and Afghanistan: Background and Analysis* (Washington: Congressional Research Service, December 2009), page 9, figure 4, "Iraq DOD Contractor Personnel by Type of Service Provided."

4. Private Security Company Association of Iraq website, available at http://www.PMSCai.org/index.html, accessed 2 May 2009.

5. Schwartz, *Department of Defense Contractors in Iraq and Afghanistan*, page 3.

6. DoD Directive 3000.05: Military Support for Stability, Security, Transition and Reconstruction (SSTR) Operations; National Security Presidential Directive 44: Management of Interagency Efforts concerning Reconstruction and Stabilization.

7. See Jason Ireland and Caroline Varin, "PMSCs and the Regulatory Environment in Iraq Post-2011," *Central European Journal of International Security Studies* 9, 1 (March 2015), pages 6–27.

8. L. Paul Bremer, *Coalition Provisional Authority Order 17: Registration Requirements for Private Security Companies (PSCSs)* (27 June 2004).

9. Bremer, *Coalition Provisional Authority Order 17*, page 4.

10. Bremer, *Coalition Provisional Authority Order 17*, page 4. The definition of "sending state" is on page 2.

11. Greg Bruno, "US Security Agreements and Iraq" (April 2010), Council on Foreign Relations website, available at http://www.cfr.org/publication/16448/. Examples taken from R. Chuck Mason, *Testimony to the US House of Representatives Committee on Foreign Affairs: Subcommittee on International Organizations, Human Rights and Oversight. Status of Forces Agreements and UN Mandates: What Authorities and Protections Do They Provide to US Personnel* (Washington: Congressional Research Service, 28 February 2007), pages 4–5.

12. Marina Caparini, "Regulating Private Military and Security Companies: The US Approach," in Andrew Alexandria, Deane-Peter Baker, and Marina Caparini, editors, *Private Military and Security Companies: Ethics, Policies and Civil-Military Relations* (Abingdon, UK: Routledge, 2008), pages 179–81.

13. Donald Rothwell, *Legal Opinion on the Status of Non-combatants and Contractors under International Humanitarian Law and Australian Law* (Sydney, Australia: Australian Strategic Policy Institute, December 2004), pages 7–10.

14. Barbara Miller, "'Example' to Be Made of Death Row Australian," *ABC News* (28 January 2010), available at http://www.abc.net.au/news/stories/2010/01/28/2803111.htm?section=world. The situation in Afghanistan is slightly different to that in Iraq, as there is no specific grant of immunity. The status of contractors is contained in an exchange of diplomatic notes between the Afghan and US governments. Although the US government's position is that these do not confer immunity from prosecution under Afghan law, a report by Human Rights First notes that this is effectively what has happened (Human Rights First, *How to End Impunity for Private Security and Other Contractors* [Washington: Human Rights First, December 2008], page 6, footnote 5).

15. Caroline Davies, "Briton Danny Fitzsimons Jailed in Iraq for Contractors' Murders," *Guardian* (28 February 2011); Tom Coghlan, "British Embassy Security Chief Bill Shaw Jailed for Two Years over Afghan 'Bribe,'" *Times* (27 April 2010).

16. Human Rights First, *Private Security Contractors at War: Ending the Culture of Impunity* (New York: Human Rights First, 2008), pages 13, 20.

17. Human Rights First, *Private Security Contractors at War*, page 20. The report quotes Erik Prince on the "window or aisle" option, but the extended version given here was in common use in Iraq and was frequently heard by the author—although not in relation to himself, he hastens to add.

18. Joshua Finer, "Contractors Cleared in Videotaped Attacks," *Washington Post* (11 June 2006).

19. Annex A to CPA Order 17 and Annex C to Multi-National Force–Iraq, Fragmentary Order (FRAGO) 09-109 (7 March 2009).

20. T. Christian Miller, "Private Security Guards in Iraq Operate with Little Supervision," *Los Angeles Times* (4 December 2005). PMSC casualty details are available in Iraq Coalition Casualty Count, "Iraq Coalition Casualties: Contractors—A Partial List," available at http://icasualties.org/Iraq/Contractors.aspx, accessed 16 December 2015.

21. Thomas W. Smith, "Protecting Civilians . . . or Soldiers? Humanitarian Law and the Economy of Risk in Iraq," *International Studies Perspectives* 9, 2 (May 2008), pages 144–64.

22. Human Rights First, *Private Security Contractors at War*, page 3.

23. "Exclusive: State Dept Emails Say Blackwater Hurting US in Iraq," *ABC News* (25 October 2007), available at http://blogs.abcnews.com/theblotter/2007/10/exclusive-state.html, accessed 12 April 2010.

24. David Johnson and John M. Broder, "FBI Says Guards Killed 14 Iraqis without Cause," *New York Times* (14 November 2007), page A1.

25. "US Judge Dismisses Charges in Iraqi Blackwater Killings," *BBC News* (31 December 2009), available at http://news.bbc.co.uk/1/hi/world/americas/8436780.stm, accessed 20 May 2015.

26. Spencer S. Shu, Victoria St. Martin, and Keith L. Alexander, "Four Blackwater Guards Found Guilty in 2007 Shootings of 31 Unarmed Civilians," *Washington Post* (22 October 2014), available at http://www.washingtonpost.com/world/national-security/verdict-expected-in-blackwater-shooting-case/2014/10/22/5a488258-59fc-11e4-bd61-346aee66ba29_story.html?hpid=z1, accessed 20 May 2015; Nicky Woolf, "Former Blackwater Guards Sentenced for Massacre of Unarmed Iraqi Civilians," *Guardian* (13 April 2015), available at http://www.theguardian.com/us-news/2015/apr/13/former-blackwater-guards-sentencing-baghdad-massacre, accessed 20 May 2015.

27. Shu, St. Martin, and Alexander, "Four Blackwater Guards Found Guilty in 2007 Shootings of 31 Unarmed Civilians."

28. Some of this section and the next is based upon an earlier article by the author, "The Future of Civil-Military Intelligence Co-operation Based on Lessons Learned in Iraq," *Intelligence and National Security* 24, 2 (2009).

29. William M. Solis, *Rebuilding Iraq: Actions Needed to Improve Use of Private Security Providers*, GAO-05-737 (Washington: Government Accountability Office, July 2005), page 22.

30. Solis, *Rebuilding Iraq*, page 22.

31. Figures obtained from http://icasualties.org/oif/Contractors.aspx.

32. Multi-National Force–Iraq, Fragmentary Order (FRAGO) 05-108, "Operationalize the RROC" (16 May 2005).

33. Reconstruction Operations Center, "Mission Brief 14 Aug 2005," PowerPoint presentation prepared by ROC operations director, Baghdad, Iraq (August 2005).

34. Reconstruction Operations Center, "Mission Brief 14 Aug 2005."

35. Special Inspector General for Iraq Reconstruction, *Compliance with Contract No. W911S0-04-C-0003* (Washington: Special Inspector General for Iraq Reconstruction, July 2008), page 6.

36. Special Inspector General for Iraq Reconstruction, *Compliance with Contract No. W911S0-04-C-0003*, pages 8, 18, 22.

37. Jonathon Finer, "Security Contractors in Iraq under Scrutiny after Shootings," *Washington Post* (10 September 2005).

38. Finer, "Security Contractors in Iraq under Scrutiny after Shootings."

39. Author's personal experience. Passing these reports from the ROC to the coalition forces in Baghdad was part of his duties while working for Aegis during 2004 and 2005.

40. Author's recollection of conversations with PMSC employees.
41. Author's own recollection from meetings with Brigadier General Horst at the time.
42. Multi-National Force–Iraq, Fragmentary Order (FRAGO) 07-428, "Armed Contractors/DOD Civilians and PMSCs" (22 December 2007).
43. Multi-National Force–Iraq, Fragmentary Order (FRAGO) 09-109, "Armed Contractors/DOD Civilians and PMSCs" (7 March 2009). Further updated by Appendix 13 to Annex C (Armed Contractor Oversight) to United States Forces—Iraq Operations Order 10-01, dated 15 January 2010.
44. Special Inspector General for Iraq Reconstruction, *Field Commanders See Improvements in Controlling and Coordinating Private Security Contractor Missions in Iraq* (Washington: Special Inspector General for Iraq Reconstruction, July 2009), page 7.
45. Special Inspector General for Iraq Reconstruction, "Field Commanders See Improvements in Controlling and Coordinating Private Security Contractor Missions in Iraq," page 5.
46. Tab C to Appendix 13 to Annex C (Armed Contractor Oversight) to United States Forces, Iraq Operational Order 10-01 (15 January 2010), pages 1–2.
47. Tab D to Appendix 13 to Annex C (Armed Contractor Oversight) to United States Forces, Iraq Operational Order 10-01 (15 January 2010).
48. Special Inspector General for Iraq Reconstruction, *Opportunities to Improve Processes for Reporting, Investigating, and Remediating Serious Incidents Involving Private Security Contractors in Iraq* (Washington: Special Inspector General for Iraq Reconstruction, April 2009), pages ii, 11, 22.
49. Special Inspector General for Iraq Reconstruction, *Quarterly Report and Semiannual to the United States Congress, July 2009* (Washington: Special Inspector General for Iraq Reconstruction, October 2009), page 155.
50. Special Inspector General for Iraq Reconstruction, *Monitoring Responsibilities for Serious Incidents Involving Private Security Contractors Once U.S. Military Forces Leave Iraq Have Not Been Determined* (Washington: Special Inspector General for Iraq Reconstruction, July 2011), page 2.
51. Author's own experience and anecdotal evidence from colleagues at the time.
52. Known as ABCA (America, Britain, Canada, and Australia), AUSCANUKUS (Australia, Canada, United Kingdom and United States), or ACGU (Australia, Canada, Great Britain, and United States) agreements.
53. United States Department of Defense, *Performance Work Statement for the Reconstruction Security Support Services (RSSS) Contract W91GDW-07-D-4021*, paragraph 3.3.3.2, CRSC Intelligence Functions (Washington: Department of Defense, 2007), pages 3–4.
54. Richard Siebert, "Re: Military/PMSC Int Co-operation Paper," email to the author (6 December 2007).
55. Major Kent Lightner, United States Army, interview with author (Baghdad, January 2008).
56. Author's experience and anecdotal evidence from colleagues at the time.
57. United States Department of Labor, Office of Workers' Compensation Programs, "Defense Base Act Case Summary by Nation," United States Department of Labor website, available at http://www.dol.gov/owcp/dlhwc/dbaallnation.htm, accessed 24 September 2015.
58. Details of the Voluntary Principles and the signatories can be found at "What Are the Voluntary Principles?" Voluntary Principle on Security + Human Rights website, available at http://www.voluntaryprinciples.org/, accessed 15 April 2010.
59. Confederation of Switzerland Department of Foreign Affairs and the International Committee of the Red Cross. *The Montreux Document on Pertinent International Legal Obligations and Good Practices for States related to Operations of Private Military and Security Companies during Armed Conflict*, UN Document A/63/467-S/2008/636 (Geneva: International Committee of the Red Cross, 2008).
60. Confederation of Switzerland Department of Foreign Affairs, *Global Code of Conduct for Respect of Human Rights and International Humanitarian Law* (Geneva: Confederation of Switzerland Department of Foreign Affairs, January 2010).

61. Confederation of Switzerland, *International Code of Conduct for Private Security Service Providers* (Geneva: Confederation of Switzerland, November 2010). Details of signatories available at http://www.icoc-psp.org/Home_Page.html, accessed 12 March 2015.

62. International Code of Conduct for Private Security Service Providers' Association, "International Code of Conduct Association," available at http://www.icoca.ch/, accessed 23 March 2015.

63. Katie Bird, "Policing Private Security," International Organization for Standardization website (12 May 2014), available at http://www.iso.org/iso/news.htm?refid=Ref1847, accessed 23 March 2015.

64. Details in British Association of Private Security Companies, "Home," available at http://www.bapsc.org.uk/?keydocuments.html, accessed 23 March 2015; and International Stability Operations Association, "ISOA Code of Conduct," available at http://www.stability-operations.org/?page=Code, accessed 23 March 2015. The BAPSC no longer has its charter available on the website.

65. Aegis Specialist Risk Management's application to join ISOA was apparently rejected at the behest of a competitor. Aegis, along with other industry professionals, concluded that this had more to do with commercial competition than anything else. See David Phinney, "From Mercenaries to Peacemakers? Scandals Confront Military Security Industry," *CorpWatch* (29 November 2005), available at http://www.corpwatch.org/article.php?id=12829, accessed April 2010.

66. Christopher Kinsey, "Private Security Companies and Corporate Social Responsibility," in Alexandria, Baker, and Caparini, *Private Military and Security Companies*, page 82.

67. Schwartz, *Department of Defense Contractors in Iraq and Afghanistan*, pages 14–16.

68. John A. Nagl, James F. Amos, Sarah Sewall, and David H. Petraeus, *The US Army/Marine Corps Counterinsurgency Field Manual. No. 3-24* (Chicago: University of Chicago Press, 2008), page 65.

Chapter Six

ISAF, Inc.?

Private Military and Security Companies and the Afghan "Surge"

David Perry

Prior to 2003, the use of armed force was widely recognized to be the purview of national militaries. In the wake of the Iraq war, both scholars and policymakers had to come to terms with the new reality that private military and security companies (PMSCs) are crucial actors on the battlefield. The shift in American and coalition forces from Iraq to Afghanistan presents an opportunity to assess the role of PMSCs in modern conflict. Similarly, a focus on PMSC use in Afghanistan affords an opportunity to examine defense privatization from a comparative perspective. Accordingly, this chapter proceeds with two primary aims: (1) to analyze the use of PMSCs in Afghanistan, particularly from the 2009 surge until the withdrawal of NATO forces; and (2) to examine and compare national approaches to the regulation and oversight of PMSCs.

There are several reasons why private sector participation in the Afghan war deserves greater scrutiny. First, after the American withdrawal from Iraq it served as the key theater of operations for Western military forces. After 2008, the number of US forces in the country more than doubled and thousands of NATO troops remained in Afghanistan under the International Security Assistance Force (ISAF) mission until local security forces assumed responsibility for Afghanistan's security in 2014. Given the pivotal role PMSCs played in the Iraq war, an analysis of their involvement in Afghanistan is warranted to determine the role the private sector played in the ultimate success or failure of the mission.

Second, Afghanistan provides an opportune theater of operations to provide a preliminary assessment of the role of PMSCs in coalition operations. Although the war in Iraq was fought with multiple coalition partners, the ISAF coalition's more robust multilateral efforts provide a better opportunity to analyze the use of PMSCs from a coalition perspective. This chapter therefore employs a comparative analysis of PMSC use by two key ISAF partners, Canada and the United States.

This comparison is undertaken for two reasons. First, it builds on the limited literature examining security privatization by analyzing the use of PMSCs by two wartime allies fighting in the same theater of operations. By doing so, it offers a meaningful comparison of national approaches to employing PMSCs in the same operating environment that will highlight any differences in national approaches. To date, examinations of PMSCs have relied on American empirical data. The novel "first image" analyses presented by Ryan Kelty, Gary Schaub, and Volker Franke in this volume provide a case in point. These chapters are instructive but their reliance on American personnel may limit their generalizability to the broader international market of contractors. Second, this comparison highlights the relevance of respective national approaches to contracting. As demonstrated below, the United States has made significant changes in how it employs PMSCs over the last 10 years, to incorporate lessons learned and best practices. Such changes in Iraq are explored in depth in chapter 5 of this volume. In contrast, other nations have unique approaches to their use of contractors. Significant differences in the use of contractors between allies thus presents added challenges to the already difficult job of integrating PMSCs into the same battle space with military actors.

Third, just as many have argued that Afghanistan was largely ignored by the Bush administration, relatively little attention has focused on the role of PMSCs in Afghanistan. In fact, much of the burgeoning literature on PMSCs concentrates on the Iraq war, and largely on American-held contracts.[1] It is therefore worth asking whether the role of PMSCs in Iraq was sui generis, a one-time and unprecedented opportunity for the private sector to participate in a poorly planned conflict, or rather a harbinger of the face of modern war. Studying the role of PMSCs in Afghanistan, particularly after the "surge" of American and NATO forces, offers an opportunity to see how the PMSCs are employed in other contemporary conflicts.

Finally, commentators both critical and supportive of the use of PMSCs have accepted that they are now a fact of military life, and that governments need to "figure out how to get better value out of them."[2] Many have argued that the extensive use of contractors in Iraq was poorly planned and arose from a process best described as "ad hoc."[3] As US Defense Secretary Robert Gates testified in 2009, the US military's use of contractors developed

> without any supervision or without any coherent strategy on how we were going to do it and without conscious decisions about what we will allow contractors to do and what we won't allow contractors to do. . . . We have not thought holistically or coherently about our use of contractors, particularly when it comes to combat environments or combat training.[4]

Thus, "prior to the wars in Iraq and Afghanistan, contracting was done on an ad-hoc basis and was not adequately incorporated into the doctrine—or culture—of the military."[5] According to James Jay Carafano, this was an inexcusable oversight by the US military, which failed to properly prepare for the shift toward contracting that occurred in the decade preceding the Iraq war. As he writes, "the military failed to iron out the kinks in the rule of land warfare, establish training and doctrine for programs like LOGCAP, or build the capacity to manage large-scale contract activities after the end of the Cold War."[6] In Iraq, Christopher Kinsey argues that this approach led contractors to be treated as operational and tactical assets, but given no consideration at the strategic level.[7]

This lack of planning has been made public by a slew of scandals related to contractor waste, fraud, and criminal activities. In several instances these had significant repercussions for the course of the war. As one commentator has noted, "uncontrolled outsourcing of the sort on display in Iraq creates more problems than it solves."[8] Yet, at the same time, there is also recognition that "strategic outsourcing" can advance national interests.[9] The lessons of previous research suggest that a more strategic approach to contracting would involve (1) ensuring contracts and contractors are properly managed and coordinated; (2) establishing an effective legal regime for contracted PMSCs; (3) providing oversight and transparency for contracts; and (4) integrating the use of PMSCs into national policy and doctrine.

In this chapter I examine the use of PMSCs in Afghanistan by Canada and the United States across these four measures. In doing so, I assess whether the use of PMSCs by Western governments has become more strategic. Over the course of the war in Iraq, the US government learned a number of lessons and subsequently made substantive progress across all four measures outlined above in its use of PMSCs in Iraq. Examining how America employs contractors in Afghanistan will indicate whether the changes made in Iraq were merely reactions to immediate problems or if they indicate more widespread changes in the US approach to contingency contracting. Similarly, analyzing Canadian practices will provide a further indication of whether the improved contracting practices in Iraq are unique to the United States or indicative of a wider shift to better planned contracting.

PMSCS IN AFGHANISTAN

The use of PMSCs in Afghanistan by Canada and the United States has been unprecedented, ranging across a wide range of services and functions. Each country held contracts with security provider firms that conducted direct security implementation and command functions; military and security consultant firms offering consulting, intelligence, and training services; and military and security support firms that provided logistics, transportation, and technical support.[10] Whereas the United States had extensive experience employing these actors, for Canada this experience was unique. The Canadian Forces (CF) began contracting for services such as strategic lift and base logistics during the 1990s, but Canada's use of PMSCs in Afghanistan far surpassed previous efforts in terms of both scale and scope.[11] Logisticians supported operations at Kandahar Airfield under the Canadian Contractor Augmentation Program (CANCAP) contract held by SNC-Lavalin-PAE, while strategic airlifters and medium lift helicopters provided by SkyLink Aviation delivered cargo into and around the theater. Canada also contracted with MacDonald, Dettwiler and Associates; Boeing; and Israeli Aerospace Industries for unmanned aerial vehicles (UAV) and others for fixed-wing surveillance.[12] Finally, in a first for the Canadian military, several Canadian bases received protection from a combination of local guards and international PMSCs.[13] While the total number of security contractors working for Canada in Afghanistan was never released, it was reported that the government spent $41 million on protection contracts between 2006 and 2010.[14] All told, available estimates indicate that well over 300 contractors worked directly for Canada at an annual cost of at least $250 million.[15]

In comparison, the number of PMSCs working for the United States in Afghanistan dwarfs their Canadian counterparts. Despite past criticism of the Bush administration's outsourcing practices, the number of American contractors in Afghanistan has increased dramatically under the Obama administration.[16] The total number of Department of Defense (DoD)–employed contractors in Afghanistan peaked at just over 117,000 in March 2012. Thus, while the 1:1 ratio of contractors to troops in Iraq has frequently been cited to mark the height of PMSCs participation in American wars, the Congressional Research Service (CRS) estimates that at one point the ratio of contractors to troops in Afghanistan surpassed this, with approximately 1.42 contractors deployed for each US serviceperson. In Afghanistan, contractors at one point comprised roughly 80 percent of the DoD workforce.[17]

The roughly 40,000-person increase in contractor force levels in 2009–2010 was largely the result of increased demands for construction and support services ahead of the surge of US forces, which required upgrades to ISAF and American operating bases, such as Kandahar Airfield and the Bagram air hub.[18] Overall, the CRS indicates that the consistently higher proportion of contractors in Afghanistan than Iraq is due to the requirements of supporting partner ISAF nations.[19] US support forces were stretched by the dual commitments in Afghanistan and Iraq, and since most troops withdrawing from the Iraqi theater are combat forces, overworked support units were hard-pressed to support the increased combat operation under the surge in Afghanistan.[20] Although the former commander of American forces in Afghanistan, General Stanley McChrystal, stated his desire to "keep [the number of] civilian contractors as small as we can,"[21] the troop surge and its rapid deployment required a substantial increase in contractor support.

Two of the PMSCs that benefited the most from the surge were Fluor and DynCorp International, who were awarded Afghanistan Task Orders under the LOGCAP IV contract. The two companies assumed responsibilities for providing base logistics support from KBR, the holder of the previous LOGCAP support contract. Fluor supported 74 bases in northern Afghanistan, providing power, water, housing, construction services, base operations, and logistics support. DynCorp provided comparable services in southern Afghanistan, and its first year of work was valued at approximately $5.9 billion over five years.[22]

AN AFGHAN FACE

The major contracts with Fluor and DynCorp notwithstanding, one of the most significant differences between the Iraqi and Afghan contracting environments was the significantly larger numbers of locally engaged personnel working on behalf of coalition forces in Afghanistan. According to the Commission on Wartime Contracting (CWC), both the DoD and the State Department employed significantly higher numbers of local personnel in Afghanistan than either third-country nationals or American citizens. As of March 2010, the DoD workforce in Iraq was comprised of 26 percent US citizens, 56 percent third-country nationals, and 18 percent local nationals (Iraqi). In comparison, Afghan figures were 14 percent, 16 percent, and 70 percent respectively, giving Afghan contracting a more distinctly local face.[23] Those figures declined significantly over time, however, with local nationals representing 37 percent of the total contractor workforce by March of 2013, but even this much lower share of local employees was much higher than in Iraq.[24] These differences are even starker when comparing the nationalities of armed PMSCs. In Iraq, only 1 percent of the armed private security contractors (PSCs) working for coalition forces were Iraqi, whereas in Afghanistan 95 percent were locals.[25] Nationality breakdowns were never made available by the Canadian government for Canadian-employed contractors, but Canada demonstrated a similar preference for hiring Afghan companies for security tasks.[26] On the other hand, the more extensive contracts for

Canadian base support arrangements primarily employed Canadian citizens because the Canadian government required that contractors working under the main supply contract hold Canadian security clearances. The protracted process for securing such clearances effectively precluded non-Canadians from supporting the Canadian military at Kandahar Airfield.[27]

The Afghan nature of US contracting is part of an American policy set forth in the 2008 National Defense Authorization Act (2008 NDAA) that mandated that the US military increase the number of contracts going to local vendors, particularly for security forces. To support this initiative, the US Joint Contracting Command Iraq/Afghanistan issued directives that newly tendered contracts for security at Afghan bases should focus on hiring guards living within 50 kilometers of the base.[28] In contrast, the Canadian military's decision to hire locally appears to be a combination of two factors. When Canada first moved into southern Afghanistan in 2005, the Provincial Reconstruction Team took over operations from an American unit that had existing contracts with Afghan guards. Not wanting to upset relations with the locals, the Canadian military simply assumed the legacy contract. Subsequent contracting practices, particularly for goods and non-security services, however, were intended to divert contract funds toward the local Afghan economy.[29] Both countries' efforts are therefore substantial improvements on the practices of coalition forces in Iraq, where the billions of dollars' worth of wartime contracts had little impact on the local economy, because they employed so few Iraqis.[30]

Even more concerning is the problem Afghan private security contractors (PSCs) present for state building in Afghanistan. Afghan President Hamid Karzai expressed frustration that locally engaged Afghans are paid more than the national police or army. Depending upon their training and qualifications, locally engaged Afghans earn between US$300 and US$600 a month providing security for coalition forces, vastly more than the $165-a-month paychecks collected by policemen. To rectify this situation, the Afghan Ministry of the Interior (MOI) imposed a salary cap on how much locally engaged Afghan security guards could be paid. This initiative was designed to dissuade Afghan National Security Forces from deserting to work for the swelling ranks of PSCs guarding coalition bases.[31] The hire-local initiative, while motivated by good intentions, ultimately undermined coalition efforts to build the Afghan government's capacity. This led US Senator Claire McCaskill to argue that "we're competing against ourselves, since . . . the most important part of this mission is to add to the police and the army."[32]

Restricting private sector salaries may also offer a means of preventing the development of a private security structure that could challenge the Afghan government's authority. In Iraq the existence of armed Iraqi PSCs is believed to have instilled a view that "loyalty is owed not to the country, but to whoever can pay a decent salary."[33] The move to put more resources into local Afghan hands therefore stood in competition with coalition efforts to increase the capacity of the government.

KARZAI'S CRACKDOWN

Just as the Blackwater security convoys became the poster boys for problem contactors in Iraq, armed security contractors in Afghanistan have been similarly problematic. In 2010, a number of incidents with Afghan PMSCs providing convoy security angered local populations. Contractors were accused of firing indiscriminately into civilian crowds, killing local civilians in Kandahar province,[34] and two of the country's largest PMSCs—Watan Risk Management and Compass Security—were banned from escorting NATO convoys between Kabul and Kandahar after a bloody confrontation.[35] In June 2010 contractors working for Watan, reportedly controlled by relatives of President Karzai, including half brother Ahmed Wali Karzai, effectively shut down Canada's signature aid project—the refurbishment of the Dahla Dam.[36] Later that month a US congressional investigation found security contractors hired to protect convoys transporting NATO supplies from Pakistan to Afghanistan were bribing the Taliban to ensure safe passage, fueling further controversy.[37] In Iraq, the work performed by various PMSCs providing security, particularly Blackwater, came under scrutiny for undermining the overall counterinsurgency campaign goals. In many of the most prominent incidents, like Nisour Square, the contractors involved were American.[38] These examples demonstrate that both host nation nationals and American PSCs were capable of insensitive behavior that tended to undermine larger campaign objectives.

Perhaps in part because of these difficulties, President Karzai decreed in August 2010 that he would disband all private security providers by the end of the year. Karzai's initial plan called for private guards to be replaced by public security forces, under the guise of reining in parallel security structures. The move threatened to end many international efforts in Afghanistan, including those of the Canadian government, leading Prime Minister Stephen Harper to concede that a ban would jeopardize plans for future civilian aid and diplomatic operations.[39] A month later, ISAF commander General David Petraeus issued contracting guidelines for NATO forces mandating, among other initiatives, greater efforts to "work with a broader range of Afghan companies."[40] Within a month, Karzai delayed the implementation of the ban, and later exempted licensed firms working for NATO, foreign embassies, the UN, and those working on development contracts.[41] Early in 2011, however, Karzai made efforts to start taxing US contractors, and accused 16 major firms of a range of violations—including weapons violations and failure to pay taxes. At the same time, he issued disbandment orders for seven other firms, including Watan Risk Management, over associations with government officials.[42] These events indicate that the practice of hiring local employees, especially for security, has at times had the unintended consequence of embroiling security concerns in local power struggles. With this overview of Afghan contracting, we can now move to assessing the use of PMSCs on the four measures outlined earlier.

LEGISLATIVE OVERSIGHT AND TRANSPARENCY

The preceding discussion of American contracting in Afghanistan has been greatly facilitated by a vigorous legislative oversight system. The Congressional Budget Office, Government Accountability Office, and CRS have issued a myriad of audits of US contracting practice dating back to the 1980s. In addition, the Special Inspector General for Iraq Reconstruction was established in 2004 to focus greater attention on Iraq contracts, and a similar body, the Special Inspector General for Afghanistan Reconstruction, was established in 2008.[43] These two offices have issued hundreds of audits and reports that complement audits from DoD, the State Department, and USAID.

As a result of this scrutiny and corresponding media coverage, several congressional committees began holding hearings midway through the Iraq war to examine American contracting practices. Following revelations of contracting abuse, and in particular after the September 2007 Nisour Square shooting of Iraqi civilians by Blackwater USA employees, Congress has taken a much greater role in monitoring contracting. At least eight separate congressional committees have held hearings about wartime contracting practices, including the bipartisan investigation of the CWC.[44] In total, the overall result is that American contracting in Afghanistan occurs under an increasingly stringent oversight regime.

Such oversight is entirely absent in Canada. Only two internal Department of National Defence audits have examined wartime contracting, and neither the Canadian Senate nor House of Commons committees on national defense have held hearings on the issue.[45] Similarly, contracting was only mentioned in passing in the single auditor-general report to focus on operations in Afghanistan.[46] Institutional differences between the American and Canadian political systems account in part for the different approaches to oversight and regulation. Whereas congressional oversight is facilitated by long-serving committee members, substantial research budgets, and the power to compel testimony before committee, Canadian legislative control over the military is much weaker.[47] The parliamentary committee system in general does not offer an avenue for meaningful study of military affairs.[48] Prime Minister Harper's decision in January 2010 to shut down Parliament in an effort to block a parliamentary committee's inquiry into CF operations in Afghanistan further weakened what little parliamentary oversight of the military existed.[49]

In Canada, the lack of civilian oversight of military contracting appears to reflect a wider pattern of civilians deferring to the military on issues concerning Afghanistan. This has effectively resulted in the cabinet abstaining from direct input into many military matters. A recent study of Canadian operations in Afghanistan found that "civilians delegated to the senior military leadership nearly all decisions, except for the decisions to deploy to particular places at particular times. . . . How the mission was to be conducted and overseen was up to Canada's Chief of the Defence Staff and his Deputy."[50] Thus, both a weak legislature and conscious decisions by the executive to give the military greater leeway to conduct operations have resulted in a weak oversight regime for Canadian contracting.

Furthermore, Canadian government reduced the transparency surrounding CF contracts, making contracting oversight and scrutiny more difficult. The names of PMSCs awarded contracts with the Canadian military were initially made public but the government stopped disclosing which firms were awarded contracts in Afghanistan.[51] While American contracting has been characterized by increasing oversight, in Canada oversight has always been lacking and transparency is waning. As a consequence, it is far more difficult to assess whether PMSCs contracted by Canada have been properly managed and controlled.

THE LEGAL REGIME

The legal regime for PMSCs operating in Afghanistan has similarities and differences with those extant in the early phases of the war in Iraq. Similarities exist because many contractors are exempt from Afghan law. The Coalition Provisional Authority infamously exempted contractors from Iraqi laws under Order 17, which effectively left contractors outside Iraqi legal purview. As a result, Iraq did not obtain primary jurisdiction over non-Iraqi contractors until the January 2009 Status of Forces Agreement for US forces went into effect. Since most contractors in Iraq were third-country nationals or Americans, jurisdiction over the bulk of the US-contracted PMSCs fell outside of host nation courts. In Afghanistan, US forces operate under two separate mandates and corresponding Status of Forces Agreements. Personnel serving under ISAF are subject to the Military Technical Agreement between NATO and Afghanistan that maintains that "all ISAF and supporting personnel are subject to the exclusive jurisdiction of their own governments."[52] Thus the bulk of American contractors in Afghanistan were exempt from Afghan law. American forces serving in support of Operation

Enduring Freedom (OEF), however, fall under a separate exchange of notes between the American and Afghan governments. Under these provisions, OEF forces were accorded a status equivalent to American diplomats, presumably exempting them from Afghan law. A Congressional Research Service review of this arrangement at the time indicated that it did "not appear to provide immunity for contractor personnel."[53] Under the subsequent Bilateral Security Agreement negotiated in 2014, however, all American contractors fall under Afghan legal jurisdiction.[54]

The status of PMSCs in Afghanistan differs from that in the early years of the Iraq war, however, with respect to their standing under the contracting nation's legal codes. For those contractors falling outside of Afghan legal jurisdiction, the US Congress has enacted several changes to the legal environment surrounding contractors. In 2004, the jurisdiction of the Military Extraterritorial Jurisdiction Act (MEJA) was expanded to federal agencies supporting DoD missions overseas. This move allowed contractors to be tried in US federal court for crimes committed abroad. The applicability of this legislation to non-DoD contractors is ambiguous, however, as it hinges on the definition of support for DoD missions. This lack of clarity led then-Senator Obama to introduce an amendment in 2007 that was intended to extend the MEJA to all agencies unambiguously, but the initiative ultimately failed.[55] More successful, however, was the 2007 NDAA, which expanded the jurisdiction of the Uniform Code of Military Justice (UCMJ) to encompass contractors, making them eligible for trial by court-martial. The military legal system is viewed as better able to try crimes committed in war zones, as opposed to the federal courts that would hear cases under the MEJA. The constitutionality of trying civilians under military law has been questioned by some scholars, however.[56]

The Canadian legal regime is somewhat different. PMSCs engaged by diplomatic missions for guard duties operate under the laws of host nations and are subject to host nation law. Similarly, all Canadian military contracts for security services in ISAF state that "contractors will be subject to the laws of Afghanistan."[57] Any contractor hired by the government of Canada to provide security services is therefore subject to Afghan law. With respect to contracts for other services, however, Canada's Status of Forces Agreement with Afghanistan makes non-Afghan contractors subject to their own nation's legal jurisdiction.[58] Any third-country national or Canadian working on a non-security contract would therefore fall outside of Afghan jurisdiction. These contractors would, however, be subject to Canada's Code of Service Discipline regardless of nationality, although none have ever been tried for offenses committed in an operational theater.[59] Thus, both countries appear, with some exceptions, to have established a legal framework for the conflict in Afghanistan where some civilian contractors operate outside of the host nation's laws. On the other hand, contractors are more thoroughly included in each country's respective legal regime.

In addition, Canada and the United States have engaged in international efforts to improve the legal and best practices regime for employing PMSCs. Both countries were original participants in the "Swiss Initiative," spearheaded by the International Committee of the Red Cross (ICRC) and the Swiss Department of Foreign Affairs, that resulted in the 17 September 2008 signing of the Montreux Document, detailed in chapter 10 of this volume. The intergovernmental document, also signed by Afghanistan, is intended to "promote respect for international humanitarian law and human rights law whenever PMSCs are present in armed conflicts."[60] While nonbinding, the document's compilation of relevant international and humanitarian laws and best practices is designed to ensure that PMSCs' involvement in armed conflict provides the maximum possible protection to individuals. Each country also signed the International Code of Conduct (ICoC) for Private Security Service Providers in November 2010. The ICoC established industry-wide standards and increased oversight and accountability.[61] For the Canadian government especially, participation in this process was a major initiative toward ensuring proper use of contractors.[62] In the spirit of the Montreux Document, the Canadian military included provisions in its contracts that PMSCs employed by Canada must adhere to all international and humanitarian law, the ICRC code of conduct, and in some instances the code of conduct espoused by the International Peace Operations Association, a US-based PMSC industry group.[63]

CONTRACT MANAGEMENT AND CONTRACTOR COORDINATION

While a proper legal regime serves to bring problem contractors to justice, effective contract management and coordination can go a long way toward ensuring that PMSCs adhere to their contracts and respect the law when performing their duties. One of the most infamous images of the Iraq war is the footage of four American contractors being mutilated by an angry mob in Fallujah. The murdered Blackwater employees entered the city while protecting a convoy that, through layers of subcontracting, was ultimately supplying the US Army through KBR's LOGCAP III contract. Their deaths highlighted two critical problems with American military contracting. First, a weak management structure and extensive subcontracting resulted in KBR hiring its own security, in contravention of its contract. Second, coordination between contractors and military units was sorely lacking. The Marines operating in Fallujah were unaware of the convoy's presence and the convoy did not receive warnings about escalating tensions in the area.[64] David Strachan-

Morris describes this as a "defining incident" in military contractor relationships, which spurred the DoD to take a number of actions to better oversee contractor movements and provide them with intelligence.[65]

Nonetheless, the shootings by another Blackwater convoy in Nisour Square three years later demonstrated that contract management was still problematic. Following the Nisour Square incident, both the State Department and DoD took steps to bring armed PMSCs under greater control. The secretary of defense issued directives reinforcing military commanders' obligations to enforce the UCMJ and their right to detain and disarm contractors engaging in inappropriate behavior. Similarly, the State Department initiated a series of steps to ensure more effective management of their security details. Most importantly, both agencies developed a December 2007 memorandum of agreement (MOA) outlining interagency operating procedures, oversight, monitoring, accountability measures, and use of force agreements, among other issues. At its root, the MOA is designed to "prevent a situation in which PSCs working for different elements of the US government follow differing policies and regulations."[66] In spite of these positive moves in Iraq, no similar agreement existed in Afghanistan for years afterward.

A similar problem exists in Afghanistan with DoD's attempt to manage its own armed contractors. The US military established an Armed Contractor Oversight Division (ACOD) in Afghanistan to "implement DOD's armed contractor policies, procedures, processes and liaison with PSCs throughout Afghanistan."[67] This unit was modeled on a similar ACOD in Iraq staffed by DoD personnel. In Afghanistan, however, the ACOD was not created until February 2009, and its operations were outsourced to the British firm Aegis. Under the terms of its contract, Aegis provides the majority of the ACOD's personnel, including the deputy director, and is responsible for maintaining the day-to-day operations of the directorate. Thus, in Afghanistan, the coordination of the most problematic PMSCs has been outsourced to another firm, with very little direct military supervision.

The coordination problems in Afghanistan persist at the most basic level: tracking contractors employed by the United States. This need is long standing. The DoD was aware as early as 1988 of the need to identify contractors providing essential services, yet a 2003 Government Accountability Office (GAO) report found the department had made limited headway in terms of identifying these services.[68] Following the Nisour Square incident, DoD, the Department of State, and USAID began collaborating on a system to share contractor data. The result is the Synchronized Predeployed and Operational Tracker (SPOT) database operated by DoD. However, due to differing criteria for logging contractors in the SPOT database, the three principal contracting agencies did "not have an accurate or consistent picture of the total number of contractor personnel in Iraq and Afghanistan."[69] Even more troubling, the system focused primarily on tracking foreign contractors, and thus worked far more effectively in Iraq, where the majority of contractors were foreign, than in Afghanistan, where most contractors were locally engaged Afghans. Without a fully operational SPOT system, American agencies continued to rely on self-reported data from contracting firms to establish the number of contractors working on their behalf.[70] As a result, the Commission on Wartime Contracting found that there was "no clear picture of who the contractors in theater are, what services they provide, which contracts they perform, and what their support costs are."[71]

The persistent problems with American contracting do not bode well for other militaries striving to improve their own contracting practices, as it has taken the US years to make these limited improvements. In 2003, the GAO recommended that DoD begin establishing a lessons-learned procedure for contracts, but a 2006 follow-up audit found no organization within the department responsible for undertaking the initiative. Only in 2007 did DoD implement a lessons-learned program. This example demonstrates that even in the face of systematic and detailed audits, contracting practices are slow to change.[72] The situation has led the CWC to note that "the effectiveness of contractor support of expanded US operations in Afghanistan [was] compromised by the failure to extract and apply lessons learned from Iraq, particularly those about poor coordination among agencies."[73]

Although the subject has not yet received significant attention from US audit agencies, coordination of PMSCs employed by other coalition partners could only exacerbate this problem. In Afghanistan, the Canadian International Development Agency and Department of Foreign Affairs and International Trade hired their own contractors, as did the Canadian military. Even within the various branches of the Canadian Armed Forces, no single body coordinated contractors. Instead, responsibility for contracting was dispersed between Canadian Operational Support Command, the logistics branch, and Canadian Expeditionary Force Command, the organization responsible for running the war.[74] Thus, in Kandahar province, where American and Canadian troops share the battle space, American soldiers must coordinate their movements with their own contractors, those employed by other American agencies, and four different Canadian contracting authorities. Factor in contractors hired by other national contingents and those working directly for NATO at Kandahar Airfield, and the coordination challenges are enormous.

These complications were apparent in Canada's contracts for aviation support in Kandahar. The Canadian military entered into a $36 million contract with SkyLink Aviation for the services of six MI-8 helicopters to support its Canadian air wing in Kandahar. This contract was held exclusively by Canada, and the contractors were "fully integrated into the military chain of command."[75] However, the helicopters themselves were not controlled centrally by the Canadian air commander, but rather considered to be contributions to NATO's pool of helicopters in southern Afghanistan.[76] An American Army unit could thus be reliant upon a private firm contracted by Canada but controlled jointly by NATO to provide it with crucial air support.

The coordination of contractors itself must occur within a wider NATO structure that has been plagued by a lack of overall coordination. At both the military and civilian levels, NATO operations in Afghanistan have been characterized by a great degree of disunity, with coalition partners operating under very different strategic, operational, and tactical frameworks and objectives.[77] The parallel command structures that separated ISAF and OEF forces until 3 October 2008 are a case in point.[78] As US Ambassador Karl Eikenberry described the situation, "it's very complex, because it's not just U.S. military, not just [the U.S. government]. It's international community and then, in some cases, just straight business interests."[79] This lack of coordination is most problematic with respect to the scores of armed contractors providing security in Afghanistan that do not fall under the NATO chain of command. According to then-ISAF commander General Stanley McChrystal, "Armed contractors don't come under ISAF. . . so it's a challenge."[80] As a result, both Canada and the US supported the Afghan MOI's initiative to license all armed contractors operating in Afghanistan. The licensing regime was a positive improvement, but proved difficult to implement. The licensing requirement was further reinforced through the provisions of the 2014 Bilateral Security Agreement between the United States and Afghanistan and the NATO Status of Forces Agreement with Afghanistan, both of which made licensing mandatory.[81]

Aside from the various coordination problems outlined above, contracting in Afghanistan has been plagued by many of the same management problems that existed in Iraq. Federal auditors have discovered almost $1 billion worth of wasteful spending in Afghanistan. The CWC's 2009 report attributed this problem to a lack of auditors and contracting staff. The CWC found only four Defense Contract Audit Agency auditors in all of Afghanistan. Similarly, only 36 percent of required Army contracting officer's representative (COR) positions for the multibillion-dollar LOGCAP IV program had been filled. As the Army's CORs are responsible for managing contracts in theater, these shortfalls meant the Army's largest contract was effectively unsupervised. Furthermore, a Special Inspector General for Afghanistan Reconstruction audit of the $15 billion Afghan Security Forces Fund devoted to training the Afghan Police and Army determined the "mechanisms necessary to ensure US funds are managed effectively and spent wisely" were missing.[82] These management problems worsened under the "buy local" provisions of the 2008 NDAA, which increased the need for contract supervision as large, omnibus contracts with Western firms were replaced by more numerous contracts with Afghan companies. CENTCOM data show that after 2008 the number of local contractors employed in Afghanistan exploded, rising from

32,000 in its August 2008 report to peak at a high of 80,725 in the CENTCOM report for the first quarter of 2010.[83]

A final management problem relates to the use of contractors with records of malfeasance and discipline problems. In 2009, the State Department allowed ArmorGroup to compete for a Kabul embassy security contract, despite having lost the previous contract due to employee misconduct. At one point, the company also held the contract to protect the Canadian embassy in Kabul.[84] Similarly, DynCorp International held multiple contracts in Afghanistan despite several government investigations.[85] Perhaps most odiously, various successor corporations and affiliates of the company formerly known as Blackwater USA continue to work in Afghanistan on contracts for both the CIA and US Joint Special Operations Command. These duties are highly classified, but reportedly included planning and conducting counterterrorism missions, supporting unmanned aerial vehicle operations, and protecting CIA forward operations bases.[86] The latter fact was made public when two Blackwater contractors were killed in an attack on a forward operating base in Khost province in 2009 that also killed several CIA officers.[87] The continued use of Blackwater affiliates was particularly troubling given the company's previous scandals and ongoing legal problems in Afghanistan, where two former employees were charged with murder.[88] The contractors were later found guilty of involuntary manslaughter in the shooting of one Afghan, but were acquitted on charges related to two other shootings, suggesting that there was a real measure of discriminate legal accountability for contractors working in Afghanistan.[89]

CONTRACTING POLICY AND DOCTRINE

Amid all of the issues surrounding the use of PMSCs, properly incorporating these private forces into national frameworks for the use of force is the most important step toward ensuring that contracting is strategic. American contracting in Iraq occurred through a series of ad hoc measures responding to a deteriorating security situation and reconstruction requirements that exceeded national capabilities. Canada's use of contractors in Afghanistan similarly began as a response to requirements that exceeded the military's capabilities, beginning with the decision to deploy CANCAP contractors to Kabul before the program had been validated.[90]

The American government, however, has taken significant steps to recognize the vital role its contractors play on military operations. The 2006 Quadrennial Defense Review (QDR) integrated contractors, active and reserve forces, and government civilians into its "Total Force" and mandated that contractors be included in operational plans and orders.[91] Adopting this policy led General David Petraeus to count "thousands of contracted security forces amongst the assets available to him to supplement the limited number of US and Iraqi troops" during the surge in Iraq.[92]

The Obama administration, however, took a series of steps to reduce American reliance on contractors.[93] Secretary of Defense Robert Gates announced initial steps toward achieving these goals by pledging to convert over 11,000 contractor positions into permanent defense civilian employees. This was to be achieved in part by reforming the government acquisition process, with an ultimate goal of increasing the civilian workforce by 20,000 personnel by 2015.[94] This "in-sourcing" initiative was launched with a goal of better balancing between mission requirements and "overall return," which presumably weighs the benefits of contractor support against its many potential costs.

With the 2010 QDR, DoD undertook a significant reevaluation of its Total Force concept, seeking a "balanced total workforce of military, government civilians, and contractor personnel that more appropriately aligns public and private sector functions, and results in better value for the taxpayer."[95] Under the 2010 QDR plan, the number of support service contractors was set to shrink to pre-2001 levels, a shift that required the contractor workforce to decrease from 39 percent to 26 percent as a proportion of the overall DoD workforce. These positions were to be replaced, "if needed, with full time government employees."[96] Publically available data suggest that such a reduction has not occurred. Both the overall number of contractor full-time equivalents and their share of the total DoD workforce increased from fiscal year 2010 to fiscal year 2012. Over this time period, the ranks of full-time contractors grew from 622,722 to 670,176, resulting in a 2 percent increase in their share of total DoD workforce.[97]

In addition to adding more government civilian positions, the 2010 QDR pledged to improve its existing Civilian Expeditionary Workforce (CEW). However, the CEW is primarily designed to provide ministerial capacity building for America's allies as part of a wider strategy of increasing training capacity. The State Department's problems generating sufficient numbers of qualified volunteers to deploy to Afghanistan indicated that finding adequate numbers of defense civilians willing to staff future contingency operations will continue to be a challenge.[98] The desire to reduce the number of contractors in the future will similarly need to be balanced with measures aimed at preserving and enhancing the All-Volunteer Force by "transitioning to sustainable rotation rates that protect the force's long-term health."[99]

For the bulk of Canada's military participation in Afghanistan, the Canadian government and Department of National Defence had no official policy regarding the use of PMSCs. Although Canadian defense policy was updated during the height of concern over armed contractor personnel, the 2008 *Canada First Defence Strategy* made no mention of PMSCs whatsoever. In this situation, Canadian defense personnel concluded that "in the absence of an overarching policy on the use of private military contractors, [policy] staff has taken the position that the Canadian Forces should at this stage strive for consistency."[100] Without a comprehensive policy framework, Canada's use of PMSCs was largely an ad hoc series of responses to operational requirements.

Similarly, at the doctrinal level, Canada has not taken any steps to recognize the role of contractors on the current battlefield. Whereas the American military has updated its doctrine on operations, logistics, and operational contract support to recognize the role of contractors, the Canadian military has taken no action. The operational doctrine published in 2005 offers only passing mention of engaging with local contractors and only in the context of purchasing local goods and services. In contrast, Canada's most recent capstone document, *Canadian Military Doctrine*, makes no mention of contractors whatsoever, and explicitly ignores contractors in its discussion of Canada's comprehensive approach to operations.[101]

This state of affairs evolved considerably with the development of a *draft* directive regarding the selection and use of PMSCs on expeditionary operations in 2012. While as of October 2015 the document had not actually been signed, it has been used in practice. The document focused on the most sensitive types of contracts, such as those for security, operation of weapons or surveillance systems, dog handling, and provision of training services.[102] It lays out numerous factors for commands to consider in deciding whether or not to contract with PMSCs, including potential costs, threat levels, implications for the local security forces and security situation, and the legal regime contractors would fall under. Of note, it specified that the Canadian military must ensure that PMSCs contracted by Canada fall under an effective legal regime. Once established, the directive will mandate effective ongoing oversight, specifically including investigations of any allegations of wrongdoing on the part of the contractor.[103] While this directive did not influence the behavior of the Canadian military until after its combat mission in Afghanistan ended, it represents a significant positive effort to provide clarity and guidance regarding decisions to use PMSCs and effectively manage contracts once in place.

CONCLUSION

For more than a decade, PMSCs have taken a leading role in the Global War on Terror. The war in Iraq demonstrated that the lone superpower can no longer engage in military operations without assistance from the private sector. Iraq also highlighted the significant trade-offs that were made to augment American military forces with PMSC support. Years after the invasion of

Iraq, the role of PMSCs on the Afghan battlefield continued to be problematic.

The preceding comparative analysis demonstrates, first and foremost, that national practices regarding PMSC use remain widely divergent, most notably with respect to the degree of oversight and transparency. Although US contracting practices remain deficient in a number of areas, the issue has garnered sufficient attention that contracting no longer flies under the congressional radar. That significant problems persist, despite this attention, is perhaps as troubling as their existence in the first place. An awareness of shortcomings with US contracting procedures did not facilitate their expeditious resolution. Canada's contracts, in contrast, faced virtually no scrutiny, making it impossible to assess whether there were any problems, and if so, whether they were resolved.

These national differences in contracting practices are meaningful in a coalition context where PMSCs working for various national contingents operate alongside each other and coalition military forces. The Canadian military has long aimed to maintain a high level of interoperability with American forces to ensure that Canada makes a meaningful contribution to allied operations.[104] Based on the available evidence, it is not apparent that Canada achieved a similar level of interoperability with its contractors. Despite adopting similar legal frameworks and practices, such as hiring locally for security, the lack of Canadian doctrine or policy regarding contractor use in particular appears to have left Canada's contracting practices at a disadvantage relative to the American military. It therefore seems appropriate to keep these national differences in mind when assessing the use of PMSCs overall.

A second issue, and one requiring greater scholarship, is the challenge of employing PMSCs in a coalition context. As demonstrated, there are substantive differences in contracting procedures even between two highly interoperable and close allies. Integrating contractors working for respective national contingents, in addition to those of multilateral organizations such as NATO, is undoubtedly a major challenge. Despite a long recognition in the United States that coordination of contracted forces is crucial, information sharing between US agencies remains limited and a common tracking system for contractors in Afghanistan took years to develop. While a full investigation was beyond the scope of this chapter, there was little to provide confidence that NATO as a whole, or even ISAF's Regional Command South, had full awareness of all the firms working in its area of operations for the military alone, never mind those working on behalf of nongovernmental actors.

Finally, the use of PMSCs in Afghanistan does not suggest that contracting has consistently become more strategic. Many improvements were made by the United States, notably in oversight regimes, legal frameworks, and the decision to hire locally. The Afghan experience with local security guards, however, demonstrated that even good decisions can have unintended consequences. By and large, throughout the conflict in Afghanistan, both Canadian and American contracts with PMSCs reflected ad hoc decision making. In Canada, this stemmed from a contracting framework that merely aimed to achieve consistency of effort. In the US, a less-than-strategic approach persisted despite incorporating contractors into operational doctrine and defense policy. Paradoxically, America's use of PMSCs reached its peak in Afghanistan, under an administration that wanted to reduce American reliance on contracting.

This tension between the imperatives of securing Afghanistan on the one hand and recalibrating America's relationship with PMSCs on the other is arguably a better indicator of the future of PMSC use than the war in Iraq. The imperatives of operational success in Afghanistan continued to dictate a heavy reliance on contractors. Troublingly, however, only limited resources were made available to ensure contracts were properly managed. As a result, as a congressional committee noted, "many of the lessons learned from Iraq may not be applied to the efforts in Afghanistan."[105] If Afghanistan is any indication, governments will continue using PMSCs as ad hoc responses to operational requirements and a strategic approach to contracting will remain elusive.

Addressing this problem will require a multinational effort to improve best practices with respect to contracting. This must begin first and foremost in the United States. As the dominant employer of PMSCs, the American military must establish an institutionalized standard for PMSC use. Much as the military establishes tactics, techniques, procedures, and doctrine for the full range of military activities, it should develop similar protocols for employing PMSCs anywhere in the world. Never again should a combatant commander conduct separate operations with dissimilar approaches to employing the contract component of the US Total Force. Until the lessons learned from contracting in Iraq can be uniformly applied elsewhere, their impact will be limited.

Similarly, until the US can achieve consistency in its use of contractors, it will be exceedingly difficult for Canada or other allies to adapt their contracting practices to ensure interoperability. While it is unrealistic to believe that nationally distinct contracting practices will disappear, aspiring to a common set of best practices should be an ultimate goal. NATO has a proven track record of establishing interoperability and common operating practices; therefore, it may prove a useful venue for establishing similar measures for contracting. If the United States can institutionalize common contracting practices and facilitate their adoption by its allies, the corporate warrior will be more effectively controlled.

NOTES

1. For literature on Iraq, specifically, see T. Christian Miller, *Blood Money: Wasted Billions, Lost Lives, and Corporate Greed in Iraq* (New York: Little, Brown and Company, 2006); Gerald Schumacher and Steve Gansen, *A Bloody Business: America's War Zone Contractors and the Occupation of Iraq* (Saint Paul: Zenith Press, 2006); Peter Singer, *Can't Win with 'Em, Can't Go to War without 'Em: Private Military Contractors and Counterinsurgency*, Policy Paper 4 (Washington: Brookings Institution, 2007); Steve Fainaru, *Big Boy Rules: America's Mercenaries Fighting in Iraq* (New York: Da Capo Press, 2008). For academic works on PMSCs more generally, see Peter Singer, *Corporate Warriors: The Rise of the Privatized Military Contractors* (Ithaca: Cornell University Press, 2003); Deborah Avant, *The Market for Force: The Consequences of Privatizing Security* (Cambridge: Cambridge University Press, 2005).

2. Max Boot, "The Mercenary Debate," *American Interest* 4 (May–June 2009), pages 37–42.

3. Peter Singer, "Outsourcing the War," *Salon* (16 April 2004), available at http://www.salon.com/2004/04/16/outsourcing_war/, accessed 11 September 2015.

4. Quoted in Moshe Schwartz, *Department of Defense Contractors in Iraq and Afghanistan: Background and Analysis* (Washington: Congressional Research Service, 2 July 2010), page 15.

5. Schwartz, *Department of Defense Contractors in Iraq and Afghanistan*, page 17.

6. James Jay Carafano, *Private Sector, Public Wars* (Westport: Praeger Security International, 2008), page 51.

7. Christopher Kinsey, *Private Contractors and the Reconstruction of Iraq: Transforming Military Logistics* (New York: Routledge, 2009).

8. Allison Stanger, *One Nation under Contract: The Outsourcing of American Power and the Future of Foreign Policy* (New Haven: Yale University Press, 2009).

9. Stanger, *One Nation under Contract*.

10. Thomas Jäger and Gerhard Kümmel, editors, *Private Military and Security Companies: Chances, Problems, Pitfalls and Prospects* (Wiesbaden: VS Verlag für Sozialwissenschaften, 2007).

11. On Canada's use of PMSCs see David Perry, "The Privatization of the Canadian Military," *International Journal* 64, 3 (Summer 2009); Christopher Spearin, "The Changing Forms and Utility of Force," *International Journal* 64, 2 (Spring 2009); Christopher Spearin, "Not a 'Real State'?" *International Journal* 60, 4 (Autumn 2005); Christopher Spearin, "International Private Security Companies and Canadian Policy," *Canadian Foreign Policy* 11, 2 (Winter 2005).

12. Department of National Defence, "Backgrounder: Strengthening the Canadian Forces and Canadian Sovereignty," BG-08.016 (Ottawa: 7 August 2008), available at http://www.forces.gc.ca/en/news/article.page?doc=strengthening-the-canadian-forces-and-canadian-sovereignty/hnps1tx, accessed 11 September 2015; David Pugliese, "Expect More Roadside Bomb Attacks, NATO," *Ottawa Citizen* (9 January 2010); Gary Schaub Jr., "JUSTAS for All? Innovation and UAVs in the Canadian Forces," *Defence Studies* 15, 2 (June 2015), page 133.

13. Mike Blanchfield and Andrew Mayeda, "Forces Enlist Former Afghan Warlord for Protection," *Ottawa Citizen* (22 November 2007); Andrew Mayeda and Mike Blanchfield, "Private Firms Rush to Fill Security Vacuum in Afghanistan," *Ottawa Citizen* (22 November 2007).

14. Murray Brewster, "Canada's Hired Guns in Afghanistan Rejected by U.S. for Unsavoury Ties," *Globe and Mail* (6 February 2011).

15. David Antonyshyn, Jan Grofe, and Don Hubert, *Beyond the Law? The Regulation of Canadian Private Military and Security Companies Operating Abroad*, National Reports Series 03/09 (Florence: European University Institute Academy of European Law, 12 February 2009); Gordon O'Connor, "Strategic Airlift Marks New Era for Canada," *Maple Leaf* (February 9, 2007), available at http://www.forces.gc.ca/site/commun/ml-fe/article-eng.asp?id=3379, accessed 14 August 2008.

16. Marcus Baram, "Cost of Private Contractors in Afghanistan Climbs to $1 Billion, as Their Numbers Multiply," *Huffington Post* (17 December 2009).

17. Schwartz, *Department of Defense Contractors in Iraq and Afghanistan*; Moshe Schwartz and Joyprada Swain, *Department of Defense Contractors in Afghanistan and Iraq* (Washington: Congressional Research Service, 13 May 2011).

18. David Axe, "Challenges Dog U.S. in Afghan War," *Washington Times* (15 October 2009).

19. Schwartz, *Department of Defense Contractors in Iraq and Afghanistan.*

20. Scott Tyson, "Support Troops Swelling U.S. Force in Afghanistan," *Washington Post* (13 October 2009).

21. Stanley A. McChrystal, "Public Address to the Conference of Defence Associations. Ottawa: December 16, 2009," transcript available at http://cda-cdai.ca/cdai/publications/comisaf, accessed 2 February 2010.

22. August Cole, "DynCorp, Fluor Win Army Jobs," *Wall Street Journal Asia* (10 July 2009).

23. Schwartz, *Department of Defense Contractors in Iraq and Afghanistan.*

24. Moshe Schwartz and Jennifer Church, *Department of Defense's Use of Contractors to Support Military Operations: Background, Analysis, and Issues for Congress*, CRS Report R43074 (Washington: Congressional Research Service, 17 May 2013).

25. Schwartz, *Department of Defense Contractors in Iraq and Afghanistan.*

26. Blanchfield and Mayeda, "Forces Enlist Former Afghan Warlord for Protection."

27. David Perry, *Purchasing Power*, unpublished PhD dissertation (Carleton University, 2015).

28. Walter Pincus, "Contractor Hirings in Afghanistan to Emphasize Locals," *Washington Post* (7 December 2009).

29. Confidential interviews with Canadian PRT officials, 2006.

30. Miller, *Blood Money.*

31. Steve Rennie, "Afghan Government to Regulate Private Security Firms," *Toronto Sun* (25 January 2010).

32. United States Senate, *Testimony: Ambassador Karl Eikenberry and COMISAF Gen Stanley McChrystal. Hearing of the Senate Armed Services Committee* (8 December 2009).

33. Jorg Friedrichs and Cornelius Friesendorf, "The Mercenary Debate," *American Interest* 4 (May–June 2009), page 48.

34. David Pugliese, "Controversial Use of Guns-for-Hire Surges in Afghanistan," *Ottawa Citizen* (5 April 2010), page A1.

35. Dexter Filkins, "Convoy Guards in Afghanistan Face an Inquiry," *New York Times* (6 June 2010).

36. Mitch Potter, "Security Standoff Stalls Canadian Dam Project in Kandahar," *Toronto Star* (9 June 2010). Also see Spearin, "The Changing Forms and Utility of Force," page 488.

37. Karen DeYoung, "U.S. Indirectly Paying Afghan Warlords as Part of Security Contract," *Washington Post* (22 June 2010), page A01.

38. Singer, *Can't Win with 'Em, Can't Go to War without 'Em.*

39. Steven Chase and John Ibbitson, "Protecting Workers Could Complicate Afghan Withdrawal," *Globe and Mail* (25 August 2010).

40. David Nakamura, "New Rules Reflect Shift in How Afghan Contracts Are Awarded," *Washington Post* (14 September 2010), page A12.

41. Alissa J. Rubin, "Afghan Government Softens Ban on Security Firms," *New York Times* (6 December 2010).

42. Joshua Partlow, "Afghan Government Accuses 16 Security Firms of Violations," *Washington Post* (8 February 2011).

43. Several of these reports are cited throughout this chapter. See also Daniel Frisk and R. Derek Trunkey, *Contractors' Support of U.S. Operations in Iraq* (Washington: Congressional Budget Office, August 2008); John Hutton, *Contingency Contracting: DOD, State, and USAID Contracts and Contractor Personnel in Iraq and Afghanistan*, GAO Report 09-19 (Washington: Government Accountability Office, 1 October 2008); United States Department of Defense, *Challenges Impacting Operations Iraqi Freedom and Enduring Freedom Reported by*

Major Oversight Organizations Beginning FY 2003 through FY 2007, Inspector General Report (Washington: Department of Defense, 18 July 2008).

44. These include the Commission on Wartime Contracting in Iraq and Afghanistan; the Senate Committee on Homeland Security and Governmental Affairs; the Senate Armed Services Committee; the Senate Committee on Foreign Relations; the Senate Committee on Appropriations; the House of Representatives Armed Services Committee; the House of Representatives Committee on Oversight and Government Reform; and the House of Representatives Committee on Foreign Affairs.

45. Department of National Defence, *Audit of the Canadian Forces Contractor Augmentation Program (CANCAP)* (Ottawa: Chief Review Services, June 2006); Canadian Department of National Defence, *Evaluation of Contracts for Transportation* (Ottawa: Chief Review Services, August 2006).

46. Office of the Auditor General of Canada, "Chapter 2: Support for Overseas Deployments—National Defence" (Ottawa: Office of the Auditor General of Canada, May 2008).

47. Spearin, "Not a 'Real State'?" pages 1108–9.

48. Janice Gross Stein and Eugene Lang, "Too Few Hilliers: The General Goes Where Ottawa Mandarins Fear to Tread," *The Walrus* (April 2008).

49. "Harper Goes Prorogue," *The Economist* (7 January 2010).

50. David Auerswald and Steve Saideman, "NATO at War: Understanding the Challenges of Caveats in Afghanistan," paper presented at the Annual Meeting of the American Political Science Association, Toronto, Ontario, 2–5 September 2009.

51. Pugliese, "Expect More Roadside Bomb Attacks, NATO."

52. Jennifer K. Elsea, *Private Security Contractors in Iraq and Afghanistan: Legal Issues* (Washington: Congressional Research Service, 7 January 2010), page 13.

53. Elsea, "Private Security Contractors in Iraq and Afghanistan," page 14.

54. *Security and Defense Cooperation Agreement between the Islamic Republic of Afghanistan and the United States of America* (30 September 2014), available at http://www.embassyofafghanistan.org/sites/default/files/documents/BSA%20ENGLISH%20AFG.pdf, accessed 30 September 2015.

55. "S. 674 (110th Congress): Transparency and Accountability in Military and Security Contracting Act of 2007," *Govtrack.us*, available at https://www.govtrack.us/congress/bills/110/s674, accessed 11 September 2015.

56. Richard Fontaine and John Nagl, *Contractors in American Conflicts*, Working Paper (Washington: Center for a New American Security, December 2009). Despite these concerns a Canadian-Iraqi contractor was successfully prosecuted in 2008 under the Uniform Code of Military Justice for stabbing a coworker in Iraq. See Ernesto Londoño, "Two U.S. Soldiers Killed as Iraqi Council Member Opens Fire after Meeting," *Washington Post* (24 June 2008).

57. Antonyshyn, Grofe, and Hubert, *Beyond the Law?* page 23.

58. Canada and the Government of the Islamic Republic of Afghanistan, *Military Technical Agreement* (18 December 2005).

59. Antonyshyn, Grofe, and Hubert, *Beyond the Law?*

60. Confederation of Switzerland Department of Foreign Affairs and the International Committee of the Red Cross, *The Montreux Document on Pertinent International Legal Obligations and Good Practices for States related to Operations of Private Military and Security Companies during Armed Conflict*, page 31, available at http://www.icrc.org/web/eng/siteeng0.nsf/htmlall/montreux-document-170908/$FILE/ICRC_002_0996.pdf, accessed 3 February 2010.

61. Anne-Marie Buzatu, "The ICOC," *Journal of International Peace Operations* 6, 4 (January–February 2011), pages 9–10.

62. Christopher Spearin, "What Montreux Means," *Canadian Foreign Policy Journal* 16, 1 (Winter 2010).

63. Andrew Mayeda, "Canadian Quietly Writes Humanitarian Law into Afghan Security Contracts," *Montreal Gazette* (27 May 2008).

64. Singer, *Can't Win with 'Em, Can't Go to War without 'Em.*

65. As detailed in chapter 5 in this volume.

66. Commission on Wartime Contracting in Iraq and Afghanistan, *At What Cost? Interim Report to Congress* (Washington: Commission on Wartime Contracting in Iraq and Afghanistan, June 2009), page 64.
67. Commission on Wartime Contracting in Iraq and Afghanistan, *At What Cost?* page 74.
68. Commission on Wartime Contracting in Iraq and Afghanistan, *At What Cost?* page 18.
69. John P. Hutton, *Contingency Contracting: Further Improvement Need in Agency Tracking of Contractor Personnel and Contracts in Iraq and Afghanistan. Statement before the Commission on Wartime Contracting in Iraq and Afghanistan*, GAO-10-187 (Washington: Government Accountability Office, 2 November 2009).
70. Hutton, *Contingency Contracting.*
71. Commission on Wartime Contracting in Iraq and Afghanistan, *At What Cost?* page 17.
72. Commission on Wartime Contracting in Iraq and Afghanistan, *At What Cost?* The CWC compiled a list of 537 reports on wartime contracting, containing 1,287 recommendations.
73. Commission on Wartime Contracting in Iraq and Afghanistan, *At What Cost?* page 5.
74. Phone interview with Canadian Operational Support Command official (8 August 2008). These organizations were subsequently subsumed under the Canadian Joint Operations Command as part of a reorganization of the military command structure, but this occurred in October 2012, after Canada's combat mission ended in July 2011.
75. Ethan Baron, "Canadian Soldiers to Fly New Choppers," Canwest News Service (17 November 2008).
76. Graeme Smith, "Canadian Air Wing Takes Flight in Afghanistan," *Globe and Mail* (18 November 2008).
77. Timo Noetzel and Sibylle Scheipers, *Coalition Warfare in Afghanistan*, Chatham House Briefing Paper 07/01 (London: Chatham House, October 2007).
78. United States Department of Defense, *Progress toward Security and Stability in Afghanistan*, report to Congress (Washington: Department of Defense, June 2009).
79. Ambassador Karl Eikenberry and General Stanley A. McChrystal, "Testimony before Hearing of the Senate Armed Services Committee on Afghanistan" (Washington: United States Senate, 8 December 2009), available at http://www.isaf.nato.int/en/article/transcripts/transcript-u.s.-senate-armed-services-committee-hearing-on-afghanistan.html, accessed 3 February 2010.
80. McChrystal, "Public Address to the Conference of Defence Associations."
81. Eikenberry and McChrystal, "Testimony before Hearing of the Senate Armed Services Committee on Afghanistan"; Mohammad Ashraf Ghani, "Presidential Decree of the President of the Islamic Republic of Afghanistan concerning the Implementation of the Bilateral Security Agreement and NATO Status of Forces Agreement" (31 December 2014), available at http://c.ymcdn.com/sites/stability-operations.site-ym.com/resource/resmgr/Advocacy/Afghan_Government__on_the_Im.pdf, accessed 30 September 2015.
82. Special Inspector General for Afghanistan Reconstruction, *Contract Oversight Capabilities of the Defense Department's Combined Security Transition Command–Afghanistan (CSTC-A) Need Strengthening*, SIGAR Audit-09-1 Contract Oversight (Washington: Special Inspector General for Afghanistan Reconstruction, 19 May 2009), page 4.
83. Office of the Assistant Secretary of Defense for Logistics and Materiel Readiness, *CENTCOM Quarterly Contractor Census Reports* (various years; last updated 2014), available at http://www.acq.osd.mil/log/PS/CENTCOM_reports.html, accessed 30 September 2015.
84. Ginger Thompson, "Official Says Contractor in Kabul May Be Ousted," *New York Times* (15 September 2009); August Cole, "U.S. Seeks New Guards in Kabul," *Wall Street Journal* (9 December 2009), page A23; Brewster, "Canada's Hired Guns in Afghanistan Rejected by U.S. for Unsavoury Ties."
85. Ellen Nakashima, "Amid Reviews, DynCorp Bolsters Ethics Practices," *Washington Post* (27 July 2009).
86. Jeremy Scahill, "Blackwater's Secret War in Pakistan," *The Nation* (23 November 2009).
87. Mark Hosenball, "Two Americans Killed in Attack on CIA Base Worked for Xe—Formerly Blackwater," *Newsweek* (6 January 2010).

88. Mike Baker, "Charged Contractors Had Checkered Military Pasts," Associated Press (25 January 2010).
89. Brock Vergakis, "Ex-Blackwater Contractors Guilty in Afghan's Death," *Washington Post* (11 March 2001).
90. David Perry, "Contractors in Kandahar, Eh?" *Journal of Military and Strategic Studies* 9, 4 (Summer 2007).
91. United States Department of Defense, *Quadrennial Defense Review Report* (Washington: Department of Defense, 6 February 2006).
92. Walter Pincus, "Security Contracts to Continue in Iraq," *Washington Post* (4 February 2007).
93. Jeff Zeleney, "Obama to Change Contract Awarding," *New York Times* (5 March 2009).
94. United States Department of Defense, *Quadrennial Defence Review Report*, page 77.
95. United States Department of Defense, *Quadrennial Defence Review Report*, page 56.
96. United States Department of Defense, *Quadrennial Defence Review Report*, page 56.
97. United States Department of Defense, *Defense Manpower Requirements Report: FY 2015* (Washington: Department of Defense, June 2014); United States Department of Defense, *Defense Manpower Requirements Report: FY 2014* (Washington: Department of Defense, August 2013); United States Department of Defense, *Defense Manpower Requirements Report: FY 2012* (Washington: Department of Defense, April 2012).
98. Karen DeYoung, "In Indiana, Practice for 'Civilian Surge' in Afghanistan," *Washington Post* (21 November 2009).
99. United States Department of Defense, *Quadrennial Defence Review Report*, page vii.
100. Murray Brewster, "Canada Lacks Policy to Rein in Hired Guns in War Zones—Critics," *Chronicle Herald* (24 June 2009).
101. Canadian Department of National Defence, *CFJP 01: Canadian Military Doctrine*, B-GJ-005-000/FP-001 (Ottawa: Department of National Defence, April 2009).
102. Canadian Department of National Defence and the Canadian Armed Forces, "Access to Information Request A-2012-000498: National Defence Directive on the Selection and Use of Private Military and Security Contractors on Deployed Operations" (Ottawa: Department of National Defence, 2012).
103. Canadian Department of National Defence and the Canadian Armed Forces, "Access to Information Request A-2012-000498."
104. Ann Griffiths, editor, *The Canadian Forces and Interoperability* (Halifax: Centre for Foreign Policy Studies, 2002).
105. Baram, "Cost of Private Contractors in Afghanistan Climbs to $1 Billion."

Chapter Seven

The UK Approach to Controlling Private Military and Security Contractors

Eugenio Cusumano and Christopher Kinsey

Since the establishment of Watchguard International, the first modern private military and security company (PMSC), the United Kingdom has harbored the growth of the world's second largest private security industry operating abroad in support of governments, international organizations, firms, and NGOs.[1] British firms such as ArmorGroup (now part of G4S), Control Risks Group, and Aegis have played a valuable role in today's strategic landscape, supporting the reconstruction of Iraq and Afghanistan, and securing the sea routes endangered by the rise of piracy. Besides hosting a sizable private military and security industry, the UK has also been characterized by a growing tendency to outsource a host of support functions ranging from the maintenance of weapons platforms and the provision of logistical support in the operational space to the performing of armed security. The British Ministry of Defence (MoD), Foreign and Commonwealth Office (FCO), and Department for International Development (DFID) have all relied on PMSCs in conducting their activities abroad. For these two reasons, an analysis of the British industry is crucial for a comprehensive understanding of the problems and tradeoffs that military and security privatization may pose to control over the use of force and how the new corporate soldiers should be regulated.

This chapter will be divided into two parts. First, we will briefly analyze the development of the British industry, presenting its origins, its main activities, and its changing relationship with the UK government. Second, we will analyze the regulatory approach promoted by British authorities. After the public uproar raised by the Sandline Affair in Sierra Leone, the need to regulate British PMSCs became a salient issue on the UK political agenda, leading to the publication by the Foreign Office of a Green Paper envisioning different regulatory options. However, government reshuffles, disagreement over the most effective way to regulate an international industry, and the transformation of the sector delayed the adoption of any decision. In 2009, the FCO finally presented its regulatory approach based on the awareness, stated by Foreign Secretary David Miliband, that PMSCs represent an "indispensable, inevitable and international industry."[2] Due to the international scope of British PMSC operations, the UK government has discarded the possibility of enforcing restrictive domestic legislation that could drive the sector offshore or underground, opting instead for a firm support for the signing of domestic and international third-party monitored codes of conduct and a responsible use of government demand as an informal regulatory tool rewarding high standards and deterring irresponsible behavior.

THE BRITISH CORPORATE SOLDIERS: HISTORY AND CHARACTERISTICS

In the course of its history, the United Kingdom has traditionally been characterized by a pronounced tendency to both purchase foreign military manpower and export its military expertise to other countries.[3] This section will analyze the development of the British private military industry and its changing relationship with the UK government.

The Private Military Industry in the UK: A Historical Overview

The purchasing of foreign military manpower has been commonplace in British history. Due to its insular geopolitical position, the legacy of the English Civil War, and its liberal political culture, British rulers came to see the raising of the standing armies that were at the core of European continental states' defense as an unnecessary and dangerous luxury.[4] The lack of a strong standing army resulted in the widespread resort to mercenaries to meet foreign policy goals.[5] The Hessian regiments employed during the American Revolution are a case in point. The hiring of paid foreigners remained a widespread practice until the Crimean War, when a Swiss, a German, and an Italian legion were employed.[6] The Royal Navy itself long remained a semi-private force, heavily reliant on merchant ships and private capital.[7] While the development of the norm of neutrality and the introduction of conscription in the periods between 1916–1918 and 1939–1962 sharply reduced the tendency to purchase military manpower, the Cold War period still saw British political elites resort to mercenaries as a covert tool of foreign policy in the developing world.[8] It was in this context that the idea to establish the first PMSCs developed.[9] Colonel David Stirling, the founder of British Special Air Service (SAS), formalized the first modern UK private military and security company, Watchguard International, in the Channel Islands in 1967. Stirling arguably devised the project of creating a commercial company performing military activities after the British intervention in Yemen, where a mixture of British and French mercenaries, some of whom were members of the SAS on leave from the military, were covertly deployed to support the forces of the Imam Al-Badr, who had been overthrown by a coup that threatened the British possession of Aden, the last remaining outpost controlling access to the Mediterranean after the loss of Suez.[10] The newly established government, however, was soon recognized by both the United States and the USSR. The 1956 Suez crisis had clearly shown that any direct military intervention could trigger unbearable diplomatic consequences if undermined by the opposition of both superpowers. For this reason, certain members of Harold Macmillan's second cabinet opted for a covert action carried out by mercenaries acting unofficially.

Together with Stirling, other former Special Forces officers also began setting up PMSCs, such as Control Risks, founded in 1975, KMS, Saladin Security, and DSL (renamed ArmorGroup and now part of G4S).[11] The experience in Yemen showed Stirling and his comrades that there was room for the creation of a private force operating for a profit in the areas of greatest interest for national authorities but where a direct British intervention could not take place. The rationale underlying the creation of Watchguard was therefore that of providing UK decision makers with a shield of plausible deniability to protect the national interest from the diplomatic consequences of using military force abroad.[12]

Although Stirling saw Watchguard as a tool of British foreign policy and identified in the Foreign Office and the Ministry of Defence its main customers, the UK government proved wary of resorting to this industry, which found its main source of revenues in commercial security and in the training of foreign armies.[13] At the end of the 1990s, the controversy raised by the combat support activities of the PMSC Sandline International in Papua New Guinea and Sierra Leone, where the firm was found in violation of a UN arms embargo, further strengthened British foreign policy officials' wariness of the industry. At the same time, however, the tightening budgetary and manpower constraints and the increased government demand for military support and security services in the wake of the global war on terror provided new business opportunities for the firms that had rejected the Sandline model, committing themselves to the provision of support services and defensive security only.[14] Indeed, many British companies proved capable of taking advantage of the growing demand for security and support services in Iraq. Control Risks, for instance, increased its revenues fifteen-fold.[15] In 2004, the British firm Aegis was awarded the largest contract for security services in Iraq, and it was renewed the following year, in spite of the controversial biography of its CEO Tim Spicer, former head of Sandline. Tasked with providing security for the green zone and devising a system for coordinating and tracking private security personnel operating in Iraq, Aegis established different Regional Operation Centres (ROCs) that would perform such functions through a computerized system relying on US military satellites.[16] After the explosion of the Iraqi private security bubble and the withdrawal of coalition troops, British firms found a new source of revenues in the provision of maritime security, providing armed teams and escorts for vessels traveling offshore between the pirate-ridden area of the Horn of Africa and the Straits of Hormuz.[17] The British private maritime industry is now the world's largest.[18] UK private security companies have also played a meaningful role in Libya, where they have supposedly supported the rebel forces in their fight against Gaddafi's military by providing tactical intelligence for NATO air strikes, helped to secure the oil infrastructure, and protected the British diplomatic mission in Benghazi.[19]

Contractor Support to UK Military Operations

While long refraining from relying on the industry for the provision of armed activities, the British Ministry of Defence has promoted the privatization of logistics to a large extent. Until the second half of the nineteenth century, logistical support to British military operations remained in the hands of commercial actors. The disastrous performance of merchant suppliers during the war in Crimea led to the establishment of in-house logistical capabilities through the creation of an all-military Land Transport Corps and Army Service Corps.[20] Contractors, however, could still be found in significant numbers, providing construction and transportation during the Anglo-Boer War and World Wars I and II.[21]

The strategic environment of the Cold War, which combined ease of logistical support through safe lines of communication, reliable host country support, and prearranged stocks of fuel and materiel with the concern that support units would have to operate under the threat of nuclear attack, reinforced the need to maintain a self-sufficient model based on the in-house provision of nearly all support activities, including laundries and bakeries.[22] In the course of the 1980s, however, this situation started to change due to the convergence of financial, ideological, operational, and technological imperatives.[23] During the Cold War already, the MoD suffered from three severe budgetary crises[24] and from a growing military manpower strain due to low retention rates and an increased unwillingness to serve in the military.[25] The electoral victory of Margaret Thatcher and her New Right created the ideological momentum for a reduction of the size and functions of the state machinery.[26] Moreover, the disappearance of the threat posed by the Soviet Union and the transition of British strategic priorities from a Cold War static defense posture to the development of leaner global expeditionary capabilities provided greater room for the involvement of the commercial sector in transportation and logistical support.[27] Initiatives like "Competing for Quality White Paper," which opened many state functions to competitive bids with private businesses, led to a constant increase in the level of private sector involvement in the provision of military support functions.[28] The New Labour's electoral victory of 1997 did not halt the privatization process. On the contrary, the Blair cabinet further increased the involvement of commercial actors into defense policies, advocated as a non-ideological response to budgetary constraints.[29] Initially limited to non-deployed activities such as home facilities management and training, contractor support eventually spilled over to deployed operations. During peace operations in the Balkans, the manpower strain of the Royal Engineers and Royal Pioneers corps resulted in the outsourcing of transportation and construction to contractors. Commercial haulers were also involved in the transportation of equipment.[30] The introduction of new and highly technological weapon systems also played a role, increasing the need for technological expertise that could no longer be found within the ranks. These technological imperatives led the UK minister of defence to recommend a partnership between the MoD and industry in the "through-life" design, development, manufacture, and support of weapon platforms.[31]

The shift from static defense to expeditionary force projection was epitomized by the 1998 Strategic Defence Review, which explicitly foresaw the possibility of contractor support to military missions overseas.[32] The following years saw the establishment of a Contractor on Deployed Operation (CONDO) policy, which first embedded contractor support into UK military doctrine, and the creation in 2004 of the CONLOG program. Similar to the US LOGCAP (Logistics Civil Augmentation Program), the British CONLOG is an umbrella contract that allows the British Permanent Joint Headquarters to purchase support services from the commercial sector.[33] In the wake of the war on terror, the CONDO policy expanded into a broader policy framework called CSO (Contractor Support to Operation).[34] A step further toward the integration of contractors into strategic planning has recently been devised through the establishment of the Total Support Concept, which sees contractors as an indispensable element of British expeditionary forces. As already stated in 2000 by the then minister of state for the armed forces, John Spellar, "MoD's objective is to incorporate the private sector so firmly into the doctrine for deployed operations that Planning Staffs and their Commanders will take it for granted that their task force will include a contract support element."[35]

Unlike the DoD, the British Ministry of Defence has not collected or publicized figures on its reliance on contracted workforce in the latest military operations. According to the only data available, collected by a private consultancy, as of the end of 2010 the UK MoD relied on 6,500–7,000 contracted personnel supporting Operations Telic (Gulf region), Herrick (Afghanistan), Calash (Indian Ocean), and Oculus (Balkans).[36] Contractor support now accounts for 40 percent of the UK total force deployed overseas.[37] Estimated annual expenditures for contractor support to deployed operations amount to about $2.6 billion.[38] Contractors have been involved in a host of services, including equipment support, food supply, transportation, personnel services, medical services, and air and maritime support.[39] In addition, commercial support "has also expanded to include much wider areas . . . than are narrowly defined as logistics,"[40] extending into sensitive tasks including intelligence, surveillance, target acquisition, and reconnaissance (ISTAR). To date, the provision of armed security by PMSCs is considered by the MoD "only in exceptional circumstances."[41] However, the use of armed contractors has become commonplace in other departments such as FCO and DFID, which are using armed contractors to provide armed protection for their diplomatic and humanitarian personnel.[42] The MoD too has indirectly become heavily reliant on armed contractors. Due to political and manpower constraints, the UK military could not provide force protection for its prime contractors transporting fuel and food supplies through Pakistan and southern Afghanistan, forcing these firms to rely on local armed security companies as subcontractors. The size and the sensitivity of contractor support are apparent in the number of fatalities. As of 2010, according to an industry investigation, over 500 MoD contractors supporting Operations Telic and Herrick have been killed since 2003.[43] Fatalities among the contracted workforce were therefore higher than casualties among military personnel, amounting to 394 uniformed personnel as of 2010.[44]

REGULATING THE INDUSTRY: THE BRITISH APPROACH

The previous section briefly reviewed the evolution of the British private military and security industry over time and how its relationship with the UK government has evolved toward increasing interdependence. This section will analyze the changing regulatory approach of the UK government, now based on a close partnership with the industry and support for self-regulation.

An Informal Regulatory System

The attempt to regulate the export of British military manpower and expertise dates back to the 1870 Foreign Enlistment Act. As a response to the evolution of the norm of neutrality, Her Majesty's Government made it an offense for a British subject to enlist in the forces of a foreign power or to recruit for such forces.[45] However, the act proved nearly impossible to enforce, leading to no condemnation.[46] The prosecution of mercenary activities conducted by British citizens was undermined by the difficulties associated with extraterritorial jurisdiction, but also restrained by the attachment to individual freedom that underlies the British political culture. As stated by the 1976 Diplock Report, released in the wake of the capture of British citizens involved in the civil war in Angola, the prohibition of mercenary activities could translate into an unwarranted interference with individual liberty. As mercenary activities could only be curbed by prohibiting certain individuals from leaving the country, anti-mercenary legislation could impact on the free movement of British citizens.[47] The British approach to regulating mercenaries was also reflected by its refusal to sign the 1989 UN Mercenary Convention.[48]

Until the late nineties, the growth of a British private security sector operating abroad did not create a demand for the formal regulation of defense services export. Unlike the US International Traffic in Arms Regulation (ITAR), the UK defense export control code does not require the licensing of contracts involving the provision of security and military training services abroad as long as no equipment is exported as part of the contract. However, the small scale and the background of the UK industry, largely composed of a network of former special operations forces personnel with a close connection to British military and policy circles, permitted the establishment of an informal regulatory environment, ensuring the consistency between PMSC activities and the UK national interest in spite of the lack of any formal obligation to notify contracts and have them approved.[49]

It was only after the scandal triggered by the Sandline Arms to Africa Affair in 1998 that the need for formal regulation of the export of combat support services came to the fore. The aftermath of Sandline's operations clearly showed the dangers of a solely informal regulatory environment and the risk that the UK government could suffer from guilt by association for the activities carried out by its private security firms abroad. As acknowledged by the 1999 Parliamentary Report of the Sierra Leone Arms Investigation, some within the Foreign Office—and particularly the British High Representative in Sierra Leone Peter Penfold—were aware of Sandline's plan.[50] While this information never reached the foreign minister in London, Sandline CEO Tim Spicer assumed he was acting with full government support.[51] The report also called for the drafting of a Foreign and Commonwealth Office Green Paper on the regulation of private military companies.[52]

Released only in 2002, the Green Paper recognized UK private military and security companies as legitimate players who can perform a positive role in international security, but it also acknowledged the need for regulation, analyzing the merits and shortcomings of six different regulatory options, namely a ban on military activities abroad, a ban on recruitment for military activity abroad, a licensing regime for military services, a system of regulation and notification, a general license for companies, and self-regulation through the creation of a voluntary code of conduct.[53] While the report did not explicitly support any of these options, in August 2002 the House of Commons Foreign Affairs Select Committee responded with a report that recommended a stringent regulation based on the creation of a licensing regime inspired by the US ITAR model, a disclosure of companies' structures and policies, and a monitoring and evaluation regime.[54] Although the secretary of state for Foreign and Commonwealth Affairs agreed to look into these recommendations[55] and a policy review took place in 2005, no explicit action followed the publication of the Green Paper in spite of considerable pressure from Parliament and civil society. Such a pressure is forcefully epitomized by the 2007 Early Day Motion 690, signed by over 100 members of Parliament who urged the government to introduce legislation,[56] and by War on Want and other NGOs' 2008 request for a judicial review in response to government's "failure to act."[57]

The Restarting of the Regulatory Debate: The Consultation Process

The regulatory process, stalled by cabinet reshuffles and lack of agreement on the feasibility and effectiveness of different regulatory options, restarted in April 2009, when the government initiated a new round of consultations with industry, academics, and civil society.[58] Although a large number of respondents recommended the establishment of some type of formal regulation, urging for the creation of a licensing system, the government maintained that it did not receive "any convincing evidence during the consultation period to suggest that a legislative approach would successfully meet its objectives."[59] It therefore opted for an approach based on the self-regulation of the industry through the establishment of domestic and international voluntary codes of conduct subject to independent, third-party monitoring.[60]

The government's choice was motivated by at least three reasons. First, at the beginning of the twenty-first century the international private military and security industry was characterized by steady change. The firms that had raised more controversy by selling direct combat support services to developing countries, notably Executive Outcomes and Sandline International, had both closed their doors to business. UK companies, on the other hand, managed to distance themselves from that model by emphasizing their commitment to defensive services and minimum use of force.[61] The determination by the industry to stay away from the provision of combat support reduced the perceived need for legislation restricting the export of military and security services. In addition, the large role and the overall good performance of UK firms during the conflict in Iraq and the lack of major incidents involving UK contractors reinforced the belief that the British industry had both a strategic and a financial relevance, and was capable of maintaining high standards of behavior and playing a vital role in support of UK interests. Finally, the existence of reputational pressures and the commercial imperative to use adherence to high professional standards as a market differentiator in an increasingly competitive sector made the British industry a firm and credible supporter of self-regulation.

Second, UK PMSCs made substantial efforts to develop corporate social responsibility and meaningful self-regulation. In 2005, the British Association of Private Security Companies (BAPSC) was launched to represent UK security firms providing armed security services overseas. Members were prescribed to abide by a charter demanding the use of weapons only for defensive purposes, the training and vetting of individual contractors, and respect for human rights legislation.[62] At the same time, a few major British firms also joined the International Peace (now Stability) Operations Association (ISOA)[63] and developed their own codes of conduct.[64] Eventually another UK interest group, Aerospace Defence and Security, took the lead in engaging with the UK government through its Security in Complex Environments Group (SCEG). In 2011, after a public tender, the SCEG was appointed as the UK government official partner in the effort to raise standards within the industry.[65] After the boom of maritime private security, a role in the regulatory process has also been played by the Security Association for the Maritime Industry (SAMI), based in London and representing a large number of UK firms involved in the maritime security business. In addition, UK firms have been strong supporters of regulatory efforts taking place at the international level, like the Swiss Initiative. About one-third of the signatories of the International Code of Conduct are based in the UK.[66] Furthermore, the British industry, represented by the SCEG, has also been involved in the drafting of the Department of Defense–sponsored standards on land-based PSCs.[67]

Third, the UK government found significant problems in the main regulatory solutions advocated by academics and NGOs, deemed to be too costly or impossible to enforce. The Green Paper already raised objections against a ban on military activity. Such a ban was considered both unfeasible due to the problems associated with extraterritorial investigation and prosecutions and undesirable, as it would deprive British citizens of a legitimate business and encroach upon their freedom of movement while at the same time denying foreign governments the possibility of purchasing the assistance needed to tackle humanitarian emergencies and legitimate security concerns.[68] A ban on the recruitment of personnel offering military support and combat alike was also considered ill-suited for the regulation of PMSCs. In its February 2009 impact assessment of other regulatory options, the FCO also called into question the possibility of establishing a licensing regime analogous to the US ITAR. The licensing of individual PMSC operations was considered problematic for various reasons. First, the government considered this option very difficult to enforce as contraventions of the license would occur outside the government's jurisdiction. In addition, the FCO maintained that regulation at the UK national level would have no influence over the wider industry, and would urge companies to relocate outside of the UK.[69] The government was also sensitive to UK firms' concern that a system of individual licenses could distort the market, affecting the competitiveness of the industry. Usually smaller than US firms, UK PMSCs see their timeliness in responding to their clients' requests as a crucial asset. Small businesses in particular could be forced to close their doors due to their lower capacity to lobby for licenses and wait for government approval.[70] The creation of a register of approved companies was also seen as problematic and potentially counterproductive. A general license, it was argued, could translate into a blank check for approved companies, inducing them to consider that any activity carried out abroad would have the UK government's seal of approval. Moreover, creating a register of approved companies could be potentially in contrast with UK competition law.[71]

The Government's Approach: International and Domestic Self-Regulation

For these reasons, the government opted for a system of self-regulation as its preferred approach. According to the FCO, the signing of independently monitored codes of conduct is the most feasible and effective solution to ensure that the industry adheres to stringent standards and reduce the risk of incidents.[72]

In addition, the UK government believes in the possibility of further encouraging high professional and ethical standards within the industry by using its contracts with PMSCs. While many have warned that PMSCs are business entities driven by corporate profit rather than public interest to emphasize the challenges posed by their activities, their commercial nature may also provide additional avenues for regulation, making them subject to a basic, extra-legal kind of pressure: consumer demand.[73] It is widely held in the literature on industrial relations that public demand can be an effective tool in the regulation of a market. The private military and security industry is no exception: since home governments are often the major customers for their services, PMSCs may "choose to abide by regulation to preserve their governmental contracts."[74] Following this line of argument, the increase in the UK government's purchasing of security and military support services increased the effectiveness of public demand as an informal tool of regulation. Moreover, the UK government has maintained that corporate social responsibility can be promoted on the two sides of the contractual relationship, arguing that "ethical corporate employers would prefer to employ PMSCs who comply with the domestic code/international standard rather than seek alternative, cheaper service providers."[75] Consistent with this approach, the FCO has been at the forefront in increasing the awareness among transnational corporations of the importance of choosing private security providers characterized by high professional standards and respect for human rights. It has done so by promoting initiatives such as the Voluntary Principles on Security and Human Rights, drafted together with the governments of the United States, Norway, and the Netherlands and some major NGOs and corporations operating in the extractive and energy sector.[76]

Finally, the UK government has maintained the need to circumvent the shortcomings of domestic regulation by supporting regulatory initiatives at the international level. Her Majesty's Government has been a firm supporter of the more nuanced and non-binding regulatory approach promoted by the Swiss Initiative, signing the Montreux Document and encouraging the signature by British PMSCs of the International Code of Conduct.[77]

While the major regulatory role to date has been played by the UK Foreign Office, working in close consultation with the Ministry of Defence and the Department for International Development, the rise of maritime private security has brought to the fore a new governmental actor in the regulatory process, namely the Department for Transport (DfT). Although initially reluctant to authorize the presence of arms onboard, in late 2011 the UK DfT came to accept the use of armed security guards on UK flagged vessels.[78] It has, however, released an interim guidance and a written ministerial statement restricting the employment of armed contractors to exceptional circumstances, specifically to the transit through the high-risk area bounded by Suez and the Straits of Hormuz. The guidance also discusses the insufficiency of unarmed security measures and the fulfillment of the latest best management practices, including appropriate training and vetting of contractors and the existence of insurance against third-party damage.[79] Under the current regulatory framework, UK vessels transiting through the high-risk area will have to obtain authorization from the Home Office for the possession of firearms. As the home state of the largest maritime private security industry, the majority of maritime insurance, and the International Maritime Organization, the UK has been the natural locus for international regulatory initiatives on maritime private security.[80] In accordance with the broader UK policy on land PSCs, the Department for Transport has therefore taken up policy leadership in calling for an international accreditation scheme for private maritime security companies.

CONCLUSION

The UK has long hosted a florid private military and security industry and increasingly relied on contractors in the provision of services such as diplomatic security and logistical support. Its government, however, has remained unwilling to establish a regulatory framework based on binding domestic legal measures. While the scandals created by Sandline International and the controversy raised by the activities of US firms like Blackwater heightened the call for further regulation by British civil society, the UK government has firmly opted for a self-regulatory approach based solely on the raising of standards within the industry. The signing of voluntary, third-party-monitored codes of conduct, reinforced by the market incentives provided by government contracts, has been considered both the most feasible and the most effective option to regulate the British private military and security industry, ensuring professionalism, respect for human rights, and consistency with the UK's national interest.

NOTES

1. Christopher Kinsey, *Corporate Soldiers and International Security: The Rise of Private Military Companies* (London: Routledge, 2006).
2. United Kingdom Foreign and Commonwealth Office, *Public Consultation on Promoting High Standards on Conduct by Private Military and Security Companies (PSCs) Internationally: Summary of Responses* (16 December 2009), page 31.
3. Traditionally, the United Kingdom military has drawn foreign military manpower from the British Commonwealth and in particular from Nepal and the Republic of Ireland. It has also exported military expertise, usually to the Middle East and the British Commonwealth through the use of contract and loan officers (United Kingdom Public Records Office, *Confidential. Subject: Advisory and General Legal Matter, Conditions of Service, Mercenaries*, Diplock Report, DEFE 24/1759).
4. Hew Strachan, *The Politics of the British Army* (Oxford: Oxford University Press, 1997); Colin McInness, *Hot War, Cold War: The British Army's Way in Warfare, 1945–95* (London: Brassey's, 1996).
5. Christopher Coker, "Outsourcing War," *Cambridge Review of International Affairs* 13, 1 (1999), page 99.
6. C. C. Bayley, *Mercenaries for the Crimea: The German, Swiss, and Italian Legions in British Service, 1854–1856* (London: McGill-Queen's University Press, 1977).
7. Coker, "Outsourcing War," page 99; Charles Tilly, *Coercion, Capital, and European States, AD 990–1992* (Cambridge: Blackwell, 1992), page 82.
8. For a detailed account of how conservative ministers used mercenaries to protect perceived UK interests in Yemen see Clive Jones, *Britain and the Yemen Civil War* (Brighton: Sussex Academic Press, 2004).
9. They harkened back to the mercantile companies that helped establish the British Empire, such as the East India Company (Kinsey, *Corporate Soldiers and International Security*, pages 38–40).
10. Alan Hoe, *David Stirling: A Biography* (London: Warner Books, 1996), pages 354–416.
11. Kinsey, *Corporate Soldiers and International Security*, pages 43–46.
12. Kinsey, *Corporate Soldiers and International Security*, pages 43–46.
13. Kinsey, *Corporate Soldiers and International Security*, pages 43–46.
14. Christopher Kinsey, *Private Contractors and the Reconstruction of Iraq: Transforming Military Logistics* (New York: Routledge, 2009); Matthew R. Uttley, "Private Contractors on Deployed Operations: The United Kingdom Experience," *Defence Studies* 4, 2 (Summer 2004), pages 145–65.
15. Eugenio Cusumano, "Policy Prospects on the Regulation of PMSCs," in Francesco Francioni and Natalino Ronzitti, editors, *War by Contract: Human Rights, Humanitarian Law, and Private Contractors* (Oxford: Oxford University Press, 2011), page 13.
16. Kinsey, *Private Contractors and the Reconstruction of Iraq*, pages 82–84; David Isenberg, *Shadow Force: Private Security Contractors in Iraq* (Westport: Praeger, 2009).

17. Donald Dominick, *After The Bubble: British Private Security Companies after Iraq*, Whitehall Paper (London: Royal United Services Institute for Defence and Security Studies, 25 July 2006).

18. James Brown, "Pirates and Privateers: Managing the Indian Ocean's Private Security Boom" (Sydney: Lowy Institute for International Policy, 2012), page 6.

19. Freedom of Information Request, 7 July 2011; Richard Norton-Taylor and Chris Stephens, "Libya: SAS Veterans Helping NATO Identify Gaddafi Targets in Misrata," *Guardian* (31 May 2011), available at http://www.guardian.co.uk/world/2011/may/31/libya-sas-veterans-misrata-rebels.

20. Tim Cross, "Logistic Support for UK Expeditionary Operations," *RUSI Journal* 145, 1 (2000), page 74.

21. Cross, "Logistic Support for UK Expeditionary Operations," page 74.

22. Cross, "Logistic Support for UK Expeditionary Operations," page 74. See also Uttley, "Private Contractors on Deployed Operations"; Kinsey, *Corporate Soldiers and International Security*.

23. Uttley, "Private Contractors on Deployed Operations."

24. McInness, *Hot War, Cold War*, page 83.

25. Hew Strachan, "The Civil-Military 'Gap' in Britain," *Journal of Strategic Studies* 26, 2 (2003), page 45.

26. Dennis Kavanagh, *Thatcherism and British Politics: The End of Consensus?* (Oxford: Oxford University Press, 1990).

27. Uttley, "Private Contractors on Deployed Operations," page 147.

28. United Kingdom Treasury, *Competing for Quality: Buying Better Public Services* (London: Her Majesty's Stationery Office, 1991).

29. Elke Krahmann, *States, Citizens and the Privatization of Security* (Cambridge: Cambridge University Press, 2010), page 95.

30. Cross, "Logistic Support for UK Expeditionary Operations," page 75.

31. Uttley, "Private Contractors on Deployed Operations," page 190.

32. United Kingdom Ministry of Defence, *Strategic Defence Review: Modern Forces for the Modern World* (London: Ministry of Defence, July 1998), paragraphs 19, 99.

33. Kinsey, *Private Contractors and the Reconstruction of Iraq*.

34. United Kingdom Ministry of Defence, *Contractor Support to Operations: Tiger Team Final Report* (London: Ministry of Defence, 16 March 2010), page 12.

35. Cited in Matthew Uttley, *Contractors on Deployed Military Operations: United Kingdom Policy and Doctrine* (Carlisle: Strategic Studies Institute, September 2005), page 1.

36. Andrew Higginson, "Contractor Support to Operations (CSO): Proactive or Reactive Support?" *RUSI Defence Systems* (2010), page 16.

37. United Kingdom Ministry of Defence, *Director Defence Support Review: Employment Mechanisms for the Total Support Force D DSR/002* (London: 14 February 2011), page 3.

38. Higginson, "Contractor Support to Operations (CSO)," page 16.

39. Kinsey, *Private Contractors and the Reconstruction of Iraq*.

40. United Kingdom Ministry of Defence, *Contractor Support to Operations*, page 5.

41. United Kingdom Ministry of Defence, *Contractor Support to Operations*, page 10.

42. Kinsey, *Private Contractors and the Reconstruction of Iraq*, page 86.

43. Higginson, "Contractor Support to Operations (CSO)," page 16.

44. See "UK Military Deaths in Afghanistan and Iraq," *BBC News*, available at http://www.bbc.co.uk/news/uk-10637526.

45. *United Kingdom Foreign Enlistment Act* (33 and 34 Vict., chapter 90, 1870).

46. Sarah Percy, *Regulating the Private Security Industry*, Adelphi Paper 384 (London: Routledge, 2006), page 34.

47. Kenneth Diplock, Derek Walker Smith, and Geoffrey de Freitas, *Report of the Committee of Privy Counsellors Appointed to Inquire into the Recruitment of Mercenaries* (London: The Stationery Office, 1976).

48. Percy, *Regulating the Private Security Industry*.

49. Deborah D. Avant, *The Market for Force: The Consequences of Privatizing Security* (Cambridge: Cambridge University Press, 2005), page 170; Kinsey, *Corporate Soldiers and*

International Security; David Shearer, *Private Armies and Military Interventions*, Adelphi Paper 316 (London: Institute of Strategic Studies, 1998).

50. United Kingdom House of Commons Foreign Affairs Committee, *Second Report: Sierra Leone* (London: The Stationery Office, 1999).

51. Tim Spicer, *An Unorthodox Soldier* (London: Mainstream Publishing, 1998).

52. United Kingdom House of Commons Foreign Affairs Committee, *Second Report: Sierra Leone*.

53. United Kingdom Foreign and Commonwealth Office, *Private Military Companies: Options for Regulation*, HC 577 (London: The Stationery Office, 12 February 2002). See also Christopher Kinsey, "Regulation and Control of Private Military Companies: The Legislative Dimension," *Contemporary Security Policy* 26, 1 (April 2005).

54. United Kingdom House of Commons Foreign Affairs Committee. *Private Military Companies: Ninth Report of Session 2001–02. Report, Together with Proceedings of the Committee, Minutes of Evidence and Appendices*, HC 922 (London: The Stationery Office, 1 August 2002), pages 20–27.

55. United Kingdom House of Commons Foreign Affairs Committee, *Response of the Secretary of State for Foreign and Commonwealth Affairs* (London: The Stationery Office, 2001–2002), page 39.

56. United Kingdom Parliament, *Early Day Motion 690: Private Military and Security Companies* (London: House of Commons, 22 January 2007), available at http://www.parliament.uk/edm/2006-07/690.

57. Leigh Day & Co. Judicial Review Letter, 18 February 2008.

58. United Kingdom Foreign and Commonwealth Office, *Public Consultation on Promoting High Standards on Conduct by Private Military and Security Companies (PSCs) Internationally*.

59. United Kingdom Foreign and Commonwealth Office, *Public Consultation on Promoting High Standards on Conduct by Private Military and Security Companies (PSCs) Internationally*, page 19.

60. United Kingdom Foreign and Commonwealth Office, *Public Consultation on Promoting High Standards on Conduct by Private Military and Security Companies (PSCs) Internationally*, page 11.

61. Kinsey, *Private Contractors and the Reconstruction of Iraq*.

62. British Association of Private Security Companies, "Home," available at http://www.bapsc.org.uk/?keydocuments=charter, accessed 5 June 2014.

63. See International Stability Operations Association, "About Us," available at http://www.stability-operations.org/?page=About, accessed 18 December 2015, as well as chapters 8 and 9 in this volume for a review of the development and functioning of ISOA.

64. See, for instance, the code of conduct of Control Risks, "Code of Ethics" (no date), available at http://www.controlrisks.com/SiteAssets/Code_Ethics.pdf, accessed 18 December 2015.

65. United Kingdom Foreign and Commonwealth Office, *Promoting High Standards in the Private Military and Security Company Industry*, written ministerial statement (21 June 2011).

66. International Code of Conduct Association, "Membership," available at http://icoca.ch/en/membership?private_security_companies=companies&op=Search&view_type=list&form_id=_search_for_members_filter_form, accessed 18 December 2015.

67. Christopher Sanderson, "International Regulatory Frameworks: The Perspective of Industry," presented to the Private Military and Security Conference, Royal United Services Institute, London, 27–28 September 2012.

68. United Kingdom Foreign and Commonwealth Office, *Private Military Companies*, page 23.

69. United Kingdom Foreign and Commonwealth Office, *Impact Assessment on Promoting High Standards of Conduct by Private Military and Security Companies (PMSCs) Internationally* (London: Foreign and Commonwealth Office, April 2009), page 3.

70. United Kingdom Foreign and Commonwealth Office, *Impact Assessment on Promoting High Standards of Conduct by Private Military and Security Companies (PMSCs) Internationally*, page 3.

71. United Kingdom Foreign and Commonwealth Office, *Impact Assessment on Promoting High Standards of Conduct by Private Military and Security Companies (PMSCs) Internationally*, page 4.

72. United Kingdom Foreign and Commonwealth Office, *Public Consultation on Promoting High Standards on Conduct by Private Military and Security Companies (PSCs) Internationally*, page 6.

73. Cusumano, "Policy Prospects on the Regulation of PMSCs," page 21.

74. Deborah D. Avant, "Selling Security: Trade-Offs in State Regulation of the Private Security Industry," in Thomas Jäger and Gerhard Kümmel, editors, *Private Military and Security Companies: Chances, Problems, Pitfalls and Prospects* (Wiesbaden: Verlag, 2007), page 421.

75. United Kingdom Foreign and Commonwealth Office, *Public Consultation on Promoting High Standards on Conduct by Private Military and Security Companies (PSCs) Internationally*, page 28. See chapter 10 in this volume for an assessment of the Montreux Document.

76. "What Are the Voluntary Principles?" Voluntary Principles on Security and Human Rights website, available at http://www.voluntaryprinciples.org/, accessed 15 April 2010.

77. United Kingdom Foreign and Commonwealth Office, *Public Consultation on Promoting High Standards on Conduct by Private Military and Security Companies (PSCs) Internationally*.

78. United Kingdom Department for Transport, *Change in UK Policy on Employing Armed Guards to Protect against Somali Piracy*, available at http://www.dft.gov.uk/news/press-releases/dft-press-20111206a/, accessed 6 December 2011.

79. United Kingdom Department for Transport, *The Use of Private Armed Guards On Board UK Registered Ships under Exceptional Circumstances to Defend against Piracy*, written ministerial statement (6 December 2011); United Kingdom Department for Transport, *Interim Guidance to UK Flagged Shipping on the Use of Armed Guards to Defend against the Threat of Piracy in Exceptional Circumstances* (November 2011; updated June 2012).

80. Brown, "Pirates and Privateers," page 13.

Chapter Eight

Industry Associations and the Regulation of Private Military and Security Companies

Surabhi Ranganathan

In the past two decades, private military and security companies (PMSCs) have grown in numbers and visibility. It is now an old joke that US operations in Iraq were best described as the "Coalition of the Billing." The name *Blackwater* is part of the popular lexicon. Far away from conflict zones, PMSC vans (of G4S) even drive through the cobbled carriageways of Cambridge. PMSCs project sophisticated corporate images: titling themselves "consultants," "risk managers," and expert purveyors of "security solutions." Their websites offer elevated service-descriptions and glossy photographs varnish the grime and danger of their daily tasks. We may claim, with some accuracy, that the days of drawing tight linkages between PMSCs and white colonial "dogs of war" are past.[1]

However, though PMSCs have successfully disowned the mercenary tag, their public acceptability falls far short of other corporate entities that we take entirely for granted. It may be that many PMSCs pose less threat to the communities in which they operate than, say, Coca-Cola.[2] Of the services that PMSCs provide, only some are proximate to the use of force—their functions include training militaries, intelligence gathering, guarding persons and property, escorting convoys, interrogation, weapons management, logistics support, catering at military bases, scanning and frisking at airports, and so forth. But the impression of their capacity for violence remains indelible: Blackwater contractors shooting civilians in Nisour Square, on 16 September 2007, is the emblematic image of their activities.[3]

PMSCs have become significant agents of states and they will likely continue to be used by them in unstable regions in the foreseeable future.

Therefore we remain focused on their continued capacity to do harm. The preferred solution to this conundrum has been to advocate for stringent regulation of PMSCs by any of the states that could serve as their principal: their home state, host state, or hiring state. As indicated in chapter 10 of this volume, there is a vast body of scholarship setting out states' regulatory obligations and proposals for their effective fulfillment.[4] Occasionally, these proposals have included suggestions for creating a supranational regulatory institution.[5] There is, of course, recognition of the gaps between hopes from and practice of state regulation, but the thrust has been on persuading states to narrow these gaps.

In contrast, industry-level efforts at self-regulation remained neglected for a long time.[6] Industry associations such as the International Stability Operations Association (ISOA), the British Association of Private Security Companies (BAPSC), and the disbanded Private Security Company Association of Iraq (PSCAI) cannot substitute for regulation by states but can complement the same. The neglect of their role not only preserved adverse perception of the PMSC industry but also impeded the development of integrated regulatory mechanisms. For example, the multi-stakeholder Swiss-ICRC Initiative for many years focused on codifying *states'* obligations and good practices vis-à-vis PMSCs.[7] Only much later did it work on a counterpart document that sets out *PMSCs'* obligations and good practices—the International Code of Conduct (ICoC) was adopted in November 2010[8] and the oversight and enforcement body, the ICoC Association, only established in September 2013. The association's certification, monitoring, and complaints procedures are still in development.

Now that multi-stakeholder efforts to scaffold industry self-regulation are finally under way, this is a good time to discuss its pitfalls and possibilities. To do so I explore the following questions: Why have we neglected to engage with the industry's initiatives toward self-regulation? What form has self-regulation taken? How may industry associations establish the credibility of their regulatory claims? And how effective have they been in their nascent regulatory role?

THE PUBLIC/PRIVATE DIVIDE

In this section, I examine some challenges of perception and practice that have led to the neglect of the possibilities inherent in industry self-regulation. Broadly, these relate to comparisons between the "private" and the "public" that conclude, invariably, that the latter must be better. On the one hand PMSC services are unfavorably compared to government-provided services, while on the other hand industry regulation suffers by comparison to state regulation.

Let us begin, first, with the specific concerns that PMSCs give rise to. The list of possible harms is indeed sobering: incidents of reckless shooting of civilians, detainee abuse, sex trafficking, and economic exploitation provide evidence of the threats that PMSCs pose to the communities in which they operate.[9] They may undermine the discipline and morale of military forces. Reports from Iraq include accounts of contractor-led rowdyism. More seriously, many contractors are experienced ex-soldiers and can upset legitimate chains of command when they serve alongside fresh military recruits, as at Abu Ghraib.[10] There is also the threat of personnel drain as higher salaries attract military members toward private sector contract work.[11] PMSCs may have a deleterious impact on states' public infrastructure—a concern reported by scholars studying PMSC operations in African states.[12] We must also keep in mind threats to PMSC personnel resulting from inadequate training, lack of briefing on rules of conduct, and improper deployment.

However, these concerns are not peculiar to PMSCs. Violations of human rights and inadequate preparation also taint the records of national militaries and peacekeeping forces: a UN internal report in 2005 listed misconduct of peacekeeping forces in Haiti, Sierra Leone, Liberia, Bosnia, Cambodia, East Timor, and the Democratic Republic of the Congo.[13] Much of the detainee abuse at Abu Ghraib took place at the hands of US Army personnel. There are similar reports of actions of UK soldiers at other detention facilities in Iraq.[14] Several corporations have no better—and often far worse—records of doing harm: Coca-Cola's example is one of many. The concerns relating to public infrastructure are surely not different in the privatization of other state functions, such as the building and maintenance of bridges, roads, and dams; the supply of water, electricity, food, and education; or the exploitation of natural resources. Yet self-regulation is an important element of the governance of these services. Ultimately, with respect to many of their functions, PMSCs are not so different from other types of corporations, so why not explore the possibilities of self-regulation?

It is sometimes argued that certain types of military and security services are not suitable for outsourcing to private contractors. The Draft Convention of the UN Working Group on Mercenaries provides that each state party must prohibit outsourcing of "inherently state functions," such as "direct participation in hostilities, waging war and/or combat operations, taking prisoners, law-making, espionage, intelligence, knowledge transfer with military, security and policing application, use of and other activities related to weapons of mass destruction, police powers, especially the powers of arrest or detention including the interrogation of detainees."[15] Several scholars too have argued that detention, interrogation, intelligence gathering, and peacekeeping should not be outsourced to contractors.[16] This has some merit, even if a walk through history soon reveals that there has never been consistent understanding on "inherent state functions." It has merit primarily because today's understanding of inherent state functions is built upon generations of struggles for states' democratic accountability in the preservation of security. Thus, there is a resonance to Chia Lehnardt's argument on peacekeeping, for she asks, "What would be left of the international community which outsources the first promise of the UN Charter to private companies?"[17]

In short, there is certainly scope for discussion on the types of activities that states could outsource to PMSCs. But this should have little bearing on the question of how to regulate PMSCs carrying out activities that they can appropriately be contracted to perform. The conflation of the two issues, to suggest that it is acceptable to outsource essential state functions if their regulation remains the preserve of the state, is a poor compromise that does not properly cater either to democratic aspirations or to the efficiency considerations that drive privatization.

Let us turn, then, to the argument that formal regulation is important because states and states alone possess the obligation, will, and capacity to regulate PMSCs. As to legal obligation, there is no denying that states, generally, have responsibility toward a wider range of interests, including other states, individuals among whom they permit or procure the operation of PMSCs, and PMSCs themselves. In addition, we could expect various mechanisms of domestic political accountability to ensure their responsiveness, somewhat, toward an even broader range of interests including human rights bodies, humanitarian agencies, and the international civil society. Arguments of states' will and capacity are also persuasive. States, after all, can bring to bear the full range of mechanisms: from contracts to criminal sanctions. Moreover, there are good reasons to expect states will wish to regulate PMSCs, because PMSCs implicate their strategic interests. For hiring and host states, this includes the impact on their public infrastructure. For host and home states it also includes direct challenge to either their authority, as in the case of Liberia, or their interests, perhaps from PMSCs undertaking undesirable contracts with hostile entities.

In contrast, there is no clear external framework that determines the scope of the industry associations' regulatory commitment. The associations owe few, if any, legal obligations to third parties, including home, host, and hiring states of PMSCs, their populations, members of their militaries, and so on. As to political obligations, it is hard to imagine what these may be for private bodies. Their private nature also raises questions about whether associations have the authority to determine and enforce standards of operation for members. On what basis may they formulate the applicable norms? Which mechanisms may they use to ensure members' compliance? And how can members ensure proper functioning of the associations? These questions are perhaps less troublesome purely within (some) domestic contexts, in which associations either operate within the legal-administrative scaffold provided by the state, or remain private clubs of limited influence. But, in the transnational context in which PMSCs operate, private institutions may come to exercise significant power without equivalent constraints. In such contexts, the above questions become critically relevant.

Even if it is natural, for the above reasons, to focus on states as the primary loci of regulation of PMSCs, there is no reason to exclude the complementary role that industry associations can play. Moreover, before we judge their limited capacities too harshly, we should be mindful of the gaps between assumption and reality that characterize state regulation, and the implications of the international context for public as well as private regulatory bodies.

To date, few states have taken even the first step of adopting legislation to regulate PMSCs. While this might soon change, due—thanks to the Montreux Document—to greater consensus on the obligations of home, host, and hiring states and mechanisms through which they can implement the same, there remain huge disparities between the enforcement capacities of different states. Monographs published by South Africa's Institute for Security Studies make the point that many African states remain without the capacity to maintain stable principal-agent relationships with the companies they hire, for they do not exercise a "choice" to outsource in any real sense, and are heavily dependent on PMSCs.[18] Moreover, PMSCs' home, host, and hiring states often all differ and this adds to the existing obstacles of lack of information, limited monitoring, and weak democratic oversight that dog their operations in conflict zones.

The aftermath of Blackwater's Nisour Square shootings illustrates this.[19] There were jurisdictional struggles between Iraq, which sought to expel Blackwater from its territory, and the United States, whose State Department renewed Blackwater's contract. Within the United States, conflicting measures were undertaken by the State Department and Department of Justice. The State Department together with the Department of Defense finalized a memorandum of understanding on appropriate rules of engagement but included neither any mention of the consequence of violating these rules, nor a reference to the Justice Department. Even as the Justice Department sought to frame charges against the contractors involved in the shootings, the State Department granted them immunity in return for information about the incident. The Justice Department tried to use this information as the basis for indictments of manslaughter, but a federal court dismissed the case, ruling that the Justice Department's use of statements given by the contractors in exchange for immunity compromised their right to a fair trial. While Blackwater did not ultimately enjoy complete impunity—the United States initiated an FBI investigation and later a joint commission with Iraq, some government departments terminated Blackwater's contracts (albeit temporarily), and the Justice Department initiated fresh prosecutions against the individuals concerned (leading to convictions seven years after the incident)—the episode reveals the collective action problems that faced both the United States and Iraq. Moreover, it is a reminder that if big scandals galvanize states into some activity, leading to reform in their legal and administrative structures, this peters out once the spotlight shifts. Before Nisour Square was Abu Ghraib, and there too, Laura Dickinson notes, the aftermath unfolded in a similar way.[20] Finally, the episode reveals that practical considerations, such as long-standing reliance on a company, can override other state imperatives.

Moreover, the international context, despite the complications it introduces as to the standards and procedures to be followed by private bodies, is one in which the concept of private regulation has great acceptance. Various forms of private regulation may be found in fields as diverse as environment protection, organ transplantation, food safety, and labor standards.[21] The example most relevant to PMSCs in conflict zones is the role of the ICRC and the Sphere Charter in regulating humanitarian agencies.[22] The acceptance of private regulation owes to the lack of international public institutions[23] and the recognition that in the international sphere even public institutions are less tightly governed by legal and political mechanisms. Instead, as I will discuss, accountability depends upon a more complex matrix of factors, including market controls, peer influences, and public reputational concerns.[24] There is no reason why these should not be similarly relevant to public and private regulatory bodies.

In sum, public/private distinctions, whether between government services and PMSCs or state and industry regulators, do not provide good reasons to exclude serious engagement with the regulatory potential of industry associations. It may, however, be argued that some reservations are justified given the potential conflict of interest between regulation and trade promotion embraced by the principal associations in the PMSC industry. This next section will discuss the implications of the joining of these two aims.

LEGITIMACY, ACCOUNTABILITY, AND EFFECTIVENESS

Should industry associations' regulatory potential be qualified by their claim to also promote contracting opportunities for their members? All the principal associations in the PMSC industry—the International Stability Operations Association (ISOA), the British Association of Private Security Companies (BAPSC), and the now-defunct Private Security Company Association of Iraq (PSCAI)—have embraced both regulation and trade promotion as their goals. Indeed, arguably, it is the latter function that motivates PMSCs to participate in their work and support them financially. The associations insist that their two functions are compatible, because better operational standards are the key to a greater market share—improved service standards will lead to greater outsourcing and their enforcement will squeeze out lower-end outfits. However, it is conceivable that the two goals may pull industry associations in different directions. For example, associations may be captured by their most powerful member firms and therefore engage in biased oversight and promotional activities. Or, given that associations have to struggle to overcome the overall negative view of the industry, this might constrain their response to particular incidents of companies' wrongdoing to avoid any damage to the image of the industry as a whole. Their choice might be between openly reviewing a company at the risk of tarnishing the industry's image and preventing a media maelstrom by suppressing information.

That industry associations may have mixed motives cannot be in itself fatal to their regulatory credibility. After all we do not dismiss *states'* regulatory potential even though the very factors that drive states to outsource military and security services may be sometimes incompatible with those that govern regulatory efforts. We do not dismiss states because we recognize them to be complex organizations, responsive to a vast range of interests and capable of exerting regulatory authority even when there may be a contradiction between their various priorities. The question is whether we can similarly view industry associations as capable of fulfilling their regulatory commitments even when these clash with their trade-promotion functions. This question is, in short, an invitation to explore whether industry associations have sufficiently demonstrated their legitimacy, accountability, and effectiveness as regulatory bodies.

Let me now introduce these concepts and their application to industry associations. In the next two sections, I will then use these concepts as lenses to examine whether and how industry associations demonstrate adequate regulatory commitment.

Legitimacy, accountability, and effectiveness are, of course, related concepts, for both accountability and effectiveness may be taken as indicators of legitimacy. We saw this above, in connection with the reasons why prominence is given to the regulatory role of states: states are seen as the legitimate regulators of PMSCs in part because they are responsible to a wide range of interests and capable of exerting control over PMSCs. Yet accountability and effectiveness do not equal legitimacy. It is possible for an entity to be an effective regulator without being considered a legitimate one, or to be perceived as legitimate even if not fully effective. Unlike effectiveness, legitimacy has a normative element. And legitimacy has a complex relationship with accountability. While we would normally expect greater accountability to imply greater legitimacy, it may be that accountability to one constituency—that is, one set of interests—makes an association less legitimate in the perception of another. Indeed, a major challenge for associations in the

PMSC industry is to balance their responsiveness to the interests of their members and third parties, when these come into conflict. It seems appropriate, therefore, to disaggregate the three factors.

Taking legitimacy first, it is reasonable to begin with Julia Black's observation that the legitimacy of any organization is socially and discursively constructed, principally by the efforts of the organization itself.[25] An organization must be able to demonstrate to its audience that its existence, its goals, actions, and decisions are justified, in order to be considered legitimate by that audience. Unfortunately, there is no simple way for it to do this. The audience of any organization will be composed of many different interests, all of whom may have different—and contradictory—perspectives on what actions, decisions, and goals are justifiable. Thus, satisfying all interests is an immensely difficult task. Indeed, building and maintaining legitimacy is a delicate art that we obviously cannot reduce to an organization's conformity to specific criteria. Even so, several scholars provide us with helpful lists of the types of legitimacy that international bodies taking on regulatory functions can claim for themselves.[26] These types emerge from detailed, in-depth studies of a range of such international bodies and suggest some indicia by which to evaluate the legitimacy of associations in the PMSC industry.

The first is their comprehensibility: the more their audience knows of their aims, structures, practices, and processes the more likely it is to find them reliable. The legitimacy of industry associations thus depends upon how well they are able to explain these aspects of their operations. Indeed, transparency has especial significance for associations in the PMSC industry, given that the dominant perception of the industry is the murkiness of PMSC operations. The second is their organizational structures: Are these sufficient to bear out the regulatory claims of the industry associations? It is important to look at the internal arrangements of the associations—to examine in particular whether they indicate sufficient internal checks and balances to ensure that associations will regularly discharge their aims and remain autonomous from the interests of specific members—as well as their external relations, namely how the associations relate to other regulatory structures and initiatives that operate within and upon the PMSC industry. The third is their process: the procedures they follow for admitting members, for persuading them to observe high standards of service, and for responding to incidents of wrongdoing.

Let us turn now to accountability and consider to whom PMSC industry associations should be accountable and how accountability is to be accomplished. It is useful to begin with Ruth Grant and Robert Keohane's two "models" of public power. Under the delegation model, recipients of power should be accountable to grantors of power; while under the participation model, an entity should be accountable to those affected by its activities.[27] Clearly, the latter model, which embraces a wider range of interests, is more appropriate to private bodies taking on regulatory functions. As to how these bodies may be made accountable, Richard Stewart describes formal mechanisms by which the relations envisaged in the delegation model may be imbued with accountability: *electoral*, *hierarchical*, *supervisory*, *fiscal*, and *legal*. In each, the body held accountable may be subject to sanctions for wrongdoing.[28] The broader category of relations embraced in the participation model calls for additional mechanisms of constraint, such as influence exercised through *participation* in an entity's operations, *market controls* maintained by its consumers, *peer norms and review* applied by others in the same industry or profession, the sway of those capable of influencing the entity's *public reputation*, or *general political influences* through activities such as lobbying. Because the remit of these influences does not extend to the capacity to impose sanctions, Stewart considers it more appropriate to term them responsiveness-promoting, rather than accountability mechanisms. However, as Keohane and Grant point out, in world politics these influences may operate more strongly upon an entity than formal mechanisms. Thus we should take note of the full range of formal and informal mechanisms to explore industry associations' accountability to their members, those affected by actions of PMSCs, and those holding a stake in their regulation.

Finally, to discuss whether industry associations can effectively regulate PMSCs, let us consider, first, the critical advantages that result from the very factors that set them apart from other regulators, namely their private character and their dual aims of regulation and trade promotion. One advantage is that as trade representatives and regulators of the PMSC industry, associations have closer links to PMSCs that enable a greater and up-to-date expertise on PMSCs' capacities and their organizational and on-ground challenges. For public bodies, in contrast, the geographical remoteness and confidentiality of PMSC operations may prove significant barriers to information. Another advantage that we can imagine industry associations to enjoy is that of greater flexibility in determining institutional arrangements and in tweaking those arrangements from time to time. Public bodies by contrast would be constrained by various bureaucratic procedures. And finally, we may expect industry associations to remain relatively insulated from the complex considerations that determine states' response to acts of wrongdoing by PMSCs. These advantages may, quite fairly, lead us to expect that industry associations could contribute to effectively regulating PMSCs not only by formulating (and leading the formulation of) well-informed standards of service and best practices for companies to follow but by persuading and guiding the companies to comply with such standards.

A study of the role(s) played by industry regulators in other industries can assist us in identifying various mechanisms through which industry associations may influence PMSCs. Andrew King and Michael Lenox usefully summarize a vast literature on this topic, to suggest three *forces* that industry associations can deploy.[29] First is coercion, through threat of sanctions such as fines, the naming and shaming of wrongdoing companies, whether among peers or publicly, and suspension or revocation of membership. The impact of such mechanism depends, of course, on the significance PMSCs attach to the associations and this in turn may depend on a number of factors: whether association membership provides access to greater contracting opportunities, whether associations receive the backing of states, and whether the mechanism itself functions in a non-arbitrary and efficient way. We will explore these factors in the next two sections. Second, associations can exert normative influence on their members. That is, they can promote the diffusion of norms and values among PMSCs and educate them on improving their standards of service. Finally, associations can channel peer pressure to encourage PMSCs to mimic industry best practices even if they do not internalize the same. Mimesis may not lead to full acceptance of the service standards reflected in the best practices, but it can ensure compliance with these standards.[30]

These, then, are the criteria upon which we can determine the legitimacy, accountability, and effectiveness of agents regulating themselves through cooperation in industry associations. It is appropriate now to make a close examination of the principal associations of the PMSC industry, as a prelude to drawing conclusions about the quality of their regulatory claims. In the next section, I will describe the background, organizational structures, and membership rules adopted by ISOA, BAPSC, and PSCAI. I will also explore the steps that they claim to have taken for better regulation of PMSCs.

THREE KEY INDUSTRY ASSOCIATIONS

I must begin this section with a caveat: information about PMSCs and industry associations changes rapidly. In the past few years, one association changed its name (ISOA was formerly the International Peace Operations Association—IPOA) and another was disbanded (PSCAI). Several companies too have changed names (Blackwater has done so twice, first calling itself Xe, now Academi); others have changed their corporate structures. Wherever relevant, I draw attention to such changes, in order to convey a sense of the dynamic nature of this industry.

ORGANIZATIONAL STRUCTURES

International Stability Operations Association

ISOA is the older of the three industry associations, and the only one established prior to 9/11 and the launch of US military operations in Afghanistan and Iraq. Its founder, Doug Brooks, an American citizen, was formerly a research fellow in political science in South Africa, where he studied the African conflicts of the 1990s. He states that in the course of his research he became convinced of the private sector's potential to contribute to the management of conflict and post-conflict situations, but equally, that states were hesitant to outsource security and military support operations. As Brooks, Koch, and Schaub discuss in chapter 9 of this volume, Brooks was driven to set up the IPOA in 2001 by an instinct that an industry association could promote professionalism, higher quality of service, and consumer confidence.[31]

Brooks has often described ISOA as nonpartisan, committed to improving industry standards, and operating independently of its members' vested interests.[32] ISOA communications emphasize that it was not set up by PMSCs, but by "individuals with backgrounds in the non-governmental, academic, and business sectors who recognized the benefits brought by the private sector to the victims of conflict."[33] They also stress that the ISOA Code of Conduct,[34] currently in its 13th iteration, is a product of consultations between international and nongovernmental organizations, human rights lawyers, and scholars.[35]

ISOA's organizational structure remains fluid. Its staff hovers between seven and nine individuals. Its work is usually divided between a board of directors and four to six task-based committees. At present, the ISOA website describes the association's work as resting on three "pillars"—government affairs, partnerships and outreach, and business development.[36] Advocacy and communication are, and have been, a major element of all three functions. Until recently, its website referred to two committees, Communications and Outreach, and Government and Advocacy, that were specifically tasked with planning and delivering strategic communications to governments, international bodies, and policymakers. Currently it offers an "Advocacy Agenda," which focuses on permanent funding from the United States and its allies for stability operations in conflict-ridden and transitioning countries, a "predictable security posture" for PMSCs in Afghanistan post–US withdrawal, and a posture for Iraq; its advocacy initiatives also include better contracting and oversight practices by governments and highlighting the creation of the ICoC and other industry standards.[37] Also in current operation are a Government and Legal Affairs Committee and a Private Security Company Committee, which develop industry positions on legislative and policy issues and best practices; a Standards, Oversight, and Compliance Committee that oversees the revision and implementation of the Code of Conduct; and a Membership Committee that recruits and approves new members.[38] Representatives of member companies serve on all committees; their composition changes annually, and most positions are filled by volunteer representatives.

A mark of the fluidity of ISOA's structure is the constant disappearance and reappearance, and modified procedures of, various committees and working groups. For example, in the 2006–2007 Annual Report of the IPOA (as ISOA was then called), an Executive Committee was mentioned as being responsible for oversight of the organization as a whole.[39] Now, this task appears to have been taken over by the board of directors. The board is now described as constituted annually and comprising seven or eight "volunteers" from among ISOA members; earlier descriptions had suggested that all members had seats on the board—making it more akin to a general assembly—and that board members were elected. Meanwhile, another former committee, the General Counsels Committee, providing a venue for private counsels of member companies to discuss "legal issues of significant import,"[40] is now set to be reestablished as a General Counsels Forum.[41]

ISOA offers membership to companies offering security services, logistics support, and equipment in conflict and post-conflict settings, irrespective of their nationality or territory of operation. Membership numbers fluctuate—ISOA had 49 members in June 2014, 51 in February 2012, and 61 in 2011. Its members are headquartered in several states, including the USA, UK, UAE, Sweden, South Africa, and Spain, and have field presence in 30 countries. Recognizing a particularly heavy presence in that region, the ISOA has started a particular "Middle East Chapter." The broad scope of ISOA's membership contrasts with that of PSCAI and BAPSC, who limit membership based on territory and nationality, respectively. But compared to the 708 companies who have signed the ICoC, the numbers remain small.

Private Security Company Association of Iraq

PSCAI was established in July 2004, as an industry initiative following the dissolution of the Iraq Coalition Provisional Authority (CPA).[42] Its—now unavailable—website described its purpose as being to "discuss and address matters of mutual interest and concern to the industry conducting operations in Iraq" and "work closely with the Iraqi Government and foster a relationship of trust and understanding." Lawrence Peter, a former US naval officer and advisor to the CPA, became the director general of PSCAI. PSCAI continued in operation for seven years, until it was "disestablished" on 31 December 2011. Its website explains:

> The PSCAI was an industry-driven response to a highly ambiguous environment in the war-torn Iraq. Now, with the complete departure of United States Forces, and the direct oversight of PSCs by the Government of Iraq, the need for the PSCAI has withered.[43]

Even while it functioned, the public portions of PSCAI's website offered little information about its structure. Its charter and code of conduct became unavailable in the later years. We do know, however, that its membership was open to all PMSCs operating in Iraq, and included about 25 companies registered in the USA, UK, Canada, South Africa, Australia, and various countries in the Middle East. Several Iraqi companies were also members.

British Association of Private Security Companies

BAPSC was launched in February 2006, "to promote the interests and regulate the activities of UK linked firms that provide armed defensive security services in countries outside the UK."[44] Like ISOA, BAPSC was established in response to a perceived need to raise standards of operation of PMSCs, but here the impetus came from companies themselves. They were motivated by the search for future contracts, in anticipation that the opportunities generated by the Iraq war would diminish.[45] Moreover, as the UK does not hire PMSCs on the same scale as the United States, there is greater competition for private sector contracts.[46] The companies possibly saw an industry association as a means to provide credible assurance of professional service and to distinguish themselves from lower-end operations.

BAPSC's website does not offer detailed information about its organization. It does, however, provide the BAPSC Charter, a composite document that lists the associations' aims and the principles governing member PMSCs. The charter affirms that BAPSC will respect human rights, the values and interests of the United Kingdom, and peace and stability of the international system. Andrew Bearpark, a former British government servant and UN official, and most recently an officeholder in the Iraq CPA, heads BAPSC. Besides Bearpark, the website mentions one other person as staff.

BAPSC membership is restricted to "UK-linked" companies providing armed security services overseas. These include services relating to the recruitment, training, equipping, coordination, or employment, directly or indirectly, of persons who bear lethal arms. BAPSC has approximately 23 members. It previously described these variously as full members, provisional members, and associate members but these categories are no longer indicated.

MEMBERSHIP

The associations' rules for admitting members, and benefits offered to members, provide important evidence of their regulatory role. Each claims to grant membership selectively, following background checks of candidates. Publicly available information indicates that ISOA requires companies to complete an application providing details of the company organization, services provided, and a sample "Past Performance Package." The ISOA website indicates that the Membership Committee vets this information, on the basis of a due diligence appraisal, putting into use the field experience of its own members, and, optionally, interviews company representatives. In a telephonic conversation some years ago, Brooks stated that the company may be asked to explain past incidents not mentioned in the application. However, he also clarified that ISOA did not have a systematic process for discovering such information.[47]

The PSCAI website had listed sections on "how to join" and "types of membership" that remained inaccessible throughout its operation.

BAPSC provides that companies interested in membership should contact the director. A section on its website, titled "Membership Criteria," remained "under construction" for many months[48] and was briefly updated[49] to specify that to be eligible, a PMSC must demonstrate legal presence in the UK, a history of providing premium private security services, and adherence to BAPSC standards, as well as provide assurance of directors' non-criminal history and compliance with corporate best practices. This section is no longer available, but when it was it indicated that BAPSC would conduct a background check using the above criteria, following which the company could apply for provisional membership. Its application would be decided by a Membership Committee. For promotion to full membership, the company was required to submit due diligence documentation according to a provided form, and complete a self-assessment workbook (no longer available). BAPSC would review these documents and visit the company before recommending a grant of full membership by the Membership Committee.

EFFORTS FOR PROMOTING BETTER STANDARDS OF SERVICE OF PMSCS

Naturally, the most important basis on which to evaluate industry associations' regulatory claims is how they are able to ensure that their members perform to high standards. I explore here the information provided by industry associations about their regulatory efforts in three respects: setting and enforcing specific codes of conduct; disseminating information about the relevant norms, values, and industry best practices; and assisting regulatory initiatives of states and other bodies.

Establishing and Enforcing Codes of Conduct

Membership provides the starting point for the application of codes of conduct to PMSCs. In order to obtain and maintain membership in good standing PMSCs must abide by, respectively, the ISOA Code of Conduct; the PSCAI Charter, Code of Conduct, and regulations; and the BAPSC Charter. These codes set out applicable standards, which include a variety of obligations. Since the PSCAI has been disbanded and its documents remained long unavailable, I will focus on the ISOA and BAPSC codes.

ISOA's code is worth describing in some detail, for it provides a good illustration of how industry associations have sought to contractually bind PMSCs to specific standards of behavior. Drafted in consultation with NGOs, human rights lawyers, and scholars, the code is periodically revised and made available in eight languages.[50] ISOA invites public comments and unsolicited suggestions for amendment for up to six months before the adoption of each new version. The current iteration, version 13.1, was adopted in October 2011. Its preamble provides that signatories will be guided by all pertinent rules of international humanitarian and human rights laws, including the Universal Declaration of Human Rights, Geneva Conventions and Additional Protocols, Convention against Torture, US Foreign Corrupt Practices Act (1977) and UK Bribery Act (2010), Chemical Weapons Convention, Voluntary Principles on Security and Human Rights (2000), Montreux Document (2008), and International Code of Conduct (2010). This is an interesting amalgamation—and application to all member PMSCs—of international legal agreements between states, domestic laws whose binding effect is otherwise dependent upon some sort of territorial or nationality linkage, and nonbinding "soft law" principles. The ISOA code then lists the following commitments, classified here by type:

- *Human rights*: PMSCs must respect human dignity; adhere to international human rights laws; minimize destruction of life and property; and operate in a responsible and prudent manner.
- *Client legitimacy*: PMSCs must work for legitimate recognized governments, international organizations, non-governmental organizations, and lawful private companies only; and refuse to engage unlawful clients, or clients actively thwarting international efforts towards peace.
- *Partner companies and sub-contractors*: PMSCs must select partners and sub-contractors with utmost diligence to ensure compliance with appropriate ethical standards and the IPOA Code.

- *Employee guarantees*: PMSCs must train personnel in accordance with clearly defined company standards, provide instruction about the applicable law, the IPOA Code, and regional sensitivities; exercise diligence to avoid hiring and subcontracting personnel who have acted in violation of humanitarian and human rights laws; and respond appropriately in situations of employee misconduct. PMSCs must also: inform employees of risks associated with employment, and of terms and significance of contracts; treat employees with dignity; ensure employees are medically fit and screened for the physical and mental requirements of their duties; render medical assistance when needed and practical; where appropriate, seek employees that are broadly representative of the local population; pay different wages based on merit and national economic differential, not racial, gender or ethnic grounds; provide health and life insurance to appropriate levels; not hire personnel below 15 years of age for continuous formal employment (and not below 18 years for employment as armed security personnel); and not deny to any employee the right to terminate employment.
- *Transparency*: PMSCs must operate with integrity and fairness; be forthcoming, with the relevant authorities, about the nature of their operations and conflicts of interest that might influence current or potential ventures; and maintain confidentiality of information.
- *Accountability*: PMSCs must support effective legal accountability for their actions and actions of employees; cooperate with official investigations into contractual and legal violations; take firm action in case employees engage in unlawful activities; support the conclusion of detailed contracts of operation specifying the mandate, restrictions, goals, benchmarks, criteria for withdrawal and accountability; not undertake offensive missions unless mandated by a legitimate authority in accordance with international law; allow safe extraction of personnel and others under their protection; and speedily and professionally comply with lawful requests from the client (or appropriate governing authorities), including withdrawal from an operation.
- *Other ethical commitments*: PMSCs in armed hostilities must: follow duly established rules of engagement; support efforts of humanitarian organizations and other entities to minimize suffering and promote reconstruction and reconciliation; and control use of arms, using only appropriate weapons common to military, security, or law-enforcement operations, and refuse illegal weapons or toxic chemicals that create long-term health problems or complicate post-conflict cleanup.

The commitments in the ISOA code are wide-ranging, yet vaguely stated. For instance, PMSCs are expected to "appropriately" respond to situations of employee misconduct, or "properly" vet employees, but there is no indication of how this is to be evaluated. Nearly all the major commitments are accompanied by an opt-out clause that qualifies their commitments "to the extent possible and subject to contractual and legal limitations"; but again, the code and related documents provide no guidance on how this phrase should be interpreted. Indeed, contracts are rarely made available to the public and, given the nature of the activities involved, it is not easy to arrive at any accurate conclusion of what is "possible." Thus, PMSCs may be able to sidestep obligations without literally violating the code.

The Standards, Oversight, and Compliance Committee deals with violations of the code. According to a previously provided enforcement mechanism, the committee would decide complaints submitted in writing by any person to the chief liaison officer, who is a nonvoting ISOA staffer. Proceedings would be kept confidential; identities of individual complainants would not be disclosed, though the name of their affiliated companies or organizations may be. Though complainants' submissions would be deemed public, they would not be made available on the website or any of ISOA's publications. Member submissions would also be deemed confidential. Sanctions specified for noncompliance would include *probation*, during which the company would remain under heightened scrutiny and/or lose voting rights, *expulsion*, or other disciplinary action (include ameliorative, but not punitive, measures). There would be a limited scope for appeals to an Appeals Task Force.[51]

The BAPSC Charter contains similar obligations, though it is a shorter document. PMSCs undertake to comply with "all rules of international, humanitarian and human rights law that are applicable as well as all relevant international protocols and conventions," and "to subscribe to and abide by the ethical codes of practice of the Association" that are not separately enumerated. The charter stresses transparent relations with the UK government and obliges members to decline contracts "that might be contrary to UK values and interests." It also asks members to decline contracts that might adversely affect the military or political balance in their territory of operation. As to the use of force, the charter requires that BAPSC members "provide security designed primarily to deter any potential aggressor and to avoid any armed exchange. This . . . allows the use of weapons to protect clients or security personnel in a defensive mode and only where there is no other way to defend against an armed attack or to effect evacuation." The website provides no details on enforcement, but its director general claims BAPSC relies upon fines, suspension, and expulsion.[52]

Disseminating Norms, Values, and Industry Best Practices

At various forums, including multi-stakeholder meetings with participants from governments and international bodies, representatives of leading

PMSCs have argued that much improvement of service standards can be achieved simply by efforts directed at clarifying the norms, values, and practices appropriate for PMSCs.[53] They claim that such information has value for their firms that already desire to display high standards of performance but need guidance on what these may be. This suggests a clear role for industry associations, among other actors, to inform, educate, and persuade companies and their employees of appropriate standards. Moreover, industry associations can provide channels for peer pressure—via feedback and naming and shaming—to coerce low-end companies that are less desirous of conforming to high service standards than leading PMSCs. In theory, such mimetic forces may be particularly effective if these companies face the threat of being squeezed out of the market by the leading companies, owing to the latter's better quality of operations.

Industry associations do recognize these aspects of their regulatory role, and contribute in several ways to disseminating information on applicable laws and best practices, and inducing companies to comply with the same. Their framework documents carry lists of relevant laws and often also provide this information in a processed form, that is, explaining the rules and procedures and bringing any changes to attention. ISOA and BAPSC conduct training programs, workshops, and simulation exercises for members. For a time ISOA provided surveys on "the State of the Industry," though no report has been issued since the second one in 2007, evidence perhaps of the ad hoc character of some initiatives that get off to a good start but then peter out. In the same vein, we might take note of the Peace Operations Institute, a think tank established by ISOA in "late 2006," but dormant since late 2007.[54] More positively, ISOA continues to regularly publish a version of its *Journal of International Peace Operations*, now as *Stability Operations* magazine. The workshops and exercises conducted by BAPSC and ISOA are among the ways of facilitating channels of peer review for their member companies. ISOA has several functioning working groups and Brooks has maintained two active online discussion groups.[55] At the local level, in Baghdad, PSCAI used to host meetings of industry representatives with local authorities and personnel from the Iraqi Ministry of Interior and US diplomatic staff.

It is fair to say that the three industry associations have undertaken several initiatives to disseminate information about appropriate norms, values, and standards and to induce companies to comply with the same. Of course, some of these have been more successful than others, and the need for the associations to persist with such efforts remains ongoing. Nevertheless, this function, more than the others, points to the huge contribution industry associations can make toward the regulation of PMSCs.

Supporting Regulatory Initiatives of States and Other Actors

An important component of the associations' activities has been to participate in and comment upon other initiatives for better governance of the industry. These include programs led by international bodies such as the ICRC—whose Swiss-ICRC Intergovernmental Initiative has resulted in the adoption of the Montreux Document and the ICoC—and the UN Working Group on mercenaries, as well as those of academic institutions, think tanks, and advocacy groups.

Most importantly, industry associations have cooperated with government initiatives to regulate PMSCs. They have provided commentary upon proposed legislation, in their home states and abroad,[56] and sponsored independent events to debate and critique applicable rules.[57] They also claim to have actively sought the introduction of specific rules and regulations: Brooks testified before the US Congress in support of the extension of the US Military Extraterritorial Jurisdiction Act to all contractors.[58] Bearpark indicates that one of BAPSC's goals has been to persuade the UK to provide an effective complaint system—perhaps an independent ombudsman—to collect, investigate, and process complaints against companies.[59] However, there has been little, if any, progress in this direction. While there are relevant mechanisms for companies operating domestically—for example, under the "Approved Contractor Scheme" run by the UK Security Industry Authority, which reports to the UK Home Office, the Security Industry Authority annually certifies companies in good standing and may withdraw "approved contractor status" as well as prosecute a company, following its own investigation of any complaints against that company[60]—such an office has not been established to investigate and scrutinize extraterritorial operations in conflict zones.

Industry associations may also facilitate PMSCs' compliance with domestic and international rules. As discussed in the previous section, they may do so by disseminating information to members, and encouraging members to maintain open and transparent relations with states and cooperate with official investigations. They also encourage compliance in more concrete ways. For example, PSCAI used to assist member companies in preparing their licensing applications to the Iraq Ministry of Interior and Kurdistan Regional Government. ISOA testified before US congressional committees.[61] The associations also provided channels for communication between members and governments.

One important question here is whether industry associations would cooperate in criminal justice proceedings against PMSCs. While their assertions in favor of the importance of better government oversight should imply the inclination to cooperate with states' efforts to prosecute companies, they do occasionally make specific statements that indicate the contrary. For example, in its enforcement mechanism, ISOA had confusingly declared that it "is not a law enforcement or judicial organization, and *will not attempt to prove the guilt or innocence of a member company in a criminal or civil legal case*."[62] In the absence of practice, it is not certain whether this statement indicates that ISOA will refuse to cooperate in a judicial proceeding.

In sum, while industry associations do cooperate actively in some ways toward "capacity building," both of states (and other bodies) for better regulation of PMSCs and of PMSCs for better compliance with regulation, their contributions thus far lack full conceptualization. This, too, as the next section will discuss, is relevant to questions of their legitimacy, accountability, and effectiveness as industry regulators.

EVALUATING THE REGULATORY ROLE OF INDUSTRY ASSOCIATIONS

Having discussed various criteria relevant to the legitimacy, accountability, and effectiveness of private regulatory bodies, and having explored the available information on organizational structures, membership rules, and regulatory initiatives of ISOA, BAPSC, and PSCAI, in this section I offer an evaluation of their regulatory claims. To do so, I use the information provided by the associations and that which can be inferred from important episodes in their dealings with specific PMSCs or states. However, because the former type of information is limited and not always easy to verify, while the latter is often anecdotal only, the evaluation provided should be regarded as preliminary. Even so, it may facilitate greater debate on the regulatory functions that associations currently perform and which they have the potential to undertake in the future. It may also suggest to the associations practices by which they can improve their claims to legitimacy, accountability, and effectiveness as regulators. My focus is on ISOA and BAPSC. Given the little information available about its activities, and its having disbanded, my references to PSCAI will be marginal. With that caveat, let us turn to legitimacy first.

LEGITIMACY

As indicated above, we may usefully examine legitimacy in terms of three criteria: comprehensibility, structures, and procedures. What do we know—and what have the associations been able to tell us—of their claims to legitimacy according to these criteria?

Comprehensibility

Comprehensibility depends foremost on the associations' transparency, and their making available to us information to demonstrate how they execute their regulatory commitments. We might borrow Daniel Esty's description of "order-based legitimacy," that is, deriving from "rules and decision-processes that are public and publicized, understandable, stable and predictable,"[63] as indicating what sort of information is valuable—that is, information about the associations' organizational structures, rules, and procedures.

ISOA's publicly circulated documents describe its management committees, staff, code of conduct, and (until lately) enforcement mechanism. Its website, annual reports, and staff-authored papers also provide much supplementary information. ISOA also promotes transparency about the industry and its regulation more generally: for example, Anna Leander and Rens van Munster point to its publication of the *Journal of International Peace Operations* as a vehicle to discuss problems of regulation and appropriate standards.[64] At the same time, it is also true that ISOA's internal arrangements and the information it makes available are subject to rapid changes and without explanation, which makes its own functioning seem nontransparent. BAPSC has made available its charter and, until lately, its membership criteria, but provides little information about its organizational structure or its procedures for reviewing and sanctioning violations of the charter. For PSCAI, public information only extended to the purpose for which it had been established; information regarding its staff, charter and code of conduct, and membership criteria remained unavailable for most of its tenure.

At the outset then, we might say that of the three, ISOA is the most comprehensible, for it makes available much more information than do the other two, while PSCAI, its operations wrapped up in mystery, is the least. However, as we shall see in the next two sections on structures and procedures, there is also plenty that we do not know or understand about ISOA.

Structures

I discuss here the associations' *internal* arrangements, exploring whether these indicate their intent to prescribe and persuade PMSCs to abide by specific standards, and their autonomy from their members' vested interests. For convenience, I will discuss the associations' external linkages, which may give further proof of the veracity of their regulatory claims, in the sections on external accountability and effectiveness.

There is little about the BAPSC that suggests the association is independent from its membership. BAPSC was established by a company-led impetus and has very few independent staff. Its charter's language conflates the association and its membership. However, previously available information on its admission process, and its director general's reference to possible sanctions against individual members, suggests that we could distinguish the collective will displayed by BAPSC's members from the vested interests of specific PMSCs. Even so, given the lack of information on its internal arrangements, its Membership Committee, or the process by which it reviews members' violations, it is difficult to attest to BAPSC's autonomy from its most powerful members.

In contrast, ISOA asserts that it was conceived and launched independently of its members and its code was formulated through consultations with a range of stakeholders. Its language also clearly portrays the association as an entity distinct from its members. An attempt to disaggregate decision making is evident in the existence of task-specific committees chaired by ISOA staff. The function of collecting complaints of violations of ISOA's code is also left to a staff member. In such ways, ISOA indicates that it is more than a collective of its members. Of course, internal arrangements are, at best, "proxies for less visible targets of evaluation such as strategies, goals and outcomes."[65] The contrasting structures of BAPSC and ISOA may show that the latter demonstrates a greater structural commitment to regulating PMSCs, but cannot be conclusive proof that it actually does so in a better way than the former.

Moreover, certain of ISOA's structural elements deserve greater scrutiny. For instance, seats on most task-specific committees, including Membership and Standards, may be had on a volunteer basis.[66] There are no institutional checks to prevent a PMSC from volunteering for seats on several committees and for years in succession. EOD Technology, Inc. (EODT), had representatives concurrently on the Executive, Standards and Membership, and Finance Committees in 2007 and 2008. In contrast, BAPSC's previously provided membership criteria indicated that its Membership Committee, at least, was elected by a General Assembly composed of the full membership of BAPSC.[67]

Procedures

Procedural legitimacy derives from the assumption that thoughtfully structured rule- and decision-making processes enable participation of all relevant stakeholders, ensure proper appreciation of norms and facts, and prevent capture by specific interests. In this respect, ISOA's procedures aim to conform to at least one administrative principle: "public participation." Its code of conduct is the result of a participatory process. It provides avenues for public suggestions for revision of the code—including submission via email and ISOA-sponsored meetings between NGOs, human rights lawyers, and scholars. We might also take note of early efforts such as simulation exercises conducted in partnership with Washington, DC–based universities to review its enforcement mechanism.[68]

However, its key procedures are not always transparent. For instance, it does not explain its membership decisions or even provide a public record of the companies that have unsuccessfully applied for membership. Possibly this is so as not to deter companies from (re)applying or because of the fear that, ironically, the revelation that a company has been refused membership would hurt the image of the industry as a whole. Even so, lack of public record creates doubts about the veracity of ISOA's procedures. Given its financial dependence upon members' annual contributions and policy of voluntary service on the Membership Committee, it is difficult to avoid the suggestion that existing members may unduly influence the selection of new members. Indeed, a controversial allegation of this type did follow the repeated denial of membership to Aegis LLC.[69] Aegis is a founding member of BAPSC and PSCAI, though admittedly its reputation is far from spotless: trophy videos of its personnel shooting at civilians are freely available on the Internet and Tim Spicer, former manager of the notorious Sandline International, which was involved in the "Arms to Africa Affair," has served as its chief executive officer.[70] However, it is not known whether either factor was relevant to ISOA's decision. Aegis' claim that it was "invited" to apply for membership each time it was refused further obscures the facts.

Similar criticisms can be leveled at ISOA's enforcement mechanism. Though ISOA claims that complainants' submissions are deemed public, it does not make them available even in redacted form. Nor does it offer public explanation for decisions of the Standards Committee. Indeed, the only occasion upon which the public may even be aware that a decision has been made is when a company has been expelled from membership, but there is no instance of this at present. ISOA's policies are probably guided by the desire to encourage PMSCs to participate in ISOA and to protect the image of the industry as a whole. However, for stakeholders, or observers at large, the secrecy surrounding ISOA's proceedings may detract from its claims of due process. Moreover, given that ISOA aims for its membership to be taken as certification of a PMSC's high standards of service, and for loss of membership to be the "commercial kiss of death,"[71] this secrecy and lack of clarity is an odd choice—and mirrors the partial, ever-changing quality of information made available about other structures and functions of ISOA.

BAPSC provides even less information about its procedures, though it did earlier indicate the criteria and processes leading up to the grant of membership. These documents also made reference to the BAPSC General Assembly, which, it was understood, maintained oversight of the association's activities. But no other details are available. Most crucially, BAPSC does not indicate the processes through which it reviews allegations of wrongdoing of its members. With respect to PSCAI, there is hardly any information available about its procedures, though its close links to the Iraqi government may indicate some degree of oversight of its activities.

The associations, in sum, provide very little information about specific aspects of their own work vis-à-vis maintaining oversight of PMSCs and enforcing regulations. They do provide much supplementary information having to do with their programs for disseminating information to PMSCs, brainstorming on the challenges they face, and forging consensus on solutions. Their legitimacy as far as these latter functions are concerned is less contestable. However, these functions provide no basis for us to have confidence in specific companies' membership in good standing, or lack thereof, beyond the assumption that membership may have made the companies somewhat better aware of relevant obligations and good practices. Moreover, as we will see in the next section, it is important to consider the interests to which the associations are most accountable, before concluding whether they may equally emphasize the norms, values, and standards relevant to all interests. It is equally conceivable that the associations would select for active promotion norms and standards that suit the interests they consider most important.

ACCOUNTABILITY

It is useful to discuss the associations' accountability under two categories: internal accountability to their members, and external accountability to various third parties. Among these, I shall discuss factors that promote the accountability of the associations to states and to organizations representative of international civil society. It may be stated up front that associations have not been accountable at all to the communities affected by PMSC operations, though this is the group that we might consider most immediately affected by the use of PMSC services. Any regard given to this group's interest is the reflection then of the (so far low) value placed upon these interests by those to whom the associations are accountable as well as the associations' own inclinations.

Internal Accountability

The industry associations can claim to be accountable to their members in many ways. To begin with, members may unsubscribe if unhappy. The associations are fiscally accountable to members for how they spend the membership fee. Further, they are made accountable through the participation of members in their functioning; for instance, ISOA members conduct the work of its task-specific committees. Possibly, peer and reputational influences operate to ensure that PMSCs seated on these committees do not abuse their positions. However, contrary to these assumptions is the view Michael Waller provides of the background to ISOA's review of Blackwater. ISOA's Standards Committee initiated this review on 8 October 2007, following the Nisour Square incident. Blackwater withdrew from ISOA on 10 October. Waller states:

> Blackwater competitors filed a complaint to initiate a review of whether or not the company had violated the code. Sources close to the issue tell Serviam that Blackwater felt some of its competitors in IPOA lodged the complaint to take advantage of the company's situation, and they did so at a time when the firm was under a State Department gag order to say almost nothing about its diplomatic security operations in Iraq. Blackwater is said to have been concerned that certain competitors would leak details of an ongoing IPOA investigation to the press to discredit the company, isolating it within the PSC sector, with the goal of picking up its nine-figure annual Iraq contract.[72]

Whatever may be said about Blackwater's own actions, this report does indicate that internal accountability—equally to all members—is not easily maintained. As discussed in chapter 9 in this volume, the ISOA took on about 20 investigations during the past 15 years. Complaints and investigations into the conduct of member firms remain confidential and only the Blackwater investigation took place in an environment in which some details were made public. Perhaps, accountability concerns are partly alleviated by the fact that ISOA committees, including Standards, are subject to the overall supervision of the elected ISOA Board of Directors. This may have prevented particular companies from so abusing the review process. However, we can reach no definite conclusion, since the only review that has been made public did not proceed.

External Accountability through Legal and Administrative Controls

It is more difficult to envisage how associations may be accountable toward communities affected by PMSC operations: national militaries, multi-stakeholder regulatory initiatives, and states. Of course, industry associations cannot act contrary to the laws of their home states, that is, states of registry. In addition to the rules applicable to trade associations in general, home states could subject these associations to additional obligations relevant to their functions via conditions attached to their regulatory licenses. These conditions could, for example, provide that these associations must follow minimum standards in scrutinizing members' service records and cooperate with government initiatives to investigate and prosecute violations. The imposition of such obligations often accompanies delegation of regulatory functions to private bodies and, in consequence, the bodies are made subject to legal and supervisory accountability. However, neither ISOA nor BAPSC has been delegated regulatory power, and thus neither is currently subject to these additional conditions.

Of course, the two associations do recognize that acceptance among some of these constituencies is important to their own legitimacy and capacity to secure greater contracting opportunities for their members. They seek to demonstrate that they are formally bound to respect a variety of interests. BAPSC's charter, for example, commits it to respect for human rights, values of the UK, and military and political balance in the territory of operation. And it has called for the appointment of an independent "ombudsman" to "verify the Association's own role and to ensure that appropriate investigative work was done."[73]

Some of the external constituencies may also have recourse to legal mechanisms—for example, PMSCs that have been arbitrarily denied membership. Indeed, there was once speculation that Aegis planned to sue ISOA for this reason.[74] Had it been brought, this suit could have clarified whether and to what extent industry associations were subject to requirements of nonarbitrariness and nondiscrimination, at least.

External Accountability through Market and Reputational Controls

Given the paucity of legal and administrative controls, industry associations may turn to market and reputational influences as evidence of their external accountability. Two market aims are relevant to industry associations: increasing each member's market share and expanding the market itself. The first requires that consumers of PMSC services prefer industry association members to nonmembers. This may come about if membership is considered to signify better service standards. It is thus in the associations' interest to be seen to follow transparent and rigorous processes for granting membership and maintaining oversight of members. It is significant that the most important PMSCs have sought membership in one or more of the associations. Important consumers like the departments of the United States government could (though currently do not) encourage transparency and rigor in associations' processes by predicating their hiring of PMSCs upon the same.

The second market aim requires that the industry itself achieve greater normative sanction. Even now, it is not acceptable for many humanitarian groups or the United Nations to employ PMSCs openly or on a significant scale. Thus an important task for industry associations is to demonstrate that the industry as a whole is responsive to various third-party interests and the first step is to prove the associations' own responsiveness to these interests. Of course the associations walk a thin line: on the one hand, external parties must be made to feel that the associations can be depended upon to reliably assess and address the conduct of PMSCs; on the other hand, associations take care not to tarnish the industry's overall image by publicizing violations (or they will lose support of their members). Thus, in the process of rendering themselves responsive to one group, they may lose their legitimacy for another.

External Accountability Driven by Systemic Forces

Industry associations may also point to systemic factors that induce them to be responsive toward third parties. According to Esty, "systemic legitimacy might take the form of a network model of governance that spreads governance responsibilities across several international bodies, leading to a multilayered system of simultaneous cooperation and competition among international organizations and national authorities."[75] These features of cooperation and competition may, for several reasons, encourage industry bodies to engage with various stakeholders in a responsible way.

First, with respect to states, industry associations have an interest not only in promoting better government regulation (as they claim they do), but also in ensuring that this government regulation takes a form that is acceptable to the industry. Therefore by demonstrating their own regulatory oversight of PMSCs, industry associations may stave off the more intrusive forms of government regulation.

Second, the regulatory landscape is dotted with nongovernmental initiatives led by advocacy groups, human rights bodies, and academics. These call upon the industry associations to explain their own role and the activities of their members at various workshops, policy-making forums, and to the media. Such interactions may encourage the associations to review their own record and to evaluate their standards, functions, and processes. As Black notes, the very fact that an organization is made to present a narrative about its activities can alter it, "to bring itself closer into accordance with the story it tells of itself."[76] Presenting to various interest groups at different levels and in multiple forums can thus only facilitate a thicker, more thoroughly vetted account of the associations' role. More tangibly, their interaction with other regulatory initiatives also provides greater information about how they must further develop their standards and procedures. For the associations, a particularly relevant development in this respect may be the adoption of the ICoC and impending conclusion of its oversight mechanisms. At present, both ISOA and BAPSC endorse the ICoC and describe it as the culmination of their own advocacy efforts. It is referenced in the ISOA's own code of conduct, and is an element of ISOA's Advocacy Agenda. BAPSC offers assistance to companies on the procedures and mechanisms for signing the ICoC. The ICoC may thus facilitate further evolution in both associations—although it may also, in time, render their role superfluous.[77]

EFFECTIVENESS

I earlier discussed several advantages that industry associations enjoyed over public bodies, including their close working relationships with PMSCs, access to on-the-ground information, and greater flexibility in adopting and revising standards, best practices, and dealing with individual companies. And the associations do put these advantages to good use in persuading PMSCs to comply with the desirable standards and assisting states' regulatory endeavors. As evidence of the former, we see that several major PMSCs now have adopted self-governance mechanisms including company codes of conduct. PMSCs also regularly attend the workshops and training sessions organized by the associations. Some companies have also sought help from industry associations in resolving particular governance issues. For instance, when EODT was embroiled in controversy because a manager was accused of obtaining contracts for service in Iraq through an illicit relationship with a US military officer and the US military was considering putting EODT on its blacklist,[78] the company turned to ISOA for advice to resolve this matter and to formulate policies to guide its personnel's interactions with the military.[79] Industry associations' contributions to policy making and implementation by government and multi-stakeholder initiatives usually take the form of discussion, testimony, and comments upon proposed legislation and codes. Occasionally, they may play a role in more directly facilitating government oversight—as PSCAI did by assisting in the Iraqi Ministry of Interior's licensing process.

Questions of industry associations' effectiveness are, of course, most pertinent in relation to their use of coercive mechanisms, such as fines, suspensions, and expulsions. Such mechanisms are only "coercive" if PMSCs highly value their association memberships. On the one hand, there is plenty to suggest that they do. Members in good standing display the associations' emblems on their websites, often referring to them as "certifications," and most PMSCs also seek membership in more than one association. Moreover, memberships do carry benefits: they promote a market perception that the relevant companies are committed to effective self-regulation. They also allow greater visibility and networking opportunities, and facilitate better public relations. On the other hand, on the occasion that an association has tried to review a member's misconduct—I refer here to ISOA's review of Blackwater in the aftermath of Nisour Square—that member chose to simply withdraw from the association. And though an ISOA staff member had previously described a company's loss of membership as the "commercial kiss of death,"[80] this consequence did not follow for Blackwater. It continued to receive US government contracts,[81] remained a PSCAI member, and later rejoined ISOA. Indeed, given that the numbers of members in all three associations have remained fluid, it is not clear that companies feel inhibited from leaving the associations. Thus it is difficult to say how concerned PMSCs currently are about the loss of their association memberships.

We might, however, take note here of various factors that could determine how much value a company places on association membership. First is whether the company enjoys an existing strong relationship with a large consumer, as Blackwater did with the US Department of State. For, even if its fallout with ISOA added to the damage done to Blackwater's public reputation by the Nisour Square incident, it did not result in loss of contracting opportunities. Second is a company's existing or continuing membership in another association. Aegis, for instance, was refused ISOA membership on several occasions but this has not affected its market position, possibly in part because it was admitted to membership by BAPSC and PSCAI. Third, the general outlook of large consumers affects how much importance any company places on continued association membership. If states, for example, do not consider membership a criterion in awarding contracts, then companies will not place value on maintaining membership, even if they initially joined an association, for whatever advantages of visibility and networking that it provided. Finally, for consumers to be inclined to be guided by industry associations, they must be aware of the reasons behind their decisions to refuse companies membership or withdraw it from them.

We may also elaborate, more generally, the factors that will prove crucial to strengthening the associations' regulatory effectiveness. First, whether industry associations can enhance the value that consumers of PMSC services place on association membership. This may be accomplished, for a start, by providing more information on their structures and processes, successes in persuading PMSCs to adopt better standards and best practices, and decisions to admit or sanction members. Such information is key to building support for associations among domestic and international civil society organizations. Industry associations must also seek greater backing from states, since as consumers, hiring states can condition contracts upon association membership in good standing, and in their sovereign capacity, home and host states can require PMSCs to abide by association codes. These forms of integration with states would also preempt any regulatory "fragmentation" that could otherwise result from the concurrent regulatory efforts of states, multi-stakeholder initiatives, and industry associations. The threat of fragmentation also arises from another quarter, namely that industry associations do not take into account each other's decisions on membership and sanctions. This was evident in the case of both Aegis and Blackwater. Such incongruities weaken the credibility of association certifications.

This leads us to the final factor, which is whether industry associations recognize their own regulatory potential. They possess the capacity to shape PMSCs' attitudes, but this is contingent upon their willingness to give priority to their regulatory functions over other activities, such as trade promotion, when these two functions come into conflict. The associations' long-term effectiveness also depends upon their efforts to evolve their role in keeping with the needs of a fast-changing regulatory landscape. For example, as earlier noted, their important function of providing standard codes of conduct may be overtaken by adoption of the ICoC. This does not mean other functions—such as disseminating information, performing background checks, reviewing incidents of misconduct, supporting and offering feedback on proposed legislation, and providing platforms for interaction between PMSCs and various stakeholders in their operations—have lost importance. It does suggest, however, that they may improve their services by devoting more attention and resources to these functions. For instance, there have been suggestions for industry associations to take the lead in establishing multi-stakeholder grievance mechanisms for those most directly affected by PMSC operations—in other words, the conflict-battered communities among which PMSCs operate.[82] Industry associations have spent the past decade establishing themselves. Now it is up to them to think creatively about the ways in which they can complement other regulatory mechanisms and use their advantage of greater operational flexibility to innovate on their role.

CONCLUSION

This chapter has explored the contribution and limits of industry associations with respect to the regulation of PMSCs. While ISOA, BAPSC, or (the former) PSCAI cannot substitute for state regulation—though in practice, state regulation may be notable for its absence only—they can, and do, complement formal regulatory initiatives. Indeed, they enjoy advantages of greater expertise, flexibility, and close relationships with members. Despite this, their regulatory claims do not receive much attention. This is because of the assumption that, as private bodies, industry associations lack sufficient legitimacy, accountability, and effectiveness as regulators. I have explored this assumption, first by outlining what these concepts signify for private regulatory bodies operating in an international context, and second, by evaluating the associations' efforts to demonstrate the credibility of their regulatory claims. These efforts have been only moderately successful, for the associations have not fully established the necessary structures and procedures; nor have they fully communicated their intent to do so. The failure to communicate is possibly the easier challenge to address, and the more crucial. The associations do recognize their flaws, but their constant changes to remedy them are often perceived as evidence of institutional unpredictability. The onus is partly on analysts and commentators as well to view and engage with these changes as proof of their regulatory evolution.

We must, of course, also keep in mind the challenges they must overcome. The primary challenge is that they combine their regulatory aim with that of representing PMSCs and promoting contracting opportunities. While the associations claim these aims are compatible, it is possible to envisage situations in which they will come into conflict, and which will thus seriously test the associations' regulatory commitment. Another challenge concerns states' failure to properly integrate the associations' decisions into their own dealings with PMSCs. While many states do invite the associations to comment on proposed legislation and provide expert testimony on PMSCs, they do not make association membership a criterion for awarding contracts. The associations' sanctions, therefore, lack bite. A final challenge is to continuously evolve their own role in keeping with the changing regulatory landscape and to extend benefits of industry regulation to those who, despite being most severely affected by PMSC operations, have been sidelined as stakeholders. This includes, for a start, the communities in which PMSCs operate. The more industry associations work to creatively realize their potential to complement formal regulation, the more likely it is that they will shape a functional path for further development of the PMSC industry as a whole.

NOTES

1. See Simon Chesterman and Chia Lehnardt, editors, *From Mercenaries to Market: The Rise and Regulation of Private Military Companies* (Oxford: Oxford University Press, 2007).
2. The Campaign to Stop Killer Coke, "About Us," available at http://killercoke.org/about.php, accessed 17 December 2015, documents charges of human rights abuses, water privatization, and labor intimidation against the Coca-Cola Company.
3. See Peter Walker, "Blackwater Guards Shot Iraqis without Provocation, Report Says," *Guardian* (8 October 2007).
4. Thorough explorations include Hannah Tonkin, *State Control over Private Military and Security Companies in Armed Conflict* (New York: Cambridge University Press, 2011); Chesterman and Lehnardt, *From Mercenaries to Market*; Michael Cottier, "Elements for Contracting and Regulating Private Security and Military Companies," *International Review of the Red Cross* 88 (2006), page 637; Fred Schreier and Mariana Caparini, *Privatising Security: Law, Practice and Governance of Private Military and Security Companies*, Occasional Paper 6 (Geneva: Geneva Centre for the Democratic Control of Armed Forces, March 2005); Caroline Holmqvist, *Private Security Companies: The Case for Regulation*, Policy Paper 9 (Stockholm: Stockholm International Peace Research Institute, January 2005).
5. Peter W. Singer, "War, Profits, and the Vacuum of Law: Privatized Military Firms and International Law," *Columbia Journal of Transnational Law* 42, 2 (Spring 2004), page 521.
6. Daphné Richemond-Barak, "Regulating War: A Taxonomy in Global Administrative Law," *European Journal of International Law* 22, 4 (November 2011), page 1027.
7. This culminated in the "Montreux Document" (Confederation of Switzerland Department of Foreign Affairs and the International Committee of the Red Cross, *The Montreux Document on Pertinent International Legal Obligations and Good Practices for States related to Operations of Private Military and Security Companies during Armed Conflict*, UN Document A/63/467-S/2008/636 [Geneva: International Committee of the Red Cross, 2008]).

8. International Code of Conduct for Private Security Service Providers' Association, "International Code of Conduct Association," available at http://www.icoca.ch/, accessed 23 March 2015.

9. Peter W. Singer, "Private Military Firms in Today's Wars," interview with Terry Gross, Centre for Global Research (24 July 2003), available at http://www.globalresearch.ca/articles/SIN307A.html, accessed 17 December 2015.

10. Steven L. Schooner, "Contractor Atrocities at Abu Ghraib: Compromised Accountability in a Streamlined, Outsourced Government," *Stanford Law and Policy Review* 16, 2 (2005), pages 549, 555.

11. Deborah D. Avant, "Private Military Companies and the Future of War," *Foreign Policy Research Association E-notes* (April 2006), available at http://www.fpri.org/enotes/200604.military.avant.privatemilitarycompanies.html.

12. Mpako H. Foaleng, "Private Military and Security Companies and the Nexus between Natural Resources and Civil Wars in Africa," in Sabelo Gumedze, *Private Security in Africa: Manifestation, Challenges and Regulation*, ISS Monograph Series 139 (November 2007), pages 39, 50.

13. Owen Bowcott, "Report Reveals Shame of UN Peacekeepers," *Guardian* (25 March 2005).

14. Ian Cobain, "Iraqi Prisoners Were Abused at 'UK's Abu Ghraib,' Court Hears," *Guardian* (6 November 2010).

15. Article 9, *Draft Convention on Private Military and Security Companies: Report of the UN Working Group on Mercenaries to the UN Human Rights Council*, A/HRC/15/25, Annex (2 July 2010).

16. Simon Chesterman and Angelina Fisher, editors, *Private Security, Public Order* (New York: Oxford University Press, 2009), page 225.

17. Chia Lehnardt, "Peacekeeping," in Chesterman and Fisher, *Private Security, Public Order*, pages 205, 221.

18. Sabelo Gumedze, "To Embrace or Not to Embrace: Addressing the Private Security Industry Phenomenon in Africa," in Gumedze, *Private Security in Africa*, page 1.

19. I have discussed this episode in greater detail in Surabhi Ranganathan, "Between Complicity and Irrelevance? Industry Associations and the Challenge of Regulating Private Security Contractors," *Georgetown Journal of International Law* 41 (2010), pages 350–53; Surabhi Ranganathan, "Constructive Constraints? Conceptual and Practical Challenges to Regulating Private Military and Security Companies," in Cedric Ryngaert and Math Noorthman, editors, *Human Security and International Law* (Cambridge, Antwerp, and Poland: Intersentia, 2014), chapter 7.

20. Laura A. Dickinson, *Outsourcing War and Peace: Preserving Public Values in a World of Privatized Foreign Affairs* (New Haven: Yale University Press, 2011), chapter 2.

21. For a typology, see A. Claire Cutler, "Private International Regimes and Inter-firm Cooperation," in Rodney Bruce Hall and Thomas J. Biersteker, editors, *The Emergence of Private Authority in Global Governance* (Cambridge: Cambridge University Press, 2002), pages 23, 33.

22. International Committee of the Red Cross, "The Fundamental Principles of the Red Cross and Red Crescent" (Geneva: International Committee of the Red Cross, 31 October 1986), available at https://www.icrc.org/eng/resources/documents/red-cross-crescent-movement/fundamental-principles-movement-1986-10-31.htm, accessed 17 December 2015; The Sphere Project, *The Core Humanitarian Standard and the Sphere Core Standards: Analysis and Comparison—Interim Guidance*, version 2 (Geneva: The Sphere Project, March 2015).

23. Benedict Kingsbury, Nico Krisch, and Richard B. Stewart, "The Emergence of Global Administrative Law," *Law and Contemporary Problems* 68, 3/4 (Summer/Autumn 2005), pages 1, 20.

24. Ruth W. Grant and Robert Keohane, "Accountability and Abuses of Power in World Politics," *American Political Science Review* 99, 1 (February 2005), page 29.

25. Julia Black, "Constructing and Contesting Legitimacy and Accountability in Poly-centric Regimes," IILJ Working Paper 2007/12 (Global Administrative Law Series).

26. Suchman refers to pragmatic, moral, and cognitive legitimacy. Pragmatic legitimacy results from the benefits that the organization is considered to provide. Moral legitimacy owes partly to the results of an organization's actions, and partly to the propriety of its procedures, its structure, and the charisma of its management. Cognitive legitimacy owes to the organization's "comprehensibility" to its audience. See Mark C. Suchman, "Managing Legitimacy: Strategic and Institutional Approaches," *Academy of Management Review* 20, 3 (July 1995), pages 571, 577–85. Esty's conception of legitimacy is similar, though his categorization is different, comprising democratic, results-based, order-based, systemic, procedural, and deliberative legitimacy. See Daniel C. Esty, "Good Governance at the Supranational Scale: Globalizing Administrative Law," *Yale Law Journal* 115, 7 (May 2006), pages 1490, 1515–22. Keohane and Buchanan offer criteria of "minimum moral acceptability," identified with an institution's respect for the most established human rights; the benefits to various constituencies from its operation; and institutional integrity, reflected by the congruence between its aims and its practices and procedures. They too suggest that an institution's *transparency* is key to evaluating its legitimacy. See Allen Buchanan and Robert O. Keohane, "The Legitimacy of Global Governance Institutions," *Ethics and International Affairs* 20, 4 (December 2006), pages 405, 419–29.

27. Grant and Keohane, "Accountability and Abuses of Power in World Politics," page 36.

28. Richard B. Stewart, "Accountability, Participation and the Problem of Disregard in Global Regulatory Governance," IILJ International Legal Theory Colloquium, NYU School of Law (7 February 2008), page 15.

29. Andrew A. King and Michael J. Lenox, "Industry Self-Regulation without Sanctions: The Chemical Industry's Responsible Care Program," *Academic Management Journal* 43, 4 (2000), pages 698, 701.

30. See Ryan Goodman and Derek Jinks, "How to Influence States: Socialization and International Human Rights Law," *Duke Law Journal* 54, 3 (December 2004), pages 635–42.

31. Telephone interview with Doug Brooks (27 May 2008).

32. See Robert Greenwald, "Robert Greenwald's Interview with Doug Brooks," available at http://iraqforsale.org/doug_brooks.php, accessed 17 December 2015; Bruce Falconer, "Doug Brooks: Blackwater's Man in Washington," *Mother Jones* (25 September 2007).

33. J. Michael Waller, "Accountability and Private Security Contractors: Visibility of Operations Is Key to Success," *Politicalwarfare.org* (10 December 2007), available at http://acmeofskill.com/2007/12/2380/, accessed 31 July 2015; see also International Stability Operations Association, "History of ISOA," available at http://www.stability-operations.org/?page=History, accessed 31 July 2015.

34. International Stability Operations Association, "ISOA Code of Conduct" (no date), available at http://www.stability-operations.org/?page=Code, accessed 31 July 2015.

35. Doug Brooks, "From Humble Beginnings in Freetown: The Origins of the Code of Conduct and Its Importance for the Industry," *Journal of International Peace Operations* 3, 5 (2007), pages 8–9.

36. International Stability Operations Association, "Our Work" (no date), available at http://www.stability-operations.org/?page=Work, accessed 31 July 2015.

37. International Stability Operations Association, "Advocacy Initiatives" (no date), available at http://www.stability-operations.org/?page=Advocacy, accessed 31 July 2015.

38. International Stability Operations Association, "Committees and Working Groups" (no date), available at http://www.stability-operations.org/?page=Committees, accessed 31 July 2015.

39. This committee was listed in the IPOA Annual Report 2006–2007. This report is no longer provided on the ISOA website.

40. This committee was also listed in the IPOA Annual Report 2006–2007.

41. International Stability Operations Association, "Committees and Working Groups."

42. CPA, vested with "powers of government temporarily in order to provide for the effective administration of Iraq during the period of transitional administration" (CPA Regulation 1 [May 16, 2003]), was dissolved on 28 June 2004.

43. Private Security Company Association of Iraq, "Effective 31 December 2011 the PSCAI Is Disestablished," available at http://www.pscai.org/, accessed 31 July 2015.

44. British Association of Private Security Companies, "Home," available at http://www.bapsc.org.uk/key_documents-charter.asp, accessed 17 December 2015.

45. See Dominick Donald, *After the Bubble: British Private Security Companies after Iraq*, Royal United Services Institute Whitehall Paper 66 (25 July 2006). Donald is a senior analyst for Aegis, a British PMSC.

46. Andrew Bearpark and Sabrina Schulz, "The Future of the Market," in Chesterman and Fisher, *Private Security, Public Order*, page 247.

47. Telephone interview with Doug Brooks (27 May 2008).

48. The link, last seen available in November 2009, was http://www.bapsc.org.uk/membership-membership_criteria.asp.

49. Dated July 2007, the relevant documents—guidelines for obtainment of membership, a form for providing due diligence documentation, and a "Self-Assessment Workbook"—were made available only in May 2008.

50. English, Arabic, German, Spanish, French, Chinese, Russian, and Swedish.

51. The "Enforcement Mechanism" was no longer available in full text by February 2012, but some details remained available until at least summer 2012.

52. Bearpark and Schulz, "The Future of the Market," page 248.

53. See Institute for International Law and Justice, New York University School of Law, "Chairman's Notes from the Greentree Workshop on Regulation of Private Military and Security Companies, 22–24 March 2007 ('Greentree Notes')," available at http://www.iilj.org/research/GreentreeNotes.asp, accessed 5 June 2014.

54. Its website is still available: http://peaceops.org/poi/index.php?option=com_content&task=view&id=12&Itemid=26.

55. The two groups are "AMPM list" (http://groups.yahoo.com/group/AMPMlist/) and "PMCs" (http://groups.yahoo.com/group/pmcs/?yguid=272748409).

56. For example, all three associations made submissions to the South African Parliament during the passage of the Prohibition of Mercenary Activity and Prohibition and Regulation of Certain Activities in an Area of Armed Conflict Act 2006.

57. See Iveta Cherneva, "IPOA Holds Capitol Hill Event on UCMJ-MEJA Debate," *Journal of International Peace Operations* 2, 5 (March/April 2007), page 6.

58. Telephone interview with Doug Brooks (27 May 2008). Also see Diana Sidakis, "Private Military Companies and State Sovereignty: Regulating Transnational Flows of Violence and Capital," in Franz von Benda-Beckman, Keebet von Benda-Beckmann, and Julia Eckert, editors, *Rule of Law and Law of Ruling: On the Governance of Law* (London: Ashgate, 2009), page 75.

59. Bearpark and Schulz, "The Future of the Market," page 248. See also "Mercenary Firms Seek Tighter Laws," *BBC News* (5 December 2007), available at http://news.bbc.co.uk/1/hi/uk/7128046.stm.

60. See Security Industry Authority, *Approved Contractor Scheme: Terms and Conditions of Approval* (London: Home Office, June 2012), available at http://www.sia.homeoffice.gov.uk/Documents/acs/sia_acs_terms.pdf, accessed 5 June 2014.

61. E.g., Doug Brooks, *Testimony on "Contracting for the Iraqi Security Forces." Hearing before the Subcommittee on Oversight and Investigations of the Committee on Armed Services, House of Representatives, 110th Congress* (Washington: Government Printing Office, 2008), pages 45–63.

62. Emphasis added. The webpage (http://www.ipoaworld.org/eng/enforcementv01eng.html) is not currently available, so it is not possible to confirm if this language subsists.

63. Esty, "Good Governance at the Supranational Scale," page 1518.

64. Anna Leander and Rens van Munster, "Private Security Contractors in Darfur: Reflecting and Reinforcing Neo-liberal Governmentality," *International Relations* 21, 2 (June 2007), page 202.

65. John W. Meyer and Brian Rowan, "Institutionalized Organizations: Formal Structure as Myth and Ceremony," in Walter W. Powell and Paul J. DiMaggio, editors, *The New Institutionalism in Organizational Analysis* (Chicago: University of Chicago Press, 1991), page 41.

66. Telephone interview with Doug Brooks (27 May 2008).

67. This was provided in the documents made available in May 2008. See Private Security Company Association of Iraq, "Effective 31 December."

68. See Tanner Ivie, "Standards Committee Holds Landmark Simulation," *Journal of International Peace Operations* 2, 1 (2006), page 21.

69. David Phinney, "From Mercenaries to Peacemakers? Scandals Confront Military Security Industry," *CorpWatch* (29 November 2005), available at http://www.corpwatch.org/article.php?id=12829, accessed April 2010.

70. For an account of Tim Spicer's career in the private military industry, see Robert Baer, "Iraq's Mercenary King," *Vanity Fair* (April 2007), http://www.vanityfair.com/politics/features/2007/04/spicer200704; see also Christopher Kinsey, *Corporate Soldiers and International Security: The Rise of Private Military Companies* (London: Routledge, 2006), pages 72–93.

71. Falconer, "Doug Brooks" (quoting Brooks).

72. Waller, "Accountability and Private Security Contractors."

73. *See* Alyson J. K. Bailes and Caroline Holmqvist, *The Increasing Role of Private Military and Security Companies*, study prepared for the European Parliament Subcommittee on Security and Defence (Brussels: Directorate General External Policies of the Union, October 2007).

74. Phinney, "From Mercenaries to Peacemakers?"

75. Esty, "Good Governance at the Supranational Scale," pages 1489–90.

76. Black, "Constructing and Contesting Legitimacy and Accountability in Poly-centric Regimes," page 24.

77. See also Ranganathan, "Constructive Constraints?" pages 175, 186–87.

78. Matt Kelley, "Army May Ban Security Firm from Contracts," *USA Today* (11 November 2007).

79. Telephone interview with Doug Brooks (27 May 2008).

80. Falconer, "Doug Brooks."

81. See Jeremy Scahill, *Blackwater: The Rise of the World's Most Powerful Mercenary Army* (London: Profile Books, 2011), pages 447–48.

82. Angelina Fisher, "Accountability to Whom?" in Chesterman and Fisher, *Private Security, Public Order*, pages 67–68.

Chapter Nine

Establishing Industry Norms

ISOA

Doug Brooks, Andrew Koch, and Gary Schaub Jr.

The stability operations industry provides a wide variety of vital services essential to international peacekeeping and conflict mitigation efforts. The most visible service of the industry is armed security, but it also includes the gamut of support services such as construction, development, and medical care. The wide variety of firms in the stability operations industry have a multiplicity of interests, requirements, and goals. However, what they have in common is that they employ civilian personnel who perform their tasks in austere and dangerous environments, and often in weak and failed states with questionable or nonexistent legal systems. The lack of stable rule of law in the areas in which they operate raises critical issues of oversight and accountability—not just for firms in the industry, but also for actors in the international community that make use of their services.

Over the past twenty-five years, the industry has expanded and contracted as related to demand, but with a long-term growth trend, and this has concerned some external observers as well as government officials responsible for hiring these firms, managing their contracts, and, if necessary, holding them accountable for their performance and adherence to appropriate legal standards. Contractors are utilized by the US Department of Defense (DoD) to free up military personnel to focus on combat missions, to provide "off the shelf" expertise on critical services such as linguistics, logistics, and base support, to quickly provide "surge capacity" for critical policies, and to construct and operate military bases cost-effectively—a capacity that DoD does not have to pay for after its actual utilization. The 2007 "Gansler Report" highlighted the reasons for DoD's use of contractors: "There is overwhelming evidence, both analytical and now historical, that many tasks can be done more effectively and less expensively by contractors."[1] Robert Gates, then the secretary of defense, agreed with the Gansler Report but repeatedly expressed concern in private and in public over the dependence of US forces on operational contract support as well as the ability of the US government to effectively track its dependence, plan for its use, and account for its operational effects.[2] These concerns were based on "the lessons learned from recent operational experience" using overseas contingency contractors in these difficult environments as well as the legal issues associated with holding firms and employees accountable for inappropriate conduct.

Secretary Gates' concerns were shared by a number of other agencies of the US government because the "whole of government" approach in Afghanistan and Iraq meant that those agencies often relied on contractors for their food, housing, security, and other support to accomplish their missions. The Department of Defense's inspector general testified before the Senate Judiciary Committee about 83 investigations into cases of war profiteering, contract fraud, kickbacks, bribery, bid rigging, product substitution, and conflicts of interest in Iraq.[3] Such allegations were aimed at American and Western firms, but also included many local firms in the area of conflict unfamiliar with the Federal Acquisition Regulations and Defense Federal Acquisition Regulations guidelines for US government contracting, leading to numerous inadvertent violations. Ultimately Congress created the United States Commission on Wartime Contracting in Iraq and Afghanistan. Its final report estimated "$31 to $60 billion" in waste, fraud, and abuse during the first decade of operations associated with military actions in Iraq, Afghanistan, and elsewhere—a sensational but questionable estimate.[4] In any case, while a significant percentage was related to contractor malfeasance, the majority of the commission's documented findings focused on waste attributable to poor government planning and coordination as well as a lack of personnel and mechanisms for conducting contract oversight.

Specific contractor-related incidents have produced results much worse than the loss of money. The most prominent event occurred in 2007 at Nisour Square in Baghdad when more than a dozen Iraqi civilians were killed by armed security contractors from Blackwater USA, working for the US Department of State. It would take seven long years for the US Department of Justice to obtain convictions of the perpetrators, but by then the political damage was done. That incident elicited a far more publicized and negative response than similar, and sometimes worse, incidents attributed to military forces, highlighting the political necessity of effective accountability for civilians operating in areas of conflict.[5]

Contractors operating in complex and insecure environments face the same ethical and legal challenges as contractors operating at home and in peacetime—as well as additional conflict-related concerns and risks to their projects and employees. Furthermore, one cannot assume that all contractors, military personnel, or government employees will operate professionally and ethically at all times—and there are bound to be some who take advantage of the turmoil and behave in less acceptable ways.[6] Ensuring proper oversight, enforcement of norms, rules, and laws, and achieving justice given the realities in which contingency contractors are employed is significantly more difficult than in peacetime environments where the facts, rules, and processes with which all operate are far clearer.

The oversight and accountability issues facing the stability operations contracting industry led the International Stability Operations Association (ISOA)[7] to coordinate and then establish a code of conduct and a monitoring organization for the industry. ISOA is the primary trade group for the contingency contractors that comprise the stability operations industry. Starting in 2000, ISOA's founder worked with nongovernmental organizations (NGOs), humanitarian groups, academics, and the association's corporate members to develop the code of conduct. Because the industry lacked sufficient oversight and regulation from states or the international community, the ISOA code has had an outsized impact on the regulation of contingency contractor firms and employees. ISOA's code of conduct has influenced the terms of contracts reached with industry firms, provided a model upon which other trade associations, such as the British Association of Private Security Companies (BAPSC), could shape their own codes, and contributed to the formation of international codes and organizations focused on encouraging more ethical and professional services in stability operations around the world.

Although the ISOA code has academic roots, it is fundamentally an effort at industry self-regulation. The broad diversity of the industry, its relatively small size, limited resources, and the wartime environment in which it developed added complexities that factored into the shape of the ultimate product. Throughout the past 15 years, ISOA has been the primary vehicle for the stability operations industry's self-regulatory efforts.

Self-regulation came into vogue as part of a wave of neoliberal policies adopted by Western nations in the 1980s and 1990s. In self-regulatory regimes, firms within an industry develop a set of standards or a code of conduct and pledge to abide by those standards. Industry self-regulation has enabled firms in many industries to address problems that concern them all, including establishing and enforcing standards of performance, controlling entry to the industry, and mitigating the uncertainty and costs that accompany operating under multiple domestic regulatory regimes. Self-regulation could enable firms to maintain their autonomy with a minimum of governmental regulation and, in theory, engage in collusive behavior vis-à-vis customers and suppliers. It could also provide legitimacy for substandard practices performed by firms that violate agreed-to norms and standards while formally subscribing to them.[8] Academic studies have shown that self-regulation regimes can be effective provided that they include mechanisms for policing violations and imposing sanctions on violators. Private security companies (PSCs)[9] and other stability operations firms have sought the ability to jointly determine the degree to which they regulate their own behavior and they have chosen to do so through industry trade associations.

In this chapter we argue that the creation of ISOA and the adoption of the ISOA Code of Conduct provided an impetus and model for more formal regulation of the stability operations industry. Additionally, we argue that ISOA and the code remain important despite changes to the international regulatory environment for stability operations. We first delve into the theory of industry self-regulation to explore the reasons that companies choose to enter into these regimes and the factors that relate to their effectiveness. We then focus on ISOA itself and its role as an informal regulator of the industry. Next we look at the ISOA code and its evolution. We then level and address some criticisms of the code. We conclude with a discussion of the new international standards set out in the Montreux Document and the International Code of Conduct for Private Security Service Providers, and the role of ISOA and the ISOA code within this more formal regulatory framework.

INDUSTRY SELF-REGULATION

Regulation of commerce has been one of the primary functions of states since the establishment of the Westphalian state system in 1648. States have utilized their position as the ultimate arbiter of social relations to encourage standards for goods and services and enforce contractual relations between private parties to facilitate economic development and efficiency.[10] State regulation increased significantly throughout the twentieth century, ameliorating market failures and managing externalities.[11] In this tradition, "regulation is instituted primarily for the protection and benefit of the public at large or some large subclass of the public."[12] The move toward neoliberal conceptions of the state in the latter part of the twentieth century facilitated legitimation of the idea that firms and industries could regulate themselves to some degree and under certain conditions.[13] Industry self-regulation entails a "regulatory process whereby [an] industry-level . . . organization (such as a trade association or a professional society) sets and enforces rules and standards relating to the conduct of firms in the industry."[14] This institutional mechanism stands apart from, and can complement, state regulatory structures. It also differs from the discipline imposed by the price mechanisms established through competition in the marketplace for different types of goods and services as well as gradations of quality.

Unlike governmental regulation, which relies upon the coercive power of the state to ensure compliance,[15] self-regulation by firms requires cooperation: firms must choose to work with one another to promote and adopt the norms, rules, and practices that go beyond their own individual adaptation to market forces. Cooperation entails the expenditure of resources—time, money, and personnel—as well as the opportunity cost of forgoing the behaviors and practices that would be outside of the common regulatory framework. Therefore, such regulation must promise—and deliver—benefits that outweigh these costs. Furthermore, cooperation may be induced by either enlightened self-interest among the firms of an industry or through their collective recognition of threats to their autonomy arising from external factors, such as the possibility of state regulation or the organization of customers or suppliers.

Indeed, industrial organization theorists such as Michael Porter have argued that firms are likely to cooperate with one another when they can gain a measure of control over the external factors that affect their overall profitability.[16] These factors include barriers to entry, competition from substitute goods and services, the relative power of customers and suppliers, and the rate of market growth. Industry cooperation could, for example, serve to erect barriers to entry for new firms or limit the suitability of substitutes by establishing standards-based licensing controlled by established firms. They could also provide a forum for collusion and cartel-like behavior to limit the level of competition between firms, reduce the ability of customers to negotiate by threatening to take their business to a competitor, and thereby extract higher prices. Finally, cooperation could provide a tool for reputation management in industries where the behaviors of one or more firms affect the perception of them all.[17]

Beyond these opportunities to influence the industry and the marketplace, industry cooperation could also act as a means of affecting the shape of governmental regulation. In domestic markets, states often negotiate the shape of regulatory regimes with those who will bear the onus of the costs. A corporate position among the firms of the industry can only strengthen their hand in these negotiations.[18] Indeed, they can lead to the "capture" of regulatory bodies by the very interests that they are responsible for policing in industries where there is a high degree of cooperation.[19] Similar solidarity can standardize governmental regulation in a transnational marketplace. Firms that conduct business in many countries face an array of regulatory schemes and pay high transactions costs to comply with the vagaries of each. Furthermore, these domestic regimes are subject to change. By establishing effective mechanisms for self-regulation within an industry, firms can discipline, affect, and gain some control over the uncertainty generated by international and domestic regulatory changes.[20] Gaining control over these uncertainties has proven to be an effective inducement for transnational industries to regulate themselves.[21]

Firms may also endure the costs of self-imposed regulatory regimes in the belief that it can help them increase their profitability over the long term.[22]

However, while promised increases in profitability through the collective management of the marketplace could induce firms to regulate themselves, the empirical record indicates that they are more likely to do so in reaction to threats to their existing level of autonomy.[23] Such threats could come from the possibility of regulation imposed by the state and from the organization of other relevant actors.[24] They can also come in the form of "civil regulation" wherein interest groups, NGOs, and other "transnational activists" use their political power and popular opinion to push industries to adopt norms and behaviors in lieu of formal regulation.[25]

Regardless of the impetus, the institutionalized cooperation that is implied by industry self-regulation requires that structures be developed for: (1) the collection of information about the industry and its environment; (2) processing of this information so as to decide the specific content of the regulatory standards that industry would impose on itself; (3) monitoring of firm behavior to check for compliance with these standards; and (4) enforcement of these standards in instances in which firm behavior is at variance. If such information-processing and decision-making mechanisms do not exist, industry self-regulation may not take place despite a rational justification for it.[26]

Industry groups such as trade associations can provide a home for these structures and make their adoption more likely.[27] Their existence is correlated with the degree of cohesion and fragmentation within an industry: greater cohesion enables the basic agreements necessary to establish them, while industry fragmentation implies a heterogeneity of interests that would reduce the chances of agreement.[28]

Once established, the effectiveness of an industry self-regulatory regime can vary significantly, depending upon how it is implemented and enforced. One important variable is the power endowed in the governing body or trade association. Trade associations that are provided with sufficient resources to monitor firm behavior are more likely to be effective than those that are not. "For instance, the standard-setting committees/task forces could be staffed either by full time employees of the industry association or by full time employees of the member firms on part time assignment to these committees/task forces. In the former case, the committee members are likely to view their primary loyalty as being to the industry as a whole rather than to any specific firms. In the latter case, just the opposite would be expected."[29] Furthermore, one could expect that the most powerful firms in the industry would be most able to endow trade associations with the resources and authority necessary to be effective—and therefore the implementation of the regulatory regime would favor their market position. However, such an asymmetry of power cannot be too great, or the implementation of the regime too biased, or else smaller firms and participants will leave the market or decline to cooperate.[30]

Likewise, the ability of a trade association or a governing body to levy sanctions against member firms for violations of the regulatory regime is key to its effectiveness. This is important but difficult to implement—and state regulation may undermine it. "Trade associations are limited as enforcers both legally and practically, since they are ultimately governed by their members. To prevent collusion antitrust legislation forbids certain types of punitive actions on the part of trade associations."[31] Of course it is important to prevent firms from using trade associations to cement their market position or other advantages, but the ability to levy sanctions is important to the functioning of a self-regulatory regime. Andrew King and Michael Lenox found that norms without enforcement are insufficient to counteract opportunism.[32]

Self-regulation that lacks an enforcement mechanism can not only fail, it can undermine the industry itself. Such regimes can "fall[] victim to . . . a disproportionate number of poor performers" and the market positions of "its members do not improve faster than nonmembers."[33] This form of adverse selection can feed upon itself as firms that provide lower quality of service will have a greater incentive to join the regulatory regime to obtain the gloss of legitimacy while endeavoring to minimize their compliance.[34] As the average quality of the service within the regime declines, higher-quality firms will value their participation less and be inclined to leave in order to avoid association with their lower-quality competitors. "Left unchecked, adverse selection will undermine self-regulatory programs as low quality firms join and reduce the differentiation benefits membership may provide."[35]

Finally, the relationship between the industry and its customers can affect the efficacy of a self-regulating regime.[36] David Garvin argues that a self-regulation scheme can be especially effective in "producer goods industries, where expert buyers play an important role."[37] These buyers "are typically better organized than buyers of consumer goods—generally, because fewer are involved—and are often able to exert considerable power. Not surprisingly, these buyers encourage standardization (through self-regulation) in their supplying industries in order to gain more accurate market information."[38] One could expand this thesis beyond just "producer goods" to any industry that is supplying a very specific good or service to a limited and organized customer base. Such customers will be "expert buyers" who are more likely to be cognizant of the standards on which their potential suppliers operate—and more likely motivated and able to enforce them through their contract negotiations and purchasing decisions. These industries will be more focused on counteracting adverse selection by including their customers in the regulatory regime.

Overall, understanding that firms in an industry have many incentives to enter into cooperative self-regulation, the variables that shape its structure and enforcement mechanisms, and the factors that determine their effectiveness is central to understanding why ISOA and the ISOA Code of Conduct were created, how the organization and the code evolved over time, and why they remain an important means for controlling private military and security firms. In the following sections, we will describe the organization and the code, their evolution, and why a dearth of appropriate international and domestic regulations, and especially enforcement, made the organization and the code vital components during the establishment of more permanent regulation in the PSC industry. Furthermore, an understanding of the limitations of self-regulatory regimes helps structure and understand criticisms of the code as well as why it remains important today despite the creation of new international standards and bodies.

ISOA: THE TRADE ASSOCIATION BEHIND THE SELF-REGULATION

The International Peace Operations Association (IPOA)—which later became the International Stability Operations Association (ISOA)—was founded in 2001. The ISOA Code of Conduct, however, dates back to late 2000 and the international peacekeeping operation in Sierra Leone where private contractors provided robust and extensive support for United Nations (UN) efforts. In 2000 Doug Brooks, the eventual founder of IPOA, made two visits to Sierra Leone and interviewed scores of people from a diversity of backgrounds—journalists, United Nations Mission in Sierra Leone (UNAMSIL) forces, nongovernmental organizations, human rights organizations, the Sierra Leonean government, trade unions, various embassies, refugees, Sierra Leonean and British soldiers, and private stability operations contractors. At the time, Sierra Leone hosted the largest peacekeeping operation in the world, with more than 17,000 UN troops, police, and staff in a country of less than four million people. Despite these numbers, the UN mission was unable to supply adequate security for the population.

It was during Mr. Brooks' second visit to Sierra Leone that he organized a two-day meeting with a group of NGOs, lawyers, and humanitarian organizations that codified some basic principles on how the private sector could be ethically utilized, how their participation could be made more transparent, and how—and to whom—firms engaged in these sorts of humanitarian operations could be held accountable. At the conclusion of his research fellowship Mr. Brooks returned to Washington, DC, where he circulated a version of the principles among a broad network of academics, human rights specialists, and policymakers. They made many suggestions and improvements and the result was a greatly enhanced document.

A number of experts, academics, and analysts suggested to Mr. Brooks that an NGO should be created to advocate for the idea that contractors could

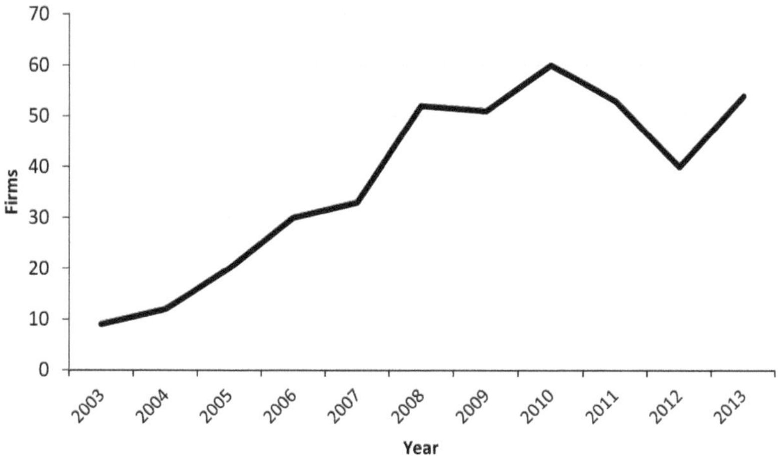

Figure 9.1. Approximate Number of IPOA/ISOA Member Firms

play a much larger role in enhancing the success of international peacekeeping and stability missions. Ultimately the NGO idea evolved into a trade association. The decision to move toward a trade association was necessary from a funding perspective and also allowed the organization to legally lobby policymakers. IPOA filed the necessary paperwork and became a 501(c)(6) association in April of 2001 with modest support from six companies with operations in Africa.[39] This early financial support was key to implementing the code of conduct drafted during the round-table exercises and these first companies served as the cornerstone of the self-regulation scheme established by IPOA. This support also allowed Mr. Brooks to begin hiring outside employees to staff this new trade association.

The momentous events of September 11, 2001, led those same companies that had first supported the new association to quickly become involved in supporting international operations in Afghanistan and, later, Iraq. They brought their subcontractors and competitors into ISOA over the next few years and the membership grew quickly (see figure 9.1). All firms were required to abide by and support the code of conduct from the beginning, and over the years the membership joined with NGO and academic partners to update and improve the document, which continues as a cornerstone of ISOA to this day.

ISOA's stated mission is to "promote high operational and ethical standards of firms active in the Peace and Stability Industry."[40] ISOA also seeks to engage with policymakers about the ever-growing value of the industry and educate the public about the private sector's role in conflict and post-conflict situations. ISOA predominantly consists of companies providing services in the field. Its membership is diverse, and includes firms at all levels of engagement. Affiliates are employed in operations ranging from base support and training to humanitarian development, security, and the removal of unexploded ordnance and landmines.

The association itself has maintained a limited independent staff throughout its existence. For years, the primary staff members were Mr. Brooks and several administrative employees who provided assistance during the public events and conferences that ISOA sponsored, helped with membership issues, coordinated committee meetings, and ran the many publications, such as the *Journal of International Peace Operations*. Volunteer personnel from member companies staffed the various committees: Membership, Government and Legal Affairs, Standards, and others. Committee membership could be time-consuming, but companies generally accepted the burden as a necessary part of responsible corporate behavior. This limited staff was partially a consequence of the funding sources that ISOA had at its disposal. These sources included publication and advertisement income, fees for an annual conference, and, most significantly, the annual dues of member firms.[41] ISOA's total revenue remained small, ranging from $110,000 in 2004 to nearly $900,000 in 2012.[42] Funding was primarily devoted to staffing, publications, and events sponsored by ISOA. ISOA's staff was never large, with no more than three full-time employees—president, director, and business development—and the association relied heavily on four to six talented interns to do much of the work. ISOA's relatively limited resources conditioned the manner in which it pursued its role as the focal point for industry self-regulation.

THE CODE: ASPIRATIONAL NORMS AND A WEAK SELF-REGULATORY FRAMEWORK

Perhaps ISOA's role providing aspirational guidance for member firms and inspiration for more formal forms of regulation from entities outside of the industry was more valuable in the long run. However, as a mechanism of industry self-regulation, the ISOA Code of Conduct faced substantial hurdles, including the heterogeneity of firms in the industry, the resources made available to ISOA to monitor compliance and investigate violations, and the ability of ISOA to enforce its code. But perhaps the most fundamental hurdle, the one that made the creation of a trade association–based code of conduct necessary, was the international and domestic legal landscape that surrounded the stability operations industry at the turn of the century.

The ISOA Code of Conduct filled an apparent void in the regulation of the blossoming contingency contracting industry. The most established piece of international law that governs conflict situations is the Geneva Conventions. The original convention classified "persons who accompany the armed forces without actually being members thereof, such as civilian members of military aircraft crews, war correspondents, supply contractors, members of labour units or of services responsible for the welfare of the armed forces, provided that they have received authorization from the armed forces which they accompany" in international conflicts (i.e., state on state) as civilian noncombatants but also granted them protections similar to those of members of the armed forces if they were captured by an opposing force.[43] But it technically did not apply to non-international conflicts or post-conflict situations.[44] The follow-on additional protocol addressed armed civilian combatants—mercenaries—in conflict. Article 47(2) of Protocol I Additional to the Geneva Conventions provides one of the more authoritative definitions of mercenaries in international humanitarian law. It states that an individual is a mercenary if he or she:

a. is specially recruited locally or abroad in order to fight in an armed conflict;
b. does, in fact, take a direct part in hostilities;
c. is motivated to take part in the hostilities essentially by the desire for private gain and, in fact is promised, by or on behalf of a Party to the conflict, material compensation substantially in excess of that promised or paid to combatants of similar ranks and functions in the armed forces of that Party;
d. is neither a national of a Party to the conflict nor a resident of territory controlled by a Party to the conflict;
e. is not a member of the armed forces of a Party to the conflict; and
f. has not been sent by a state which is not a Party to the conflict on official duty as a member of its armed forces.[45]

This definition requires that all facets be fulfilled in order for the mercenary label to apply and is therefore so restrictive as to be inapplicable to all but a very few persons. Furthermore, its narrow scope fails to address other private actors in the conflict zone.

The International Convention against the Recruitment, Use, Financing and Training of Mercenaries of 1989 was approved by the UN General Assembly but did not take effect until 20 October 2001.[46] It likewise adopts a very narrow definition of the people whose behavior it seeks to regulate, leaving out the vast majority of contractors, although it does prohibit state signatories from recruiting, training, or financing mercenaries.[47]

On a regional level, the 1977 Organization of African Unity's[48] Convention for the Elimination of Mercenarism in Africa entered into force in 1985.[49] To date 30 members of the African Union have ratified the convention. However, despite the fact that the convention's intent was to eliminate the continued threat of mercenaries to African nations, it permits African states to hire non-nationals to perform security functions and fails to regulate the behavior of other types of contractors.

At the turn of the twenty-first century, the Geneva Convention and the African Union Convention were the primary instruments of international law that were related to the regulation of the use of stability operations contractors in conflict zones.[50] They failed to cover the wide array of actors and functions that were being permitted by state actors—indeed, encouraged—and thus some have argued that these formal laws created confusion and in some ways were more of a hindrance than a help to the proper regulation of the industry.[51] It was not until 2008 and 2009 that many of these issues were addressed, but certainly not resolved, by the Montreux Document and the Interpretive Guidance of the International Committee of the Red Cross, which provided more nuanced interpretations of these issues based upon the functions performed by civilians accompanying the armed forces.[52]

The domestic legal environment for stability operations was equally underdeveloped at the turn of the century. Consider the cases of three leading states: South Africa, the United States, and the United Kingdom. As argued in chapter 2 of this volume, South Africa only had a prohibition on members of the South African military from engaging in "mercenary" activity under the Defence Act of 1957. The government led by the African National Congress extended this prohibition to all South African civilians and entities, except by explicit approval, under the Foreign Military Assistance Act of 1998 (FMA). Additionally, the government attempted to extend this regulation to all forms of organized conflict behavior by South African civilians under a proposed 2010 amendment to the South African Citizenship Act of 1995. These efforts were oriented more toward prohibiting mercenary activity than regulating the behavior of the wider variety of actors conducting stability operations activities that were active in Africa throughout the 1990s and early 2000s.

In the United States, the Uniform Code of Military Justice (UCMJ) and the Military Extraterritorial Jurisdiction Act (MEJA) were the primary sets of law regulating the behavior of PSCs. Each required some amendment before it could be applied to all contractors. The MEJA, which was adopted in 2000, was originally applicable only to contractors working for the US Department of Defense.[53] After the scope of the requirement for private contactors in Iraq became apparent to US policymakers, MEJA was expanded in 2007, with the support of ISOA, to allow American authorities to prosecute all contractors working in support of DoD missions.[54] More specifically, the extension included "persons employed by or accompanying the armed forces" in conflict zones, excluding only local nationals. Under MEJA, the US government could now prosecute private contractors in its employ for breaches of international criminal law, filling the jurisdictional void left by international criminal legislation, and thereby extending many of the criminal laws of the United States to foreign jurisdictions. But even with this additional attention and focus, it proved difficult to enforce—as the eight years between the events of Nisour Square and the conviction of four armed security personnel working for Blackwater attests.[55]

Finally, as argued in chapter 7, British policymakers slowly came to realize the shift in the nature of these private actors and the need to regulate them between Sandline International's involvement in the "Arms to Africa Affair" of 1998 and the release of the Green Paper in 2002.[56] Despite this, the British government failed to adopt formal regulations and ultimately chose an approach based upon industry self-regulation—as detailed in chapter 8 in this volume.

AN EXEMPLAR

Given the nebulous nature of the international and domestic legal landscape that faced the industry in the early 2000s, ISOA developed and implemented the code of conduct as a means of elevating ethical and professional standards critical to effective international peacekeeping, stability operations, and disaster relief. The code was designed to have a normative impact on the industry. The idea was that ethical behavior by industry firms and employees would increase the value of the services performed on behalf of clients, benefit international missions, and stimulate new business and greater industry growth as the international community gained confidence in the proficiency and professionalism of the firms that were members of ISOA.

As the stability operations industry continued to grow in the number of firms and range of services offered, the nature of the conflicts in which they were engaged changed and the domestic and international regulatory environment in which they operated developed further. Because of these changes the needs of—and expectations for—private firms transformed. Contingency contractors were providing a variety of different services to clients during this period, including logistical services, equipment provision, remote site medical facilities management, expeditionary support, and armed security services. The balance of tasks performed by the industry shifted in response to the demands of their clients. The wide variety of services provided created potential conflicting interests for the association's member firms, thus it was in the best interest of the association to develop a code that would encompass norms that all firms could abide by.

The ambition of the ISOA code was to provide members with an ethical framework with which to facilitate their services in conflict and post-conflict zones and recognition for operating with higher ethical and professional standards. It was hoped that this would improve their standing with both current and potential clients, and thus increase their future business opportunities. In particular, the code outlines the responsibilities of member companies in the fields of human rights, ethics, arms, personnel safety, workplace regulations relating to clients, employees and subcontractors, and rules for the use of force, control, transparency, and accountability, as well as enforcement of the code. Signatories are also obliged to observe applicable international humanitarian and human rights laws, protocols, and conventions. The documents specifically referenced in the preamble today include the Universal Declaration of Human Rights, the Geneva Convention and its Additional Protocol, the Montreux Document on Private Military and Security Companies, and the International Code of Conduct for Private Security Service Providers.[57]

The code also evolved with the constantly changing industry and external contexts in order to retain its relevance. Today, the ISOA code is in its 13th iteration.[58] Each revised version included improvements and clarifications coming from many different sources. A variety of stakeholders, such as transnational humanitarian organizations, government representatives, and academics, participated in a structured process to revise the code. Such a process was intended to enhance legitimacy and confidence in the result.

MONITORING AND ENFORCING NORMS

ISOA focused a good deal of its energy on ensuring that its code of conduct remained relevant and accepted by its members, their clients, and other stakeholders. But could ISOA enforce it? As discussed above, ISOA faced significant hurdles as the industry's regulatory body. ISOA simply did not have enough financial or human resources to systematically monitor the thousands of projects that member and nonmember firms were participating in around the world. Instead ISOA relied on outside organizations and individuals to monitor the firms operating in these austere environments and act as "fire alarms" if they observed violations of the code.[59] As stated on the ISOA website: "The ISOA Enforcement Mechanism allows any person or organization to lodge a complaint against an ISOA member company or organization for violations of the ISOA Code of Conduct."[60] Through a simple web form at the end of the web page ISOA allows easy access for concerned individuals or organizations to lodge a complaint based on an observed violation of the ISOA code by a member company. Because ISOA did not have the ability to be a monitoring or an investigatory body, the burden of proof rested with the complainant. ISOA did reassure the complainant that his or her complaint was being funneled to an independent member of the trade association for review and action, rather than an employee of a member firm. The website states: "Your complaint will be directed to the Chief Liaison Officer of the Standards Committee, who is an employee of ISOA and is not affiliated with any company."[61]

Once gathered, the body of evidence compiled by the complainant would be evaluated by the volunteers of the Standards Committee. The peer-review nature of the process ensured that judgments were rendered on ethical, rather than legal, grounds. Thus the members of the Standards Committee were free to interpret the letter of the code so as to enforce its spirit when rendering judgments. Because these judgments rested on a shared understanding of the intent and spirit of the code, ISOA utilized annual simulations based on possible complainant scenarios to keep knowledge of the code high for the standards enforcement committee. These simulations also sought to keep the code up-to-date. The simulations allow a varied selection of stakeholders to engage productively with one another and they specifically included representatives from humanitarian organizations, academic institutions, and governments. Representatives from vastly divergent fields had the opportunity to work together in a cooperative, noncompetitive setting to foster an appreciation for one another's concerns and requirements. Overall, the standards simulation promoted a cross-disciplinary exchange of practices and knowledge, helped socialize the norms and values of the industry to its members and other stakeholders, and resulted in not only a better standards enforcement mechanism, but also a more comprehensive and effective code.[62]

The Standards Compliance and Oversight Procedure (SCOPe) became a means of standards enforcement.[63] It was codified in Article 14, section 2 of the code in September 2009. Once a transgression had been reported by a third party and the Standards Committee evaluated the complaint, it could choose to impose requirements for change on the violator. In its first decade of operation ISOA received numerous complaints against member firms from outside organizations that served as informal monitors for ISOA and the code. For the most part these complaints fell into four areas: (1) Performance or Contractual; (2) Criminal; (3) Labor; and (4) Ethical. Despite receiving a large number of complaints, ISOA recognized that there were more appropriate venues for recourse when it came to performance/contractual, criminal, and labor disputes—and that a trade association has little standing in such issues. Especially during cases of criminal misconduct, ISOA's policy was to stand aside and ensure cooperation and/or noninterference with relevant legal and enforcement authorities. ISOA's Standards Committee did reserve the right to address a complaint on an ethical level after legal processes had run their course. It is important to note that all complaints made to and investigations by ISOA were kept confidential unless information on the investigation was released by the member firm or the original complainant. Between 2004 and 2013, ISOA chose to process approximately 20 complaints using the SCOPe, and the vast majority of these were regarding ethical issues.[64]

Article 14 section 2 of the code outlined the sanctions available to ISOA for member firms who violated its terms. The primary goal of the compliance procedure is to modify behavior that caused the violation in the first place and therefore enforcement was geared toward stipulating the steps that a member firm must take to return to compliance with the code. The most serious sanction that can be imposed is expulsion from ISOA, but the goal was to improve the industry, not to banish the bad actors. Member firms under investigation by either ISOA or an outside body could suspend their membership in ISOA, thus mooting the SCOPe's ability to enforce the code but essentially having the same effect as expulsion. For example, "when Blackwater USA was under investigation by what was then the IPOA following the September 2007 Nisour Square incident, Blackwater simply announced that it was putting its IPOA membership on hold."[65] While some observers implied that Blackwater escaped punishment by leaving the association, in fact the decision may also be seen as one part of the backlash that led to the firm's decline and ultimate sale, and there were many within the company who later privately expressed their dismay at learning of the departure from IPOA. With Blackwater outside of the trade association IPOA had no further influence on the firm's behavior, although its clients could and did.[66]

AN EFFECTIVE SELF-REGULATION REGIME?

Given ISOA's fairly limited monitoring, investigative, and enforcement capabilities, we would expect the code to be a weak instrument of self-regulation for the industry. The industry self-regulation literature clearly points to the pitfalls of a trade association that lacks a dedicated staff to monitor and enforce its code of conduct. ISOA mitigated this weakness within the constraints of limited resources by decentralizing the monitoring effort to concerned individuals and organizations, and made it easier for these actors to file a compliant against a member firm. Furthermore, it ensured that the chief liaison officer of the Standards Committee was an employee of the trade association itself and not a volunteer from a member company. Despite the limits, these monitoring mechanisms did capture many breaches of the code of conduct and served to socialize expectations and norms throughout the industry.

Furthermore, ISOA strengthened its ability to establish and enforce industry norms through the involvement of knowledgeable customers of the services provided by the industry. While ISOA itself lacked sufficient ability to enforce norms of conduct on firms in and outside of the association, it could act as a fire alarm for the industry's customers as well as governmental entities that could enforce legal sanctions. Indeed, ISOA's practice of informing complainants of more appropriate bodies to whom they could direct their concerns was but one way that it leveraged knowledgeable and powerful customers to enforce industry norms.

For instance, the Afghan government in 2003 followed the recommendation of the United Nations and mandated that all private security companies abide by the ISOA Code of Conduct as a condition of licensure. The requirement demonstrated appreciation for the code as a benchmark of best practices globally. While security firms were not required to be members of ISOA in order to be eligible for operations—which limited ISOA's ability to promote compliance—the requirement created a business opportunity for firms that could demonstrate that they abided by the code.

Finally, did the inability of ISOA to effectively sanction violators prove counterproductive to the industry as a whole? Did poorly performing firms take advantage of the prestige and legitimacy that signing up for the code provided without intending to abide by its provisions? The ISOA policy was to be as inclusive as possible with new members with the goal of ensuring industry-wide agreement on standards. It is quite difficult to determine if ISOA suffered from the adverse selection problem given the constantly changing industry environment, the addition and subtraction of many firms over the years of ISOA's existence, and the size and complexity of some member firms. What can be determined is that ISOA mitigated the problems of adverse selection through its vetting process for new member firms. The primary reason that firms were rejected for membership during this process was a lack of transparency about their business activities and ownership. Despite this, some ISOA member firms, like all large contractors even in peacetime environments, were fined by the United States government over this period for a variety of issues,[67] but this should not lead one to believe that these were inherently poorly performing firms or firms that desired a shield for their activities. While ISOA may have experienced some minor adverse selection issues, they were not debilitating to the functioning of the organization or the code.

A more significant criticism falls on the industry resourcing of the association. IPOA, and later ISOA, was positioned to serve as an independent monitor and enforcer of the code following the introduction of the standards enforcement mechanism. However, ISOA is an association within a small industry and never had the financial or human resources to properly staff a robust monitoring, compliance, and enforcement network. Instead the Standards Committee had to rely on a variety of disparate external monitors and only had a limited ability to analyze the information submitted when the association was notified of a potential violation. The expense of such a monitoring network involving trained and experienced personnel deploying to areas of conflict would cost many times ISOA's entire budget. Industry self-regulation theorists would likely argue that, through this lack of funding, the member firms deliberately kept ISOA weak and prevented it from developing into an independent organization with the ability to effectively monitor and enforce. While keeping this potential criticism in mind, there is no evidence that the industry members purposefully kept the association from becoming more independent or more powerful. On the contrary, ISOA member firms were remarkably supportive of the ICoC developments that subsequently addressed this issue.

Despite steps taken to strengthen ISOA and its code, fundamentally they do present an example of what economists would categorize as weak industry self-regulation. The stability operations industry was and is very heterogeneous: composed of a large and ever-changing number of firms performing a wide variety of services and functions for a diverse set of clients across the world. Therefore, it has proved difficult to reach a critical mass of firms willing to cooperate to reach a consensus around a regulatory regime to advance all of their interests. It was also difficult to endow ISOA with sufficient resources to permit it to effectively monitor firm performance, investigate transgressions, and enforce involuntary sanctions against violators. Indeed, the panoply of sanctions available to ISOA were quite limited and some have judged the reputational effects of expulsion or voluntary withdrawal after a key incident to be small—at least in the case of firms as large and influential as Blackwater. ISOA's inclusive membership policies benefited industry self-regulation, but may have meant some firms dropped out rather than comply with the standards their peers had developed. Overall, while ISOA and its code would be considered a fundamentally weak form of industry self-regulation by some analysts, they were effective in their own way. They were taken seriously by member companies who contributed to their development and promptly addressed allegations in complaints, and ultimately they demonstrated the industry's recognition of the value of an internationally recognized code of conduct. The ISOA code also inspired more powerful international actors to start working on the problem of regulating the stability operations industry with a special focus on private military and security contractors. Finally, firms in the industry demonstrated a high degree of willingness to enact such institutions to ensure effectiveness and legitimacy, which perhaps reflected their years of association with ISOA and the success of its educational and socialization processes.

NEW INTERNATIONAL STANDARDS AND THE CONTINUED RELEVANCE OF THE ISOA CODE

The stability operations industry had recognized that external regulation could serve an important sorting function, requiring a level of professionalism that would squeeze out the "bottom feeders"—companies unable or unwilling to ensure compliance. The code established by ISOA was an overt attempt by members of the industry to achieve tighter regulation and more ethical practice within the industry through external supervision. However, the code is a non-punitive measure that applies only to affiliate firms. Thus enhanced regulation, with realistic means of enforcement, was the logical next step.

Therefore, in its role as an advocate for improved oversight and regulation, ISOA played a central part in the establishment of the Montreux Document on Private Military and Security Companies by way of the Swiss Initiative,[68] the follow-on International Code of Conduct (ICoC),[69] and the International Code of Conduct Association (ICoCA), which governs the ICoC. Much of the ICoC is based on what the ISOA was able to accomplish with its code. Additionally, ISOA was instrumental as both a partner and a model for the establishment of the ICoCA. Like the ISOA Code of Conduct before them, the Montreux Document, the ICoC, and the ICoCA benefit the private sector by improving the quality and required standards for participation. The ability of firms to meet international expectations and adhere to law is greater when these are clearly articulated, while more effective enforcement makes it difficult for marginal, low-end companies to compete.

While the establishment of these new international standards has been a huge step forward for the industry, an important role remains for ISOA and the ISOA Code of Conduct. First, and most important, the Montreux Document, the ICoC, and the ICoCA are specifically focused on firms that provide security services (PSCs). As explained above, the stability operations industry is quite diverse. The new International Code of Conduct for Private Security Service Providers is groundbreaking but it does not apply directly to the rest of the stability operations industry. While the PSCs represent the relatively small segment of the larger industry (5–20 percent) that human rights analysts, lawyers, and governments are most concerned with, maintaining industry-wide representation and standards continues to have significant value. Other members of the community need the guidelines set out in the code and potential clients of these non-PSCs still require some method to differentiate bad actors and to ensure that they are getting a best-of-breed company.

Second, while the new international standards have much stronger institutional mechanisms to monitor and punish bad actors, it remains important for companies to self-regulate and peer-regulate. Keeping the code and the trade association active allows ISOA's members to address problems proactively within the industry and work with members in violation of the code to ensure that they are on a path to addressing the issues that caused the problems with their operations in the first place. Neil Gunningham and Joseph Rees highlight the significant amount of positive pressure put on organizations that sign up for self-regulatory regimes.[70] The positive pressure of the code on ISOA members creates an environment where members are encouraged to abide by the code or risk the consequences not only from any new international standards body that may cover their small part of the stability operations industry, but also from other trade association members and the ISOA itself. Together, self-regulation and formal regulation can be remarkably effective.

Thus we see ISOA and its code continuing to play an important part in helping to govern the actions of stability operations contractors. The introduction of new international standards and an association that can actively govern, monitor, and enforce sanctions provides ISOA's self-regulation regime with the outside group that industry self-regulation theorists say is needed to be successful. It behooves ISOA to continue to work closely with the ICoCA to ensure that both organizations are in harmony on issues relating to stability operations contractors as a whole and not just private military and security contractors. ISOA should also ensure that it continues to work with governments, NGOs, humanitarian interest groups, and others to guarantee the code remains relevant and valuable to companies and clients alike. Keeping the ISOA Code of Conduct up-to-date and in force for its members and the larger stability operations industry is a leadership role that the trade association should embrace.

CONCLUSION

The coincidence of the end of the Cold War, an increase in the demand for organized forces that could provide security and stability to societies that lacked sufficient capabilities to secure themselves, and the decrease in the willingness of more advanced and capable states to deploy their own personnel to deal with these humanitarian crises produced conditions conducive to the emergence of private sector firms that could and would meet these needs. The growth in the stability operations industry throughout the past 25 years and its utilization by states, international organizations, and NGOs indicated the mutual development of a market for these services. That growth did not prove to be unproblematic, as providers and consumers of these services attempted to meet their own needs and objectives within a set of norms, regulations, and laws that had been developed prior to the formation of this market. These new agents required a means of establishing norms and standards of performance that would be consonant with the demands made upon them by their potential principals and the structures within which even they would be held accountable.

ISOA was founded in the middle of this upsurge in the establishment of firms and interest in the industry. The association was created with the specific goal of advancing the standards of the stability operations industry so that the private sector could become more accepted, provide better services, and therefore improve the success of international peace and stability operations. IPOA, and later ISOA, strived to ensure sound and ethical professionalism and transparency in the conduct of contingency contractors through the establishment of its code of conduct. ISOA recognized that there was a large hole in the regulation of the stability operations industry and saw the opportunity to establish an industry self-regulation regime based on the lessons learned from the involvement of contingency contractors during the 1990s and early 2000s. The resulting regime was cemented in the ISOA Code of Conduct. In order to make the code as useful as possible, ISOA ensured that there was a transparent multi-stakeholder process during the evolution of the document. It actively reached out not only to the industry, but also to policymakers, clients, NGOs, scholars, and the public to create a more effective industry self-regulation regime.

The code was generally successful in mitigating many of the concerns expressed by industry self-regulation theorists. Through iterations, the code developed corrective guidelines for violators and successfully ran a relatively independent standards enforcement mechanism that was able to modify firm behavior when necessary. ISOA did encounter difficulty mitigating the problem of adverse selection, although there is little empirical evidence that this caused difficulties in the practice of revising the code or the performance of the Standards Compliance and Oversight Procedure. While there were some firms that were helped back into compliance by ISOA or reprimanded by a government authority for various infractions, for the most part these were not systemic cases that would indicate that these firms were inherently poor performers. Furthermore, the self-regulation regime did suffer from a lack of financial and human resources. Without a more substantial investment by member firms, or perhaps a significantly larger industry, ISOA was never in a position to become the independent monitoring and enforcement organization that many outside observers were demanding.

The ISOA Code certainly had a significant level of success, yet there remained a need and a desire for a more established regulatory system that was independent of the industry but inclusive enough to embrace industry, governments, NGOs, and other stakeholders. As an inspiration and model for the further development of means of regulation for the industry, the ISOA code excelled. With the leadership of select governments, NGOs, contingency contractors, and, importantly, ISOA, a new international standard setting and enforcement system was created. The resulting system, established with the Montreux Document, the ICoC, and the ICoCA, has helped to fill the regulatory hole left by the unsystematic patchwork of international and domestic laws as well as the structural limitations of the ISOA code. Necessarily, these new standard setting and enforcement bodies do not represent the entire stability operations industry, thus we continue to see a need for ISOA to remain active in standard setting and for its code to remain up-to-date. Finally, ISOA needs to ensure that its code and the standards that it continues to set are in harmony with those established by the new standard setting bodies. These are roles that ISOA should embrace moving forward.

APPENDIX 1: THE ISOA CODE OF CONDUCT, VERSION 1, ADOPTED 1 APRIL 2001

ISOA members providing military services undertake their profession with a deep sense of responsibility. They are well aware of the immense potential of their services and strive to ensure their capabilities are not misused. The members believe that private firms are ultimately more accountable, transparent and candid about their motivations than similar military organizations operated by states. The companies strongly believe that relevant restrictions and controls are appropriate in the provision of these services in order that they be utilized for the greatest benefit of humanity.

Members of ISOA are pledged to the following principles in all their operations:

Human Rights

In all their operations, signatories will strictly adhere to all relevant international laws and protocols in regards to human rights. They will take every practicable measure to minimize loss of life. Signatories who are engaged in combat will follow all relevant international laws and protocols in the propagation of that conflict, and will seek a swift and beneficial conclusion.

Transparency

Signatories engaged in peace operations pledge to be open and forthcoming in terms of the nature of their operations and in terms of the corporate ties and connections that might in any way be perceived as influencing their current or potential operations. Signatories support the use of trained independent observers and neutral oversight of all their operations.

Accountability

Signatories support effective legal and financial accountability for their actions and the actions of company employees. Signatories pledge to support official investigations into allegations of contractual or human rights violations.

Clients

Signatories pledge to work only for legitimate governments, international organizations, and non-governmental organizations. Signatories will refuse to engage clients that are actively thwarting international efforts towards peace.

Control

In undertaking peace operations, signatories pledge to adhere to the control of their client, to modify contractual obligations when appropriate, and to speedily withdraw from a conflict if so requested.

Ethics

Signatories pledge to go beyond the minimum legal requirements, and support additional ethical imperatives that are essential for effective peace operations.

Rules of Engagement

Signatories that may become involved in combat situations will have appropriate "Rules of Engagement" negotiated with their clients before deployment, and will work with their client to do any necessary modifications. All rules should emphasize restraint and caution to minimize casualties and damage.

Civil Society and Reconstruction

Signatories recognize that the services they provide are necessary for ending conflicts but not sufficient in themselves. Therefore, signatories pledge to work closely with groups and organizations specializing in reconciliation and reconstruction to bring conflicts to a permanent and just end.

Support of International Organizations and NGOs

Signatories pledge to support the work of other international organizations and non-governmental organizations working to mitigate or end conflicts.

Increasingly chaotic conflicts have made such work increasingly difficult and hazardous. Where feasible, signatories will offer necessary security, aid, and even rescue and evacuation if required.

Arms Control

While signatories may be required to use military weapons for their activities, these weapons will only be obtained legally via regular international protocols. Signatories using weapons pledge to put the highest emphasis on removing all weapons and ammunition introduced by the members into an operation. Signatories pledge to work closely with legitimate international authorities in post-conflict disarmament and micro-disarmament operations removing small arms and landmines that have aggravated and helped to perpetuate conflicts. Signatories refuse to utilize illegal weapons, landmines, toxic chemicals or weapons that could create long-term health problems or complicate post-conflict cleanup.

Confidentiality

While signatories may have confidential contracts unrelated to international peace operations, they pledge to ensure that these contracts do not compromise their ethics. If appropriate, neutral, independent observers may be utilized to confirm that no conflict of interest issues exist.

Quality

Signatories pledge to utilize fully trained and prepared international personnel in all their operations. Local personnel will be vetted, properly trained and supervised.

APPENDIX 2: THE ISOA CODE OF CONDUCT, VERSION 13, ADOPTED 20 OCTOBER 2011

Preamble: Purpose

This Code of Conduct seeks to establish consistent ethical standards for members of International Stability Operations Association operating in complex environments so that they may contribute their valuable services for the benefit of international peace and human security.

Additionally, Signatories will be guided by all pertinent rules of international humanitarian and human rights laws including as set forth in:

Universal Declaration of Human Rights (1948)
Geneva Conventions (1949)

Convention Against Torture (1975)
Protocols Additional to the Geneva Conventions (1977)
Foreign Corrupt Practices Act (1977)
Chemical Weapons Convention (1993)
Voluntary Principles on Security and Human Rights (2000)
Montreux Document on Private Military and Security Companies (2008)
International Code of Conduct for Private Security Providers (2010)
UK Bribery Act (2010)

Signatories are pledged to the following principles in all of their operations:

1. Human Rights, Property and the Environment

1.1. Signatories shall respect the dignity of all human beings and adhere to all applicable international humanitarian and human rights laws.

1.2. Signatories shall take appropriate measures to minimize loss of life and destruction of property and cultural elements, and harm to the environment.

2. Transparency

2.1. Signatories shall operate with integrity, honesty and fairness.

2.2. Signatories shall, to the extent possible and subject to contractual and legal limitations, be open and forthcoming on the nature of their operations and any conflicts of interest that might reasonably be perceived as influencing their current or potential ventures.

2.3. Nothing contained in this Code of Conduct shall require Signatories to disclose information in violation of: applicable law; contractually required confidentiality; or any legally recognized privilege.

3. Accountability

3.1. Signatories, understanding the unique nature of the complex environments in which many of their operations take place, fully recognize the importance of clear and operative lines of accountability to ensure effective peace and stability operations and to the long-term viability of the industry.

3.2. Signatories shall support effective legal accountability to relevant authorities for their actions and the actions of their personnel. Signatories shall proactively address infractions, and to the extent possible and subject to contractual and legal limitations, cooperate with official investigations into allegations of contractual violations and breaches of international humanitarian and human rights laws.

3.3. Signatories shall take legally appropriate action if their personnel engage in unlawful activities. For serious infractions signatories should report such offences to the relevant authorities.

4. Clients

4.1. Signatories shall only work for legitimate, recognized governments, international organizations, non-governmental organizations and lawful private companies.

5. Safety

5.1. Signatories, recognizing the often high level of risk inherent to operations in complex environments, shall strive to operate in a safe, responsible, conscientious and prudent manner and shall make their best efforts to ensure that their personnel adhere to these principles.

6. Personnel

6.1. Personnel: Rights

6.1.1. Signatories shall act responsibly and ethically toward their personnel and provide instruction on applicable legal framework(s) and guidelines on ethical conduct.

6.1.2. Signatories shall ensure that personnel are fully informed of risk associated with their employment, as well as terms, conditions and significance of their contracts in accordance with clearly defined company standards.

6.1.3. Payment of different wages to various nationalities shall be based on merit and national economic differential, and shall not be based on racial, gender or ethnic grounds.

6.1.4. Signatories shall not retain the personal travel documents of their personnel against their will.

6.1.5. Signatories shall always respect the right of personnel to terminate their employment.

6.2. Personnel: Resourcing

6.2.1. Signatories shall conduct all reasonable due diligence when vetting personnel to be fit, medically and psychologically, to perform their duties according to the terms of their contract.

6.2.2. Signatories shall, where appropriate, seek personnel that are broadly representative of the local population, while respecting the age-minimum standard of 15 years of age as defined by the International Labor Organization Minimum Age Convention (1973) for hiring. In the hiring of armed security personnel, Signatories shall respect the age-minimum standard of 18 years of age as defined by the Optional Protocol to the United Nations Convention on the Rights of the Child on the Involvement of Children in Armed Conflict (1989).

6.3. Signatories shall provide their personnel with requisite equipment and materials along with proper supervision and training to compel them to conduct themselves humanely with honesty, integrity, objectivity and diligence and to not violate international humanitarian and human rights laws.

6.4. Signatories shall speedily and professionally comply with lawful requests from the client for cancellation of a contract and for safe extraction of deployed personnel.

6.5. Signatories shall not engage or allow their personnel to engage in the act of trafficking in persons.

6.6. Signatories shall not engage in sexual exploitation or abuse.

7. Insurance

7.1. Foreign and local personnel shall be provided with health and life insurance policies appropriate to their wage structure and the level of risk of their service as required by law.

8. Control

8.1. Signatories shall endorse the use of detailed contracts specifying the mandate, restrictions, goals, benchmarks, criteria for withdrawal and accountability for the operation.

8.2. Operations shall be predicated on missions mandated by a legitimate authority in accordance with international law.

9. Ethics

9.1. Signatories shall be responsible for establishing a corporate culture that promotes awareness of and adherence by all personnel to the principles of this code.

10. Support of International Organizations, Non-Governmental Organizations and Civil Society

10.1. Signatories recognize that the services relief organizations provide are necessary for ending conflicts and alleviation of associated human suffering.

10.2. Signatories shall, to the extent possible and subject to contractual and legal limitations, support the efforts of international organizations, humanitarian and non-governmental organizations and other entities working to minimize human suffering and support reconstructive and reconciliatory goals of peace and stability operations.

11. Rules for the Use of Force

11.1. Signatories that could potentially become involved in armed hostilities shall have appropriate Rules for the Use of Force established with their clients before deployment, and shall work with their clients to make any necessary modifications should threat levels or the political situation merit change.

11.2. All Rules for the Use of Force shall be in compliance with international humanitarian and human rights laws and emphasize appropriate restraint and caution to minimize casualties and damage, while preserving a person's inherent right of self-defense.

12. Weapons Accountability

12.1. Signatories using weapons shall emphasize on accounting for and controlling all weapons and ammunition utilized during an operation and for ensuring their legal and proper accounting and disposal at the end of a contract.

12.2. Signatories shall refuse to utilize illegal weapons, toxic chemicals or weapons that could create long-term health problems or complicate post-conflict cleanup and will limit themselves to appropriate weapons common to military, security or law enforcement operations.

12.3. Signatories shall only obtain weapons through legal channels and shall not engage in illicit arms trading, and shall comply with United Nations arms embargos.

13. Partner Companies and Subcontractors

Due to the nature of complex environments, Signatories often employ the services of partner companies and subcontractors to fulfill the duties of their contract, therefore:

13.1. Signatories shall select partner companies and subcontractors with the utmost care and due diligence to ensure that they comply with all appropriate ethical standards, including the ISOA Code of Conduct.

13.2. Signatories shall encourage the recognition of and compliance with the standards contained within the ISOA Code of Conduct by partner companies, subcontractors and the industry as a whole.

14. Application and Enforcement

14.1. This Code of Conduct is the official code of ISOA. Signatories shall maintain the standards laid down in the ISOA Code of Conduct in addition to the standards and provisions of Signatories' codes of conduct.

14.2. The enforcement of the ISOA Code of Conduct is guided by the ISOA Enforcement Mechanism, the complaint system available to the public at-large. Signatories who fail to uphold any provision contained in this Code may be subject to dismissal from ISOA.

14.3. Signatories shall endeavor to inform personnel, clients and subcontractors of the ISOA Code of Conduct and ISOA Enforcement Mechanism. Signatories shall endeavor to publicize both to local communities.

14.4. Signatories shall have an effective mechanism for personnel to internally report suspected breaches of international humanitarian and human rights laws and violations of other applicable laws or the ISOA Code of Conduct. Signatories shall not retaliate against any person who reports in good faith and on reasonable grounds such suspected violations.

NOTES

1. Jacques S. Gansler, David Berteau, David M. Maddox, David R. Oliver Jr., Leon E. Salomon, George T. Singley III, George Sears, Kristi Crear, Karl Ellcessor, Dave Mabee, Jill Stiglich, and Jana Weston, *Urgent Reform Required: Army Expeditionary Contracting*, Report of the Commission on Army Acquisition and Program Management in Expeditionary Operations (Washington: Office of the Assistant Secretary of the Army for Acquisition, Logistics, and Technology, 2007), page 13, available at http://www.acq.osd.mil/dpap/contingency/reports/docs/gansler_commission_report_final_report_20071031.pdf.

2. Sue Pleming and Andrew Grey, "Gates Takes Swipe at Security Contractors in Iraq," Reuters (19 October 2007), available at http://www.reuters.com/article/2007/10/19/us-iraq-usa-blackwater-idUSN1842593420071019, accessed 3 August 2015; Robert M. Gates, "Strategic and Operational Planning for Operational Contract Support (OCS) and Workforce Mix," memorandum for the secretaries of the military departments et al. (Washington: Office of the Secretary of Defense, 24 January 2011), page 1.

3. *Testimony of Thomas F. Gimble, "Combatting War Profiteering: Are We Doing Enough to Investigate and Prosecute Contracting Fraud in Iraq?" Hearing before the Committee on the Judiciary, United States Senate* (20 March 2007).

4. Commission on Wartime Contracting in Iraq and Afghanistan, *Transforming Wartime Contracting: Controlling Costs, Reducing Risks. Final Report to Congress* (Washington: Commission on Wartime Contracting in Iraq and Afghanistan, August 2011), page 1; Center for Effective Government, "CWC's Final Report: Make Investments in Contracting Oversight" (13 September 2011), available at http://www.foreffectivegov.org/node/11850, accessed 30 September 2015. The Commission on Wartime Contracting did not provide the data it used to support its numbers and sealed its research and work-related documents for 20 years. See Nathan Hodge, "Panel's War-Waste Records Sealed as Work Ends," *Wall Street Journal* (30 September 2011), available at http://www.wsj.com/articles/SB10001424052970204226204576603060868379444, accessed 1 October 2015. In a subsequent interview with a former lead staffer of the commission, Brooks asked, "Was there enough information to accurately estimate the $31 to $60 billion numbers?" The former staffer responded, "Not to the quality required for an audit. One would have to evaluate specific contract data that we did not have available" (Doug Brooks, telephone interview with a former lead staff member of the Commission on Wartime Contracting, conducted 1 October 2015).

5. "Blackwater Incident: What Happened," *BBC News* (8 December 2008), available at http://news.bbc.co.uk/2/hi/7033332.stm, accessed 16 August 2015. Additional military incidents include 24 Iraqi civilians killed in Haditha in 2005 and up to 19 Afghan civilians in Shinwar in 2007. See CNN Library, "Haditha Killings Fast Facts," *CNN.com* (14 March 2015), available at http://edition.cnn.com/2013/10/30/world/meast/haditha-killings-fast-facts/, accessed 30 September 2015); David Zucchino, "Unit Cleared in Afghan Killings," *Los Angeles Times* (24 May 2008).

6. For recent cases see Julia Harte, "U.S. Military Personnel Have Been Convicted of $50 Million Worth of Crimes in Iraq and Afghanistan," Center for Public Integrity website (5 May 2015), available at http://www.publicintegrity.org/2015/05/05/17268/us-military-personnel-have-been-convicted-50-million-worth-crimes-iraq-and, accessed 1 October 2015; "Army Sergeant Pleads Guilty in Scheme to Defraud the Military; Army Sergeant and Co-conspirators Stole More than One Million Gallons of Fuel," *FBI.gov* (23 September 2014), available at https://www.fbi.gov/charlotte/press-releases/2014/army-sergeant-pleads-guilty-in-scheme-to-defraud-the-military, accessed 1 October 2015; Jim McElhatton, "How a Contracting Official Scammed More than $30M," *Federal Times* (1 April 2013), available at http://www.federaltimes.com/article/20130401/ACQUISITION02/304010001/How-contracting-official-scammed-more-than-30M?odyssey=tab%7Ctopnews%7Cimg%7CAcquisition, accessed 1 October 2015; "U.S. Marine Pleads to Taking $150K in Bribes in Iraq," *Seattle Times* (7 December 2012), available at http://www.seattletimes.com/nation-world/us-marine-pleads-to-taking-150k-in-bribes-in-iraq/, accessed 1 October 2015; David Lee, "Army Major Took 'Gratuities' in Iraq," *Courthouse News* (10 April 2012), available at http://www.courthousenews.com/2012/04/10/45466.htm, accessed 1 October 2015; Samuel Rubenfeld, "Former Major Sentenced in Defense Contractor Bribery Case," *Wall Street Journal* (6 January 2012), available at http://blogs.wsj.com/corruption-currents/2012/01/06/former-major-sentenced-in-defense-contractor-bribery-case/, accessed 1 October 2015; John Kell, "Ex-Army Employee Pleads Guilty to Taking Bribes," *MarketWatch* (19 September 2011), available at http://www.marketwatch.com/story/ex-army-employee-pleads-guilty-to-taking-bribes-2011-09-19, accessed 1 October 2015; Adam Klasfeld, "Army Captain Gets Three Years for Taking Bribes," *Courthouse News* (17 August 2011), available at http://www.courthousenews.com/2011/08/17/39061.htm, accessed 1 October 2015; John E. Mulligan, "Bribery Case in San Diego Has Parallels to Rhode Island," *Providence Journal* (3 July 2011), available at http://www.ocnus.

net/artman2/publish/Dark_Side_4/Navy-Bribery-Case-In-San-Diego-Has-Parallels-To-Rhode-Island.shtml, accessed 1 October 2015; Gidget Fuentes, "Officer Gets 6 Years in Iraq Contracting Scheme," *Marine Corps Times* (7 February 2011), available at http://archive.marinecorpstimes.com/article/20110207/NEWS/102070315/Officer-gets-6-years-in-Iraq-contracting-scheme, accessed 1 October 2015.

7. ISOA was originally the International Peace Operations Association (IPOA). It was rebranded in 2010 as the International Stability Operations Association (ISOA).

8. Susan Bisom-Rapp, "Bulletproofing the Workplace: Symbol and Substance in Employment Discrimination Law Practice," *Florida State University Law Review* 26, 4 (Summer 1999).

9. In this chapter we have deliberately chosen to use the term "private security company" to refer to companies providing services to protect "nouns"—people, places, and things—as this is the terminology used in the International Code of Conduct and because it more carefully delineates the vital line in international law between civilians and recognized "privileged combatants" in conflict environments. The Montreux Document uses the term "private military and security company," and although imperfect, it has become the generally accepted academic term.

10. Adam Smith, *The Wealth of Nations, Books IV–V* (New York: Penguin, 2000).

11. Alfred Pigou, *The Economics of Welfare* (London: Macmillan, 1938); Thomas K. McGraw, "Regulation in America: A Review Article," *Business History Review* 49, 2 (Summer 1975); Joseph Stiglitz, *Whither Socialism?* (Cambridge: MIT Press, 1989); Edward L. Glaeser and Andrei Schleifer, "The Rise of the Regulatory State," *Journal of Economic Literature* 16, 2 (June 2003).

12. George J. Stigler, "The Theory of Economic Regulation," *Bell Journal of Economics and Management Science* 2, 1 (Spring 1971), page 3. Critics such as Stigler, Huntington, and Kolko have argued that regulation has also been intended to protect and benefit minority interests, particularly specific privileged groups. See Samuel P. Huntington, "The Marasmus of the ICC: The Commission, the Railroads, and the Public Interest," *Yale Law Review* 61, 467 (April 1952); Gabriel Kolko, *Railroads and Regulation 1877–1916* (New York: W. W. Norton & Company, 1970); and Gabriel Kolko, *The Triumph of Conservatism: A Reinterpretation of American History, 1900–1916* (New York: The Free Press, 1963).

13. Giandomenico Majone, "The Rise of the Regulatory State in Europe," *West European Politics* 17, 3 (1994); Richard H. Pildes and Cass R. Sunstein, "Reinventing the Regulatory State," *University of Chicago Law Review* 62, 1 (Winter 1995); Michael Moran, "Review Article: Understanding the Regulatory State," *British Journal of Political Science* 32, 2 (April 2002).

14. Anil K. Gupta and Lawrence J. Lad, "Industry Self-Regulation: An Economic, Organizational, and Political Analysis," *Academy of Management Review* 8, 3 (1983), page 417.

15. Stigler, "The Theory of Economic Regulation," pages 3–4.

16. Michael E. Porter, *Competitive Strategy: Techniques for Analyzing Industries and Competitors* (New York: The Free Press, 1980).

17. Andrew A. King, Michael J. Lenox, and Michael L. Barnett, "Strategic Responses to the Reputation Commons Problem," in Andrew J. Hoffman and Marc J. Ventresca, editors, *Organizations, Policy and the Natural Environment: Institutional and Strategic Perspectives* (Palo Alto: Stanford University Press, 2001).

18. Stigler, "The Theory of Economic Regulation," pages 10–13.

19. Stigler, "The Theory of Economic Regulation," *passim*; McGraw, "Regulation in America," pages 162–64; Ernesto Dal Bó, "Regulatory Capture: A Review," *Oxford Review of Economic Policy* 22, 2 (Summer 2006).

20. Virginia Haufler, *A Public Role for the Private Sector* (Washington: The Carnegie Endowment for International Peace, 2013), pages 1–2.

21. Haufler, *A Public Role for the Private Sector*, pages 1–2.

22. Haufler, *A Public Role for the Private Sector*, pages 1–2.

23. Gupta and Lad, "Industry Self-Regulation," page 421.

24. Gupta and Lad, "Industry Self-Regulation," page 421.

25. Haufler, *A Public Role for the Private Sector*, pages 1–2; David Levi-Faur, "Regulation," in George Thomas Kurian, editor in chief, *The Encyclopedia of Political Science*, volume 5: *R–Z* (Washington: CQ Press, 2011), page 1445.
26. Gupta and Lad, "Industry Self-Regulation," page 421.
27. Gupta and Lad, "Industry Self-Regulation," page 422.
28. Gupta and Lad, "Industry Self-Regulation," page 422.
29. Gupta and Lad, "Industry Self-Regulation," page 422.
30. Gupta and Lad, "Industry Self-Regulation," page 422.
31. Andrew A. King and Michael J. Lenox, "Industry Self-Regulation without Sanctions: The Chemical Industry's Responsible Care Program," *Academy of Management Journal* 43, 4 (August 2000), page 713. Also see David A. Garvin, "Can Industry Self-Regulation Work?" *California Management Review* 25, 4 (Summer 1983).
32. King and Lenox, "Industry Self-Regulation without Sanctions," page 713.
33. King and Lenox, "Industry Self-Regulation without Sanctions," page 713.
34. Michael J. Lenox and Jennifer Nash, "Industry Self-Regulation and Adverse Selection: A Comparison across Four Trade Association Programs," *Business Strategy and the Environment* 12, 6 (November/December 2003).
35. Lenox and Nash, "Industry Self-Regulation and Adverse Selection," page 2.
36. Garvin, "Can Industry Self-Regulation Work?" page 45.
37. Garvin, "Can Industry Self-Regulation Work?" page 45.
38. Garvin, "Can Industry Self-Regulation Work?" page 45.
39. The founding members of IPOA included Sandline, AirScan Inc., PAE Group, MPRI, ArmorGroup North America, and International Charter Inc. of Oregon.
40. International Stability Operations Association, "About Us" (no date), available at http://www.stability-operations.org/?page=About, accessed 16 August 2015.
41. The sources of income for ISOA are identified in tax filings from 2012. ISOA tax filings can be found at Pro Publica, "International Peace Operations Association," ProPublica Nonprofit Explorer, available at https://projects.propublica.org/nonprofits/organizations/542033637, accessed 17 August 2015.
42. According to tax filings, total revenue was $110,522 in 2004 and peaked in 2012 at $899,182.
43. Chapter 2, Article 13, subsection 4, and Chapter 3, Article 4, subsection 4 (United Nations, *Geneva Conventions of 12 August, 1949 and Protocols Additional to the Conventions* [12 August 1949], available at http://www.un-documents.net/gc.htm, accessed 12 August 2015).
44. Giulio Bartolini, "Private Military and Security Contractors as 'Persons Who Accompany the Armed Forces,'" in Fracesco Francioni and Natalino Ronzitti, editors, *War by Contract: Human Rights, Humanitarian Law, and Private Contractors* (Oxford: Oxford University Press, 2011), pages 219–20; Lindsey Cameron and Vincent Chetail, *Privatizing War: Private Military and Security Companies under Public International Law* (Cambridge: Cambridge University Press, 2013), pages 418–19; Emily Crawford, *Identifying the Enemy: Civilian Participation in Armed Conflict* (Oxford: Oxford University Press, 2015), page 164.
45. *Article 47 of Additional Protocol One to the Geneva Convention* (8 June 1977), available at https://www.icrc.org/ihl/WebART/470-750057, accessed 12 August 2015.
46. United Nations General Assembly, *International Convention against the Recruitment, Use, Financing and Training of Mercenaries* (4 December 1989), available at http://www.un.org/documents/ga/res/44/a44r034.htm, accessed 31 July 2015.
47. International Committee of the Red Cross, "Summary: International Convention against the Recruitment, Use, Financing and Training of Mercenaries, 4 December 1989," available at https://www.icrc.org/ihl/INTRO/530?OpenDocument, accessed 14 September 2015.
48. The Organization of African Unity was the precursor organization to the African Union.
49. 1977 Convention for the Elimination of Mercenarism in Africa (XXXIX) Annex II rev. 3, OAU CM/817 (OAU Mercenaries Convention), which entered into force on 22 April 1985. To date 30 members of the African Union have ratified the convention.
50. The UN passed the International Convention against the Recruitment, Use, Financing and Training of Mercenaries in 1989 and it came into force in 2001. However, the document

was generally an amalgamation of earlier international laws (i.e., the Additional Protocol to the Geneva Convention and the OAU's Convention for the Elimination of Mercenaries in Africa) and thus carried the same problems of defining mercenaries, enforcing the restrictions on state use of mercenaries, and a pure focus on armed mercenaries rather than the entire stability operations industry (International Committee of the Red Cross, "Summary.")

51. Christopher Kinsey, "International Law and the Control of Mercenaries and Private Military Companies," *Cultures and Conflits* 52 (2004), available at http://conflits.revues.org/11502, accessed 23 September 2015; Anna Leander, "Existing International Instruments and Mechanisms," paper presented at the Latin America and Caribbean Regional Consultation on the Effects of the Activities of Private Military and Security Companies on the Enjoyment of Human Rights: Regulation and Oversight, organized by the UN Working Group on the use of Mercenaries/Special Procedures assumed by the Office of the High Commissioner on Human Rights, Panama (17–18 December 2007), available at http://openarchive.cbs.dk/bitstream/handle/10398/6992/wp%202007-4.pdf?sequence, accessed 23 September 2015.

52. Bartolini, "Private Military and Security Contractors as 'Persons Who Accompany the Armed Forces,'" page 221.

53. US Code Title 18, Chapter 212, section 3261(a)(1): Military Extraterritorial Jurisdiction, available at https://www.law.cornell.edu/uscode/text/18/3261, accessed 16 August 2015.

54. International Peace Operations Association, "IPOA Endorsement of H.R. 2740, 'MEJA Expansion and Enforcement Act of 2007,'" press release (2 October 2007).

55. Spencer S. Hsu and Victoria St. Martin, "Four Blackwater Guards Sentenced in Iraq Shootings of 31 Unarmed Civilians," *Washington Post* (13 April, 2015), available at http://www.washingtonpost.com/local/crime/four-blackwater-guards-sentenced-in-iraq-shootings-of-31-unarmed-civilians/2015/04/13/55b777e0-dee4-11e4-be40-566e2653afe5_story.html, accessed 9 July 2015.

56. For the complexities of the "Arms to Africa Affair," see Christopher Kinsey, *Corporate Soldiers and International Security: The Rise of Private Military Companies* (London: Routledge, 2006), pages 72–93, as well as Laura Silber and David Wighton, "UN Lawyers Rule on Sierra Leone Arms," *Financial Times* (23 May 1998), and James Bone, "Sandline Is Given Support by UN," *Times* (London) (25 May 1998).

57. The last two international agreements were added later following their creation. International Stability Operations Association, "ISOA Code of Conduct Version 13," (20 October 2011), available at http://www.stability-operations.org/?page=Code, accessed 16 August 2015.

58. International Stability Operations Association, "ISOA Code of Conduct Version 13."

59. Matthew D. McCubbins and Thomas Schwartz, "Congressional Oversight Overlooked: Police Patrols versus Fire Alarms," *American Journal of Political Science* 28, 1 (February 1984), page 166; Peter D. Feaver, *Armed Servants: Agency, Oversight, and Civil-Military Relations* (Cambridge: Harvard University Press, 2003), page 80.

60. International Stability Operations Association, "How to Submit a Standards Complaint" (no date), available at http://www.stability-operations.org/?page=Standards_Complaint, accessed 24 September 2015.

61. International Stability Operations Association, "How to Submit a Standards Complaint."

62. For example, the addition of clause 6.9 to the "ISOA Code of Conduct Version 13," obliging signatories to refrain from employing any personnel less than 15, and in the case of armed security personnel 18 years of age, was a direct result of these simulations. These minimum ages echo the standards set by the International Labor Organization Minimum Age Convention and the Optional Protocols to the United Nations Convention on the Rights of the Child, respectively.

63. Until the ISOA code was superseded by the ICoC, it was the main tool for handling complaints regarding industry behavior.

64. Recollection of Doug Brooks, former president of the International Stability Operations Association.

65. Molly Dunigan, *Victory for Hire: Private Security Companies' Impact on Military Effectiveness* (Palo Alto: Stanford University Press, 2011), pages 167–68.

66. Dunigan, *Victory for Hire*, pages 167–68; Associated Press, "Blackwater Chief: I Was 'Thrown Under the Bus': Contractor's Founder Says Secret CIA Program Revealed for Politi-

cal Reasons," *NBC News* (2 December 2009), available at http://www.nbcnews.com/id/34242158/ns/us_news-security/t/blackwater-chief-i-was-thrown-under-bus/#.VgRnSo-qpBc, accessed 24 September 2015.

67. According to the Project on Government Oversight several member firms including DynCorp, Academi (formerly Blackwater), and PAE have all been fined for misconduct related to government contracting (Project on Government Oversight, "Federal Contractor Misconduct Database," available at http://www.contractormisconduct.org/contractors, accessed 25 September 2015).

68. IPOA released a statement on the completion of the Montreux Document in which it stated, "IPOA was honored to be a part of the process and we see the agreement as an affirmation of the global value of ethical private sector operations in conflict, post-conflict and disaster relief operations" (J. J. Messner, "IPOA Welcomes Montreux Agreement on Private Security Companies" [17 September 2008], available at http://www.reports-and-materials.org/sites/default/files/reports-and-materials/IPOA-welcomes-Montreux-agreement-17-Sep-2008.pdf, accessed 25 September 2015).

69. ISOA also released a joint statement with two other industry associations (the Pan-African Security Association and the British Association of Private Security Companies) in support of the establishment of the ICoC. The statement highlights the role of the industry in creating the new international standards and encourages its members and other members of the industry to immediately sign on to the new international standard. See Chris Greyling, Doug Brooks, and Andrew Bearpark, "Industry Statement" (30 September 2010), available at http://business-humanrights.org/sites/default/files/media/documents/industry-pmsc-code-30-sep-2010.pdf, accessed 25 September 2015.

70. Neil Gunningham and Joseph Rees, "Industry Self-Regulation: An Institutional Perspective," *Law and Policy* 19, 4 (October 1997), page 363.

Chapter Ten

The Montreux Document

The Legal Significance of a Non-legal Instrument

Ian Ralby

It is not often that the most legally significant instrument in a given field is expressly not a legal instrument. But the field of private security is unusual in many respects. The 2008 "Montreux Document" was the first major international undertaking to address the use of companies that offer security services for hire.[1] A number of initiatives have sought to bolster the accountability of armed contractors in the years since the Montreux Document was first signed, but it remains the only initiative focused on the interaction between states and the industry.[2] While the Document's text restates existing international legal obligations and provides states with "good practices" concerning their engagement with "private military and security companies" (PMSCs), the Document has international legal significance in two key respects. First, it is the most credible and extensive clarification of the legal twilight surrounding the PMSC industry. Second, and most importantly, it is likely over time to form the basis of customary international law regarding the use of PMSCs. Despite its own protestations, therefore, the Montreux Document should be seen to have inherent and growing international legal significance.

THE MONTREUX DOCUMENT

In 2006, the International Law Division of the Swiss Federal Department of Foreign Affairs and the International Committee for the Red Cross (ICRC) initiated the so-called Swiss Initiative to address the perceived accountability gap in the use and operation of companies offering security services in conflict zones.[3] Eighteen key countries collaborated via four expert meetings and five intergovernmental sessions over the next two years to first identify the existing international legal obligations surrounding the industry and suggest what "good practices" states should adopt when interacting with the industry.[4] The participating countries were Afghanistan, Angola, Australia, Austria, Canada, China, France, Germany, Iraq, Poland, Russia, Sierra Leone, South Africa, Sweden, Switzerland, Ukraine, the United Kingdom, and the United States—essentially the countries with the strongest ties to PMSCs.[5] On 17 September 2008, 17 of those states—Russia backed out the day before the proceedings concluded—endorsed the Montreux Document on Pertinent International Legal Obligations and Good Practices for States related to Operations of Private Military and Security Companies during Armed Conflict.[6] Now, with 53 states and 3 international organizations—the European Union (EU), North Atlantic Treaty Organization (NATO), and the Organization for Security and Cooperation in Europe (OSCE)—"participating" in the Montreux Document,[7] it is the most widely accepted international agreement on the subject of private armed contracting.

According to its preface, the Document "recalls existing legal obligations of States and PMSCs and their personnel . . . and provides States with good practices to promote compliance with international humanitarian law and human rights law during armed conflict."[8] It is expressly non-binding and explicitly neither creates nor alters any legal obligations.[9] Participating states and organizations specify that they do not seek to endorse the use of PMSCs, but rather to use multilateral collaboration in order to clarify what laws and practices should guide states and other contracting entities[10] when the decision to use a PMSC has been made.[11] Importantly, the preface also makes it clear that the principles of the Document are not limited to armed conflict settings and not exclusively applicable to states.[12] It encourages cooperation between states in the implementation of the Document, suggesting that the realization of the Document's aims will be an ongoing process.[13] Additionally, part of that cooperation includes working with PMSCs.

WHAT ARE PRIVATE MILITARY AND SECURITY COMPANIES?

This entire volume could be filled with analysis of the various terms that are used to label private military, private security, and armed contracting activity. Fortunately for the present analysis, however, the Montreux Document provides the most widely endorsed definition of the term "private military and security companies," or PMSCs. They are

> private business entities that provide military and/or security services, irrespective of how they describe themselves. Military and security services include, in particular, armed guarding and protection of persons and objects, such as convoys, buildings and other places; maintenance and operation of

weapons systems; prisoner detention; and advice to or training of local forces and security personnel.[14]

It bears noting, however, that many companies within the industry as well as some of the participating states object to the inclusion of the word "military" in the definition.[15] Their argument is that they only provide defensive security services under the laws of self-defense and defense of others.[16] While that may be the case, the Montreux Document applies to companies offering a broad array of services that, as the above definition indicates, includes activities beyond protection of people or even property.

The international accountability initiatives that have sprung forth from the Montreux Document—including the International Code of Conduct for Private Security Service Providers (ICoC) and its governing association (ICoCA), the American National Standards Institute Private Security Company (ANSI PSC) standards, and the forthcoming International Organization for Standardization (ISO) standards—have all applied to a more limited array of actors than the PMSCs addressed in the Montreux Document. Indeed, companies that maintain and operate weapons systems, provide prisoner detention services, and train local forces are expressly excluded from these other initiatives.[17] This analysis, therefore, will use the terminology and definition provided by the Montreux Document.

As many continue to refer to PMSCs as "mercenaries," it is important to take a moment to distinguish these two different sets of private actors involved in conflict. Mercenaries have been defined under international law in a number of instruments, including an African Union convention,[18] Additional Protocol I to the Geneva Conventions,[19] and a 1989 United Nations convention[20] that outlaws the recruitment, use, financing, and training of mercenaries (which will be discussed further below). The definitions contained in the various international legal instruments, however, are lengthy, with numerous sub-parts, and require that all elements be met. PMSCs are considered to fall "outside the full domain of all of these existing legal regimes."[21] Furthermore, as one commentator boldly put it: "any mercenary who cannot exclude himself from th[ose] definition[s] deserves to be shot—and his lawyer with him."[22] The present analysis will not delve into the distinctions between mercenaries and PMSCs, but maintains, throughout, that the two terms are neither synonymous nor interchangeable.

THE STATUS OF THE MONTREUX DOCUMENT

The Montreux Document is part of a growing body of "soft law" initiatives. Contrasted with "hard law," which refers to binding legal commitments, "soft law" is often used to characterize quasi-legal instruments like the Montreux Document that, while not binding, nevertheless indicate a desire on the part of states to clarify how they should conduct themselves. Soft law is a controversial term, as some legal practitioners and scholars do not believe in its existence.[23] It is unquestionable, however, that the Montreux Document is not a treaty, convention, or other traditional instrument, but does nevertheless constitute an agreement between states. The terminology used to describe and explain the Montreux Document indicates a concerted effort for it not to be mistaken for a hard law instrument. States are not signatories, they do not ratify it, and it is not "in effect." Instead, states "participate" in it. This nuance underscores the soft law, or at least non-binding nature of the Document.

As noted, significant analysis could be devoted to distinguishing *PMSCs* from *mercenaries*, but a brief comparison between the uptake of the Montreux Document versus the UN Mercenary Convention provides some insight into the former's significance. On 4 December 1989, the General Assembly made good on its commitment to outlaw mercenary activity by producing the International Convention against the Recruitment, Use, Financing and Training of Mercenaries.[24] The UN Mercenary Convention, as it is known, did not, however, take effect until 20 October 2001, as it took those 12 years to garner sufficient support. Since 1989, only 33 of the 193 member states of the United Nations have ratified the UN Mercenary Convention.[25] Since 2008, 52 states and 3 major intergovernmental organizations have signed to participate in the Montreux Document.[26] The lack of support for the UN Convention and the speed with which the Montreux Document—which tacitly legitimizes the existence and operation of PMSCs—has been embraced indicates that state practice favors the acceptance of PMSCs over banning mercenaries. Furthermore, 13 states have signed both documents, indicating that these states understand PMSCs as being fundamentally different from the mercenaries outlawed by the UN convention. The growing support for the Montreux Document certainly suggests increasing international consensus surrounding its content—with regard to both the legal obligations and "good practices." But the non-binding nature of it also helps account for the speed with which it has been adopted. This analysis, therefore, explores the hard law effects of this soft law instrument.

On its terms, the Montreux Document applies to armed conflict settings. While PMSCs continue to be used in both international and non-international armed conflicts, the industry has become involved in a wide variety of contexts around the world, many of which are complex or hostile, but not armed conflicts. the Document notes that many of the provisions drawn from international humanitarian law only apply in the context of armed conflict, but the participating states suggest nevertheless that many of the good practices, in particular, can apply to other contexts in which PMSCs are hired.[27] Notably, however, the onus of compliance falls on the voluntary action of the states, as "each State is responsible for complying with the obligations it has undertaken pursuant to international agreements to which it is a party, subject to any reservations, understandings and declarations made, and to customary international law."[28] The value of the Document, therefore, lies in identifying what obligations do exist in the context of private military and security contracting. Taking this broader construction of the document, the analysis will not consider the Montreux Document to be limited in relevance only to armed conflict settings.

STRUCTURE OF THE ANALYSIS

This analysis explores the legal significance of the Montreux Document in its two most significant areas: (1) the clarification it provides regarding the application of international law to PMSC contracting, and (2) the potential it has to form the basis of binding customary international law. It does not, however, herald the initiative as resolving the issue of accountability for PMSCs. On the contrary, it suggests that the Montreux Document provides a valuable starting point for a process that will need to continue indefinitely. Wherever possible, the analysis points out the shortcomings of the Montreux Document, but highlights what has been done thus far to remedy any such problems.

An analysis of the Document's section on legal obligations helps elucidate its substance and its role in clarifying legal consensus surrounding the PMSC industry. This first part, among other things, notes the importance of having clarification as to the status of armed contractors under international humanitarian law and highlights that, though endorsed by states, the Document also provides legal guidance to PMSCs. It also points out some of the gaps that have arisen since 2008, particularly with regard to "manpower states," which are not included along with contracting, home, and territorial states in the Document.

In the second part, the analysis explores the Document's potential role in creating customary international law, examining in some depth the portions relating to "good practices." Some of those good practices are also examined insofar as they contribute to legal clarity. Ultimately, the main conclusion of the analysis argues that the Montreux Document may already be contributing to the creation of customary international law. It goes so far as to suggest that, given the number of participating states, there appears to be customary international law developing around the acceptability of using PMSCs.

The analysis concludes by arguing that this non-legal, non-binding document might ultimately have as much international legal significance as if it had been a multilateral treaty or convention. It reasons that, from an international law standpoint, no initiative since the Montreux Document compares to it in legal significance. The conclusion emphasizes that, while imperfect, the Montreux Document remains the most important development to date in the quest to resolve the legal twilight that continues to surround the private military and security industry.

PART I: LEGAL CLARIFICATION

The legal clarification provided by the Montreux Document is the primary focus of the first 27 paragraphs, grouped under the heading "Part One." Part One focuses on the existing laws pertaining to PMSCs and breaks them into six categories: those applicable to (1) contracting states, (2) territorial states, (3) home states, (4) all other states, (5) PMSCs and their personnel, and finally (6) the relevant laws of superior responsibility. To clarify, contracting states are the ones that hire PMSCs, territorial states are those on whose territory PMSCs operate, and home states are the ones in which PMSCs are registered as businesses. According to the publicity surrounding the Montreux Process, "The Montreux Document is the first international document to describe international law as it applies to the activities of private military and security companies (PMSCs) whenever these are present in the context of an armed conflict."[29] While this assessment is true in some regards, it is important to remember that states, not PMSCs, are the signatories of the Montreux Document. So the principal focus and value of the Document is in clarifying international legal principles, parameters, and guidance with regard to how states should interact with the industry. It only clarifies to a limited extent, therefore, principles, parameters, and guidance for the industry itself. With that in mind, there are some important provisions worth noting.

General Obligations

According to the Montreux Document, contracting states, territorial states, home states, and all other states are advised that they have an obligation "to ensure respect for international humanitarian law"[30] and "are responsible to implement their obligations under international human rights law."[31] Furthermore, contracting states, territorial states, home states, and all other states "have an obligation to enact any legislation necessary to provide effective penal sanctions for persons committing, or ordering to be committed, grave breaches of the Geneva Conventions and, where applicable, Additional Protocol I."[32] These provisions unequivocally restate the bodies of law under which the various interested states must operate. Furthermore, they remind participating states of their obligation to ensure their domestic laws adequately incorporate international legal principles and provide functional criminal penalties when the international laws are violated. While these general provisions do not provide substantive guidance on the interpretation of international laws vis-à-vis PMSCs, other provisions go into greater specificity.

Contracting Responsibility

The Document establishes that contracting states retain their international legal obligations even after contracting with a PMSC[33] and thus cannot outsource to PMSCs what they cannot legally do themselves.[34] While seemingly obvious, this provision is extremely important in light of criticism suggesting that states use PMSCs to avoid legal obligations.[35] The Document furthermore establishes that states have an affirmative duty to monitor the PMSCs with which they contract,[36] to punish any violations of international law,[37] and to amend their national legal systems to provide penal remedies for any PMSCs that violate the Geneva Conventions or Additional Protocol I.[38] This obligation is not a one-off, so the requirement of legal reform requires that states continually work to ensure that domestic legislation adequately satisfies international obligations, even as the activities of the industry evolve and change. Contracting states also, according to the Montreux Document, have a responsibility to provide reparations to parties injured by PMSCs as the result of violations of international humanitarian law and international human rights law.[39] These provisions clearly establish an obligation on the part of contracting states to proactively address these matters of accountability and seem to be consistent with the "Respect, Protect, Remedy" framework promoted by the United Nations in its Guiding Principles on Business and Human Rights.[40]

State Responsibility

One of the most significant provisions of the Document in terms of legal clarification pertains to the responsibility of contracting states for the actions of the PMSCs they hire. Paragraph 7 of the "Legal Obligations" section reads:

> Although entering into contractual relations does not in itself engage the responsibility of Contracting States, the latter are responsible for violations of international humanitarian law, human rights law, or other rules of international law committed by PMSCs or their personnel where such violations are attributable to the Contracting State, consistent with customary international law, in particular if they are:
>
> a. incorporated by the State into its regular armed forces in accordance with its domestic legislation;
> b. members of organized armed forces, groups or units under a command responsible to the State;

c. empowered to exercise elements of governmental authority if they are acting in that capacity (i.e. are formally authorized by law or regulation to carry out functions normally conducted by organs of the State); or
d. in fact acting on the instructions of the State (i.e. the State has specifically instructed the private actor's conduct) or under its direction or control (i.e. actual exercise of effective control by the State over a private actor's conduct).[41]

This paragraph explains, according to the states principally involved in the private military and security industry, how the actions of PMSCs can be attributed to the states that hire them. Without even delving into the nuances of state responsibility,[42] this provision provides agreement between states as to how the relationship between contracting states and PMSCs should be treated. Indirectly, this also helps illuminate the various functions a PMSC can have and the various ways such companies can take on responsibilities traditionally held by states.

Individual Responsibility

The final paragraph of the "Legal Obligations" section also further clarifies the responsibility of states that hire PMSCs, as well as the directors and officers of the PMSCs themselves.[43] Whereas paragraph 7 focused on the responsibility of states for the actions of PMSCs, this paragraph establishes individual criminal liability for acts committed by the personnel of PMSCs. Contractual relations alone do not suffice to create such liability according to this provision. In order for a superior, whether within a PMSC, within the client government, or within a nonstate client that has hired the PMSC, to be individually liable for the acts of a contractor, he or she must exercise control over the contractor. Again, this provision provides important guidance to PMSCs, albeit indirectly, as to how their personnel can incur liability, and thereby, how they should seek to avoid or limit that liability. Furthermore, it serves as a warning to states regarding the exercise of control over the acts of a PMSC. By making military or civilian government personnel individually liable for the criminal conduct of a PMSC under their control, they place a heavy burden on state officials to ensure the lawful actions of such contractors. It also clarifies that individuals cannot avoid responsibility for PMSC misconduct on account of their position or role within a client organization.

PMSC Responsibility

With regard to PMSCs themselves, paragraphs 22–26 of the "Legal Obligations" section are most directly relevant in terms of guiding the conduct of the industry. Paragraph 23 provides clear direction for the personnel of PMSCs: "The personnel of PMSCs are obliged to respect the relevant national law, in particular the national criminal law, of the State in which they operate, and, as far as applicable, the law of the States of their nationality."[44] At any given time under normal circumstances, an individual should be able to determine the law of the state in which he or she operates as well as the law of the state of his or her nationality, even if he or she has to hire a lawyer to do so. This provision, therefore, provides useful guidance that is understandable without substantial extrapolation. Problems may arise, however, when there is no guidance given as to what to do when the rule of law has collapsed in the state in which PMSCs are operating, or when there is a conflict between that state's laws and those of another relevant jurisdiction like that of the contracting state or of the contractor's nationality. So difficult questions remain unanswered.

The other four paragraphs in this section similarly suffer from a failure to address the full complexity of international law, but are nevertheless helpful in providing some clarification. Paragraph 22 reads: "PMSCs are obliged to comply with international humanitarian law or human rights law imposed upon them by applicable national law, as well as other applicable national law such as criminal law, tax law, immigration law, labor law, and specific regulations on private military or security services."[45] The Montreux Document does not take on the mammoth task of interpreting how or even when international humanitarian law, either customary or treaty-based, applies to PMSCs. Indeed, relatively little work has been done to delve into the legal nuance surrounding the industry.[46] The caveat added to the mention of human rights law, "imposed upon them by applicable national law," makes the human rights component of this provision somewhat more intelligible. That said, what laws are "applicable" may be difficult to interpret in the contexts in which PMSCs operate.

This is an industry that had only self-imposed industry guidelines that could lead to established standards or practices at the time the Montreux Document was written[47] and has few credible sources of official guidance on how to operate within international law to this day. Indeed, the Montreux Document set out to start the process of resolving that very uncertainty. While the Montreux Document provides a general formula for determining what human rights law applies, the difficulty is that it might not always be clear for a PMSC, especially one registered in state A, working on a contract for state B in state C with personnel from state D, to determine how to apply that formula in practice.

Applying IHL to PMSCs

While it is all well and good that international humanitarian law (IHL) applies to PMSCs—a fact that is indisputable, since IHL applies universally within armed conflict settings—the difficult question is determining where

PMSCs, a relatively new entity in world affairs, fit into treaties and customs that do not account for their existence. The Montreux Document does offer some guidance. "The status of the personnel of PMSCs is determined by international humanitarian law, on a case by case basis, in particular according to the nature and circumstances of the functions in which they are involved."[48] This provision provides a starting point and methodology for determining the status of a PMSC contractor in the midst of an armed conflict. It does not, however, clarify how that determination should actually be made. In other words, this provision does not provide criteria for evaluating whether the individuals are protected civilians, unprotected civilians, members of militias and other volunteer corps, contractors accompanying the armed forces, or possessing of some other status.

The next paragraph skips over the status determination process and examines the legal protections attributed to PMSC personnel when they are operating in civilian status. "If they are civilians under international humanitarian law, the personnel of PMSCs may not be the object of attack, unless and for such time as they directly participate in hostilities."[49] Direct participation in hostilities is a difficult matter to interpret. While the ICRC has published its Interpretive Guidance on the matter, those interpretations, particularly with regard to PMSCs, are not universally shared. While there is some consensus that self-defense—the principal activity of PMSCs—does not constitute direct participation in hostilities, the lack of universal agreement means that this provision of the Document, like many of the others, is too vague to provide consistent guidance. But it is, again, an important starting point and useful for identifying where problematic legal issues are likely to arise.

Paragraph 26 of the Montreux Document, on the other hand, provides the most important guidance for interpreting how international humanitarian law applies to PMSCs. This paragraph, more than any other in the Montreux Document, explains how PMSCs fit into the existing law of armed conflict. It reads:

> The personnel of PMSCs:
>
> a. are obliged, regardless of their status, to comply with applicable international humanitarian law;
> b. are protected as civilians under international humanitarian law, unless they are incorporated into the regular armed forces of a State or are members of organized armed forces, groups or units under a command responsible to the State; or otherwise lose their protection as determined by international humanitarian law;
> c. are entitled to prisoner of war status in international armed conflict if they are persons accompanying the armed forces meeting the requirements of article 4A(4) of the Third Geneva Convention;

d. to the extent they exercise governmental authority, have to comply with the State's obligations under international human rights law;
e. are subject to prosecution if they commit conduct recognized as crimes under applicable national or international law.[50]

In terms of providing clarity, this provision shows that PMSCs can have a range of statuses and can have prisoner of war protection in certain circumstances. It also establishes that their default status is as protected civilians, unless that status is mitigated or altered under the circumstances. Additionally, it places an emphasis on their following IHL regardless of their status and furthermore opens the door to their exercising quasi-official governmental status with regard to human rights obligations. The danger is that it leaves quite a few uncertainties. For example, when would PMSC personnel be deemed members of organized armed forces? Would that only be a de jure determination or would it also include de facto incorporation? Could a PMSC itself be considered an organized armed group? Under what circumstances, besides the direct participation in hostilities, might the contractors lose their protection under IHL? Indeed, the Montreux Document may raise as many, if not more, questions than it answers.

Perhaps not surprisingly, this paragraph has been the focus of extensive commentary and critique. What is surprising, however, is that much of that commentary and criticism lacks rigor and is rife with inaccuracies. For example, one commentator wrote: "Among other obligations, the Montreux Document guarantees PMC personnel POW status (provided they comply with article 4(A) of the Third Geneva Convention), and thus stands in stark contrast to Protocol I."[51] First, it is not clear why PMSC personnel having prisoner of war status in certain circumstances stands in stark contrast to Additional Protocol I. Such a statement indicates that the commentator believes PMSC personnel to be equivalent to mercenaries who, under Article 47 of Additional Protocol I, do not have such status—a confusion that is inconsistent with sound legal analysis.[52] Further, the Montreux Document, as discussed above, only mentions prisoner of war status for PMSCs when they act as persons accompanying the armed forces under Article 4(A) of the Third Geneva Convention. Nothing in the Montreux Document requires PMSC personnel to "comply" with Article 4(A)—a strange notion to begin with, since compliance with a list of statuses does not make sense.

Similarly, esteemed international criminal law scholar Cherif Bassiouni has written, "The Document avoids defining contractors as combatants or non-combatants, a move probably designed to have the document provide a more functional than political approach to the role of civilian contractors in combat zones."[53] Though the Document does not mention combatant status specifically, paragraph 26 does establish PMSCs as protected civilian non-combatants in most cases and clarifies that they can, under the proper circumstances, have combatant status and that they can do things to lose civilian protections. Jamie Williamson of the ICRC even recognizes that very point in an analysis of direct participation in hostilities.[54]

Conclusion

This brisk review of the some of the key legal portions of the Montreux Document highlights a few important elements. First, the Document places responsibilities on participating states to proactively engage in legislative processes to ensure that existing international legal obligations are adequately translated into domestic law. Second, it provides some clarity regarding interpretation of international law with regard to the use and operation of PMSCs. Third, while it flags a number of legal issues, it does not delve into some of the more complex nuances of them. It is limited, therefore, in the guidance it provides to states. Further work to establish international consensus on certain legal complexities will be needed. Finally, it sets a solid stage for future undertakings to delve into the legal challenges and nuances that remain unaddressed. In other words, the Document does not answer all the questions that would provide complete legal clarity, but it does offer a good starting point for honing the international consensus around the legal matters relevant to the PMSC industry.

PART II: THE BASIS OF CUSTOMARY LAW

Understanding the Montreux Document's potential role in developing customary international law requires at least a basic understanding of how international law is made. The statute of the International Court of Justice establishes four principal sources of international law:

1. Treaties and conventions.
2. Custom.
3. The laws of civilized nations.
4. Jurisprudence of courts and treatises of experts.[55]

While some commentators seem to believe a convention is the only way to adequately address the accountability issues of the private security industry,[56] they often fail to recognize that there are other processes, already in motion, that may provide, over time, the legal clarity needed for the industry to be a functional, legal, and reliable contributor to international security.

Customary international law is born of state practice.[57] The International Law Association defines it as being "created and sustained by the constant and uniform practice of states in circumstances that give rise to the legitimate expectation of similar conduct in the future."[58] By prescribing a uniform and mutually agreed approach to interacting with the PMSC industry, the Montreux Document could form the basis of customary international law. In other words, if states consistently and continually adhere to the principles and prescriptions of the Montreux Document, particularly out of a sense of obligation, then customary international law will form around the Document's content. Having reviewed the Document's portion on legal obligations in part 1, it is necessary to review the good practices section to explore what new international law may arise out of adherence to the Montreux Document.

Good Practices

The term "best practices" is commonly found as an indication of the expected standard within a given field. Similar to the emphasis on states "participating" in the Document instead of "ratifying" it, the use of the term "good practices" in the Montreux Document highlights the novelty and uncertainty surrounding the PMSC industry. In other words, states were content to articulate good practices, but they were not willing to declare them "best practices," as best practice would require greater time and experience to ascertain. As in the legal section, the good practices are divided among those for contracting states, those for territorial states, and those for home states. In contrast to the legal section, however, no sections focus specifically on the industry itself or the laws of superior responsibility.

Contracting States

The section on contracting states begins by asserting that states must first assess what they may and may not outsource.[59] Certain services presumably fall within the exclusive ambit of the state, and therefore the state may not contract with a PMSC to perform those services. The provision, however, does not clarify where to draw the line, but seems to indicate that direct participation in hostilities would be impermissible, as it notes that "in determining which services may not be contracted out, contracting states take into account factors such as whether a particular service could cause PMSC personnel to become involved in direct participation in hostilities."[60] While this provision is a useful reminder that not all services can be outsourced, it does not provide much guidance on how to determine what services would be permissible versus impermissible for a PMSC to perform on behalf of the contracting state.

The next several provisions pertain to the "procedure of selection and contracting of PMSCs." Essentially, the Document instructs that contracting states must perform due diligence before hiring a PMSC. While not expressly referenced, it is likely that current interpretation of these provisions will encourage consideration of the due diligence approach promoted by UN Special Rapporteur on Business and Human Rights John Ruggie in the UN

Guiding Principles on Business and Human Rights.[61] The Document suggests that, ultimately, there must be transparency in the relationship between the contracting state and the PMSC. Paragraph 4 details various ways in which this transparency can be achieved. This section provides contracting states with valuable guidance on what to do when selecting a PMSC.

The section setting forth the "criteria for the selection of PMSCs" provides remarkably detailed and practical advice, covering everything from prior records to financial stability to training standards. This portion of the Montreux Document is evidently based on the experiences gleaned from a relatively unregulated private military and security industry. It requires that contracting states ensure that the equipment and weapons used by the company are obtained legally; that the contracting state ensure that the PMSC's personnel are trained in national and international law; that the PMSC have not participated in any violations of international humanitarian law or human rights law, or at least have remedied any past violations; that the PMSC have the financial stability to fulfill its contract and pay any liabilities it may incur; that the PMSC have all the proper licenses; that the PMSC abide by labor laws and look after the welfare of its employees and contractors, and so on.[62] Indeed, paragraphs 5–13 contain the most direct guidance of any part of the Montreux Document and the most direct guidance in any international instrument to date concerning the responsibilities when hiring a PMSC. It is not surprising that these provisions are later referenced in other parts of the Document.

As helpful in some respects as these provisions may be, the question arises: How? How are states to verify this information with virtually no domestic and, as yet, no international infrastructure for recording or preserving the necessary information? As there is no central body that adjudicates violations of IHL and as states are often unable to pursue action on such violations, verifying violations of IHL is quite difficult. Equally, confirming that the PMSC has sufficient financial stability to ensure that it can pay for any liabilities it might incur is impracticable, since the range of liabilities is immense and rife with uncertainty. These pragmatic barriers to the best practices of the Montreux Document inhibit its potential effectiveness and even the ICoCA has not yet provided adequate remedy. That said, it is a good aspiration toward which to work.

The guidance as well as the challenges inherent in paragraphs 5–13 are incorporated into many of the remaining good practices. In establishing the contract between the state and the PMSC, for example, the Document instructs that the criteria of paragraphs 5–13 should be included. The focus is on ensuring the preeminence of national and international law, and to do so, the contracting state should consider contractual provisions addressing

a. past conduct (good practice 6);
b. financial and economic capacity (good practice 7);
c. possession of required registration, licenses or authorizations (good practice 8);
d. personnel and property records (good practice 9);
e. training (good practice 10);
f. lawful acquisition and use of equipment, in particular weapons (good practice 11);
g. internal organization and regulation and accountability (good practice 12);
h. welfare of personnel (good practice 13).[63]

Though these provisions incorporate by reference the uncertainty discussed above, the guidance provided is, from a theoretical standpoint, quite useful. The subsequent provisions on the termination of contracts, the contractual arrangements surrounding selection and hiring of subcontracted PMSCs, requirements regarding identification of PMSC personnel, pricing and payment arrangements, and consultative agreements with the territorial state or states are likewise of substantial value and utility.[64] Even if they do not provide specifics, they provide a set of ingredients necessary for states to include when contracting with PMSCs.

Focusing more on some of the legal significance of the Document, the section on "monitoring compliance and ensuring accountability" provides advice to contracting states regarding the treatment of PMSCs in their national laws.[65] It advocates that the states institute laws that address criminal and noncriminal matters, and institute administrative frameworks for regulatory oversight, building on a number of provisions from the "Legal Obligations" portion of the Document. Since these provisions are fundamental to the present analysis, it is worth examining them in their entirety.

Paragraph 19 focuses on criminal law, not just for individual contractors, but for the corporate entities employing them as well. It advocates that contracting states seek

> to provide for criminal jurisdiction in their national legislation over crimes under international law and their national law committed by PMSCs and their personnel and, in addition, to consider establishing:
>
> a. corporate criminal responsibility for crimes committed by the PMSC, consistent with the Contracting State's national legal system;
> b. criminal jurisdiction over serious crimes committed by PMSC personnel abroad.[66]

The recommendations of this paragraph mean that contracting states should actually amend their laws in order to be able to exercise criminal jurisdiction over both the employees of a PMSC with which it has contracted and the PMSC itself. It suggests, for example, that UK courts should have criminal jurisdiction over the American or even Peruvian employees of a US PMSC with which it has contracted. Furthermore, the UK courts should have criminal jurisdiction over the US PMSC as a corporate entity with an independent capacity for criminal activity. The clarification of such jurisdiction would help substantially to reduce one of the principal areas of legal twilight surrounding PMSCs. It would certainly establish more stringent relations between state principals and their agents. Essentially, this provision recommends that states adopt long-arm criminal statutes that allow for prosecution of crimes committed abroad, regardless of nationality.

This recommended criminal jurisdiction would apply to crimes defined under international law, as well as in the contracting state's domestic law. This means that contracting states would have to resolve any complications in their own legal systems that could potentially hinder a criminal prosecution of a noncitizen or nonresident corporation for international crimes committed on foreign territory. Currently, such complications form a substantial barrier to successful prosecutions in most states. Even procedural concerns and evidentiary issues relating to the collection and admissibility of evidence must therefore be addressed. These recommendations, therefore, propose a rather extensive undertaking.

The Document goes on to make similar recommendations regarding non-criminal matters:

> To provide for non-criminal accountability mechanisms for improper or unlawful conduct of PMSCs and their personnel, including:
>
> a. contractual sanctions commensurate to the conduct, including:
>
>   a. immediate or graduated termination of the contract;
>   b. financial penalties;
>   c. removal from consideration for future contracts, possibly for a set time period;
>   d. removal of individual wrongdoers from the performance of the contract;
>
> b. referral of the matter to competent investigative authorities;
> c. providing for civil liability, as appropriate.[67]

This paragraph also requires new legislation specifically targeted at decreasing twilight in national law surrounding the use and operation of PMSCs in noncriminal contexts. Subsection (a) is uncontroversial, as it draws on standard contract laws and indeed seeks more to set the terms of the contract than to amend a legal system. It does, however, implicitly require some form of data collection, as contracting states are expected to keep track of companies based on their past performance. Subsection (b) is a simple recommendation that straddles criminal and noncriminal measures, and essentially suggests that the contracting state be prepared to refer the PMSC to investigating entities such as the police or tax agencies. It is not entirely clear, however, what parameters this subsection attempts to set.

Finally, subsection (c) is both important and ambiguous. Whereas the section on criminal law clarified, albeit in broad terms, what the contracting states needed to do, this provision leaves a great deal of uncertainty as to how a state should proceed. Providing civil liability could mean anything from clarifying the laws of vicarious corporate liability to instituting civil penalties for specific conduct by PMSCs. The word "appropriate" is highly ambiguous, as this is a new field, with few precedents, and virtually no guidance or agreed-upon standards. The Montreux Document is the first articulated set of guidelines, so it does not help much that in attempting to clarify issues of civil accountability—one of the most, if not the most contentious issue—the Document advises contracting states to take "appropriate" action.

Having now recommended substantial amendments to national criminal law and civil law to account for the nature of PMSCs, the Document proceeds to suggest that states also adopt administrative mechanisms for dealing with the operation of these companies.[68] Again, the drafters opted to use "appropriate" as a means of characterizing the measures that the contracting state must take. Additionally, the provisions themselves are rather vague as to what is actually necessary. Some sort of accountability mechanism needs to be put in place, and it needs to be adequately resourced; it needs to provide training, information sharing, and oversight. But there is no sense of how such a mechanism might actually be set up, or how it would work. Since there is no precedent for one it will be a challenge to successfully develop one on these principles alone. Again, however, it is an important step to have an agreement between the states as to the ingredients necessary for moving forward with how to resolve the issues of accountability surrounding PMSCs. There may be a number of different approaches, but at least there is some consensus as to what is required.

Territorial States

While the first 23 paragraphs of good practices in the Montreux Document center on the obligations of contracting states, the next 29 paragraphs focus on the obligations of territorial states. These would be states like Iraq, Afghanistan, Sierra Leone, Colombia, and others—many of which would be collapsed, failed, or otherwise in a situation where the rule of law had broken down. In summarizing the obligations, the Document establishes that "Territorial States should evaluate whether their domestic legal framework is adequate to ensure that the conduct of PMSCs and their personnel is in conformity with relevant national law, international humanitarian law and human rights law or whether it needs to establish further arrangements to regulate the activities of PMSCs."[69] The one acknowledgment of the difficulties such states face is that the Document suggests that territorial states may accept information from the contracting state concerning the PMSC's ability to conduct itself in a manner consistent with domestic and international laws. Seeing as most collapsed and failed states will not be able to fulfill the obligations or adhere to the best practices described in the Montreux Document, it is not worth spending the time on a close analysis of the entire section, but as Afghanistan has shown, not all states amid armed conflict are unable to take measures to regulate PMSCs.

At the outset, territorial states are charged with determining what activities PMSCs may legally engage in on their territory.[70] Again, direct participation in hostilities seems to be a threshold point. Once such a determination is made, the territorial states should then institute, manage, and oversee a licensing and authorization program to ensure that PMSCs are approved to perform the services in which they engage.[71] Paragraphs 26–29 deal with the procedure of authorizing PMSCs to act, and paragraphs 30–39 address the specific criteria the territorial state should use in determining whether to authorize the PMSC. These criteria are similar and at times identical to those provided to contracting states in determining whether the PMSCs were suitable for hiring. Yet there are even more criteria. While the aims are laudable, it is difficult to conceive of how these territorial states, as a practical matter, would even be able to engage in the kind of background investigation required. The introduction to the section on territorial states indicates that, in light of the challenges faced by such states, they may accept information from contracting states about the PMSCs. Given that the Montreux Document pertains to armed conflict settings, the only way that territorial states could adhere to these requirements would be to cooperate and rely upon the contracting state. This proposes, therefore, a strange dynamic concerning the licensing procedure within the territorial state. Furthermore, what if, as in Sierra Leone, the contracting state and the territorial state are one and the same? Such a dynamic effectively eliminates the possibility of serious accountability on the part of the PMSC. Perhaps even more challenging: What happens if, as in the early stages of Iraq, the contracting state is at war with the territorial state? Information sharing on PMSCs in such circumstances appears impossible or untenable.

In addition to suggesting territorial states set maximum numbers for PMSC personnel and equipment, and require the companies to post bond, paragraphs 40–42 further establish that the territorial state should refer to the criteria of paragraphs 30–39 in formalizing the authorization. Paragraph 40 is even a near copy of paragraph 14, which establishes what contracting states should include in a contract and lists past conduct, personnel records, and training among other things.[72] This is an extensive and challenging undertaking for a state that perhaps does not have a functioning electricity grid or control over its own capital city.

The term "appropriate" continues to characterize the advice given in the next several paragraphs to territorial states. Territorial states should have in place "appropriate rules on the use of force and firearms by PMSCs and their personnel"[73] and "appropriate rules on the possession of weapons by PMSCs and their personnel."[74] These various paragraphs on safety procedure again provide nice ideals, but such ideals are hard to imagine being practiced in most territorial states. Additionally, it is hard to assess, given the unique nature of conflict, what "appropriate" weapons regulations would be. These good practices therefore leave a great deal of discretion to the state in which the conflict is located and seem to actually be better suited to non-armed conflict settings.

In the final section on territorial states, "Monitoring compliance and ensuring accountability," the Montreux Document encourages territorial states to take similar legal measures as contracting states. In other words, territorial states should amend their laws to account for criminal and noncriminal jurisdiction over the actions of PMSCs. Additionally, they should oversee the authorization program that allows PMSCs to operate in the country. While such recommendations might seem reasonable, no state will normally plan to be the host of an armed conflict; and when it is a host, amending its laws to account for PMSCs will rarely constitute a top priority. In other words, these extensive recommendations really only apply to a very few states that might possibly be in a position to take them on board despite the turmoil within their boundaries. Again, this entire section seems better suited to guiding the conduct of states that are not engaged in armed conflict.

Home States

The final portion of the good practices part of the Montreux Document provides a series of recommendations for home states. These last 20 paragraphs principally reiterate the sorts of suggestions directed at both contracting and territorial states in the previous sections. In the introduction to this portion of the Document, the limitations of the advice given are noted: "It is recognised that other good practices for Regulation—such as regulation of standards through trade associations and through international cooperation—will also provide guidance for regulating PMSCs, but have not been elaborated here."[75]

The introduction continues, however, to advocate essentially an audit and rethinking of the domestic legal regimes surrounding PMSCs: "In this understanding, Home States should evaluate whether their domestic legal framework, be it central or federal, is adequately conducive to respect for relevant international humanitarian law and human rights law by PMSCs and their personnel, or whether, given the size and nature of their national private military and security industry, additional measures should be adopted to encourage such respect and to regulate the activities of PMSCs."[76]

Finally, the introduction advocates that home states look to the laws of contracting and territorial states for guidance on regulatory regimes. Between the placement of this section as the last portion of the Document, and several suggestions that home states cooperate with other relevant states, it seems the drafters of the Montreux Document see home states not as taking the lead on the regulation of PMSCs, but as the least important of the various states involved with the industry. Given that the home states have immense leverage over PMSCs—as the authority best placed to limit or control the services their country exports—this advice is, much like the section on territorial states, out of sync with reality.

In general, the Document advocates that home states develop an authorization program in which they use a series of criteria to determine whether PMSCs should be allowed to offer their services within those states.[77] The criteria are essentially the same as those used by territorial states in their authorization schemes and by contracting states in determining whether to enter a contract.[78] The home state should also adapt its laws to account for criminal and noncriminal jurisdiction over PMSCs and to create other administrative oversight.[79] Those states should also monitor and oversee the licensing and authorization program and implement various compliance measures.[80] And they should have "appropriate" accountability mechanisms in place to address weapons purchase, ownership, and use.[81] Besides the notion that home states should "harmonize their authorization system and decisions with those of other States and take into account regional approaches relating to authorization systems,"[82] there is nothing surprising or novel in this portion of the Document.

Conclusion

These good practices were developed by collaboration between states, the ICRC, and high-level international experts. The industry had not been, and perhaps still has not been, in operation long enough to discern if those practices are actually best practices or merely good ones. As a result, this guidance is based on a mix of what is necessary, what is ideal and feasible, and what is ideal, but not yet realistic. In other words, these practices constitute a blend of the achievable and the aspirational. The criticism in this analysis points out what is perhaps not clear on account of legal uncertainty and what is not yet possible on account of the immaturity of the accountability infrastructure surrounding the industry. None of that criticism, however, detracts from the great benefit that the guidance in the Montreux Document provides. If states follow that guidance out of a sense of obligation, and recent studies suggest they are,[83] then that routine practice based on the Document will begin to form customary international law over time. That law would then become binding, even on the states that have not chosen to participate in the Montreux Document. Consequently, the good practices section of the Document may ultimately have greater legal effect than the legal obligations section.

COMMENTARY AND GENERAL ANALYSIS

It is easy to criticize the Montreux Document for all the things it does not do. It does not resolve all issues of accountability for the private military and security industry. It also does not dispel all the legal twilight or uncertainty surrounding the industry. It does not close the gaps of practice between legal systems that may make it difficult for states and other actors to achieve comprehensive accountability. The legal section does not delve into the complex nuances of legal obligations incumbent upon states or do much to interpret the international legal obligations of the industry itself. Indeed, many of the most challenging legal questions pertaining to PMSCs under international law are left unanswered by the Montreux Document. And the good practices section does not provide a comprehensive or enforceable "how to" guide to addressing all issues that may arise in private military and security contracting.

But it is more important to recognize what the Montreux Document does and will continue to do. As the previous two sections argue, the Document helps clarify the consensus surrounding the application of international law to the use and operation of PMSCs and provides a starting point for the development of international custom. Indeed, the contrast between the number of states that have signed the UN Mercenary Convention and the number of states and organizations that participate in the Montreux Document—together with the overlap between those two lists of states—helps indicate that there may be growing custom with regard to the recognition of PMSCs as acceptable, legal actors within the field of international security. Perhaps even more importantly, evidence suggests that states are working to incorporate the principles and practices of the Montreux Document into their national law and policy, and are taking their commitment to the Montreux Document seriously.[84]

To fully appreciate the value of the Document, however, it is worth reviewing some of the key criticisms of it beyond those articulated above. Amol Mehra, in a rather extensive and pointed critique, argues that "although the goal of the Montreux Document is to clarify the pertinent international legal obligations under international humanitarian law and human rights law, it lacks either a concrete and clear categorization of applicable laws, or the enforcement mechanisms necessary to address violations."[85] While such concrete and clear categorization would theoretically be helpful, it is unrealistic given the complexity of the legal twilight surrounding the industry. Many of the legal clarifications provided by the Montreux Document are subtle and perhaps undetectable to those who are not intimately engaged with the nuances of international law. The Document does not provide what Mehra wishes, but doing so would require oversimplifying the legal complexities. Furthermore, the Document does indicate that the appropriate mechanism for addressing violations would be the domestic courts of the interested states and encourages states to proactively invigorate their national capacity on this front. Thus, this critique seems more aimed at international legal complexity than at actual shortcomings of the Montreux Document.

Mehra further criticizes the limited scope of the Document given that armed conflicts only constitute a portion of the settings in which PMSCs operate, and armed guarding only constitutes one of the services PMSCs provide.[86] First, the ICRC and Swiss Foreign Ministry were focusing on armed conflict settings because that was the context of greatest concern. Second, the *lex specialis* of international humanitarian law needed to be addressed and interpreted with regard to these "new" actors in conflict. Third, the ICRC's focus is armed conflict settings, so it makes sense that it would be focused on that context. Fourth, the definition of PMSCs in the Document is much broader than armed guarding as it includes training of other forces, the maintenance and operation of weapons systems, and other activities that have actually not been covered by any of the other accountability initiatives to date. Finally and most importantly, the Document does suggest, as noted, that the principles—particularly the good practices—are relevant in non-armed conflict contexts, as well. This criticism, therefore, is inconsistent with the actual content of the Document.

Mehra proceeds to also criticize the Document for not conforming to the "framework for corporate activity and human rights" developed by John Ruggie in the UN Guiding Principles on Business and Human Rights.[87] As Mehra writes:

> By choosing to create its own framework, the Montreux Document in effect creates a separate way of examining PMSCs even though they are themselves business entities. This choice is unfortunate because it undermines the effort towards consistency in the drafting of international obligations. Consistency is important to ensure the uniform application of common principles to corporate entities, and to minimise any confusion over applicable obligations.[88]

Essentially, Mehra questions the legitimacy and position of the Montreux Document in international affairs, suggesting that while it is backed by some important states, it falls outside recognized international structures. Other commentary on the Document further develops this argument but is largely countered, as Nigel White points out, by the fact that the ICRC was not only involved, but at the helm of the initiative to produce the Document, thereby lending it considerable credibility.[89] Additionally, the Montreux Document does not need to reference the Ruggie framework in order to be consistent with it. As noted above, many of the legal clarifications and good practices provided are completely consistent with the main tenets of the UN Guiding Principles on Business and Human Rights, which weren't even published until three years after the Document. Incidentally, Mehra's current role as a member of the Board of Directors of the ICoC Association, which derives from the Montreux Document, suggests he has perhaps changed his position or at least does not feel these criticisms are fatal to the credibility of the initiative.

In a more optimistic and positive tone, Mehra also writes that "if State parties do adopt the Montreux Document in significant numbers, it may gain the dimension of becoming 'soft law,' and through influencing the practice of States, could become binding customary international law. In other words, to the extent that the Montreux Document and its contents are adopted by States, it may acquire a firmer root in the legal realm."[90] While there are several inaccuracies with this statement, the point is nevertheless valid. States are not parties to the Montreux Document, and given its status as an international agreement, it does not need to "become" soft law; it already is. That said, Mehra is right that the Montreux Document seems to be growing firmer legal roots and becoming legally significant in new ways.

James Cockayne, an informal advisor to the Montreux Process, wrote one of the most extensive early reviews of the Document. He finds that it has five key areas of significance: (1) "a very public reaffirmation by a diverse group of states, including the United States, of the applicability of international humanitarian law (IHL) and human rights to contemporary armed conflict";[91] (2) "an important statement of lex lata regarding states' existing duties to protect human rights and to ensure respect for international humanitarian law (IHL), when dealing with PMSCs";[92] (3) "a snapshot of the current common ground among key states on the question of states' obligations to regulate the extraterritorial conduct of business entities more generally";[93] (4) "soft standards in the form of 73 'good practices,' which may lay the foundation for further practical regulation of PMSCs through contracts, codes of conduct, national legislation, regional instruments and international standards";[94] and (5) "reveal[ing] the tension between two international regulatory approaches that are increasingly relevant to conflict and security: a state-backed approach that emphasizes a patchwork of hard law obligations; and an industry-backed approach that encourages cross-jurisdictional regulatory harmonization to reduce transaction costs and help secure industry investments."[95] These milestones are somewhat vitiated by the shortcomings Cockayne elaborates upon in his article.

Ultimately, Cockayne finds three key weaknesses in the Document: (1) "the Document proves unwieldy—and has notable lacunae—as a guide for PMSCs as to the conduct they ought engage in";[96] (2) "further work may need to be done to flesh out state and corporate due diligence obligations, on the basis of the Montreux Document's provisions";[97] and (3) "more could be done to build on the rather fragmented treatment of remedial arrangements in the Montreux Document."[98] In general, Cockayne warns that the Montreux Document might engender apathy or complacency with regard to the effort to improve regulation of and increase the legal clarity surrounding the industry. In other words, if states considered the Document the solution to all the problems, it is unlikely that they would push forward with continuing to address the problems. These criticisms have largely been addressed by the processes that have sprung forth from the Document, as they have helped clarify the standards and obligations for PMSCs, provided states with a means of assessing PMSCs in the due diligence process, and created a mechanism to ensure that remedial arrangements do not fall through the cracks. More could be done and is being done, but it does not seem that apathy will stifle onward progress. Cockayne concludes, however, that the Montreux Document "has the potential to provide the basis for other forms of more enforceable regulation."[99] And it has.

The ICoC, ICoCA, PSC Standards Series, and ISO Standards all reference the Montreux Document as a normative statement of international consensus. As these various initiatives, and others, are all aimed at the accountability of PMSCs themselves, their potential legal effect is limited. In other words, while they may contribute to presumptions of negligence in some domestic courts, they cannot ever rise to the level of being customary international law, as they do not provide guidance for state action. Furthermore, while they are in no way limited to armed conflict settings, none of them address the services included in the Document's definition of PMSCs that aren't "security services." Finally, these largely voluntary, business-oriented processes do not all fit together into a completely coherent framework. Rather, they form a patchwork of obligations incumbent on PMSCs themselves.[100] So while the Montreux Document may have limited direct effect on the operation of PMSCs, its real effect is on guiding the conduct of states and is therefore far more significant with regard to international law.

One final feature to note is the Montreux Document Forum, which was initiated in September 2013. Essentially a collaborative exercise among the participating states and organizations of the Montreux Document, the forum provides an incredibly useful venue for ensuring that the legal clarifications and promoted good practices of the Document remain consistent with international consensus and relevant to the actual operations of the industry. As this forum is nascent, it is hard to predict what functions it may have, but it does provide a potential venue for updating and adapting international approaches to the industry.

CONCLUSION

The Montreux Document is not perfect and does not solve the issue of international accountability for PMSCs. But perfection was never its goal, as indicated by the use of the term "good" rather than "best" when prescribing practices for states. And solving the issue of international accountability was never considered a possible outcome. Rather, the aim was to start a process of developing international consensus on how to address the private military and security industry. The Document provides some clear, as well as subtle, guidance to states, and to a lesser degree to the industry, on what international legal obligations exist and how they should be applied to the contracting and operations of PMSCs. Ultimately, however, the section on good practices may prove to be more legally significant than the section on legal obligations, as it may serve as the basis for the development of binding customary international law.

Looking ahead, there are a number of implications that can be drawn from this analysis. They include:

- *Customary international law is forming and will form around the Montreux Document.* It does appear that customary international law is forming around the Montreux Document and more will likely form as states, over time, consistently adhere to the practices promoted by the Document out of a sense of obligation. At a minimum, there seems to be customary law forming over the international recognition of PMSCs as an acceptable actor, distinct from mercenaries.
- *A treaty or convention is not currently needed and could be a mistake.* A treaty or convention does not appear to be the best approach to addressing ongoing concerns that PMSCs lack accountability. As the PMSC industry continues to mature and evolve, and as the use of PMSCs continues to move in different directions, the posture of states toward the industry will need to adapt as well. The advantage of customary international law is that it is flexible and born of states' best practices. In the case of international custom based on the Montreux Document, the starting point for those practices would be derived from recommended approaches proffered by leading international legal experts.
- *Better coordination between multi-stakeholder accountability initiatives and state processes is needed.* The various accountability initiatives aimed

at PMSCs themselves need better coordination with state-based approaches to regulation and policy. The Montreux Document Forum may provide a venue for clarifying how the patchwork of initiatives should be understood to work together in concert with both international and national laws.

- *Expert legal clarification is needed.* Further and ongoing clarification of international legal nuances is needed. While individual experts can conduct such work in isolation, there needs to be a focal point for states to digest this expert interpretation, form consensus around it, and integrate it into national law and policy. The Montreux Document Forum is not currently configured for this purpose, but it could serve as a useful locus for developing this capacity.
- *Assistance to states with incorporating international obligations and practices is needed.* States will need ongoing assistance with incorporating international legal obligations and agreed good practices relating to PMSCs into domestic law and policy. Again, no mechanism for such assistance currently exists, but states could collectively create such capacity, potentially within the Montreux Document Forum.

There are certainly more possible extrapolations from this analysis, but these five points provide an indication of what may be next for states in their efforts to develop accountability and international legal clarity regarding the PMSC industry. Notwithstanding the criticism levied or the follow-on progress that is still needed, this analysis holds that the Montreux Document remains the most legally significant instrument to date concerning private military and security companies.

NOTES

1. Confederation of Switzerland Department of Foreign Affairs and the International Committee of the Red Cross, *The Montreux Document on Pertinent International Legal Obligations and Good Practices for States related to Operations of Private Military and Security Companies during Armed Conflict*, UN Document A/63/467-S/2008/636 (Geneva: International Committee of the Red Cross, 2008), available at http://www.eda.admin.ch/psc (hereinafter "Montreux Document").

2. See, e.g., International Code of Conduct Association, *The International Code of Conduct for Private Security Service Providers* (Geneva: International Code of Conduct Association, 2010), available at http://icoc-psp.org/; International Code of Conduct Association, *Articles of Association of the International Code of Conduct Association* (Geneva, 2013), available at http://www.icoca.ch/en/articles_of_association; American National Standards Institute, *Management System for Quality of Private Security Company Operations: Requirements with Guidance*, ANSI/ASIS PSC.1-2012 (Alexandria: ASIS International, 5 March 2012).

3. Simon Chesterman, "Lawyers, Guns and Money: The Governance of Business Activities in Conflict Zones," *Chicago Journal of International Law* 11, 1 (Summer 2010), page 334.

4. Confederation of Switzerland Department of Foreign Affairs, "The Montreux Document on Private Military and Security Companies" (5 May 2015), available at http://www.eda.admin.ch/psc, accessed 31 July 2015.

5. Montreux Document.
6. Confederation of Switzerland Department of Foreign Affairs, "The Montreux Document on Private Military and Security Companies."
7. Confederation of Switzerland Department of Foreign Affairs, "Participating States of the Montreux Document" (8 April 2015), available at http://www.eda.admin.ch/eda/en/home/topics/intla/humlaw/pse/parsta.html, accessed 31 July 2015.
8. Montreux Document, preface ¶ 2.
9. Montreux Document, preface ¶ 3.
10. Montreux Document, preface ¶ 8.
11. Montreux Document, preface ¶ 7.
12. Montreux Document, preface ¶¶ 5, 8.
13. Montreux Document, preface ¶ 6.
14. Montreux Document, preface ¶ 9(a).
15. Discussion at the First Meeting of the Security in Complex Environments Group, Aerospace Defense Security Group, Ltd. (13 January 2011).
16. Sarah Percy, "Morality and Regulation," in Simon Chesterman and Chia Lehnardt, editors, *From Mercenaries to Market: The Rise and Regulation of Private Military Companies* (Oxford: Oxford University Press, 2007), pages 12–14; United Kingdom Foreign and Commonwealth Office, *Private Military Companies: Options for Regulation*, HC 577 (London: The Stationery Office, 12 February 2002), ¶ 9.
17. International Code of Conduct Association, *The International Code of Conduct for Private Security Service Providers*, ¶ 7.
18. Organization of African Unity, *Convention for the Elimination of Mercenarism in Africa (Opened for Signature) 3 July 1977*, OAU Document CM/817 (29), Annex 2, Article 1 (3rd revision 1977) (entered into force 22 April 1985).
19. *Protocol Additional to the Geneva Conventions of 12 August 1949, and Relating to the Protection of Victims of International Armed Conflicts (Protocol I)*, Article 47 (8 June 1977), 1125 UNTS 17512, available at http://www.icrc.org/ihl.nsf/FULL/470?OpenDocument (hereinafter "Additional Protocol I").
20. United Nations, *International Convention against the Recruitment, Use, Financing and Training of Mercenaries* (4 December 1989), UN Treaty Series 2163 (A/RES/44/34), Article 1 (hereinafter "UN Mercenary Convention").
21. Peter W. Singer, "War, Profits, and the Vacuum of Law: Privatized Military Firms and International Law," *Columbia Journal of Transnational Law* 42, 2 (Spring 2004), page 532.
22. Geoffrey Best, *Humanity in Warfare: The Modern History of the International Law of Armed Conflicts* (London: Weinenfeld and Nicolson, 1980), pages 374–75, note 83.
23. Andrew T. Guzman and Timothy L. Meyer, "International Soft Law," *Journal of Legal Analysis* 2, 1 (Spring 2010), pages 171, 172.
24. UN Mercenary Convention.
25. UN Mercenary Convention.
26. Confederation of Switzerland Department of Foreign Affairs, "Participating States of the Montreux Document."
27. Montreux Document, preface ¶ 5.
28. Montreux Document, part 1 (2008) .
29. Confederation of Switzerland Department of Foreign Affairs, "The Montreux Document on Private Military and Security Companies."
30. Montreux Document, part 1 ¶¶ 3, 9, 14, 18.
31. Montreux Document, part 1 ¶¶ 4, 10, 15, 19.
32. Montreux Document, part 1 ¶¶ 5, 11, 16, 20.
33. Montreux Document, part 1 ¶ 1.
34. Montreux Document, part 1 ¶ 2.
35. See, e.g., James R. Coleman, "Constraining Modern Mercenarism," *Hastings Law Journal* 55, 6 (June 2004), pages 1493, 1537.
36. Montreux Document, part 1 ¶¶ 3–4, 6.
37. Montreux Document, part 1 ¶¶ 3–4, 6.
38. Montreux Document, part 1 ¶ 5.

39. Montreux Document, part 1 ¶ 8.
40. United Nations Office of the High Commissioner for Human Rights, *Guiding Principles on Business and Human Rights: Implementing the United Nations "Protect, Respect and Remedy" Framework* (New York: United Nations, 2011).
41. Montreux Document, part 1 ¶ 7.
42. "Draft Articles on Responsibility of States for Internationally Wrongful Acts, with Commentaries," in *Report of the International Law Commission on the Work of its Fifty-third Session, UN GAOR, 56th Sess., Supp. No. 10, at 43,* UN Document A/56/10 (New York: United Nations, 2001).
43. Montreux Document, part 1 ¶ 27.
44. Montreux Document, part 1 ¶ 23.
45. Montreux Document, part 1 ¶ 22.
46. See, e.g., Ian Ralby, "Private Military Companies and the *Jus ad Bellum*," in Marc Weller, editor, *The Oxford Handbook of the Use of Force in International Law* (Oxford: Oxford University Press, 2015).
47. As discussed in chapters 8 and 9 in this volume.
48. Montreux Document, part 1 ¶ 24.
49. Montreux Document, part 1 ¶ 25.
50. Montreux Document, part 1 ¶ 26(b).
51. Adam Ebrahim, "Going to War with the Army You Can Afford: The United States, International Law, and the Private Military Industry," *Boston University International Law Journal* 28, 1 (Spring 2010), page 213.
52. Percy, "Morality and Regulation," pages 12–14.
53. M. Cherif Bassiouni, "Legal Status of Forces in Iraq from 2003–2008," *Chicago Journal of International Law* 11, 1 (Summer 2010), pages 1, 23.
54. Jamie Williamson, "Challenges of Twenty-first Century Conflicts: A Look at Direct Participation in Hostilities," *Duke Journal of Comparative and International Law* 20, 3 (Spring 2010), pages 457, 465.
55. Statute of the International Court of Justice, Article 38(1)(b).
56. José Luis Gómez del Prado, rapporteur, *Report of the Working Group on the Use of Mercenaries as a Means of Violating Human Rights and Impeding the Exercise of the Right of Peoples to Self-Determination*, UN Document A/HRC/15/25 (New York: United Nations, 2 July 2010).
57. Statute of the International Court of Justice, Article 38(1)(b).
58. International Law Association, "Statement of Principles Applicable to the Formation of General Customary International Law," adopted by Resolution No. 16/2000, London Conference,section 1(i).
59. Montreux Document, part 1 ¶ 1.
60. Montreux Document, part 1 ¶ 1.
61. United Nations Office of the High Commissioner for Human Rights, *Guiding Principles on Business and Human Rights*.
62. Montreux Document, part 2 ¶¶ 5–13.
63. Montreux Document, part 2 ¶ 14.
64. Montreux Document, part 2 ¶¶ 14–18.
65. Montreux Document, part 2 ¶¶ 19–23.
66. Montreux Document, part 2 ¶ 19.
67. Montreux Document, part 2 ¶ 20.
68. Montreux Document, part 2 ¶ 21.
69. Montreux Document, part 2, "B. Good Practices for Territorial States."
70. Montreux Document, part 2 ¶ 24.
71. Montreux Document, part 2 ¶ 25.
72. Montreux Document, part 2 ¶ 40 (2008) .
73. Montreux Document, part 2 ¶ 43.
74. Montreux Document, part 2 ¶ 44.
75. Montreux Document, part 2, "C. Good Practices for Home States."
76. Montreux Document, part 2, "C. Good Practices for Home States."

77. Montreux Document, part 2 ¶¶ 54–59.
78. Montreux Document, part 2 ¶¶ 60–66.
79. Montreux Document, part 2 ¶¶ 71–72.
80. Montreux Document, part 2 ¶¶ 68–69.
81. Montreux Document, part 2 ¶ 55.
82. Montreux Document, part 2 ¶ 56.
83. Rebecca DeWinter-Schmitt, editor, *Montreux Five Years On: An Analysis of State Efforts to Implement Montreux Document Legal Obligations and Good Practices* (Barcelona: Adjuntament de Barcelona, 2013).
84. DeWinter-Schmitt, *Montreux Five Years On*.
85. Amol Mehra, "Bridging the Accountability Gaps: The Proliferation of Private Military and Security Companies and Ensuring Accountability for Human Rights Violations," *Pacific McGeorge Global Business and Development Law Journal* 22, 2 (2010), pages 323, 329.
86. Mehra, "Bridging the Accountability Gaps," pages 323, 328.
87. Mehra, "Bridging the Accountability Gaps," pages 323, 329.
88. Mehra, "Bridging the Accountability Gaps," pages 323, 329.
89. Nigel D. White, "The Privatization of Military and Security Functions and Human Rights: Comments on the U.N. Working Group's Draft Convention," *Human Rights Law Review* 11, 1 (2011), pages 133, 134.
90. Mehra, "Bridging the Accountability Gaps," pages 323, 329.
91. James Cockayne, "Regulating Private Military and Security Companies: The Content, Negotiation, Weaknesses and Promise of the Montreux Document," *Journal of Conflict and Security Law* 13, 3 (Winter 2008), page 403.
92. Cockayne, "Regulating Private Military and Security Companies," page 403.
93. Cockayne, "Regulating Private Military and Security Companies," page 403.
94. Cockayne, "Regulating Private Military and Security Companies," page 404.
95. Cockayne, "Regulating Private Military and Security Companies," page 404.
96. Cockayne, "Regulating Private Military and Security Companies," page 427.
97. Cockayne, "Regulating Private Military and Security Companies," page 427.
98. Cockayne, "Regulating Private Military and Security Companies," page 427.
99. Cockayne, "Regulating Private Military and Security Companies," page 427 .
100. Ian Ralby, "Accounting for Private Security," *Fletcher Security Review* 2, 1 (January 2015).

Chapter Eleven

Contractor Identity

Military Professional Practice and the Evolution of the Modern Soldier

Volker Franke

On 13 April 2015, a federal judge sentenced a former employee of the now-defunct private security company Blackwater Worldwide to life in prison and three others to 30-year prison sentences for killing 14 unarmed civilians in a Baghdad traffic circle in 2007.[1] The verdict overturned a 2010 decision dismissing all charges against the security guards based on claims they had acted in self-defense when their convoy, tasked with rushing American VIPs through the crowded streets of the Iraqi capital, came under attack.[2] The April 2015 verdict brought a legal end to an incident that had been the tip of the spear in a series of violent episodes involving private military and security companies (PMSCs) at the height of the Iraq war that had stoked anger and hostility among the Iraqi government and people.[3]

Further marring the reputation of these actors were frequent tales of waste, fraud, and overbilling.[4] Repeatedly, media reports portrayed security contractors as gun-slinging, Rambo-type warriors interested primarily in seeking adventure and making a quick buck. David Isenberg observed at the time that "nowadays, people tend to label anyone who carries a gun while not a member of the regular military establishment a mercenary. Such people are supposedly uncontrollable rogues who commit unspeakable atrocities and wreak havoc."[5] Following the Nisour Square shooting incident, even the US government became critical of its own practice. As then–secretary of defense Robert Gates told reporters at the Pentagon in 2007, "There have been instances where, to put it mildly, the Iraqis have been offended and not treated properly." Gates went on to say, "Those kinds of activities work at cross purposes to our larger mission in Iraq."[6]

In a January 2011 memorandum intended to institutionalize procedures to better "view, account, and plan for contracted . . . support in the contingency environment," Gates outlined the challenge:

> At the height of Operation IRAQI FREEDOM, contractor numbers well exceeded the military footprint; a similar situation is occurring in support of Operation ENDURING FREEDOM. I do not expect this to change now or in future contingency operations. Although there is historic precedence for contracted support to our military forces, I am concerned about the risks introduced by our current level of dependency, our future total force mix, and the need to better plan for OCS [operational contract support] in the future.[7]

But contracting is big business that has become a necessary component to support the resource-heavy way America fights its wars. In Afghanistan and Iraq alone, the number of contractors has more than doubled the number of uniformed personnel on the ground at various points over the past decade. While there were only about 5,000 contractors in Iraq in March 2015, down from more than 160,000 during the height of the fighting, the 39,600 contractors supporting their training and advising mission, 14,200 of whom are American citizens, dwarfed the 10,000 US troops deployed in Afghanistan.[8] Although most of these contractors are unarmed, media attention still largely focuses on the shooters—the men who carry and use weapons. But are they indeed the gun-toting mercenary loners interested primarily in personal gain they are portrayed to be? Or is there a sense of professionalism, a shared corporate identity, emerging among the members of the booming security industry?

In this chapter, I intend to answer these questions by examining the social identity, occupational self-conceptions, and motivations of individuals who provide armed services in post-conflict environments under contract by PMSC firms. Although the US Congress and the international community have adopted a series of legal norms controlling the private security sector, the industry still relies heavily on self-regulation for monitoring the behavior of its members in the field. While outlining the primary approaches to date intended to formally regulate the industry, I also examine the merits and limitations of informal regulation through social group norms and identifications. To set the stage for this analysis, I briefly introduce social identity theory and its impact on the forming of professional identity. Next, following a discussion of military professionalism, I develop a typology of military identities based on degrees of formal and informal regulation associated with each identity. Since armed security contractors take on military operational responsibilities, I present the findings of a survey of security contractors conducted in 2009 that explores the extent to which their values and attitudes embrace military professionalism or point to the emergence of a unique corporate identity. I conclude with some observations for the future of outsourcing security functions to the private sector and the utility of using contractors in peace and stability operations.

THE CONCEPT OF IDENTITY

Most generally, identity represents "the process by which the person seeks to integrate his [*sic*] various statuses and roles, as well as his diverse experiences, into a coherent image of self."[9] Individuals draw on multiple, sometimes even competing sub-identities (e.g., religious, political, social, ethnic, or occupational) to derive their self-conceptions. These sub-identities become consequential for behavior in situations when their salience is invoked.[10] A person's various sub-identities form specific links between the self and his or her membership in social groups. John Hofman specified salience as the probability by which a sub-identity is remembered and activated in a given context.[11] Prolonged salience upgrades the sub-identity in the "prominence hierarchy," thereby enhancing its "centrality" and the degree to which it connects with other sub-identities. The more central a sub-identity is to an individual's self-conception and the more interconnected it is with other sub-identities, the more committed the individual will be to preserving and enhancing that identity and to displaying attitudes, values, and social behaviors consistent with it.

In the present context, the concept of "social identity" refers to "that part of individuals' self-concept which derives from knowledge of their membership in a social group (or groups) together with the value and emotional significance attached to that membership."[12] Theories of social identity are typically based on three premises:

1. people are motivated to create and maintain a positive self-concept;
2. the self-concept derives largely from group identifications; and
3. people establish positive social identities through normative comparisons between favorable in-groups and unfavorable out-groups.[13]

Social identity research has demonstrated that individuals tend to invoke their group identifications in many decision contexts, since the norms, values, stereotypes, and behavior patterns associated with a particular identity provide a sense of certainty and may inform their choice among decision alternatives.[14]

PROFESSIONAL IDENTITY

A professional, Morris Janowitz explained, "as a result of prolonged training, acquires a skill which enables him to render a specialized service."[15] Janowitz further conjectured that "a profession is more than a group with special skill, acquired through intensive training. A professional group develops a sense of group identity and a system of internal administration. Self-administration—often supported by state intervention—implies the growth of a body of ethics and standards of performance."[16] As part of an individual's overall identity structure, professional identity reflects the expression of his or her self-perception as a social carrier of the values, norms, skills, and behaviors that define his or her professional in-group. The stronger an individual's sense of professional identity the more probable it is that this identity will serve as a central cognitive resource to incite and sustain motivation, render work meaningful, and shape behavior amid the complex and fluid demands of today's occupational environments. To society, Robert Kennedy argued, professionals provide "reliable fixed standards (of health, of justice, of truth, etc.) in situations where the facts are murky. . . . They represent the best a particular community is able to muster in response to new challenges."[17] Nearly a century ago, sociologist Edward Alsworth Ross explained, in "The Making of the Professions":

> One will hesitate to commit one's dearest interests to such men unless one has ground for believing them to be worthy of trust. There is need, therefore, that callings of this confidential character be restricted to men of honor acting with reference to a high standard. . . . The expert cannot raise the tone of his calling unless he is shielded from the withering competition of bunglers, quacks and charlatans.[18]

But, Ross argued further, simply excluding the unfit from the practice of a profession was insufficient. Instead, it was central for professions to attract "men of good breeding and high spirit, for it is such men who will contribute most to set and fix the exacting standard of professional conduct."[19] For Ross, true professionals are never motivated primarily by economic interests. "The natural effect of fencing the field and attracting into it superior men is the growth of *the professional spirit*, which is the very antithesis of the commercial spirit. In a true profession the pursuit of gain is subordinated to the aim of service."[20] Professional identity comprises three key elements:

1. *Specialized knowledge* accumulated over time and built up by experience, analysis, and insight from predecessors in the field. It is knowledge that "penetrates the root of the matter and gives its possessor an understanding not only of *how* things are, but also *why* they are that way."[21]

2. *Motivation/commitment to service*. This includes service to one's professional community, that is, a public promise to fulfill one's professional

responsibilities and perform one's tasks according to principles and accepted practices defined by the discipline. Moreover, professionals "commit themselves to use their specialized knowledge principally to serve others and not primarily to serve themselves."[22]

3. *Decision autonomy/control.* Professionals are granted liberty to choose concrete goals and specific courses of action with little to no interference or within fairly expansive and flexible boundaries. Kennedy explains that "the conditions in which problems present themselves in real life are inherently unpredictable, and so it is not possible to develop routines and detailed plans for coping with every contingency. Instead, we rely upon people who thoroughly understand the principles that lie at the foundation of successful solutions to craft a workable plan within the context in which the problem occurs."[23] This argument implies that the more unpredictable or unknowable a situation is, the less behavior can be regulated formally through standard operation procedures or predetermined rules of engagement. Consequently, the more individuals in complex and volatile contexts will rely on invoking the values and principles associated with their salient (professional) identities.[24]

The expectation is that, in conditions of uncertainty, professionals apply prudence and sound judgment based on their professional education, training, and experience. The underlying assumption (or hope) is that vetted professionals will be able to respond to emerging challenges reliably, effectively, and efficiently while being committed first and foremost to the well-being of those they serve—especially in complex and uncertain contexts where formal regulation may not exist, may not be appropriate, or may be difficult to implement and enforce. Based on the evolution of the profession of arms since World War II, I develop a typology of military identity in the following section as a baseline for assessing the professional self-conception of private security contractors.

THE PROFESSION OF ARMS

A poster child for illustrating the elements of professional or corporate identity has been the military: officers and soldiers adhere to a unique ethos that distinguishes them from professionals in other occupations.[25] Nearly six decades ago, Samuel Huntington described military professionals as experts trained in the "management of violence" and noted that military professionals were not motivated by financial gain but by patriotism and service to society.[26] Early social psychologists had already demonstrated that individuals adopt cognitive patterns for framing reality from their membership in groups and these function as "social carriers" of values and normative thought patterns.[27] The 1993 US Army operations manual, for instance, described the values that shape military identity very generally as "proper subordination to political authority, loyalty, duty, selfless service, courage, integrity, respect for human dignity, and a sense of justice."[28] Although these values have long been at the heart of military identity, the idea of what it means to be a soldier has changed over the course of the last half century. For the purpose of this chapter, I distinguish among the following five types of military professionals (see table 11.1 for a summary):

1. *Militarist*: Developed during World War II, Harold Lasswell's theory of the "garrison state" envisioned a society run by the "specialists of violence."[29] In the context of an all-out war, even management and administrative skills were needed to "translate the complicated operations of modern life into every relevant frame of reference—the frame of fighting effectiveness as well as pecuniary profit."[30] Believing the world to be in a more or less permanent state of conflict, Lasswell conjectured that the military elite would eventually subordinate the masses and enlist them in a total war effort.[31] In the garrison state, two central values motivate military professionals: service and personal glory.

2. *Traditional Warrior*: Contending Lasswell's argument that the military professional preferred war over peace, Huntington argued that the military professional "is afraid of war. He wants to prepare for war. But he is never ready to fight a war."[32] Nevertheless, Huntington acknowledged that soldiers typically believed in the permanence, irrationality, weakness, and evil in human nature. As a traditional warrior, "the military man is held to believe that peace is stultifying and that conflict and war develop man's highest moral and intellectual qualities; he favors aggressive and bellicose national policies. He is also thought to be opposed to democracy and to desire the organization of society on the basis of the chain of command."[33] Distinguishing between military professionals primarily charged with combat and command and those responsible for technical and logistical support, Huntington argued that the latter group did not represent traditional warriors since their expertise contained both the management of violence and technical or other professional knowledge not unique to the military.[34] Committed above all to preserving the security of the state, traditional warriors operate in a state of constant preparation for war, favoring the use of force to ensure victory. Overall, Huntington concluded, the professional ethic of the traditional warrior is essentially a combination of realism and conservatism.[35]

3. *Constabulary Soldier*: Like Huntington, Morris Janowitz viewed military professionals first and foremost as managers of violence. Yet changes in the military's operational environment required soldiers to also fulfill noncombat roles and become "more skilled in techniques of organization, in the management of morale and negotiation," and to "develop a capacity for public relations."[36] Janowitz acknowledged that professional soldiers might resist identifying with constabulary duties because they were likely to view

these police-like activities as less prestigious and less honorable than traditional combat tasks.[37] Consequently, he proposed a distinction between two types of military professionals: (1) "heroic leaders" or "absolutists" who embodied traditional notions of militarism and glory, resembling Huntington's traditional warrior; and (2) "military managers" or "pragmatists" who concerned themselves primarily with the rational and scientific conduct of war. In line with Huntington, Janowitz noted that absolutists viewed war as the most fundamental basis of international relations and believed political objectives were to be gained through victory. By contrast, constabulary soldiers approached warfare as only one instrument of international politics alongside ideological, diplomatic, and economic means.

4. *Postmodern Peace Soldier*: With the end of the Cold War, the debate surrounding military professionalism and the self-conception of soldiers and officers received renewed attention. Conceptions of military identity, military roles and missions, and models of civilian control required such peculiar adaptation in the context of peace and stability operations that Charles Moskos and others described the early-twenty-first-century American military as "postmodern," characterized by five fundamental organizational traits: (1) increased coordination and communication between the civilian and military spheres; (2) a reduction of the rigid differences within the services regarding rank and role (i.e., combat versus service support); (3) a shift in understanding of the military's purpose to include stabilization and peace operations; (4) the need to seek mission legitimacy from the United Nations, NATO, or other supranational organizations; and (5) the internationalization of military forces, as nations increasingly sought to build coalitions to solve international problems.[38]

5. *Mercenary*: Specialists in the application and management of violence for whom profit maximization is a more important motivator than public service may seek opportunities to employ their skills outside the auspices of their respective state. Hence, at the extreme end of the professional spectrum we find the classic mercenary whose interest in profit maximization exceeds any national allegiances or service obligations. Defined most generally, a mercenary is a professional soldier hired by a foreign state to take part in armed conflict. He is not a national or a party to the conflict and is "motivated to take part in the hostilities essentially by the desire for private gain and, in fact, is promised, by or on behalf of a party to the conflict, material compensation substantially in excess of that promised or paid to combatants of similar ranks and functions in the armed forces of that Party."[39]

Table 11.1 summarizes the five types of military professionals, each resembling notions of professionalism based on specialized skill sets, motivations, control mechanisms, and value orientations.

Table 11.1. Characteristics of Military Professional Practice

Type of Military Professional	Specialized Knowledge	Motivation/Service Commitment	Decision Autonomy/ Control	Values
Militarist	Combat (management of violence)	Service to country Pursuit of glory	Chain of command High degree of formal control	War > peace Patriotism Nationalism Military honor Above politics
Traditional Warrior	Combat and command Maximum use of force	Security of the state Military honor Pursuit of glory Sense of brotherhood Intense group loyalty	Chain of command High degree of formal control	Peace > war Readiness for war Patriotism Opposed to international law and regulation Realism and conservatism Victory orientation
Constabulary Soldier	Rational and scientific conduct of war Combat and peacekeeping Combat support (logistics) Minimum use of force Management of morale and negotiation	Service to the nation Code of honor Sense of brotherhood Transferability of skills to civilian sector	Civilian supremacy Formal and informal control Civil-military relations	Peace > war Seeks viable international relations Support for economics and diplomatic policy options Belief in the legitimacy of peace operations Political responsibility
Postmodern Peace Soldier	Combat Peace enforcement Peacekeeping Peacebuilding Managing transitions Cultural sensitivity	Economic incentives and educational benefits Service to country/ people in need	Democratic (national and international, formal and informal) control Recognition of supranational authority Civil-military cooperation	Peace > war Globalism Support of international law/regulation
Mercenary	Combat	Profit	Employer (government or private) Little formal control	War > peace Self-interest Non-patriotic

PRIVATE SECURITY CONTRACTORS AND MILITARY PROFESSIONALS

Which, if any, of these military professionals do security contractors resemble? On the one hand, industry representatives suggest that contractors employed by private military and security companies bear a resemblance to the constabulary or postmodern peace soldier.[40] Yet most media categorize them as mercenaries. This simply reflects the multifaceted nature of the industry. In a 2009 study, Volker Franke and Marc von Boemcken[41] distinguished five types of services provided by security firms based on their relative distance from an assumed front line in the context of armed conflict:

1. *Armed operative combat support* is performed in immediate proximity to the battlefield and includes the active and armed participation in offensive war-fighting activities. Firms offering such services usually function as force multipliers for their clients, who typically include weak or fragile states with relatively low military capabilities.[42]

2. *Armed security services* require readiness to engage in fighting. Tasks include (1) static security, that is, protecting fixed sites such as housing areas, oil pipelines, reconstruction work sites, or government buildings; (2) convoy security, that is, escorts for vehicle convoys moving equipment, supplies, or people through a combat theater; and (3) personal security details, providing full-time protective security to high-ranking officials.[43]

3. *Unarmed operative combat support* services are performed in close proximity to the battlefield and/or have an immediate impact on activities therein. Services include establishing and managing command, control, and communications operations, and providing security-related surveillance.

4. *Military and/or security-related consultancy and training* services typically assist a client's armed forces with intelligence, threat analyses, and military training.

5. Finally, *military support services* include secondary military functions (e.g., logistics, intelligence, technical support, supply, and transportation) that are far removed from the front line and have little direct impact on the battlefield. Military support services make up the lion's share of military outsourcing, freeing up a client's military personnel to focus on core combat functions.[44] For instance, of the approximately 114,000 Department of Defense (DoD) contractors deployed in Iraq in September 2009, fewer than 10 percent (11,162) provided armed security services.

Given that much of the controversy surrounding the use of contractors in combat and stability operations revolves around the provision of armed combat or armed security services, I focus the following discussion of formal and informal control on individuals employed by firms providing armed security services. I explore whether those individuals have formed a coherent professional identity and, if so, the extent to which that identity resembles characteristics of professional military practice outlined in table 11.1.

CONTROLLING THE PRIVATE SECURITY INDUSTRY

Reports of waste, fraud, and contractor misbehavior suggest under-regulation of the private security industry. This section explores mechanisms for regulating individual and group behavior through social control: the formal use of positive or negative sanctions or through informal intersubjective internalization of norms and values. When the concept of social control was first introduced at the turn of the twentieth century, it emphasized society's need for "social integration into common value systems" in response to trends of increasing individualism tearing at the social fabric of communities.[45] The idea of social control was initially conceived as individuals' ability to harmonize their desires with those of the larger society—to "assume the attitudes of others who are involved with them in a common endeavor"[46] —and modify their behavior accordingly.[47] Social control, Ross explained, refers to the "ascendancy over the aims and acts of the individual which is exercised on behalf of the group. . . . It is kept up partly by definite organs, formally constituted and supported by the will of society, and partly by informal spontaneous agencies that, consciously or unconsciously, serve the social interest and function under constant supervisions from above. . . . Control harmonizes clashing activities by checking some and stimulating others."[48]

Formal and informal control mechanisms operate side by side and, depending on the degree of internalization and the kinds of values in question, one may either bolster, weaken, or substitute for the other. Which formal and informal control mechanisms exist regulating the private security industry? To what extent are these internalized and supported by individual contractors? The remainder of the chapter will explore these questions.

Formal Regulation

Formal regulation refers to the issuance and enforcement of legal prescriptions, drawing an authoritative distinction between the permitted and the prohibited. In general, contractors operating in Iraq and Afghanistan are subject to three types of formal regulation: international laws of war and UN Security Council resolutions specific to the area of operations, US law, and the domestic law of the respective host country.[49] Since the beginning of the US occupation in Iraq in 2003 contractor activities became subject to increasing formal regulation.[50] During the initial phase of the occupation, contractors operating on behalf of US agencies were regulated by orders issued by the Coalition Provisional Authority (CPA). For instance, CPA Order 3 (December 2003) required weapons-carrying contractors to obtain a weapons permit and restricted the legitimate range of weapons.[51] CPA Order 17 (June 2004) prohibited contractors from joining coalition forces in "combat operations except in self-defense or in defense of persons as specified in [their] contracts."[52] It also exempted contractors from Iraqi laws for acts related to their contracts. In January 2009, however, jurisdiction over US defense contractors came to be governed by the Withdrawal Agreement that granted Iraqi authorities "primary jurisdiction over U.S. Defense contractors and their employees who are not citizens of Iraq or who habitually reside there."[53]

In addition to provisions regulating the specific domestic operational context, US nationals or members of the armed forces are regulated by the War Crimes Act of 1996 and civilian employees of the Department of Defense may be prosecuted under the 2000 Military Extraterritorial Jurisdiction Act (MEJA) for felonies "if committed within the special maritime and territorial jurisdiction of the United States."[54] In response to the 2007 Nisour Square shootings, formal mechanisms to regulate the industry and the behavior of individual contractors tightened considerably:[55]

- In 2007 Congress passed the MEJA Expansion and Enforcement Act (HR 2740), subjecting all contractors working for the US government in war zones to the jurisdiction of US criminal law. In a first application of this act in December 2008, four Blackwater guards were charged with manslaughter for their involvement in the Nisour Square shootings.[56] In January 2010, however, the judge dismissed the indictment on the basis that the prosecution had built its case on statements by the defendants that had been improperly compelled by State Department investigators during the investigation of the incident.[57] New charges were brought against them in October 2013 and in April 2015 a federal judge sentenced one of the shooters to life in prison and three others to 30-year prison sentences.[58]
- In March 2008, the Department of Defense extended the jurisdiction of the Uniform Code of Military Justice (UCMJ) to also cover "any illegal activities by Department of Defense civilian employees and DoD contractor personnel overseas with our Armed Forces."[59]
- In September 2008, 17 states, including the United States, finalized the so-called Montreux Document, the first international document to describe international law as it applies to the activities of private military and security companies whenever these are present in the context of an armed conflict.[60] The number of signatories to the Montreux Document has increased considerably since 2008, but as discussed in chapter 10 of this volume, the non-binding nature of the document still very much limits its enforceability.

- In January 2009, the Iraqi government lifted the immunity of contractors to local law, thus making it possible for Iraqi authorities to criminally prosecute security contractors for unlawful behavior.
- Following the departure of United States forces from Iraq in December 2011, the Iraqi government began regulating foreign PMSCs under Iraqi law, including officially requiring permissions to operate, vehicle registrations, and weapons licenses restricting certain weapons and types of ammunition.[61]

The question of whether and to what extent any of these regulatory mechanisms apply to security contractors will ultimately depend on their legal status. Assuming, for instance, that the definition of "mercenary" applies as customary international law in peace and stability operations, third-party contractor personnel who are non-coalition nationals might be considered mercenaries. While more than three-fourths (77 percent) of the armed security contractors operating in Iraq in September 2009 were third-party nationals, 90 percent of armed contractors in Afghanistan were local nationals.[62] The question of what it means to "take an active part in hostilities" is central to deciding whether to categorize security contractors as combatants or civilians in combat, yet what constitutes "participating in armed conflict" is neither fully settled nor easy to determine. Jennifer Elsea observed that "because contract employees fall outside the military chain of command, even those who appear to meet the criteria of combatants could be at risk of losing their right to be treated as POW if captured by the enemy."[63] A 2009 guidance issued by the International Committee of the Red Cross (ICRC) concluded: "All armed actors [in international armed conflict] showing a sufficient degree of military organization and belonging to a party to the conflict must be regarded as part of the armed forces of that party."[64] Under this view, the incorporation into the armed forces of a party to the conflict will assign combatant status to contractors. Otherwise, they are considered civilians for the purpose of international law.

Besides legal accountability, political oversight also seems to have improved markedly as, for instance, the theater rules of engagement (ROE) apply to security contractors and coalition military personnel alike. In addition, the Departments of State and Defense agreed to extend their oversight responsibilities. The DoD established an Armed Contractor Oversight Division in 2007 and "significantly [increased] the number of Defense Contracting Management Agency personnel."[65] At the same time, the State Department has taken steps to improve on-site monitoring of contractor activities through, for instance, video surveillance of privately protected convoys.[66]

Informal Regulation

Informal regulation refers to the norms, rules, and values that are internalized by individuals as a central element of their very sense of "selfness" and identity. As a consequence, behavior is guided through continual *self*-surveillance and *self*-regulation instead of the threat of external sanctions.[67] Distinguishing professional from material interests, Ross asserted almost a century ago that "while in the true profession the practitioner is made into a faithful servant of society by control from within, the business corporation is not to be made such save by control from without."[68]

Informal regulation is a fundamentally intersubjective process, in that identity is—above all—a *social* matter, for one arrives at a sense of selfhood predominantly through the identification with others.[69] When informal regulation is effective, individuals will voluntarily conform to an intersubjectively shared system of rules and values, which, in turn, influences their social identity and shapes and constrains or provokes certain behavior. Behavior influenced by group values may be desirable or undesirable, as group pressures may incite disrespectful or abusive conduct. For instance, the infamous 1992 torture and killing of a Somali youth by Canadian peacekeepers and the Abu Ghraib prisoner abuses serve as grave illustrations of informal group cultures urging aggressive behavior.[70] In theory, informal control may well exist in the absence of formal laws and disciplinary practices and may provide order and predictability in an otherwise more or less "anarchical" environment but, as these examples illustrate, informal control does not always only restrain behavior.

Most commonly, however, informal regulation extends and intensifies formal regulatory practices.[71] As a result, control is effectively maximized if both formal and informal regulation reinforce each other. By contrast, when rules, norms, and values are not internalized, formal regulation is considerably weakened. For instance, in complex operational contexts where the rules of engagement (i.e., formal regulation) are ambiguous or nonexistent, behavior may be controlled by the norms and values that constitute the identity invoked in that situation (i.e., informal regulation).[72] By contrast, Gary Schaub shows elsewhere in this volume that accepting contractors as legitimate members of the profession of arms may reduce role ambiguity, thereby motivating behavior to be more or less consistent with that of the military in-group.

Employed as a decision heuristic, social identity may result in undesirable outcomes, as in cases of contractor misconduct. Social psychologists tend to explain these phenomena as results of cognitive biases that distort reality, because individuals attempt to master new situations through the application of familiar perceptions and behavior patterns that may not fit the context.[73] Empirical research on cognitive inconsistencies suggests that individuals may try to reduce uncertainty and overcome identity tensions by bolstering the stature of the in-group and of in-group norms, attitudes, and behaviors either through derogation of the out-group or by redefining the prototypicality of the situational context.[74] For instance, combat soldiers may need to create psychological distance from the enemy—for example, by pretending to play a game—in order to apply deadly force.[75] In other instances, soldiers may justify decisions to use force by claiming to act in pursuit of some greater good (e.g., restore peace and democracy, terminate an unjust regime, or end human suffering).[76]

Recognizing the utility of informal regulation under conditions of operational uncertainty, the security industry has begun to provide strong incentives for companies to monitor their employees' behavior and adopt self-regulating mechanisms. For instance, the International Stability Operations Association (ISOA), an umbrella organization representing the interests of the "peace and stability operations industry," developed a voluntary code of conduct calling on members to respect human rights; operate with integrity, honesty, and fairness; recognize and support legal accountability; work only for legitimate and recognized governments, international and nongovernmental organizations, and lawful private companies; and ensure adequate training and vetting of their personnel.[77] Former ISOA president Doug Brooks explained: "It is critical the international community be proactive in ensuring that the companies doing this work in conflict and post-conflict environments and among highly vulnerable populations are the most professional and ethical available."[78] As of July 2015, the ISOA served a total of 56 corporate members, all of whom have signed its code of conduct and have pledged to abide by the ethical standards established therein. Self-regulation seems an attractive choice for many companies. ISOA membership has more than doubled since 2006.[79]

Recognizing the need for self-regulation, the industry has adopted comprehensive regulatory mechanisms raising the bar on vetting and training future employees and on prescribing acceptable behavioral standards for the field. A vice-president of a US-based security firm explained, "As in many industries, there is a lot of hype early on. And if it is a rapidly growing industry, there may be problems with vetting early on as well. But the market has weeded out those companies that have not behaved ethically, legally or morally. At my company, we have a very detailed vetting system. We use psychometric tools for selecting employees, which help us determine whether they fit in the culture and how they will operate under stress. We are confident that we can weed out potential problem employees."[80]

CONTRACTOR SELF-IMAGE

Given the discussion of formal and informal control and the legal status of contractors, how do individuals working for the private security industry view themselves? In what dimensions, if any, do they resemble the different conceptions of military professionalism discussed earlier? In 2009, Marc von Boemcken and I conducted a first survey and empirical test of the motivations, values, and attitudes of security contractors, using a sample of more than 200 American contractors with at least one deployment to a conflict region.

The initial intent of this research was to survey a broad range of contractors providing armed security services in post-conflict settings. Because of contractual prohibitions against surveying contractors on active deployment, we administered the survey to the members of the CivPol Alumni Association, a nonprofit organization whose members are typically American police officers who completed at least one tour of duty on contract in a conflict region. Usually, these police officers receive a leave of absence from their regular jobs and are recruited to participate in international civilian police activities and local police development programs in countries around the world. At the time of survey administration, the CivPol Alumni Association sponsored some 1,400 active members, all of whom received an email from the association president with a link to the Security Contractor Survey and a request to complete the survey online at their convenience. With this approach, it was impossible to identify respondents, thus ensuring the anonymity of all information provided on the survey. Between March and May of 2009, 355 active CivPol Alumni Association members followed the email link and responded to at least part of the survey (a 25 percent response rate). In all, 223 respondents answered every question on the survey and were included in the data analysis.

All respondents in the sample were US citizens with a law enforcement background and the vast majority were male (216, or 96.9 percent), white (77.5 percent), and married (77.1 percent). All respondents had completed at least high school, almost half (49.8 percent) held undergraduate degrees, and 15.7 percent held graduate degrees. Almost two-thirds (136, or 61.5 percent) of respondents had served in the military, and four in five of those (108) had been directly involved in combat. Of the respondents with a military background, almost all had served as enlisted personnel (95 percent) and nearly three-fourths (71 percent) were discharged at the ranks of E4–E6 (corporal or sergeant). At the time of survey administration, respondents had an average of 4.7 years of experience working for the private security industry, with a median of three years. About one-quarter of respondents (23.7 percent) had less than 2 years of private security work experience, 44.9 percent had worked 2–5 years, 23.7 percent had worked 5–10 years, and 16 respondents

(7.7 percent) had worked for more than 10 years in the private security sector. Almost one-third of respondents (69, or 30.9 percent) reported that their job required them to "engage in actual fighting/security detail or security protection" and more than three-quarters (171, or 76.7 percent) reported providing advisory and training services (multiple responses were possible to this question).[81]

The survey asked respondents to rank their motivations for working as a private security contractor, indicate their level of specialized knowledge and their commitment to and investment in their job, and respond to a series of statements about ethical conduct in the field that were derived directly from the code of conduct promoted by the International Stability Operations Association. In terms of specialized knowledge, slightly more than half (51.4 percent) of respondents felt that "civilian contractors performing in combat roles should be regarded as military professionals." Generally, respondents showed value orientations very similar to those of American soldiers and officers, which may, in part, be the result of their prior professional socialization in the military. For instance, contractors were slightly more patriotic than respondents in a recent sample of American officers and showed levels of warriorism most resembling those of combat support officers.[82] These results suggest that contractors identify largely with the constabulary roles assigned to them in peace and stability operations.

In order to assess stereotypical contractor traits, I explored respondents' levels of individualism/self-centeredness, social dominance orientation, and masculinity. The results confirmed the earlier findings that the surveyed contractors do not fit media stereotypes. Overall, contractors scored fairly low on Machiavellianism, a scale measuring a series of hypothetical personality traits that self-interested individuals who are effective in controlling others should possess. These traits include a relative lack of affect in interpersonal relationships, little concern with conventional morality, and a focus on getting things done over compromising.[83] In line with these findings, contractors also showed low levels of social dominance orientation, that is, the desire to establish and maintain the superiority of their own group over other groups.[84] Finally, given the high-risk, male-only context of armed security provision, we would expect contractors to display elevated levels of aggression, dominance, adventure, and risk taking. Using a shortened version of the Brannon Masculinity Scale to measure these traits, the data showed average masculinity scores, with three-quarters of contractors stating they were not bothered "when a man does something that I consider feminine" and one-third disagreeing that a man should "look somewhat tough" and that men should "not show pain."[85]

While nearly half of officers in a recent study felt that "peacekeeping and other non-combat activities should be central to the military's functions," only 4 in 10 (39.8 percent) contractors agreed.[86] These findings suggest that a considerable portion of contractors in our sample perceived the military and its role in terms of the militarist or traditional warrior images outlined in table 11.1. However, this is not how respondents on average viewed themselves. Clearly distinguishing between their professional responsibilities as contractors and the roles performed by the military, almost 8 in 10 respondents (78.0 percent) agreed that "there are certain functions performed by military personnel that should not be performed by a civilian contractor" and two-thirds (65.9 percent) disagreed with the statement that there are no military functions that "cannot be performed by a civilian contractor." At the same time, nearly 9 in 10 respondents (89.7 percent) were very certain that "civilian contractors deployed abroad should be protected by the same international treaties as the armed forces." The sample was evenly split in their opinion of whether (39.2 percent) or not (41.9 percent) "civilian contractors employed by the enemy in a combat zone should be regarded as unlawful combatants."

Moreover, almost two-thirds of contractors (60.5 percent) said they had not expected to engage in actual fighting when they decided to sign on with a security firm. The fact that their experience on the ground in fighting, security detail, or security protection did not significantly affect their attitudes suggests values and motivations more closely resembling those of the constabulary or postmodern peace soldier. Although we did not assess decision autonomy in our empirical study, the fact that 90 percent of respondents thought they should be protected by international law suggests that they recognize supranational authority and control mechanisms analogous to those regulating postmodern peace soldiers.

Contrary to the mercenary archetype of the military professional, we found only one-quarter of respondents to be highly motivated by prospects of monetary gain. Moreover, only one in five cited "seeking adventure and excitement" as a prime motivator for their choice of occupation. Instead, respondents overwhelmingly mentioned the opportunity to face and meet new challenges and to help others as most important motivators. Consistent with earlier findings that many contractors wished to be "proud" of what they did, to do "something worthwhile," to help other people,[87] our results suggest that there is a strong interest on the part of the contractors to be considered professionals in the provision of security. Again, these findings, in conjunction with contractors' high levels of job engagement, satisfaction, and identification with constabulary roles, reflect a professional commitment to police-like functions, but less so to warrior-like peace enforcement roles. Moreover, they suggest a desire for the development of a corporate identity reflecting specialized skills in the provision of tactical services in peace operations. Further research should examine this dynamic more closely for contractors from different occupational, cultural, and national backgrounds and from different firms working for a range of contracting agencies.

In sum, the sparse empirical evidence to date suggests that contractors engaged in the provision of armed security services view their professional identity as distinct from, yet closely related to, that of military professionals, particularly those resembling constabulary and postmodern types. At the same time, the responses to our survey indicate concern about the current ambiguous status of contractors in international law. While most thought that certain roles ought to remain the prerogative of soldiers, a majority felt they should be regarded as military professionals when engaged in combat. The data at hand is inconclusive as to whether this perception is attributable to the fact that their operational responsibilities resemble most closely those of military professionals or simply that no other clearly identifiable comprehensive corporate identity exists to date for security contractors.

Nevertheless, these results indicate that weapons-carrying contractors do not view themselves as, nor do they want to be compared to, classical mercenaries. Their law enforcement background seemed to prepare respondents in our sample very well for constabulary roles and their level of job engagement indicates a high correlation between specialized skills and motivation for their operational responsibilities. In order to measure the effectiveness of informal control mechanisms, we examined respondents' level of adherence to the ethical standards set forth in the ISOA Code of Conduct. We found that virtually all respondents agreed that it was important to "respect the dignity of all human beings and adhere to relevant international law," to "minimize loss of life and destruction of property," to investigate violations of human rights and humanitarian law, and to take action against unlawful activities. Literally every respondent also agreed that "integrity, honesty and fairness are key guiding principles for anyone deployed in a contingency operation."

In general, the standards promoted by the private security industry resemble the characteristics that make up a profession: specialized skills (the management and application of violence, at least for contractors providing armed security services); motivation (adventure, service, profit); decision autonomy absent specified standard operating procedures; and professional values. However, the extent to which members of the "contractor guild" have internalized these traits—and, as a result, the extent to which informal social control is effective—has not yet been examined systematically across the industry.

SECURITY CONTRACTOR: TOWARD A CORPORATE IDENTITY

In his farewell address to the nation on 17 January 1961, President Dwight D. Eisenhower warned of the dangers of the military-industrial complex: "The potential for the disastrous rise of misplaced power exists and will persist.

We must never let the weight of this combination endanger our liberties or democratic processes."[88]

With more contractors than military personnel operating in Iraq and Afghanistan and with a sizable number of them performing armed security provision services, Eisenhower's half-century-old warning takes on a remarkable new meaning. Many media reports and much of the academic research that has accompanied the rapid rise of the private security industry have portrayed contractors as self-interested and undisciplined mercenaries with few to no moral inhibitions and little to no concern for ethical conduct. Although a range of formal regulatory measures are in place, there is considerable concern over the effectiveness of their implementation. At present, much of the industry still relies on informal control mechanisms, such as the ISOA Code of Conduct. Although our empirical analysis here shows strong adherence to ISOA's ethical standards,[89] future research will need to validate the effectiveness of informal control for security contractors from different national, cultural, organizational, and professional backgrounds.

To some, the rise of the PMSC industry "signal[s] a powerful new realignment of forces that speak to novel ways of seeing the world. They may result in new legal doctrines, or new paradigms of governance, and new ways of fighting wars. In the midst of the agitation they cause, they may signal a shift in the larger environment that nurtures them. It could be that PMSCs are in fact powerful adaptations to under-analyzed institutional or cultural trends . . . wherein established laws and customs are breaking down, and new practices are emerging. These organizations are not necessarily lawless, or without governing principles, but they may seem to appear out of nowhere."[90]

But our findings suggest more continuity than disruption. Modern-day security contractors do not resemble the militarists or mercenaries of old; their identity and operational responsibilities resemble largely those of constabulary or postmodern peace soldiers. The empirical evidence available to date suggests that a large number of security contractors perceived their occupation as contractors as a logical continuation of their previous military careers and a majority thought they should be regarded as military professionals.[91]

These still-preliminary results point to a desire for the development and recognition of a professional identity among contractors. However, the lack of regulatory enforcement mechanisms combined with the highly fragmented nature of the industry, its multitude of firms, heterogeneous labor pool, and short-cycle deployment rotations has made it difficult for the industry to forge a common corporate identity through coherent and consistent professional socialization, training, and educational experiences. Although the nature of the operational tasks performed by contractors encourages small-group cohesion, it does not necessarily foster the development of a distinct professional identity. Unlike the military, there is no enforced conformity in all aspects of life for civilian contractors over an extended period of time that could forge such a common identity.[92]

The current lack of a corporate identity among security contractors may explain the difficulties in regulating the industry effectively through formal control mechanisms. Furthermore, the lack of a common professional identity also demonstrates the virtues of informal control and the need for further internalization of ethical standards and professional norms and values.[93] This need is immense given the diversity of individual contractors in terms of professional/military, national, and cultural background and firms working for a wide range of contracting agencies, which hampers the development of a concise, coherent, and comprehensive professional security contractor identity.

Outsourcing increasingly dominates military operations, and notions of free market capitalism have convinced many political leaders that private actors motivated by profit are more efficient and effective than public actors motivated by a diffuse sense of the common good. However, the profit motive may get in the way of a company's—and by extension its employees'—commitment to serving a greater good and, by extension, to developing a professional identity. Almost a century ago, Ross warned:

> Some want to foster the professional spirit in occupations in which it is quite incapable of producing the hoped-for benefits. It is too much to expect one to put quality of service above gain when one is the employee of a man who prefers gain to service. . . . When, therefore, in the production of any service, capital comes to be a factor so prominent that the capitalist hires labor instead of the laborer hiring capital, we shall have a business rather than a profession.[94]

Although one may not reasonably expect a change in capitalist corporate culture anytime soon, recent evidence indicates that there is a strong interest on the part of the security industry as well as individual contractors to be considered members of the profession of arms.[95] Considering the private security industry as a quasi-profession for the provision of tactical services would allow the consolidation and reinforcement of shared norms and values that could serve more effectively in regulating it both formally and informally. Nearly 100 years ago, Charles Boston observed, "An early training in the best traditions of the profession will not only discourage such [dishonorable] tendencies in the individual, but will tend also to create a general professional atmosphere in which it will be too uncomfortable for the guileful to live."[96]

With the continuing rapid rise of the security industry, it behooves us to heed President Eisenhower's warning that "we can no longer risk emergency improvisation of national defense."[97] At a time when enforcement of formal control mechanisms is still sporadic and inconsistent, informal control becomes pivotal to ensuring the effective and efficient delivery of operational services. Recognizing the private security industry as a quasi-profession for the provision of tactical services will boost informal control and, in the long run, may allow also for the strengthening of formal regulation. The private security industry is here to stay; recognizing it as a quasi-profession will likely enhance democratic control and accountability of a sector currently lacking effective regulation.

NOTES

1. Spencer S. Hsu and Victoria St. Martin, "Four Blackwater Guards Sentenced in Iraq Shootings of 31 Unarmed Civilians," *Washington Post* (13 April 2015), available at http://www.washingtonpost.com/local/crime/four-blackwater-guards-sentenced-in-iraq-shootings-of-31-unarmed-civilians/2015/04/13/55b777e0-dee4-11e4-be40-566e2653afe5_story.html, accessed 9 July 2015.

2. Matt Apuzzo, "Judge Cites Gov't Missteps, Tosses Blackwater Case," Associated Press (1 January 2010), available at http://www.wenatcheeworld.com/news/2010/jan/01/judge-cites-missteps-tosses-blackwater-case/, accessed 27 January 2010.

3. A congressional investigation following the incident revealed that "Blackwater has been involved in at least 195 'escalation of force' incidents in Iraq since 2005 that involved the firing of shots by Blackwater forces." See United States House of Representatives, Committee on Oversight and Government Reform, Memorandum (Washington: United States House of Representatives, 1 October 2007), page 1, available at http://oversight.house.gov/documents/20071001121609.pdf, accessed 30 March 2009. In February 2009, Blackwater replaced its management and changed its name to Xe Services, LLC. A a group of investors later bought the former Blackwater training facilities in security service provider and renamed it Academi. On its website, the new firm distances itself from Blackwater and its original owner, Erik Prince, and in order to "help oversee and guide the company's award-winning governance and compliance efforts" it hired a new senior management team and formed a bipartisan board of directors, which includes former attorney general John Ashcroft, retired admiral Bobby Inman, and former White House counsel Jack Quinn. For further detail see the official Academi website at https://www.academi.com/pages/about-us, accessed 9 July 2015.

4. Cf. T. Christian Miller, "Military Suspends Firm Accused of Overbilling in Iraq," *Los Angeles Times* (9 October 2004), available at http://articles.latimes.com/2004/oct/09/world/fg-custer9, accessed 15 August 2009; Jason M. Lure, "How a Contractor Cashed In on Iraq," *Legal Times* (4 March 2005); Nathan Hodge, "Study Finds Extensive Waste in War Contracting," *Wall Street Journal* (1 September 2011), available at http://www.wsj.com/articles/SB10001424053111904716604576542703010051380, accessed 19 July 2015. See also Doug Brooks and Mackenzie Duelge, "Ethical Lessons on Maximizing Private Contractor Value in Afghanistan and Iraq," in Volker Franke and Robert H. Dorff, editors, *Conflict Management and "Whole of Government": Useful Tools for U.S. National Security Strategy?* (Carlisle: US Army War College, Strategic Studies Institute, 2012).

5. David Isenberg, *Shadow Force: Private Security Contractors in Iraq* (Westport: Praeger, 2009), page 5. For instance, author Jeremy Scahill termed the rapid rise of the private security industry a "mercenary revolution." See Jeremy Scahill, "The Mercenary Revolution: Flush with Profits from the Iraq War, Military Contractors See a World of Business Opportunities," *Indypendent* (10 August 2007), available at http://www.indypendent.org/2007/08/10/the-mercenary-revolution-flush-with-profits-from-the-iraq-war-military-contractors-see-a-world-of-business-opportunities/, accessed 4 February 2010.

6. Sue Pleming and Andrew Grey, "Gates Takes Swipe at Security Contractors in Iraq," Reuters (19 October 2007), available at http://www.reuters.com/article/2007/10/19/us-iraq-usa-blackwater-idUSN1842593420071019, accessed 3 August 2015.

7. Robert M. Gates, "Strategic and Operational Planning for Operational Contract Support (OCS) and Workforce Mix," memorandum for the secretaries of the military departments et al. (Washington: Office of the Secretary of Defense, 24 January 2011), page 1.

8. Paul McLeary, "US Looking for Contractors to Help in Iraq," *Defense News*, 9 March 2015, available at http://www.defensenews.com/story/defense/2015/03/09/us-private-contractor-iraq-isis/24654439/, accessed 19 July 2015. See also Molly Dunigan, "A Lesson from Iraq: How to Outsource War to Private Contractors," *Christian Science Monitor* (19 March 2013), available at http://www.csmonitor.com/Commentary/Opinion/2013/0319/A-lesson-from-Iraq-war-How-to-outsource-war-to-private-contractors, accessed 19 July 2015.

9. A. Epstein, *Ethos and Identity* (London: Tavistock, 1978), page 101.

10. Sheldon Stryker, "Identity Salience and Role Performance: The Relevance of Symbolic Interaction Theory for Family Research," *Journal of Marriage and the Family* 30, 4 (November 1968), pages 558–64.

11. John E. Hofman, "Social Identity and Intergroup Conflict: An Israeli View," in Wolfgang Stroebe, Arie W. Kruglanski, Daniel Bar-Tal, and Miles Hewstone, editors, *The Social Psychology of Intergroup Conflict: Theory, Research and Applications* (Berlin, Heidelberg, and New York: Springer Verlag, 1988), pages 89–102.

12. Henri Tajfel, *Differentiation between Social Groups: Studies in the Social Psychology of Intergroup Relations* (London: Academic Press, 1978), page 63.

13. See Volker Franke, *Preparing for Peace: Military Identity, Value Orientation, and Professional Military Education* (Westport: Praeger, 1999).

14. See Dominic Abrams and Michael A. Hogg, *Social Identity and Social Cognition* (Oxford: Blackwell, 1999); Michael A. Hogg, "Intergroup Processes, Groups Structure and Social Identity," in W. P. Robinson, editor, *Social Groups and Identities: Developing the Legacy of Henri Tajfel* (Oxford: Butterworth-Heinemann, 1996); Michael A. Hogg and Dominic Abrams, *Social Identifications: A Social Psychology of Intergroup Relations and Group Processes* (London and New York: Routledge, 1988); Muzafer Sherif, O. J. Harvey, B. Jack White, William R. Hood, and Carolyn W. Sherif, *The Robbers Cave Experiment: Intergroup Conflict and Cooperation* (Middletown, CT: Wesleyan University Press, 1988); Jim Sidanius, "The Psychology of Group Conflict and the Dynamics of Oppression: A Social Dominance Perspective," in Shanto Iyengar and William J. McGuire, editors, *Explorations in Political Psychology* (Durham and London: Duke University Press, 1993); Jim Sidanius and Hillary Haley, "Person-Organization Congruence and the Maintenance of Group-Based Social Hierarchy: A Social Dominance Perspective," *Group Processes and Intergroup Relations* 8, 2 (April 2005); Paul M. Sniderman, Richard A. Brody, and Philip E. Tetlock, *Reasoning and Choice: Explorations in Political Psychology* (Cambridge, New York, Melbourne, and Sydney: Cambridge University Press, 1991).

15. Morris Janowitz, *The Professional Soldier: A Social and Political Portrait* (New York: The Free Press, 1960), page 5.

16. Janowitz, *The Professional Soldier*, page 6.

17. Robert G. Kennedy, "Why Military Officers Must Have Training in Ethics," *International Society for Military Ethics* (2000).

18. Edward Alsworth Ross, "The Making of Professions," *International Journal of Ethics* 27, 1 (1916), page 67.

19. Ross, "The Making of Professions," page 68.

20. Ross, "The Making of Professions," page 69.

21. Kennedy, "Why Military Officers Must Have Training in Ethics," page 2.

22. Kennedy, "Why Military Officers Must Have Training in Ethics," page 3.

23. Kennedy, "Why Military Officers Must Have Training in Ethics," pages 3–4.

24. See Volker Franke, "The Social Identity of Peacekeeping," in Thomas W. Britt and Amy B. Adler, editors, *The Psychology of the Peacekeeper: Lessons from the Field* (Westport: Praeger, 2003).

25. Ross, "The Making of Professions."

26. Samuel P. Huntington, *The Soldier and the State: The Theory and Politics of Civil-Military Relations* (Cambridge: Belknap Press of Harvard University Press, 1957).

27. Karl Mannheim, "Conservative Thought," in Kurt H. Wolff, editor, *From Karl Mannheim* (New York: Oxford University Press, 1971), pages 132–222.

28. United States Department of the Army, *Field Manual (FM) 100-5: Operations* (Washington: Department of the Army, Headquarters, 1993), pages 1–2.

29. Harold D. Lasswell, "The Garrison State," *American Journal of Sociology* 46, 4 (January 1941).

30. Lasswell, "The Garrison State," page 458.

31. Lasswell, "The Garrison State," page 443.

32. Huntington, *The Soldier and the State*, page 69.

33. Huntington, *The Soldier and the State*, page 60.

34. "They belong to the officer corps in its capacity as an administrative organization of the state, but not in its capacity as a professional body" (Huntington, *The Soldier and the State*, page 12).

35. See also Peter D. Feaver and Richard Kohn, editors, *Soldiers and Civilians: The Civil-Military Gap and American National Security* (Cambridge: MIT Press, 2001); Franke, *Preparing for Peace*; Karen O. Dunivin, "Military Culture: Change and Continuity," *Armed Forces and Society* 20, 4 (1994).

36. Janowitz, *The Professional Soldier*, page 10.

37. See also Volker Franke and Karen Guttieri, "Picking Up the Pieces: Are Officers Ready for Nation Building?" *Journal of Political and Military Sociology* 37, 1 (2009); Franke, "The Social Identity of Peacekeeping"; David R. Segal, "Five Phases of United Nations Peacekeeping: An Evolutionary Typology," *Journal of Political and Military Sociology* 23 (Summer 1995); Christopher Dandeker, "A Farewell to Arms? The Military and the Nation-State in a Changing World," in James Burk, editor, *The Military in New Times: Adapting Armed Forces to a Turbulent World* (Boulder, San Francisco, and Oxford: Westview, 1994).

38. Charles C. Moskos, John Allen Williams, and David R. Segal, editors, *The Postmodern Military: Armed Forces after the Cold War* (New York: Oxford University Press, 2000); see also Franke and Guttieri, "Picking Up the Pieces."

39. *Protocol Additional to the Geneva Conventions of 12 August 1949, and Relating to the Protection of Victims of International Armed Conflicts (Protocol I)* (8 June 1977).

40. See Moshe Schwartz and Jennifer Church, *Department of Defense's Use of Contractors to Support Military Operations: Background, Analysis, and Issues for Congress*, CRS Report R43074 (Washington: Congressional Research Service, 17 May 2013); Doug Brooks, "Messiahs or Mercenaries? The Future of International Private Military Services," *International Peacekeeping* 7, 4 (Winter 2000), pages 135–36. See also the discussion of norm adoption by contractors in chapter 12 in this volume.

41. Volker Franke and Marc von Boemcken, *Attitudes, Values and Self-Conception of Private Security Contractors in Iraq: An Exploratory Study*, Final Research Report, German Peace Research Foundation (Bonn: Bonn International Center for Conversion, 2009).

42. With plenty of highly skilled individuals with military training looking for employment and a rapidly expanding global security market, companies offering combat and combat support services blossomed in the mid-1990s. Early success stories included South African–based Executive Outcomes, whose engagement forced negotiations in Angola and facilitated the end of fighting in Sierra Leone. It is important to note that the market share for firms providing these types of classical mercenary services has been steadily declining since the late 1990s. For further detail see Marc von Boemcken, "Outsourcing the State? Security Governance and the Privatization of Military Functions," in Michael Brzoska, editor, *Bonn International Center for Conversion: Conversion Survey 2005* (Baden-Baden: Nomos, 2005); Herbert Wulf, *Internationalizing and Privatizing War and Peace* (Basingstoke: Palgrave Macmillan, 2005); David Keen, *Conflict and Collusion in Sierra Leone* (London and New York: James Currey Publishers, 2005).

43. See Moshe Schwartz, *The Department of Defense's Use of Private Security Contractors in Afghanistan and Iraq: Background, Analysis, and Options for Congress*, CRS Report R40835 (Washington: Congressional Research Service, 19 January 2010).

44. See Gerhard Kümmel, "Die Privatisierung der Sicherheit: Fluch oder Segen? Postheroische Gesellschaft, Überlasteter Staat und Private Sicherheits- und Militärunternehmen," *SOWI Arbeitspapier* 137 (Potsdam: Sozialwissenschaftliches Institut der Bundeswehr, October 2004).

45. Mathieu Deflem, "The Concept of Social Control: Theories and Application," paper presented at the International Conference on "Charities as Instruments of Social Control in Nineteenth-Century Britain," Université de Haute Bretagne (Rennes 2), France (22–23 November 2007), page 1; Francis Fukuyama, "The Great Disruption," *Atlantic Monthly* 283, 5 (May 1999).

46. George H. Mead, "The Genesis of the Self and Social Control," *International Journal of Ethics* 35, 3 (April 1925), page 275.

47. See Edward Alsworth Ross, *Social Control: A Survey of the Foundations of Order* (New York: Macmillan, 1901); George H. Mead, *Mind, Self, and Society from the Standpoint of a Social Behavioralist* (Chicago and London: University of Chicago Press, 1934).

48. Edward Alsworth Ross, "Social Control," *American Journal of Sociology* 1, 5 (March 1896), page 519.

49. A discussion and detailed list of international and domestic regulations for the private security industry is provided by the University of Denver's Private Security Monitor. See http://psm.du.edu/index.html, accessed 19 July 2015.

50. In this context see chapter 5 in this volume.

51. L. Paul Bremer, *Coalition Provisional Authority Order 3 (Revised): Weapons Control*, CPA/ORD/31 December 2003/3, available at http://www.iraqcoalition.org/regulations/20031231_AORD3;REV__AMD_.pdf, accessed 1 February 2011.

52. L. Paul Bremer, *Memorandum Number 17: Registration Requirements for Private Security Companies (PSCSs)*, CPA/MEM/26 June 2004/17, page 11.

53. Jennifer K. Elsea, *Private Security Contractors in Iraq and Afghanistan: Legal Issues* (Washington: Congressional Research Service, 7 January 2010), page 13.

54. Elsea, *Private Security Contractors in Iraq and Afghanistan*, page 22.

55. Aside from these domestic and international legal controls, private security firms are also accountable to the War Crimes Act of 1996, Victims of Trafficking and Violence Protection Act of 2000, anti-torture statute, Defense Trade Controls Act, Arms Export Control Act, Gun Control Act, Export Administration Regulations, International Traffic in Arms Regulations, Defense Base Act, Foreign Corruption Practices Act, Federal Aviation Regulations, Defense Federal Acquisition Regulations (DFAR), and General Orders of the Central Command, Multi-National Corps–Iraq and Combined Joint Task Force (CJTF) 76. For further detail see Isenberg, *Shadow Force*, chapter 6.

56. Ginger Thompson and James Risen, "Plea by Blackwater Guard Helps Indict Others," *New York Times* (8 December 2008), available at http://www.nytimes.com/2008/12/09/washington/09blackwater.html, accessed 10 April 2010.

57. For further detail see Elsea, *Private Security Contractors in Iraq and Afghanistan*.

58. Sari Horwitz, "New Charges Brought against Former Blackwater Guards in Baghdad Shooting," *Washington Post* (17 October 2013); Hsu and St. Martin, "Four Blackwater Guards Sentenced in Iraq Shootings of 31 Unarmed Civilians ."

59. Quoted in Elsea, *Private Security Contractors in Iraq and Afghanistan*, page 29; see also Isenberg, *Shadow Force*.

60. As discussed in chapter 10, the Montreux Document is the product of an initiative launched cooperatively by the Swiss government and the International Committee of the Red Cross. It was developed in a series of meetings between 2006 and 2008 with the participation of experts from 17 governments and in consultation with representatives of civil society and of the private military and security industry. The document reaffirms the obligation of states to ensure that private military and security companies operating in armed conflicts comply with international humanitarian and human rights law. The document lists some 70 recommendations, derived from good state practice, including verifying the track record of companies and examining the procedures they use to vet their staff. The text of the document is available at http://www.icrc.org/web/eng/siteeng0.nsf/htmlall/montreux-document-170908/$FILE/Montreux-Document-eng.pdf, accessed 2 June 2009.

61. Jason Ireland and Caroline Varin, "PMSCs and the Regulatory Environment in Iraq Post-2011," *Central European Journal of International and Security Studies* 9, 1 (2015), available at http://static.cejiss.org/data/uploaded/1425974229319946/Article%2001.pdf, accessed 19 July 2015.

62. See Schwartz and Church, *Department of Defense's Use of Private Security Contractors in Afghanistan and Iraq*.

63. Elsea, *Private Security Contractors in Iraq and Afghanistan*, pages 5–6.

64. International Committee of the Red Cross, "Interpretative Guidance on the Notion of Direct Participation in Hostilities under International Humanitarian Law" (2009), available at http://www.icrc.org/Web/eng/siteeng0.nsf/htmlall/direct-participation-report_res/$File/direct-participation-guidance-2009-icrc.pdf, accessed 13 March 2010.

65. Jennifer K. Elsea and Nina M. Serafino, *Private Security Contractors in Iraq: Background, Legal Status, and Other Issues*, CRS Report for Congress RL32419 (Washington: Congressional Research Service, 21 June 2007), page 42.

66. Elsea and Serafino, *Private Security Contractors in Iraq*.

67. See Deflem, "The Concept of Social Control"; Michel Foucault, "Prison Talk," in Colin Gordon, editor, *Power/Knowledge: Selected Interviews and Other Writings, 1972–1977* (Brighton: Harvester Press, 1980); Nancy Fraser, "Foucault on Modern Power: Empirical Insights and Normative Confusions," *PRAXIS International* 3 (1981).

68. Ross, "The Making of Professions," page 81.

69. See Henri Tajfel and John C. Turner, "An Integrative Theory of Intergroup Conflict," in William G. Austin and Stephen Worchel, editors, *The Social Psychology of Intergroup Relations* (Monterey, CA: Brooks/Cole, 1979).

70. See Volker Franke, "Resolving Identity Tensions: The Case of the Peacekeeper," *Journal of Conflict Studies* 19, 2 (1999); Donna Winslow, *The Canadian Airborne Regiment in Somalia: A Socio-cultural Inquiry* (Ottawa: Canadian Government Publishing, 1997).

71. See Michel Foucault (Michel Senellart, editor), *Security, Territory, Population: Lectures at the Collège de France* (Basingstoke: Palgrave Macmillan, 2007).

72. See Franke, "The Social Identity of Peacekeeping."

73. Daniel Kahneman, Paul Slovic, and Amos Tversky, editors, *Judgment under Uncertainty: Heuristics and Biases* (Cambridge: Cambridge University Press, 1982).

74. See Abrams and Hogg, *Social Identity and Social Cognition*; Eleanor Rosch, "Principles of Categorization," in E. Rosch and B. B. Lloyd, editors, *Cognition and Categorization* (Hillsdale, NJ: Erlbaum, 1978); Henri Tajfel, *Human Groups and Social Categories* (Cambridge: Cambridge University Press, 1981).

75. Benedict Carey, "Psychologists Explain Iraq Airstrike Video," *New York Times* (7 April 2010), available at http://www.nytimes.com/2010/04/08/world/08psych.html, accessed 10 April 2010.

76. See Franke, "The Social Identity of Peacekeeping."

77. For a detailed discussion of the evolution of the ISOA Code of Conduct see chapter 9 in this volume. The latest version of the ISOA Code of Conduct is available at http://www.stability-operations.org/?page=CodeofConduct_131&hhSearchTerms=%22code+and+conduct%22, accessed 19 July 2015. In a similar fashion, the British Association of Private Security Companies (BAPSC) has committed itself to upholding ethical criteria in its charter. See chapter 8 of this volume as well as http://www.bapsc.org.uk/?keydocuments=charter, accessed 5 February 2012.

78. Doug Brooks, "From Humble Beginnings in Freetown: The Origins of the Code of Conduct and Its Importance for the Industry," *Journal of International Peace Operations* 3, 5 (2007), pages 8–9, available at http://ipoaworld.org/eng/codeofconducthistory.html, accessed 23 February 2010.

79. For a current listing of all members see http://www.stability-operations.org/search/newsearch.asp, accessed 19 July 2015.

80. Interview with the author on background (26 March 2009).

81. Volker Franke and Marc von Boemcken, "Guns for Hire: Motivations and Self-Perception of Private Security Contractors," *Armed Forces and Society* 37, 4 (October 2011), pages

725–42; Franke and Boemcken, *Attitudes, Values and Self-Conception of Private Security Contractors in Iraq*.

82. See Franke and Guttieri, "Picking Up the Pieces."

83. See Richard Christie and Florence Geis, *Studies in Machiavellianism* (New York and London: Academic Press, 1970).

84. See Sidanius, "The Psychology of Group Conflict and the Dynamics of Oppression," pages 183–219.

85. Robert Brannon and Samuel Juni, "A Scale for Measuring Attitudes about Masculinity," *Psychological Dimensions* 14 (1984), pages 6–7.

86. Franke and Guttieri, "Picking Up the Pieces."

87. Robert Young Pelton, *Licensed to Kill: Hired Guns in the War on Terror* (New York: Crown Publishers, 2006), page 179.

88. Dwight D. Eisenhower, "Farewell Address, January 17, 1961," available at http://www.eisenhower.archives.gov/education/bsa/citizenship_merit_badge/speeches_national_historical_importance/farewell_address.pdf, accessed 30 July 2015.

89. See Franke and Boemcken, *Attitudes, Values and Self-Conception of Private Security Contractors in Iraq*.

90. Kateri Carmola, *Private Security Contractors and New Wars: Risk, Law, and Ethics* (New York: Routledge, 2010), page 38.

91. Franke and Boemcken, *Attitudes, Values and Self-Conception of Private Security Contractors in Iraq*.

92. Gary Schaub Jr. and Volker Franke, "Contractors as Military Professionals?" *Parameters* 39, 4 (Winter 2009–2010).

93. See also chapter 9 in this volume.

94. Ross, "The Making of Professions," page 78.

95. See chapters 12 and 13 in this volume for discussions of barriers contractors face to acceptance into the military in-group.

96. Quoted in Ross, "The Making of Professions," page 78.

97. Eisenhower, "Farewell Address."

Chapter Twelve

Brothers in Arms?

Identity, Military Professionals, and Armed Contractors

Gary Schaub Jr.

Contractors are ubiquitous on today's battlefields. Their numbers consistently equaled or surpassed the number of military personnel deployed during the wars in Iraq and Afghanistan.[1] Roughly 17 percent of these personnel have been classified as private security contractors by the Department of Defense (DoD).[2] Although contractors have accompanied American military forces into theaters of war in large numbers in the past, the use of armed civilian personnel has reached all-time highs. The highest recorded number of private security personnel used by DoD in any conflict in the history of the United States was reached in June 2012 with 28,686 private security contractor personnel in Afghanistan.[3]

These personnel are necessary. Neither the DoD nor the Department of State would be able to execute their missions in Afghanistan and Iraq without PMSCs.[4] This is the result of several trends that have encouraged the United States government to substitute civilian contractors for military personnel for the past few decades.[5] In particular, the shift to an all-volunteer military force while maintaining a traditional system of compensation based upon rank as opposed to skill has made it difficult to develop and retain personnel with esoteric skill sets—that is, beyond core military competencies—within the military. Furthermore, congressionally mandated limits to the size of the military services make it difficult for them to expand and contract in response to demands placed on them. Demand induced the private sector to supply what was needed when it was needed and to further build demand.

But are these personnel as reliable as the military personnel that they have effectively replaced? Are they controllable? Numerous incidents documented elsewhere suggest not.[6] Over the past decade, there have been numerous parallel efforts to institutionalize control over these private entities. At the international level, the Montreux Document of September 2008 provides a compendium of the formal legal norms and informal business, administrative, and regulatory practices that states have agreed ought to guide PMSC (private military and security company) behavior.[7] At the level of the industry, the International Stability Operations Association (ISOA, formerly IPOA, the International Peace Operations Association) mandates adherence to its code of conduct for all member firms and has in place a mechanism to investigate violations by the personnel of member firms and provide incentives to bring member companies back into compliance.[8] For instance, Blackwater USA withdrew from IPOA three weeks after its employees killed 17 Iraqi civilians in 2007, reportedly due to IPOA's impending investigation.[9] At the national level, the United States government has taken actions to increase its oversight and ability to legally control the behavior of contractors, including establishing congressional committees on wartime contracting, revising the Military Extraterritorial Jurisdiction Act (MEJA) to cover the contractors of agencies other than the Department of Defense supporting DoD missions, and expanding the Uniform Code of Military Justice to cover DoD contractors in overseas combat zones.[10] Finally, at the institutional level, the Department of Defense has long regarded contractors as part of the "Total Force"—which also includes active duty military members, reserve military members, and DoD civilians.[11] The idea is to enable the DoD to overcome "challenges that stem from the department's failure to fully integrate operational contract support within DOD, including planning for the use of contractors, training military personnel on the use of contractor support, accurately tracking contractor use, and establishing measures to ensure that contractors are accountable."[12]

As the DoD makes progress integrating civilian contractors at the institutional level, it may have an additional effect: socializing them into the Total Force and thereby inducing them to adopt the norms and behaviors of other "Total Force" components—the active duty military in particular. A raft of recent literature suggests that employees will be more likely to adhere to norms of behavior when they have developed an identity that encompasses such norms than when they are provided with external motivators such as monetary incentives that require monitoring and evaluation.[13] Therefore, to the degree that socialization of PMSC personnel is possible, it would provide an additional way to control the corporate warrior.

I focus on a key factor that affects the likelihood that Western PMSC personnel will adopt the norms of the military personnel whom they supplement: the degree to which they are accorded status as members of the military profession by members of the military profession. The greater their acceptance into the profession of arms the more likely they will behave like military professionals.[14] I draw upon two aspects of identity—role and social—to form hypotheses about the manner and degree to which these contractors may be accepted as brothers in arms.[15] I utilize the responses of 985 elite field-grade officers collected annually from 2007 to 2010 to assess these hypotheses. I find that evoking different aspects of identity in these officers leads to differential rates of acceptance of contractors as members of the professional military in-group.

In particular, I find that officers have a strong social identity vis-à-vis civilian contractors, but it is permeable. Civilian contractors placed in the functional military role of armed combatants overcome their out-group status with many officers along multiple dimensions, particularly with regard to their status as combatants under international law.

I therefore conclude that if inculcating a professional military identity in PMSC personnel is key to influencing their behavior, to make it more consonant with that expected of the military personnel they effectively replace, then a concerted effort to socialize them into the norms of behavior and attitudes of military professionals ought to be undertaken at the company, industry, national, and international level. These parallel efforts should focus on the obligations and rights of combatants and noncombatants in warfare. Not only is this the area in which their involvement has drawn the most attention but it is also the place where military professionals are most likely to accept these private actors as legitimate brothers-in-arms.[16]

In the sections that follow, I discuss identity theory to establish the framework within which the analysis takes place. I then provide an analysis of the manner and degree to which the officers in my sample accord civilian contractors status as military professionals. I conclude the analysis with recommendations to enhance the identification of contractors with the military profession so as to increase the likelihood that they will adhere to appropriate norms of behavior.

IDENTITIES AND THE MILITARY PROFESSION

How do officers view PMSC personnel? How might officer views affect contractor behavior? I turn to identity theory to address these questions. Identity theory posits that individuals are self-aware, exist within a social structure, and interact with others. Being self-aware implies the ability to see oneself as an object and behave toward oneself as one would behave toward others. In so doing, people recognize that they are unique individuals, that they are members of groups, and that they occupy roles in the social structure. They then derive various conceptions of themselves, or identities, from these bases: personal, group, and role. "In general, one's identities are composed of the self-views that emerge from the reflexive activity of self-categorization or identification in terms of membership in particular groups or roles."[17] A "social identity is a person's knowledge that he or she belongs to a social category or group."[18] A role identity is a person's internalized expectations of the attitudes and behaviors associated with a social position.[19] Finally, personal identity is based upon "idiosyncratic personality attributes that are not shared with other people"[20] and "the set of meanings that define the person as a unique individual rather than as a role-holder or group member."[21] As such, personal identity is outside of the current research question and therefore discussed only in passing.

Although the bases for these identities differ, they "all operate the same way. Identities from each basis have identity standards that serve as the reference and guide behavior in situations."[22] Social identity derives from a person's identification with a social group. When a person identifies with a group, they do so because they believe that they share characteristics with or resemble group members. "In real life, and particularly for social categories, we tend to represent categories as fuzzy sets of attributes where members have a 'family resemblance.'"[23] This "resemblance" is refined through comparison, resulting in an identity standard or "group prototype" that embodies "exemplary members (actual group members who best embody the group) or ideal types (an abstraction of group features)."[24] These prototypes "chart the contours of social groups and tell us not only what characterizes a group but also how that group is different from other groups."[25] They maximize similarities among the in-group and differences with the out-group and so are polarizing images. This is known as the "metacontrast principle" and it produces accentuated barriers between groups on myriad dimensions.[26] Among these barriers are tendencies to view in-group members positively and out-group members negatively.[27] Likewise, "the core of a [role] identity is the categorization of the self as an occupant of a role, and the incorporation, into the self, of the meanings and expectations associated with that role and its performance. . . . These expectations and meanings form a set of standards that guide behavior."[28] Hence, occupants of the same role share a role identity standard and so can be categorized as members of the same group.

These identities guide behavior as part of the identity verification process. As a person interacts with others, he or she receives information about how he or she is being perceived. "Whether it is a role, social, or person[al] identity, individuals act to control perceptions of who they are in a situation to match the feedback they receive in the situation."[29] When this information confirms that they are acting in accord with their identity standard, the positive feedback boosts their self-esteem.[30] When they perceive that they are not being seen as acting in accord with their identity standard, this dissonance causes stress that lowers self-esteem.[31] Confirmation of one's identity standard also reinforces the behavior associated with this standard. Failure to have one's behavior perceived as in accord with one's identity standard leads to an overcorrection in behavior in the short term, impelling behaviors far more in accord with the stereotypical prototype than the person's own adaptation of it. Prolonged dissonance can cause a person to leave the situation, adapt, or abandon the identity standard itself so as to relieve the dissonant feedback.[32] Thus feedback that affirms or conflicts with a person's identity standards, be they personal, role, or social, has a significant effect on subsequent behavior.

Encounters with people who are accepted as being members of a group, occupiers of a role (or counter-role[33]), or embodying certain individualistic traits that reflect one's identity standards likely provide significant feedback with regard to one's behavior and identity. Indeed, "the strongest confirmation that one is a group member may come from acceptance by others in the group."[34] On the other hand, rejection by members of a group would be strong disconfirmation of one's identity and provoke short-term overcorrection and long-term adaptation or abandonment of the identity or the situation.

IDENTITY STANDARDS OF MILITARY PROFESSIONALS

Given this, what are the identity standards against which prototypical members of the military profession—elite officers—are likely to determine who is a member of the profession? What are the fuzzy sets of attributes associated with the core role and social identities of military professionals?

The role identity standard encompasses the position of the military professional in society and is focused on the functions performed by its members. The core functions of military professionals are the planning, organizing, and employment of military force. Although military professionals perform other functions—such as administration, supply, maintenance, legal, medical, and religious support—it is the art of war and the management of violence that is at the heart of the profession.[35] The social identity standard defines who is a member of the in-group of military professionals.[36] Title 10 of the US Code defines this as active duty members of a regular component of the armed forces: the Army, Navy, Air Force, Marine Corps, and Coast Guard.[37] International treaties that define members of the armed forces of a state as privileged combatants that enjoy certain rights and bear certain responsibilities for their conduct enhance this legal definition. Combining these two results in a core professional identity standard that would be an active duty officer in a position of command in the combat arms. Samuel Huntington explicitly limited the military profession to these officers.[38] These role and social identities thus form the prototype against which membership in the profession of arms can be judged.

Although private military and security contractor personnel are institutionally separate from members of the military profession, they can bear more than a passing resemblance to these identity standards. Contract employees have performed the functions of combat and command. In Iraq, PMSC personnel constituted the second-largest armed force in the country, behind only the US military.[39] These civilians have used force to protect persons and property and have planned and participated in clandestine raids led by elite special forces and CIA operatives.[40] Contract personnel have long been regarded as part of the Total Force, and a US Defense Science Board report repeatedly characterized civilian defense services firms as the "fifth force provider in addition to the four services."[41] In addition, although the status of armed contractors under international law is unclear,[42] "conduct that violates international obligations is attributable to a State if it is committed by the government of the State or any of its political subdivisions, or by any official, employee, or agent operating within the scope of authority of any of these governments, or under color of such authority."[43] Thus PMSC personnel perform in roles that are similar to those of military professionals and are in many ways insinuated within the institution of the Department of Defense and the military services.

Given these attributes, as well as others, it has been argued that there is a basis for including contractors within the profession of arms.[44] In particular, we might expect that armed contractors performing in combat roles would have a very strong resemblance to the military professional role prototype. This functional resemblance may encourage PMSC personnel to adopt the social identity of a military professional, as shown in chapter 11 in this volume. It may also persuade officers to include these contractors in the profession of arms, thereby providing positive feedback on their group status and encouraging them to emulate in-group behaviors. In the next sections, I address the degree to which officers accept contractors along the multiple dimensions that constitute the prototype of the military professional.

ANALYSIS: POPULATION AND SAMPLE

In order to assess the manner and degree to which officers accept contractors as military professionals, I report the responses of 985 elite officers to 12 items pertaining to civilian contractors on the Officer Strategic Leadership Survey. This survey was administered to officers attending Air Command and Staff College, the School of Advanced Air and Space Studies, and the Air War College in May 2007, 20 August–10 September 2008, 1–16 October

Table 12.1. Officer Strategic Leadership Survey Sample by Service

	Air Force	Army	Marine	Navy	Coast Guard	Total
Sample	757 (77%)	84 (9%)	32 (3%)	103 (11%)	4 (0.5%)	980

2009, and September 2010.[45] Officers from the Naval War College were surveyed in June 2007. These officers are not just a convenient population to sample from: attendance in a resident professional military education (PME) program has proven to be a reliable institutional indicator of an officer's potential for advancement into the ranks of the elite. "These officers come from the pool of military leaders that shape the military profession in America and function as the custodians of military culture over time."[46] However, care must be taken. While the sample is representative of the schools from which it was drawn, it is not representative of all "elite" officers or the officer corps in general, primarily due to an overrepresentation of air force officers and an underrepresentation of officers from the other services.[47] But as shown in table 12.1, which presents the distribution of officers by service in the sample, this does not mean that significant numbers of officers from other services were not surveyed.

Respondents were directed to consider Western contractors organically attached to military units or acting as private security forces in support of Western military operations.[48] I utilize their responses to 12 items to make assessments of the degree to which officers grant contractors role or group identity status as military professionals. The responses to these items are compiled in table 12.2 and are discussed more thoroughly in the subsequent sections.

ANALYSIS: EVOKING ROLE AND SOCIAL IDENTIFICATION WITH ARMED CONTRACTORS

First, officers were asked about the perceived efficacy of contracting out support functions. Support functions do not directly involve command or combat and therefore are not central to the role prototype of the military professional. Indeed, these functions have been most extensively privatized for the longest period of time. We might therefore expect that civilian contractors who perform these functions are considered to be members of a nonmilitary out-group and consequently evaluated negatively by officers. As can be seen in table 12.2, only 39 percent of officers agreed or strongly agreed with the statement that "the privatization of military support functions, such as logistics and maintenance, has been beneficial to military effectiveness in my country," while 36 percent disagreed, and a quarter were neutral. Privatization of support functions in particular has been justified by its efficacy[49] and yet these officers displayed ambivalence toward its value.[50] This suggests contractors are not viewed in an overwhelmingly positive light—as we might expect of an out-group.

Second, we asked whether "civilian contractors do their jobs more effectively than uniformed personnel could." This question was designed to more

Table 12.2. Officer Responses, 2007–2010[a]

Item	Strongly Agree	Agree	Neutral	Disagree	Strongly Disagree	Total N
The privatization of military support functions, such as logistics and maintenance, has been beneficial to military effectiveness in my country.	4%	35%	24%	28%	8%	975
Civilian contractors do their jobs more effectively than uniformed personnel could.	<1%	4%	25%	52%	19%	975
There are certain functions performed by military personnel that *should never* be performed by a civilian contractor.	61%	32%	3%	2%	2%	971
There are no functions performed by military personnel that, in principle, *cannot* be performed by a civilian contractor.	2%	8%	5%	44%	42%	975
Civilian contractors performing in combat roles should be regarded as military professionals.	4%	28%	17%	36%	15%	971
Civilian contractors performing in combat support roles should be regarded as military professionals.	2%	19%	16%	46%	18%	258
The use of civilian contractors in combat roles is compatible with military ethos.	<1%	20%	26%	38%	16%	972

directly elicit a social categorization response from the officers, wherein the positive characteristics of the in-group (military members) should be emphasized and favorably compared with those of the out-group (civilian contractors).[51] As expected, 71 percent of officers identified with their in-group and disagreed with the notion that civilian contractors are more effective, as opposed to less than 5 percent who agreed and 25 percent who were neutral. This can be seen in table 12.2. The shift in responses from the previous question, from performance in general to performance by group members, shows that social identity is stronger among military professionals than role identity when judged against the out-group of civilian contractors.

Next, we wanted to directly evoke the social identity of the officers by eliciting their judgment as to whether "there are certain functions performed by military personnel that *should never* be performed by a civilian contractor." By phrasing the question in normative, as opposed to empirical, terms, we expected to isolate role identity from social identity and tap officers' views of the legitimacy of their professional identity. In so doing we expected that officer judgments would more precisely capture their social identity. As seen in table 12.2, we found that 93 percent of officers believed that there are functions that only military members ought to perform, 3 percent were neutral, and 4 percent disagreed. It is clear that this normative question required respondents to evaluate contractors in terms of the social prototype of the military professional and the vast majority of officers deemed them to be members of the out-group.

Fourth, we asked whether "there are no functions performed by military personnel that, in principle, *cannot* be performed by a civilian contractor." This question was designed to evoke an empirical assessment of the general level of skill, expertise, and competence that respondents attributed to civilian contractors when performing in a military role. Responses should tap both role identity and social identity: positive responses indicate that the out-group of civilian contractors are not so distant that they are deemed functionally incompetent and that they can be perceived as filling any and all military roles. The responses shown in table 12.2 indicate that civilian contractors are deemed to be members of the social and role out-group: 10 percent of officers agreed that there are no functions that cannot be performed by contractors, another 5 percent were neutral, and 86 percent judged that there were indeed functions that could not be performed by civilian contractors. This suggests that the vast majority of officers do not see civilian contractors as embodying the role prototype of the military professional. The slight shift in responses from the previous question, from 93 percent to 86 percent, here shows that social identity is stronger among military professionals than role identity.

But what happens when we posit that the out-group closely resembles the role prototype of the in-group? How do officers evaluate the differences between themselves and civilian contractors when this out-group is narrowed to armed civilian contractors performing in a combat role? We asked a series of questions to tap different dimensions of the social identity prototype of military professionals while holding role constant.

First, we directly asked respondents whether "civilian contractors performing in combat roles should be regarded as military professionals." By asking about social out-group members performing in the core military role, this question provides the ability to again assess the relative strength of social and role identities in these military professionals. Table 12.2 shows that 32 percent of officers judged contractors in an armed combat role to be military professionals while 51 percent judged that they were not—and 17 percent were neutral. The 21–28 percent increase in the acceptance of contractors compared to the responses to the discrete functional and normative questions discussed above is striking. It confirms that officers' conception of the military profession is a function of both social and role identity and that outgroup members that embody the role identity prototype of the in-group can dilute the social identity of its members.

The role of armed combatant is central to the identity of military professionals, yet military professionals also perform support functions and these are sometimes not regarded as core military functions.[52] Indeed, support functions such as logistics, maintenance, and transportation have been the areas where civilian contractors have most penetrated the military. Yet these remain key career fields for military personnel. Therefore, we wanted to compare the degree to which support functions evoked the ideal military professional as a social identity. We asked whether "civilian contractors performing in combat support roles should be regarded as military professionals." As seen in table 12.2, we found that 21 percent of officers accorded civilian contractors performing support functions status as military professionals—11 percent fewer than for combat functions—while 64 percent did not accord them such status—13 percent more. These responses confirm that the combat role is central to the military's professional identity. And when compared to the responses with regard to military functions, they suggest that characterizing the out-group as performing a military role, even one that is not central to the role identity standard, softened these officers' conception of the scope and limits of their in-group.

To further explore this phenomenon, we asked whether "the use of civilian contractors in combat roles is compatible with military ethos." Given that the military ethos would characterize the exemplar of this group, we might expect that responses would be similar to those regarding armed civilians as military professionals. Table 12.2 shows that almost 21 percent of officers agreed that civilian contractors in combat roles would be compatible with military ethos—a bit of a decline from the 32 percent that granted these contractors professional status. Fifty-four percent disagreed, which is practically equivalent to the 51 percent that declined to give armed contractors in combat roles professional status, and 26 percent were neutral. Such responses suggest that presenting the in-group prototype in a normative manner evokes a stronger social identity response than presenting the out-group empirically—that is, "civilian contractors performing in combat roles."

I also approached this interaction of role and social identity by introducing a legal component. Uniformed military personnel are recognized as a privileged group under international law: they are legal combatants. This legal component constitutes an important aspect of the social identity of a military professional, as it defines who can legally kill and destroy property on behalf of the state. Civilians in general, including those who accompany the armed forces, are not so privileged.[53] As Albert Biderman put it, "it is 'combatant' that the uniform signifies. Its function is to distinguish . . . those who may kill and be killed from the bystanders."[54] Those who engage in hostilities "incur the risk of being an unlawful combatant,"[55] are committing a crime under local laws and international law, and "forfeit [their] protection from being made the object of direct attack."[56] This legal distinction therefore provides another basis for assessing the degree to which contractors assuming the role of an armed combatant softens the social identity of military officers. We asked whether "civilian contractors performing in combat roles and employed by *Western* governments in a combat zone should be regarded as combatants, not civilians, under international law." Table 12.3 shows that 75 percent of respondents agreed, 14 percent disagreed, and 11 percent were neutral.

This flies in the face of what many international law experts would assume. Department of Defense "regulations reflect considerable diligence in attempting to distinguish such contractors from combatants."[57] *Joint Publication 4-0, Doctrine for Logistic Support of Joint Operations* indicates that "in *all* instances, *contractor employees cannot lawfully perform military functions* and should not be working in scenarios that involve military combat operations where they might be conceived of as combatants."[58] This stance is reflected in the views of military lawyers, such as then US Air Force (USAF) Majors Lisa Turner and Lynn Norton, who argued in 2001 that "contractor personnel of an armed force are non-combatant civilians and *must never* take part in hostilities."[59] Fellow USAF Reserve lawyer, then Major Michael Guillory, agreed: "no civilian can ever lawfully directly participate in hostilities."[60] At that time the US Army and the USAF had regulations that prohibited contractors from being armed or wearing uniforms that were similar in appearance to those of military members except in extenuating circumstances.[61] Clearly, line officers have a different view than either policymakers or military lawyers.

We also asked whether "civilian contractors performing in combat roles and employed by the *enemy* in a combat zone should be regarded as combatants, not civilians, under international law." As can be seen in table 12.3, 78 percent of respondents agreed, 11 percent disagreed, and 10 percent were

Table 12.3. Officer Responses, 2007–2010[a]

Item	Strongly Agree	Agree	Neutral	Disagree	Strongly Disagree	Total N
Civilian contractors performing in combat roles and employed by *Western* governments in a combat zone should be regarded as combatants, not civilians, under international law.	22%	53%	11%	9%	5%	259
Civilian contractors performing in combat roles and employed by the *enemy* in a combat zone should be regarded as combatants, not civilians, under international law.	23%	55%	10%	7%	4%	258
Civilian contractors employed by the enemy in a combat zone should be regarded as unlawful combatants.	11%	31%	21%	31%	7%	974
Civilian contractors employed by Western governments in a combat zone should be regarded as unlawful combatants.	9%	27%	22%	34%	8%	971
Civilian contractors and military members deployed to a combat zone should be treated equally under international law.	15%	44%	10%	24%	7%	259

a. The items with far fewer responses were added to the survey in 2010.

neutral. The significant degree of agreement with this proposition, regardless of whether the armed contractor is performing a combat role for a Western government or for an adversary, suggests that "combatant" evokes a role identity far more than a social identity for these officers.

In order to capture the social identity within this legal distinction, we asked whether officers included civilian contractors in the group of lawful or unlawful combatants. "Unlawful combatants" is not a standard term in international law, although the Third Geneva Convention defines combatants who are privileged in that they cannot be held personally accountable for violating civilian laws when acting in accordance with the laws and customs of war. Rather, the term was defined in US law in the 2006 Military Commissions Act.[62] It defined "unlawful combatant" as "(i) a person who has engaged in hostilities or who has purposefully and materially supported hostilities against the United States or its co-belligerents who is not a lawful enemy combatant (including a person who is part of the Taliban, al-Qaida, or associated forces)."[63] It seemed possible that officers would accord combatant status to armed contractors performing in a combat role but deny them the legitimacy of legal status, reserving it for themselves and other members of the military in-group. We therefore asked about contractors employed by the enemy: "Civilian contractors employed by the enemy in a combat zone should be regarded as unlawful combatants." We found that officer views were ambivalent: 38 percent regarded them as lawful combatants, 42 percent grouped them as unlawful combatants, and 21 percent were neutral. This can be seen in table 12.3.

We also asked if "civilian contractors employed by Western governments in a combat zone should be regarded as unlawful combatants." Table 12.3 reveals an officer corps whose collective views were ambivalent: 42 percent regarded them as lawful combatants, 36 percent grouped them as unlawful combatants, and 22 percent were neutral. The similarity of responses suggests that the officers see "contractors" as a stronger identity for civilians employed on the battlefield than "Western" or "enemy." And while officers in general are unsure whether armed contractors in combat roles should or should not be members of the privileged in-group of legal combatants, they are more discriminating (by roughly 38 percent) than when according them status as combatants. This suggests that "lawfulness" taps an important aspect of the social identity of military professionals.

Finally, we asked whether "civilian contractors and military members deployed to a combat zone should be treated equally under international law." This would establish parity if not identity between the military in-group and the civilian out-group and remove one basis for distinguishing between the two. We found that 59 percent of respondents agreed, 31 percent disagreed, and 10 percent were neutral. These responses fall squarely between those regarding combatant status: at least 78 percent of officers believe that civilian contractors in combat roles ought to be considered combatants under international law and only 42 percent believe that they ought to be considered legal combatants. These responses, shown in table 12.3, suggest that equal treatment under international treaties does not evoke a strong social identity response.

CONCLUSION

How do elite military professionals categorize private military and security company contractors in relation to themselves? In general, the officers in my sample clearly differentiated between their in-group and the out-group of contractors. They evinced ambivalence toward the efficacy of contracted support (39 versus 36 percent), they clearly evaluated uniformed personnel as more effective than contracted civilians (71 versus 5 percent) as well as more broadly capable at performing military functions (86 versus 10 percent), and they were quite emphatic with regard to who should perform military functions (93 versus 4 percent). This evidence suggests that officers have a very strong sense of social identity and this feeds an almost equally strong sense of role identity. They clearly differentiate themselves from the out-group of PMSC personnel. This is consistent with the metacontrast principle and supports the findings of previous studies that demonstrated the effects of social categorization theory[64] in relations between military and civilian personnel.[65]

Yet social and role identities are constructed along multiple dimensions. These may not be entirely consistent with one another, especially when being drawn across the domains of role and social identity. Civilian contractors working for private military and security companies in theaters of war have taken on roles formerly filled by military professionals. In particular, many have been armed and placed in positions where they have engaged in combat—and this is well known by the officers surveyed. Positing this role identity for PMSC personnel to isolate role from social identity in the mind of respondents had a significant effect on the permeability of the boundary between the military professional in-group and the civilian contractor out-group. Thirty-two percent of officers accorded these civilians status as military professionals and 21 percent agreed that allowing civilians in combat roles was compatible with military ethos—significant increases from the 4 percent who believed that civilians should be allowed to perform in a military role.

More importantly, the military profession is one that is defined by law in contrast with the rest of the civilian population, unlike most social groups. They have a privileged status in national and international law. They are permitted to engage in acts that are prohibited for other groups, including civilian contractors that accompany the armed forces into a combat area. When presented with this contrast, officers still accepted armed civilians in combat roles far more readily than one would expect: 75–78 percent agreed that they should be regarded as combatants rather than civilians—regardless of who they are fighting for; 38–42 percent regarded them as legal combatants; and 59 percent believed that they ought to be treated equally with military members under international law. These results demonstrate that the de facto boundaries of the military profession are permeable and that elite officers are not universally opposed to accepting privately employed civilian brethren into the profession of arms.

In international law, the area in which formal regulation of corporate warriors arguably requires the most progress, officers are willing to see these new combatants incorporated into existing frameworks of control. This may reflect their operational experience. Classifying civilian contractors in combat roles as combatants would simplify matters greatly at the tactical level. Any civilian engaging in hostilities would forfeit his or her protection from direct attack under international humanitarian law and could be lawfully targeted by American personnel. Likewise, any civilian accompanying the armed forces of either side would be privileged if captured, eliminating legal ambiguities that have led to debacles such as Abu Ghraib.[66] And all would be subject to the precepts of international humanitarian law, thereby removing many of the aspects of "lawfare" that have complicated military operations.[67] Incorporating armed PMSC personnel performing combat roles more fully into the legal regime may increase officers' acceptance of them as brothers in arms, thereby increasing the likelihood that these civilians will behave as military professionals and observe the precepts of international humanitarian law.

Beyond such legal reforms, which are likely to not be supported by the scholars and practitioners of international humanitarian law,[68] the relative openness of officers to accepting armed PMSC personnel as members of the profession in terms of their status as combatants suggests that this is an area ripe for pursuing identity development among civilian contractors. Individual PMSC companies, industry trade associations such as ISOA, and governments ought to require education and training in the appropriate conduct of persons performing in the roles of armed combatants in conflict just as it is required for military professionals. The adoption of these aspects of the behavior and attitudes of military professionals by civilian contractors would be welcomed and reinforced by members of the military profession. This would buttress the basis of acceptance that already exists within the officer corps based upon the role identity of these contractors. In this way, the basis for a professional culture among these private actors that has been found to already exist[69] could be built and sustained.

NOTES

1. See Moshe Schwartz, *The Department of Defense's Use of Private Security Contractors in Afghanistan and Iraq: Background, Analysis, and Options for Congress*, CRS Report R40835 (Washington: Congressional Research Service, 21 February 2011), pages 8 and 12, figures 3 and 7.

2. "The National Defense Authorization Act for Fiscal Year 2008 (P.L. 110-181 Sec. 864) defined private security functions as the guarding of personnel, facilities, or property, and any other activity for which contractors are required to be armed. . . . In June 2010, DOD stopped providing data on armed versus unarmed personnel. As a result, PSC data used in this report includes both armed and unarmed PSC personnel. . . . Historically, the percentage of armed PSC personnel working for DOD was 90% or greater" (Schwartz, *The Department of Defense's Use of Private Security Contractors*, pages 2, 6).

3. Heidi M. Peters, Moshe Schwartz, and Lawrence Kapp, *Department of Defense Contractor and Troop Levels in Iraq and Afghanistan: 2007–2014* (Washington: Congressional Research Service, 22 July 2015), page 3, table 2.

4. Schwartz, *The Department of Defense's Use of Private Security Contractors*, page 5.

5. See Peter W. Singer, *Corporate Warriors: The Rise of the Privatized Military Industry* (Ithaca: Cornell University Press, 2003); Deborah D. Avant, *The Market for Force: The Consequences of Privatizing Security* (Cambridge: Cambridge University Press, 2005); Allison Stanger, *One Nation under Contract: The Outsourcing of American Power and the Future of Foreign Policy* (New Haven: Yale University Press, 2009); Christopher Kinsey, *Private Contractors and the Reconstruction of Iraq: Transforming Military Logistics* (London: Routledge, 2009); David Isenberg, *Shadow Force: Private Security Contractors in Iraq* (Westport: Praeger, 2009); Trevor Taylor, "Review Article: Private Security Companies in Iraq and Beyond," *International Affairs* 87, 2 (2011).

6. See T. X. Hammes, "Private Contractors in Conflict Zones: The Good, the Bad, and the Strategic Impact," *Strategic Forum* 260 (November 2010); Peter W. Singer, *Can't Win with 'Em, Can't Go to War without 'Em: Private Military Contractors and Counterinsurgency*, Policy Paper 4 (Washington: Brookings Institution, September 2007); Molly Dunigan, *Victory for Hire: Private Security Companies' Impact on Military Effectiveness* (Palo Alto: Stanford University Press, 2011).

7. As discussed in chapter 10 in this volume.

8. As discussed in chapter 9 in this volume.

9. International Peace Operations Association, "IPOA Press Release on Blackwater USA" (5 October 2007), available at http://ipoaworld.org/eng/press/132-20071005blackwaterusa.html; Bruce Falconer, "IPOA Smackdown: Dyncorp vs. Blackwater," *Mother Jones* (12 November 2007), available at http://motherjones.com/mojo/2007/11/ipoa-smackdown-dyncorp-vs-blackwater.

10. See chapter 6 in this volume.

11. United States Department of Defense, *Quadrennial Defense Review Report* (Washington: Department of Defense, 6 February 2006), page 75.

12. William M. Solis, *Warfighter Support: Cultural Change Needed to Improve How DOD Plans for and Manages Operational Contract Support. Statement of William M. Solis, Director, Defense Capabilities and Management. Testimony before the Subcommittee on National Security and Foreign Affairs, Committee on Oversight and Government Reform, House of Representatives* (Washington: Government Accountability Office, 29 June 2010), page 0.

13. See George A. Akerlof and Rachel E. Kranton, "Economics and Identity," *Quarterly Journal of Economics* 115, 3 (August 2000); John B. Davis, *The Theory of the Individual in Economics: Identity and Value* (New York: Routledge, 2003); George A. Akerlof and Rachel E. Kranton, "Identity, Supervision, and Work Groups," *American Economic Review Papers and Proceedings* 98, 2 (May 2008); George A. Akerlof and Rachel E. Kranton, *Identity Economics: How Our Identities Shape Our Work, Wages, and Well-Being* (Princeton: Princeton University Press, 2010).

14. In this manner, this work complements that of Ryan Kelty in "Citizen Soldiers and Civilian Contractors: Soldiers' Unit Cohesion and Retention Attitudes in the 'Total Force,'"

Journal of Political and Military Sociology 37, 2 (Winter 2009), as well as in chapter 13 in this volume.

15. See Gary Schaub Jr. and Volker Franke, "Contractors as Military Professionals?" *Parameters* 39, 4 (Winter 2009–2010), and chapter 11 in this volume for complementary discussions of how contractors view themselves in relation to the military profession.

16. Other stakeholders, such as lawyers who study and practice international humanitarian law, may be less likely to accept armed PMSC contract personnel as legitimate in this context. Future research ought to systematically collect and analyze their views.

17. Jan E. Stets and Peter J. Burke, "Identity Theory and Social Identity Theory," *Social Psychology Quarterly* 63, 3 (2000), page 226.

18. Stets and Burke, "Identity Theory and Social Identity Theory," page 225.

19. Peter J. Burke and Jan E. Stets, *Identity Theory* (Oxford: Oxford University Press, 2009), page 114.

20. Michael A. Hogg, "Social Identity Theory," in Peter J. Burke, editor, *Contemporary Social Psychological Theory* (Palo Alto: Stanford University Press, 2006), page 115.

21. Burke and Stets, *Identity Theory*, page 124.

22. Burke and Stets, *Identity Theory*, page 112.

23. Michael A. Hogg, "Social Categorization, Depersonalization, and Group Behavior," in Michael A. Hogg and R. Scott Tindale, editors, *Blackwell Handbook of Social Psychology: Group Processes* (Malden: Blackwell Publishers, 2002), page 60.

24. Michael A. Hogg, *The Social Psychology of Group Cohesiveness: From Attraction to Social Identity* (Washington Square: New York University Press, 1992), page 200.

25. Hogg, "Social Identity Theory," page 118.

26. Hogg, "Social Categorization, Depersonalization, and Group Behavior," page 60; Burke and Stets, *Identity Theory*, pages 118–19; S. Alexander Haslam, Penelope J. Oakes, John C. Turner, and Craig McGarty, "Social Categorization and Group Homogeneity: Changes in the Perceived Applicability of Stereotype Content as a Function of Comparative Context and Trait Favourableness," *British Journal of Social Psychology* 34, 2 (June 1995).

27. Henri Tajfel and John C. Turner, "An Integrative Theory of Intergroup Conflict," in William G. Austin and Stephen Worchel, editors, *The Social Psychology of Intergroup Relations* (Monterey, CA: Brooks/Cole, 1979), pages 33–47; Kate J. Reynolds, John C. Turner, and S. Alexander Haslam, "When Are We Better than Them and They Worse than Us? A Closer Look at Social Discrimination in Positive and Negative Domains," *Journal of Personality and Social Psychology* 78, 1 (January 2000); Hogg, "Social Identity Theory," page 118.

28. Stets and Burke, "Identity Theory and Social Identity Theory," page 225.

29. Burke and Stets, *Identity Theory*, page 112.

30. Self-esteem has three components that correspond with each type of identity: verifying one's personal identity increases feelings of authenticity, verifying one's group identity increases feelings of self-worth, and verifying one's role identity increases feelings of self-efficacy (Burke and Stets, *Identity Theory*, page 129).

31. Burke and Stets, *Identity Theory*, page 80.

32. Burke and Stets, *Identity Theory*, pages 66, 181. Also see George J. McCall and J. L. Simmons, *Identities and Interactions* (New York: The Free Press, 1978), for an interactionist account of the manner in which the prominence and salience of identities are affected by feedback.

33. Burke and Stets, *Identity Theory*, pages 115–16.

34. Stets and Burke, "Identity Theory and Social Identity Theory," page 233.

35. Harold D. Lasswell, "The Garrison State," *American Journal of Sociology* 46, 4 (January 1941), page 455; Morris Janowitz, *The Professional Soldier: A Social and Political Portrait* (New York: The Free Press, 1960), chapter 1; Samuel P. Huntington, *The Soldier and the State: The Theory and Politics of Civil-Military Relations* (Cambridge: Belknap Press of Harvard University Press, 1957); Samuel P. Huntington, "Power, Expertise, and the Military Profession," *Daedalus* 92 (Fall 1963), page 785; Donald J. Campbell and Kathleen M. Campbell, "Soldiers as Police Officers/Police Officers as Soldiers: Role Evolution and Revolution in the United States," *Armed Forces and Society* 36, 2 (January 2010), page 328.

36. One of the traditional aspects of a profession is licensure by the state.

37. Title 10 also includes members of the Army and Air National Guard when in federal service, but generally National Guard forces are more akin to the reserves than the active duty force.

38. Huntington, *The Soldier and the State*, pages 13–18.

39. These figures refer only to individuals employed by *non-Iraqi* security companies. See Cindy Cleveland, *Contractors' Support of U.S. Operations in Iraq* (Washington: Congressional Budget Office, August 2008).

40. James Risen and Mark Mazetti, "Blackwater Guards Tied to Secret Raids by the C.I.A.," *New York Times* (11 December 2009), page 1.

41. *Report of the Defense Science Board Task Force on Institutionalizing Stability Operations within DoD* (Washington: Office of the Under Secretary of Defense for Acquisition, Technology, and Logistics, September 2005), pages 14, 31, 33, 38, 49.

42. Hence the burgeoning literature discussing their status in the field of international law.

43. Jennifer K. Elsea, Moshe Schwartz, and Kennon H. Nakamura, *Private Security Contractors in Iraq: Background, Legal Status, and Other Issues* (Washington: Congressional Research Service, updated 29 September 2008), page 14, note 52.

44. David R. Segal and Karin De Angelis, "Changing Conceptions of the Military as a Profession," in Suzanne C. Nielsen and Don M. Snider, editors, *American Civil-Military Relations: The Soldier and the State in a New Era* (Baltimore: Johns Hopkins University Press, 2009), page 212; Schaub and Franke, "Contractors as Military Professionals?"; Gary Schaub Jr., "Civilian Combatants, Military Professionals? American Officer Judgments," *Defence Studies* 10, 3 (Autumn 2010). On the other hand, the February 2012 *Strategic Direction to the Joint Force* of chairman of the Joint Chiefs of Staff General Martin Dempsey drew the boundaries more tightly: "We are a Profession of Arms. . . . Membership is inclusive, encompassing every Soldier, Sailor, Airman, Marine, and Coast Guardsman—Active and Reserve, military and DoD civilian, office and enlisted (Martin Dempsey, *Strategic Direction to the Joint Force* [Washington: Joint Chiefs of Staff, 6 February 2012], pages 8–9).

45. The survey was exempted from human experimentation requirements by the Air Force Research Labs Wright Site Institutional Research Board on 28 June 2006 (protocol F-WR-2006-0057-E). It was approved annually by the Air University Institutional Assessment office and the commandants of each school. It was approved by the dean of students of the Naval War College. All US students were sent an email invitation with an embedded link to a web-based survey built using Inquisite. Their consent to participate was gained when they proceeded to the survey website. They were able to not respond to any question with which they were not comfortable and were able to discontinue at any time.

46. Peter D. Feaver, Richard Kohn, and Lindsay P. Cohn, "The Gap between Military and Civilian in the United States in Perspective," in Peter D. Feaver and Richard Kohn, editors, *Soldiers and Civilians: The Civil-Military Gap and American National Security* (Cambridge: MIT Press, 2001), pages 6–7.

47. The leadership of sister service institutions whose student populations would have corrected this bias were repeatedly approached but declined to participate. For the period 2007–2010, the service breakdown for the officer corps was 31 percent USAF, 36 percent Army, 24 percent Navy, and 9 percent Marine Corps. For the ranks sampled, major through colonel, the breakdown was 33 percent USAF, 35 percent Army, 24 percent Navy, and 7 percent Marine Corps. Percentages compiled from United States Department of Defense, *Population Representation in the Military Services* (Washington: Office of the Under Secretary of Defense for Personnel and Readiness, annually).

48. "For this survey, 'civilian contractors' are defined as those who are either organically attached to military units (such as mechanics or IT specialists) or those who operate as private security forces (such as Blackwater security personnel) in support of Western military operations, not those who provide unskilled support services (cooking, cleaning, maintaining grounds) and do not work directly with military units. The civilians we would like you to think about are not locals, such as Iraqis or Afghanis, but from Western countries including the United States, Europe, Australia, and South Africa."

49. Stanger, *One Nation under Contract*, *passim*.

50. This finding supports that of Kelty, "Citizen Soldiers and Civilian Contractors," and Lindy Heinecken, "Discontent within the Ranks? Officers' Attitudes toward Military Employment and Representation—A Four-Country Comparative Study," *Armed Forces and Society* 35, 3 (April 2009).

51. Hogg, "Social Identity Theory," page 118.

52. Huntington limited the concept of a military professional to officers in the combat arms. (Huntington, *The Soldier and the State*, pages 12, 17–18).

53. Although Article 4.1.4 of the Third Geneva Convention specifies that civilians who have non-combat support roles with the military and who carry a valid identity card issued by the military they support are to be accorded the protections of prisoners of war if captured during a conflict.

54. Albert D. Biderman, "What Is Military?" in Sol Tax, editor, *The Draft: A Handbook of Facts and Alternatives* (Chicago: University of Chicago Press, 1967), page 124.

55. Lisa L. Turner and Lynn G. Norton, "Civilians at the Tip of the Spear," *Air Force Law Review* 51 (2001), page 26.

56. Turner and Norton, "Civilians at the Tip of the Spear," page 27.

57. Jack M. Beard, "The Geneva Boomerang: The Military Commissions Act of 2006 and U.S. Counterterror Operations," *American Journal of International Law* 101, 1 (January 2007), page 66.

58. *Joint Publication 4-0, Doctrine for Logistic Support of Joint Operations* (Washington: Joint Chiefs of Staff, 6 April 2000), page V-I, emphasis added.

59. Turner and Norton, "Civilians at the Tip of the Spear," page 26.

60. Michael E. Guillory, "Civilianizing the Force: Is the United States Crossing the Rubicon?" *Air Force Law Review* 51 (2001), page 134.

61. Guillory, "Civilianizing the Force," pages 128–29.

62. Public Law 109-366; Title 10, US Code sections 948–49. The term was in use prior to this law. See Turner and Norton, "Civilians at the Tip of the Spear," *passim*; Michael H. Hoffman, "Terrorists Are Unlawful Belligerents, Not Unlawful Combatants: A Distinction with Implications for the Future of International Humanitarian Law," *Case Western Reserve Journal of International Law* 34, 2 (2002).

63. As well as "a person who, before, on, or after the date of the enactment of the Military Commissions Act of 2006, has been determined to be an unlawful enemy combatant by a Combatant Status Review Tribunal or another competent tribunal established under the authority of the President or the Secretary of Defense."

64. Hogg, "Social Categorization, Depersonalization, and Group Behavior," page 60; Burke and Stets, *Identity Theory*, pages 118–19.

65. Kelty, "Citizen Soldiers and Civilian Contractors"; Heinecken, "Discontent within the Ranks?"

66. On the involvement of civilian contractors in Abu Ghraib, see Glenn J. Voelz, *Managing the Private Spies: Use of Commercial Augmentation for Intelligence Operations*, Discussion Paper 14 (Washington: Joint Military Intelligence College Press, June 2006), and Laura A. Dickinson, *Outsourcing War and Peace: Preserving Public Values in a World of Privatized Foreign Affairs* (New Haven: Yale University Press, 2011).

67. Charles J. Dunlap Jr., "Lawfare: A Decisive Element of 21st-Century Conflicts?" *Joint Force Quarterly* 54, 3 (Fall 2009); Charles J. Dunlap Jr., "Does Lawfare Need an Apologia?" *Case Western Reserve Journal of International Law* 43, 1–2 (2011).

68. Many oppose altering the current distinctions between combatant and civilian—and few support doing so. For opposition see Michael N. Schmitt, "Humanitarian Law and Direct Participation in Hostilities by Private Contractors or Civilian Employees," *Chicago Journal of International Law* 5, 2 (2004); Emanuela-Chiara Gillard, "Business Goes to War: Private Military/Security Companies and International Humanitarian Law," *International Review of the Red Cross* 38, 863 (2006); Renée de Nevers, "Private Security Companies and the Laws of War," *Security Dialogue* 40, 2 (2009). For support, see Daphné Richemond-Barak, "Private Military Contractors and Combatancy Status under International Humanitarian Law," presented to Conference on Complementing IHL: Exploring the Need for Additional Norms to Govern Contemporary Conflict Situations, Jerusalem, 1–3 June 2008.

69. Volker Franke and Marc von Boemcken, *Attitudes, Values, and Professional Self-Conception of Private Security Contractors in Iraq: An Exploratory Study* (Bonn: Bonn International Center for Conversion, August 2009); Schaub and Franke, "Contractors as Military Professionals?"; chapter 11 in this volume.

Chapter Thirteen

A Boots'-Eye View of Civilian Contractors

Ryan Kelty

Much has been written in the journalistic and academic literature in recent years on issues surrounding civilian contracting in the military.[1] With respect to the use of civilian contractors several broad trends are clear. First, the US military's reliance on civilians to augment uniformed personnel is a question of degree rather than a simple dichotomous "yes, we use them" versus "no, we don't use them." The American military tradition has, since the beginning, relied on civilians.[2] From the iconic camp followers of early military conflicts in the Republic to the more highly structured and routinized use of civilians during the large-scale expeditionary conflicts of the twentieth century, civilians have played critical roles in the mobilization and prosecution of America's wars. However, the first Gulf War that began in January 1991 marked a turning point in the use of civilians by the United States as "force multipliers" in war fighting, a trend that accelerated with US involvement in Iraq and Afghanistan beginning in 2003. By 2007 contractors comprised more than half of the US military's total force.[3]

A 2007 federal commission convened to examine military outsourcing in Operation Enduring Freedom (OEF) and Operation Iraqi Freedom (OIF) concluded that the US military "does not yet fully recognize the impact of contractors in expeditionary operations on mission success."[4] This report focused on structural issues related to outsourcing military functions. The assessment of the micro-level effects is conspicuously absent in federal assessments and this omission leads to the same conclusion—we don't yet know the impact contractors are having at this level. Few have published on these micro-level dynamics. This chapter will examine the attitudes of military personnel and civilian employees of the Department of the Army toward the civilian contractors with whom they worked during their overseas deployment in support of OIF and OEF (in Afghanistan).

This chapter shares a focus on the micro-level examination of civilian contractors and their impact on military operations (and the military as an institution) with chapters 11 and 12 in this volume. There are several key characteristics that distinguish this chapter from the two preceding, providing a unique contribution to the overall discussion of this volume.

One key difference is that the data presented in this chapter come from enlisted US Army soldiers, whereas chapter 12 surveyed US Air Force officers and chapter 11 presented data from armed security contractors. A second distinction is at the level of defining "warrior." Chapters 11 and 12 define warriors as those with guns; the so-called trigger pullers. In this chapter, "warrior" is used in a more generic sense to reflect the range of military specialties that comprise forward deployed military units. The contractors military personnel are asked to consider include those who are organically attached to their unit and perform comparable duties to the military personnel. Respondents were specifically instructed that those who cook, clean, or perform routine building and grounds maintenance are *not* part of the contactor population under consideration. This definition of warrior allows for a more inclusive assessment of the effect of private contractors on military personnel and the organization as a whole. Finally, the emphases on social roles and role identities in the preceding chapters are not extended in the current chapter. Rather, as a central framework for understanding the effects of contractors the current chapter uses the concept of social comparisons and attitudes toward contractors across several highly salient work-related factors as foundations for assessing the impacts of contractor integration. This chapter, along with the previous two in this volume, addresses the gap in knowledge of contractor effects at the micro level of analysis and discusses implications for mechanisms by which to control contractors.

THE EFFECT OF CONTRACTORS

Civilian contractors are employed to increase the flexibility, effectiveness, and efficiency of an organization by streamlining the full-time workforce and allowing it to focus on the core mission or specialty of the organization.[5] Despite these motivations, assessments of civilian contractors, both objective and subjective, reveal that employing them is not necessarily achieving the intended goals.[6]

Indeed, incorporating contractors into an organization's structure may negatively impact social-psychological, structural, and economic outcomes. Prior studies show that full-time employees see the loss of jobs due to downsizing and/or contracting as a source of instability.[7] The ambiguity of contractors' status can also foster unease among full-time employees, as well as tension between full-time employees and contractors.[8] For example, with regard to the military, to whom does the civilian contractor answer and take directives? Will a given civilian contractor remain with his or her military peers when they are deployed—especially to a war zone? What are contractors' job descriptions and can they perform duties not specifically itemized in their contract's scope of work? Depending on how questions such as these are answered, organizational effectiveness, efficiency, cost saving, and even morale may be negatively impacted. Contracting is not simply a means of improving (hopefully) organizational outcomes of efficiency and effectiveness. It is also a form of organizational change that can dramatically alter social relations, self-perceptions, and attitudes among members of the organization.

Let us not omit from the discussion the benefit most often cited in using contractors: cost-effectiveness. Assessments of contracting out work by the federal government indicate that anticipated cost savings have not been clearly achieved. For example, citing a multitude of hidden costs in employing contractors, Albert Robbert argues that the military's reliance on civilian contractors is essentially as expensive as hiring servicemen and women, and could actually increase project costs.[9] While civilian contractors may "cost less as a rule, some of the savings are wiped out by the need for more oversight of contractor performance,"[10] as well as overhead charges to execute the contracts. The fact that the monetary impact of introducing contractors into the federal workforce is not well understood is reflected in the Government Accountability Office (GAO) conclusion: "We cannot convincingly prove nor disprove that the results of federal agencies' contracting out decisions have been beneficial and cost-effective."[11]

In a more recent GAO report, additional concerns were raised about some of the challenges posed by civilian contractors. For example, no systematic laws or regulations constrain contractors with regard to conflict of interest, accepting travel and gifts, using nonpublic information for personal gain, having contact with future employers, or misusing one's position to provide preferential treatment to a private interest.[12] Additionally, the GAO has found that there are large hidden costs in using civilian contractors in the present system. It estimates that in fiscal year 2004 alone over $3.3 billion in tax debt was owed by Department of Defense (DoD) civilian contracting agencies, 45 percent ($1.5 billion) of which was due to unpaid corporate income tax, and another 37 percent ($1.2 billion) due to unpaid payroll taxes.[13] There is no evidence among the mounting evaluations of civilian contractor use that they unequivocally reduce costs in operating our military. Indeed, much of the extant data indicates that contractors, on balance, increase the monetary cost of military operations in addition to the associated organizational and social challenges they present. These social and social-psychological dimensions of civilian contracting in the US military are discussed in the following sections.

CONTRACTORS IN THE WORKPLACE

When President Barack Obama took office he began to redirect the federal government's use of OMB A-76, the legislation governing federal outsourcing. All new OMB A-76 studies through fiscal year 2009 were suspended when the president signed into law the FY 2009 Omnibus Appropriations Act on 2 July 2009.[14] Obama clearly has a different orientation toward contracting work previously performed by government personnel than his predecessor. The 2010 Quadrennial Defense Review (QDR) also reflects the Obama administration's departure from the Bush administration, calling for a deliberate assessment of current and future military (Total Force) manpower requirements, with an eye toward reducing the number of military contractors. According to the 2010 QDR:

> This [assessment] will ensure that the Department has the right workforce size and mix (military/civilian/contractor) with the right competencies. This assessment will be enterprise-wide, enabling the Department to better recruit and retain personnel with the most-needed skills. . . . In keeping with the Administration's goal of reducing the government's dependence on contractors, the Department introduced its in-sourcing initiative in the FY 2010 budget.[15]

The 2010 QDR under the Obama administration emphasizes the need for the recruitment and retention of competently trained individuals to man the total military workforce. President Obama's in-sourcing plan called for a reduction in the number of support service contractors working for the Department of Defense through 2014 (a five-year timeline) with the target of reestablishing their pre–September 11, 2001, level of approximately one-quarter of the total military workforce, down from their current level of 39 percent. Full-time civilian DoD employees would be used to augment any manpower needs arising from the downsizing of the contractor workforce.[16] A 2014 GAO report found that the DoD had thus far fallen short in its efforts to implement a five-year systematic strategic realignment of its workforce (i.e., the mix of contractors, federal civilians, and uniformed personnel).[17] While these formal mechanisms seek to control the number and type of contractors working for the military, they leave unaddressed the micro-dynamics of the phenomenon—ones that affect the contractors as well as the service members and DoD civilians with whom they work. These micro-dynamics and their implications for informal control of contractors are of central interest in this chapter.

CIVILIAN CONTRACTORS AND MILITARY PERSONNEL

At its foundation, hiring independent contractors or contracting firms institutionalizes a separateness among employees; this separateness by its very nature precludes equality. In addition to tangibles such as benefits, office space, and the like, unequal status lends itself to coloring perceptions about those in the "other" group. Natural comparisons between group members fueled by ambiguity and potential threats to one's own status, performance, job security, or physical safety can lead to segregation by worker status and generalized negative attitudes toward the "other" group. Thus, while introducing contractors into an organization inevitably has an impact on workers of both statuses, context matters with regard to which category of employees appears more advantaged or disadvantaged by the structural arrangement.

Despite the increased numbers of civilian contractors and growing range of jobs they performed in the US wars in Afghanistan and Iraq, there has been little empirical examination of the effects this manpower strategy has had on service members who work alongside contractors. In addition to the work presented in chapters 11 and 12 in this volume, a handful of other studies have examined military outsourcing from a micro-level perspective.

Social comparisons with civilian contractors and civilian mariners were shown to have significant negative effects on retention attitudes of both soldiers and sailors.[18] These negative effects were not direct, but operated indirectly through their impact on job satisfaction and organizational commitment. One key finding was that the negative effects of contractors on retention were not influenced by the amount of exposure soldiers had to contractors. Rather, the mere presence of contractors in the unit was enough to produce feelings of relative deprivation that led to reduced propensity to remain in service.

Ryan Kelty and Irving Smith examined racial, gender, and marital status differences in enlisted soldiers' attitudes toward contractors, as well as social comparisons with contractors.[19] They found more agreement than divergence in attitudes across these social categories. Hispanic soldiers viewed contractors more negatively than non-Hispanic soldiers, and white soldiers were significantly more likely than black soldiers to view contractors as relatively advantaged over soldiers. Neither attitudes toward contractors nor level of contact with contractors significantly impacted retention, but social comparisons were observed to negatively impact intent to remain in service indirectly through satisfaction and commitment. These data have small sample sizes of Hispanics and African Americans, so results should be viewed cautiously.

A cross-national comparative study of attitudes toward military employment found that a minority of officers agreed that civilianization and outsourcing in the military enhances operational effectiveness.[20] Only 16 percent of British officers agreed that civilian outsourcing benefited the military, with slightly higher numbers of Canadian (20 percent) and German (24 percent) officers voicing support. South African officers had a more positive view of civilian integration, with 43 percent stating it enhanced military effectiveness, though Lindy Heinecken notes that civilianization and outsourcing in the military is in its infancy in this country. This study of mid-level officers included a single variable related to civilian contracting. This important work should motivate additional studies to examine a more robust suite of variables related to outsourcing and their effects on readiness and retention.

A final study using data from National Guard soldiers recently returned to the eastern United States from a 15-month deployment at a military detention facility demonstrated that when comparing oneself to the contractors with whom one works, soldiers report that contractors are better off.[21] These feelings of relative deprivation among soldiers have direct negative effects on perceived unit cohesion and general attitudes toward contractors. Soldiers' general attitudes toward contractors did not significantly affect perceived unit cohesion, though the total indirect effect of general attitudes toward contractors on retention was significant. These four studies are consistent in demonstrating that the integration of civilian contractors is having negative impacts on critical outcome variables for the military: cohesion, commitment to the military, and attitudes toward retention.

METHODOLOGICAL NOTES

The data presented in this chapter were collected from two Army combat arms units: one infantry (n = 348) and one combat aviation (n = 191).[22] The infantry battalion surveyed in this study was located in the southeastern United States and had recently returned from a 12-month deployment in Iraq. During their deployment these infantry soldiers worked with contractors whose specializations ranged from mechanics who repaired their armored vehicles, to computer technicians, to private security who secured the forward operating base at which these soldiers were stationed.

The army combat aviation squadron was stationed outside of the continental United States but not in a combat theater. The civilian contractors who worked with this squadron performed duties that were previously done by uniformed army personnel. The integration of civilian contractors with this squadron was well established, having been initiated well before any of the current military or civilian personnel arrived on post.

The surveys included the following definition to focus and contextualize respondents' responses to contractor-related questions:

> For this survey "civilian contractors" are defined as those civilians who are either organically attached to military units (e.g., mechanics, IT specialists) or

> those who operate as private security forces (e.g., Blackwater security personnel) in support of the US military. For this survey the term "civilian contractors" *does not* refer to the more general unskilled support personnel who cook, clean, and maintain physical grounds who are not working directly with military units.

This study examines variables across two domains: social comparisons with contractors and attitudes toward contractors. Social comparisons and attitudes toward contractors were each operationalized using multiple-item scales. The social comparisons scale includes 17 items that were modeled on Faye Crosby's *Working Women and Relative Deprivation* and Mady Segal's analysis of the military and the family as greedy institutions.[23] The literature on job satisfaction was used to inform additional job-related characteristics that are identified as most salient by workers and likely to be used by respondents as points of comparison with civilian contractors. Respondents rated their attitude on a five-point Likert-type scale ranging from "much greater for myself" to "much greater for civilian contractors" with a neutral midpoint. Several items were reverse-coded for analysis so that higher values would consistently equate to more positive social comparisons for soldiers.

Soldiers' attitudes toward contractors[24] were measured using 15 items that refer to both salient characteristics of civilian coworkers brought into the "Total Force" (e.g., level of commitment, expertise, work ethic) and specifically to the espoused benefits offered by proponents of federal outsourcing (e.g., organizational flexibility, cost savings, improving morale, freeing soldiers up to perform core military duties).[25] Response categories range from "disagree strongly" to "agree strongly" using a six-point Likert-type scale. Scale reliability for this measure is strong, indicating the various items are tightly clustered around a common underlying construct.

Single-item measures were used to assess several additional experiences with and attitudes toward civilian contractors. Soldiers were asked how much contact they had with contractors during their current assignment. Responses to this item ranged from "never" to "daily" using a seven-point scale. Service personnel were also asked to rate the attractiveness of working as a civilian contractor after leaving the service using a five-point Likert-type scale ranging from "very unattractive" to "very attractive." Attitudes about whether soldiers view contractors as part of the Total Force were measured using a six-point Likert-type scale ranging from "strongly disagree" to "strongly agree."

EXPOSURE TO CONTRACTORS

Initial analyses focused on descriptive data examining soldiers' level of contact with contractors (figure 13.1). Nearly one-quarter of the soldiers (23 percent) reported never working with a contractor during deployment, with another 31 percent saying they did so less than once a week. Despite the heavy presence of contractors working with both the infantry and combat aviation units included in this study, less than a quarter of soldiers (23 percent) indicated that they interacted with contractors on a daily basis. These results suggest a high level of variation in soldier exposure to contractors as part of their daily job duties. It is likely that one's military specialty has much to do with potential interaction with contractors in the course of performing one's duties—current data does not allow us to test this hypothesis. Even so, more than three-quarters of soldiers report having at least some interaction with contractors in the course of performing their jobs. This high level of visibility (if not direct interaction) normalizes contractor integration with military units.

Many civilian contractors have prior military experience. This suggests that many soldiers may have friends and acquaintances who have left the service to become civilian contractors. Within this sample, a plurality of soldiers (43.6 percent) report that they do not have any friends who have left the Army to become a civilian contractor, although 20 percent report five or more friends who have separated to become contractors (figure 13.2). Taken together, approximately 56 percent of the soldiers surveyed indicate that they have at least one friend who has left the Army to work as a civilian contractor. Of those who know friends who have left to become a contractor, most know three or fewer friends who have done so. Given the massive growth in the hiring of contractors and the media's portrayal of contractors as seemingly all having military backgrounds, the relatively low level of exposure to friends who have left to work as contractors seems surprising. Still, a major-

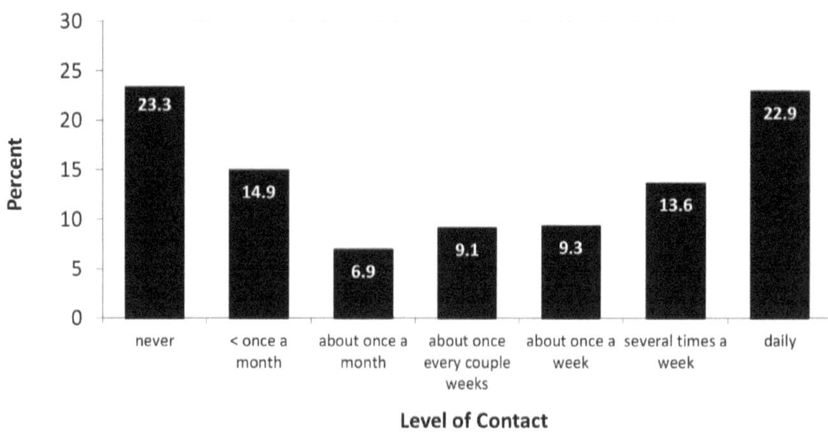

Figure 13.1. Soldiers' Level of Contact with Civilian Contractors (*n* = 537)

ity of the soldiers surveyed reported knowing at least one person who has intentionally left the Army to pursue work as a civilian contractor.

While measures of how much contact soldiers have with contractors and how many of one's friends in uniform have left the Army to work as contractors assess soldiers' experiences, whether or not contractor integration is viewed positively or negatively is an attitudinal question. The next series of data presents numerous attitudinal outcomes from soldiers related to the integration of civilian contractors with military units.

SOLDIERS' SOCIAL COMPARISONS WITH CONTRACTORS

Social comparisons are measures that assess the degree to which one individual feels he or she (or his/her group) fares, positively or negatively, relative to a referent individual (or group). In the context of the data presented here, social comparisons can be interpreted as indicators of soldiers' recognition of contractors' status as part of the "in-group" versus an "out-group" in terms of being a cohesive, integral part of the Total Force.

The distribution of responses to social comparison items is summarized in table 13.1. Among the results for favorable aspects, the clear pattern is that soldiers perceive contractors to be advantaged across nearly all variables examined. For example, a strong majority of soldiers see contractors as advantaged on pay (92.5 percent greater for contractors versus 3.2 percent greater for soldiers), the ability to negotiate the terms of their contract (84.2 percent versus 3.0 percent), and the level of autonomy enjoyed in their job (70 percent versus 8.1 percent). Among the favorable work-related variables,

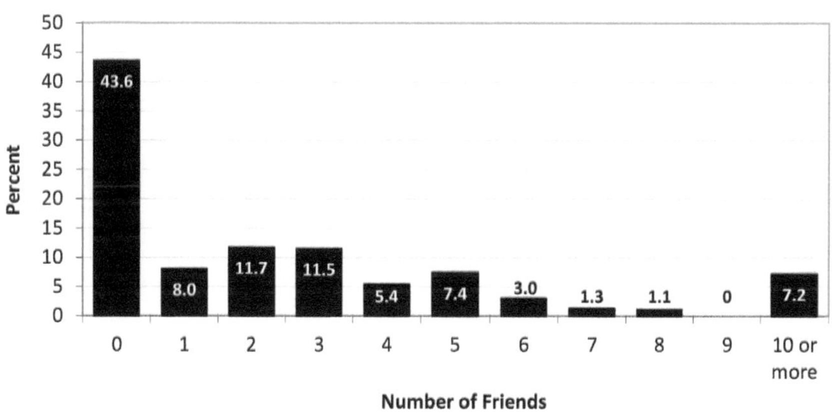

Figure 13.2. Number of Friends Who Have Left to Become Contractors (*n* = 536)

only benefits and ability to contribute to society through one's work clearly favor soldiers.

Soldiers also feel deprived relative to contractors due to greater presence of negative outcomes such as risk of injury or death (63.0 percent greater for soldiers versus 8.4 percent greater for contractors), amount of control one's employer has over its employees (50.1 percent versus 25.2 percent), negative impacts of one's employment on one's family (64.0 percent versus 9.8 percent), time required to be away from family (65.1 percent versus 6.9 percent), and hours worked per day (71.2 percent versus 12.7 percent). The strong and consistent pattern that emerges from the unfavorable aspects of work, again, documents soldiers' perceptions that contractors represent a distinct group from soldiers, even if the DoD includes contractors as part of the Total Force from an organizational perspective. The huge disparities present in perceptions of burden sharing for the most negative aspects of military work suggest that soldiers clearly distinguish themselves from contractors in terms of selfless sacrifice, which is a hallmark of "real" military service. This result is consistent with Gary Schaub's finding, in chapter 12 of this volume, of Air Force officers' perception of contractors as an out-group.

Another important pattern is that more than half of the items examined (9 of 17) revealed more than a third of soldiers indicated equality between groups. This highlights a general tendency toward ambivalence toward contractors seen among these respondents. Of the three items with a majority of soldiers selecting equality between soldiers and contractors, the balance of non-neutral responses favors contractors for perceptions of positive relations with peers and gaining a feeling of accomplishment from one's work. The third item with a majority indicating parity between soldiers and contractors, the ability to contribute to society through one's work, is one of only two items examined that are perceived to clearly favor soldiers among the non-neutral responses (25.5 percent greater for soldiers versus 13.5 percent greater for contractors; the other item is benefits). Surprisingly, given the military's emphasis on excellence in leadership, a larger proportion of soldiers perceived quality of leadership in contracting organizations to be greater than in the Army (33.8 percent for contractors versus 26.3 percent for soldiers). Soldiers also reported equivalent levels of leadership support to complete tasks for soldiers and contractors (21.4 percent and 22.9 percent, respectively).

Overall, these results indicate perceptions among soldiers that contractors are advantaged relative to soldiers on numerous highly salient aspects of work. The huge disparity in perceived pay between soldiers and contractors, in combination with the other perceived benefits accrued by contractors over soldiers, supports the conclusion that soldiers perceive contractors to be a structurally distinct group from military personnel. Moreover, the powerful

Table 13.1. Soldiers' Social Comparisons with Civilian Contractors

Item	Greater for Soldiers	Equal for Each Group	Greater for Contractors
Positive Work-Related Items [a]	%	%	%
Pay	3.2	4.3	92.5
Benefits	34.8	36.7	28.5
Level of job autonomy	8.1	21.9	70.0
Variety in job tasks	28.4	37.5	34.2
Opportunities for promotion	33.5	33.8	32.7
Quality of leaders in one's organization	26.3	40.0	33.8
Positive relationship with peers	14.1	57.4	28.5
Ability to negotiate employment contract	3.0	12.8	84.2
The degree to which one's organization cares for employees	15.0	38.5	46.4
Gain feeling of accomplishment from one's work	20.2	57.3	22.5
Ability to contribute to society through one's work	25.1	61.4	13.5
Leader support to facilitate job completion	21.4	55.6	22.9
Negative Work-Related Items [b]	%	%	%
Risk of injury or death	63.0	28.5	8.4
Amount of control employer has over employee behavior	50.1	24.7	25.2
Negative impacts on family	64.0	26.2	9.8
Time required to be away from family	65.1	28.0	6.9
Hours worked per day	71.2	16.1	12.7

a. Higher values indicate perceptions of greater relative advantage.
b. Higher values indicate perceptions of greater relative deprivation.

and consistent pattern of viewing contractors as more advantaged on unfavorable aspects of work suggests that the sacrifices of war fighting, not solely the organizational conditions under which they serve, are more favorable for contractors compared to soldiers.

Though contractors are structurally integrated in the military and job descriptions may overlap among individuals in these two groups, these results suggest that the mere presence of contractors, in itself, may not legitimate them as actors in the Total Force. Another way to assess whether contractors are viewed as legitimate actors within a "Total Force" concept is to examine soldiers' explicit attitudes toward contractors' contributions to the war effort.

ATTITUDES TOWARD CIVILIAN CONTRACTORS

Attitudes toward contractors were measured using multiple indicators as a way to more robustly understand soldiers' views of the effects civilian contractors have at the organizational and individual level in the military. Results demonstrate a general pattern of ambivalence toward civilian contractors (table 13.2). Attitudes appear ambivalent in that there was a mixture of positive attitudes toward the roles and abilities of contractors, but negative feelings about contractors in terms of cost-effectiveness and both how long and how hard contractors work. A strong majority of respondents (greater than 80 percent) agree that contractors increase military effectiveness, organizational efficiency, and flexibility to meet missions. Similarly, a majority indicated that contractors free up military personnel to focus on the "real" war-fighting duties and do not feel that contractors have a negative impact on soldiers' morale. In addition, nearly 70 percent of soldiers studied indicated that they don't mind working with contractors, they view contractors as having high levels of expertise, and they are impressed with contractors' abilities. More than two-thirds reported that contractors have similar motivation and commitment levels for their work as do soldiers.

Despite these positive regards, there is relatively *little* support for the most often cited motivation for using civilian contractors. Only 20 percent view contractors as more cost-effective than soldiers. Further, less than half of the soldiers indicated agreement with the notion that the military should contract out jobs to civilians if civilians are able to do the job just as well as soldiers. Thus, although soldiers indicate an openness to working with contractors, recognize the expertise that they have, and can see a purpose in their use, when it comes to the central issues of cost and whether or not contractors *should* be used, soldiers in general do not have positive attitudes toward contractors.

If we apply the typology outlined by Volker Franke in chapter 11 of this volume, the data on soldiers' attitudes toward contractors, in combination with soldiers' social comparisons data, suggest that contractors are postmodern military professionals. Recall that the data presented here asked soldiers to think about the contractors who worked with their unit or private security forces working in their area of operations in support of allied operations—not the so-called "ash and trash" contractors who maintain the grounds or who provide cooking and cleaning services on base.[26] While soldiers' atti-

Table 13.2. Soldier Agreement with Statements about Civilian Contractors

Item	Total
Positively Worded Items	**% agree**
Contractors allow military to operate more effectively	84.4
Contractors are important because they free up soldiers to train for and perform the real war-fighting duties	81.6
Contractors increase efficiency of the Army	81.6
Contractors are less expensive to employ than soldiers	20.4
The use of contractors increases the flexibility of the Army in striving to achieve its core missions	84.1
Contractors work just as long as soldiers	32.1
Contractors work just as hard as soldiers	45.5
Contractors perform at least to the same level of expertise that I do	70.4
I am impressed with the abilities of contractors	76.0
Negatively Worded Items [a]	**% disagree**
As a soldier in the US Army, I am uncomfortable working with contractors	63.4
I would prefer not to work with contractors	78.8
Contractors decrease morale among soldiers	80.4
The Army should not use its personnel to perform duties that contractors can do just as well as soldiers	47.9
By having soldiers serve alongside contractors performing comparable duties, it encourages soldiers to leave the service	34.6
Contractors are less committed than soldiers to the work they perform	68.7
Contractors are less motivated than I am to do a good job	66.5

a. Since items are negatively worded, responses of "disagree" indicate more positive feelings toward contractors.

tudes and experiences reported in this chapter point toward contractors as postmodern military professionals, they also pose serious questions about the extent to which contractors are viewed as legitimate actors within the US military's Total Force. Several social theorists suggest that identities are only legitimated through a social process that reflects acceptance of a given identity of an individual or group.[27] Thus, it is not enough for contractors to claim an identity as part of the US military's Total Force (via postmodern military professionalism) to legitimate these identities. They must also be accepted by military personnel who are a significant reference group among those in the profession of arms within which contractors are seeking legitimacy as part of the US military's Total Force.

To assess the degree to which soldiers do indeed legitimate contractors as part of the Total Force, they were asked the question directly: "Do you consider civilian contractors to be members of the US military's Total Force?"[28] The distribution of soldiers' attitudes on this question is skewed, with nearly two-thirds (63.4 percent) reporting that they consider contractors part of the Total Force (figure 13.3). Thus, it appears that a majority of soldiers view contractors as working toward military mission success in an integrated, interdependent relationship with military personnel. But differences between soldiers in the infantry and aviation units are apparent. Additional analysis that tested the difference between mean scores among soldiers in each unit surveyed revealed that soldiers in the combat aviation unit were significantly more likely than the infantry soldiers surveyed to view contractors as part of the Total Force.[29]

The differences in perceptions of contractors as part of the Total Force between units may be due in part to the different missions of the units, where the units were operating when surveyed, or the types of contractors associated with each unit. The current data do not allow for testing these potential effects, but clearly motivate a need to better understand what may be producing the variation between groups on whether or not contractors are viewed as legitimate members of our military's Total Force. Understanding what contributes to legitimization of civilian contractors among service personnel is important not simply for reasons of developing identity—it extends to the critical aspects of both formal and informal control of contractors. In terms of formal control, this legitimization provides social and political support for

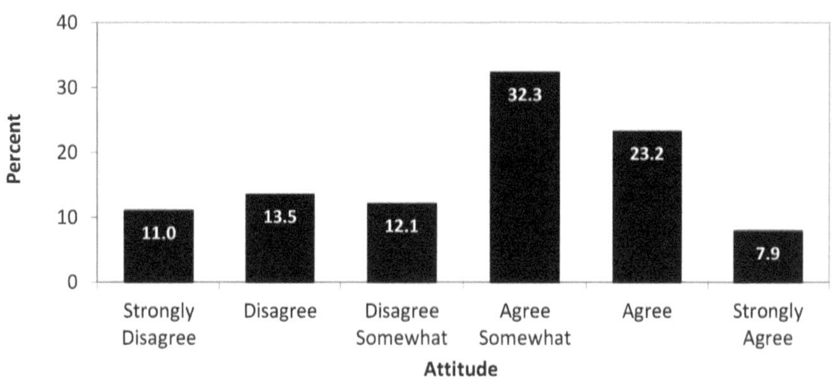

Figure 13.3. "I consider civilian contractors to be members of the US military's Total Force." (*n* = 535)

clarifying contractors' roles, responsibilities (including rules of engagement), and accountability. Informally, supporting contractors' identities through legitimating them as part of the Total Force will encourage self-regulation among contractors via the internalized role identities and the role expectations that accompany them.

Soldiers' attitudes toward working as civilian contractors once they separate from the Army are summarized in figure 13.4. Soldiers are overwhelmingly positive in their attitude about potentially working as a civilian contractor: 70 percent say it is either an attractive or very attractive option and less than 10 percent have a negative view toward working as a contractor. These results correspond with the prior findings on soldiers' social comparisons with contractors (table 13.1, above) that demonstrate a clear view that contractors garner better work-related benefits and are exposed to less risk than military personnel while also contributing to society through their work.

It is clear that many contractors who work in direct support of operations are perceived to bring the technical training, experience, and leadership that they gained from military service. Some argue that, in addition to these skills and abilities, military veterans who work as contractors also bring with them the moral-ethical socialization and training acquired during their time in the military. The argument here is that since so many of the contractors being integrated with military units are veterans of the military themselves, they add to and reinforce these important characteristics—providing additional levels of informal control within the ranks of civilian contractors. To the extent that these characteristics are transferred as hoped, it would help address some of the issues of controlling contractor behavior, though this remains an empirical question.

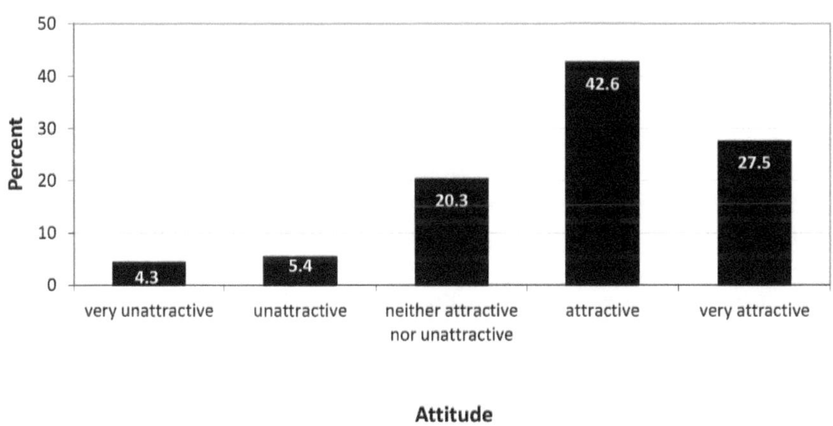

Figure 13.4. Soldiers' Attitudes toward Becoming a Contractor (*n* = 538)

Analysis to determine whether soldiers' attitudes toward working as a contractor are dependent on their intentions to remain in service beyond their current obligation found a significant relationship.[30] Specifically, those soldiers who are planning to leave the Army following their current enlistment or who are neutral regarding their military future are significantly *less* likely than expected to view contractor work positively. Those who are planning to stay in the Army beyond their current obligation demonstrated no significant patterns in their attitudes toward working as a contractor.

THE WAY FORWARD: IMPLICATIONS AND RECOMMENDATIONS FOR CONTROLLING CONTRACTORS

The US military has always relied on civilians when it has engaged in military operations. Federal mandates requiring all government agencies to competitively source jobs based on cost-effectiveness and increased emphasis on a market, as opposed to a public service, orientation laid the foundation for the current explosion in civilian contracting with the military. Despite this explosive growth in military outsourcing, little attention has been given in the literature to how this dramatic change in "Total Force" military manning affects military personnel. The data presented in this chapter help to address this gap in our understanding of the effects of integrating civilian contractors with military units.

Overall results indicate significant levels of relative deprivation and discontent among soldiers within a broader context of ambivalence toward contractors. Soldiers don't appear to mind working with contractors, and they recognize that contractors have valuable knowledge and skills, increase the military's flexibility and effectiveness, and allow uniformed personnel to focus on the core duties of war fighting. Yet contractors are viewed as significantly more advantaged across the range of job characteristics studied—especially pay. Moreover, there is a clear sense among soldiers that contractors are not cost-effective, and they are not perceived to work as hard or for as many hours during the day as do soldiers. The irony of the inverse relationship observed among these key variables—that contractors cost more but work fewer hours and less hard—is keenly felt and frequently expressed by soldiers.

Subjective attitudes of individuals may differ from "objective" reality. To the extent that perceptions of reality frame people's orientations to their world and motivate actions within that (perceived) world, these subjective attitudes represent an important force guiding soldiers' actions and attitudes. In prior studies, attitudes toward contractors have been shown to have negative effects on perceived unit cohesion, job satisfaction, commitment to the military, and intentions to remain in military service (i.e., retention).[31]

Whether or not their subjective attitudes and perceptions are objectively accurate, they nonetheless create realities on the ground that significantly impact individuals and the military organization as a whole. Additional research is needed to better understand these different effects across various groups and contexts. This is true in particular for understanding the unique organizational position and experiences of our Guard and Reserve servicemen and women given the dramatic increase in their mobilization and deployment in OEF and OIF—a trend likely to continue in the twenty-first century.

Cost savings, flexibility, and efficiency and effectiveness are the most often cited motivations for the increased use of civilian contractors as a manpower strategy. This study suggests mixed results on these key outcomes and provides insight into more general attitudes toward contractors and the effects of having contractors as a comparison group within the military's "Total Force." Nearly a third of soldiers indicate neutral-to-negative attitudes toward contractors with respect to how comfortable it is to work with them, how hard they work, and how motivated and committed they are. Finally, less than half of soldiers believe that, just because contractors can do the work as well as soldiers, those jobs should be performed by contractors. This cluster of findings both indirectly and directly calls into question whether we should engage in this manpower practice if important indicators of success are only partially met at best.

These data demonstrate a clear need to gain administrative control over a system built reactively without clear definitions, guidance, oversight, or means of assessing intended and unintended outcomes. The ad hoc nature that characterized the dramatic increase in civilian contractor use by the military in recent decades favors the contracting industry in terms of momentum, lack of clear goals and definitions, and the pure economic realities of cost-prohibitiveness in regaining internal capacity to perform jobs that have been contracted out in many cases. Soldiers are not merely interested in getting a job done well, they are also interested in doing things the right way, and these data suggest that the integration of contractors muddies the waters somewhat with respect to equity, accountability, trust, and legitimacy. These findings suggest a need for more systematic assessment of contractor effects (benefits as well as challenges) and a greater emphasis on resourcing monitoring and administering. Possible examples of this would include enhanced contract oversight and enforcement through both increased numbers of contracting officers and more comprehensive regulations, as well as discussing options to give military commanders greater control over contractor actions through application of both positive and negative sanctions.

There are real social-psychological costs associated with the decision to integrate civilian contractors in military units. These costs express themselves directly, as well as through secondary and tertiary effects that impact many of the variables traditionally included in cost-benefit analyses. For example, perceptions of leadership likely play a role in soldiers' retention decisions. Leadership is traditionally viewed as a strength within the Army, but those surveyed in this study considered leadership within the contracting companies to be on par with Army leadership, creating no competitive advantage on this variable to remain in service versus working for a contracting company. Improving leadership within the Army, and educating soldiers as to "actual" leadership advantages provided by the Army, could reduce the appeal of contracting. Improving leadership will help control the power of the contract industry as a pull for military personnel to leave the service (recall that 70 percent of soldiers responded that working as a contractor was either an "attractive" or "very attractive" option).

Cost-benefit assessments of the use of contractors rather than military personnel need to include the social-psychological effects of contractor integration. For example, future research should examine the effects of contractors on the morale and readiness of our military. This line of research should also include spousal attitudes toward contractors and support for their military husband or wife working as a contractor since prior work has documented a significant effect of spousal attitudes toward service member commitment to the military.[32] The development and implementation of *best practices* can only be achieved through proper discussion and assessment. Assessment of benefits and challenges of integrating contractors in military units provides additional opportunities to control civilian contractors through systematic observation with an eye toward optimizing military operations at home and abroad.

Finally, taking steps to reduce the perceived relative advantage of contractors may produce several positive controls over contractors. For example, if perceived discrepancies can be reduced through changes in policies, education, or training, military personnel will be more likely to reflect positive appraisals of contractors that would more strongly legitimate their presence as members of the Total Force. Theory on social identity and identity salience would suggest that the more salient one's identity, the more likely one is to act in ways consistent with that identity. If the military (and contracting companies) can foster a stronger "brother/sister in arms" identity among contractors and between contractors and military personnel, it will enhance the informal controls that would prescribe behaviors and attitudes that are less at odds with military personnel and organizational goals of the military. This is a tough task, though, given the self-interest that underlies corporate motives and the organizational and legal constraints these private companies place on their employees.

While better pay, more autonomy, and less time away from family would be welcomed by military personnel, they would not present any direct control over contractors, since these changes would not affect contractors' own outcomes. However, by closing the gap between contractors and service personnel on some of the more salient job characteristics, it may moderate some of the potential damage done by contractors' attitudes and behaviors that translate into feelings of relative deprivation among military personnel. In this sense, it might be possible to control the impact contractors are having on military personnel indirectly through equalizing work conditions between the two groups. By the same token, highlighting those aspects of the military that provide relative advantage for service members may be beneficial in moderating the effects of contractors at the individual and organizational levels of the military. However, this poses challenges, since it simultaneously sharpens distinctions between the two groups—something that is not particularly fruitful in fostering the more "military-friendly" social identities and associated role behaviors among contractors.

The findings and recommendations presented here, in conjunction with past and future research in this area, will help to motivate, frame, and inform discussions within the military and at the national level toward identifying the best way to control (or at least moderate) the negative effects of using contractors as part of the Total Force.

NOTES

1. The research presented in this chapter was supported by a grant from the United States Military Academy's Dean's Faculty Enhancement Fund. The views expressed in this chapter are those of the author and not necessarily those of the United States Military Academy, the Department of the Army, or the Department of Defense.

2. Peter W. Singer, *Corporate Warriors: The Rise of the Privatized Military Industry* (Ithaca: Cornell University Press, 2003); Janice E. Thomson, *Mercenaries, Pirates, and Sovereigns: State-Building and Extraterritorial Violence in Early Modern Europe* (Princeton: Princeton University Press, 1994).

3. Jacques S. Gansler, David Berteau, David M. Maddox, David R. Oliver Jr., Leon E. Salomon, George T. Singley III, George Sears, Kristi Crear, Karl Ellcessor, Dave Mabee, Jill Stiglich, and Jana Weston, *Urgent Reform Required: Army Expeditionary Contracting*, report of the Commission on Army Acquisition and Program Management in Expeditionary Operations (Washington: Office of the Assistant Secretary of the Army for Acquisition, Logistics, and Technology, 2007).

4. Gansler, Berteau, Maddox, Oliver, Salomon, Singley, Sears, Crear, Ellcessor, Mabee, Stiglich, and Weston, *Urgent Reform Required.*

5. Chris Edwards, "Moving Public Work to the Private Sector," *Philadelphia Inquirer* (24 November 2002), available at http://www.cato.org/publications/commentary/moving-public-work-private-sector, accessed 27 March 2015; Lindy Heinecken, "Outsourcing Public Security: The Unforeseen Consequences for the Military Profession," *Armed Forces and Society* 40, 4 (October 2014), pages 625–46; James F. Kennedy, Daniel T. Holt, Mark A. Ward, and Michael T. Rehg, "The Influence of Outsourcing on Job Satisfaction and Turnover Intentions of Technical Managers," *Human Resource Planning* 25, 1 (March 2002); Andreas Kruck, "Theorising the Use of Private Military Security Companies: A Synthetic Perspective," *Journal of International Relations and Development* 17, 1 (January 2014); Paul C. Light, *The True Size of Government* (Washington: Brookings Institution Press, 1999).

6. L. Nye Stevens, *Government Contractors: An Overview of the Federal Contracting-Out Program. Statement of L. Nye Stevens, Director of Planning and Reporting, General Govern-*

ment Division, GAO/T-GGD-95-131 (Washington: General Accounting Office, March 1995); Singer, *Corporate Warriors*.

7. James Baron and David Kreps, *Strategic Human Resources: Frameworks for General Managers* (New York: John Wiley & Sons, 1999), page 9; Leonard Wong and Jeffrey McNally, "Downsizing the Army: Some Policy Implications Affecting the Survivors," *Armed Forces and Society* 20, 2 (Winter 1994), pages 199–216.

8. Victor J. Callan, "Individual and Organizational Strategies for Coping with Organizational Change," *Work and Stress* 7, 1 (1993); Ryan Kelty and Alex Bierman, "Ambivalence on the Front Lines: Perceptions of Contractors in Iraq and Afghanistan," *Armed Forces and Society* 39, 1 (January 2013); Adrian Nelson, Cary L. Cooper, and Paul R. Jackson, "Uncertainty amidst Change: The Impact of Privatization on Employee Job Satisfaction and Well-Being," *Journal of Occupational and Organizational Psychology* 68, 1 (March 1995).

9. Albert A. Robbert, quoted in Gordon Towbridge, "DOD Lacks Funds to Turn Jobs Over to Civilians: Plan On Hold unless Billions Added to Budget," *Federal Times* (20 October 2003), page 10.

10. Albert A. Robbert, quoted in Towbridge, "DOD Lacks Funds to Turn Jobs Over to Civilians," page 11.

11. Stevens, *Government Contractors*, page i.

12. United States General Accounting Office, *Defense Contracting: Additional Personal Conflict of Interest Safeguards Needed for Certain DOD Contractor Employees*, GAO-08-169 (Washington: General Accounting Office, March 2008).

13. Joseph A. Christoff, *Securing, Stabilizing, and Rebuilding Iraq. Progress Report: Some Gains Made, Updated Strategy Needed* (Washington: General Accounting Office, June 2008).

14. Christina Erling and Enid Doggett, *President Obama Signs Bill into Law to Stop A-76 Privatization Studies through FY2009* (Washington: American Federation of Government Employees, 12 March 2009).

15. United States Department of Defense, *Quadrennial Defense Review* (Washington: Department of Defense, 2010), page 55, available at http://www.defense.gov/qdr/QDR%20as%20of%2029JAN10%201600.pdf.

16. United States Department of Defense, *Quadrennial Defense Review*.

17. Charles S. Clark, "Pentagon's Plan for Civilian Workforce Falls Short, GAO Finds," *Government Executive* (11 July 2014), available at http://www.govexec.com/defense/2014/07/pentagons-plan-civilian-workforce-falls-short-gao-finds/88507/, accessed 18 July 2014.

18. Ryan Kelty and David R. Segal, "The Civilianization of the U.S. Military: Army and Navy Case Studies of the Effects of Civilian Integration on Military Personnel," in Thomas Jäger and Gerhard Kümmel, editors, *Private Military and Security Companies: Chances, Problems, Pitfalls, and Prospects* (Wiesbaden: VS Verlag für Sozialwissenschaften, 2007); Ryan Kelty, "The Navy's Maiden Voyage: Effects of Integrating Sailors and Civilian Mariners on Deployment," *Armed Forces and Society* 34, 4 (Summer 2008), pages 536–64.

19. Ryan Kelty and Irving Smith, "Racial, Ethnic and Gender Differences in Soldiers' Attitudes toward Civilian Contractors," poster presented at the Defense Equal Opportunity Management Institute's Sixth Biennial EO/EEO Research Symposium, Cocoa Beach, Florida (January 2007).

20. Lindy Heinecken, "Discontent within the Ranks? Officers' Attitudes toward Military Employment and Representation—A Four-Country Comparative Study," *Armed Forces and Society* 35, 3 (Spring 2009), pages 477–500.

21. Ryan Kelty, "Citizen Soldiers and Civilian Contractors: Soldiers' Unit Cohesion and Retention Attitudes in the 'Total Force,'" *Journal of Political and Military Sociology* 37, 2 (Winter 2009), pages 1–27.

22. Samples sizes for the various analyses may differ from these totals due to item non-response on some items.

23. Faye J. Crosby, *Relative Deprivation and Working Women* (New York: Oxford University Press, 1982); Mady W. Segal, "The Military and the Family as Greedy Institutions," *Armed Forces and Society* 13, 1 (Fall 1986), pages 9–38.

24. Respondents were not asked what specific jobs contractors performed in working with their units; rather, they were instructed to keep in mind the definition of "civilian contractor"

used for the study (presented in the prior paragraph) when responding to survey items. In addition, on the social comparison scale, they were instructed to make comparisons with contractors who performed the same or comparable duties as themselves.

25. George W. Bush, *The President's Management Agenda* (Washington: Office of Management and Budget, 2002), page 14, available at http://www.whitehouse.gov/omb/budget/fy2002/mgmt.pdf, accessed 4 May 2003; Light, *The True Size of Government*.

26. The private security forces who carry weapons and operate outside of secure operating bases discussed by other authors in this volume may be considered mercenary—but may equally likely be considered postmodern military professionals.

27. See, for example, Charles Horton Cooley, *Human Nature and the Social Order* (New York: Scribner's, 1902); Erving Goffman, *Presentation of Self in Everyday Life* (Garden City, NY: Anchor, 1959); George H. Mead, *Mind, Self, and Society from the Standpoint of a Social Behaviorist* (Chicago: University of Chicago Press, 1934/1962).

28. The 2010 Quadrennial Defense Review refers to the Total Defense Workforce, comprised of three distinct groups: military personnel, Department of Defense civilian personnel, and civilian contractors.

29. $\chi^2 = 11.490, p < .05$. Traditional significance levels begin with a p-value of .05 or lower.

30. $\chi^2 = 14.443, p < .01$.

31. Kelty, "The Navy's Maiden Voyage"; Kelty, "Citizen Soldiers and Civilian Contractors"; Kelty and Segal, "The Civilianization of the U.S. Military."

32. Chris Bourg and Mady W. Segal, "The Impact of Family Supportive Policies and Practices on Organizational Commitment to the Army," *Armed Forces and Society* 25, 4 (Summer 1999), pages 633–52.

Chapter Fourteen

Weaving a New Tapestry

Controlling Corporate Warriors

Gary Schaub Jr.

> Disciplined armed forces . . . are the political program of the rational utopia, of the society which is both orderly and free; orderly because every member and every act is dedicated to the attainment of a common goal, free because every soldier either is a free contracted volunteer or has consciously accepted his role as part of the broader social contract to which he adheres. [1]

In this volume we have discussed and analyzed a phenomenon that is still emerging. States are increasingly choosing to acquire coercive capacities from private actors rather than producing them themselves. Although the private production of coercive capacities was common in previous centuries, states worked diligently to assert monopoly control over the institutions of coercion within their territories and reinforced the legitimacy of doing so through a collective oligopoly with other states. These institutions were designed to minimize the elemental problem facing all societies: controlling those proficient in violence and harnessing their skills for the good of the community. States developed processes to socialize and indoctrinate their warriors in an ethos of public service explicitly linked to citizenship and constructed rules and regulations to direct their behavior. To support this modern model of military manning, states built all-encompassing hierarchical institutions to monitor and discipline their military's actions, monopolized their legitimate employment opportunities for warriors, forged their military and their soldiers into a national symbol and instrument of the state, and collaborated with other states to legitimate the entire process.

Over the past quarter century, states that successfully built and sustained such institutions felt secure enough to revisit their choice between producing and procuring many aspects of their coercive capacities. The neoliberal theories of economics that permeated Western public policy suggested that efficiencies could be gained by shifting from making to buying.[2] Temporarily leasing the services of personnel with the requisite skills promised several advantages:

- It would reduce military manpower costs directly through force structure reductions, paying temporary employees only when actually employed.[3] In particular, expenditures on noncash and deferred compensation would be reduced.[4]
- It would reduce military manpower costs indirectly through reductions in administering force structure.[5]
- It would allow remaining military personnel to focus on military core competencies.
- The use of personnel for whom support services are core competencies, including former military members who performed those functions while in uniform, would improve the quality of ancillary services.[6]
- It would simplify the process of increasing the workforce or reassigning personnel, particularly in time-sensitive contingencies, thereby increasing responsiveness, agility, and flexibility.[7]
- It would further reduce costs because market forces discipline private sector firms to maximize efficiency in their structure and performance.[8]

Overall, it was presumed that outsourcing would decrease costs and increase the effectiveness of military forces by permitting each type of agent to focus on its core competencies. While it has proven difficult and controversial to engage in direct cost-effectiveness comparisons between services supplied by military and contractor personnel,[9] the entire endeavor was premised upon core coercive capacities remaining the province of the state and its multidimensional tapestry of control.[10]

At the same time, security demands upon these states shifted from defending themselves against their similarly developed neighbors to projecting stability into areas where the state consolidation process has been less successful.[11] Private military and security companies (PMSCs) became involved in weak and unstable states in three ways. First, weak, unstable, and less-developed states such as Angola, Sierra Leone, and Papua New Guinea availed themselves of foreign PMSCs to fight their internal enemies and consolidate state power in a manner reminiscent of Italian city-states of the sixteenth century.[12] Second, strong and stable states contracted with PMSCs to assist weaker states in these endeavors, as in the cases of Croatia and Bosnia-Herzegovina.[13] Third, PMSC personnel accompanied the regular military personnel of strong states when they intervened in weaker and less stable ones, as in the cases of Iraq and Afghanistan discussed in the introduction.

Yet aggressive outsourcing of support services in peacetime deprived the military of many strong states of the ability to support their operations in wartime. This issue became much more salient when civilian contractors joined regular military forces on the battlefield. Much of the contract oversight and regulatory machinery used to monitor and enforce contracts was designed for domestic services provided in peacetime. It was not well suited for such tasks in an expeditionary environment.[14] As the use of contractors in such environments increased dramatically in the 2000s, even well-developed bureaucracies could not keep up[15] and the weak institutions of the states in which they operated were unable to fill the gap.[16]

Such gaps existed in the entire tapestry of institutions developed to control, direct, and manage PMSCs in comparison to the armed forces. They introduced uncertainties that undermined the effective management and purposive use of military force by the state. As we argued in the introduction, these uncertainties concerned the degree of overlap between the relational and functional preferences of states and their new PMSC agents, the oversight and enforcement mechanisms that can be used by states to encourage—if not ensure—that PMSCs behave in ways that accord with state preferences, and the ability of PMSC personnel to substitute for state military forces. States have attempted to adapt existing structures to deal with these uncertainties and our contributors have approached these efforts with skeptical eyes.

In the following sections, I synthesize the insights in the preceding chapters with regard to the three uncertainties that the resort to private actors introduces to the state's ability to control and meaningfully utilize violence: that deriving from the divergence of preferences between the state and PMSCs, the looser oversight and enforcement mechanisms used to discipline the behavior of PMSCs, and the degree to which PMSC personnel are suitable substitutes for regular military personnel. I then turn to the gaps that remain in the tapestry of control that states have woven to regain their collective oligopoly over the legitimate use of force internationally and offer brief suggestions for addressing them. Finally, I conclude with a summary of the overall argument of the volume: that the different efforts taken by states have resulted in an uneven patchwork of mechanisms to shape the preferences of PMSCs and their personnel, to oversee their activities, and to discipline their behavior; that the lack of harmonization has contributed to the underdevelopment of these mechanisms; and that further efforts must be made to effectively control the corporate warrior.

CONVERGENT OR DIVERGENT PREFERENCES?

As we argued in the introduction, the essence of statehood is the ability of a governing regime to assert a monopoly over the legitimate use of physical force within its territory and the recognition of its independence among other states.[17] When states turned to the market to procure the coercive services of private actors, we argued, they introduced a substantial uncertainty into their ability to control those agents. This derived from the divergence between the preference of the state to ensure its own security and the preferences of the PMSC to make a profit. Given the instability of weak states and their vulnerability to the use of mercenaries in the past, many states and observers feared that PMSCs might pose a serious threat to the political leadership of such states.[18] Such dangers arising from divergent relational preferences were quite salient in weak and unstable states. As David Perry argued in chapter 6, the utilization of locally staffed and, at times, locally owned PMSCs by international actors in Afghanistan led President Hamid Karzai to attempt to disband and absorb these groups into a state structure to ensure his government's monopoly over the legitimate use of force. That effort failed and was replaced by a licensing regime that took hold only because the United States and NATO's International Security Assistance Force (ISAF) required the PMSCs that they employed to be locally licensed by the Afghan government. Without the external assistance, the multiplicity of armed actors outside of the government's control in Afghanistan would have posed an even larger challenge to its ability to govern.

President Karzai's reaction was not atypical. As our volume shows, states have reacted differently to the challenge that PMSCs may pose to the state's control over the means of organized violence. On the one hand, as Shannon Bosch, Marelie Maritz, and Matthew Kimble argued in chapter 2, South Africa built its entire approach to PMSCs to guard itself and its neighbors against this danger. The local genesis of the industry during a time when the African National Congress (ANC) was attempting to consolidate power after the transition to majority rule induced the government to adopt a rigid and restrictive approach to these new actors. Would the existence of a well-organized, well-trained, and well-equipped group of military personnel who had formerly fought against the men and women of the ANC pose a threat to the new government? Would it pose dangers to their neighbors—dangers for which they could be blamed? Assured in the knowledge that the key to statehood was maintaining a monopoly over the use of organized violence and seeing no viable alternative approach, the South African government chose to treat PMSCs and their employees as mercenaries and effectively moved to prohibit them and their activities. Yet its nascent judicial system demonstrated an inability to enforce these prohibitions in practice. It progressively drafted layers of restrictions on the ability of individuals to be employed by private entities to effectively criminalize mercenary-like activities, yet could not grasp the innovation of the corporate form that these new actors had adopted. Its poorly functioning regulatory scheme has highlighted the gap between the government's desires and its capabilities. Weak enforcement institutions and an inability to successfully prosecute violators undermined the legitimacy of the South African approach. The challenges increased as South African PMSCs moved offshore and other states adopted a more relaxed attitude toward PMSCs and focused on developing regulatory frameworks. By declining to adopt the good practices for home states indicated in the Montreux Document, it has effectively accepted a poorly regulated but still prominent PMSC industry based in its territory and populated by South African nationals. The South African approach also presented difficulties in gaining effective cooperation from neighboring states to enforce its preferred restrictions. Rather, it persists in promoting less tolerant international approaches to these private actors to the detriment of its own diplomatic success.

On the other hand, some states have not reacted to the challenge that PMSCs supposedly pose for state control over organized violence. In chapter 3, Guy Seidman argued that Israel has not yet privatized security to any appreciable level given the relationship between its society and its armed forces. The strong communal tradition of the Israeli polity, its reliance on near-universal national military service, and its broad definition of military functions have made significant manpower available for state purposes at below-market rates and therefore muted demand for private military and security services. Indeed, to the extent that they are used, it is in a domestic security context, such as the control of border crossings. Israel lacks, for example, a legal framework to regulate the activities of its citizens or nationals abroad.[19] Therefore, the control of private military actors, either corporate or individual, has not motivated the Israeli government to react to, nor engage proactively, issues of controlling PMSCs and their agents.

Indeed, potential challenges to the political control of force arising from incongruent relational preferences with PMSCs have been minimized for strong and stable states by their practice of using them as auxiliary forces in expeditionary operations to help construct viable institutions in weak states. When deployed in distant lands, they pose little threat to the contracting state's monopoly over the legitimate use of force. As discussed in conjunction with figure 1.4 in chapter 1, PMSCs remain in these states for a period of time to provide services that these states cannot yet provide effectively for themselves.[20] Although some worry that they could utilize their position to perpetuate demand for their services unnecessarily,[21] there has yet to be an instance of a PMSC overthrowing the government of a weak state that it was assisting.

This practice is also reflected in the use of PMSCs in maritime commerce. Christopher Spearin argued in chapter 4 that the United States in particular has encouraged private commercial shipping companies to undertake greater responsibility for their own protection when shipping goods through potentially insecure waters such as those around the Horn of Africa or the Straits of Malacca. They have done so because traditional navies are structured to interact with other navies, not to police the sea lanes against the small crafts operated by modern pirates. Their capabilities are thus inappropriate to the task and they have sought to off-load it to the private sector. Yet the maritime environment poses its own challenges to controlling PMSCs. These include the reluctance of shipping companies to develop the oversight and enforcement mechanisms necessary to control PMSCs on their vessels, the necessity to hire high-quality and trustworthy personnel, and existing international law designed to limit violent private behavior on the high seas. Spearin concluded that the regime that states have built to control piracy and violence on the high seas reduces the incentives to resort to private security actors in the first place. In essence, PMSCs in the maritime environment pose little threat to the state's monopoly over the use of force. As a result, to the degree that states and shippers express concern, it is centered upon the functional preferences of PMSCs.

In chapter 1 we highlighted that it is in the functional preferences of contracting with PMSCs that states primarily face the problem of *adverse selection.*[22] States want to select an agent that is capable of delivering the desired outcome in an acceptable manner and at a reasonable cost. Collecting information about the agents offering their services is costly in time and effort—and the nature of the market for force made the task even more difficult. Indeed, the lack of an authoritative registry of PMSCs hinders state due diligence when selecting, contracting, and authorizing PMSCs.[23] Furthermore, the market for security is inscrutable: the buyer and seller have difficulty discerning the quality of the services to be offered beforehand.[24] Without the ability to distinguish between goods and services, "cost of distinguishing the good from the bad, the best from the rest, the bogus from the authentic," buyers and sellers have difficulty settling on a fair price—let alone a quality agent.[25] How have states and PMSCs gone about addressing this potential market failure?

The preceding chapters have highlighted that the weight of this effort has fallen on PMSCs that claim to deliver quality services. PMSCs have made three types of efforts to supply information to state principals about the quality of services that they offer. The first is the association of the PMSC and its personnel with the state's military. As argued in chapter 1 and in chapters 11, 12, and 13, PMSCs such as Executive Outcomes, MPRI, and Blackwater have utilized the previous military experience of their leadership and employees to signal that their services provide an acceptable substitute for the functions previously provided by regular military forces.[26] Furthermore, such firms have argued that they share a common interest in the outcome with their clients, beyond the letter of their contractual obligations. They can demonstrate this commitment in many ways, such as accepting a smaller profit margin than permitted by law,[27] partially integrating themselves into the command structures of their client's military,[28] and continuing to perform their duties even when the going gets tough and the client defaults on its end of the contractual agreement.[29] In these ways, some PMSCs attempted to develop a niche "coalition" market wherein principals and agents share a sense of solidarity and common interests.[30]

The second way to signal quality is to provide proxy symbols that enable principals to differentiate between good and bad firms. As Doug Brooks, Andrew Koch, and Gary Schaub argued in chapter 9, firms in the industry had an incentive to cooperate with one another to establish and enforce standards of performance and control entry to the market so as to separate themselves from firms providing substandard services. Trade associations such as the International Stability Operations Association (ISOA), the British Association of Private Security Companies (BAPSC), and the now defunct Private Security Company Association of Iraq (PSCAI) could provide a venue for firms to collect data about their services, set standards, enforce them, and grant a seal of approval to those that consistently meet the agreed-upon standards. In the case of the PMSC market, membership in one of these trade associations served as an indicator of companies that abided by its code of conduct—one measure of quality service. The degree of information conveyed by such symbols depends upon the difficulty of acquiring them. ISOA, BAPSC, and PSCAI provided such symbols and had mechanisms of differing quality for policing their value that were recognized by states and international organizations alike. Yet, as Surabhi Ranganathan argued in chapter 8, the limited ability of industry trade associations to set, monitor, and enforce agreed practices among their members hampered their potential as regulatory agencies. So did the lack of universal membership, since the signaling effect of revoking the membership of a violator is muted when legitimate PMSCs are permitted to operate without being members of an industry association.[31] The degree to which contracting states require PMSCs to be members in good standing—either as a provision within individual contracts or through general legislation—will increase the ability of these trade associations to enforce their codes of conduct and more credibly signal quality service. In the ideal, ejection from the trade association for a violation would disqualify the company (and any derivative entities) from eligibility for future business for some period of time. But this would require industry associations to be stronger and better resourced than they have been heretofore.

The third approach taken by PMSCs to signal quality has been establishing a brand-name reputation through a record of efficient, effective, and unproblematic service. Reputations can play an outsized role in markets where the quality of goods and services is difficult to judge beforehand. They spare firms "from repeating the burden of proof at every transaction" and "shelter [such firms] from competitive threats."[32] As discussed in chapter 1 and in chapter 2 on South Africa by Bosch, Maritz, and Kimble, Executive Outcomes established a reputation for effectiveness very quickly and valued that asset highly. Indeed, it avoided becoming problematic by accepting risk to avoid civilian casualties in its operations, engaged in policing actions not called for in its contract, and thereby "created popularity with civilians."[33] Likewise, Blackwater's reputation for effectiveness sustained it through many problems that caught the public's attention, from the slaughtering of its personnel in Fallujah in 2004 through the Nisour Square incident where 17 civilians were killed and 18 injured. As Blackwater's founder, Erik Prince, noted, "regardless of what was happening in Iraq, [the] State [Department] suddenly needed our help in Afghanistan—and beyond."[34] Still, events in Iraq did cause reputational difficulties and Blackwater rebranded itself as Xe to wipe the slate clean. As Prince put it, "if the PR nightmare was going to doom Blackwater, then 'Blackwater' had to go."[35] Indeed, eventually Blackwater's leadership changed and Prince himself left the company in order to rehabilitate the business.[36]

Such changes, however, also highlight the limits of reputation as a signaling device. Blackwater survived in other forms. "I wasn't thrilled with the idea," wrote Prince. "But if customers like Raytheon wanted that built-in deniability—a way to hire us while also being able to later claim, 'We didn't know it was Blackwater!'—I thought it best to let them have it."[37] Peter Singer argued that the ability to reinvent themselves is "perhaps the final advantage that private firms have, even in death."[38] Nothing binds them to any particular name, geographic location for incorporation, services to be provided, leadership, or employees.[39] The same holds for individual employees, who can reenter the labor pool after causing a disruption and/or being disciplined for poor behavior. Although individuals are more vulnerable to a negative reputation, the cadre–independent contractor structure of many PMSCs makes transparency difficult especially in a competitive market. At each level, reputation can be diffused, the shadow of the future can be shortened, and redemption can be obtained far more easily than for states and their military personnel. Such processes can make it difficult for states to follow the "good practices" specified in the Montreux Document to perform due diligence before selecting a PMSC. As Ian Ralby argues in chapter 10, mechanisms and institutions for regulating PMSCs and controlling their behavior must improve their ability to recall past performance or the problems of adverse selection will continue to haunt the industry.

MONITORING AND ENFORCEMENT?

Ryan Kelty and I argued in the introductory chapter that procuring services from private actors in the market utilizes a different set of oversight and enforcement mechanisms than those used to control the armed forces. In general, these are less developed and introduce additional uncertainties into the state-PMSC relationship. The analyses of American, Canadian, and British regulation of the expeditionary PMSC operations provided by David Strachan-Morris, David Perry, and Eugenio Cusumano and Christopher Kinsey indicate that regulatory efforts by these states did not provide sufficient performance data to overcome the information deficiencies of the market. These states suffered from a common belief that their well-developed and effective processes for selecting, monitoring, and controlling private agents in other spheres would be sufficient in an expeditionary environment.[40] Yet negotiating a cost-effective contract that delivers the best value for money and ensuring that goods and services are delivered as agreed is but one small part of that oversight challenge.[41] Even basic information was deficient. The United Kingdom did not systematically collect statistics on the value of contracts or data on contractor personnel deployed on operations until 2003.[42] The US Department of Defense (DoD) did not track the number of private security contractors (PSCs) deployed with its military forces until 2007.[43] Officials continued to express dismay and "concern" over their inability to oversee and manage the vast increase in contracts well into 2015.[44]

Beyond acquiring such basic situational awareness, ensuring appropriate behavior during the performance of services required significantly more effort than governments anticipated. But the United States undertook these efforts and, as the leading user of PMSCs, it developed the most comprehensive system to monitor and enforce laws and norms upon them. It has carried out a comprehensive review of its operational contracting practices and has implemented specific guidance for them.[45] No other states have done this, including Canada and the United Kingdom, both of which share the American penchant for engaging the services of PMSCs at home and abroad. Furthermore, the United States has undertaken significant efforts to define inherently governmental functions that should remain the province of state authorities with a significant degree of nuance.[46] It has "a fairly restrictive procedure for issuing licenses to entities that export military or defense services," a "rather robust regulatory system" for selecting and contracting with PMSCs, and "a complex system for overseeing and monitoring PMSCs and their personnel" that reflect the "good practices" of the Montreux Document.[47] The extension of the Military Extraterritorial Jurisdiction Act (MEJA) to contractors working for other entities in support of DoD objectives and the extension of the Uniform Code of Military Justice (UCMJ) to civilians employed overseas by the armed forces in 2008 greatly enhanced the ability of the United States to hold PMSC personnel accountable. Yet the challenge of extraterritoriality still poses challenges to American efforts to hold PMSC personnel and firms responsible for criminal behavior committed abroad.

Indeed, military commanders found themselves bereft of the tools that they needed to monitor the activities of these private actors, to direct or command their behavior, and to enforce those orders through their normal chain of command. US Army policy explicitly states that "contractor employees are *not* under the direct supervision of military personnel in the chain-of-command."[48] "A military commander can influence contractor employees' behavior through the contracting officer and the contractor's desire to have a satisfied customer, but the commander has limited direct control over any one employee."[49] Furthermore, they lacked the tools to discipline aberrant behavior. "Military commanders have less control over civilians and contractors than over military personnel who commit crimes during a conflict. . . . [T]here is no general mechanism for the military to try DoD civilians or contractors who are not retired service members for crimes committed during undeclared wars."[50] Instead, they must be turned over to the civilian justice system, where significant hurdles to effective enforcement remain.

The experiences of the US military in Iraq also led to the introduction of oversight mechanisms to monitor the performance of contractors in their day-to-day responsibilities. As Strachan-Morris explained in his chapter on battlefield relations between PMSCs and military personnel, the DoD recognized the issue fairly quickly. It established Reconstruction Operations Centers in 2004 to coordinate the movements of PMSCs in areas controlled by the US military and facilitate the sharing of intelligence. In 2008, the establishment of Contractor Operations Centers (CONOCs) at divisional headquarters further improved visibility of PMSCs, enabling more effective oversight, as well as a quicker military response in the event of incidents involving contractors and the local population. Subsequent regulations have also improved PMSC accountability by requiring them to report serious incidents, and the DoD established an Armed Contractor Oversight Division (ACOD) to investigate such incidents. In 2009 an ACOD was created for Afghanistan—and its operation immediately contracted out to a PMSC. These institutions enabled PMSCs to plan their movements to avoid potential trouble spots, reduced the likelihood of armed confrontations with the civilian population, and reduced the number of friendly fire incidents.[51] Strachan-Morris argues that these solutions eventually proved viable primarily because they fostered informal relations between the participants on the ground. In this, his findings complement those of Molly Dunigan, who found that co-deployment of regular military forces and PMSCs in Iraq and Afghanistan decreased military effectiveness when they were not integrated into a transparent chain of command and thus able to work out coordination issues.[52] Despite such lessons, he argues that these theater oversight mechanisms and more effective command and control arrangements have not been institutionalized or incorporated into American (or allied) doctrine. Therefore they may have to be created yet again when the next contingency operation strains the capacities of regular military forces.

In chapter 6, David Perry further argued that Canada has not yet developed a comprehensive system to regulate PMSCs. No single entity controls or coordinates contractors or contracts. It relies upon ad hoc vetting of companies and personnel by international missions, the Canadian Forces, and Canadian military intelligence in its contract award process.[53] Likewise, monitoring and enforcement are decentralized, with personnel on site responsible for monitoring performance, investigating alleged misconduct, and referring cases to appropriate authorities for action.[54] Those authorities include the host state, depending upon the Status of Forces Agreement reached with it, and the home state of the employee. Furthermore, the conduct of PMSC personnel that accompany Canadian armed forces abroad is subject to the Code of Service Discipline, regardless of their nationality, and alleged violators can be held accountable within the military justice system.[55] Thus Canada has developed a system for addressing issues of extraterritoriality, but it has never been put to the test.[56]

Canada's efforts to establish a more effective legal regime and regulatory mechanisms to ensure proper management and coordination of contracts and contractors, provide oversight and transparency for contracts, and integrate the use of PMSCs into national policy and doctrine foundered for lack of attention. Indeed, parliamentary interest in these issues decreased over time. The Canadian Forces' efforts to develop a doctrine to govern the use and control of PMSCs in expeditionary operations have remained on the drafting board since 2012. This lack of urgency ensures that significant gaps in the tapestry of control will remain into the future.

Still, the Canadian efforts compare favorably to the lenient approach of the United Kingdom. The United Kingdom has not clarified the functions that it considers to be inherently governmental and therefore immune to privatization. It does not require licensing to operate abroad or to be eligible to contract with the government.[57] Cusumano and Kinsey argued in chapter 7 that the purchasing of foreign military manpower has been commonplace in British history and was not considered problematic until the informal coordination between the Foreign and Commonwealth Office and the PMSC Sandline International resulted in a scandal. This was sufficient to prompt the Commonwealth Office to formally consider different regulatory schemes in its 2002 Green Paper, but not to take action. British officials judged direct regulation too costly and prohibitively difficult to implement and instead chose to rely upon "old boy networks" and the "nod and wink business practice approach" to convey regulatory guidance.[58] The lack of further scandal enabled the government to work with the industry to help it regulate itself and to support the efforts of international bodies to provide regulatory guidance. The United Kingdom is relying on the International Code of Conduct Association (ICoCA) to provide independent certification and monitoring of PMSCs.[59] Its Foreign and Commonwealth Office relies upon its contracts with PMSCs to regulate their behavior, although the publicly available terms of these are vague.[60] UK PMSCs operating for other clients—which constitute the majority—are monitored by third parties and there is no centralized authority with responsibility for receiving complaints, let alone investigating violations or pursuing enforcement actions.[61] Finally, the United Kingdom has asserted extraterritorial authority over a limited number of serious criminal activities perpetrated by British nationals and some contractors accompanying its armed forces, but has yet to begin considering mechanisms for expanding those areas or accountability to PMSCs themselves.[62] This laissez-faire attitude differs substantially from that of Canada and the United States. Given that these states often deploy their military forces together in expeditionary operations, Perry concluded that their ability to operate effectively together has been—and will continue to be—challenged unless and until they harmonize their approaches to controlling PMSCs in expeditionary operations.

Beyond the challenges of harmonization in the name of operational effectiveness, Brooks, Koch, and Schaub argued in chapter 9 that the variation in domestic regulation across relevant states presents a host of additional challenges to monitoring and control. Overly stringent regulations and controls may drive PMSCs (or their derivatives) offshore to more lax regulatory environments. Differences can permit PMSCs to select a home state with the form and type of regulation that best suits their interests. Indeed, Bosch, Maritz, and Kimble argued in chapter 2 that this is what happened with the South African PMSC industry. States should be encouraged to harmonize their approaches to national regulation to reduce this potential through trade associations as well as through international agreements such as the Montreux Document, as that is its foremost purpose.

Indeed, as Ralby argues in chapter 10, the Montreux Document provides guidance regarding criminal and non-criminal matters, as well as administrative frameworks for regulatory oversight that build on the legal obligations of states outlined in the document. These include establishing corporate criminal responsibility for PMSCs, establishing national criminal jurisdiction over serious crimes committed by PMSC personnel abroad, and establishing graduated penalties for improper and unlawful conduct by states that contract with PMSCs. It asks states where PMSCs operate to consider whether their judicial systems and legal frameworks are sufficient to enforce appropriate behavior among PMSC personnel, including determining which activities are permissible. These suggestions are intended to decrease twilight in national law surrounding the use and operation of PMSCs in non-criminal contexts and, Ralby argues, are likely to require the auditing of domestic legal regimes, crafting new legislation to fill any gaps and strengthen areas of weakness. In particular, in the case of territorial states, emphasis must be placed on building the effective institutions of governance that they likely lack and that account for the presence of the PMSCs in the first place.

In the absence of such harmonization—and uniformly strong justice systems—the most significant legal challenges to be overcome are those posed by extraterritoriality, even for strong and stable states with well-developed justice systems. PMSCs have been increasingly used in an expeditionary manner, which makes it difficult for a contracting or home state to monitor and enforce its domestic regulatory regime when it comes to operations abroad. This holds true whether the PMSC is working for the state or for other entities, such as private corporations, nongovernmental organizations, or international organizations. Companies have muted incentives to bring any bad behavior of which they become aware to the attention of the relevant authorities and, absent a resulting tactical engagement that comes to the attention of the home or contracting state's military forces (as in the case of the US CENTCOM Reconstruction Operations Centers [ROCs] in Iraq), states have thus far relied upon third-party reports to hear about aberrant activity. Furthermore, actual enforcement of even flagrant violations with dire consequences has proven problematic. As shown in the numerous attempts of South Africa to prosecute violations of its Foreign Military Assistance Act and the seven-year-long cases against the Blackwater employees who killed and injured civilians in Nisour Square, it is extremely difficult to enforce domestic regulatory frameworks and laws on activities taken in other countries. Beyond the ambiguities inherent in any regulatory scheme or individual case, difficulties include sustaining the expense of timely investigations, securing witness testimony, and collecting and transporting evidence through a proper chain of custody. Without the institutional wherewithal to undertake such efforts, establishing extraterritorial jurisdiction over PMSC behavior may be largely symbolic and lacking functional enforcement.

In this context it must be further noted that registration of a PMSC in one state need not imply a license to operate in any state or for any client. The states that hire and permit PMSCs to operate within their territory have some ability to dictate the certifications, licenses, and conditions that must be met. As mentioned above, these mechanisms can serve as useful signaling devices. Sarah Percy argues that "at its best, all regulation (as opposed to a ban) will be able to do is to draw a sharp distinction between the good, the bad and the ugly, and ensure that state contracts only go to legitimate companies."[63] But perhaps that is sufficient for shaping the market if the primary states that hire PMSCs never hire companies that fail to meet their regulatory requirements, denying them the most lucrative and legitimate portions of the market. It may even be sufficient for territorial states to deny them permission to operate. Blackwater suffered a key blow when Iraq denied it a license in January 2009 and the State Department accepted that ruling.[64] Furthermore, such a sorting mechanism should provide incentives to induce companies at the margin to improve the quality of their services. Encouraging appropriate and effective behavior, not simply punishing the bad, is a key function of any regulatory regime.

At the international level, the Montreux Document has provided the basis for separating PMSCs from mercenaries—the contemporary "good" actors from the historically "bad" ones. As Ralby argued in chapter 10, the parties to the document have enabled a distinction between legitimate and illegitimate private suppliers of organized violence. This is clearly a necessary first step that states must take if they are to adapt the international regime that has legitimated the state oligopoly over the legitimate use of force to accommodate these new actors. Doing so permits states to supplement their military forces with private organizations when necessary, while not accepting the legitimacy of all armed private actors.[65] Such differentiation can reinforce the power of states to determine the actors that are permitted to organize, train, and equip personnel so as to wield or support the wielding of organized violence within their territorial jurisdiction. Consensus on these points could provide a degree of protection for states with weak institutions that fear the potential of predatory PMSCs.

The Montreux Document highlights the obligations of PMSC personnel to respect all applicable national and international laws. It also asserts that the military, governmental, and private superiors of those personnel can be held accountable if those operating under their authority commit "serious crimes," albeit with differential levels of responsibility. Yet it is not a binding legal commitment like treaties and international conventions. As Ralby contends, it does not entirely dispel the "legal twilight" surrounding the use of PMSCs. Nor does it "close the gaps" between the manner in which states approach regulating the industry. It also fails to provide specific standards against which signatory states can be held accountable. Finally, it does not provide for a monitoring and enforcement regime.

Ralby argues that it is part of a growing body of "soft law" initiatives that indicate a desire on the part of states to clarify how they should conduct themselves. As such, its force comes from its assemblage and clarification of relevant agreements and customary international law. Ralby makes the case that this is a strength rather than a weakness. Soft law offers an effective way to deal with uncertainty, initiating processes that can evolve over time as actors encounter new issues and develop new approaches to resolving them. Treaties and conventions can be too rigid to adapt to fairly rapidly evolving phenomena such as the market for force, he argues, and states have yet to adapt their own practices, legal codes, and regulatory regimes to effectively account for it. Locking in formal obligations now, as the South African approach has attempted to do, would prematurely stifle creative means of dealing with the problem in favor of the then-current state of the art.

In all of these areas, the Montreux Document lacks the precision and weight that the formal laws of armed conflict bring to bear upon states and their armed forces. As with most "soft law" efforts it relies upon third parties to monitor performance and interest national authorities in enforcing applicable legal sanctions when required.[66] In this it differs little from the ISOA Code of Conduct as discussed by Brooks, Koch, and Schaub. Still, by prescribing an approach to interacting with the PMSC industry it provides a basis from which customary international law can form. The soft law generated by the Montreux Document thereby addressed an important gap at a crucial time and provides for a process for further developing solutions. And it did so much more quickly than would be possible through the negotiation and ratification of an international convention on the use of PMSCs. But it only begins to provide a means to dispel the uncertainties that imperfect monitoring and enforcement bring into the relationship between states and their new coercive agents.

SUITABLE SUBSTITUTES FOR MILITARY PERSONNEL?

The third and final uncertainty that the resort to private actors introduces to the state's ability to control and meaningfully utilize violence concerns whether the personnel employed by PMSCs are inclined to perform their duties in ways that complement and substitute for the military forces of the state. As discussed in the introductory chapter, these private corporate actors have not adopted the mechanisms of total institutions in order to indoctrinate, socialize, and professionalize their management or personnel. Doing so would reduce their appeal as efficient substitutes. Nor are they greedy institutions that develop all-encompassing relations with their personnel, including the promise of a long-term career relationship that serves as a key inducement to discipline behavior. Indeed, their lightweight management structures and use of temporary employees requires them to place great stock in the quality and professionalism of the labor pool from which they draw their employees. Do these personnel possess the qualities of military professionals? Do they demonstrate the behavioral skill sets and identities that can provide confidence that the tasks for which they are responsible will be carried out in a dependable manner?

Throughout this volume, our contributors have devoted their attention to the many individuals working for PMSCs who have a Western military background and who many have argued[67] have been socialized into a common military culture, both formal and informal. Such personnel would be familiar with national and international law and the restraints on military activity due to regulations and norms, and they may have developed strong notions of military professionalism, honor, and ethos. As Kelty argued in chapter 13, such employees likely retain the "moral-ethical socialization" that they acquired while in uniform. These values and habits should influence their decisions while they execute the duties that they have been contracted to perform.

In their chapters, Victor Franke, Schaub, and Kelty utilized survey methods to assess the validity of these sorts of claims. In chapter 11, Franke surveyed 223 American security contractors, two-thirds of whom had served in the US military, 95 percent as enlisted personnel. He found that they showed value orientations very similar to military personnel, being motivated by patriotism and altruism rather than the opportunity for personal gain, and that they experienced high levels of job engagement and satisfaction. Personality-wise, they showed low desire for social dominance, average masculinity scores, and levels of "warriorism" most resembling those of combat support personnel rather than those in the combat arms. Furthermore, they emphasized adherence to international law and humanitarian principles even when these could place them in an ambiguous legal status, as reflected in their split views regarding whether their counterparts on the other side of a conflict ought to be regarded as legal combatants and the 10 percent of respondents who did not believe that they themselves should have protected status under international law.

Franke's survey found evidence of a nascent professional identity among the sample. Within his typology of different types of military professionals, he found that their self-conceptions of professional identity most resembled those of the constabulary soldier and the postmodern peace soldier. This captured the types of tasks that they performed as PMSC personnel and demonstrated the degree to which role identity informs professional identity. They were more likely than the field-grade officers surveyed by Schaub in chapter 12 to exclude "peacekeeping and other non-combat activities" from the military's core functions, and 60 percent had not expected to engage in actual fighting when they decided to sign on with a PMSC. Thus they themselves indicated that their role and functions are conceptually different than those of military personnel. Indeed, half recognized that they were not members of the military profession and over three-quarters acknowledged that there were functions that civilians such as themselves ought not perform. They therefore recognized their separation from the military.

This separation can prove to be problematic, undermining the foundational identity that PMSCs rely upon to maintain disciplined and effective behavior in the absence of significant socialization, management, and oversight of behavior in the field. It is not enough for PMSC personnel to claim an identity as a military professional, regardless of the type, to legitimate their identity. As Kelty and Schaub argue, identities are legitimated through a social process that reflects acceptance of a given identity by others. Indeed, we argued in the introductory chapter that the role and social identities of military personnel are reinforced through almost every aspect of their existence: uniforms, rituals, emblems, and oaths, as well as interactions with others that elicit and reinforce their identity.[68] To sustain a professional identity, PMSC personnel must be accepted as military professionals by military personnel since they constitute their primary reference group. Legitimization would provide social and political support for clarifying the roles of contractors, their responsibilities, and accountability. Furthermore, it would encourage self-regulation among contractors as they internalize the role identities and the role expectations that accompany them. Degradation of these processes of feedback, legitimation, and internalization can erode the ability of contractors to sustain whatever residue of a military identity they brought with them into the private sector. Does the identity feedback that civilian contractors receive from the military members with whom they interact help sustain or degrade the "military" identity of PMSC contractors? The findings of Schaub and Kelty suggest that the feedback loop that could sustain such an identity is fragmented at best.

Kelty used the concept of social comparisons and attitudes toward contractors across several highly salient work-related factors as the foundation for assessing these questions and the impact of contractor integration among uniformed personnel. Among his sample of 539 soldiers from Army combat arms units, he found significant levels of relative deprivation and discontent among soldiers within a broader context of ambivalence toward contractors. Soldiers don't appear to mind working with contractors, and they recognize that contractors have valuable knowledge and skills, increase the military's flexibility and effectiveness, and allow the military to focus on the core duties of war fighting. Yet contractors are viewed as significantly more advantaged across the range of job characteristics—especially pay. These attitudes not only reduce soldier morale through perceptions of relative deprivation, but they also indicate that contractors may encounter significant barriers to acceptance as members of the military in-group, and therefore be less likely to adopt the desirable norms and behaviors implied by a military identity. Indeed, a third of the soldiers surveyed did not consider civilian contractors part of the "Total Force."

Schaub drew upon two aspects of identity—role and social—to assess the manner and degree to which contractors may be accepted as brothers in arms by a sample of 985 elite field-grade officers collected during the height of American contracting in Iraq and Afghanistan. He found that evoking different aspects of identity in these officers led to differential rates of acceptance of contractors as members of the professional military in-group. Large majorities of officers expressed ambivalence at best about the effectiveness and capabilities of civilian contractors. They overwhelmingly judged that there were military functions that civilian contractors could not and ought not perform because of their status. They clearly had negative views of contractors as a social group. Yet their views of contractors were more positive when their role identity was evoked. In particular, civilian contractors placed in the functional military role of armed combatants overcame their out-group status with many officers along multiple dimensions, particularly with regard to their status as combatants under international law—regardless of which side of the conflict they were on. On the other hand, contractors performing support roles were less likely to be accepted as military professionals since they were functionally further from the ideal type. This suggests that different types of contractors evoke different responses from those with whom they interact and will receive different degrees of positive reinforcement of their professional identity.

Additional research in the field supports the claim that the heterogeneity of the PMSC marketplace will generate different types of identities among contractor personnel. In the only study of its kind, Scott Fitzsimmons found that there are substantial differences across the cultures of individual PMSC firms, even among those drawn from the same labor pool and performing similar duties in similar circumstances for the same client.[69] Fitzsimmons found that DynCorp "maintained a military culture that encourage[d] far less violent behavior" and maintained rules of engagement more stringent than those imposed by the Department of State or the Coalition Provisional Authority, encountered insurgents far less frequently, was attacked far less frequently, yet suffered significantly more casualties per encounter with insurgents than Blackwater—despite performing similar duties under similar conditions.[70] Blackwater, on the other hand, "maintained a relatively bellicose military culture that placed strong emphasis on norms encouraging its personnel to exercise personal initiative, a proactive use of force and an exclusive approach to security, which, together, motivated its personnel to use violence quite freely against anyone suspected of posing a threat."[71] This culture arguably derived from the US Navy SEAL culture of its founder, Erik Prince, and other key Blackwater personnel.[72] Blackwater used a "brief (approximately 164 hours) but rigorous training and indoctrination program" to instill these norms and expectations in its personnel.[73] Such cohesion within firms—despite the loose organizational structure that characterizes their cadre-contractor arrangements—and distinctions in culture across them suggests that regarding all PMSC personnel with military backgrounds as "similar" is a mistake, and that some may develop the professional identity of the postmodern peace soldier while others may develop that of the traditional warrior depending upon their duties and the socialization efforts of their employers.

The inference to be drawn is that the assumption within the literature that most Western PMSC employees bring with them a uniform and stable professional identity is blithe. Furthermore, it suggests that if inculcating a particular professional identity in PMSC personnel is key to influencing the behavior of civilian contract personnel to make it more consonant with that expected of the military personnel they replace, then a concerted effort to socialize them into the normative behaviors and attitudes of military professionals ought to be undertaken at the company, industry, national, and international level. Indeed, such programs ought to take advantage of the different types of PMSC services offered, as well as the base identity that contractors in each of those fields likely hold, and work to reinforce those identities so that common understandings of role expectations can be developed and shared among civilian contractors and the military personnel with whom they will work. Key aspects of the industry itself, those that focus on training military forces and inculcating professionalism in them, ought to be focused on PMSC personnel as well, as part of an effort to increase the quality of services and decrease the likelihood of problematic behavior—at least among Western nationals. Requiring such training can increase the quality of the employment pool and provide an additional measure of confidence in the likelihood that they will comport themselves professionally.

BARE THREADS IN THE TAPESTRY

Taken as a whole, the arguments presented by the contributors to this volume suggest that the decision taken by an increasing number of states to legitimize and utilize private actors to perform coercive tasks on their behalf is a trend that will likely be a key characteristic of military action in the twenty-first century. Furthermore, the contributors have argued that even leading states with strong institutions and regulatory cultures were unprepared to meet the scale and scope of the demands that the use of these actors imposed upon them. Individual states have varied in the manner in which they have framed this issue, the speed with which they have reacted to it, and the measures that they have taken. The industry itself has grown and evolved over the past 25 years. It began as a dichotomous market of firms that provided combat services to weak states and firms populated by personnel drawn mostly from Western militaries that primarily offered discrete support services to their home state's military. It has become a globalized market for force comprised of multinational firms of greatly varying size, form, and quality, offering a spectrum of combat, policing, and support functions, and populated by personnel drawn from many nations, including the fragile states in which they operate on behalf of intervening powers. Voluntary trade associations have formed to develop and promulgate industry standards that filled the gap while states adjusted, but resourcing their ability to monitor and enforce those standards has not been a priority for industry firms, even when a state such as the United Kingdom has deliberately deferred such tasks to them. Finally, the community of stakeholders—states, industry firms, international organizations, and nongovernmental organizations—have collaborated to build "soft law" institutions at the international level, utilizing the Montreux Document as their foundation. Each of these macro-level developments provides some ability to address the challenges raised by the wide-scale use of private actors by states to perform functions that they had heretofore considered their province alone. Yet this tapestry of control is not woven nearly as tightly as that for state armed forces. Gaps remain and in this final section I review some of the most pressing and offer illustrative suggestions for addressing them.

Personnel

The discussion above raises one further issue regarding PMSC personnel that has yet to be addressed in depth: that of non-Western personnel employed by PMSCs servicing contracts with Western states.[74] As the industry grew and many more firms entered the marketplace, homogeneity of employees became harder to manage. In particular, PMSCs came to rely more and more on third-country nationals and local employees from the host nation for their manpower as the expeditionary operations in which they participated persisted much longer and required more extensive development than anticipated. In fact, the United States and its allies pursued a deliberate policy of hiring host nation nationals to increase local participation in many aspects of potential governance and economic structures in Iraq and Afghanistan.[75] As shown in figures 14.1 and 14.2, CENTCOM data demonstrate that American PMSC personnel were greatly outnumbered by those of the host nation and third countries in both Iraq and Afghanistan from 2007 forward.[76]

The third-country nationals that made up this workforce hailed from states as diverse as Nepal, Peru, Bulgaria, Ukraine, Chile, Honduras, Colombia, Uganda, and South Africa.[77] In Iraq, US nationals averaged 38 percent of the PMSC workforce between September 2007 and December 2015 (figure 14.1). In Afghanistan, they averaged 33 percent from September 2007 through September 2015 (figure 14.2). More significantly for the state control of violence, the mix of American and other nationals was even more lopsided for personnel assigned to core tasks such as "personal security, convoy security, and static security missions" in an armed or unarmed capacity.[78] US nationals comprised an average of 9.3 percent of PSC personnel in Iraq from 2007 to 2015 (figure 14.3), while they averaged 7.5 percent in Afghanistan (figure 14.4).[79]

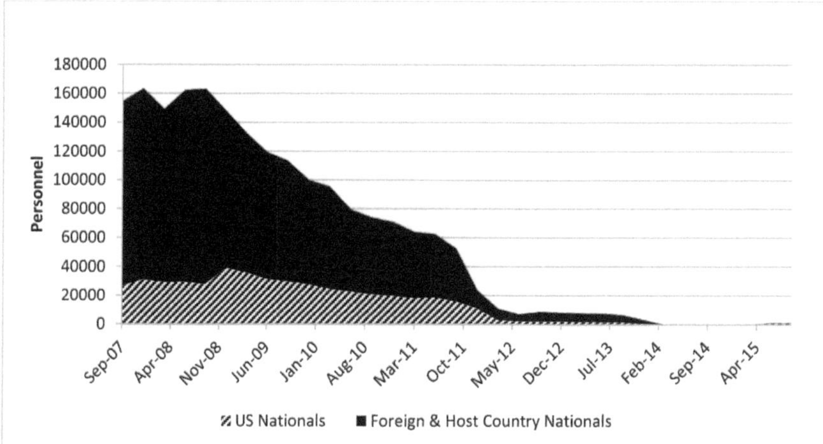

Figure 14.1. Iraq PMSC Personnel 2007–2015

Such a multinational workforce produces considerable barriers to the formation of a professional identity, ethos, and culture among employees. Beyond obvious differences in language, nationality, and ethnicity, the cultural barriers to be overcome to forge a common identity are significant. They include differences in (a) the respect and deference given to superiors by a subordinate, (b) proclivities toward individual or collective identity, and (c) tendencies toward comfort with uncertainty and risk.[80] Moreover, the transient nature of employment in theater, the heterogeneity of employers, and the lack of a coherent multinational structure to provide stable expectations, identities, and mechanisms for deconfliction, coordination, cooperation, and the building of trust further hamper the formation of a common identity.[81]

Although developing and maintaining a coherent identity through selective recruitment and training was one of the primary objectives of PMSCs such as Executive Outcomes, MPRI, and Blackwater, the ability of the vast majority of firms to meet the surge in demand for their services in Iraq, Afghanistan, and beyond precluded these sorts of investments.[82] Without such efforts it will prove difficult to place much stock in the assumption that the recruitment pool for PMSC personnel will yield professionals with a disposition toward any coherent identity beyond that formed in response to the incentive structures in which they find themselves as private military and security contractors.

States can facilitate socialization and training processes through the conditions that they include in their contracts with PMSCs. They can require that the core personnel of the firms that they hire be screened for past criminal activities or past dismissal from previous employment due to misconduct[83]

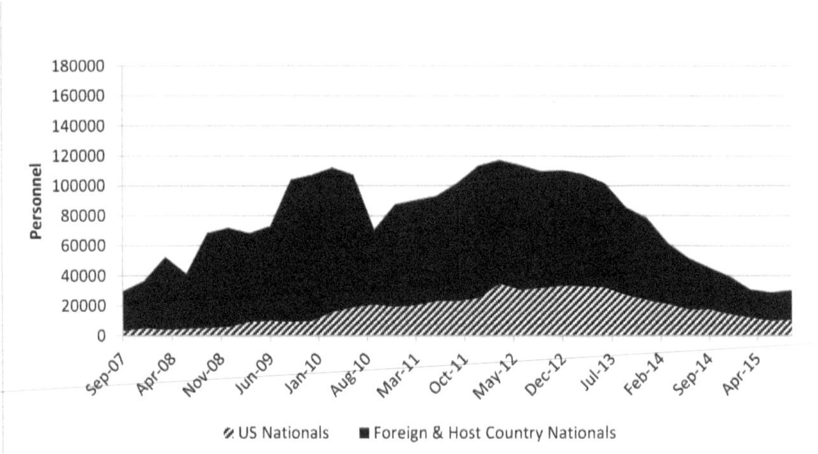

Figure 14.2. Afghanistan PMSC Personnel 2007–2015

and that they be licensed to perform the tasks that will be assigned—particularly those that may involve the use of force[84] —and they can show a preference for firms that have pursued targeted recruitment of personnel who have previously served in the armed forces of an advanced and stable state if they will be deployed in expeditionary operations. Such incentives could help screen out bad actors and reward firms that minimize the dangers of adverse selection when hiring personnel. States and firms can develop and implement joint training programs prior to deployment to familiarize military, civil service, and private contractor personnel with one another as well as the rules of engagement and their appropriate roles within the larger purpose of their operations.[85] Such training programs could mirror those for multinational peacekeeping missions[86] and could even provide a basis for reinforcing a professional ethos, if not necessarily an identity, among the contractors.

Monitoring and Enforcement

Monitoring the activities of PMSCs, evaluating their performance, and enforcing laws and norms of behavior upon them and their personnel are primarily the responsibility of the states that hire them, although the states in which they are incorporated and in which they operate share such responsibilities. The Montreux Document places responsibilities on participating states to ensure that existing international legal obligations are adequately translated into domestic law, military regulations, administrative orders, and other regulatory mechanisms.

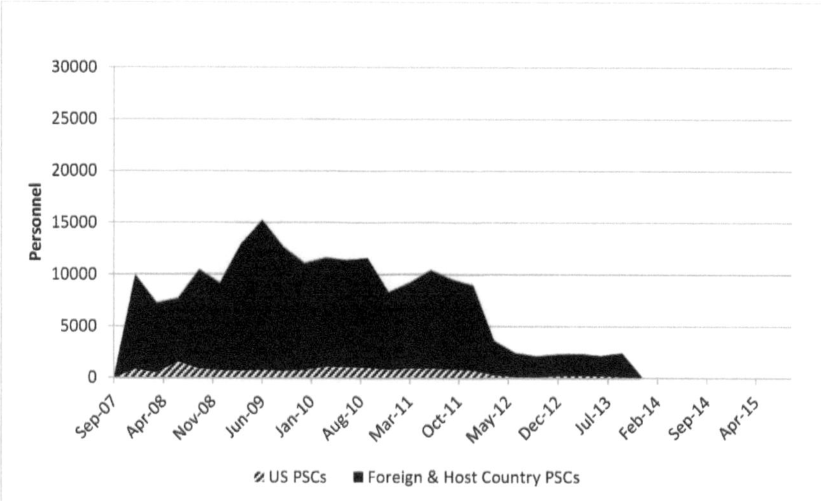

Figure 14.3. Iraq PSC Personnel 2007–2015

Yet as the contributors to this volume make clear, individual states have varied in the manner in which they have framed their approach to PMSC regulation, the speed with which they have recognized and reacted to the challenges that they pose, and the measures that they have taken. Although this volume focused on only five states, it offers some lessons for how states may improve their control over the coercive capacities of these actors.

In general, the heterogeneity of national approaches to regulating PMSCs provides for significant gaps in the tapestry of control. States overcame this difficulty with regard to their military forces by harmonizing their approaches. They should do so with regard to PMSCs. First, all states should undertake the effort to define inherently governmental functions that should not be performed by private entities for themselves. This will define the scope of the industry, which remains a key ambiguity for determining which actors and services require regulation. Then harmonization of national approaches to defining core state functions should be a priority—particularly among close allies such as the United States, Canada, and the United Kingdom whose military forces routinely operate together in expeditionary environments. Furthermore, all of the states should make efforts to implement the standards and good practices that have been agreed upon in the Montreux Document. They provide a basis for further harmonization of domestic approaches that can enable more consistent monitoring and enforcement of laws and norms applicable to PMSCs. This concerted international effort to standardize approaches to controlling military contractors is essential in an

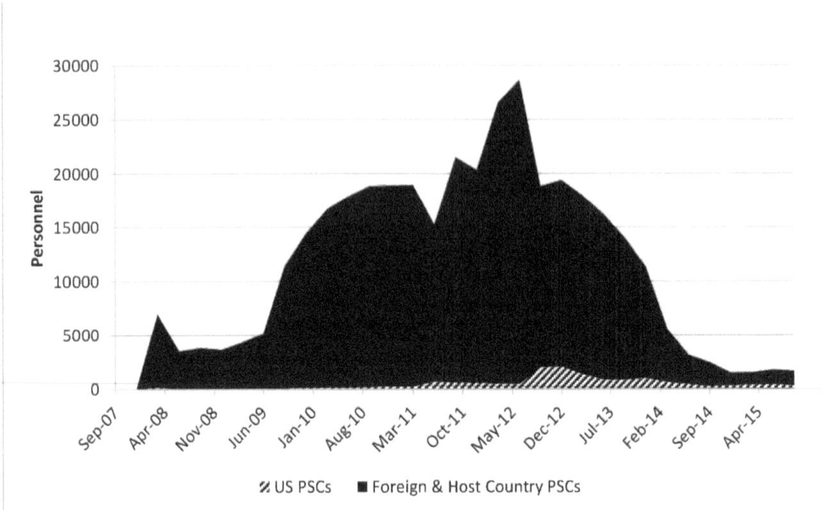

Figure 14.4. Afghanistan PSC Personnel 2007–2015

age of joint operations and multinational forces engaged in conflict, as well as in peacekeeping and humanitarian operations. Such efforts can be pursued through programs in security sector reform and building partner capacity, whether they are bilateral or multilateral in nature, commencing on an as-needed basis in response to particular issues that arise during operations or institutionalized through the procedures of international organizations such as NATO or the United Nations. Providing multiple avenues for harmonization and incentivizing compliance can only accelerate the building of mechanisms that can consistently address controlling PMSCs.

Convergent and Divergent Preferences

Finally, we come back to the problem of preference divergence between state principals and their private agents. In many ways the consequences of divergence in functional preferences have to be addressed through better selection of agents, better monitoring of their behavior, better provision of incentives for appropriate behavior, and more effective punishment of behavior that is inappropriate, ineffective, or illegal. Yet the ultimate difficulties that PMSCs may cause derive from potential divergences in their relational preferences—in particular, whether they can be trusted to not use their coercive capacities against the interests of the state.

In this, the weight of 25 years of experience suggests that PMSCs do not pose a direct threat to the security of the states that hire them—even in weak and unstable states experiencing significant security challenges. Consider the case of Executive Outcomes, which remained loyal to its employers in Angola and Sierra Leone in the 1990s. It performed its duties as contracted, did not switch sides, did not threaten the government, and did not shirk from combat.[87] Furthermore, neither the company nor its personnel became involved in the several coup plots that took place in Sierra Leone in 1996; rather, it reportedly forestalled planned coups prior to the 1996 elections.[88] It did, however, fail to intervene to protect the regime of President Valentine Strasser when his chief of defense, Brigadier General Julius Maada Bio, overthrew him in a coup.[89] Singer contends that Executive Outcomes "did approve of the coup" because it considered Bio "easier to work with"[90] and Deborah Avant argues that the company "in effect supported the plotters by refusing to tie its continued work in the country to Strasser's regime."[91] Loyalty to the state differs from loyalty to a particular leader, however, and by performing its contracted duties Executive Outcomes exercised the nonpartisan attitude of a professional military. Its volitional agnosticism, however, does demonstrate that its loyalty was not of the same quality as one may expect from military forces in strong and stable states with reliable mechanisms for the peaceful transfer of political power—which Sierra Leone was not.

On the other hand, PMSCs were involved in a few attempted regime changes in Africa. In Sierra Leone, President Ahmad Tejan Kabbah assumed the office in an election overseen by the military regime led by Bio a month after his coup, but was ousted by another coup led by other officers the following year.[92] Kabbah hired Sandline International to help reinstall him in power. These efforts were successful, but did cause political ramifications for Great Britain and demonstrated that PMSCs could pose a threat to those who held power, whether legitimately or not.[93] Likewise, the 2004 "Wonga coup" in Equatorial Guinea was an externally financed attempt to replace that state's leader with an exiled political figure through the use of elements of PMSCs.[94] Such instances demonstrate that private foreign forces can play an important role in internal struggles for power in weak and unstable states. But in neither of these cases had the PMSC been hired by the state or regime that it targeted. Rather, in these instances the regime's opponents had hired them and these PMSCs acted faithfully on their client's behalf.

Finally, an increasingly urgent issue that has not been directly dealt with in national and international approaches to PMSCs is their use by private companies, such as multinational corporations, particularly those operating in weak states. Many companies have found it to be in their interests to maintain operations in parts of the world where state authorities have been unable or unwilling to provide effective governance and security. In the past such companies helped finance state institutions that would provide security in general or for their operations in particular.[95] Financing from such external sources decreases the dependence of the state on the support of its local population and increases its receptivity to the interests of foreign investors, often leading to skewed state priorities, corruption, and instability.[96] It also has significant long-run implications for the consolidation of state institutions, at least if these processes follow lines similar to those of European states.[97]

The emergence of PMSCs has provided these multinational actors an alternative source of security, one that reduces or eliminates their need to deal directly with state authorities and also curbs the state's need to be responsive to its citizens. This could be good or bad from the standpoint of justice—many oppressive regimes have received foreign support in return for local protection and, deprived of that support, become more dependent upon their populations for resources and, perhaps, more accommodating to their interests.[98] But from the standpoint of sovereignty, it ensures that they do not exercise priority in some respects over all other organizations operating within their territory.[99] Addressing the challenges to weak states posed by well-resourced transnational actors that have purchased coercive capacities is beyond the scope of the present volume—as well as the majority of the literature addressing PMSCs. But I raise it here to note that the regulation of domestic and international security firms requires significant attention from states and scholars alike.

That said, given that foreign-based PMSCs would be the most likely to pose a danger to weak and unstable states (if not their populations), the home states of such firms could more uniformly restrict the clientele of PMSCs based in their territory and subject to their jurisdiction, as the United States has done and South Africa has attempted to do. Requiring permission to work for an overseas client—to export their services abroad—would subject PMSCs to governmental review and remove the burden of determining the legitimacy of their clients from their shoulders. Subjecting violators to harsh criminal penalties could reduce the fear that PMSCs will lend credible military capabilities to nonstate actors such as terrorist groups, narcotics traffickers, and other transnational criminal organizations.[100] Harmonization of national statutes through the Montreux Document process could further formalize the norm and enable states to gain better control over the market for force. Furthermore, states can prevent themselves from contracting with PMSCs on behalf of nonstate actors. Removing the PMSCs from their policy toolbox when they desire to assist favored nonstate groups will require significant discipline, particularly when the deniability of the action would be efficacious in the short run. States have demonstrated such restraint in the past with regard to covert actions and can apply the same principles to their use of PMSCs.[101] Indeed, institutionalizing norms of restraint will be necessary for all aspects of regaining state control over the legitimate use of force.

CONTROLLING THE CORPORATE WARRIOR?

Will the market for force continue into the future? The answer would appear to be yes. The structural conditions that enabled the market in the first place continue to operate. Strong and stable states continue to shift responsibility for the provision of public goods and services to the private sector. Large numbers of skilled personnel separate or retire from military forces every year. There continues to be a large demand for auxiliaries to accompany the military forces of Western powers as they intervene to stabilize territories where governance is lacking and threats are produced. The use of contractors to build partner capacity in states with weak security institutions has become standard practice.[102] As Strachan-Morris noted in chapter 5, the Department of Defense in 2009 elevated stability operations to equal status with major combat operations in joint doctrine and directed the military to "collaborate with other U.S. Government agencies and with foreign governments and security forces, international governmental organizations, nongovernmental organizations, *and private sector firms* as appropriate to plan, prepare for, and conduct stability operations."[103] As Percy noted, "the twenty-first century market for force is a state-to-state-based exchange of private violence, whereby private assistance for training and reconstruction is sent from strong states to weak, and where strong states use private force to supplement their own forces."[104]

Furthermore, the use of private actors to supply military services is no longer novel. More states have become comfortable procuring public services from private vendors and this includes placing private civilian contractors in a position to utilize force for offensive purposes. While mobile security services like those provided to diplomats epitomize this function, it extends beyond: PMSC personnel are involved in almost all aspects of unmanned aerial vehicle operation, for instance, including verifying targets and piloting them in combat air patrols.[105] Contracts have been routinely awarded for decades, bureaucratic procedures have been developed and utilized for years, and many large multinational defense companies have diversified their offerings to provide a range of services that would take tremendous efforts for state militaries to reabsorb. Indeed, the faltering of US Secretary of Defense Robert Gates' in-sourcing initiative highlights the difficulties of reversing the privatization trend in the military.[106]

In the end, it is clear that the ability of political authorities to exercise meaningful control over organized violence and to utilize it for the collective good continues to evolve. Political leaders worked earnestly over centuries to consolidate the power to legitimately use coercion in their hands. They found they could do so in the context of clearly specified territorial boundaries and exclusive agreements with the leaders of other such entities: states. Those states undertook building institutions that would co-opt, socialize, and indoctrinate individuals possessed of martial skills and inclinations. They found producing the people and institutions that would wield violence on their behalf to be a more effective option than permitting other entities to develop such capabilities and then procuring their services in the market. Yet, by the end of the twentieth century, key strong and stable states found that many of the services produced by these institutions and personnel were no longer unique to the military and could be procured from private entities at a lower cost—especially when overhead was considered. Indeed, they could permit the development of a market for these services precisely because they had established institutions that enabled them to be confident in their ability to do so without threatening their sovereign control over the legitimate use of organized force. Once demand and supply increased in the context of the post–Cold War security environment, market dynamics encouraged the diversification of the offerings of these private entities, bringing them closer and closer to the core of tasks performed by state military institutions and personnel, including providing military assistance, operational support, intelligence services, static and dynamic security, and even combat.

The development of this market was not followed by the building of support, control, and regulatory mechanisms that would enable states to ensure tight control over the private agents that performed military services on their behalf. The past quarter century has been characterized by the attempt by states, the international community, PMSCs, nongovernmental organizations, and individuals to negotiate with one another to erect such institutions on the fly. The analyses provided in this volume have addressed these attempts. Efforts to date have resulted in an incomplete, multilayered tapestry of formal and informal mechanisms of control that include degree of professionalization of the individual contractor and his acceptance by the regular military forces of states, efforts of the industry to regulate and socialize its own firms and employees, military command-and-control arrangements on the battlefield, and the laws and regulations imposed upon the industry by key states, as well as efforts at the international level to guide states in their relations with these new private entities and to clarify the obligations of all under international law. It is clear that efforts to control private military companies and their agents must progress further before they can begin to approach the carefully constructed social, normative, institutional, legal, and ideological mechanisms that states have built to control their own military forces. Until they do, the uncertainties involved in procuring coercive services from private agents will remain and meaningful control over them will be less total than that exercised over state military forces. The development of the tapestry of institutions intended to control the corporate warrior is a dynamic process that must continue for the indefinite future to ensure the power and stability of the state—and security and social justice for the citizens from whom the state derives its power and whom it protects.

NOTES

1. Maury D. Feld, *The Structure of Violence: Armed Forces as Social Systems* (Beverly Hills: Sage, 1977), page 16.

2. Jeffrey R. Henig, Chris Hamnett, and Harvey B. Feigenbaum, "The Politics of Privatization: A Comparative Perspective," *Governance* 4, 1 (October 1988); Harvey B. Feigenbaum and Jeffrey R. Henig, "The Political Underpinnings of Privatization: A Typology," *World Politics* 46, 2 (January 1994).

3. Frank Camm, "How to Decide When a Contractor Source Is Better to Use than a Government Source," in Christopher Kinsey and Malcolm Patterson, editors, *Contractors and War: The Transformation of United States' Expeditionary Operations* (Palo Alto: Stanford University Press, 2012), pages 233–34.

4. Noncash and deferred benefits account for 50–60 percent of military compensation in the United States. See Carla Tighe Murray, *Evaluating Military Compensation* (Washington: Congressional Budget Office, June 2007), page 13. As Erik Prince put it, "at Blackwater, none of that applied, starting with the obvious. We hired contractors and let them go as needed—the concept of job security never really applied. We offered no regular salary or overtime to the contractors, and we didn't cover their Medicare, Social Security, or federal income taxes. There wasn't a retirement plan, health insurance, life insurance, or paid sick leave available, much less paid vacation. And Blackwater wasn't paying for anyone's college education" (Erik Prince with Davin Coburn, *Civilian Warriors: The Inside Story of Blackwater and the Unsung Heroes of the War on Terror* [New York: Portfolio/Penguin, 2013], page 185).

5. Matthew Goldberg, J. Michael Gilmore, Adebayo Adedeji, Daniel Frisk, Carla Tighe Murray, R. Derek Trunkey, David Newman, Jo Ann Vines, and Frances Lussier, *Logistic Support for Deployed Military Forces* (Washington: Congressional Budget Office, October 2005), pages 23–24; Cathy Downes, "Military Manpower: Strategic Asset, Liability or Non-entity?" *Defence Economics* 2, 4 (1991); Todd Sandler and Keith Hartley, *The Economics of Defense* (Cambridge: Cambridge University Press, 1999), page 158.

6. Goldberg, Gilmore, Adedeji, Frisk, Murray, Trunkey, Newman, Vines, and Lussier, *Logistic Support for Deployed Military Forces*, pages 23–24; Philip A. Odeen, chairman, *Report of the Defense Science Board Task Force on Outsourcing and Privatization* (Washington: Office of the Under Secretary of Defense for Acquisition and Technology, August 1996), page 17.

7. Odeen, *Report of the Defense Science Board Task Force on Outsourcing and Privatization*, page 17; Katherine E. McCoy, "Beyond Civil-Military Relations: Reflections on Civilian Control of a Private, Multinational Workforce," *Armed Forces and Society* 36, 4 (July 2010), page 676; Goldberg, Gilmore, Adedeji, Frisk, Murray, Trunkey, Newman, Vines, and Lussier, *Logistic Support for Deployed Military Forces*, page 24; Camm, "How to Decide When a Contractor Source Is Better to Use than a Government Source," page 237.

8. Odeen, *Report of the Defense Science Board Task Force on Outsourcing and Privatization*, page 17; Matthew Uttley, *Contractors on Deployed Military Operations: United Kingdom Policy and Doctrine* (Carlisle: Strategic Studies Institute, September 2005), page 11; McCoy, "Beyond Civil-Military Relations," page 676. Such efficiency usually was gained by not offering employees noncash compensation.

9. Daniel Frisk and R. Derek Trunkey, *Contractors' Support of U.S. Operations in Iraq* (Washington: Congressional Budget Office, August 2008); William M. Solis, *Warfighter Support: A Cost Comparison of Using State Department Employees versus Contractors for Security Services in Iraq*, GAO-10-266R (Washington: Government Accountability Office, 4 March 2010); Goldberg, Gilmore, Adedeji, Frisk, Murray, Trunkey, Newman, Vines, and Lussier, *Logistic Support for Deployed Military Forces*; Prince with Coburn, *Civilian Warriors*, pages 183–89; Charles M. Smith, *War for Profit: Army Contracting vs. Supporting the Troops* (New York: Algora Publishing, 2012); Jacques S. Gansler, David Berteau, David M. Maddox, David R. Oliver Jr., Leon E. Salomon, George T. Singley III, George Sears, Kristi Crear, Karl Ellcessor, Dave Mabee, Jill Stiglich, and Jana Weston, *Urgent Reform Required: Army Expeditionary Contracting. Report of the Commission on Army Acquisition and Program Management in Expeditionary Operations* (Washington: Office of the Assistant Secretary of the Army

for Acquisition, Logistics, and Technology, 2007); United States Senate Committee on Armed Services, *The Department of Defense's Management of Costs under the Logistics Civil Augmentation Program (LOGCAP) Contract in Iraq* (Washington: Government Printing Office, 19 April 2007).

10. Philip A. Odeen, "Memorandum for Chairman, Defense Science Board: Final Report of the Defense Science Board Task Force on Outsourcing and Privatization. August 27, 1996," in Odeen, *Report of the Defense Science Board Task Force on Outsourcing and Privatization.*

11. John Lewis Gaddis, "Toward the Post–Cold War World," *Foreign Affairs* 70, 2 (Spring 1991); Max Singer and Aaron Wildavsky, *The Real World Order: Zones of Peace/Zones of Turmoil* (Chatham, NJ: Chatham House, 1993); G. John Ikenberry, "The Myth of Post–Cold War Chaos," *Foreign Affairs* 75, 3 (May/June 1996); Henry A. Kissinger, *Does America Need a Foreign Policy? Toward a Diplomacy for the 21st Century* (New York: Simon & Schuster, 2001).

12. David Isenberg, *Soldiers of Fortune Ltd.: A Profile of Today's Private Sector Corporate Mercenary Firms* (Washington: Center for Defense Information, November 1997); David Shearer, *Private Armies and Military Intervention*, Adelphi Paper 316 (London: International Institute for Strategic Studies, 1998), pages 34–55; Ian Douglas, "Fighting for Diamonds: Private Military Companies in Sierra Leone," in Jakkie Cilliers and Peggy Mason, editors, *Peace, Profit or Plunder? The Privatisation of Security in War-Torn African Societies* (Pretoria: Institute for Security Studies, 1999); Deborah D. Avant, *The Market for Force: The Consequences of Privatizing Security* (Cambridge: Cambridge University Press, 2005), pages 95–98; Simon Chesterman and Chia Lehnardt, "Introduction," in Simon Chesterman and Chia Lehnardt, editors, *From Mercenaries to Market: The Rise and Regulation of Private Military Companies* (Oxford: Oxford University Press, 2007).

13. Shearer, *Private Armies and Military Intervention*, pages 56–63; Avant, *The Market for Force*, page 104; Bruce E. Stanley, *Outsourcing Security: Private Military Contractors and U.S. Foreign Policy* (Lincoln: Potomac Books, 2015), pages 82–92; John Ashbrook and Spencer D. Bakich, "Storming to Partition: Croatia, the United States, and Krajina in the Yugoslav War," *Small Wars and Insurgencies* 21, 4 (December 2010), pages 538–40.

14. Jacques S. Gansler and William Lucyshyn, "Contractors Supporting Military Operations: Many Challenges Remain," in Christopher Kinsey and Malcolm Patterson, editors, *Contractors and War: The Transformation of United States' Expeditionary Operations* (Palo Alto: Stanford University Press, 2012), pages 282, 286.

15. James Jay Carafano, *Private Sector, Public Wars* (Westport: Praeger Security International, 2008), pages 83–85; Neal Curtin, *Military Operations: Contractors Provide Vital Services to Deployed Forces but Are Not Adequately Addressed in DoD Plans*, GAO-03-695 (Washington: General Accounting Office, June 2003); Gansler and Lucyshyn, "Contractors Supporting Military Operations," pages 282–86.

16. Avant, *The Market for Force*, pages 59–65; Christine Bakker, *Private Military and Security Companies: Positive Human Rights Obligations of the Host State*, EUI Working Paper 2009/20 (Florence: European University Institute Academy of European Law, 2009).

17. H. H. Gerth and C. Wright Mills, translators and editors, *From Max Weber: Essays in Sociology* (New York: Oxford University Press, 1946), pages 82–83; Hedley Bull, *The Anarchical Society: A Study of Order in World Politics* (London: Macmillan, 1977), pages 8–9.

18. Douglas, "Fighting for Diamonds"; Avant, *The Market for Force*, pages 95–98; Anna Leander, "The Market for Force and Public Security: The Destabilizing Consequences of Private Military Companies," *Journal of Peace Research* 42, 5 (September 2005); Chesterman and Lehnardt, "Introduction."

19. Yaël Ronen, "Israel: Going Private—The Use and Regulation of Private Military and Security Companies in Situations of Armed Conflict," in Christine Bakker and Mirko Sossai, editors, *Multilevel Regulation of Military and Security Contractors: The Interplay between International, European and Domestic Norms* (Oxford: Hart Publishing, 2011).

20. Don Mayer, "Peaceful Warriors: Private Military Security Companies and the Quest for Stable Societies," *Journal of Business Ethics* 89, supplement 4 (2009); Rachel Zedeck, "Private Military/Security Companies, Human Security, and State Building in Africa," *African Security Review* 16, 4 (December 2007).

21. Leander, "The Market for Force and Public Security"; Anna Leander, *Eroding State Authority? Private Military Companies and the Legitimate Use of Force* (Rome: Centro Militare di Studi Strategici, 2006); Anna Leander and Rens van Munster, "Private Security Contractors in Darfur: Reflecting and Reinforcing Neo-liberal Governmentality," *International Relations* 21, 2 (June 2007); Anna Leander, "The Paradoxical Impunity of Private Military Companies: Authority and the Limits to Legal Accountability," *Security Dialogue* 41, 5 (October 2010).

22. Terry M. Moe, "The New Economics of Organization," *American Journal of Political Science* 28, 4 (November 1984), pages 754–55; Oliver E. Williamson, *Markets and Hierarchies* (New York: The Free Press, 1975).

23. Rebecca DeWinter-Schmitt, editor, *Montreux Five Years On: An Analysis of State Efforts to Implement Montreux Document Legal Obligations and Good Practices* (Barcelona: Adjuntament de Barcelona, 2013), *passim*.

24. Diego Gambetta, "Inscrutable Markets," *Rationality and Society* 6, 3 (July 1994), page 354; Christopher Kinsey, *Corporate Soldiers and International Security: The Rise of Private Military Companies* (London: Routledge, 2006), page 158.

25. Gambetta, "Inscrutable Markets," page 354.

26. On Executive Outcomes see Shearer, *Private Armies and Military Intervention*, page 41. On MPRI see Peter W. Singer, *Corporate Warriors: The Rise of the Privatized Military Industry* (Ithaca: Cornell University Press, 2003), page 120. On Blackwater see Erik D. Prince, "How Blackwater Serves America," *Wall Street Journal* (16 December 2008), page 23.

27. Prince argues that Blackwater's "billing rate included a 10.4 percent profit margin—well below the allowable 15 percent on cost-plus deals" (Prince with Coburn, *Civilian Warriors*, page 187).

28. Elizabeth Rubin, "An Army of One's Own," *Harper's Magazine* (February 1997).

29. Executive Outcomes undertook operations on behalf of the government in Sierra Leone despite its inability to pay at that time given the devastation caused by the civil war (Herbert M. Howe, "Private Security Forces and African Stability: The Case of Executive Outcomes," *Journal of Modern African Studies* 36, 2 [June 1998], page 314). Singer argues, however, that Executive Outcomes' sister company, London-based Branch-Heritage Group, "agreed to bankroll the operation in exchange for future diamond mining concessions in the Kono region" (Singer, *Corporate Warriors*, page 112).

30. Ulrich Petersohn, "The Social Structure of the Market for Force," *Cooperation and Conflict* 50, 2 (June 2014), page 272.

31. Sarah Percy, *Regulating the Private Security Industry*, Adelphi Paper 384 (London: Routledge, 2006), page 59.

32. Gambetta, "Inscrutable Markets," page 355.

33. Petersohn, "The Social Structure of the Market for Force," page 274; Howe, "Private Security Forces and African Stability," page 316.

34. Prince with Coburn, *Civilian Warriors*, page 294.

35. Prince with Coburn, *Civilian Warriors*, page 292.

36. Prince with Coburn, *Civilian Warriors*, pages 305–7.

37. Prince with Coburn, *Civilian Warriors*, page 293.

38. Singer, *Corporate Warriors*, page 118.

39. Simon Chesterman and Chia Lehnardt, "Conclusion," in Simon Chesterman and Chia Lehnardt, editors, *From Mercenaries to Market: The Rise and Regulation of Private Military Companies* (Oxford: Oxford University Press, 2007), page 254.

40. J. Eric Fredland, "Outsourcing Military Force: A Transactions Cost Perspective on the Role of Military Companies," *Defence and Peace Economics* 15, 3 (June 2004), page 216.

41. Karolina Maclachlan and Hilary Hurd, "How Corruption Undermines NATO Operations," *Defense One* (2 December 2015), available at http://www.defenseone.com/ideas/2015/12/how-corruption-undermines-nato-operations/124148/, accessed 3 December 2015.

42. Uttley, *Contractors on Deployed Military Operations*, pages 9–10.

43. Moshe Schwartz, *The Department of Defense's Use of Private Security Contractors in Afghanistan and Iraq: Background, Analysis, and Options for Congress*, CRS Report R40835 (Washington: Congressional Research Service, 21 February 2011), page 6.

44. General Peter W. Chiarelli, Vice Chief of Staff, US Army, "Selection and Training of Contracting Officer's Representatives (CORs)" (Washington: Office of the Vice Chief of Staff of the United States Army, 2 March 2010); United States Senate Committee on Armed Services, *Inquiry into the Role and Oversight of Private Security Contractors in Afghanistan: Report with Additional Views* (Washington: Government Printing Office, 28 September 2010); Commission on Wartime Contracting in Iraq and Afghanistan, *Transforming Wartime Contracting: Controlling Costs, Reducing Risks. Final Report to Congress* (Washington: Commission on Wartime Contracting in Iraq and Afghanistan, August 2011); Michael Macagnone, "DOD IG Finds Oversight of Contract Deficiencies Falls Short," Law360 (2 October 2015), available at http://www.law360.com/articles/710093/dod-ig-finds-oversight-of-contract-deficiencies-falls-short, accessed 25 November 2015.

45. Maclachlan and Hurd, "How Corruption Undermines NATO Operations."

46. Camm, "How to Decide When a Contractor Source Is Better to Use than a Government Source," details the comprehensive series of requirements for choosing a private supplier over government agency provision.

47. Rebecca DeWinter-Schmitt, "Executive Summary," in DeWinter-Schmitt, *Montreux Five Years On*, page 8.

48. United States Department of the Army, *Army Regulation 715-9: Contractors Accompanying the Force* (Washington: Department of the Army, 29 October 1999), page 13; Gansler and Lucyshyn, "Contractors Supporting Military Operations," pages 282–86.

49. Goldberg, Gilmore, Adedeji, Frisk, Murray, Trunkey, Newman, Vines, and Lussier, *Logistic Support for Deployed Military Forces*, page 9.

50. Goldberg, Gilmore, Adedeji, Frisk, Murray, Trunkey, Newman, Vines, and Lussier, *Logistic Support for Deployed Military Forces*, pages 9–10.

51. Also see Ulrich Petersohn, "The Effectiveness of Contracted Coalitions: Private Security Contractors in Iraq," *Armed Forces and Society* 39, 3 (July 2013), especially figure 2, page 477.

52. Molly Dunigan, *Victory for Hire: Private Security Companies' Impact on Military Effectiveness* (Palo Alto: Stanford University Press, 2011), pages 54–62, 68–71.

53. David Antonyshyn, Jan Grofe, and Don Hubert, *Beyond the Law? The Regulation of Canadian Private and Security Companies Operating Abroad*, National Reports Series 03/09 (Florence: European University Institute Academy of European Law, 12 February 2009), page 23.

54. Antonyshyn, Grofe, and Hubert, *Beyond the Law?* page 23.

55. Antonyshyn, Grofe, and Hubert, *Beyond the Law?* page 25.

56. No civilian contractors have been tried by courts-martial for offenses committed in an operational theater, however (Antonyshyn, Grofe, and Hubert, *Beyond the Law?* page 27).

57. Annie O'Reilly and Karinne Coombes, "Meeting the Legal Obligations and Good Practices of the Montreux Document: The United Kingdom," in DeWinter-Schmitt, *Montreux Five Years On*, page 61. For a comprehensive accounting of US laws and regulations specifically tailored to the provision of private security services, see the letter from Eileen Chamberlain Donahoe, ambassador to the United Nations and other international organizations in Geneva, "Letter to Ms. Faiza Patel, Chair-Rapporteur, Working Group on the Use of Mercenaries" (2 July 2012), available at http://www.ohchr.org/Documents/Issues/Mercenaries/WG/Law/USA/CoverLetter.pdf, accessed 12 December 2015.

58. Kinsey, *Corporate Soldiers*, page 154.

59. O'Reilly and Coombes, "Meeting the Legal Obligations and Good Practices of the Montreux Document," pages 62–63.

60. O'Reilly and Coombes, "Meeting the Legal Obligations and Good Practices of the Montreux Document," pages 64, 79–81.

61. O'Reilly and Coombes, "Meeting the Legal Obligations and Good Practices of the Montreux Document," pages 79–80.

62. O'Reilly and Coombes, "Meeting the Legal Obligations and Good Practices of the Montreux Document," pages 110–12.

63. Percy, *Regulating the Private Security Industry*, page 39.

64. Prince with Coburn, *Civilian Warriors*, pages 283–84.

65. Percy, *Regulating the Private Security Industry*, page 50; Chesterman and Lehnardt, "Conclusion," pages 251–52; James Larry Taulbee, "Myths, Mercenaries and Contemporary International Law," *California Western International Law Journal* 15, 2 (1985), page 347.

66. Eyal Benvenisti, "Towards a Typology of Informal International Lawmaking Mechanisms and Their Distinct Accountability Gaps," in Joost Pauwelyn, Ramses Wessel, and Jan Wouters, editors, *Informal International Lawmaking* (Oxford: Oxford University Press, 2015), page 299.

67. Petersohn, "The Effectiveness of Contracted Coalitions," page 471. This claim does not extend to third-country nationals or host nation nationals, however, and they constitute the vast majority of the PMSC workforce.

68. Nathan Joseph and Nicholas Alex, "The Uniform: A Sociological Perspective," *American Journal of Sociology* 77, 4 (January 1972); Talcott Parsons, *The Social System* (New York: The Free Press, 1951); Robert K. Merton, *Social Theory and Social Structure* (New York: The Free Press, 1957); Neal Gross, Ward S. Mason, and Alexander W. McEachern, *Explorations in Role Analysis* (New York: Wiley, 1958); Peter J. Burke and Jan E. Stets, *Identity Theory* (Oxford: Oxford University Press, 2009); Michael A. Hogg, *The Social Psychology of Group Cohesiveness: From Attraction to Social Identity* (Washington Square: New York University Press, 1992).

69. Scott Fitzsimmons, *Private Security Companies during the Iraq War: Military Performance and the Use of Deadly Force* (London: Routledge, 2016).

70. Fitzsimmons, *Private Security Companies during the Iraq War*, pages 3–4.

71. Fitzsimmons, *Private Security Companies during the Iraq War*, page 4.

72. Fitzsimmons, *Private Security Companies during the Iraq War*, pages 83–84.

73. Fitzsimmons, *Private Security Companies during the Iraq War*, page 83.

74. For noteworthy exceptions, see Petersohn, "The Effectiveness of Contracted Coalitions"; McCoy, "Beyond Civil-Military Relations"; Amanda Chisholm, "Marketing the Gurkha Security Package: Colonial Histories and Neoliberal Economies of Private Security," *Security Dialogue* 45, 4 (August 2014).

75. John A. Nagl, James F. Amos, Sarah Sewall, and David H. Petraeus, *The US Army/Marine Corps Counterinsurgency Field Manual*, number 3-24 (Chicago: University of Chicago Press, 2007), pages 169, 282; T. X. Hammes, "Private Contractors in Conflict Zones: The Good, the Bad, and the Strategic Impact," *Strategic Forum* 260 (November 2010), page 4.

76. Data for figures 14.1 and 14.2 are drawn from the following sources: For data from September 2007 to December 2013 for Iraq and December 2014 for Afghanistan, see Heidi M. Peters, Moshe Schwartz, and Lawrence Kapp, *Department of Defense Contractor and Troop Levels in Iraq and Afghanistan: 2007–2014* (Washington: Congressional Research Service, 22 July 2015), pages 5–6, tables 3–4. For data in 2015, see United States Deputy Assistant Secretary of Defense for Program Support, *Contractor Support of U.S. Operations in the USCENTCOM Area of Responsibility* (Washington: Department of Defense, quarterly), posted at the Private Security Monitor, "Data and Statistics: CENTCOM Data," Sié Chéou-Kang Center for International Security and Diplomacy of the University of Denver website, available at http://psm.du.edu/articles_reports_statistics/data_and_statistics.html, accessed 19 December 2015.

77. McCoy, "Beyond Civil-Military Relations," page 677.

78. United States Deputy Assistant Secretary of Defense for Program Support, *Contractor Support of U.S. Operations in the USCENTCOM Area of Responsibility* (Washington: Department of Defense, October 2015), page 2.

79. Data for figures 14.3 and 14.4 are drawn from the following sources: For data from September 2007 to December 2013 for Iraq and December 2014 for Afghanistan, see Peters, Schwartz, and Kapp, *Department of Defense Contractor and Troop Levels in Iraq and Afghanistan*, pages 5–6, tables 3–4. For data in 2015, see United States Deputy Assistant Secretary of Defense for Program Support, *Contractor Support of U.S. Operations in the USCENTCOM Area of Responsibility* (quarterly).

80. Geert H. Hofstede, *Culture's Consequence: International Differences in Work-Related Values* (Beverly Hills: Sage, 1980); Efrat Elron, Boas Shamir, and Eyal Ben-Ari, "Why Don't They Fight Each Other? Cultural Diversity and Operational Unity in Multinational Forces,"

Armed Forces and Society 26, 1 (Fall 1999), pages 77–79, especially table 2, which provides scores on these variables for 26 countries.

81. Elron, Shamir, and Ben-Ari, "Why Don't They Fight Each Other?" pages 84–90.

82. McCoy, "Beyond Civil-Military Relations," page 679–81.

83. United States General Accounting Office, *Rebuilding Iraq: Actions Still Needed to Improve Use of Private Security Providers*, GAO-06-865 (Washington: General Accounting Office, June 2006), page 15; Confederation of Switzerland Department of Foreign Affairs and the International Committee of the Red Cross, *The Montreux Document on Pertinent International Legal Obligations and Good Practices for States related to Operations of Private Military and Security Companies during Armed Conflict*, UN Document A/63/467-S/2008/636 (Geneva: International Committee of the Red Cross, 2008), page 17, available at http://www.eda.admin.ch/psc, accessed 5 May 2015.

84. Montreux Document, page 17.

85. Dunigan, *Victory for Hire*, page 160.

86. Elron, Shamir, and Ben-Ari, "Why Don't They Fight Each Other?" pages 87–88. Such institutions are plentiful. The International Association of Peacekeeping Training Centres had 266 institutional members as of August 2015 ("IAPTC Membership," International Association of Peacekeeping Training Centres website, available at http://www.iaptc.org/iaptc-membership/, accessed 10 December 2015).

87. Howe, "Private Security Forces and African Stability," page 317.

88. Howe, "Private Security Forces and African Stability," page 317; Singer, *Corporate Warriors*, pages 113–14.

89. Avant, *The Market for Force*, page 89.

90. Singer, *Corporate Warriors*, pages 113–14.

91. Avant, *The Market for Force*, page 97.

92. Singer, *Corporate Warriors*, pages 114–15.

93. As discussed in chapter 7.

94. As discussed in chapter 2.

95. Avant, *The Market for Force*, page 184.

96. Avant, *The Market for Force*, pages 181–84.

97. Charles Tilly, "Reflections on the History of European State-Making," in Charles Tilly, editor, *The Formation of States in Western Europe* (Princeton: Princeton University Press, 1975).

98. Everett C. Dolman, *The Warrior State: How Military Organization Structures Politics* (New York: Palgrave Macmillan, 2004).

99. Charles Tilly, *Coercion, Capital, and European States, AD 990–1992* (Cambridge: Blackwell, 1992), page 19.

100. This has not always been the case as it requires agreement on consistent definitions of these actors. For instance, Singer argues that "in the late 1990s, a number of firms targeted the lucrative market of training young Muslims who were being recruited globally to join radical groups engaged in jihads," particularly those in Bosnia and Chechnya that received the sympathy and acquiescence of many Western states (Singer, *Corporate Warriors*, page 181). Also see Juan Carlos Zarate, "The Emergence of a New Dog of War: Private International Security Companies, International Law, and the New World Order," *Stanford Journal of International Law* 34 (Winter 1998), page 147.

101. William Michael Reisman and James E. Baker, *Regulating Covert Action: Practices, Contexts, and Policies of Covert Coercion Abroad in International and American Law* (New Haven: Yale University Press, 1992).

102. Indeed, according to the Defense Security Cooperation Agency of the Department of Defense, security assistance consists of "a group of programs, authorized by law, through which the U.S. Department of Defense (DoD) or commercial contractors provide defense articles and services in support of national policies and objectives" (Christopher Paul, Colin P. Clarke, Beth Grill, Stephanie Young, Jennifer D. P. Moroney, Joe Hogler, and Christine Leah, *What Works Best When Building Partner Capacity and under What Circumstances?* [Santa Monica: RAND Corporation, 2013], page 8).

103. Michèle Flournoy, "Department of Defense Directive 3000.5: Stability Operations" (Washington: Office of the Secretary of Defense, 16 September 2009), page 2, emphasis added.

104. Sarah Percy, *Mercenaries: The History of a Norm in International Relations* (Oxford: Oxford University Press, 2007), page 235.

105. Kyle Mizokami, "The U.S. Air Force Is Using Civilians to Fly Drones in Combat Theaters," *Popular Mechanics* (1 December 2015), available at http://www.popularmechanics.com/military/weapons/news/a18377/the-us-air-force-is-using-civilians-to-fly-drones/, accessed 10 December 2015; Gary Schaub Jr., "JUSTAS for All? Innovation and UAVs in the Canadian Forces," *Defence Studies* 15, 2 (June 2015), pages 133–34; David Isenberg, "Predator Military Contractors: Privatizing the Drones," *Huffington Post* (18 December 2012), available at http://www.huffingtonpost.com/david-isenberg/contractors-privatizing-the-drones_b_1976650.html, accessed 6 August 2015; Abigail Fielding-Smith, Crofton Black, Alice Ross, and James Ball, "Revealed: Private Firms at Heart of US Drone Warfare," *Guardian* (30 July 2015), available at http://www.theguardian.com/us-news/2015/jul/30/revealed-private-firms-at-heart-of-us-drone-warfare, accessed 12 August 2015.

106. Matthew Weigelt, "Insourcing Failed, DOD's Gates Says. Now What?" *FCW* (10 August 2010), available at https://fcw.com/articles/2010/08/10/gates-insourcing-did-not-work.aspx, accessed 15 November 2015; Loren Thompson, "Pentagon Insourcing Binge Begins to Unravel," *Forbes* (7 March 2011), available at http://www.forbes.com/sites/beltway/2011/03/07/pentagon-insourcing-binge-begins-to-unravel/, accessed 15 November 2015; Brenda S. Farrell, *Defense Workforce: DOD Needs to Better Oversee Insourcing Data and Align Insourcing Efforts with Strategic Workforce Plans*, GAO-12-319 (Washington: General Accountability Office, February 2012); Kate M. Manuel and Jack Maskell, *Insourcing Functions Performed by Federal Contractors: Legal Issues*, R41810 (Washington: Congressional Research Service, 22 February 2013).

Bibliography

Abadi, Jacob. *Israel's Quest for Recognition and Acceptance in Asia: Garrison State Diplomacy* (London: Frank Cass, 2004).
Abrahams, David. "Brief Legal Commentary on PMSCs in South Africa" (2008), available at http://psm.du.edu/media/documents/national_regulations/countries/africa/south_africa/south_africa_legal_commentary_by_david_abrhams_2008-english.pdf, accessed 13 August 2015.
Abrahamsson, Bengt. *Military Professionalization and Political Power* (Beverly Hills: Sage, 1972).
Abrams, Dominic, and Michael A. Hogg. *Social Identity and Social Cognition* (Oxford: Blackwell, 1999).
Abrisketa, Joana. "Blackwater: Mercenaries and International Law," *Fundación para las Relaciones Internacionales y el Diálogo Exterior (FRIDE)* (October 2007).
Academi. "About Us," available at https://www.academi.com/pages/about-us, accessed 9 July 2015.
Adam, Udi. "Transcript of The Future Structuring of Israel's Defense Industries," seminar held at the Fisher Institute for Air and Space Strategic Studies (12 September 2004), available in Hebrew at http://www.fisherinstitute.org.il/?CategoryID=23&ArticleID=121, accessed 8 August 2015.
The Additional Protocol I to the Geneva Conventions, available at http://www.icrc.org/ihl/intro/470, accessed 16 June 2015.
Aharoni, Yair. "The Changing Political Economy of Israel," *Annals of the American Academy of Political and Social Science* 555, 1 (January 1998).
Ahmadou, Nadia, and Sabelo Gumedze. *Seminar Report on the Prohibition of Mercenary Activities and Regulation of Certain Activities in Areas of Armed Conflict Act 27 of 2006* (Pretoria: Institute for Security Studies, 22 May 2008), available at http://www.iss.co.za/uploads/RPSSREPFIN.pdf, accessed 6 June 2015
Akerlof, George A., and Rachel E. Kranton. "Economics and Identity," *Quarterly Journal of Economics* 115, 3 (August 2000).
Akerlof, George A., and Rachel E. Kranton. *Identity Economics: How Our Identities Shape Our Work, Wages, and Well-Being* (Princeton: Princeton University Press, 2010).
Akerlof, George A., and Rachel E. Kranton. "Identity, Supervision, and Work Groups," *American Economic Review Papers and Proceedings* 98, 2 (May 2008).
Albright, Madeleine, with Bill Woodward. *Madam Secretary: A Memoir* (New York: Miramax Books, 2003).
Allan, Trevor R. S. *Constitutional Justice: A Liberal Theory of the Rule of Law* (Oxford: Oxford University Press, 2001).

American National Standards Institute. *Management System for Quality of Private Security Company Operations: Requirements with Guidance. ANSI/ASIS PSC.1-2012* (Alexandria: ASIS International, 5 March 2012).

Amstrdmski, Saul. "Kahlon, Netanyahu, and Others: Locker Recommendations Will Not Be Implemented in the Near Term," *Calcalist* (4 August 2015), available in Hebrew at http://www.calcalist.co.il/local/articles/0,7340,L-3666068,00.html, accessed 8 August 2015.

Analysis of Eight Francophone African Countries: National Legislation on PMSCs (New York: United Nations Office of the High Commissioner for Human Rights, no date), available at http://www.ohchr.org/EN/Issues/Mercenaries/WGMercenaries/Pages/NationalLegislationStudies.aspx, accessed 6 June 2015.

Anna Stoil, Rebecca. "Orlev Calls to Thwart Tamir's 40% Cut to National Service," *Jerusalem Post* (21 May 2008).

Antonyshyn, David, Jan Grofe, and Don Hubert. *Beyond the Law? The Regulation of Canadian Private and Security Companies Operating Abroad.* National Reports Series 03/09 (Florence: European University Institute Academy of European Law, 12 February 2009).

Apuzzo, Matt. "Judge Cites Gov't Missteps, Tosses Blackwater Case," Associated Press (1 January 2010), available at http://www.wenatcheeworld.com/news/2010/jan/01/judge-cites-missteps-tosses-blackwater-case/, accessed 27 January 2010.

Arlosoroff, Meirav. "Brodet: Slashing Army Training Was Wrong," *Ha'aretz* (30 March 2007).

Arlosoroff, Meirav. "Locker IDF Reforms: More Money, More Transparency," *Ha'aretz* (22 July 2015).

Arlosoroff, Meirav. "The Most Exciting, Screwed-Up Country in the World," *Ha'aretz* (11 May 2010).

Arlosoroff, Meirav. "Soft Landing Israel Teaches the World a Lesson in Economics," *Ha'aretz* (15 September 2009).

"Army Sergeant Pleads Guilty in Scheme to Defraud the Military; Army Sergeant and Co-conspirators Stole More than One Million Gallons of Fuel," *FBI.gov* (23 September 2014), available at https://www.fbi.gov/charlotte/press-releases/2014/army-sergeant-pleads-guilty-in-scheme-to-defraud-the-military, accessed 1 October 2015.

Article 47 of Additional Protocol One to the Geneva Convention (8 June 1977), available at https://www.icrc.org/ihl/WebART/470-750057, accessed 12 August 2015.

Ashbrook, John, and Spencer D. Bakich. "Storming to Partition: Croatia, the United States, and Krajina in the Yugoslav War," *Small Wars and Insurgencies* 21, 4 (December 2010).

Ashkenazi, Eli. "After 100 Years, the Kibbutz Movement Has Completely Changed," *Ha'aretz* (7 January 2010).

Ashkenazi, Eli. "Degania A, First Kibbutz in Israel, to Undergo Privatization," *Ha'aretz* (17 February 2007).

Asmal, Kader, and John Peter. "Proposed Citizen Law Is an Erosion of Rights," *Business Day Live* (4 August 2010), available at http://www.bdlive.co.za/articles/2010/08/04/kader-asmal-nd-john-peter-proposed-citizen-law-is-an-erosion-of-rights;jsessionid=24E3F3651E4AA70ED5E956683BCF5E4A.present1.bdfm, accessed 24 July 2015.

Associated Press. "Blackwater Chief: I Was 'Thrown under the Bus': Contractor's Founder Says Secret CIA Program Revealed for Political Reasons," *NBC News* (2 December 2009), available at http://www.nbcnews.com/id/34242158/ns/us_news-security/t/blackwater-chief-i-was-thrown-under-bus/#.VgRnSo-qpBc, accessed 24 September 2015.

Auerswald, David, and Steve Saideman. "NATO at War: Understanding the Challenges of Caveats in Afghanistan," paper presented at the Annual Meeting of the American Political Science Association, Toronto, Ontario, 2–5 September 2009.

Avant, Deborah D. "Are the Reluctant Warriors Out of Control? Why the U.S. Military Is Averse to Responding to Post–Cold War Low-Level Threats," *Security Studies* 6, 2 (Winter 1996/1997).

Avant, Deborah D. "Conflicting Indicators of 'Crisis' in American Civil-Military Relations," *Armed Forces and Society* 24, 3 (Spring 1998).

Avant, Deborah D. *The Market for Force: The Consequences of Privatizing Security* (Cambridge: Cambridge University Press, 2005).

Avant, Deborah D. "Private Military Companies and the Future of War," *Foreign Policy Research Association E-notes* (April 2006), http://www.fpri.org/enotes/200604.military.avant.privatemilitarycompanies.html.

Avant, Deborah D. "Selling Security: Trade-Offs in State Regulation of the Private Security Industry," in Thomas Jäger and Gerhard Kümmel, editors, *Private Military and Security Companies: Chances, Problems, Pitfalls and Prospects* (Wiesbaden: Verlag, 2007).

Axe, David. "Challenges Dog U.S. in Afghan War," *Washington Times* (15 October 2009).

Azulai, Yuval, and Lilach Weissman. "Cabinet Sets Up Company to Move IDF Bases to South," *Globes* (1 April 2015), available in Hebrew at http://www.globes.co.il/en/article-cabinet-sets-up-company-to-move-idf-bases-to-south-1000998342, accessed 15 August 2015.

Bacevich, Andrew J. *The New American Militarism: How Americans Are Seduced by War* (Cambridge: Oxford University Press, 2005).

Baer, Robert. "Iraq's Mercenary King," *Vanity Fair* (April 2007), available at http://www.vanityfair.com/politics/features/2007/04/spicer200704, accessed 17 December 2015.

Bailes, Alyson J. K., and Caroline Holmqvist. *The Increasing Role of Private Military and Security Companies.* Study prepared for the European Parliament Subcommittee on Security and Defence (Brussels: Directorate General External Policies of the Union, October 2007).

Baker, Deane-Peter. "To Whom Does a Private Military Commander Owe Allegiance?" in Paolo Tripodi and Jessica Wolfendale, editors, *New Wars and New Soldiers: Military Ethics in the Contemporary World* (Surrey: Ashgate, 2011).

Baker, Deane-Peter, and Sabelo Gumedze. "Private Military/Security Companies and Human Security in Africa," *African Security Review* 16, 4 (2007).

Baker, Mike. "Charged Contractors Had Checkered Military Pasts," Associated Press (25 January 2010).

Bakker, Christine. *Private Military and Security Companies: Positive Human Rights Obligations of the Host State.* EUI Working Paper 2009/20 (Florence: European University Institute Academy of European Law, 2009).

The Baltic and International Maritime Council. "BIMCO's Position: Piracy, Armed Robbery, Kidnapping, Torture and Murder at Sea," available at http://www.bimco.org/Viewpoint/03_Piracy.aspx, accessed 12 September 2012.

The Baltic and International Maritime Council. "Guidance on Rules for the Use of Force (RUF) by Privately Contracted Armed Security Personnel (PCASP) in Defence of a Merchant Vessel (MV)" (no date), available at https://www.bimco.org/~/media/Chartering/Document_Samples/Sundry_Other_Forms/Sample_Copy_Guidance_on_the_Rules_for_the_Use_of_Force.ashx, accessed 14 October 2015.

Baram, Marcus. "Cost of Private Contractors in Afghanistan Climbs to $1 Billion, as Their Numbers Multiply," *Huffington Post* (17 December 2009).

Barnett, Corelli. "The Education of Military Elites," *Journal of Contemporary History* 2, 3 (July 1967).

Baron, Ethan. "Canadian Soldiers to Fly New Choppers," Canwest News Service (17 November 2008).

Baron, James, and David Kreps. *Strategic Human Resources: Frameworks for General Managers* (New York: John Wiley & Sons, 1999).

Bartolini, Giulio. "Private Military and Security Contractors as 'Persons Who Accompany the Armed Forces,'" in Fracesco Francioni and Natalino Ronzitti, editors, *War by Contract: Human Rights, Humanitarian Law, and Private Contractors* (Oxford: Oxford University Press, 2011).

"Basic Law: The Military," available at http://www.knesset.gov.il/laws/special/eng/basic11_eng.htm, accessed 15 August 2015.

Bassiouni, M. Cherif. "Legal Status of Forces in Iraq from 2003–2008," *Chicago Journal of International Law* 11, 1 (Summer 2010).

Bassok, Moti. "Cabinet Approves 88 Billion Budget for 2015," *Ha'aretz* (8 October 2014).

Bassok, Moti. "Defense Budget to Grow, Education Spending to Shrink," *Ha'aretz* (30 September 2009).

Bassok, Moti. "Locker Does Less to Trim Army Spending than It Seems," *Ha'aretz* (24 July 2015), available at http://www.haaretz.com/beta/.premium-1.667562, accessed 15 August 2015.

Bayley, C. C. *Mercenaries for the Crimea: The German, Swiss, and Italian Legions in British Service, 1854–1856* (London: McGill-Queen's University Press, 1977).

Bearce, David H. "Institutional Breakdown and International Cooperation: The European Agreement to Recognize Croatia and Slovenia," *European Journal of International Relations* 8, 4 (December 2002).

Beard, Jack M. "The Geneva Boomerang: The Military Commissions Act of 2006 and U.S. Counterterror Operations," *American Journal of International Law* 101, 1 (January 2007).

Bearpark, Andrew, and Sabrina Schulz. "The Future of the Market," in Simon Chesterman and Chia Lehnardt, editors, *From Mercenaries to Market : The Rise and Regulation of Private Military Companies* (New York: Oxford University Press, 2007).

Bebler, Anton. "Slovenia's Smooth Transition," *Journal of Democracy* 13, 1 (January 2002).

Bellamy, Alex J. *Global Politics and the Responsibility to Protect: From Words to Deeds* (London: Routledge, 2010).

Ben-Eliezer, Uri. "Post-Modern Armies and the Question of Peace and War: The Israeli Defense Forces in the 'New Times,'" *International Journal of Middle East Studies* 36, 1 (February 2004).

Bensahel, Nora, Olga Oliker, Keith Crane, Rick Brennan Jr., Heather S. Gregg, Thomas Sullivan, and Andrew Rathmell. *After Saddam: Prewar Planning and the Occupation of Iraq* (Santa Monica: RAND Corporation, 2008).

Benvenisti, Eyal. "Towards a Typology of Informal International Lawmaking Mechanisms and Their Distinct Accountability Gaps," in Joost Pauwelyn, Ramses Wessel, and Jan Wouters, editors, *Informal International Lawmaking* (Oxford: Oxford University Press, 2015).

Bessner, Daniel, and Eric Lorber. "Toward a Theory of Civil-Military Punishment," *Armed Forces and Society* 38, 4 (October 2012).

Best, Geoffrey. *Humanity in Warfare: The Modern History of the International Law of Armed Conflicts* (London: Weinenfeld and Nicolson, 1980).

Betts, Richard K. "Are Civil-Military Relations Still a Problem?" in Suzanne C. Nielsen and Don M. Snider, editors, *American Civil-Military Relations: The Soldier and the State in a New Era* (Baltimore: Johns Hopkins University Press, 2009).

Betts, Richard K. *Soldiers, Statesmen, and Cold War Crises* (Cambridge: Harvard University Press, 1977).

Bhagavan, M. R. *Angola's Political Economy, 1975–1985* (Uppsala: Scandinavian Institute of African Studies, 1986).

Biderman, Albert D. "What Is Military?" in Sol Tax, editor, *The Draft: A Handbook of Facts and Alternatives* (Chicago: University of Chicago Press, 1967).

Bird, Katie. "Policing Private Security," International Standards Organisation website (12 May 2014), available at http://www.iso.org/iso/news.htm?refid=Ref1847, accessed 23 March 2015.

Birnhack, Michael D. "Book Review: Privacy in Context," *Jurimetrics: The Journal of Law, Science, and Technology* 51, 4 (Summer 2011), page 463.

Bisom-Rapp, Susan. "Bulletproofing the Workplace: Symbol and Substance in Employment Discrimination Law Practice," *Florida State University Law Review* 26, 4 (Summer 1999).

Bjelaja, Mile, and Ozren Žunec. "The War in Croatia, 1991–1995," in Charles W. Ingrao and Thomas Allan Emmert, editors, *Confronting the Yugoslav Controversies: A Scholars' Initiative* (West Lafayette, Indiana: Purdue University Press, 2009).

Black, Julia. "Constructing and Contesting Legitimacy and Accountability in Poly-centric Regimes." IILJ Working Paper 2007/12 (Global Administrative Law Series).

"Blackwater Incident: What Happened," *BBC News* (8 December 2008), available at http://news.bbc.co.uk/2/hi/7033332.stm, accessed 16 August 2015.

Blackwater USA: Hearing before the Committee on Oversight and Government Reform, House of Representatives, One Hundred Tenth Congress (October 2, 2007). Serial number 110-89 (Washington: Government Printing Office, 2008), available at https://house.resource.org/110/org.c-span.201290-1.1.pdf.

Blanchfield, Mike, and Andrew Mayeda. "Forces Enlist Former Afghan Warlord for Protection," *Ottawa Citizen* (22 November 2007).

Bone, James. "Sandline Is Given Support by UN," *Times* (London) (25 May 1998).

Bookmiller, Kirsten Nakjavani. *The United Nations* (New York: Chelsea House, 2008).

Boot, Max. "The Mercenary Debate," *American Interest* 4 (May–June 2009), pages 37–42.

Bosch, Shannon. *The Combatant Status of Private Military and Security Contractors in International Armed Conflicts, in Light of the International Humanitarian Law Notion of Civilian Direct Participation in Hostilities*, PhD thesis (Durban: University of KwaZulu-Natal, 2013).

Bosch, Shannon, and Marelie Maritz. "South African Private Security Contractors Active in Armed Conflicts: Citizenship, Prosecution and the Right to Work." *Potchefstroom Electronic Law Journal* 14, 7 (2011).

Bourg, Chris, and Mady W. Segal. "The Impact of Family Supportive Policies and Practices on Organizational Commitment to the Army," *Armed Forces and Society* 25, 4 (Summer 1999).

Bowcott, Owen. "Report Reveals Shame of UN Peacekeepers," *Guardian* (25 March 2005).

Brabazon, James. *My Friend the Mercenary: A Memoir* (New York: Grove Press, 2011).

Brannon, Robert, and Samuel Juni. "A Scale for Measuring Attitudes about Masculinity," *Psychological Dimensions* 14 (1984).

Branovic, Zeljko. *The Privatisation of Security in Failing States: A Quantitative Assessment.* Occasional Paper 24 (Geneva: Geneva Centre for the Democratic Control of Armed Forces, April 2011).

Bremer, L. Paul. *Coalition Provisional Authority Order 1: De- Ba`athification of Iraqi Society* (16 May 2003).

Bremer, L. Paul. *Coalition Provisional Authority Order 3 (Revised): Weapons Control* (31 December 2003), available at http://www.iraqcoalition.org/regulations/20031231_AORD3;REV__AMD_.pdf, accessed 1 February 2011.

Bremer, L. Paul. *Coalition Provisional Authority Order 17: Registration Requirements for Private Security Companies (PSCSs)* (27 June 2004).

Brewster, Murray. "Canada Lacks Policy to Rein in Hired Guns in War Zones: Critics," *Chronicle Herald* (24 June 2009).

Brewster, Murray. "Canada's Hired Guns in Afghanistan Rejected by U.S. for Unsavoury Ties," *Globe and Mail* (6 February 2011).

British Association of Private Security Companies. "Home," available at http://www.bapsc.org.uk/key_documents-charter.asp, accessed 17 December 2015.

British Broadcasting Company. "British Military Deaths in Iraq" (21 July 2010), available at http://www.bbc.co.uk/news/uk-10637526, accessed 17 December 2015.

Broder, John M. "State Dept. Official Resigns; Oversaw Blackwater and Other Private Guards," *New York Times* (25 October 2007), available at http://www.nytimes.com/2007/10/25/washington/25griffin.html?_r=0, accessed 14 October 2015.

Brodet Commission. *Doch ha-Va'adah Libchinal Taktziv ha-Bitacho* (Jerusalem, 2007).

Bromley, Mark. *United Nations Arms Embargoes: Their Impact on Arms Flows and Target Behavior. Case Study: Former Yugoslavia, 1991–96* (Stockholm: Stockholm International Peace Research Institute, 2007).

Bronner, Ethan. "Issues Stand before Israel in Joining Elite Group," *New York Times* (20 January 2010).

Brooks, Doug. "From Humble Beginnings in Freetown: The Origins of the Code of Conduct and Its Importance for the Industry," *Journal of International Peace Operations* 3, 5 (2007).

Brooks, Doug. "Messiahs or Mercenaries? The Future of International Private Military Services," *International Peacekeeping* 7, 4 (Winter 2000).

Brooks, Doug. *Testimony on " Contracting for the Iraqi Security Forces." Hearing before the Subcommittee on Oversight and Investigations of the Committee on Armed Services , House of Representatives, 110th Congress* (Washington: Government Printing Office, 2008).

Brooks, Doug. "Write a Cheque, End a War," *Conflict Trends* 6 (July 2000).

Brooks, Doug, and Mackenzie Duelge. "Ethical Lessons on Maximizing Private Contractor Value in Afghanistan and Iraq," in Volker Franke and Robert H. Dorff, editors, *Conflict*

Management and "Whole of Government": Useful Tools for U.S. National Security Strategy? (Carlisle: U.S. Army War College, Strategic Studies Institute, 2012).

Brown, James. "Pirates and Privateers: Managing the Indian Ocean's Private Security Boom" (Sydney: Lowy Institute for International Policy, 2012).

Bruno, Greg. "US Security Agreements and Iraq," Council on Foreign Relations website, available at http://www.cfr.org/publication/16448/.

Buchanan, Allen, and Robert O. Keohane. "The Legitimacy of Global Governance Institutions," *Ethics and International Affairs* 20, 4 (December 2006).

Bull, Hedley. *The Anarchical Society: A Study of Order in World Politics* (London: Macmillan, 1977).

Bures, Oldrich. "Private Military Companies: A Second Best Peacekeeping Option?" *International Peacekeeping* 12, 4 (Winter 2005).

Burke, Peter J., and Jan E. Stets. *Identity Theory* (Oxford: Oxford University Press, 2009).

Bush, George W. *The President's Management Agenda* (Washington: Office of Management and Budget, 2002), available at http://www.whitehouse.gov/omb/budget/fy2002/mgmt.pdf, accessed 4 May 2003.

Bush, George W. "The President's News Conference. October 17, 2007," *The American Presidency Project*, available at http://www.presidency.ucsb.edu/ws/index.php?pid=75943, accessed 18 October 2015.

Buzan, Barry, and Richard Little. *International Systems in World History: Remaking the Study of International Relations* (Oxford: Oxford University Press, 2000).

Buzatu, Anne-Marie. "The ICOC," *Journal of International Peace Operations* 6, 4 (January–February 2011).

Callan, Victor J. "Individual and Organizational Strategies for Coping with Organizational Change," *Work and Stress* 7, 1 (1993).

Cameron, Lindsey, and Vincent Chetail. *Privatizing War: Private Military and Security Companies under Public International Law* (Cambridge: Cambridge University Press, 2013).

Camm, Frank. "How to Decide When a Contractor Source Is Better to Use than a Government Source," in Christopher Kinsey and Malcolm Patterson, editors, *Contractors and War: The Transformation of United States' Expeditionary Operations* (Palo Alto: Stanford University Press, 2012).

The Campaign to Stop Killer Coke. "About Us," available at http://killercoke.org/about.php, accessed 17 December 2015.

Campbell, Donald J., and Kathleen M. Campbell. "Soldiers as Police Officers/Police Officers as Soldiers: Role Evolution and Revolution in the United States," *Armed Forces and Society* 36, 2 (January 2010).

Canada and the Government of the Islamic Republic of Afghanistan. *Military Technical Agreement* (18 December 2005).

Canadian Department of National Defence. *Audit of the Canadian Forces Contractor Augmentation Program (CANCAP)* (Ottawa: Chief Review Services, June 2006).

Canadian Department of National Defence. "Backgrounder: Strengthening the Canadian Forces and Canadian Sovereignty," BG-08.016 (Ottawa: 7 August 2008), available at http://www.forces.gc.ca/en/news/article.page?doc=strengthening-the-canadian-forces-and-canadian-sovereignty/hnps1tx, accessed 11 September 2015.

Canadian Department of National Defence. *CFJP 01: Canadian Military Doctrine.* B-GJ-005-000/FP-001 (Ottawa: Department of National Defence, April 2009).

Canadian Department of National Defence. *Evaluation of Contracts for Transportation* (Ottawa: Chief Review Services, August 2006).

Canadian Department of National Defence and the Canadian Armed Forces. "Access to Information Request A-2012-000498: National Defence Directive on the Selection and Use of Private Military and Security Contractors on Deployed Operations" (Ottawa: Department of National Defence, 2012).

Cancian, Mark. "Contractors: The New Element of Military Force Structure," *Parameters* 38, 3 (Autumn 2008).

Capaccio, Tony. "Petraeus Urges Ships to Use Armed Guards," *Boston Globe* (25 April 2009), available at http:www.boston.com/news/nation/washington/articles/2009/04/25/petraeus_urges_ships_to_use_armed_guards/, accessed 22 October 2015.

Caparini, Marina. "Regulating Private Military and Security Companies: The US Approach," in Andrew Alexandria, Deane-Peter Baker, and Marina Caparini, editors, *Private Military and Security Companies: Ethics, Policies and Civil-Military Relations* (Abingdon, UK: Routledge, 2008).

Carafano, James Jay. *Private Sector, Public Wars* (Westport: Praeger Security International, 2008).

Carey, Benedict. "Psychologists Explain Iraq Airstrike Video," *New York Times* (7 April 2010), available at http://www.nytimes.com/2010/04/08/world/08psych.html, accessed 10 April 2010.

Carforio, Giuseppe, editor. *The European Cadet: Professional Socialisation in Military Academies—A Crossnational Study* (Baden-Baden: Nomos Verlagsgesellschaft, 1998).

Carmola, Kateri. *Private Security Contractors and New Wars: Risk, Law, and Ethics* (New York: Routledge, 2010).

Carter, Ashton. *Department of Defense Instruction 3020.50: Private Security Contractors (PSCs) Operating in Contingency Operations* (Washington: Department of Defense, 22 July 2009).

Center for Effective Government. "CWC's Final Report: Make Investments in Contracting Oversight" (13 September 2011), available at http://www.foreffectivegov.org/node/11850, accessed 30 September 2015.

Chase, Steven, and John Ibbitson. "Protecting Workers Could Complicate Afghan Withdrawal," *Globe and Mail* (25 August 2010).

Chemerinsky, Erwin. "Rethinking State Action," *Northwest University Law Review* 80, 3 (Fall 1985).

Cherneva, Iveta. "IPOA Holds Capitol Hill Event on UCMJ-MEJA Debate," *Journal of International Peace Operations* 2, 5 (March/April 2007).

Chesterman, Simon. "Lawyers, Guns and Money: The Governance of Business Activities in Conflict Zones," *Chicago Journal of International Law* 11, 1 (Summer 2010).

Chesterman, Simon, and Angelina Fisher, editors. *Private Security, Public Order* (Oxford: Oxford University Press, 2009).

Chesterman, Simon, and Chia Lehnardt. "Conclusion," in Simon Chesterman and Chia Lehnardt, editors, *From Mercenaries to Market: The Rise and Regulation of Private Military Companies* (Oxford: Oxford University Press, 2007).

Chesterman, Simon, and Chia Lehnardt. "Introduction," in Simon Chesterman and Chia Lehnardt, editors, *From Mercenaries to Market: The Rise and Regulation of Private Military Companies* (Oxford: Oxford University Press, 2007).

Chesterman, Simon, and Chia Lehnardt, editors. *From Mercenaries to Markets: The Rise and Regulation of Private Military Companies* (Oxford: Oxford University Press, 2007).

Chiarelli, Peter W. "Selection and Training of Contracting Officer's Representatives (CORs)" (Washington: Office of the Vice Chief of Staff of the United States Army, 2 March 2010).

Chisholm, Amanda. "Marketing the Gurkha Security Package: Colonial Histories and Neoliberal Economies of Private Security," *Security Dialogue* 45, 4 (August 2014).

Chollet, Derek H. *The Road to the Dayton Accords: A Study of American Statecraft* (New York: Palgrave Macmillan, 2005).

Christie, Richard, and Florence Geis. *Studies in Machiavellianism* (New York and London: Academic Press, 1970).

Christoff, Joseph A. *Securing, Stabilizing, and Rebuilding Iraq. Progress Report: Some Gains Made, Updated Strategy Needed* (Washington: General Accounting Office, June 2008).

Cilliers, Jakkie. "Security and Transition in South Africa," *Journal of Democracy* 6, 4 (1995).

Cilliers, Jakkie, and Ian Douglas. "The Military as Business: Military Professional Resources, Incorporated," in Jakkie Cilliers and Peggy Mason, editors, *Peace, Profit and Plunder? The Privatisation of Security in War-Torn Societies* (Pretoria: Institute for Security Studies, 1999).

Cilliers, Jackie, and Richard Cornwell. "Africa: From the Privatization of Security to the Privatization of War?" in Jakkie Cillers and Peggy Mason, editors, *Peace, Profit or Plunder? The Privatisation of Security in War-Torn African Societies* (Pretoria: Institute for Security Studies, 1999).

Clarence-Smith, W. G. "Review Article: Class Structure and Class Struggles in Angola in the 1970s," *Journal of Southern African Studies* 7, 1 (October 1980).

Clark, Charles S. "Pentagon's Plan for Civilian Workforce Falls Short, GAO Finds," *Government Executive* (11 July 2014), available at http://www.govexec.com/defense/2014/07/pentagons-plan-civilian-workforce-falls-short-gao-finds/88507/, accessed 18 July 2014.

Cleveland, Cindy. *Contractors' Support of U.S. Operations in Iraq* (Washington: Congressional Budget Office, August 2008).

CNN Library. "Haditha Killings Fast Facts," *CNN.com* (14 March 2015), available at http://edition.cnn.com/2013/10/30/world/meast/haditha-killings-fast-facts/, accessed 30 September 2015.

Coase, Ronald "The Nature of the Firm," *Economica* 4, 16 (November 1937), pages 386–405.

Cobain, Ian. "Iraqi Prisoners Were Abused at 'UK's Abu Ghraib,' Court Hears," *Guardian* (6 November 2010).

Cockayne, James. "Regulating Private Military and Security Companies: The Content, Negotiation, Weaknesses and Promise of the Montreux Document," *Journal of Conflict and Security Law* 13, 3 (Winter 2008).

Coghlan, Tom. "British Embassy Security Chief Bill Shaw Jailed for Two Years over Afghan 'Bribe,'" *Times* (27 April 2010).

Cohen, Eliot A. *Supreme Command: Soldiers, Statesmen, and Leadership in Wartime* (New York: The Free Press, 2002).

Cohen, Gil. "IDF Expanding Net of Recruits but 1 in 6 Won't Finish Service," *Ha'aretz* (9 December 2014).

Cohen, Gil. "Ya'alon: Proposed IDF Reforms 'a Gamble on the Lives of Israeli Citizens,'" *Ha'aretz* (21 July 2015).

Cohen, Roger. "U.S. Cooling Ties to Croatia after Winking at Its Buildup," *New York Times* (28 October 1995).

Cohen, Stuart A. "From Integration to Segregation: The Role of Religion in the IDF," *Armed Forces and Society* 25, 3 (Spring 1999).

Cohen, Stuart A. *Israel and Its Army: From Cohesion to Confusion* (London: Routledge, 2008).

Cohen, Stuart A. "The Israel Defense Forces (IDF): From a 'People's Army' to a 'Professional Military'—Causes and Implications," *Armed Forces and Society* 21, 2 (Winter 1995).

Cohn, Lindsay P. "It Wasn't in My Contract: Security Privatization and Civilian Control," *Armed Forces and Society* 37, 3 (July 2011).

Coker, Christopher. "Outsourcing War," *Cambridge Review of International Affairs* 13, 1 (1999).

Cole, August. "DynCorp, Fluor Win Army Jobs," *Wall Street Journal Asia* (10 July 2009).

Cole, August. "U.S. Seeks New Guards in Kabul," *Wall Street Journal* (9 December 2009).

Coleman, James R. "Constraining Modern Mercenarism," *Hastings Law Journal* 55, 6 (June 2004).

Combined Maritime Forces Public Affairs. "Super Tanker Attacked in Arabian Sea." Story number NNS081117-07 (17 November 2008), http://www.navy.mil/search/display.asp?story_id=40943.

Commission on Wartime Contracting in Iraq and Afghanistan. *At What Cost? Interim Report to Congress* (Washington: Commission on Wartime Contracting in Iraq and Afghanistan, June 2009).

Commission on Wartime Contracting in Iraq and Afghanistan. *Transforming Wartime Contracting: Controlling Costs, Reducing Risks. Final Report to Congress* (Washington: Commission on Wartime Contracting in Iraq and Afghanistan, August 2011).

Comparative Analysis of the Regulation of Private Military and Security Companies in Eight Asian Countries (New York: United Nations Office of the High Commissioner for Human Rights, no date), available at http://www.ohchr.org/EN/Issues/Mercenaries/WGMercenaries/Pages/NationalLegislationStudies.aspx, accessed 6 June 2015.

Confederation of Switzerland. *International Code of Conduct for Private Security Service Providers* (Geneva: Confederation of Switzerland, November 2010), available at http://www.icoca.ch/en/articles_of_association.

Confederation of Switzerland Department of Foreign Affairs. *Global Code of Conduct for Respect of Human Rights and International Humanitarian Law* (Geneva: Confederation of Switzerland Department of Foreign Affairs, January 2010).

Confederation of Switzerland Department of Foreign Affairs. "The Montreux Document on Private Military and Security Companies" (5 May 2015), available at http://www.eda.admin.ch/psc, accessed 31 July 2015.

Confederation of Switzerland Department of Foreign Affairs. "Participating States of the Montreux Document" (8 April 2015), available at http://www.eda.admin.ch/eda/en/home/topics/intla/humlaw/pse/parsta.html, accessed 31 July 2015.

Confederation of Switzerland Department of Foreign Affairs and the International Committee of the Red Cross. *The Montreux Document on Pertinent International Legal Obligations and Good Practices for States related to Operations of Private Military and Security Companies during Armed Conflict*. UN Document A/63/467-S/2008/636 (Geneva: International Committee of the Red Cross, 2008) .

Control Risks. "Code of Ethics" (no date), available at http://www.controlrisks.com/SiteAssets/Code_Ethics.pdf, accessed 18 December 2015.

"Controversial Blackwater Security Firm Gets Iraq Contract Extended by State Dept," *CBS News* (30 January 2009), available at http://www.cbsnews.com/news/us-nixes-blackwater-contract-for-iraq/, accessed 14 October 2015.

Cooley, Charles Horton. *Human Nature and the Social Order* (New York: Scribner's, 1902).

Corder, Mike, and Slobodan Lekic. "Dutch Navy Under Fire for 'Idiotic' Catch and Release of Somali Pirates," *Chicago Tribune* (21 April 2009).

Cornish, Paul. "Myth and Reality: US and UK Approaches to Casualty Aversion and Force Protection," *Defence Studies* 3, 2 (May 2003).

Coser, Lewis A. *Greedy Institutions: Patterns of Undivided Commitment* (New York: The Free Press, 1974).

Cottier, Michael. "Elements for Contracting and Regulating Private Security and Military Companies," *International Review of the Red Cross* 88 (2006).

Cottle, Eddie. "Will the ANC Government Ever Prosecute South Africans Serving in the Israeli Defence Force?" South African Civil Society Information Service (21 April 2015), available at http://www.sacsis.org.za/site/article/2355, accessed 2 September 2015.

Cotton, Sarah K., Ulrich Petersohn, Molly Dunigan, Q. Burkhart, Megan Zander-Cotugno, Edward O'Connell, and Michael Webber. *Hired Guns: Views about Armed Contractors in Operation Iraqi Freedom* (Santa Monica: RAND Corporation, 2010).

Crawford, Beverly. "Explaining Defection from International Cooperation: Germany's Unilateral Recognition of Croatia," *World Politics* 48, 4 (July 1996).

Crawford, Beverly. "German Foreign Policy and European Political Cooperation: The Diplomatic Recognition of Croatia in 1991," *German Politics and Society* 13, 2 (Summer 1995).

Crawford, Emily. *Identifying the Enemy: Civilian Participation in Armed Conflict* (Oxford: Oxford University Press, 2015).

"Croatian Atrocities Being Forgotten," *CBC Report* (21 July 2003), available at http://www.globalresearch.ca/articles/CHO307D.html, accessed 6 October 2015.

Crook, John. "Contemporary Practice of the United States Relating to International Law," *American Journal of International Law* 107, 1 (January 2013).

Crosby, Faye J. *Relative Deprivation and Working Women* (New York: Oxford University Press, 1982).

Cross, Tim. "Logistic Support for UK Expeditionary Operations," *RUSI Journal* 145, 1 (2000).

Cullen, Patrick Jerome. *Private Security in International Politics: Deconstructing the State's Monopoly of Security Governance*, unpublished PhD thesis (London: London School of Economics and Political Science, 2009).

Curtin, Neal. *Military Operations: Contractors Provide Vital Services to Deployed Forces but Are Not Adequately Addressed in DoD Plans*. GAO-03-695 (Washington: General Accounting Office, June 2003).

Cusumano, Eugenio. "Policy Prospects on the Regulation of PMSCs," in Francesco Francioni and Natalino Ronzitti, editors, *War by Contract: Human Rights, Humanitarian Law, and Private Contractors* (Oxford: Oxford University Press, 2011).

Cusumano, Eugenio, and Christopher Kinsey. "Bureaucratic Interests and the Outsourcing of Security: The Privatization of Diplomatic Protection in the United States and the United Kingdom," *Armed Forces and Society* 41, 4 (October 2015).

Cutler, A. Claire. "Private International Regimes and Inter-firm Cooperation," in Rodney Bruce Hall and Thomas J. Biersteker, editors, *The Emergence of Private Authority in Global Governance* (Cambridge: Cambridge University Press, 2002).

Daalder, Ivo H. *Getting to Dayton: The Making of America's Bosnia Policy* (Washington: Brookings Institution, 2000).

Dal Bó, Ernesto. "Regulatory Capture: A Review," *Oxford Review of Economic Policy* 22, 2 (Summer 2006).

Dandeker, Christopher. "A Farewell to Arms? The Military and the Nation-State in a Changing World," in James Burk, editor, *The Military in New Times: Adapting Armed Forces to a Turbulent World* (Boulder, San Francisco, and Oxford: Westview, 1994).

Davies, Caroline. "Briton Danny Fitzsimons Jailed in Iraq for Contractors' Murders," *Guardian* (28 February 2011).

Davis, John B. *The Theory of the Individual in Economics: Identity and Value* (New York: Routledge, 2003).

Dawood v Minister of Home Affairs 2000 3 South Africa 936 (CC), paragraph 53.

Deflem, Mathieu. "The Concept of Social Control: Theories and Application," paper presented at the International Conference on "Charities as Instruments of Social Control in Nineteenth-Century Britain," Université de Haute Bretagne (Rennes 2), France (22–23 November 2007).

Del Prado, Jose Gomez. "Mercenaries, Private Military and Security Companies and International Law," lecture, University of Wisconsin Law School (31 January 2008).

Del Prado, José Luis Gómez, rapporteur. *Report of the Working Group on the Use of Mercenaries as a Means of Violating Human Rights and Impeding the Exercise of the Right of Peoples to Self-Determination.* UN Document A/HRC/15/25 (New York: United Nations, 2 July 2010).

Demeter, Karl (Angus Malcolm, translator). *The German Officer-Corps in Society and State: 1650–1945* (New York: Frederick A. Praeger, 1965).

Dempsey, Martin. *Strategic Direction to the Joint Force* (Washington: Joint Chiefs of Staff, 6 February 2012).

De Nevers, Renée. "Private Security Companies and the Laws of War," *Security Dialogue* 40, 2 (2009).

De Normann, Roderick. "Operation Storm: Attack on the Krajina," *Jane's Intelligence Review* (November 1995).

DeWinter-Schmitt, Rebecca. "Executive Summary," in Rebecca DeWinter-Schmitt, editor, *Montreux Five Years On: An Analysis of State Efforts to Implement Montreux Document Legal Obligations and Good Practices* (Barcelona: Adjuntament de Barcelona, 2013).

DeWinter-Schmitt, Rebecca. "A New Twist to Management Standards, Bringing in Human Rights," *Private Security Monitor* (Summer 2014), available at http://psm.du.edu/commentary/index.html, accessed 4 December 2014.

DeWinter-Schmitt, Rebecca, editor. *Montreux Five Years On: An Analysis of State Efforts to Implement Montreux Document Legal Obligations and Good Practices* (Barcelona: Adjuntament de Barcelona, 2013).

DeYoung, Karen. "In Indiana, Practice for 'Civilian Surge' in Afghanistan," *Washington Post* (21 November 2009).

DeYoung, Karen. "U.S. Indirectly Paying Afghan Warlords as Part of Security Contract," *Washington Post* (22 June 2010), page A01.

Dickinson, Laura A. *Outsourcing War and Peace: Preserving Public Values in a World of Privatized Foreign Affairs* (New Haven: Yale University Press, 2011).

Diplock, Kenneth, Derek Walker Smith, and Geoffrey de Freitas. *Report of the Committee of Privy Counsellors Appointed to Inquire into the Recruitment of Mercenaries* (London: The Stationery Office, 1976).

Doder, Dusko. "Yugoslavia: New War, Old Hatreds," *Foreign Policy* 91 (Summer 1993).

Dolman, Everett C. *The Warrior State: How Military Organization Structures Politics* (New York: Palgrave, 2004).

Donahoe, Eileen Chamberlain. "Letter to Ms. Faiza Patel, Chair-Rapporteur, Working Group on the Use of Mercenaries" (2 July 2012), available at http://www.ohchr.org/Documents/Issues/Mercenaries/WG/Law/USA/CoverLetter.pdf, accessed 12 December 2015.

Donahue, John. *The Privatization Decision: Public Ends, Private Means* (New York: Basic Books, 1989).

Donald, Dominick. *After the Bubble: British Private Security Companies after Iraq*. Royal United Services Institute Whitehall Paper 66 (London: Royal United Services Institute for Defence and Security Studies, 25 July 2006).

Dornbusch, Sanford M. "The Military Academy as an Assimilating Institution," *Social Forces* 33, 4 (May 1955).

Douglas, Ian. "Fighting for Diamonds: Private Military Companies in Sierra Leone," in Jakkie Cilliers and Peggy Mason, editors, *Peace, Profit or Plunder? The Privatisation of Security in War-Torn African Societies* (Pretoria: Institute for Security Studies, 1999).

Downes, Cathy. "Military Manpower: Strategic Asset, Liability or Non-entity?" *Defence Economics* 2, 4 (1991).

Downes, Cathy. *Special Trust and Confidence: The Making of an Officer* (New York: Routledge, 2013).

Downing, Brian M. *The Military Revolution and Political Change: Origins of Democracy and Autocracy in Early Modern Europe* (Princeton: Princeton University Press, 1992).

"Draft Articles on Responsibility of States for Internationally Wrongful Acts, with Commentaries," in *Report of the International Law Commission on the Work of Its Fifty-third Session, UN GAOR, 56th Sess., Supp. No. 10, at 43*. UN Document A/56/10 (New York: United Nations, 2001).

Draft Convention on Private Military and Security Companies: Report of the UN Working Group on Mercenaries to the UN Human Rights Council. A/HRC/15/25, Annex (2 July 2010).

Drury, Ian. "Ex-Cabinet Minister Paul Boateng Becomes a Director of a Private Military Firm after Lobbying to Water Down Anti-mercenary Legislation," *Mail Online* (9 November 2009), available at http://www.dailymail.co.uk/news/article-1226269/Paul-Boateng-director-private-military-firm-lobbying-water-anti-mercenary-laws.html, accessed 6 June 2015.

Drutschmann, Sebastian. "Informal Regulation: An Economic Perspective on the Private Security Industry," in Thomas Jäger and Gerhard Kümmel, editors, *Private Military and Security Companies: Chances, Problems, Pitfalls and Prospects* (Wiesbaden: VS Verlag für Sozialwissenschaften, 2007).

Dunigan, Molly. "A Lesson from Iraq: How to Outsource War to Private Contractors," *Christian Science Monitor* (19 March 2013), available at http://www.csmonitor.com/Commentary/Opinion/2013/0319/A-lesson-from-Iraq-war-How-to-outsource-war-to-private-contractors, accessed 19 July 2015.

Dunigan, Molly. *Victory for Hire: Private Security Companies' Impact on Military Effectiveness* (Palo Alto: Stanford University Press, 2011).

Dunigan, Molly, Carrie M. Farmer, Rachel M. Burns, Alison Hawks, and Clause Messan Setodji. *Out of the Shadows: The Health and Well-Being of Private Contractors Working in Conflict Environments* (Santa Monica: RAND Corporation, 2013).

Dunivin, Karen O. "Military Culture: Change and Continuity," *Armed Forces and Society* 20, 4 (1994).

Dunlap, Charles. "Civilianizing Military Justice? Sorry, It Can't—and Shouldn't—Work," *War on the Rocks* (8 October 2015).

Dunlap, Charles J., Jr. "Does Lawfare Need an Apologia?" *Case Western Reserve Journal of International Law* 43, 1–2 (2011).

Dunlap, Charles J., Jr. "Lawfare: A Decisive Element of 21st-Century Conflicts?" *Joint Force Quarterly* 54, 3 (Fall 2009).
Durch, William J. "The Cuban Military in Africa and the Middle East: From Algeria to Angola," *Studies in Comparative Communism* 11, 1–2 (Spring–Summer 1978).
Ebrahim, Adam. "Going to War with the Army You Can Afford: The United States, International Law, and the Private Military Industry," *Boston University International Law Journal* 28, 1 (Spring 2010).
Edwards, Chris. "Moving Public Work to the Private Sector," *Philadelphia Inquirer* (24 November 2002), available at http://www.cato.org/publications/commentary/moving-public-work-private-sector, accessed 27 March 2015.
Eikenberry, Karl, and Stanley A. McChrystal. "Testimony before Hearing of the Senate Armed Services Committee on Afghanistan" (Washington: United States Senate, 8 December 2009), available at http://www.isaf.nato.int/en/article/transcripts/transcript-u.s.-senate-armed-services-committee-hearing-on-afghanistan.html, accessed 3 February 2010.
Eisendorfer, Arnold, and Martin S. Bergmann. "The Factor of Maturity in Officer Selection," *Psychiatry* 9, 1 (1946).
Eisenhower, Dwight D. "Farewell Address, January 17, 1961," available at http://www.eisenhower.archives.gov/education/bsa/citizenship_merit_badge/speeches_national_historical_importance/farewell_address.pdf, accessed 30 July 2015.
Elis, Niv. "Israel Military Industries Moving Ahead with Privatization," *Jerusalem Post* (5 March 2015).
Elron, Efrat, Boas Shamir, and Eyal Ben-Ari. "Why Don't They Fight Each Other? Cultural Diversity and Operational Unity in Multinational Forces," *Armed Forces and Society* 26, 1 (Fall 1999).
Elsea, Jennifer K. *Private Security Contractors in Iraq and Afghanistan: Legal Issues* (Washington: Congressional Research Service, 7 January 2010).
Elsea, Jennifer K., and Nina M. Serafino. *Private Security Contractors in Iraq: Background, Legal Status, and Other Issues.* CRS Report for Congress RL32419 (Washington: Congressional Research Service, 21 June 2007).
Elsea, Jennifer K., Moshe Schwartz, and Kennon H. Nakamura, *Private Security Contractors in Iraq: Background, Legal Status, and Other Issues* (Washington: Congressional Research Service, updated 29 September 2008).
Endweld, Miri, Daniel Gotleib, and Refaela Cohen. *Poverty and Inequality in Income Distribution in Israel, 2006/7: Main Findings* (National Insurance Institute, Research and Planning Administration, February 2008).
Engbrecht, Shawn. *America's Covert Warriors: Inside the World of Private Military Contractors* (Washington: Potomac Books, 2010).
Epstein, A. *Ethos and Identity* (London: Tavistock, 1978).
Epstein, Alek D., and Michael Uritsky. "Questioning the Role of Army in Nation-Building: The Development of Critical Discourse on Civil-Military Relations in Israel," in Constantine P. Danopoulos, Dhirendra Vajpeyi, and Amir Bar-Or, editors, *Civil-Military Relations, Nation Building, and National Identity: Comparative Perspectives* (Westport: Praeger, 2004).
Erbel, Mark, and Christopher Kinsey. "Privatizing Military Logistics," in Rita Abrahamsen and Anna Leander, editors, *Routledge Handbook of Private Security Studies* (New York: Routledge, 2016).
Erling, Christina, and Enid Doggett. *President Obama Signs Bill into Law to Stop A-76 Privatization Studies through FY2009* (Washington: American Federation of Government Employees, 12 March 2009).
Erwin, Sandra I. "War on Somali Pirates: Big Business and Growing," *National Defense Magazine* (14 August 2012), available at http://www.nationaldefensemagazine.org/blog/Lists/Posts/Post.aspx?ID=868, accessed 22 October 2015.
Esty, Daniel C. "Good Governance at the Supranational Scale: Globalizing Administrative Law," *Yale Law Journal* 115, 7 (May 2006).

"Etienne Kabila Charged in South Africa for DR Congo 'Plot,'" *BBC News* (12 February 2013), available at http://www.bbc.com/news/world-africa-21432981, accessed 8 June 2015.

Evans, Gareth, and Mohamed Sahnoun, chairmen. *The Responsibility to Protect: Report of the International Commission on Intervention and State Sovereignty* (Ottawa: International Development Research Centre, December 2001).

Evans, Michael. "The Front-Line States, South Africa and Southern African Security: Military Prospects and Perspectives," *Zambezia* 12 (1984/1985).

"Exclusive: State Dept Emails Say Blackwater Hurting US in Iraq," *ABC News* (25 October 2007), available at http://blogs.abcnews.com/theblotter/2007/10/exclusive-state.html, accessed 12 April 2010.

Fabricius, Peter. "Mercenaries Turning Tide in Nigeria," *IOL News* (12 April 2015), available at http://www.iol.co.za/news/africa/sadf-mercenaries-turning-tide-in-nigeria-1.1843796#.VXSklM-qqko, accessed 3 June 2015.

Fabricius, Peter. "Strange Chapter in South Africa-Congo Saga Ends," *Star* (24 February 2015), available at http://www.iol.co.za/the-star/strange-chapter-in-South Africa-congo-saga-ends-1.1823026#.VXSkmc-qqko, accessed 5 June 2015.

Fainaru, Steve. *Big Boy Rules: America's Mercenaries Fighting in Iraq* (New York: Da Capo Press, 2008).

Falconer, Bruce. "Doug Brooks: Blackwater's Man in Washington," *Mother Jones* (25 September 2007).

Falconer, Bruce. "IPOA Smackdown: Dyncorp vs. Blackwater," *Mother Jones* (12 November 2007), available at: http://motherjones.com/mojo/2007/11/ipoa-smackdown-dyncorp-vs-blackwater.

Fallows, James. *Blind into Baghdad: America's War in Iraq* (New York: Vintage Books, 2006).

Farquha, Scott C., editor. *Back to Basics: A Study of the Second Lebanon War and Operation CAST LEAD* (Fort Leavenworth: US Army Combined Arms Center, 2009).

Farrell, Brenda S. *Defense Workforce: DOD Needs to Better Oversee Insourcing Data and Align Insourcing Efforts with Strategic Workforce Plans.* GAO-12-319 (Washington: General Accountability Office, February 2012).

Farrell, Theo. *The Sources of Military Change: Culture, Politics, Technology* (Boulder: Lynne Rienner Publishers, 2002).

Feaver, Peter D. *Armed Servants: Agency, Oversight, and Civil-Military Relations* (Cambridge: Harvard University Press, 2003).

Feaver, Peter D. "The Civil-Military Problematique: Huntington, Janowitz, and the Problem of Civilian Control," *Armed Forces and Society* 23, 2 (Winter 1996).

Feaver, Peter D. "Civil-Military Relations," in Nelson W. Polsby, editor, *Annual Review of Political Science* 2 (1999).

Feaver, Peter D., and Richard Kohn, editors. *Soldiers and Civilians: The Civil-Military Gap and American National Security* (Cambridge: MIT Press, 2001).

Feaver, Peter D., Richard Kohn, and Lindsay P. Cohn. "The Gap between Military and Civilian in the United States in Perspective," in Peter D. Feaver and Richard Kohn, editors, *Soldiers and Civilians: The Civil-Military Gap and American National Security* (Cambridge: MIT Press, 2001).

Feigenbaum, Harvey B., and Jeffrey R. Henig. "The Political Underpinnings of Privatization: A Typology," *World Politics* 46, 2 (January 1994).

Feld, Maury D. *The Structure of Violence: Armed Forces as Social Systems* (Beverly Hills: Sage, 1977).

Fielding-Smith, Abigail, Crofton Black, Alice Ross, and James Ball. "Revealed: Private Firms at Heart of US Drone Warfare," *Guardian* (30 July 2015), available at http://www.theguardian.com/us-news/2015/jul/30/revealed-private-firms-at-heart-of-us-drone-warfare, accessed 12 August 2015.

Filkins, Dexter. "Convoy Guards in Afghanistan Face an Inquiry," *New York Times* (6 June 2010).

Finer, Jonathon. "Security Contractors in Iraq under Scrutiny after Shootings," *Washington Post* (10 September 2005).

Finer, Joshua. "Contractors Cleared in Videotaped Attacks," *Washington Post* (11 June 2006).

Finer, Samuel E. "State- and Nation-Building in Europe: The Role of the Military," in Charles Tilly, editor, *The Formation of National States in Western Europe* (Princeton: Princeton University Press, 1975).

Fisher, Angelina. "Accountability to Whom?" in Simon Chesterman and Angelina Fisher, editors, *Private Security, Public Order* (New York: Oxford University Press, 2009).

Fishman, Alex. "The Opening Shot of the Battle for the Defense Budget," *ynetnews.com* (25 July 2015), available at http://www.ynetnews.com/articles/0%2c7340%2cL-4683778%2c00.html, accessed 8 August 2015.

Fitzgerald, John A. "Changing Patterns of Officer Recruitment at the US Naval Academy," *Armed Forces and Society* 8, 1 (Fall 1981).

Fitzsimmons, Scott. *Private Security Companies during the Iraq War: Military Performance and the Use of Deadly Force* (London: Routledge, 2016).

Fleitz, Frederick H. *Peacekeeping Fiascoes of the 1990s: Causes, Solutions, and U.S. Interests* (Westport: Praeger, 2002).

Flournoy, Michèle. "Department of Defense Directive 3000.5: Stability Operations" (Washington: Office of the Secretary of Defense, 16 September 2009).

Foaleng, Mpako H. "Private Military and Security Companies and the Nexus between Natural Resources and Civil Wars in Africa," in Sabelo Gumedze, *Private Security in Africa: Manifestation, Challenges and Regulation*. ISS Monograph Series 139 (November 2007).

Fontaine, Richard, and John Nagl. *Contractors in American Conflicts*. Working Paper (Washington: Center for a New American Security, December 2009).

Foucault, Michel. "Prison Talk," in Colin Gordon, editor, *Power/Knowledge: Selected Interviews and Other Writings, 1972–1977* (Brighton: Harvester Press, 1980).

Foucault, Michel (Michel Senellart, editor). *Security, Territory, Population: Lectures at the Collège de France* (Basingstoke: Palgrave Macmillan, 2007).

Franke, Volker. *Preparing for Peace: Military Identity, Value Orientation, and Professional Military Education* (Westport: Praeger, 1999).

Franke, Volker. "Resolving Identity Tensions: The Case of the Peacekeeper," *Journal of Conflict Studies* 19, 2 (1999).

Franke, Volker. "The Social Identity of Peacekeeping," in Thomas W. Britt and Amy B. Adler, editors, *The Psychology of the Peacekeeper: Lessons from the Field* (Westport: Praeger, 2003).

Franke, Volker, and Karen Guttieri. "Picking Up the Pieces: Are Officers Ready for Nation Building?" *Journal of Political and Military Sociology* 37, 1 (2009).

Franke, Volker, and Marc von Boemcken. *Attitudes, Values, and Professional Self-Conception of Private Security Contractors in Iraq: An Exploratory Study* (Bonn: Bonn International Center for Conversion, August 2009).

Franke, Volker, and Marc von Boemcken. "Guns for Hire: Motivations and Self-Perception of Private Security Contractors," *Armed Forces and Society* 37, 4 (October 2011).

Frankel, Rafael D. "The Loud Awakening of Israel's Secular Middle Class," *The Atlantic* (8 August 2011), available at http://www.theatlantic.com/international/archive/2011/08/the-loud-awakening-of-israels-secular-middle-class/243263/, accessed 7 August 2015.

Franklin, Sarah. "South African and International Attempts to Regulate Mercenaries and Private Military Companies," *Transnational Law and Contemporary Problems* 17, 2 (Winter 2008).

Fraser, Nancy. "Foucault on Modern Power: Empirical Insights and Normative Confusions," *PRAXIS International* 3 (1981).

Fredland, J. Eric. "Outsourcing Military Force: A Transactions Cost Perspective on the Role of Military Companies," *Defence and Peace Economics* 15, 3 (June 2004).

Friedrichs, Jorg, and Cornelius Friesendorf. "The Mercenary Debate," *American Interest* 4 (May–June 2009), page 48.

Frisk, Daniel, and R. Derek Trunkey. *Contractors' Support of U.S. Operations in Iraq* (Washington: Congressional Budget Office, August 2008).

Fuentes, Gidget. "Officer Gets 6 Years in Iraq Contracting Scheme," *Marine Corps Times* (7 February 2011), available at http://archive.marinecorpstimes.com/article/20110207/NEWS/102070315/Officer-gets-6-years-in-Iraq-contracting-scheme, accessed 1 October 2015.

Fukuyama, Francis. "The Great Disruption," *The Atlantic Monthly* 283, 5 (May 1999).

Gaddis, John Lewis. "Toward the Post–Cold War World," *Foreign Affairs* 70, 2 (Spring 1991).

Gambetta, Diego. "Inscrutable Markets," *Rationality and Society* 6, 3 (July 1994).

Gansler, Jacques S., and William Lucyshyn. "Contractors Supporting Military Operations: Many Challenges Remain," in Christopher Kinsey and Malcolm Patterson, editors, *Contractors and War: The Transformation of United States' Expeditionary Operations* (Palo Alto: Stanford University Press, 2012).

Gansler, Jacques S., David Berteau, David M. Maddox, David R. Oliver Jr., Leon E. Salomon, George T. Singley III, George Sears, Kristi Crear, Karl Ellcessor, Dave Mabee, Jill Stiglich, and Jana Weston. *Urgent Reform Required: Army Expeditionary Contracting.* Report of the Commission on Army Acquisition and Program Management in Expeditionary Operations (Washington: Office of the Assistant Secretary of the Army for Acquisition, Logistics, and Technology, 2007).

Garvin, David A. "Can Industry Self-Regulation Work?" *California Management Review* 25, 4 (Summer 1983).

Gaston, Erica. "Mercenarism 2.0? The Rise of the Modern Private Security Industry and Its Implications for International Humanitarian Law Enforcement," *Harvard International Law Journal* 49, 1 (Winter 2008).

Gates, Robert M. "Strategic and Operational Planning for Operational Contract Support (OCS) and Workforce Mix," memorandum for the secretaries of the military departments et al. (Washington: Office of the Secretary of Defense, 24 January 2011).

Gaul, Matthew J. "Regulating the New Privateers: Private Military Service Contracting and the Modern Marque and Reprisal Clause," *Loyola of Los Angeles Law Review* 31, 4 (June 1998).

George, Edward. *The Cuban Intervention in Angola, 1965–1991: From Che Guevara to Cuito Cuanavale* (London: Frank Cass, 2005).

Gerth, H. H., and C. Wright Mills, translators and editors. *From Max Weber: Essays in Sociology* (New York: Oxford University Press, 1946).

Ghani, Mohammad Ashraf. "Presidential Decree of the President of the Islamic Republic of Afghanistan concerning the Implementation of the Bilateral Security Agreement and NATO Status of Forces Agreement" (31 December 2014), available at http://c.ymcdn.com/sites/stability-operations.site-ym.com/resource/resmgr/Advocacy/Afghan_Government__on_the_Im.pdf, accessed 30 September 2015.

Gillard, Emanuela-Chiara. "Business Goes to War: Private Military/Security Companies and International Humanitarian Law," *International Review of the Red Cross* 38, 863 (2006).

Gilroy, Curtis L., and Cindy Williams, editors. *Service to Country: Personnel Policy and the Transformation of Western Militaries* (Cambridge: MIT Press, 2006).

Gimble, Thomas F. *Testimony of Thomas F. Gimble, "Combatting War Profiteering: Are We Doing Enough to Investigate and Prosecute Contracting Fraud in Iraq?" Hearing before the Committee on the Judiciary, United States Senate* (20 March 2007).

Glaeser, Edward L., and Andrei Schleifer. "The Rise of the Regulatory State," *Journal of Economic Literature* 16, 2 (June 2003).

Glanz, James, and Alissa J. Rubin. "Blackwater Shootings 'Murder,' Iraq Says," *New York Times* (8 October 2007), available at http://www.nytimes.com/2007/10/08/world/middleeast/08blackwater.html?, accessed 14 October 2015.

Gleijeses, Piero. "Moscow's Proxy? Cuba and Africa 1975–1988," *Journal of Cold War Studies* 8, 2 (Spring 2006).

Glenny, Misha. *The Fall of Yugoslavia: The Third Balkan War*, 3rd revised edition (New York: Penguin, 1996).

Gloystein, Henning, and Jonathan Saul. "Germany Wants Armed Guards on Europe Ships as Piracy Costing Billions of Dollar a Year," Reuters (23 August 2011), available at http://www.alarabiya.net/articles/2011/08/23/163755.html, accessed 1 October 2015.

Goffman, Erving. "The Characteristics of Total Institutions," in *Symposium on Preventive and Social Psychiatry, Walter Reed Army Institute of Research, Washington, D.C. 15–17 April 1957* (Washington: Government Printing Office, 1958).
Goffman, Erving. *Presentation of Self in Everyday Life* (Garden City, NY: Anchor, 1959).
Goldberg, Matthew, J. Michael Gilmore, Adebayo Adedeji, Daniel Frisk, Carla Tighe Murray, R. Derek Trunkey, David Newman, Jo Ann Vines, and Frances Lussier. *Logistic Support for Deployed Military Forces* (Washington: Congressional Budget Office, October 2005).
Goldfield, Stephen. *Garrison State: Israel's Role in U.S. Global Strategy* (San Francisco: Palestine Focus Publications, 1985).
Goldman, Emily O., and Richard B. Andres. "Systemic Effects of Military Innovation and Diffusion," *Security Studies* 8, 4 (Summer 1999).
Goodman, Ryan, and Derek Jinks. "How to Influence States: Socialization and International Human Rights Law," *Duke Law Journal* 54, 3 (December 2004).
Gordon, Michael R., and Bernard E. Trainor. *Cobra II: The Inside Story of the Invasion and Occupation of Iraq* (New York: Pantheon Books, 2006).
Grant, Ruth W., and Robert Keohane. "Accountability and Abuses of Power in World Politics," *American Political Science Review* 99, 1 (February 2005).
Greenwald, Robert. "Robert Greenwald's Interview with Doug Brooks," available at http://iraqforsale.org/doug_brooks.php, accessed 17 December 2015.
Greyling, Chris, Doug Brooks, and Andrew Bearpark. "Industry Statement" (30 September 2010), available at http://business-humanrights.org/sites/default/files/media/documents/industry-pmsc-code-30-sep-2010.pdf, accessed 25 September 2015.
Griffiths, Ann, editor. *The Canadian Forces and Interoperability* (Halifax: Centre for Foreign Policy Studies, 2002).
Gross, Neal, Ward S. Mason, and Alexander W. McEachern. *Explorations in Role Analysis* (New York: Wiley, 1958).
Grotius, Hugo. *The Free Sea* (Indianapolis: The Liberty Fund, Inc., 2004).
Guillory, Michael E. "Civilianizing the Force: Is the United States Crossing the Rubicon?" *Air Force Law Review* 51 (2001).
Gumedze, Sabelo. *Addressing the Use of Private Security and Military Companies at the International Level.* ISS Paper 206 (Pretoria: Institute for Security Studies, November 2009), available at http://www.issafrica.org/publications/papers/addressing-the-use-of-private-security-and-military-companies-at-the-international-level, accessed 6 June 2015.
Gumedze, Sabelo. *The Need for an International Code of Conduct for Private Security Actors in Africa* (Pretoria: Institute for Security Studies, 24 February 2012), available at https://www.issafrica.org/iss-today/the-need-for-an-international-code-of-conduct-for-private-security-actors-in-africa, accessed 27 July 2015.
Gumedze, Sabelo. "Pouring Old Wine into New Bottles? The Debate around Mercenaries and Private Military and Security Companies," *Elimination of Mercenarism in Africa: A Need for a New Continental Approach* (Pretoria: International, July 2008).
Gumedze, Sabelo. "To Embrace or Not to Embrace: Addressing the Private Security Industry Phenomenon in Africa," in Sabelo Gumedze, *Private Security in Africa: Manifestation, Challenges and Regulation*. ISS Monograph Series 139 (November 2007).
Gumedze, Sabelo. "Towards the Revisions of the 1977 OAU/AU Convention on the Eliminations of Mercenarism in Africa," *African Security Review* 16, 4 (2007).
Gunningham, Neil, and Joseph Rees. "Industry Self-Regulation: An Institutional Perspective," *Law and Policy* 19, 4 (October 1997).
Gupta, Anil K., and Lawrence J. Lad. "Industry Self-Regulation: An Economic, Organizational, and Political Analysis," *Academy of Management Review* 8, 3 (1983).
Gurría, Angel. "Presentation of the Labour Market and Social Policy Review of Israel: Remarks by Angel Gurría, OECD Secretary-General, at the Roundtable with Israel's Finance Minister Yuval Steinitz. Prime Minister's Office in Jerusalem, 19 January 2010," available at http://www.oecd.org/israel/presentationofthelabourmarketandsocialpolicyreviewofisrael.htm, accessed 15 August 2015.
Gutierrez, Pedro Ruz, and E. A. Torriero. "U.S. Pilots Risk Their Lives in Colombia's Drug War," *Fort Lauderdale Sun Sentinel* (19 September 2000), available at http://articles.sun-

sentinel.com/2000-09-19/news/0009190123_1_pilot-error-daredevil-pilots-colombia/2, accessed 19 October 2015.

Guzman, Andrew T., and Timothy L. Meyer, "International Soft Law," *Journal of Legal Analysis* 2, 1 (Spring 2010).

Hacket, John. *The Profession of Arms* (London: Times Publishing Company, 1963).

Halberstam, David. *War in a Time of Peace: Bush, Clinton, and the Generals* (New York: Scribner, 2001).

Haltiner, Karl W. "Athens versus Sparta: The New Missions and the Future of Military Education in Europe," in Harry Kirkels, Wim Klinkert, and Rene Moelker, editors, *NL ARMS: Netherlands Annual Review of Military Studies* (Breda: Netherlands Defence Academy, 2003).

Haltiner, Karl W., and Tibor Szvircsev Tresch. "New Trends in Civil-Military Relations: The Decline of Conscription in Europe," in Alise Weibull and Abrahamsson Bengt, editors, *The Heritage and the Present: From Invasion Defence to Mission Oriented Organization* (Karlstad: Digitaltryck, 2008).

Hammer, Anders Sømme. *The Control of Private Security Companies: A Study of the Relationship between the United States and Private Actors in Plan Colombia*, master's thesis (Oslo: University of Oslo, May 2006).

Hammes, T. X. "Private Contractors in Conflict Zones: The Good, the Bad, and the Strategic Impact," *Strategic Forum* 260 (November 2010).

Hanieh, Adam. "From State-Led Growth to Globalization: The Evolution of Israeli Capitalism," *Journal of Palestine Studies* 32, 4 (Summer 2003).

Harding, Jeremy. "The Mercenary Business: 'Executive Outcomes,'" *Review of African Political Economy* 24, 71 (March 1997).

Harel, Amos. "Discarding Their Uniform Thought," *Ha'aretz* (6 August 2004).

Harel, Amos. "IDF Facing Shortage of New Soldiers," *Ha'aretz* (24 February 2012).

Harel, Amos. "More than Half of Israel's Security Cabinet Wants Say in Defense Budget," *Ha'aretz* (27 July 2015).

"Harper Goes Prorogue," *The Economist* (7 January 2010).

Harte, Julia. "U.S. Military Personnel Have Been Convicted of $50 Million Worth of Crimes in Iraq and Afghanistan," Center for Public Integrity website (5 May 2015), available at http://www.publicintegrity.org/2015/05/05/17268/us-military-personnel-have-been-convicted-50-million-worth-crimes-iraq-and, accessed 1 October 2015.

Hartley, Keith. "The All-Volunteer Force: An Economic Perspective," in Gwyn Harries-Jenkins, editor, *Recruitment to the All-Volunteer Force* (Fort Belvoir: US Army Institute for the Behavioral and Social Sciences, March 2001).

Haslam, S. Alexander, Penelope J. Oakes, John C. Turner, and Craig McGarty. "Social Categorization and Group Homogeneity: Changes in the Perceived Applicability of Stereotype Content as a Function of Comparative Context and Trait Favourableness," *British Journal of Social Psychology* 34, 2 (June 1995).

Haufler, Virginia. *A Public Role for the Private Sector* (Washington: The Carnegie Endowment for International Peace, 2013).

Hedgpeth, Dana. "State Department to Renew Deal with Blackwater for Iraq Security," *Washington Post* (5 April 2008), available at http://www.washingtonpost.com/wp-dyn/content/article/2008/04/04/AR2008040403449.html, accessed 14 October 2015.

Heimer, Franz-Wilhelm. *The Decolonization Conflict in Angola, 1974–76: An Essay in Political Sociology* (Geneva: Institut Universitaire de Hautes Études Internationales, 1979).

Heinecken, Lindy. "Discontent within the Ranks? Officers' Attitudes toward Military Employment and Representation—A Four-Country Comparative Study," *Armed Forces and Society* 35, 3 (April 2009).

Heinecken, Lindy. "Outsourcing Public Security: The Unforeseen Consequences for the Military Profession," *Armed Forces and Society* 40, 4 (October 2014).

Hendershot, Chris. "The Commercial Military and Security Services Industry: A Canadian Consideration?" in Rosalind Warner, editor, *Unsettled Balance: Ethics, Security, and Canada's International Relations* (Vancouver: University of British Columbia Press, 2015).

Henderson, Christian. "Non-state Actors and the Use of Force," in Math Noortmann, August Reinisch, and Cedric Ryngaert, editors, *Non-state Actors in International Law: Studies in International Law* (Oxford: Hart Publishing, 2015).

Henig, Jeffrey R., Chris Hamnett, and Harvey B. Feigenbaum. "The Politics of Privatization: A Comparative Perspective," *Governance* 4, 1 (October 1988).

Hermann, Tamar, Ella Heller, Chanan Cohen, Gilad Be'ery, and Yuval Lebel. *The Israeli Democracy Index 2014* (Jerusalem: The Israel Democracy Institute, 2014).

Herspring, Dale R. *The Pentagon and the Presidency: Civil-Military Relations from FDR to George W. Bush* (Lawrence: University Press of Kansas, 2005).

Higginson, Andrew. "Contractor Support to Operations (CSO): Proactive or Reactive Support?" *RUSI Defence Systems* (2010).

Hill, J. L. "The Five Faces of Freedom in American Political and Constitutional Thought," *Boston College Law Review* 45, 3 (2004).

Hodge, Nathan. "Army for Hire," *Slate* (31 August 2006), available at http://www.slate.com/articles/news_and_politics/foreigners/2006/08/army_for_hire.html, accessed 6 June 2015.

Hodge, Nathan. "Panel's War-Waste Records Sealed as Work Ends," *Wall Street Journal* (30 September 2011), available at http://www.wsj.com/articles/SB10001424052970204226204576603060868379444, accessed 1 October 2015.

Hodge, Nathan. "Study Finds Extensive Waste in War Contracting," *Wall Street Journal* (1 September 2011), available at http://www.wsj.com/articles/SB10001424053111904716604576542703010051380, accessed 19 July 2015.

Hoe, Alan. *David Stirling: A Biography* (London: Warner Books, 1996).

Hoffman, Frank G. "Neo-classical Counterinsurgency?" *Parameters* 37, 2 (Summer 2007).

Hoffman, Michael H. "Terrorists Are Unlawful Belligerents, Not Unlawful Combatants: A Distinction with Implications for the Future of International Humanitarian Law," *Case Western Reserve Journal of International Law* 34, 2 (2002).

Hofman, John E. "Social Identity and Intergroup Conflict: An Israeli View," in Wolfgang Stroebe, Arie W. Kruglanski, Daniel Bar-Tal, and Miles Hewstone, editors, *The Social Psychology of Intergroup Conflict: Theory, Research and Applications* (Berlin, Heidelberg, and New York: Springer Verlag, 1988).

Hofstede, Geert H. *Culture's Consequence: International Differences in Work-Related Values* (Beverly Hills: Sage, 1980).

Hogg, Michael A. "Intergroup Processes, Groups Structure and Social Identity," in W. P. Robinson, editor, *Social Groups and Identities: Developing the Legacy of Henri Tajfel* (Oxford: Butterworth-Heinemann, 1996).

Hogg, Michael A. "Social Categorization, Depersonalization, and Group Behavior," in Michael A. Hogg and R. Scott Tindale, editors, *Blackwell Handbook of Social Psychology: Group Processes* (Malden: Blackwell Publishers, 2002).

Hogg, Michael A. "Social Identity Theory," in Peter J. Burke, editor, *Contemporary Social Psychological Theory* (Palo Alto: Stanford University Press, 2006).

Hogg, Michael A. *The Social Psychology of Group Cohesiveness: From Attraction to Social Identity* (Washington Square: New York University Press, 1992).

Hogg, Michael A., and Dominic Abrams. *Social Identifications: A Social Psychology of Intergroup Relations and Group Processes* (London and New York: Routledge, 1988).

Holbrooke, Richard. *To End a War* (New York: Random House, 1998).

Holmqvist, Caroline. *Private Security Companies: The Case for Regulation.* SIPRI Policy Paper 9 (Stockholm: Stockholm International Peace Research Institute, January 2005).

Honig, Jan Willem, and Norbert Both. *Srebrenica: Record of a War Crime* (New York: Penguin, 1997).

Horowitz, Dan. "Is Israel a Garrison State?" *Jerusalem Quarterly* 4 (1977).

Horwitz, Joshua, and Casey Anderson. "Taking Gun Rights Seriously: The Insurrectionist Idea and Its Consequences," *Albany Government Law Review* 1, 2 (2008).

Horwitz, Sari. "New Charges Brought against Former Blackwater Guards in Baghdad Shooting," *Washington Post* (17 October 2013).

Hosenball, Mark. "Two Americans Killed in Attack on CIA Base Worked for Xe—Formerly Blackwater." *Newsweek* (6 January 2010).

Houreld, Katharine. "Security Firms Join Somali Piracy Fight," *San Francisco Chronicle* (26 October 2008).

Howe, Herbert M. "Private Security Forces and African Stability: The Case of Executive Outcomes," *Journal of Modern African Studies* 36, 2 (June 1998).

Hsu, Spencer S., and Victoria St. Martin. "Four Blackwater Guards Sentenced in Iraq Shootings of 31 Unarmed Civilians," *Washington Post* (13 April 2015), available at http://www.washingtonpost.com/local/crime/four-blackwater-guards-sentenced-in-iraq-shootings-of-31-unarmed-civilians/2015/04/13/55b777e0-dee4-11e4-be40-566e2653afe5_story.html, accessed 9 July 2015.

Hsu, Spencer S., Victoria St. Martin, and Keith L. Alexander. "Four Blackwater Guards Found Guilty in 2007 Iraq Shootings of 31 Unarmed Civilians," *Washington Post* (22 October 2014), available at https://www.washingtonpost.com/world/national-security/verdict-expected-in-blackwater-shooting-case/2014/10/22/5a488258-59fc-11e4-bd61-346aee66ba29_story.html, accessed 11 August 2015.

Human Rights Council. *Annual Report of the Working Group on the Use of Mercenaries as a Means of Violating Human Rights and Impeding the Exercise of the Right of Peoples to Self-Determination.* A/HRC/15/25 (New York: United Nations Office of the High Commissioner for Human Rights, 2 July 2010).

Human Rights First. *How to End Impunity for Private Security and Other Contractors* (Washington: Human Rights First, December 2008).

Human Rights First. *Private Security Contractors at War: Ending the Culture of Impunity* (New York: Human Rights First, 2008).

Huntington, Samuel P. "The Marasmus of the ICC: The Commission, the Railroads, and the Public Interest," *Yale Law Review* 61, 467 (April 1952).

Huntington, Samuel P. "Power, Expertise, and the Military Profession," *Daedalus* 92 (Fall 1963).

Huntington, Samuel P. "Reforming Civil-Military Relations," *Journal of Democracy* 6, 4 (1995).

Huntington, Samuel P. *The Soldier and the State: The Theory and Politics of Civil-Military Relations* (Cambridge: Belknap Press of Harvard University Press, 1957).

Hutson, Terry. "Piracy: BIMCO to Prepare Armed Guards on Ships Contract," *Ports and Ships Maritime News* (23 November 2011), available at http://www.ports.co.za/news/news_2011_11_23_01.php, accessed 14 October 2015.

Hutton, John. *Contingency Contracting: DOD, State, and USAID Contracts and Contractor Personnel in Iraq and Afghanistan.* GAO Report 09-19 (Washington: Government Accountability Office, 1 October 2008).

Hutton, John P. *Contingency Contracting: Further Improvement Need in Agency Tracking of Contractor Personnel and Contracts in Iraq and Afghanistan. Statement before the Commission on Wartime Contracting in Iraq and Afghanistan.* GAO-10-187 (Washington: Government Accountability Office, 2 November 2009).

Ikenberry, G. John. "The Myth of Post–Cold War Chaos," *Foreign Affairs* 75, 3 (May/June 1996).

"IMO Approves Further Interim Guidance on Privately Contracted Armed Security Personnel," intersessional meeting of the Maritime Security and Piracy Working Group of the Maritime Safety Committee, 13–15 September 2011, briefing 47 (16 September 2011), available at http://www.imo.org/mediacentre/pressbriefings/pages/47-piracyguidance.aspx, accessed 12 December 2011.

Institute for International Law and Justice, New York University School of Law. "Chairman's Notes from the Greentree Workshop on Regulation of Private Military and Security Companies, 22–24 March 2007 ('Greentree Notes')," available at http://www.iilj.org/research/GreentreeNotes.asp, accessed 5 June 2014.

International Association of Peacekeeping Training Centres. "IAPTC Membership," International Association of Peacekeeping Training Centres website, available at http://www.iaptc.org/iaptc-membership/, accessed 10 December 2015.

International Code of Conduct Association. *Articles of Association of the International Code of Conduct Association* (Geneva, 2013), available at http://www.icoca.ch/en/articles_of_association.

International Code of Conduct Association. *The International Code of Conduct for Private Security Service Providers* (Geneva: International Code of Conduct Association, 2010), available at http://icoc-psp.org/.

International Code of Conduct Association. "Membership," available at http://icoca.ch/en/membership?private_security_companies=companies&op=Search&view_type=list&form_id=_search_for_members_filter_form, accessed 18 December 2015.

International Code of Conduct for Private Security Service Providers' Association. International Code of Conduct Association website, available at http://www.icoca.ch/, accessed 23 March 2015.

International Committee of the Red Cross. "The Fundamental Principles of the Red Cross and Red Crescent" (Geneva: International Committee of the Red Cross, 31 October 1986), available at https://www.icrc.org/eng/resources/documents/red-cross-crescent-movement/fundamental-principles-movement-1986-10-31.htm, accessed 17 December 2015.

International Committee of the Red Cross. "Interpretative Guidance on the Notion of Direct Participation in Hostilities under International Humanitarian Law" (2009), available at http://www.icrc.org/Web/eng/siteeng0.nsf/htmlall/direct-participation-report_res/$File/direct-participation-guidance-2009-icrc.pdf, accessed 13 March 2010.

International Committee of the Red Cross. "Summary: International Convention against the Recruitment, Use, Financing and Training of Mercenaries, 4 December 1989," available at https://www.icrc.org/ihl/INTRO/530?OpenDocument, accessed 5 September 2015.

International Convention against the Recruitment, Use, Financing and Training of Mercenaries, General Assembly Resolution 44/34. UN Document A/RES/44/34, Article 1 (4 December 1989).

International Law Association, "Statement of Principles Applicable to the Formation of General Customary International Law," adopted by Resolution No. 16/2000, London Conference (2000), section 1(i).

International Peace Operations Association. "IPOA Endorsement of H.R. 2740, 'MEJA Expansion and Enforcement Act of 2007,'" press release (2 October 2007).

International Peace Operations Association. "IPOA Press Release on Blackwater USA" (5 October 2007), available at: http://ipoaworld.org/eng/press/132-20071005blackwaterusa.html.

International Stability Operations Association. "About Us," *International Stability Operations Association* website (no date), available at http://www.stability-operations.org/?page=About, accessed 16 August 2015, 18 December 2015.

International Stability Operations Association. "Advocacy Initiatives" (no date), available at http://www.stability-operations.org/?page=Advocacy, accessed 31 July 2015.

International Stability Operations Association. "Committees and Working Groups" (no date), available at http://www.stability-operations.org/?page=Committees, accessed 31 July 2015.

International Stability Operations Association. "History of ISOA" (no date), available at http://www.stability-operations.org/?page=History, accessed 31 July 2015.

International Stability Operations Association. "How to Submit a Standards Complaint" (no date), available at http://www.stability-operations.org/?page=Standards_Complaint, accessed 24 September 2015.

International Stability Operations Association. "ISOA Code of Conduct" (no date), available at http://www.stability-operations.org/?page=Code, accessed 23 March 2015, 31 July 2015.

International Stability Operations Association. "ISOA Code of Conduct Version 13" (20 October 2011), available at http://www.stability-operations.org/?page=Code, accessed 16 August 2015.

International Stability Operations Association. "Our Work" (no date), available at http://www.stability-operations.org/?page=Work, accessed 31 July 2015.

Iraq Coalition Casualty Count. "Iraq Coalition Casualties: Contractors—A Partial List," available at http://icasualties.org/Iraq/Contractors.aspx, accessed 16 December 2015.

Ireland, Jason, and Caroline Varin. "PMSCs and the Regulatory Environment in Iraq Post-2011," *Central European Journal of International Security Studies* 9, 1 (March 2015), available at http://static.cejiss.org/data/uploaded/1425974229319946/Article%2001.pdf, accessed 19 July 2015.

Isenberg, David. "MPRI Couldn't Read Minds: Let's Sue Them," *Huffington Post* (19 August 2010).

Isenberg, David. "Predator Military Contractors: Privatizing the Drones," *Huffington Post* (18 December 2012), available at http://www.huffingtonpost.com/david-isenberg/contractors-privatizing-the-drones_b_1976650.html, accessed 6 August 2015.

Isenberg, David. *Shadow Force: Private Security Contractors in Iraq* (Washington: Cato Institute, 16 February 2009), available at http://www.cato.org/pub_display.php?pub_id=9979, accessed 3 April 2010.

Isenberg, David. *Shadow Force: Private Security Contractors in Iraq* (Westport: Praeger, 2009).

Isenberg, David. *Soldiers of Fortune Ltd.: A Profile of Today's Private Sector Corporate Mercenary Firms* (Washington: Center for Defense Information, November 1997).

Israeli Defense Forces. "IDF to Follow McKinsey and Co.'s Recommendations for Efficiency" (25 November 2009), available at http://www.idf.il/1283-11888-en/Dover.aspx, accessed 15 August 2015.

Ivie, Tanner. "Standards Committee Holds Landmark Simulation," *Journal of International Peace Operations* 2, 1 (2006).

Jacobs, Philip C. "South Africa's New Counter-Mercenary Law," *Strategic Review for Southern Africa* 30, 1 (May 2008).

Jäger, Thomas, and Gerhard Kümmel, editors. *Private Military and Security Companies: Chances, Problems, Pitfalls and Prospects* (Wiesbaden: VS Verlag für Sozialwissenschaften, 2007).

Jakobsen, Peter Viggo. "Myth-Making and Germany's Unilateral Recognition of Croatia and Slovenia," *European Security* 4, 3 (Autumn 1995).

James, W. Martin, III. *A Political History of the Civil War in Angola: 1974–1990* (New Brunswick: Transaction Publishers, 2011).

Janowitz, Morris. "Military Elites and the Study of War," *Conflict Resolution* 1, 1 (March 1957).

Janowitz, Morris. *The Professional Soldier: A Social and Political Portrait* (New York: The Free Press, 1960).

Jennings, Kathleen M. *Armed Services: Regulating the Private Military Industry.* Fafo Report 532 (Oslo: Fafo, 2006).

Joenniemi, Perti, editor. *The Changing Face of European Conscription* (Aldershot: Ashgate, 2006).

Johnson, David, and John M. Broder. "FBI Says Guards Killed 14 Iraqis without Cause," *New York Times* (14 November 2007).

Johnson, David E. *Hard Fighting: Israel in Lebanon and Gaza* (Santa Monica: RAND Corporation, 2011).

Johnston, Les. "Transnational Private Policing: The Impact of Global Commercial Security," in J. W. E. Sheptycki, editor, *Issues in Transnational Policing* (London: Routledge, 2000).

Joint Publication 4-0: Doctrine for Logistic Support of Joint Operations (Washington: Joint Chiefs of Staff, 6 April 2000).

Jones, Clive. *Britain and the Yemen Civil War* (Brighton: Sussex Academic Press, 2004).

Joseph, Nathan, and Nicholas Alex. "The Uniform: A Sociological Perspective," *American Journal of Sociology* 77, 4 (January 1972).

Joubert, Marie Sophie. "Private Security Firms Benefit from Piracy," *France 24* (30 November 2008), available at http://www.france24.com/en/20081130-private-security-firms-benefit-piracy-somalia-military-blackwater, accessed 5 May 2010.

Juma, Laurence. "Privatisation, Human Rights and Security: Reflections on the Draft International Convention on Regulation, Oversight and Monitoring of Private Military and Security Companies," *Law, Democracy and Development* 15 (2011).

Juster, Kenneth I. "Discussant," in Meena Bose and Rosanna Perotti, editors, *From Cold War to New World Order: The Foreign Policy of George H. W. Bush* (Westport: Greenwood Press, 2002).

Kahneman, Daniel, Paul Slovic, and Amos Tversky, editors. *Judgment under Uncertainty: Heuristics and Biases* (Cambridge: Cambridge University Press, 1982).

Kaunda v The President of the Republic of South Africa 2005 (3) South Africa 235 (CC) Chaskalson CJ, paragraphs 38–40.

Kavanagh, Dennis. *Thatcherism and British Politics: The End of Consensus?* (Oxford: Oxford University Press, 1990).

Keen, David. *Conflict and Collusion in Sierra Leone* (London and New York: James Currey Publishers, 2005).

Kell, John. "Ex-Army Employee Pleads Guilty to Taking Bribes," *MarketWatch* (19 September 2011), available at http://www.marketwatch.com/story/ex-army-employee-pleads-guilty-to-taking-bribes-2011-09-19, accessed 1 October 2015.

Kelley, Matt. "Army May Ban Security Firm from Contracts," *USA Today* (11 November 2007).

Kelty, Ryan. "Citizen Soldiers and Civilian Contractors: Soldiers' Unit Cohesion and Retention Attitudes in the 'Total Force,'" *Journal of Political and Military Sociology* 37, 2 (Winter 2009).

Kelty, Ryan. "The Navy's Maiden Voyage: Effects of Integrating Sailors and Civilian Mariners on Deployment," *Armed Forces and Society* 34, 4 (Summer 2008).

Kelty, Ryan, and Alex Bierman. "Ambivalence on the Front Lines: Perceptions of Contractors in Iraq and Afghanistan," *Armed Forces and Society* 39, 1 (January 2013).

Kelty, Ryan, and David R. Segal. "The Civilianization of the U.S. Military: Army and Navy Case Studies of the Effects of Civilian Integration on Military Personnel," in Thomas Jäger and Gerhard Kümmel, editors, *Private Military and Security Companies: Chances, Problems, Pitfalls, and Prospects* (Wiesbaden: VS Verlag für Sozialwissenschaften, 2007).

Kelty, Ryan, and Irving Smith. "Racial, Ethnic and Gender Differences in Soldiers' Attitudes toward Civilian Contractors," poster presented at the Defense Equal Opportunity Management Institute's Sixth Biennial EO/EEO Research Symposium, Cocoa Beach, Florida (January 2007).

Kemp, Kenneth W., and Charles Hudin. "Civil Supremacy over the Military: Its Nature and Limits," *Armed Forces and Society* 19, 1 (Fall 1992).

Kennedy, James F., Daniel T. Holt, Mark A. Ward, and Michael T. Rehg. "The Influence of Outsourcing on Job Satisfaction and Turnover Intentions of Technical Managers," *Human Resource Planning* 25, 1 (March 2002).

Kennedy, Robert G. "Why Military Officers Must Have Training in Ethics," *International Society for Military Ethics* (2000).

Keohane, Robert O., and Joseph S. Nye Jr. *Power and Interdependence* (New York: Longman Publishing Group, 2001).

Kidane, Won. "The Status of Private Military Contractors under International Humanitarian Law," *Denver Journal of International Law and Policy* 38, 3 (Summer 2010).

Kilcullen, David. *Counterinsurgency* (New York: Oxford University Press, 2010).

Kimmerling, Baruch. "Patterns of Militarism in Israel," *European Journal of Sociology* 34, 2 (November 1993).

King, Andrew A., and Michael J. Lenox. "Industry Self-Regulation without Sanctions: The Chemical Industry's Responsible Care Program," *Academic Management Journal* 43, 4 (2000).

King, Andrew A., Michael J. Lenox, and Michael L. Barnett. "Strategic Responses to the Reputation Commons Problem," in Andrew J. Hoffman and Marc J. Ventresca, editors, *Organizations, Policy and the Natural Environment: Institutional and Strategic Perspectives* (Palo Alto: Stanford University Press, 2001).

Kingsbury, Benedict, Nico Krisch, and Richard B. Stewart. "The Emergence of Global Administrative Law," *Law and Contemporary Problems* 68, 3/4 (Summer/Autumn 2005).

Kinsey, Christopher. *Corporate Soldiers and International Security: The Rise of Private Military Companies* (London: Routledge, 2006).

Kinsey, Christopher. "International Law and the Control of Mercenaries and Private Military Companies," *Cultures and Conflits* 52 (2004), available at http://conflits.revues.org/11502, accessed 23 September 2015.
Kinsey, Christopher. *Private Contractors and the Reconstruction of Iraq: Transforming Military Logistics* (London: Routledge, 2009).
Kinsey, Christopher. "Private Security Companies and Corporate Social Responsibility," in Andrew Alexandria, Deane-Peter Baker, and Marina Caparini, editors, *Private Military and Security Companies: Ethics, Policies and Civil-Military Relations* (Abingdon, UK: Routledge, 2008).
Kinsey, Christopher. "Regulation and Control of Private Military Companies: The Legislative Dimension," *Contemporary Security Policy* 26, 1 (April 2005).
Kinsey, Christopher. "Transforming Supplying War: Considerations and Rationales behind Contractor Support to Future UK Overseas Military Operations in the 21st Century," *International Journal* 69, 4 (December 2014).
Kissinger, Henry A. *Does America Need a Foreign Policy? Toward a Diplomacy for the 21st Century* (New York: Simon & Schuster, 2001).
Klasfeld, Adam. "Army Captain Gets Three Years for Taking Bribes," *Courthouse News* (17 August 2011), available at http://www.courthousenews.com/2011/08/17/39061.htm, accessed 1 October 2015.
Klein, Yael. "Defense Minister Ya'alon: 'The Locker Commission Report Is Superficial and Unbalanced,'" *JerusalemOnline.com* (21 July 2015), available at http://www.jerusalemonline.com/news/politics-and-military/politics/israeli-defense-minister-condemns-locker-commission-report-14763, accessed 8 August 2015.
Klein, Zeev. "Central Bureau of Statistics: The Second Lebanon War Will Cut Israel's GDP in 2006 by 0.7%, or NIS 5 billion," *Globes* (20 September 2006).
Kolko, Gabriel. *Railroads and Regulation 1877–1916* (New York: W. W. Norton & Company, 1970).
Kolko, Gabriel. *The Triumph of Conservatism: A Reinterpretation of American History, 1900–1916* (New York: The Free Press, 1963).
Korsk, Noa. "Tel Aviv and Netanya Security Systems Will Pay Tens of Millions for Construction of Luxury Towers," *Ha'aretz* (16 May 2010), available in Hebrew at http://www.haaretz.co.il/hasite/spages/1169088.html, accessed 8 August 2015.
Kourvetaris, George A., and Betty A. Dobratz. "Social Recruitment and Political Orientations of the Officer Corps in a Comparative Perspective," *Pacific Sociological Review* (1973).
Krahmann, Elke. "Conceptualizing Security Governance," *Cooperation and Conflict* 38, 1 (March 2003).
Krahmann, Elke. *States, Citizens and the Privatization of Security* (Cambridge: Cambridge University Press, 2010).
Kraska, James. *Contemporary Maritime Piracy: International Law, Strategy, and Diplomacy at Sea* (Santa Barbara: Praeger, 2011).
Krasner, Stephen D. *Sovereignty: Organized Hypocrisy* (Princeton: Princeton University Press, 1999).
Kruck, Andreas. "Theorising the Use of Private Military Security Companies: A Synthetic Perspective," *Journal of International Relations and Development* 17, 1 (January 2014).
Kümmel, Gerhard. "Die Privatisierung der Sicherheit: Fluch oder Segen? Postheroische Gesellschaft, Überlasteter Staat und Private Sicherheits—und Militärunternehmen," *SOWI Arbeitspapier* 137 (Potsdam: Sozialwissenschaftliches Institut der Bundeswehr, October 2004).
Kyzer, Liel. "Israel Set to Become OECD's Poorest Member," *Ha'aretz* (20 January 2010).
Lahav, Avital. "Locker Committee Recommends Freezing Defense Budget for Five Years," *ynetnews.com* (21 July 2015), available at http://www.ynetnews.com/articles/0,7340,L-4682560,00.html, accessed 8 August 2015.
Lang, Kurt. *Military Institutions and the Sociology of War: A Review of the Literature with Annotated Bibliography* (Beverly Hills: Sage, 1972).
Lappin, Yaakov, and Yonah Jeremy Bob. "Locker Commission Calls for Massive IDF Budget Cuts Across-the-Board," *Jerusalem Post* (21 July 2015).

Lasswell, Harold D. *Essays on the Garrison State* (New Brunswick: Transaction Publishers, 1997).

Lasswell, Harold D. "The Garrison State," *American Journal of Sociology* 46, 4 (January 1941).

The Law of Armed Conflict: Basic Knowledge (Geneva: International Committee of the Red Cross, June 2002).

Law Society of South Africa. "Before the Parliamentary Portfolio Committee on Home Affairs. Re: Submissions by the Law Society of South Africa in Re: SA Citizenship Amendment Bill 2010" (no date), available at http://pmg-assets.s3-website-eu-west-1.amazonaws.com/docs/100817pchomelssa_0.pdf, accessed 13 August 2015.

Leander, Anna. *Eroding State Authority? Private Military Companies and the Legitimate Use of Force* (Rome: Centro Militare di Studi Strategici, 2006).

Leander, Anna. "Existing International Instruments and Mechanisms," paper presented at the Latin America and Caribbean Regional Consultation on the Effects of the Activities of Private Military and Security Companies on the Enjoyment of Human Rights: Regulation and Oversight. Organized by the UN Working Group on the Use of Mercenaries/Special Procedures assumed by the Office of the High Commissioner for Human Rights, Panama (17–18 December 2007), available at http://openarchive.cbs.dk/bitstream/handle/10398/6992/wp%202007-4.pdf?sequence=, accessed 23 September 2015.

Leander, Anna. "The Market for Force and Public Security: The Destabilizing Consequences of Private Military Companies," *Journal of Peace Research* 42, 5 (September 2005).

Leander, Anna. "The Paradoxical Impunity of Private Military Companies: Authority and the Limits to Legal Accountability," *Security Dialogue* 41, 5 (October 2010).

Leander, Anna, and Rens van Munster. "Private Security Contractors in Darfur: Reflecting and Reinforcing Neo-liberal Governmentality," *International Relations* 21, 2 (June 2007).

Lee, David. "Army Major Took 'Gratuities' in Iraq," *Courthouse News* (10 April 2012), available at http://www.courthousenews.com/2012/04/10/45466.htm, accessed 1 October 2015.

Lehnardt, Chia. "Peacekeeping," in Simon Chesterman and Angelina Fisher, editors, *Private Security, Public Order* (New York: Oxford University Press, 2009).

Leigh Day & Co. Judicial Review Letter, 18 February 2008.

Lenox, Michael J., and Jennifer Nash. "Industry Self-Regulation and Adverse Selection: A Comparison across Four Trade Association Programs," *Business Strategy and the Environment* 12, 6 (November/December 2003).

Le Roux, Len. "South African Mercenary Legislation Enacted," Institute for Security Studies website (21 January 2008), available at https://www.issafrica.org/topics/peacekeeping-and-conflict-management/21-jan-2008-iss-today-south-african-mercenary-legislation-enacted, accessed 10 July 2015.

Lett, Dan. "Practicalities of Pirate Prosecution Raises Questions," *Winnipeg Free Press* (22 May 2009), available at http://www.winnipegfreepress.com/breakingnews/Prosecution-of-pirates--45858172.html, accessed 1 October 2015.

Levi-Faur, David. "Regulation," in George Thomas Kurian, editor in chief, *The Encyclopedia of Political Science*, volume 5: *R–Z* (Washington: CQ Press, 2011).

Levy, Yagil. "Military-Society Relations: The Demise of the 'People's Army,'" in Guy Ben-Porat, Yagil Levy, Schlomo Mizrahi, Ayre Naor, and Erez Tzfadia, editors, *Israel since 1980* (Cambridge: Cambridge University Press, 2008).

Levi, Yagil, and Shlomo Mizrahi. "Alternative Politics and the Transformation of Society-Military Relations: The Israeli Experience," *Administration and Society* 40, 1 (March 2008).

Lifshitz, Yaacov. *The Economics of Producing Defense: Illustrated by the Israeli Case* (Dordrecht: Kluwer, 2003).

Light, Paul C. *The True Size of Government* (Washington: Brookings Institution Press, 1999).

Linz, Juan J., and Alfred Stepan. *Problems of Democratic Transition and Consolidation: Southern Europe, South America, and Post-Communist Europe* (Baltimore: Johns Hopkins University Press, 1996).

Lis, Jonathan. "To Craft Defense Budget, Netanyahu to Compare Panel's Report with Military's Plan," *Ha'aretz* (28 July 2015).

Lobo-Guerrero, Luis. *Insuring Security: Biopolitics, Security and Risk* (London: Routledge, 2010).

Londoño, Ernesto. "Two U.S. Soldiers Killed as Iraqi Council Member Opens Fire after Meeting," *Washington Post* (24 June 2008).

Londregan, John B., and Keith T. Poole. "Poverty, the Coup Trap, and the Seizure of Executive Power," *World Politics* 42, 2 (January 1990).

Lovell, John P. "Professionalism and the Service Academies," *American Behavioral Scientist* 19, 5 (May/June 1976).

Luckey, John R., Valerie Bailey Grasso, and Kate M. Manuel. *Inherently Governmental Functions and Department of Defense Operations: Background, Issues, and Options for Congress*. R40641 (Washington: Congressional Research Service, 15 June 2009).

Lure, Jason M. "How a Contractor Cashed In on Iraq," *Legal Times* (4 March 2005).

Lytton, Christopher H. "Blood for Hire: How the War in Iraq Has Reinvented the World's Second Oldest Profession," *Oregon Review of International Law* 8 (Summer 2006).

Macagnone, Michael. "DOD IG Finds Oversight of Contract Deficiencies Falls Short," Law360 (2 October 2015), available at http://www.law360.com/articles/710093/dod-ig-finds-oversight-of-contract-deficiencies-falls-short, accessed 25 November 2015.

Maclachlan, Karolina, and Hilary Hurd. "How Corruption Undermines NATO Operations," *Defense One* (2 December 2015), available at http://www.defenseone.com/ideas/2015/12/how-corruption-undermines-nato-operations/124148/, accessed 3 December 2015.

Majone, Giandomenico. "The Rise of the Regulatory State in Europe," *West European Politics* 17, 3 (1994).

Makhubu, Ntando. "Five DRC 'Rebels' Freed," *IOL News* (21 February 2015), available at http://www.iol.co.za/news/crime-courts/five-drc-rebels-freed-1.1821749#.VXSiA8-qqko, accessed 5 June 2015.

Malan, Mark, and Jakkie Cilliers. "Mercenaries and Mischief: The Regulation of Foreign Military Assistance Bill." Occasional Paper 25 (Pretoria: Institute for Security Studies, September 1997).

Manby, Bronwyn. *Citizenship Law in Africa: A Comparative Study*, 2nd edition (New York: Open Society Foundations, 2010).

Mancini, Marina, Faustin Ntoubandi, and Thilo Marauhn. "Old Concepts and New Challenges: Are Private Contractors the Mercenaries of the Twenty-first Century?" in Francesco Francioni and Natalino Ronzotti, editors, *War by Contract: Human Rights, Humanitarian Law and Private Contractors* (Oxford: Oxford University Press, 2011).

Mandel, Robert. *Armies without States: The Privatization of Security* (Boulder: Lynne Rienner Publishers, 2002).

Mandel, Robert. "Fighting Fire with Fire: Privatizing Counterterrorism," in Russell D. Howard and Reid L. Sawyer, editors, *Defeating Terrorism: Shaping the New Security Environment* (Guilford: McGraw-Hill/Dushkin, 2004).

Mannheim, Karl. "Conservative Thought," in Kurt H. Wolff, editor, *From Karl Mannheim* (New York: Oxford University Press, 1971).

Manuel, Kate M., and Jack Maskell. *Insourcing Functions Performed by Federal Contractors: Legal Issues*. R41810 (Washington: Congressional Research Service, 22 February 2013).

Marley, David F. *Modern Piracy: A Reference Handbook* (Santa Barbara: ABC-CLIO, 2010).

Martin, Gary. "A Safe Pair of Hands," *The Phrase Finder*, available at http://www.phrases.org.uk/meanings/309350.html, accessed 9 August 2015.

Masland, John W., and Laurence I. Radway. *Soldiers and Scholars: Military Education and National Policy* (Princeton: Princeton University Press, 1957).

Mason, R. Chuck. *Testimony to the US House of Representatives Committee on Foreign Affairs: Subcommittee on International Organizations, Human Rights and Oversight. Status of Forces Agreements and UN Mandates: What Authorities and Protections Do They Provide to US Personnel* (Washington: Congressional Research Service, 28 February 2007).

Mathieu, Fabien, and Nick Dearden. "Corporate Mercenaries: The Threat of Private Military and Security Companies," *Review of African Political Economy* 34, 114 (December 2007).

Mayeda, Andrew. "Canadian Quietly Writes Humanitarian Law into Afghan Security Contracts," *Montreal Gazette* (27 May 2008).

Mayeda, Andrew, and Mike Blanchfield. "Private Firms Rush to Fill Security Vacuum in Afghanistan," *Ottawa Citizen* (22 November 2007).

Mayer, Don. "Peaceful Warriors: Private Military Security Companies and the Quest for Stable Societies," *Journal of Business Ethics* 89, supplement 4 (2009).

McAllister, Ian, and Hugh Smith. "Selecting the Guardians: Recruitment and Military Values in the Australian Corps," *JPMS: Journal of Political and Military Sociology* 17, 1 (Summer 1989).

McCall, George J., and J. L. Simmons. *Identities and Interactions* (New York: The Free Press, 1978).

McChrystal, Stanley A. "ISAF Commander's Counterinsurgency Guidance" (Kabul: Headquarters International Security Assistance Force, 2009).

McChrystal, Stanley A. "Public Address to the Conference of Defence Associations. Ottawa: December 16, 2009." Transcript available at http://cda-cdai.ca/cdai/publications/comisaf, accessed 2 February 2010.

McChrystal, Stanley A. "Tactical Directive" (Kabul: Headquarters International Security Assistance Force, 2 July 2009).

McCormick, David. *The Downsized Warrior: America's Army in Transition* (New York: New York University Press, 1998).

McCoy, Katherine E. "Beyond Civil-Military Relations: Reflections on Civilian Control of a Private, Multinational Workforce," *Armed Forces and Society* 36, 4 (July 2010).

McCubbins, Matthew D., and Thomas Schwartz. "Congressional Oversight Overlooked: Police Patrols versus Fire Alarms," *American Journal of Political Science* 28, 1 (February 1984).

McElhatton, Jim. "How a Contracting Official Scammed More than $30M," *Federal Times* (1 April 2013), available at http://www.federaltimes.com/article/20130401/ACQUISITION02/304010001/How-contracting-official-scammed-more-than-30M?odyssey=tab%7Ctopnews%7Cimg%7CAcquisition, accessed 1 October 2015.

McGraw, Thomas K. "Regulation in America: A Review Article," *Business History Review* 49, 2 (Summer 1975).

McInness, Colin. *Hot War, Cold War: The British Army's Way in Warfare, 1945–95* (London: Brassey's, 1996).

McLaughlin, Mark C. "Assessing the Effectiveness of Deliberate Force: Harnessing the Political-Military Connection," in Robert C. Owen, editor, *Deliberate Force: A Case Study in Effective Air Campaigning. Final Report of the Air University Balkans Air Campaign Study* (Maxwell Air Force Base: Air University Press, January 2000).

McLeary, Paul. "US Looking for Contractors to Help in Iraq," *Defense News*, 9 March 2015, available at http://www.defensenews.com/story/defense/2015/03/09/us-private-contractor-iraq-isis/24654439/, accessed 19 July 2015.

McNeill, William H. *The Pursuit of Power: Technology, Armed Force and Society since AD 1000* (Chicago: University of Chicago Press, 1982).

Mead, George H. "The Genesis of the Self and Social Control," *International Journal of Ethics* 35, 3 (April 1925).

Mead, George H. *Mind, Self, and Society from the Standpoint of a Social Behaviorist* (Chicago: University of Chicago Press, 1934/1962).

Mehra, Amol. "Bridging the Accountability Gaps: The Proliferation of Private Military and Security Companies and Ensuring Accountability for Human Rights Violations," *Pacific McGeorge Global Business and Development Law Journal* 22, 2 (2010).

Mehta, Aaron. "US Ships Still Monitoring Iranian Flotilla," *Defense News* (23 April 2015), available at http://www.defensenews.com/story/defense/policy-budget/warfare/2015/04/23/iran-ships-yemen-houthi-us-navy-flotilla-roosevelt/26241855/, accessed 28 September 2015.

"Mercenary Firms Seek Tighter Laws," *BBC News* (5 December 2007), available at http://news.bbc.co.uk/1/hi/uk/7128046.stm, accessed 17 December 2015.

Meredith, Martin. *The Fate of Africa: From the Hopes of Freedom to the Heart of Despair—A History of Fifty Years of Independence* (New York: PublicAffairs, 2005).

Merton, Robert K. *Social Theory and Social Structure* (New York: The Free Press, 1957).

Messner, J. J. "IPOA Welcomes Montreux Agreement on Private Security Companies" (17 September 2008), available at http://www.reports-and-materials.org/sites/default/files/reports-and-materials/IPOA-welcomes-Montreux-agreement-17-Sep-2008.pdf, accessed 25 September 2015.

Messner, J. J. "Working towards Effective Legislative and Regulatory Solutions for the Private Security Industry in Africa," in Sabelo Gumedze, editor, *Elimination of Mercenarism in Africa: A Need for a New Continental Approach* (Pretoria: Institute for Security Studies, 2008).

Mettraux, Guénaël. *The Law of Command Responsibility* (New York: Oxford University Press, 2009).

Meyer, John W., and Brian Rowan. "Institutionalized Organizations: Formal Structure as Myth and Ceremony," in Walter W. Powell and Paul J. DiMaggio, editors, *The New Institutionalism in Organizational Analysis* (Chicago: University of Chicago Press, 1991).

Middleton, Roger. *Piracy in Somalia: Threatening Global Trade, Feeding Local Wars.* Chatham House Briefing Paper, AFP BP 08/02 (London: Chatham House, October 2008).

Miewald, Robert D. "Weberian Bureaucracy and the Military Model," *Public Administration Review* 30, 2 (March/April 1970).

Miller, Barbara. "'Example' to Be Made of Death Row Australian," *ABC News* (28 January 2010), available at http://www.abc.net.au/news/stories/2010/01/28/2803111.htm?section=world, accessed 12 April 2010.

Miller, T. Christian. *Blood Money: Wasted Billions, Lost Lives, and Corporate Greed in Iraq* (New York: Little, Brown and Company, 2006).

Miller, T. Christian. "Military Suspends Firm Accused of Overbilling in Iraq," *Los Angeles Times* (9 October 2004), available at http://articles.latimes.com/2004/oct/09/world/fg-custer9, accessed 15 August 2009.

Miller, T. Christian. "Private Security Guards in Iraq Operate with Little Supervision," *Los Angeles Times* (4 December 2005). PMSC casualty details available at http://www.icasualties.org/Iraq/Contractors.aspx, accessed April 2010.

Mills, C. Wright. *The Power Elite* (New York: Oxford University Press, 1959).

Minter, William. "The US and the War in Angola," *Review of African Political Economy* 18, 50 (1991).

Mintz, Alex. "Military-Industrial Linkages in Israel," *Armed Forces and Society* 12, 1 (Fall 1985).

Mirovsky, Arik, and Amitai Ziv. "Israeli Army Eats Up Land, Air and Radio Frequencies, Says Special Panel," *Ha'aretz* (22 July 2015).

Mizokami, Kyle. "The U.S. Air Force Is Using Civilians to Fly Drones in Combat Theaters," *Popular Mechanics* (1 December 2015), available at http://www.popularmechanics.com/military/weapons/news/a18377/the-us-air-force-is-using-civilians-to-fly-drones/, accessed 10 December 2015.

Mjøsetand, Lars, and Stephen Van Holde. "Killing for the State, Dying for the Nation," in Lars Mjøsetand and Stephen Van Holde, editors, *The Comparative Study of Conscription in the Armed Forces* (Amsterdam: JAI, 2002).

Moe, Terry M. "The New Economics of Organization," *American Journal of Political Science* 28, 4 (November 1984).

Moran, Michael. "Review Article: Understanding the Regulatory State," *British Journal of Political Science* 32, 2 (April 2002).

Morris, Ben S. "Officer Selection in the British Army, 1942–1945," *Occupational Psychology* 23, 4 (October 1949).

Moskos, Charles C., John Allen Williams, and David R. Segal, editors. *The Postmodern Military: Armed Forces after the Cold War* (New York: Oxford University Press, 2000).

Mueller, Karl. "The Demise of Yugoslavia and the Destruction of Bosnia: Strategic Causes, Effects, and Responses," in Robert C. Owen, editor, *Deliberate Force: A Case Study in Effective Air Campaigning. Final Report of the Air University Balkans Air Campaign Study* (Maxwell Air Force Base: Air University Press, January 2000).

Mulligan, John E. "Bribery Case in San Diego Has Parallels to Rhode Island," *Providence Journal* (3 July 2011), available at http://www.ocnus.net/artman2/publish/Dark_Side_4/

Navy-Bribery-Case-In-San-Diego-Has-Parallels-To-Rhode-Island.shtml, accessed 1 October 2015.

Multi-National Force–Iraq. Fragmentary Order (FRAGO) 05-108, "Operationalize the RROC" (16 May 2005).

Multi-National Force–Iraq. Fragmentary Order (FRAGO) 07-428, "Armed Contractors/DOD Civilians and PMSCs" (22 December 2007).

Multi-National Force–Iraq. Fragmentary Order (FRAGO) 09-109, "Armed Contractors/DOD Civilians and PMSCs" (7 March 2009).

Murithi, Tim. "The South Africa Defence Review: A Contrarian Perspective." South Africa Foreign Policy Initiative, Policy Brief 4 (5 July 2012).

Murray, Carla Tighe. *Evaluating Military Compensation* (Washington: Congressional Budget Office, June 2007).

Nagl, John A., James F. Amos, Sarah Sewall, and David H. Petraeus. *The US Army/Marine Corps Counterinsurgency Field Manual*, number 3-24 (Chicago: University of Chicago Press, 2008).

Nakamura, David. "New Rules Reflect Shift in How Afghan Contracts Are Awarded," *Washington Post* (14 September 2010), page A12.

Nakashima, Ellen. "Amid Reviews, DynCorp Bolsters Ethics Practices," *Washington Post* (27 July 2009).

National Assembly of South Africa Questions for Written Reply to Minister Jeff Radebe (Minister of Justice and Constitutional Development), Issued by Parliament (3 September 2013), available at http://www.politicsweb.co.za/archive/2006-prohibition-of-mercenary-activities-act-not-y, accessed 24 June 2015.

Nevin, Tom. "South Africa's Second Army," *African Business* 46, 392 (December 2012).

Nelson, Adrian, Cary L. Cooper, and Paul R. Jackson. "Uncertainty amidst Change: The Impact of Privatization on Employee Job Satisfaction and Well-Being," *Journal of Occupational and Organizational Psychology* 68, 1 (March 1995).

Nesbitt, Prexy. "Terminators, Crusaders and Gladiators: Western (Public and Private) Support for RENAMO and UNITA," *Review of African Political Economy* 15, 43 (1988).

Nichols, Louis B. "The Justice of Military Justice," *William and Mary Law Review* 12, 3 (1971).

Nitzan, Jonathan, and Shimshon Bichler. *The Global Political Economy of Israel: From War Profits to Peace Dividends* (London: Pluto Press, 2002).

Noetzel, Timo, and Sibylle Scheipers. *Coalition Warfare in Afghanistan.* Chatham House Briefing Paper 07/01 (London: Chatham House, October 2007).

Norton-Taylor, Richard, and Chris Stephens. "Libya: SAS Veterans Helping NATO Identify Gaddafi Targets in Misrata," *Guardian* (31 May 2011), available at http://www.guardian.co.uk/world/2011/may/31/libya-sas-veterans-misrata-rebels.

Notholt, Stuart A. "Review: *The Decolonization of Portuguese Africa: Metropolitan Revolution and the Dissolution of Empire* by Norrie MacQueen; *Mozambique since Independence: Confronting Leviathan* by Margaret Hall, Tom Young," *African Affairs* 97, 387 (April 1998).

Nozick, Robert. *Anarchy, State, and Utopia* (New York: Basic Books, 1974).

O'Brien, Kevin A. "PMCs, Myths and Mercenaries: The Debate on Private Military Companies," *RUSI Journal* 145 (2000).

O'Connor, Gordon. "Strategic Airlift Marks New Era for Canada," *Maple Leaf* (February 9, 2007), available at http://www.forces.gc.ca/site/commun/ml-fe/article-eng.asp?id=3379, accessed 14 August 2008.

Odeen, Philip A. "Memorandum for Chairman, Defense Science Board: Final Report of the Defense Science Board Task Force on Outsourcing and Privatization. August 27, 1996," in Philip A. Odeen, chairman, *Report of the Defense Science Board Task Force on Outsourcing and Privatization* (Washington: Office of the Under Secretary of Defense for Acquisition and Technology, August 1996).

Odeen, Philip A., chairman. *Report of the Defense Science Board Task Force on Outsourcing and Privatization* (Washington: Office of the Under Secretary of Defense for Acquisition and Technology, August 1996).

Oelofs, Louis. "Court Hears Details of Alleged E Guinea Coup Plot," *Mail and Guardian Online* (14 February 2007).

Office of the Assistant Secretary of Defense for Logistics and Materiel Readiness. *CENTCOM Quarterly Contractor Census Reports* (various years; last updated 2014), available at http://www.acq.osd.mil/log/PS/CENTCOM_reports.html, accessed 30 September 2015.

Office of the Auditor General of Canada. "Chapter 2: Support for Overseas Deployments—National Defence" (Ottawa: Office of the Auditor General of Canada, May 2008).

Oliver, Jonathan. "Lobbying Row as Ex-Minister Paul Boateng Lands Defence Firm Job," *Sunday Times* (8 November 2009), available at http://www.timesonline.co.uk, accessed 6 June 2015.

O'Malley, Pat. "Risk and Responsibility," in Andrew Barry, Thomas Osborne, and Nikolas Rose, editors, *Foucault and Political Reason: Liberalism, Neo-liberalism, and Rationalities of Government* (Chicago: University of Chicago Press, 1996).

O'Reilly, Annie, and Karinne Coombes. "Meeting the Legal Obligations and Good Practices of the Montreux Document: The United Kingdom," in Rebecca DeWinter-Schmitt, editor, *Montreux Five Years On: An Analysis of State Efforts to Implement Montreux Document Legal Obligations and Good Practices* (Barcelona: Adjuntament de Barcelona, 2013).

Organization for Economic Cooperation and Development. "Israel's Accession to the OECD," available at http://www.oecd.org/israel/israelsaccessiontotheoecd.htm, accessed 7 August 2015.

Organization of African Unity. *Convention for the Elimination of Mercenarism in Africa (Opened for Signature) 3 July 1977*. OAU Document CM/817 (29), Annex 2, Article 1 (3rd revision 1977) (entered into force 22 April 1985).

Ortiz, Carlos. "Regulating Private Military Companies: States and the Expanding Business of Commercial Security Provision," in Libby Assassi, Duncan Wigan, and Kees Van der Pijl, editors, *Global Regulation Managing Crises after the Imperial Turn* (Basingstoke: Palgrave Macmillan, 2004).

Osler, David, and Mike Grinter. "Owners Hire Armed Guards to Secure Ships against Pirates," *Lloyd's List* (12 September 2008), available at http://lloydslist.com/ll/news/owners-hire-armed-guards-to-secure-ships-against-pirates/20017570367.htm, accessed 22 October 2015.

Paczulla, Jutta. "The Long, Difficult Road to Dayton: Peace Efforts in Bosnia-Herzegovina," *International Journal* 60, 1 (Winter 2004–2005).

Palomba, Junio V. "Private Military and Security Companies and the Pursuit of Legitimacy," *E-international Relations* (2 October 2009), available at http://www.e-IR.info/?p=2450, accessed 4 June 2015.

Parsons, Talcott. *The Social System* (New York: The Free Press, 1951).

Partlow, Joshua. "Afghan Government Accuses 16 Security Firms of Violations," *Washington Post* (8 February 2011).

Paterson, Mark, rapporteur. "The South African Defence Review of 2012: Problems, Progress, and Prospects." Centre for Conflict Resolution Policy Brief 11 (3 May 2012).

Patterson, Malcolm Hugh. "Private Military and Security Companies and the International Trade in Small Arms and Light Weapons," in Andrew T. H. Tan, editor, *The Global Arms Trade: A Handbook* (London: Routledge, 2014).

Paul, Christopher, Colin P. Clarke, and Beth Grill. *Victory Has a Thousand Fathers: Sources of Success in Counterinsurgency* (Santa Monica: RAND Corporation, 2010).

Paul, Christopher, Colin P. Clarke, Beth Grill, Stephanie Young, Jennifer D. P. Moroney, Joe Hogler, and Christine Leah. *What Works Best When Building Partner Capacity and under What Circumstances?* (Santa Monica: RAND Corporation, 2013).

Pech, Khareen. "Executive Outcomes: A Corporate Conquest," in Jakkie Cillers and Peggy Mason, editors, *Peace, Profit or Plunder? The Privatisation of Security in War-Torn African Societies* (Pretoria: Institute for Security Studies, 1999).

Pelton, Robert Young. *Licensed to Kill: Hired Guns in the War on Terror* (New York: Crown Publishers, 2006).

Percy, Sarah. *Mercenaries: The History of a Norm in International Relations* (Oxford: Oxford University Press, 2007).

Percy, Sarah. "Morality and Regulation," in Simon Chesterman and Chia Lehnardt, editors, *From Mercenaries to Market: The Rise and Regulation of Private Military Companies* (Oxford: Oxford University Press, 2007).

Percy, Sarah. *Regulating the Private Security Industry.* Adelphi Paper 384 (London: Routledge, 2006).

Pereira, Anthony W. "The Neglected Tragedy: The Return to War in Angola, 1992–93," *Journal of Modern African Studies* 32, 1 (March 1994).

Perrin, Benjamin. *Modern Warfare: Armed Groups, Private Militaries, Humanitarian Organizations, and the Law* (Vancouver: University of British Columbia Press, 2012).

Perrin, Benjamin. *On the Edges of Conflict: Humanitarian Assistance and the Private Security Debate—An International Humanitarian Law Perspective* (no publisher, no date), available at http://www.croixrouge.ca/cmslib/general/oteoc_ben_perrin.pdf, accessed 15 December 2014.

Perry, David. "Contractors in Kandahar, Eh?" *Journal of Military and Strategic Studies* 9, 4 (Summer 2007).

Perry, David. "The Privatization of the Canadian Military," *International Journal* 64, 3 (Summer 2009).

Perry, David. *Purchasing Power*, unpublished PhD dissertation (Carleton University, 2015).

Peters, Heidi M., Moshe Schwartz, and Lawrence Kapp. *Department of Defense Contractor and Troop Levels in Iraq and Afghanistan: 2007–2014* (Washington: Congressional Research Service, 22 July 2015).

Petersohn, Ulrich. "The Effectiveness of Contracted Coalitions: Private Security Contractors in Iraq," *Armed Forces and Society* 39, 3 (July 2013).

Petersohn, Ulrich. "The Social Structure of the Market for Force," *Cooperation and Conflict* 50, 2 (June 2014).

Pham, J. Peter. "Somali Pirates Undeterred by Naval Build-Up, but Risks Heightened," *World Defense Review* (2 April 2009).

Phinney, David. "From Mercenaries to Peacemakers? Scandals Confront Military Security Industry," *CorpWatch* (29 November 2005), available at http://www.corpwatch.org/article.php?id=12829, accessed April 2010.

Pickering, Jeffrey, and Emizet F. Kisigani. "The International Military Intervention Dataset: An Updated Resource for Conflict Scholars," *Journal of Peace Research* 46, 4 (July 2009).

Pigou, Alfred. *The Economics of Welfare* (London: Macmillan, 1938).

Pildes, Richard H., and Cass R. Sunstein. "Reinventing the Regulatory State," *University of Chicago Law Review* 62, 1 (Winter 1995).

Pincus, Walter. "Contractor Hirings in Afghanistan to Emphasize Locals," *Washington Post* (7 December 2009).

Pincus, Walter. "Security Contracts to Continue in Iraq," *Washington Post* (4 February 2007).

"Piracy: Issues Arising from the Use of Armed Guards" (London: Ince & Co. International LLP, 2011).

Pitney, John T., Jr., and John-Clark Levin. *Private Anti-piracy Navies: How Warships for Hire Are Changing Maritime Security* (Plymouth: Lexington Books, 2014).

Pleming, Sue, and Andrew Grey. "Gates Takes Swipe at Security Contractors in Iraq," Reuters (19 October 2007), available at http://www.reuters.com/article/2007/10/19/us-iraq-usa-blackwater-idUSN1842593420071019, accessed 3 August 2015.

Ploch, Lauren, Christopher M. Blanchard, Ronald O'Rourke, R. Chuck Mason, and Rawle O. King. *Piracy Off the Horn of Africa.* CRS Report for the US Congress, R4-528 (Washington: Congressional Research Service, 24 April 2009).

"PM Orders NIS 2.4b. to Restock IDF," *Jerusalem Post* (10 February 2009).

Porter, Michael E. *Competitive Strategy: Techniques for Analyzing Industries and Competitors* (New York: The Free Press, 1980).

Potgieter, De Wet, and Khadija Pate. "Congo Rebels, a Kabila Family Affair?" *Daily Maverick* (12 February 2013), available at http://www.dailymaverick.co.za/article/2013-02-11-congo-rebels-a-kabila-family-affair#.VXnmzKbN7dk, accessed 6 June 2015.

Potter, Mitch. "Security Standoff Stalls Canadian Dam Project in Kandahar," *Toronto Star* (9 June 2010).

Powell, Jonathan. "Determinants of the Attempting and Outcome of Coups d'État," *Journal of Conflict Resolution* 56, 6 (December 2012).

Prince, Erik, with Davin Coburn. *Civilian Warriors: The Inside Story of Blackwater and the Unsung Heroes of the War on Terror* (New York: Portfolio/Penguin, 2013).

Prince, Erik D. "How Blackwater Serves America," *Wall Street Journal* (16 December 2008).

Private Security Company Association of Iraq website, available at http://www.PMSCai.org/index.html, accessed 2 May 2009.

Private Security Company Association of Iraq. "Effective 31 December 2011 the PSCAI Is Disestablished," available at http://www.pscai.org/, accessed 31 July 2015.

Project on Government Oversight. "Federal Contractor Misconduct Database," available at http://www.contractormisconduct.org/contractors, accessed 25 September 2015.

Pro Publica. "International Peace Operations Association," ProPublica Nonprofit Explorer, available at https://projects.propublica.org/nonprofits/organizations/542033637, accessed 17 August 2015.

Protocol Additional to the Geneva Conventions of 12 August 1949, and Relating to the Protection of Victims of International Armed Conflicts (Protocol I), Article 47 (8 June 1977), 1125 UNTS 17512, available at http://www.icrc.org/ihl.nsf/FULL/470?OpenDocument.

Pugliese, David. "Controversial Use of Guns-for-Hire Surges in Afghanistan," *Ottawa Citizen* (5 April 2010).

Pugliese, David. "Expect More Roadside Bomb Attacks, NATO," *Ottawa Citizen* (9 January 2010).

Raenette Taljaard. "Implementing South Africa's Regulation of Foreign Military Assistance Act," in Alan Bryden and Marina Caparini, editors, *Private Actors and Security Governance* (London: Transactions Publishers, 2006).

Raghavan, Sudarsan, and Thomas E. Ricks. "Private Security Puts Diplomats, Military at Odds in Iraq Fuel Debate," *Washington Post* (26 September 2007), available at http://www.washingtonpost.com/wp-dyn/content/article/2007/09/25/AR2007092502675.html, accessed 14 October 2015.

Ralby, Ian. "Accounting for Private Security," *Fletcher Security Review* 2, 1 (January 2015).

Ralby, Ian. "A Brief Explanation of the Private Security Regulatory Initiatives: UN Initiatives," I.R. Consilium website (17 April 2014), available at http://irconsilium.com/a-brief-explanation-of-the-private-security-regulatory-initiatives-u-n-inititatives, accessed 4 June 2015.

Ralby, Ian. "Private Military Companies and the *Jus ad Bellum*," in Marc Weller, editor, *The Oxford Handbook of the Use of Force in International Law* (Oxford: Oxford University Press, 2015).

Ramet, Sabrina P. *The Three Yugoslavias: State-Building and Legitimation, 1918–2005* (Indiana University Press, 2006).

Ranganathan, Surabhi. "Between Complicity and Irrelevance? Industry Associations and the Challenge of Regulating Private Security Contractors," *Georgetown Journal of International Law* 41 (2010).

Ramet, Sabrina Petra. "Slovenia's Road to Democracy," *Europe-Asia Studies* 45, 5 (1993).

Ranganathan, Surabhi. "Constructive Constraints? Conceptual and Practical Challenges to Regulating Private Military and Security Companies," in Cedric Ryngaert and Math Noorthman, editors, *Human Security and International Law* (Cambridge, Antwerp, and Poland: Intersentia, 2014).

Rapoport, Meron. "Outsourcing the Checkpoints," *Ha'aretz* (2 October 2007).

Ravid, Barak. "OECD Entrance Is 'Seal of Approval,' Netanyahu Says," *Ha'aretz* (10 May 2010).

Reconstruction Operations Center. "Mission Brief 14 Aug 2005," PowerPoint presentation prepared by ROC operations director, Baghdad, Iraq (August 2005).

Record, Jeffrey. "Collapsed Countries, Casualty Dread, and the New American Way of War," *Parameters* 32, 2 (Summer 2002).

Record, Jeffrey. "Force-Protection Fetishism: Sources, Consequences, and (?) Solutions," *Aerospace Power Journal* (Summer 2000).

Reisman, William Michael, and James E. Baker. *Regulating Covert Action: Practices, Contexts, and Policies of Covert Coercion Abroad in International and American Law* (New Haven: Yale University Press, 1992).

Rennie, Steve, "Afghan Government to Regulate Private Security Firms," *Toronto Sun* (25 January 2010).

Report of the Defense Science Board Task Force on Institutionalizing Stability Operations within DoD (Washington: Office of the Under Secretary of Defense for Acquisition, Technology, and Logistics, September 2005).

Republic of South Africa, Department of Defence, Briefing to the Security and Constitutional Affairs Select Committee, Prohibition of Mercenary Activities and Regulation of Certain Activities in Countries of Armed Conflict Bill [B42B-2005] (Cape Town: National Assembly, 7 September 2006).

Resende-Santos, Joao. "Anarchy and the Emulation of Military Systems: Military Organization and Technology in South America, 1870–1914," in Benjamin Frankel, editor, *Realism: Restatements and Renewal* (London: Frank Cass, 1996).

Reyes, Brian. "First Sea Lord Warns of al-Qa'eda Plot to Target Merchant Ships," *Lloyd's List* (5 August 2004).

Reynolds, Kate J., John C. Turner, and S. Alexander Haslam. "When Are We Better than Them and They Worse than Us? A Closer Look at Social Discrimination in Positive and Negative Domains," *Journal of Personality and Social Psychology* 78, 1 (January 2000).

Rich, Roland. "Recognition of States: The Collapse of Yugoslavia and the Soviet Union," *European Journal of International Law* 36, 1 (1993).

Richemond-Barak, Daphné. "Private Military Contractors and Combatancy Status under International Humanitarian Law," presented to Conference on Complementing IHL: Exploring the Need for Additional Norms to Govern Contemporary Conflict Situations, Jerusalem, 1–3 June 2008.

Richemond-Barak, Daphné. "Regulating War: A Taxonomy in Global Administrative Law," *European Journal of International Law* 22, 4 (November 2011).

Ricks, Thomas E. *Fiasco: The American Military Adventure in Iraq* (New York: Penguin, 2006).

Rinat, Zafrir. "How Did IDF Gain Control over Half of the Country?" *Ha'aretz* (17 November 2008), available at http://www.haaretz.com/print-edition/business/how-did-idf-gain-control-over-half-of-the-country-1.257326, accessed 15 August 2015.

Ripley, Tim, and Paul Beaver. "Analysis: Operation Storm," *Jane's Sentinel: The Balkans Newsletter* 2, 8 (no date).

Risen, James, and Mark Mazetti. "Blackwater Guards Tied to Secret Raids by the C.I.A.," *New York Times* (11 December 2009).

Risen, James, and Timothy Williams. "U.S. Looks for Blackwater Replacement in Iraq," *New York Times* (29 January 2009), available at http://www.nytimes.com/2009/01/30/world/middleeast/30blackwater.html, accessed 14 October 2015.

Roberts, Adam. *The Wonga Coup: Guns, Thugs and a Ruthless Determination to Create Mayhem in an Oil-Rich Corner of Africa* (London: Profile Books, 2009).

Rochlin, Jim. "Plan Colombia and the Revolution in Military Affairs: The Demise of the FARC," *Review of International Studies* 37, 2 (April 2011).

Rona, Gabor. "Remarks by Gabor Rona, UN Working Group on the Use of Mercenaries, Montreux +5 Conference 11–13 December 2013," United Nations Office of Human Rights, Office of the High Commissioner, available at http://www.ohchr.org/EN/NewsEvents/Pages/DisplayNews.aspx?NewsID=14105&LangID=E, accessed 3 July 2015.

Ronen, Yaël. "Israel: Going Private—The Use and Regulation of Private Military and Security Companies in Situations of Armed Conflict," in Christine Bakker and Mirko Sossai, editors, *Multilevel Regulation of Military and Security Contractors: The Interplay between International, European and Domestic Norms* (Oxford: Hart Publishing, 2011).

Rosch, Eleanor. "Principles of Categorization," in E. Rosch and B. B. Lloyd, editors, *Cognition and Categorization* (Hillsdale, NJ: Erlbaum, 1978).

Rosemann, Nils. *Code of Conduct: Tool for Self-Regulation for Private Military and Security Companies*. Occasional Paper 15 (Geneva: Geneva Centre for the Democratic Control of Armed Forces, 2008).

Rosky, Clifford J. "Force, Inc.: The Privatization of Punishment, Policing, and Military Force in Liberal States," *Connecticut Law Review* 36, 3 (Spring 2004).

Ross, Edward Alsworth. "The Making of Professions," *International Journal of Ethics* 27, 1 (1916).

Ross, Edward Alsworth. "Social Control," *American Journal of Sociology* 1, 5 (March 1896).

Ross, Edward Alsworth. *Social Control: A Survey of the Foundations of Order* (New York: Macmillan, 1901).

Rotberg, Robert I. "Failed States, Collapsed States, Weak States: Causes and Indicators," in Robert I. Rotberg, editor, *State Failure and State Weakness in a Time of Terror* (Washington: Brookings Institution and World Peace Foundation, 2003), page 3.

Rothwell, Donald. *Legal Opinion on the Status of Non-combatants and Contractors under International Humanitarian Law and Australian Law* (Sydney: Australian Strategic Policy Institute, December 2004).

Rubenfeld, Samuel. "Former Major Sentenced in Defense Contractor Bribery Case," *Wall Street Journal* (6 January 2012), available at http://blogs.wsj.com/corruption-currents/2012/01/06/former-major-sentenced-in-defense-contractor-bribery-case/, accessed 1 October 2015.

Rubin, Alissa J. "Afghan Government Softens Ban on Security Firms," *New York Times* (6 December 2010).

Rubin, Elizabeth. "An Army of One's Own," *Harper's Magazine* (February 1997).

Ryu, Alisha. "Shipping Industry Mulls Hiring Private Security to Fight Piracy," *Voice of America* (22 October 2008), available at http://voanews.com/english/2008-10-22-voa42.cfm?renderforprint=1, accessed 25 June 2009.

"S. 674 (110th Congress): Transparency and Accountability in Military and Security Contracting Act of 2007," *Govtrack.us*, available at https://www.govtrack.us/congress/bills/110/s674, accessed 11 September 2015.

Salzman, Zoe. "Private Military Contractors and the Taint of a Mercenary Reputation," *International Law and Politics* 40 (2008).

Sanderson, Christopher. "International Regulatory Frameworks: The Perspective of Industry," presented to the Private Military and Security Conference, Royal United Services Institute, London, 27–28 September 2012.

Sandler, Todd, and Keith Hartley. *The Economics of Defense* (Cambridge: Cambridge University Press, 1999).

Sandoz, Yves. "Private Security and International Law," in Jakkie Cilliers and Peggy Mason, editors, *Peace, Profit or Plunder? The Privatisation of Security in War-Torn African Societies* (Pretoria: Institute for Security Studies, 1999).

Sassi, Kimo. "Committee Opinion: Private Military and Security Firms and the Erosion of the State Monopoly on the Use of Force," European Parliamentary Assembly, Committee on Legal Affairs and Human Rights (Strasbourg: European Parliamentary Assembly, 27 January 2009), available at http://assembly.coe.int/nw/xml/XRef/Xref-DocDetails-EN.asp?fileid=12076&lang=EN&search=InByaXZhdGUgY29udHJhY3RvcnMiIA, accessed 15 August 2015.

Scahill, Jeremy. *Blackwater: The Rise of the World's Most Powerful Mercenary Army* (London: Profile Books, 2011).

Scahill, Jeremy. *Blackwater: The Rise of the World's Most Powerful Mercenary Army*, revised and updated edition (New York: Nation Books, 2008).

Scahill, Jeremy. "Blackwater's Secret War in Pakistan," *The Nation* (23 November 2009).

Scahill, Jeremy. "Iraq Withdrawal? Obama and Clinton Expanding US Paramilitary Force in Iraq," *The Nation* (22 July 2010).

Scahill, Jeremy, "The Mercenary Revolution: Flush with Profits from the Iraq War, Military Contractors See a World of Business Opportunities," *Indypendent* (10 August 2007), available at http://www.indypendent.org/2007/08/10/the-mercenary-revolution-flush-with-profits-from-the-iraq-war-military-contractors-see-a-world-of-business-opportunities/, accessed 4 February 2010.

Schaub, Gary, Jr. "Civilian Combatants, Military Professionals? American Officer Judgments," *Defence Studies* 10, 3 (Autumn 2010).

Schaub, Gary, Jr. "JUSTAS for All? Innovation and UAVs in the Canadian Forces," *Defence Studies* 15, 2 (June 2015).

Schaub, Gary, Jr., and Volker Franke. "Contractors as Military Professionals?" *Parameters* 39, 4 (Winter 2009–2010).

Scheimer, Michael. "Separating Private Military Companies from Illegal Mercenaries in International Law: Proposing an International Convention for Legitimate Military and Security Support that Reflects Customary International Law," *American University International Law Review* 24, 3 (2009).

Schmitt, Michael N. "Humanitarian Law and Direct Participation in Hostilities by Private Contractors or Civilian Employees," *Chicago Journal of International Law* 5, 2 (2004).

Schmitter, Phillippe C. "Liberation by Golpe: Retrospective Thoughts on the Demise of Authoritarian Rule in Portugal," *Armed Forces and Society* 2, 1 (November 1975).

Schooner, Steven L. "Contractor Atrocities at Abu Ghraib: Compromised Accountability in a Streamlined, Outsourced Government," *Stanford Law and Policy Review* 16, 2 (2005).

Schooner, Steven L. "Why Contractor Fatalities Matter," *Parameters* 38, 3 (Autumn 2008).

Schooner, Steven L., and Collin D. Swan. "Contractors and the Ultimate Sacrifice," *Service Contractor* (September 2010).

Schreier, Fred, and Marina Caparini. *Privatising Security: Law, Practice and Governance of Private Military and Security Companies.* Occasional Paper 6 (Geneva: Geneva Centre for the Democratic Control of Armed Forces, March 2005).

Schumacher, Gerald, and Steve Gansen. *A Bloody Business: America's War Zone Contractors and the Occupation of Iraq* (Saint Paul: Zenith Press, 2006).

Schwartz, Moshe. *Department of Defense Contractors in Iraq and Afghanistan: Background and Analysis* (Washington: Congressional Research Service, December 2009).

Schwartz, Moshe. *Department of Defense Contractors in Iraq and Afghanistan: Background and Analysis* (Washington: Congressional Research Service, 2 July 2010).

Schwartz, Moshe. *The Department of Defense's Use of Private Security Contractors in Afghanistan and Iraq: Background, Analysis, and Options for Congress.* CRS Report R40835 (Washington: Congressional Research Service, 19 January 2010).

Schwartz, Moshe. *The Department of Defense's Use of Private Security Contractors in Afghanistan and Iraq: Background, Analysis, and Options for Congress.* CRS Report R40835 (Washington: Congressional Research Service, 21 February 2011).

Schwartz, Moshe, and Jennifer Church. *Department of Defense's Use of Contractors to Support Military Operations: Background, Analysis, and Issues for Congress.* CRS Report R43074 (Washington: Congressional Research Service, 17 May 2013).

Schwartz, Moshe, and Joyprada Swain. *Department of Defense Contractors in Afghanistan and Iraq* (Washington: Congressional Research Service, 13 May 2011).

Security and Constitutional Affairs Select Committee Department. "Prohibition of Mercenary Activities and Regulation of Certain Activities in Countries of Armed Conflict Bill [B42B-2005]: Briefing," Parliamentary Monitoring Group (7 September 2006), available at https://pmg.org.za/committee-meeting/7298/, accessed 10 July 2015.

Security and Defense Cooperation Agreement between the Islamic Republic of Afghanistan and the United States of America (30 September 2014), available at http://www.embassyofafghanistan.org/sites/default/files/documents/BSA%20ENGLISH%20AFG.pdf, accessed 30 September 2015.

Security Industry Authority. *Approved Contractor Scheme: Terms and Conditions of Approval* (London: Home Office, June 2012), available at http://www.sia.homeoffice.gov.uk/Documents/acs/sia_acs_terms.pdf, accessed 5 June 2014.

Segal, David R. "Five Phases of United Nations Peacekeeping: An Evolutionary Typology," *Journal of Political and Military Sociology* 23 (Summer 1995).

Segal, David R., and Karin De Angelis. "Changing Conceptions of the Military as a Profession," in Suzanne C. Nielsen and Don M. Snider, editors, *American Civil-Military Rela-*

tions: The Soldier and the State in a New Era (Baltimore: Johns Hopkins University Press, 2009).

Segal, Mady W. "The Military and the Family as Greedy Institutions," *Armed Forces and Society* 13, 1 (Fall 1986).

Seidman, Guy, and Eyal Nun. "Women, the Military and the Court: Israel at 2001," *Southern California Review of Law and Women's Studies* 11, 1 (Fall 2001).

Senor, Dan, and Saul Singer. *Start-Up Nation: The Story of Israel's Economic Miracle* (New York: Random House, 2011).

"Severo Moto, condenado a 63 años de cárcel por el intento de golpe de Estado en Guinea Ecuatorial," *El Pais Internacional* (26 November 2004), available at http://internacional.elpais.com/internacional/2004/11/26/actualidad/1101423606_850215.html, accessed 10 July 2015.

Sewall, Sarah. "Modernizing US Counterinsurgency Practice: Rethinking Risk and Developing a National Strategy," *Military Review* 86, 5 (September–October 2006).

Shapiro, Andrew J. "Turning the Tide on Somalia Piracy: Remarks to the Atlantic Council," Department of State Bureau of Public Affairs (26 October 2012), available at http://www.state.gov/t/pm/rls/rm/199927.htm, accessed 22 October 2015.

Shearer, David. "Outsourcing War," *Foreign Policy* (Fall 1998).

Shearer, David. *Private Armies and Military Interventions*. Adelphi Paper 316 (London: Institute of Strategic Studies, 1998).

Sheffer, Gabriel. "Has Israel Really Been a Garrison Democracy? Sources of Change in Israel's Democracy," *Israel Affairs* 3, 1 (1996).

Sherif, Muzafer, O. J. Harvey, B. Jack White, William R. Hood, and Carolyn W. Sherif. *The Robbers Cave Experiment: Intergroup Conflict and Cooperation* (Middletown, CT: Wesleyan University Press, 1988).

Sherman, Edward F. "Military Justice without Military Control," *Yale Law Review* 82, 7 (June 1973).

Shiffer, Zalman F. "Money and Inflation in Israel: The Transition of an Economy to High Inflation," *Federal Reserve Bank of St. Louis Review* 64, 7 (August/September 1982).

"Shippers Weigh Armed Response to Somali Piracy," *Hellenic Shipping News Worldwide* (4 June 2009), available at http://www.hellenicshippingnews.com/index.php?option=com_content&task=view&id=50445&Itemid=79>&task=view&id=50445&Itemid=79, accessed 5 May 2010.

Shorrock, Tim. *Spies for Hire: The Secret World of Intelligence Outsourcing* (New York: Simon & Schuster, 2008).

Shtrasler, Nehemia. "Privatization Is Good," *Ha'aretz* (8 November 2009).

Shu, Spencer S., Victoria St. Martin, and Keith L. Alexander. "Four Blackwater Guards Found Guilty in 2007 Shootings of 31 Unarmed Civilians," *Washington Post* (22 October 2014), available at http://www.washingtonpost.com/world/national-security/verdict-expected-in-blackwater-shooting-case/2014/10/22/5a488258-59fc-11e4-bd61-346aee66ba29_story.html?hpid=z1, accessed 20 May 2015.

Sidakis, Diana. "Private Military Companies and State Sovereignty: Regulating Transnational Flows of Violence and Capital," in Franz von Benda-Beckman, Keebet von Benda-Beckmann, and Julia Eckert, editors, *Rule of Law and Law of Ruling: On the Governance of Law* (London: Ashgate, 2009).

Sidanius, Jim. "The Psychology of Group Conflict and the Dynamics of Oppression: A Social Dominance Perspective," in Shanto Iyengar and William J. McGuire, editors, *Explorations in Political Psychology* (Durham and London: Duke University Press, 1993).

Sidanius, Jim, and Hillary Haley. "Person-Organization Congruence and the Maintenance of Group-Based Social Hierarchy: A Social Dominance Perspective," *Group Processes and Intergroup Relations* 8, 2 (April 2005).

Silber, Laura, and Allan Little. *Yugoslavia: Death of a Nation* (New York: Penguin, 1997).

Silber, Laura, and David Wighton. "UN Lawyers Rule on Sierra Leone Arms," *Financial Times* (23 May 1998).

Silverstein, Ken. "Mercenary, Inc?" *Washington Business Forward* (26 April 2001).

Silverstein, Ken, and Daniel Burton-Rose. *Private Warriors* (New York: Verso, 2000).

Simons, Marlise. "Mladic Arrives in the Hague," *New York Times* (31 May 2011).
Singer, Max, and Aaron Wildavsky. *The Real World Order: Zones of Peace/Zones of Turmoil* (Chatham, NJ: Chatham House, 1993).
Singer, Peter W. *Can't Win with 'Em, Can't Go to War without 'Em: Private Military Contractors and Counterinsurgency.* Policy Paper 4 (Washington: Brookings Institution, September 2007).
Singer, Peter W. *Corporate Warriors: The Rise of the Privatized Military Industry* (Ithaca: Cornell University Press, 2003).
Singer, Peter W. "Outsourcing the War," *Salon* (16 April 2004), available at http://www.salon.com/2004/04/16/outsourcing_war/, accessed 11 September 2015.
Singer, Peter W. "Private Military Firms in Today's Wars," interview with Terry Gross, Centre for Global Research (24 July 2003), available at http://www.globalresearch.ca/articles/SIN307A.html, accessed 17 December 2015.
Singer, Peter W. *The Private Military Industry and Iraq: What Have We Learned and Where to Next?* Policy Paper for the Geneva Centre for the Democratic Control of Armed Forces (Geneva: Geneva Centre for the Democratic Control of Armed Forces, November 2004).
Singer, Peter W. "War, Profits, and the Vacuum of Law: Privatized Military Firms and International Law," *Columbia Journal of Transnational Law* 42, 2 (Spring 2004).
Singer, Peter. "Humanitarian Principles, Private Military Agents: Implications of the Privatized Military Industry for the Humanitarian Community," *Brown Journal of World Affairs* 13, 1 (Fall/Winter 2006).
Smith, Adam. *The Wealth of Nations, Books IV–V* (New York: Penguin, 2000).
Smith, Charles M. *War for Profit: Army Contracting vs. Supporting the Troops* (New York: Algora Publishing, 2012).
Smith, David. "South Africa Mercenaries Are 'Giving Boko Haram a Hiding,'" *Mail and Guardian* (17 April 2015), available at http://mg.co.za/article/2015-04-16-South Africa-mercenaries-turn-the-tide-in-nigeria, accessed 3 June 2015.
Smith, Eugene B. "The New Condottieri and US Policy: The Privatization of Conflict and Its Implications," *Parameters* (Winter 2002–2003).
Smith, Graeme. "Canadian Air Wing Takes Flight in Afghanistan," *Globe and Mail* (18 November 2008).
Smith, Hugh. "What Costs Will Democracies Bear? A Review of Popular Theories of Casualty Aversion," *Armed Forces and Society* 31, 4 (Summer 2005).
Smith, Thomas W. "Protecting Civilians . . . or Soldiers? Humanitarian Law and the Economy of Risk in Iraq," *International Studies Perspectives* 9, 2 (May 2008).
Smyser, W. R. *The Humanitarian Conscience: Caring for Others in the Age of Terror* (New York: Palgrave Macmillan, 2003).
Sniderman, Paul M., Richard A. Brody, and Philip E. Tetlock. *Reasoning and Choice: Explorations in Political Psychology* (Cambridge, New York, Melbourne, and Sydney: Cambridge University Press, 1991).
Snyder, William P. "Officer Recruitment for the All-Volunteer Force: Trends and Prospects," *Armed Forces and Society* 10, 3 (Spring 1984).
Soeters, Joseph L., Alise Weibull, and Donna Winslow. "Military Culture," in Giuseppe Caforio, editor, *Handbook of the Sociology of the Military* (New York: Kluwer Academic, 2004).
Solis, William M. *Rebuilding Iraq: Actions Needed to Improve Use of Private Security Providers.* GAO-05-737 (Washington: Government Accountability Office, July 2005).
Solis, William M. *Warfighter Support: A Cost Comparison of Using State Department Employees versus Contractors for Security Services in Iraq.* GAO-10-266R (Washington: Government Accountability Office, 4 March 2010).
Solis, William M. *Warfighter Support: Cultural Change Needed to Improve How DOD Plans for and Manages Operational Contract Support. Statement of William M. Solis, Director, Defense Capabilities and Management. Testimony before the Subcommittee on National Security and Foreign Affairs, Committee on Oversight and Government Reform, House of Representatives* (Washington: Government Accountability Office, 29 June 2010).
Sortor, Ronald E. *Army Active/Reserve Mix: Force Planning for Major Regional Contingencies* (Santa Monica: RAND Corporation, 1995).

South Africa Department of Defence. *South Africa Defence Review 2014* (Pretoria: Ministry of Defence, 2014), available at http://www.gov.za/sites/www.gov.za/files/defencereview_2014_ch10-13.pdf, accessed 6 June 2015.

South African Press Association. "Arrest SA 'Mercenaries,' says Defence Boss," *IOL News* (29 January 2015), available at http://www.iol.co.za/news/africa/arrest-South Africa-mercenaries-says-defence-boss-1.1810571#.VXS4os-qqkp, accessed 3 June 2015.

South African Press Association. "DRC Coup Plot Accused Denies Guilt," IOL News (5 August 2014), available at http://www.iol.co.za/news/crime-courts/drc-coup-plot-accused-denies-guilt-1730979, accessed 14 April 2016.

South African Press Association. "DRC Coup Plot Continues," *IOL News* (11 August 2014), available at http://www.iol.co.za/news/crime-courts/drc-coup-plot-trial-continues-1.1733776#.VXSiCc-qqko, accessed 5 June 2015.

"South Africa to Strip Soldiers Abroad of Citizenship?" *DefenceWeb* (6 August 2010), available at http://www.defenceweb.co.za/index.php?option=com_content&view=article&id=9204:South Africa-to-strip-soldiers-abroad-of-citizenship&catid=54:Governance&Itemid=118, accessed 6 June 2015.

Spearin, Christopher. "The Changing Forms and Utility of Force," *International Journal* 64, 2 (Spring 2009).

Spearin, Christopher. *Humanitarian Non-governmental Organizations and International Private Security Companies: The "Humanitarian" Challenges of Moulding a Marketplace.* Policy Paper 16 (Geneva: Center for the Democratic Control of the Armed Forces, 2007).

Spearin, Christopher. "International Private Security Companies and Canadian Policy," *Canadian Foreign Policy* 11, 2 (Winter 2005).

Spearin, Christopher. "Not a 'Real State'?" *International Journal* 60, 4 (Autumn 2005).

Spearin, Christopher. "Private Security Companies and Humanitarians: A Corporate Solution to Securing Humanitarian Spaces?" *International Peacekeeping* 8, 1 (Spring 2001).

Spearin, Christopher. "A Private Security Solution to Somali Piracy? The U.S. Call for Private Security Engagement and the Implications for Canada," *Naval War College Review* 63, 4 (Fall 2010).

Spearin, Christopher. "What Montreux Means," *Canadian Foreign Policy Journal* 16, 1 (Winter 2010).

Special Inspector General for Afghanistan Reconstruction. *Contract Oversight Capabilities of the Defense Department's Combined Security Transition Command–Afghanistan (CSTC-A) Need Strengthening.* SIGAR Audit-09-1 Contract Oversight (Washington: Special Inspector General for Afghanistan Reconstruction, 19 May 2009).

Special Inspector General for Iraq Reconstruction. *Compliance with Contract No. W911S0-04-C-0003* (Washington: Special Inspector General for Iraq Reconstruction, July 2008).

Special Inspector General for Iraq Reconstruction. *Field Commanders See Improvements in Controlling and Coordinating Private Security Contractor Missions in Iraq* (Washington: Special Inspector General for Iraq Reconstruction, July 2008).

Special Inspector General for Iraq Reconstruction. *Field Commanders See Improvements in Controlling and Coordinating Private Security Contractor Missions in Iraq* (Washington: Special Inspector General for Iraq Reconstruction, July 2009).

Special Inspector General for Iraq Reconstruction. *Monitoring Responsibilities for Serious Incidents Involving Private Security Contractors Once U.S. Military Forces Leave Iraq Have Not Been Determined* (Washington: Special Inspector General for Iraq Reconstruction, July 2011).

Special Inspector General for Iraq Reconstruction. *Opportunities to Improve Processes for Reporting, Investigating, and Remediating Serious Incidents Involving Private Security Contractors in Iraq* (Washington: Special Inspector General for Iraq Reconstruction, April 2009).

Special Inspector General for Iraq Reconstruction. *Quarterly and Semiannual Report to the United States Congress, July 2009* (Washington: Special Inspector General for Iraq Reconstruction, October 2009).

The Sphere Project. *The Core Humanitarian Standard and the Sphere Core Standards: Analysis and Comparison—Interim Guidance*, version 2 (Geneva: The Sphere Project, March 2015).

Spicer, Tim. *An Unorthodox Soldier* (London: Mainstream Publishing, 1998).

Spindler, G. Dearborn. "The Military: A Systematic Analysis," *Social Forces* 27, 1 (October 1948).

Spruyt, Hendrick. *The Sovereign State and Its Competitors: An Analysis of Systems Change* (Princeton: Princeton University Press, 1994).

Stanger, Allison. *One Nation under Contract: The Outsourcing of American Power and the Future of Foreign Policy* (New Haven: Yale University Press, 2009).

Stanley, Bruce E. *Outsourcing Security: Private Military Contractors and U.S. Foreign Policy* (Lincoln: Potomac Books, 2015).

Starkman, Rotem. "The Profligate Israeli Army Will Fight Criticism with Every Weapon It Has," *Ha'aretz* (23 July 2015).

Status Report on Anglophone Africa: Comprehensive Study and Analysis of National Legislation (New York: United Nations Office of the High Commissioner for Human Rights, no date), available at http://www.ohchr.org/EN/Issues/Mercenaries/WGMercenaries/Pages/NationalLegislationStudies.aspx, accessed 6 June 2015.

Stein, Janice Gross, and Eugene Lang. "Too Few Hilliers: The General Goes Where Ottawa Mandarins Fear to Tread," *The Walrus* (April 2008).

Stephens, Bret. "Why Don't We Hang Pirates Anymore?" *Wall Street Journal* (25 November 2008).

Stets, Jan E., and Peter J. Burke. "Identity Theory and Social Identity Theory," *Social Psychology Quarterly* 63, 3 (2000).

Stevens, L. Nye. *Government Contractors: An Overview of the Federal Contracting-Out Program. Statement of L. Nye Stevens, Director of Planning and Reporting, General Government Division.* GAO/T-GGD-95-131 (Washington: General Accounting Office, March 1995).

Stewart, Richard B. "Accountability, Participation and the Problem of Disregard in Global Regulatory Governance," IILJ International Legal Theory Colloquium, NYU School of Law (7 February 2008).

Stigler, George J. "The Theory of Economic Regulation," *Bell Journal of Economics and Management Science* 2, 1 (Spring 1971).

Stiglitz, Joseph. *Whither Socialism?* (Cambridge: MIT Press, 1989).

Stockholm International Peace Studies Institute. "Military Expenditure by Country as Percentage of Government Spending, 1988–2014," available at http://www.sipri.org/research/armaments/milex/milex_database, accessed 9 August 2015.

Strachan, Hew. "The Civil-Military 'Gap' in Britain," *Journal of Strategic Studies* 26, 2 (2003).

Strachan, Hew. *The Politics of the British Army* (Oxford: Oxford University Press, 1997).

Strachan-Morris, David. "The Future of Civil-Military Intelligence Co-operation Based on Lessons Learned in Iraq." *Intelligence and National Security* 24, 2 (2009).

Strickey, Stephen S. "'Anglo-American' Military Justice Systems and the Wave of Civilianization: Will Discipline Survive?" *Cambridge Journal of International and Comparative Law* 2, 4 (2013).

Stryker, Sheldon. "Identity Salience and Role Performance: The Relevance of Symbolic Interaction Theory for Family Research," *Journal of Marriage and the Family* 30, 4 (November 1968).

Suchman, Mark C. "Managing Legitimacy: Strategic and Institutional Approaches," *Academy of Management Review* 20, 3 (July 1995).

The Supreme Court Sitting as the High Court of Justice. *H.C.J. 2605/05 Academic Center for Law and Business, Human Rights Division v Minister of Finance* (Jerusalem: 19 November 2009).

Tajfel, Henri. *Differentiation between Social Groups: Studies in the Social Psychology of Intergroup Relations* (London: Academic Press, 1978).

Tajfel, Henri. *Human Groups and Social Categories* (Cambridge: Cambridge University Press, 1981).

Tajfel, Henri, and John C. Turner. "An Integrative Theory of Intergroup Conflict," in William G. Austin and Stephen Worchel, editors, *The Social Psychology of Intergroup Relations* (Monterey, CA: Brooks/Cole, 1979).

Taljaard, Raenette. "Implementing South Africa's Regulation of Foreign Military Assistance Act," in Alan Bryden and Marina Caparini, editors, *Private Actors and Security Governance* (London: Transactions Publishers, 2006).

Taulbee, James Larry. "Myths, Mercenaries and Contemporary International Law," *California Western International Law Journal* 15, 2 (1985).

Taussig-Rubbo, Mateo. "Outsourcing Sacrifice: The Labor of Private Military Contractors," *Yale Journal of Law and Humanities* 21, 1 (Winter 2009).

Taylor, Trevor. "Review Article: Private Security Companies in Iraq and Beyond," *International Affairs* 87, 2 (2011).

Thompson, Ginger. "Official Says Contractor in Kabul May Be Ousted," *New York Times* (15 September 2009).

Thompson, Ginger, and James Risen. "Plea by Blackwater Guard Helps Indict Others," *New York Times* (8 December 2008), available at http://www.nytimes.com/2008/12/09/washington/09blackwater.html, accessed 10 April 2010.

Thompson, Loren. "Pentagon Insourcing Binge Begins to Unravel," *Forbes* (7 March 2011), available at http://www.forbes.com/sites/beltway/2011/03/07/pentagon-insourcing-binge-begins-to-unravel/, accessed 15 November 2015.

Thomson, Janice E. *Mercenaries, Pirates, and Sovereigns: State-Building and Extraterritorial Violence in Early Modern Europe* (Princeton: Princeton University Press, 1994).

Thurnher, Jeffrey S. "Drowning in Blackwater: How Weak Accountability over Private Security Contractors Significantly Undermines Counterinsurgency Efforts," *The Army Lawyer* (July 2008).

Tilly, Charles. *Coercion, Capital, and European States, AD 990–1992* (Cambridge: Blackwell, 1992).

Tilly, Charles. "Reflections on the History of European State-Making," in Charles Tilly, editor, *The Formation of States in Western Europe* (Princeton: Princeton University Press, 1975).

"Timeline: E Guinea Coup Plot," *BBC News* (3 November 2009), available at http://news.bbc.co.uk/2/hi/africa/4170589.stm, accessed 6 June 2015.

Tonkin, Hannah. *State Control over Private Military and Security Companies in Armed Conflict* (New York: Cambridge University Press, 2011).

Towbridge, Gordon. "DOD Lacks Funds to Turn Jobs Over to Civilians: Plan on Hold Unless Billions Added to Budget," *Federal Times* (20 October 2003).

Tsagourias, Nicholas. "Non-state Actors and the Use of Force," in Jean d'Aspermont, editor, *Participants in the International Legal System: Multiple Perspectives on Non-state Actors in International Law* (Abington: Routledge, 2011).

Turkel, Gerald. "The Public/Private Distinction: Approaches to the Critique of Legal Ideology," *Law and Society Review* 22, 4 (1988).

Turner, Lisa L., and Lynn G. Norton. "Civilians at the Tip of the Spear," *Air Force Law Review* 51 (2001).

Tvedten, Inge. *Angola: Struggle for Peace and Reconstruction* (Boulder: Westview, 1997).

Tvedten, Inge. "U.S. Policy towards Angola since 1975," *Journal of Modern African Studies* 30, 1 (March 1992).

Tyson, Scott. "Support Troops Swelling U.S. Force in Afghanistan," *Washington Post* (13 October 2009).

"UK Military Deaths in Afghanistan and Iraq," BBC News, available at http://www.bbc.co.uk/news/uk-10637526.

"Undercover Cop Testifies in DRC Coup Plot Trial," *News 24* (11 August 2014), available at http://www.news24.com/SouthAfrica/News/Undercover-cop-testifies-in-DRC-coup-plot-trial-2014081, accessed 10 June 2015.

United Kingdom Department for Transport. *Change in UK Policy on Employing Armed Guards to Protect against Somali Piracy*, available at http://www.dft.gov.uk/news/press-releases/dft-press-20111206a/, accessed 6 December 2011.

United Kingdom Department for Transport. *Interim Guidance to UK Flagged Shipping on the Use of Armed Guards to Defend against the Threat of Piracy in Exceptional Circumstances* (November 2011; updated June 2012).

United Kingdom Department for Transport. *The Use of Private Armed Guards On Board UK Registered Ships under Exceptional Circumstances to Defend against Piracy*, written ministerial statement (6 December 2011).

United Kingdom Foreign and Commonwealth Office. *Consultation on Promoting High Standards of Conduct by Private Military and Security Companies (PMSCs) Internationally* (London: The Stationery Office, 2009), available at http://www.fco.gov.uk, accessed 28 May 2015.

United Kingdom Foreign and Commonwealth Office. *Impact Assessment on Promoting High Standards of Conduct by Private Military and Security Companies (PMSCs) Internationally* (London: Foreign and Commonwealth Office, April 2009).

United Kingdom Foreign and Commonwealth Office. *Private Military Companies: Options for Regulation.* HC 577 (London: The Stationery Office, 12 February 2002).

United Kingdom Foreign and Commonwealth Office. *Promoting High Standards in the Private Military and Security Company Industry*, written ministerial statement (21 June 2011).

United Kingdom Foreign and Commonwealth Office. *Public Consultation on Promoting High Standards on Conduct by Private Military and Security Companies (PMSCs) Internationally: Summary of Responses* (16 December 2009).

United Kingdom Foreign Enlistment Act (33 and 34 Vict., chapter 90, 1870).

United Kingdom House of Commons Foreign Affairs Committee. *Private Military Companies: Ninth Report of Session 2001–02. Report, Together with Proceedings of the Committee, Minutes of Evidence and Appendices.* HC 922 (London: The Stationery Office, 1 August 2002).

United Kingdom House of Commons Foreign Affairs Committee. *Response of the Secretary of State for Foreign and Commonwealth Affairs* (London: The Stationery Office, 2001–2002).

United Kingdom House of Commons Foreign Affairs Committee. *Second Report: Sierra Leone* (London: The Stationery Office, 1999).

United Kingdom Ministry of Defence. *Contractor Support to Operations: Tiger Team Final Report* (London: Ministry of Defence, 16 March 2010).

United Kingdom Ministry of Defence. *Director Defence Support Review: Employment Mechanisms for the Total Support Force D DSR/002* (London: 14 February 2011).

United Kingdom Ministry of Defence. *Strategic Defence Review: Modern Forces for the Modern World* (London: Ministry of Defence, July 1998).

United Kingdom Parliament. *Early Day Motion 690: Private Military and Security Companies* (London: House of Commons, 22 January 2007).

United Kingdom Public Records Office. *Confidential. Subject: Advisory and General Legal Matter, Conditions of Service, Mercenaries*. Diplock Report, DEFE 24/1759.

United Kingdom Treasury. *Competing for Quality: Buying Better Public Services* (London: Her Majesty's Stationery Office, 1991).

United Nations. *Geneva Conventions of 12 August 1949 and Protocols Additional to the Conventions* (12 August 1949), available at http://www.un-documents.net/gc.htm, accessed 12 August 2015.

United Nations. "Growth in United Nations Membership, 1945–Present," United Nations website, available at http://www.un.org/en/members/growth.shtml, accessed 18 October 2015.

United Nations. *International Convention against the Recruitment, Use, Financing and Training of Mercenaries.* UN Treaty Series 2163 (A/RES/44/34).

United Nations General Assembly. *International Convention against the Recruitment, Use, Financing and Training of Mercenaries* (4 December 1989), available at http://www.un.org/documents/ga/res/44/a44r034.htm, accessed 31 July 2015.

United Nations International Criminal Tribunal for the Former Yugoslavia. "The Conflicts," International Criminal Tribunal for the Former Yugoslavia website, available at http://www.icty.org/sid/322, accessed 6 October 2015.

United Nations Office of the High Commissioner for Human Rights. *Guiding Principles on Business and Human Rights: Implementing the United Nations 'Protect, Respect and Remedy' Framework* (New York: United Nations, 2011).

United Nations Office of the High Commissioner for Human Rights. "UN Working Group on Mercenaries to Launch Study on the Use of Private Military and Security Companies by the UN" (18 March 2013), available at http://www.ohchr.org/EN/NewsEvents/Pages/DisplayNews.aspx?NewsID=13154&LangID=E, accessed 13 August 2015.

United Nations Office of the High Commissioner for Human Rights. "Working Group on the Use of Mercenaries as a Means of Violating Human Rights and Impeding the Exercise of the Right of Peoples to Self Determination," available at http://www.ohchr.org/EN/Issues/Mercenaries/SRMercenaries/Pages/SRMercenariesIndex.aspx, accessed 18 February 2015.

United States Department of Defense. *Challenges Impacting Operations Iraqi Freedom and Enduring Freedom Reported by Major Oversight Organizations Beginning FY 2003 through FY 2007*. Inspector General Report (Washington: Department of Defense, 18 July 2008).

United States Department of Defense. *Defense Manpower Requirements Report: FY 2012* (Washington: Department of Defense, April 2012).

United States Department of Defense. *Defense Manpower Requirements Report: FY 2014* (Washington: Department of Defense, August 2013).

United States Department of Defense. *Defense Manpower Requirements Report: FY 2015* (Washington: Department of Defense, June 2014).

United States Department of Defense. *Performance Work Statement for the Reconstruction Security Support Services (RSSS) Contract W91GDW-07-D-4021* (Washington: Department of Defense, 2007).

United States Department of Defense. *Population Representation in the Military Services* (Washington: Office of the Under Secretary of Defense for Personnel and Readiness, annually).

United States Department of Defense. *Progress toward Security and Stability in Afghanistan*, report to Congress (Washington: Department of Defense, June 2009).

United States Department of Defense. *Quadrennial Defense Review* (Washington: Department of Defense, 2010).

United States Department of Defense. *Quadrennial Defense Review Report* (Washington: Department of Defense, 6 February 2006).

United States Department of Defense, Office of the Deputy Under Secretary of Defense (Logistics and Materiel Readiness). *Contractor Support of U.S. Operations in USCENTCOM AOR, Iraq, and Afghanistan* (Washington: Department of Defense, May 2009).

United States Department of Labor, Office of Workers' Compensation Programs. "Defense Base Act Case Summary by Nation," United States Department of Labor website, available at http://www.dol.gov/owcp/dlhwc/dbaallnation.htm, accessed 24 September 2015.

United States Department of the Army. *Army Regulation 715-9: Contractors Accompanying the Force* (Washington: Department of the Army, 29 October 1999).

United States Department of the Army. *Field Manual (FM) 100-5: Operations* (Washington: Department of the Army, Headquarters, 1993).

United States Deputy Assistant Secretary of Defense for Program Support. *Contractor Support of U.S. Operations in the USCENTCOM Area of Responsibility* (Washington: Department of Defense, quarterly), posted at the Private Security Monitor, "Data and Statistics: CENTCOM Data," Sié Chéou-Kang Center for International Security and Diplomacy of the University of Denver website, available at http://psm.du.edu/articles_reports_statistics/data_and_statistics.html, accessed 19 December 2015.

United States Forces, Iraq. *Operations Order 10-01* (15 January 2010).

United States General Accounting Office. *Defense Contracting: Additional Personal Conflict of Interest Safeguards Needed for Certain DOD Contractor Employees.* GAO-08-169 (Washington: General Accounting Office, March 2008).

United States General Accounting Office. *Military Operations: Contractors Provide Vital Services to Deployed Forces but Are Not Adequately Addressed in DoD Plans*. GAO-03-695 (Washington: General Accounting Office, June 2003).

United States General Accounting Office. *Rebuilding Iraq: Actions Still Needed to Improve Use of Private Security Providers*. GAO-06-865 (Washington: General Accounting Office, June 2006).

United States House of Representatives Committee on Oversight and Government Reform. Memorandum (Washington: United States House of Representatives, 1 October 2007), available at http://oversight.house.gov/documents/20071001121609.pdf, accessed 30 March 2009.

United States Navy. "Naval Power 21 . . . a Navy Vision" (Washington: Department of the Navy, October 2002).

United States Senate. *Testimony: Ambassador Karl Eikenberry and COMISAF Gen Stanley McChrystal. Hearing of the Senate Armed Services Committee* (8 December 2009).

United States Senate Committee on Armed Services. *The Department of Defense's Management of Costs under the Logistics Civil Augmentation Program (LOGCAP) Contract in Iraq* (Washington: Government Printing Office, 19 April 2007).

United States Senate Committee on Armed Services. *Inquiry into the Role and Oversight of Private Security Contractors in Afghanistan: Report with Additional Views* (Washington: Government Printing Office, 28 September 2010), available at https://www.congress.gov/111/crpt/srpt345/CRPT-111srpt345.pdf, accessed 6 June 2015.

"U.S. Ambassador Praises Blackwater Bodyguards," *USA Today* (26 October 2007), available at http://usatoday30.usatoday.com/news/world/iraq/2007-10-26-iraq-news_N.htm, accessed 15 October 2015.

US Code Title 18, Chapter 212, S. 3261(a)(1): Military Extraterritorial Jurisdiction, available at https://www.law.cornell.edu/uscode/text/18/3261, accessed 16 August 2015.

"US Judge Dismisses Charges in Iraqi Blackwater Killings," *BBC News* (31 December 2009), available at http://news.bbc.co.uk/1/hi/world/americas/8436780.stm, accessed 20 May 2015.

"U.S. Marine Pleads to Taking $150K in Bribes in Iraq," *Seattle Times* (7 December 2012), available at http://www.seattletimes.com/nation-world/us-marine-pleads-to-taking-150k-in-bribes-in-iraq/, accessed 1 October 2015.

"US Warships Head to Yemeni Waters; Could Block Iran Weapons," *Stars and Stripes* (21 April 2015), available at http://japan.stripes.com/news/us-warships-heads-yemeni-waters-could-block-iran-weapons, accessed 28 September 2015.

Uttley, Matthew. *Contractors on Deployed Military Operations: United Kingdom Policy and Doctrine* (Carlisle: Strategic Studies Institute, September 2005).

Uttley, Matthew R. "Private Contractors on Deployed Operations: The United Kingdom Experience," *Defence Studies* 4, 2 (Summer 2004).

Vergakis, Brock. "Ex-Blackwater Contractors Guilty in Afghan's Death," *Washington Post* (11 March 2001).

Verkuil, Paul R. *Outsourcing Sovereignty: Why Privatization of Government Functions Threatens Democracy and What We Can Do about It* (New York: Cambridge University Press, 2007).

Vines, Alex. *Well Oiled: Oil and Human Rights in Equatorial Guinea* (New York: Human Rights Watch, July 2009).

Voelz, Glenn J. *Managing the Private Spies: Use of Commercial Augmentation for Intelligence Operations*. Discussion Paper 14 (Washington: Joint Military Intelligence College Press, June 2006).

Von Boemcken, Marc. "Outsourcing the State? Security Governance and the Privatization of Military Functions," in Michael Brzoska, editor, *Bonn International Center for Conversion: Conversion Survey 2005* (Baden-Baden: Nomos, 2005).

Wakelam, Randall. "One Officer Factory: The Royal Military College and Officer Education since 1955," *Historical Studies in Education* 26, 1 (Spring 2014).

Walker, Clive, and Dave Whyte. "Contracting Out War? Private Military Companies, Law and Regulation in the United Kingdom," *International and Comparative Law Quarterly* 54, 3 (July 2005).

Walker, Peter. "Blackwater Guards Shot Iraqis without Provocation, Report Says," *Guardian* (8 October 2007).

Wallace, William, and Katrina Mason. "Africa's Soldiers of Fortune Join Fight against Boko Haram," *Financial Times* (26 March 2015), available at http://www.ft.com/cms/s/0/4cda876e-d2e8-11e4-a792-00144feab7de.html#axzz45phBwmeP, accessed 14 April 2016.

Waller, J. Michael. "Accountability and Private Security Contractors: Visibility of Operations Is Key to Success," *Politicalwarfare.org* (10 December 2007), available at http://acmeofskill.com/2007/12/2380/, accessed 31 July 2015.

Ward, Daniel. "Assessing Force Protection Risk," *Military Review* 77, 6 (November–December 1997).

Webber, Mark. "Soviet Policy in Sub-Saharan Africa: The Final Phase," *Journal of Modern African Studies* 30, 1 (March 1992).

Weigelt, Matthew. "Insourcing Failed, DOD's Gates Says. Now What?" *FCW* (10 August 2010), available at https://fcw.com/articles/2010/08/10/gates-insourcing-did-not-work.aspx, accessed 15 November 2015.

Weiler-Polak, Dana. "Poll: Nearly 50% of Israelis Fear State Is Pushing Them into Poverty," *Ha'aretz* (17 November 2009).

Weintraub, Jeff. "The Theory and Politics of the Public/Private Distinction," in Jeff Weintraub and Krishan Kumar, editors, *Public and Private in Thought and Practice: Perspectives on a Grand Dichotomy* (Chicago: University of Chicago Press, 1997).

Weissman, Lilach. "PM to Decide on Locker Report Defense Cuts," *Globes* (23 July 2015), available in Hebrew at http://www.globes.co.il/en/article-netanyahu-to-decide-on-locker-report-1001055175, accessed 8 August 2015.

"What Are the Voluntary Principles?" Voluntary Principles on Security and Human Rights website, available at http://www.voluntaryprinciples.org/, accessed 15 April 2010.

White, Nigel D. "The Privatization of Military and Security Functions and Human Rights: Comments on the U.N. Working Group's Draft Convention," *Human Rights Law Review* 11, 1 (2011).

Whyte, Dave. "Lethal Regulation: State-Corporate Crime and the United Kingdom Government's New Mercenaries," *Journal of Law and Society* 30, 4 (December 2003), pages 575–600.

Wilkinson, Tracy. "U.N. Troops Held as Human Shield: Bosnia—Ukrainian Peacekeepers in Zepa 'Safe Area' Detained by Serbs to Ward Off NATO Air Strikes. Rebel Advance Slows as Government Soldiers Strongly Resist," *Los Angeles Times* (18 July 1995).

Williams, Stanley B., and Harold J. Leavitt. "Methods of Selecting Marine Corps Officers," in George A. Kelley, editor, *New Methods in Applied Psychology* (College Park: University of Maryland Press, 1947).

Williamson, Jamie. "Challenges of Twenty-first Century Conflicts: A Look at Direct Participation in Hostilities," *Duke Journal of Comparative and International Law* 20, 3 (Spring 2010).

Williamson, Oliver E. *Markets and Hierarchies* (New York: The Free Press, 1975).

Winslow, Donna. *The Canadian Airborne Regiment in Somalia: A Socio-cultural Inquiry* (Ottawa: Canadian Government Publishing, 1997).

Winthrop, William. *Military Law and Precedents*, 2nd edition (Washington: Government Printing Office, 1920).

Wong, Leonard, and Jeffrey McNally. "Downsizing the Army: Some Policy Implications Affecting the Survivors." *Armed Forces and Society* 20, 2 (Winter 1994).

Woodward, Susan L. *Balkan Tragedy: Chaos and Dissolution after the Cold War* (Washington: Brookings Institution Press, 1995).

Woolf, Nicky. "Former Blackwater Guards Sentenced for Massacre of Unarmed Iraqi Civilians," *Guardian* (13 April 2015), available at http://www.theguardian.com/us-news/2015/apr/13/former-blackwater-guards-sentencing-baghdad-massacre, accessed 20 May 2015.

Wright, George V. "US Foreign Policy and Destabilisation in Southern Africa," *Review of African Political Economy* 16, 45–46 (1989).

Wulf, Herbert. *Internationalizing and Privatizing War and Peace* (Basingstoke: Palgrave Macmillan, 2005).

Zamparelli, Steven J. "Contractors on the Battlefield: What Have We Signed Up For?" *Air Force Journal of Logistics* 23, 3 (Fall 1999).

Zarate, Juan Carlos. "The Emergence of a New Dog of War: Private International Security Companies, International Law, and the New World Order," *Stanford Journal of International Law* 34 (Winter 1998).

Zedeck, Rachel. "Private Military/Security Companies, Human Security, and State Building in Africa," *African Security Review* 16, 4 (December 2007).

Zeleney, Jeff. "Obama to Change Contract Awarding," *New York Times* (5 March 2009).

Zemanek, Karl. "Armed Attack," in Rüdiger Wolfrum, director, *Max Planck Encyclopedia of Public International Law* (October 2013), available at http://opil.ouplaw.com/view/10.1093/law:epil/9780199231690/law-9780199231690-e241, accessed 1 November 2015.

Zrahiya, Zvi. "Defense Budget for 2014 Tops 70 Billion Shekels," *Ha'aretz* (7 December 2014).

Zucchino, David. "Unit Cleared in Afghan Killings," *Los Angeles Times* (24 May 2008).

Zunec, Ozren. "Democracy in the 'Fog of War': Civil-Military Relations in Croatia," in Constantine P. Danopoulos and Daniel Zirker, editors, *Civil-Military Relations in the Soviet and Yugoslav Successor States* (Boulder: Westview, 1996).

Index

About the Editors and Contributors

Gary Schaub Jr. is a senior researcher at the Centre for Military Studies, Department of Political Science, at the University of Copenhagen. Prior to assuming that position in December 2011, he was an assistant professor in the Department of Strategy at the United States Air Force Air War College. Dr. Schaub was previously a research fellow at the Air Force Research Institute, a visiting assistant professor at the School of Advanced Air and Space Studies, and a MacArthur Scholar in Arms Control, Disarmament, and International Security at the University of Illinois–Urbana. His publications include scholarly articles in *Political Psychology*, *Strategic Studies Quarterly*, *Parameters*, *Defence Studies*, *International Studies Review*, *International Journal*, and *Refuge*; chapters in books published by Oxford University Press, Ashgate, CQ Press, Air University Press, and St. Martin's; reports for the Danish Ministry of Defence; and opinion pieces in the *New York Times*, *Washington Times*, *Pittsburgh Post-Gazette*, and *Air Force Times*.

Ryan Kelty is an associate professor and chair of the Department of Sociology at Washington College. Previously he served as assistant professor in the Department of Behavioral Sciences and Leadership at the United States Military Academy, and was an instructor and research associate at the Center for Research on Military Organization at the University of Maryland. His research has been published in *Social Psychology Quarterly*, *Armed Forces and Society*, *Journal of Political and Military Sociology*, and *The Future of Children*, as well as chapters in several edited volumes. Dr. Kelty has consulted with various military organizations on issues related to civilian contractors, civil-military relations, and diversity, including the US Army and Navy and NATO's research group on Military and Civilian Personnel Work Culture and Relations in Defense Organizations. He holds a PhD in sociology from the University of Maryland and a BA in sociology and Eastern religions from Middlebury College.

CONTRIBUTORS

Shannon Bosch is an admitted attorney and senior lecturer at the University of KwaZulu-Natal (UKZN) School of Law in South Africa. She holds a BA (Hons) LLB from the University of Natal, South Africa, and an LLM in international law from Cambridge University (as DFID Commonwealth and Mandela Magdalene Scholar). She graduated with a PhD from UKZN, and her thesis dealt with, among other topics, private military and security contractors. Dr. Bosch sits on the editorial board of the *African Yearbook of International Humanitarian Law* and publishes extensively in the area of international humanitarian law. Her publications on the private security industry include "Private Security Contractors and Neutral Relief Workers: An Unlikely Marriage?" *African Yearbook on International Humanitarian Law* (2013); "Private Military and Security Contractors: A Face-Off with the Notion of Direct Participation in Hostilities in International Armed Conflicts," *Journal of Juridical Science* 37, 2 (2012); "Private Security Contractors and State Responsibility," *Comparative and International Law Journal of Southern Africa* 41, 4 (2008); and "Private Security Contractors and International Humanitarian Law: A Skirmish for Recognition in International Armed Conflicts," *African Security Studies* 16, 4 (2007).

Doug Brooks is president emeritus of the International Stability Operations Association (ISOA), a trade association he founded and developed, which focuses on advancing the global role of the industry in supporting international efforts in conflict, after conflict, humanitarian rescue, and disaster relief environments. The ISOA works with multiple stakeholders from academia, think tanks, industry, government, and nongovernmental organizations to develop and negotiate international codes, norms, standards, and guidelines for private sector operations in stability operations. Mr. Brooks has testified before the US Congress and South African Parliament and at many UN functions. He has appeared on Al Jazeera, the BBC, CBS News, NBC News, Fox News, CNN International, National Public Radio, *The Diane Rehm Show*, the Voice of America, SABC in South Africa, and *PBS NewsHour*. He has lectured at Georgetown University; South African Defense College; the Inter-American Defense College at Fort McNair; George C. Marshall Center in Garmisch, Germany; and the United States Military Academy at West Point. He has authored numerous articles, book chapters, and op-eds that have appeared in leading media including the *Washington Post*, the *New York Times*, and the Johannesburg *Star*. A native of Indiana,

Mr. Brooks earned a BA in history from Indiana University and an MA in history from Baylor University, with additional doctoral studies at the Graduate School of Public and International Affairs, University of Pittsburgh. He previously worked as a teacher in Kambuzuma Township in Harare, Zimbabwe; the Library of Congress; the National Archives; and the Institute of International Education. Before founding ISOA, he was an academic fellow at the South African Institute for International Affairs in Johannesburg in 1999–2000.

Eugenio Cusumano is a lecturer in international relations at the Baltic Defence College. He holds an MA in international relations from the University of Bologna and a PhD in political and social sciences from the European University Institute. Before joining the Baltic Defence College, he was a Fulbright-Schuman Scholar at the Korbel School of International Studies, University of Denver, and a visiting lecturer at the University of Maastricht. He is coeditor, with Christopher Kinsey, of *Diplomatic Security: A Comparative Analysis* (forthcoming), and has published in *Armed Forces and Society, International Peacekeeping*, and a volume from Oxford University Press.

Volker Franke is an associate professor of conflict management at Kennesaw State University. He was previously an associate professor of political science and international studies at McDaniel College and director of research at the Bonn International Center for Conversion. Currently, Dr. Franke serves on the Scientific Advisory Board of the German Foundation for Peace Research. From 1998 to 2007, he was director and managing editor of the National Security Studies Case Studies Program at Maxwell School of Citizenship and Public Affairs Syracuse University. Dr. Franke holds a PhD in political science from Syracuse University's Maxwell School, a master of public administration from North Carolina State University, and an MA in political science and sociology from Johannes Gutenberg University in Mainz, Germany. He is the author of *Preparing for Peace: Military Identity, Value Orientations, and Professional Military Education* (1999) and more than 30 journal articles, book chapters, case studies, and research reports on issues related to peace and security studies, conflict management, civil-military relations, development policy, and social identity. He is also the editor of *Terrorism and Peacekeeping: New Security Challenges* (2005) and *Security in a Changing World: Case Studies in U.S. National Security Management* (2002).

Matthew Kimble is a candidate attorney at Stirling Attorneys in Durban, South Africa. He earned an LLB LLM (by research) from the University of

KwaZulu-Natal and his research has focused on issues surrounding private military and security companies.

Christopher Kinsey is a reader in business and international security in the Defence Studies Department at King's College London. Previously he was an Economic and Social Research Council Postdoctoral Fellow at the Department of International Politics, University of Wales, Aberystwyth, where he also received his doctoral degree, which examined the impact of private security in international politics, and his MS in economics. He is the author of *Corporate Soldiers and International Security: The Rise of Private Military Companies* (2006), *Private Contractors and the Reconstruction of Iraq: Transforming Military Logistics* (2009), and *Contractors and War: The Transformation of United States' Military and Stabilization Operations* (2011); has published in *European Security*, *Armed Forces and Society*, *Human Rights and International Legal Discourse*, *Journal of Military History*, *Journal of Contemporary European Research*, *Cambridge Review of International Affairs*, *Journal of Modern African Studies*, *Defence Studies*, and *Conflict, Security and Development*; and has contributed chapters to a number of volumes.

Andrew N. Koch is an MA Candidate at the Fletcher School of Law and Diplomacy at Tufts University, concentrating in international security studies and international business relations. Prior to the Fletcher School he worked in management consulting. He holds a BA with high distinction in foreign affairs and history from the University of Virginia.

Marelie Maritz holds an LLB LLM (cum laude, specializing in international law) from the University of Pretoria in South Africa. Ms. Maritz has been a lecturer at the University of Kwazulu-Natal School of Law in Durban, South Africa; an intern for the Institute for Security Studies in Pretoria, South Africa, in its Security Sector Governance Programme; and an academic assistant at the University of Pretoria. Her work has been published in the *Potchefstroom Electronic Law Journal*.

David Perry is a doctoral student in political science at Carleton University. His dissertation research analyzes the privatization of defense and security in the United States, Canada, and Great Britain, focusing on the use of private military firms on international operations. He was previously the deputy director of Dalhousie University's Centre for Foreign Policy Studies. He holds a BA in political science and history from Mount Allison University and an MA in political science from Dalhousie University.

Ian M. Ralby has been intimately involved in both national and international efforts to develop codes, standards, and mechanisms of accountability for the private security industry. He is founder and executive director of I.R. Consilium and adjunct professor of maritime law and security at the Africa Center for Strategic Studies at National Defense University in Washington, DC, as well as a retained expert for both the United Nations and NATO. He holds both an MPhil and a PhD from St. John's College, Cambridge, a JD from William and Mary School of Law, and both a BA and an MA from the University of Maryland, Baltimore County. He lectures frequently around the world and has published in an array of mainstream and academic publications, including the *Huffington Post*, *Fletcher Security Review*, *Georgetown Journal of International Law*, and *The Oxford Handbook of the Use of Force in International Law*.

Surabhi Ranganathan is assistant professor at Warwick University, where she teaches international law. She was previously a junior research fellow at King's College, Cambridge and the Lauterpacht Centre for International Law, and a program officer and institute fellow at the Institute for International Law and Justice, New York University. Author of the monograph *Strategically Created Treaty Conflicts and the Politics of International Law* (2014), she is also assistant editor of *The Cambridge Companion to International Law* (2012) and *The British Yearbook of International Law*. She holds a PhD from St. John's College, Cambridge, where she was a Gates Scholar; an LLM from New York University, where she was a Vanderbilt Scholar; and a BA LLB from the National Law School of India University, Bangalore.

Guy Seidman has been on faculty at the Radzyner School of Law since 1999. A graduate of Tel-Aviv University (LLB, 1989; LLM, 1995) and Northwestern University of Chicago (LLM, 1997; SJD, 1999), Professor Seidman has visited and taught at various institutions in Israel, Europe, and the United States, including the University of Chicago, Northwestern University, Boston University, and the Max Planck Institute at Heidelberg. He is primarily interested in administrative law and comparative law and the cross between the two. A former officer of the Israeli Judge Advocate General's Corps, Professor Seidman pursues other teaching and research interests including military law as well as medical law. He has written extensively in his fields of research. Notable recent publications include "Who Are You, the Israeli Administrative Law? In View of Daphne Barak-Erez's Book *Adminstrative Law*" *51 Hapraklit* (May 2012); *The Origins of the Necessary and Proper Clause* (coauthored with Gary Lawson, Geoffrey Miller, and Robert Natelson, 2010), and "Is a Flat-Line a Good Thing? On the Privatization of Israel's Healthcare System," *American Journal of Law and Medicine* 36 (2010).

Christopher Spearin is an associate professor in the Department of Defence Studies of the Royal Military College of Canada. He holds a PhD from the University of British Columbia. His work has been published in a number of edited books and in a variety of forums, including *Canadian Foreign Policy, Canadian Military Journal, Civil Wars, Contemporary Security Policy, Human Security Bulletin, International Peacekeeping, International Journal, International Politics, Journal of Conflict Studies, Journal of International Criminal Justice, Naval War College Review, Oxford Analytica, Parameters, Security Dialogue, Small Wars and Insurgencies*, and *World Defence Systems*. Dr. Spearin is the yearly contributor on Canadian foreign and defense policy in the long-standing *Canadian Annual Review of Politics and Public Affairs*.

David Strachan-Morris is a lecturer in intelligence and security in the Department of Politics and International Relations at the University of Leicester. Previously he worked as a political and security risk analyst in the private sector and served in the British Army. He holds a PhD from the University of Wolverhampton, awarded in 2011. Recent publications include "The Intelligence Cycle in the Corporate World: Bespoke or Off the Shelf," in *Understanding the Intelligence Cycle* (2013); "From the Banana Wars to the Three Block War: Warrior Scholars in the US Marine Corps," in *Warrior Scholars in Counterinsurgency* (2013); "Threat and Risk: What Is the Difference and Why Does It Matter?" *Intelligence and National Security* 27, 2 (April 2012); and "Leadership Decapitation: Al Qa'ida in Iraq as a Case Study," *RUSI Journal* 155, 4 (2010). His first book, on the US Marine Corps counterinsurgency strategy in Vietnam, is forthcoming in 2016.

www.ingramcontent.com/pod-product-compliance
Ingram Content Group UK Ltd.
Pitfield, Milton Keynes, MK11 3LW, UK
UKHW012034150926
475560UK00001B/10

9 781442 260214